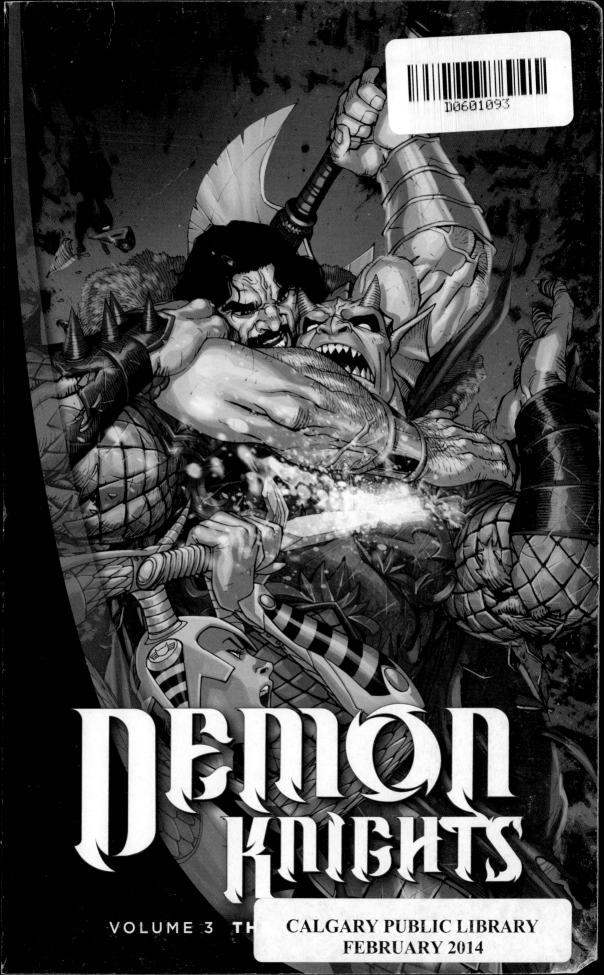

DEMON
KNIGHTS

VOLUME 3 TH

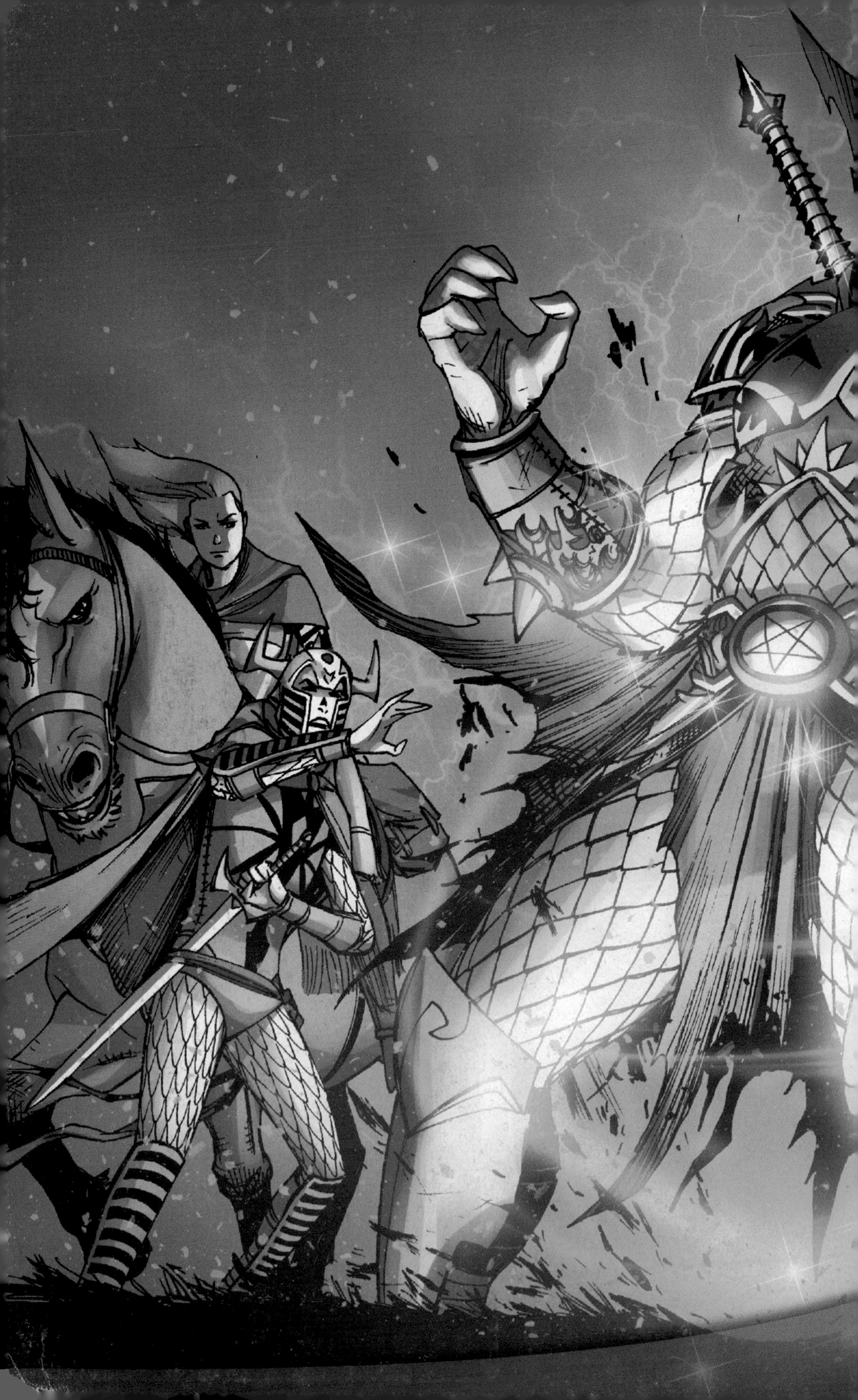

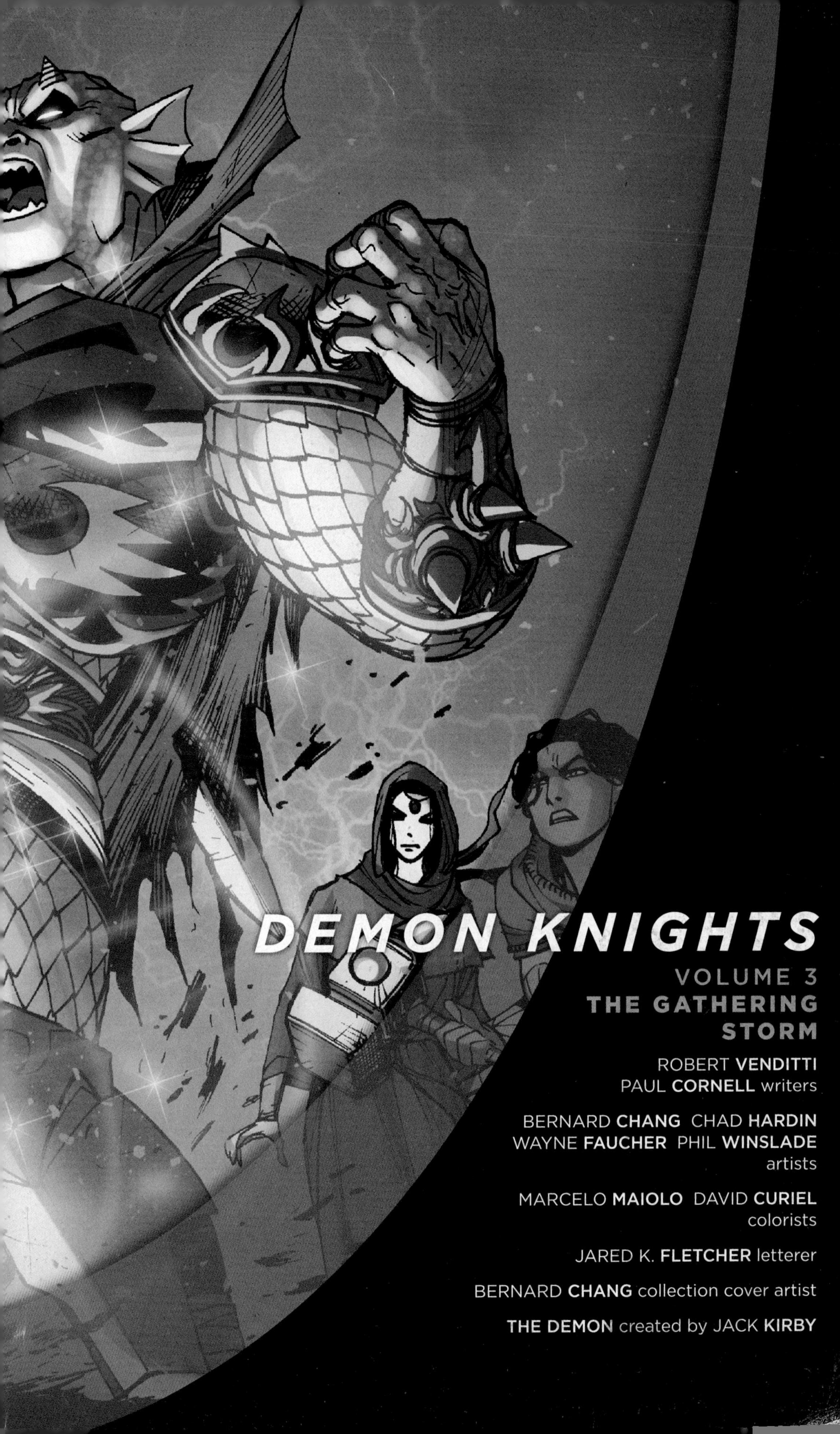

DEMON KNIGHTS

VOLUME 3
THE GATHERING STORM

ROBERT **VENDITTI**
PAUL **CORNELL** writers

BERNARD **CHANG** CHAD **HARDIN**
WAYNE **FAUCHER** PHIL **WINSLADE**
artists

MARCELO **MAIOLO** DAVID **CURIEL**
colorists

JARED K. **FLETCHER** letterer

BERNARD **CHANG** collection cover artist

THE DEMON created by JACK **KIRBY**

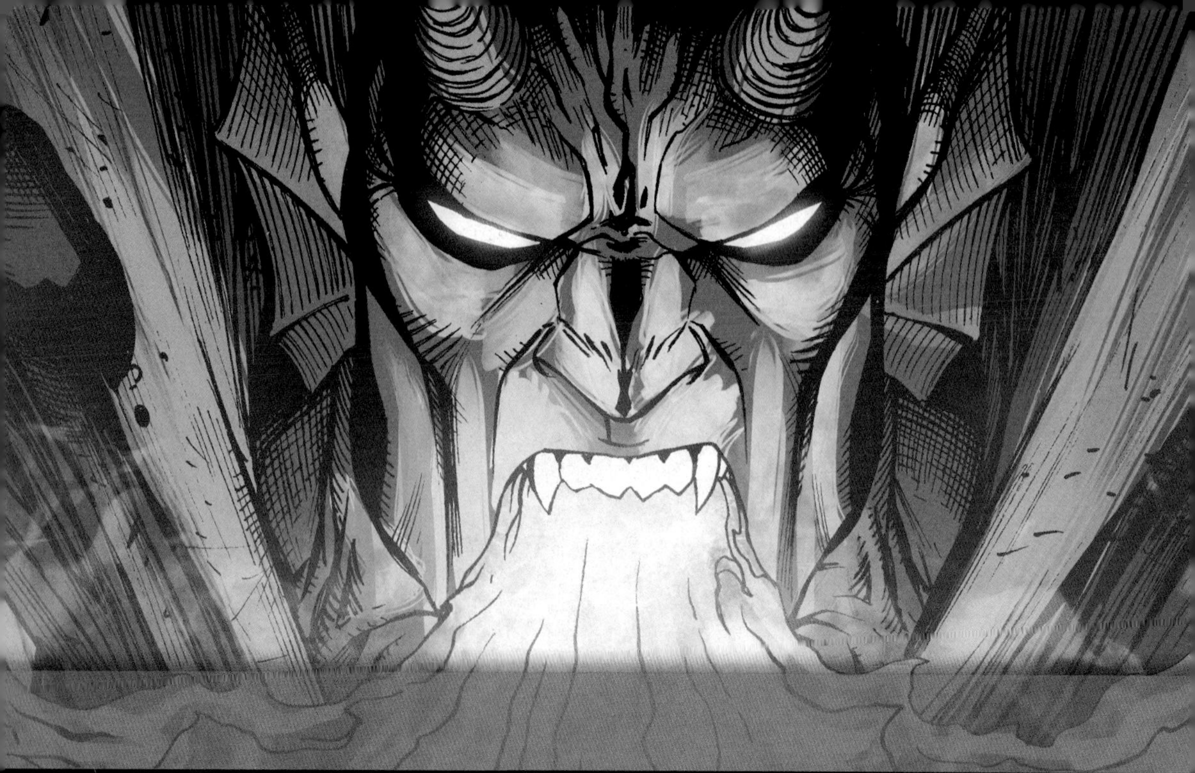

JOEY CAVALIERI CHRIS CONROY Editors - Original Series KYLE ANDRUKIEWICZ Assistant Editor - Original Series
ROBIN WILDMAN Editor ROBBIN BROSTERMAN Design Director - Books ROBBIE BIEDERMAN Publication Design

BOB HARRAS Senior VP - Editor-in-Chief, DC Comics

DIANE NELSON President DAN DIDIO and JIM LEE Co-Publishers GEOFF JOHNS Chief Creative Officer
JOHN ROOD Executive VP - Sales, Marketing and Business Development AMY GENKINS Senior VP - Business and Legal Affairs
NAIRI GARDINER Senior VP - Finance JEFF BOISON VP - Publishing Planning
MARK CHIARELLO VP - Art Direction and Design JOHN CUNNINGHAM VP - Marketing
TERRI CUNNINGHAM VP - Editorial Administration ALISON GILL Senior VP - Manufacturing and Operations
HANK KANALZ Senior VP - Vertigo and Integrated Publishing JAY KOGAN VP - Business and Legal Affairs, Publishing
JACK MAHAN VP - Business Affairs, Talent NICK NAPOLITANO VP - Manufacturing Administration SUE POHJA VP - Book Sales
COURTNEY SIMMONS Senior VP - Publicity BOB WAYNE Senior VP - Sales

DEMON KNIGHTS VOLUME 3: THE GATHERING STORM

DC Comics, 1700 Broadway, New York, NY 10019
A Warner Bros. Entertainment Company.
Printed by RR Donnelley, Salem, VA, USA.
12/13/13. First Printing.
ISBN: 978-1-4012-4269-5

Library of Congress Cataloging-in-Publication Data

Cornell, Paul, author.
Demon Knights. Volume 3, The Gathering Storm / Paul Cornell, Robert Venditti, [illustrated by] Bernard Chang.
pages cm. — (The New 52!)
ISBN 978-1-4012-4269-5 (pbk.)
1. Graphic novels. I. Venditti, Robert, author. II. Chang, Bernard, illustrator. III. Title. IV. Title: Gathering Storm.
PN6728.D435C69 2014
741.5'973—dc23
2013035965

SUSTAINABLE FORESTRY INITIATIVE
Certified Chain of Custody
At Least 20% Certified Forest Content
www.sfiprogram.org
SFI-01042
APPLIES TO TEXT STOCK ONLY

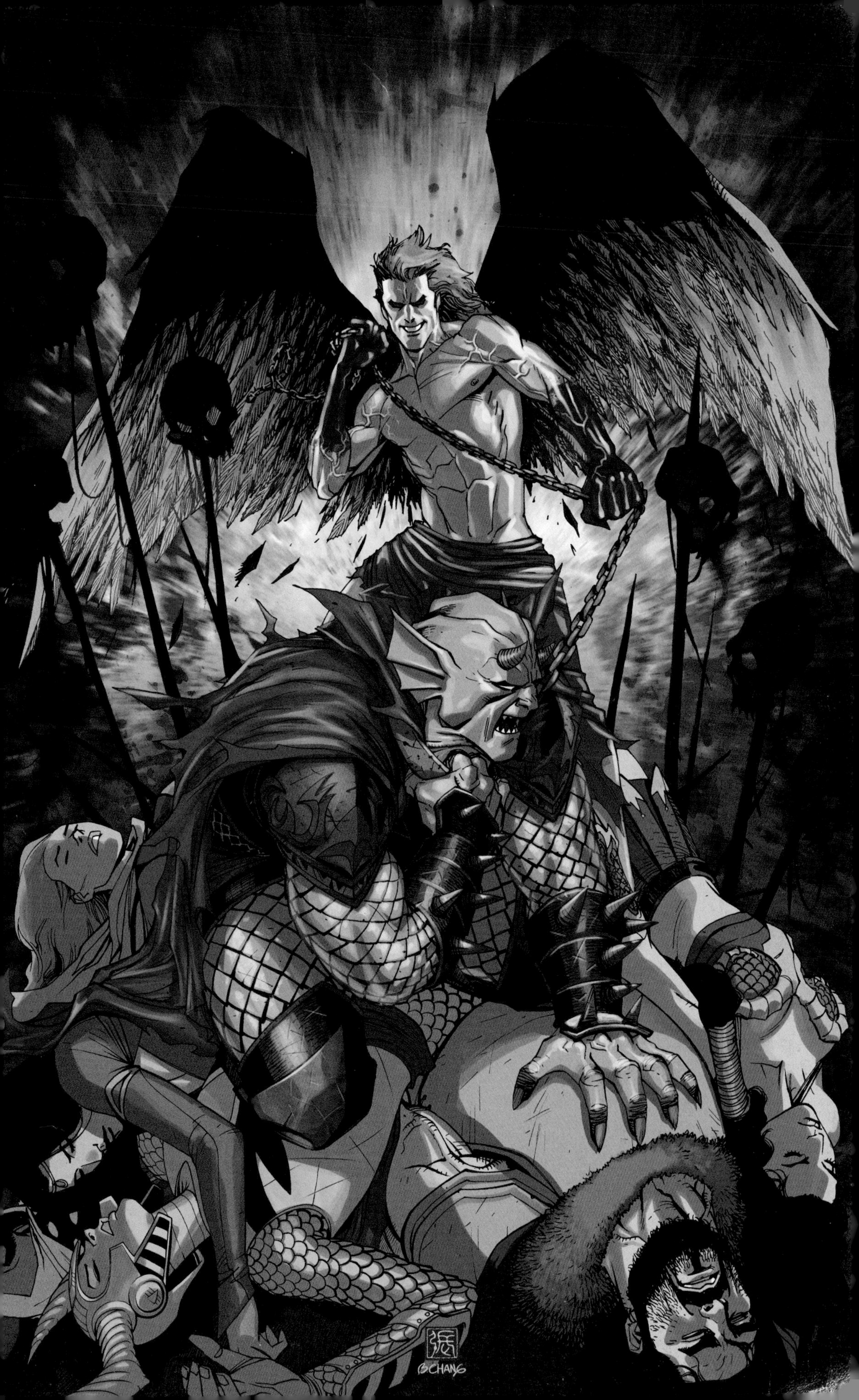
BCHANG

PAUL CORNELL
writer

BERNARD CHANG
artist

BERNARD CHANG
cover artist

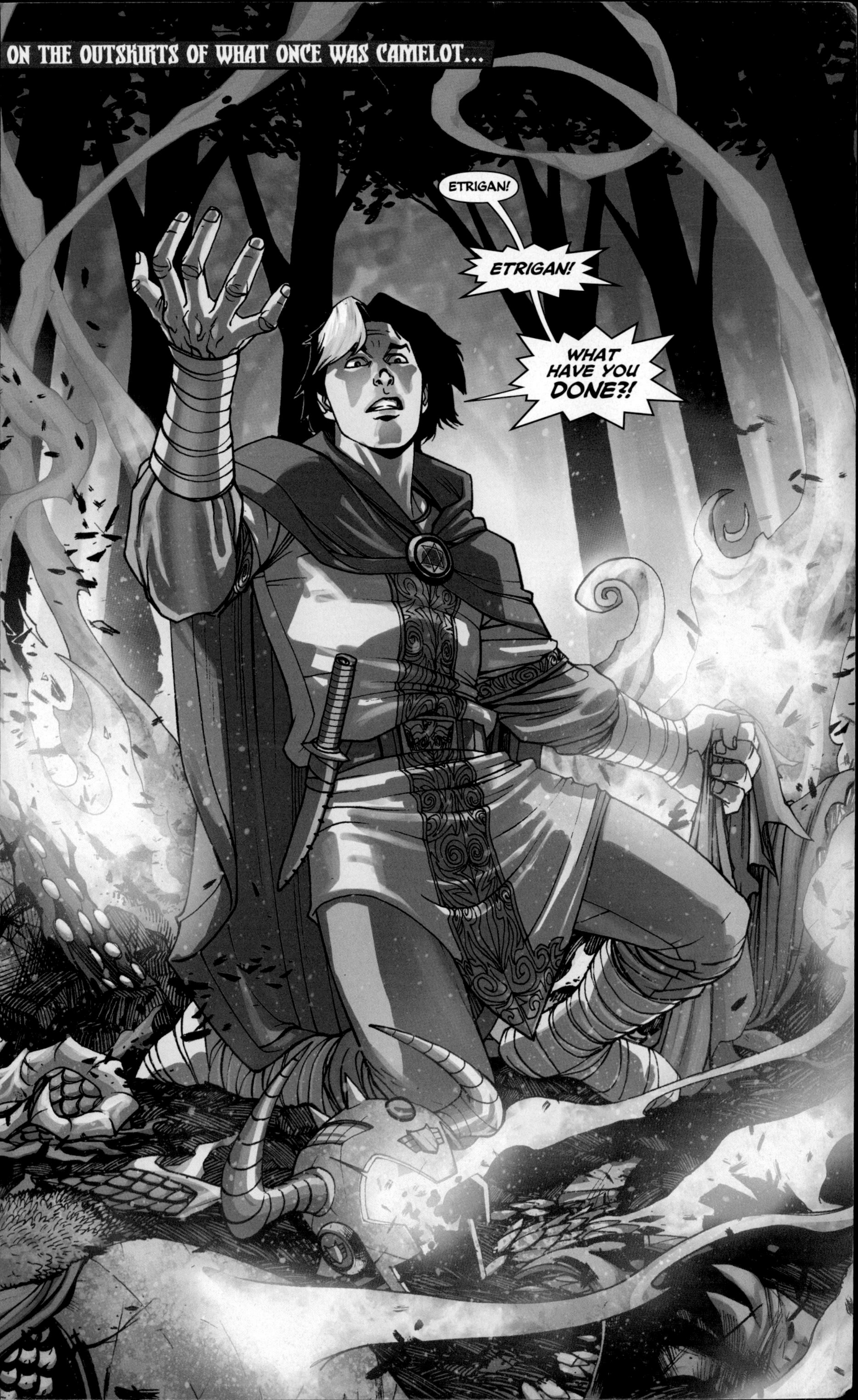
ON THE OUTSKIRTS OF WHAT ONCE WAS CAMELOT...
ETRIGAN!
ETRIGAN!
WHAT HAVE YOU DONE?!

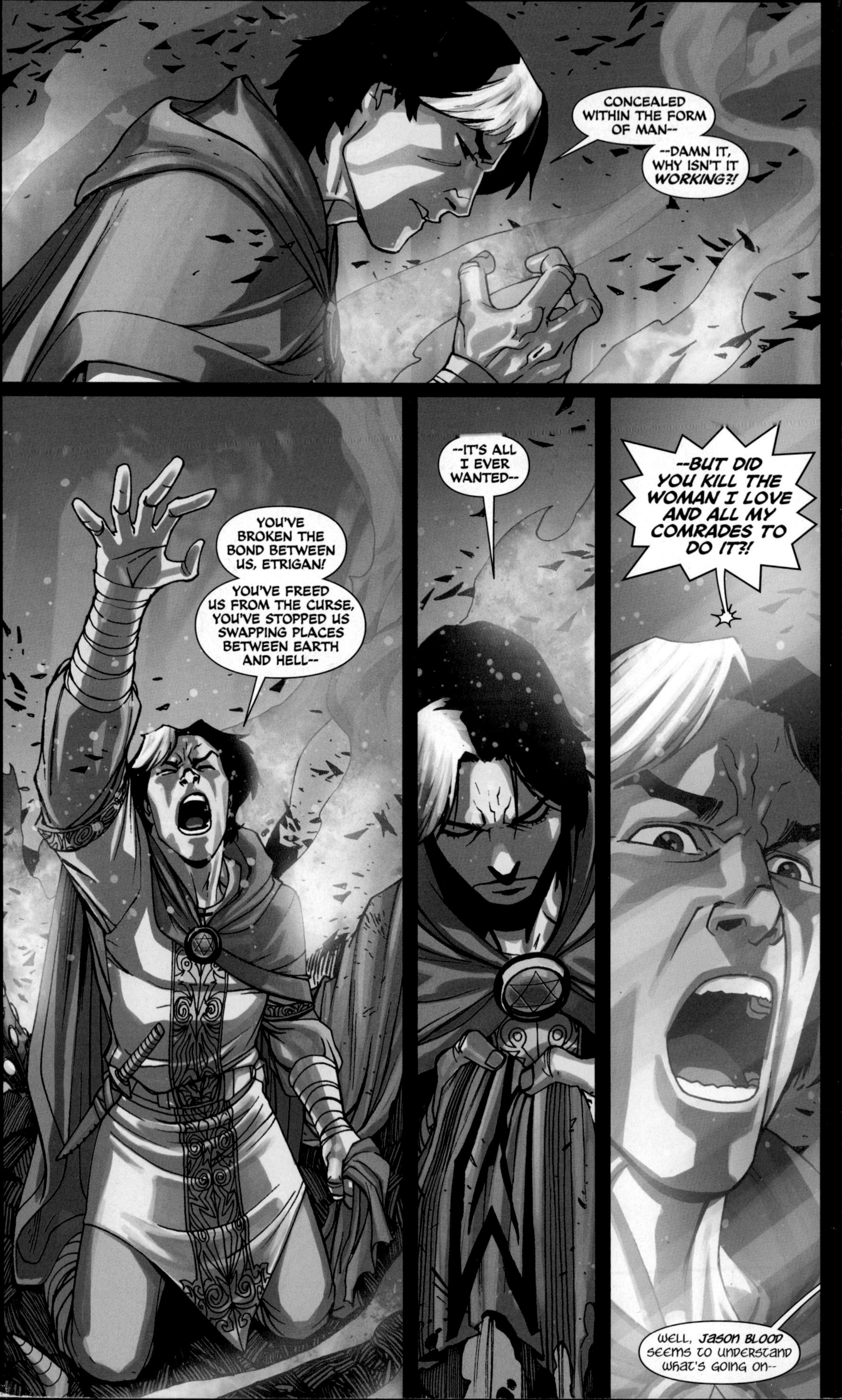
CONCEALED WITHIN THE FORM OF MAN--
--DAMN IT, WHY ISN'T IT WORKING?!
YOU'VE BROKEN THE BOND BETWEEN US, ETRIGAN!
YOU'VE FREED US FROM THE CURSE, YOU'VE STOPPED US SWAPPING PLACES BETWEEN EARTH AND HELL--
--IT'S ALL I EVER WANTED--
--BUT DID YOU KILL THE WOMAN I LOVE AND ALL MY COMRADES TO DO IT?!
WELL, JASON BLOOD SEEMS TO UNDERSTAND WHAT'S GOING ON--

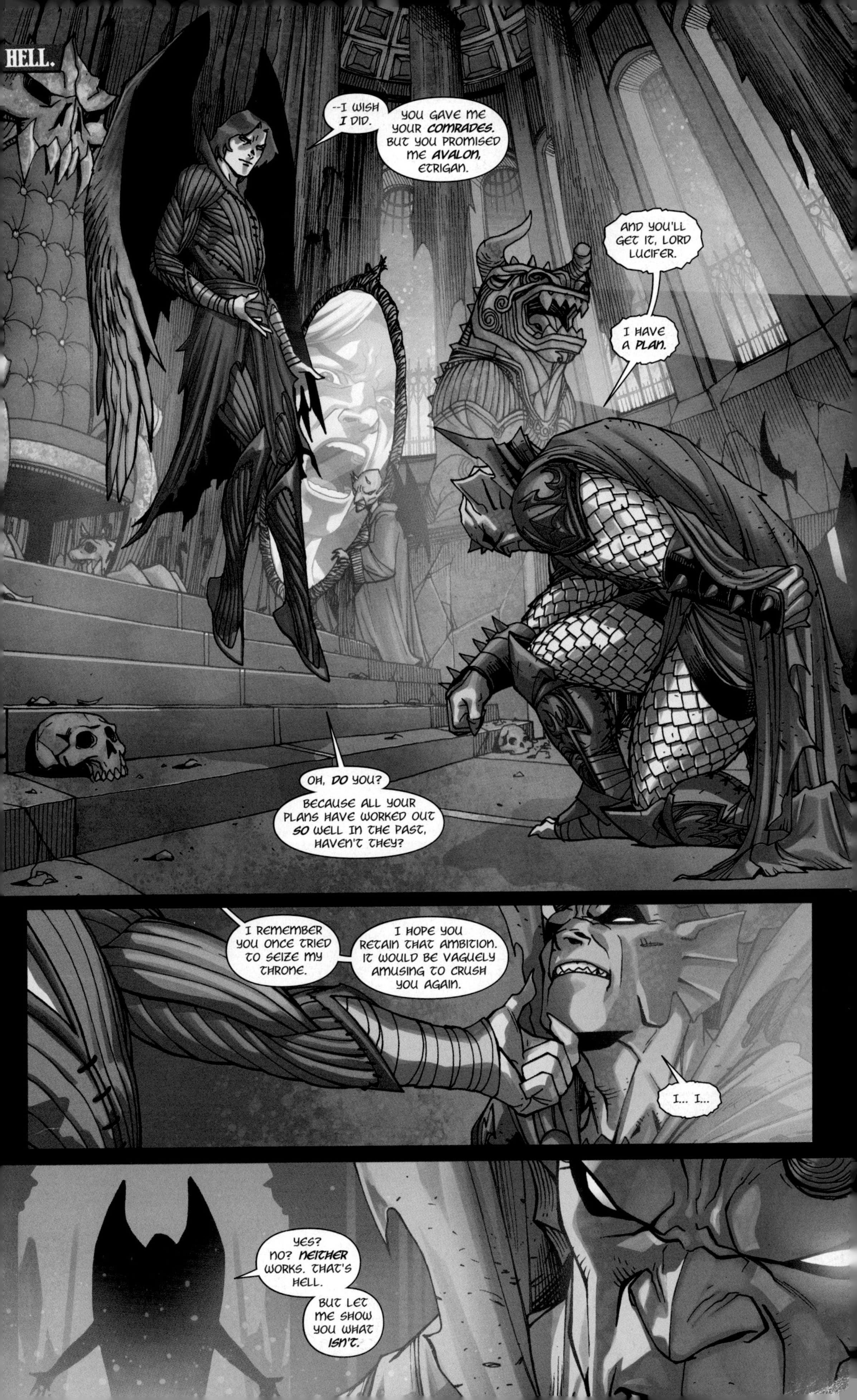
HELL.
--I WISH I DID.
YOU GAVE ME YOUR COMRADES. BUT YOU PROMISED ME AVALON, ETRIGAN.
AND YOU'LL GET IT, LORD LUCIFER.
I HAVE A PLAN.
OH, DO YOU?
BECAUSE ALL YOUR PLANS HAVE WORKED OUT SO WELL IN THE PAST, HAVEN'T THEY?
I REMEMBER YOU ONCE TRIED TO SEIZE MY THRONE.
I HOPE YOU RETAIN THAT AMBITION. IT WOULD BE VAGUELY AMUSING TO CRUSH YOU AGAIN.
I... I...
YES? NO? NEITHER WORKS. THAT'S HELL.
BUT LET ME SHOW YOU WHAT ISN'T.

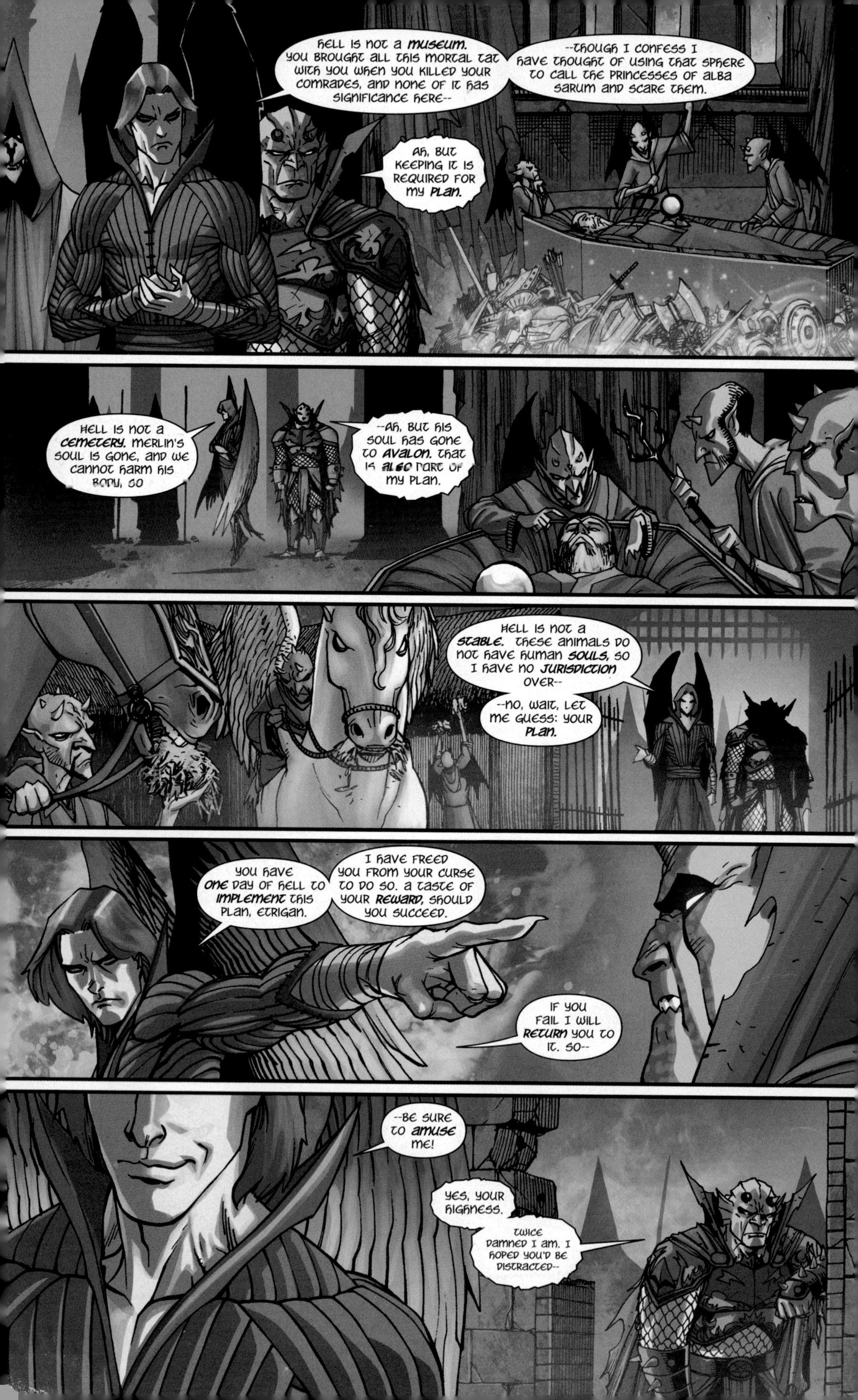
HELL IS NOT A MUSEUM. YOU BROUGHT ALL THIS MORTAL TAT WITH YOU WHEN YOU KILLED YOUR COMRADES, AND NONE OF IT HAS SIGNIFICANCE HERE--
--THOUGH I CONFESS I HAVE THOUGHT OF USING THAT SPHERE TO CALL THE PRINCESSES OF ALBA SARUM AND SCARE THEM.
AH, BUT KEEPING IT IS REQUIRED FOR MY PLAN.
HELL IS NOT A CEMETERY. MERLIN'S SOUL IS GONE, AND WE CANNOT HARM HIS BODY, SO
--AH, BUT HIS SOUL HAS GONE TO AVALON. THAT IS ALSO PART OF MY PLAN.
HELL IS NOT A STABLE. THESE ANIMALS DO NOT HAVE HUMAN SOULS, SO I HAVE NO JURISDICTION OVER--
--NO, WAIT, LET ME GUESS: YOUR PLAN.
YOU HAVE ONE DAY OF HELL TO IMPLEMENT THIS PLAN, ETRIGAN.
I HAVE FREED YOU FROM YOUR CURSE TO DO SO. A TASTE OF YOUR REWARD, SHOULD YOU SUCCEED.
IF YOU FAIL I WILL RETURN YOU TO IT. SO--
--BE SURE TO AMUSE ME!
YES, YOUR HIGHNESS.
TWICE DAMNED I AM. I HOPED YOU'D BE DISTRACTED--

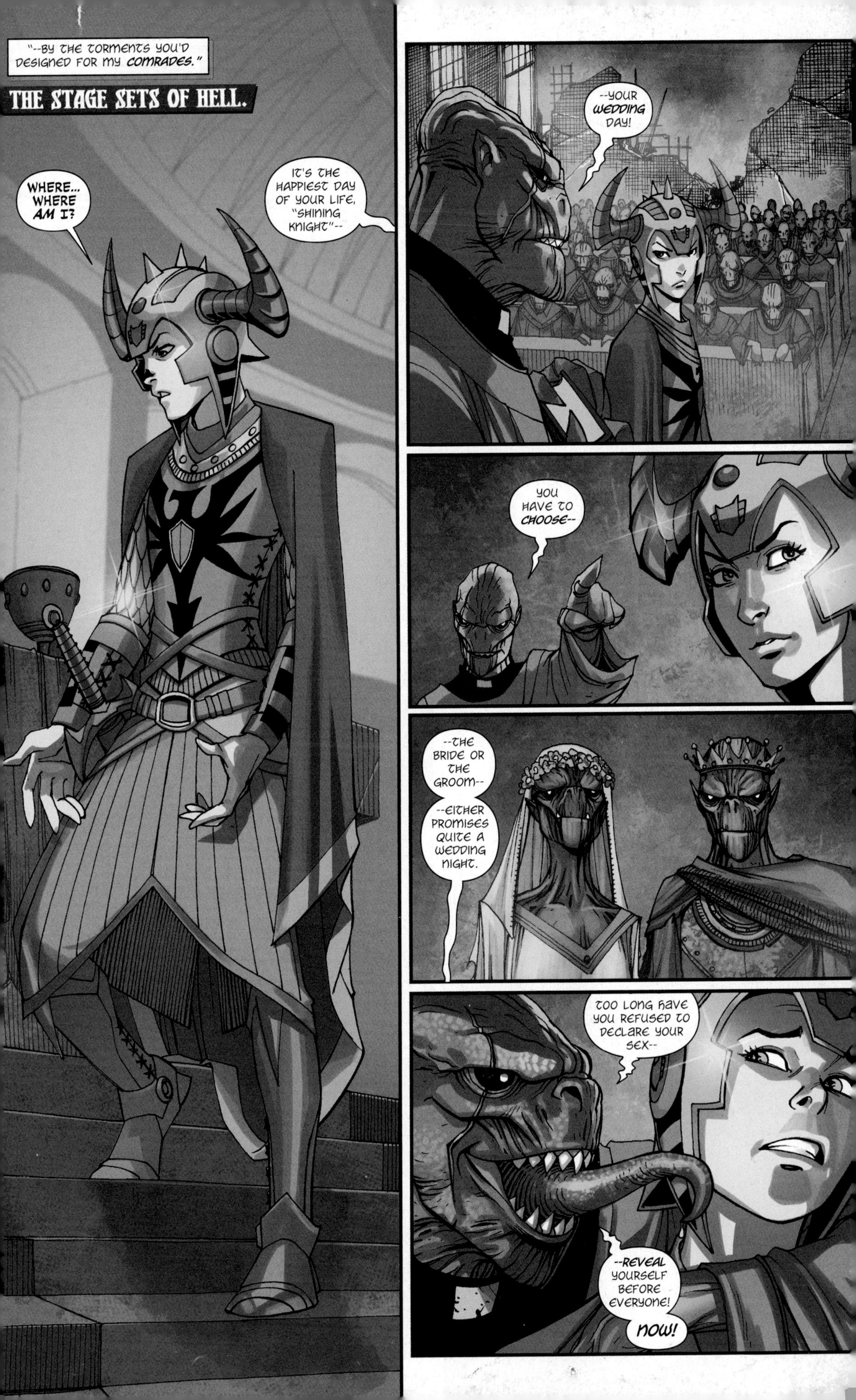
"--BY THE TORMENTS YOU'D DESIGNED FOR MY COMRADES."
THE STAGE SETS OF HELL.
WHERE... WHERE AM I?
IT'S THE HAPPIEST DAY OF YOUR LIFE, "SHINING KNIGHT"--
--YOUR WEDDING DAY!
YOU HAVE TO CHOOSE--
--THE BRIDE OR THE GROOM--
--EITHER PROMISES QUITE A WEDDING NIGHT.
TOO LONG HAVE YOU REFUSED TO DECLARE YOUR SEX--
--REVEAL YOURSELF BEFORE EVERYONE!
NOW!

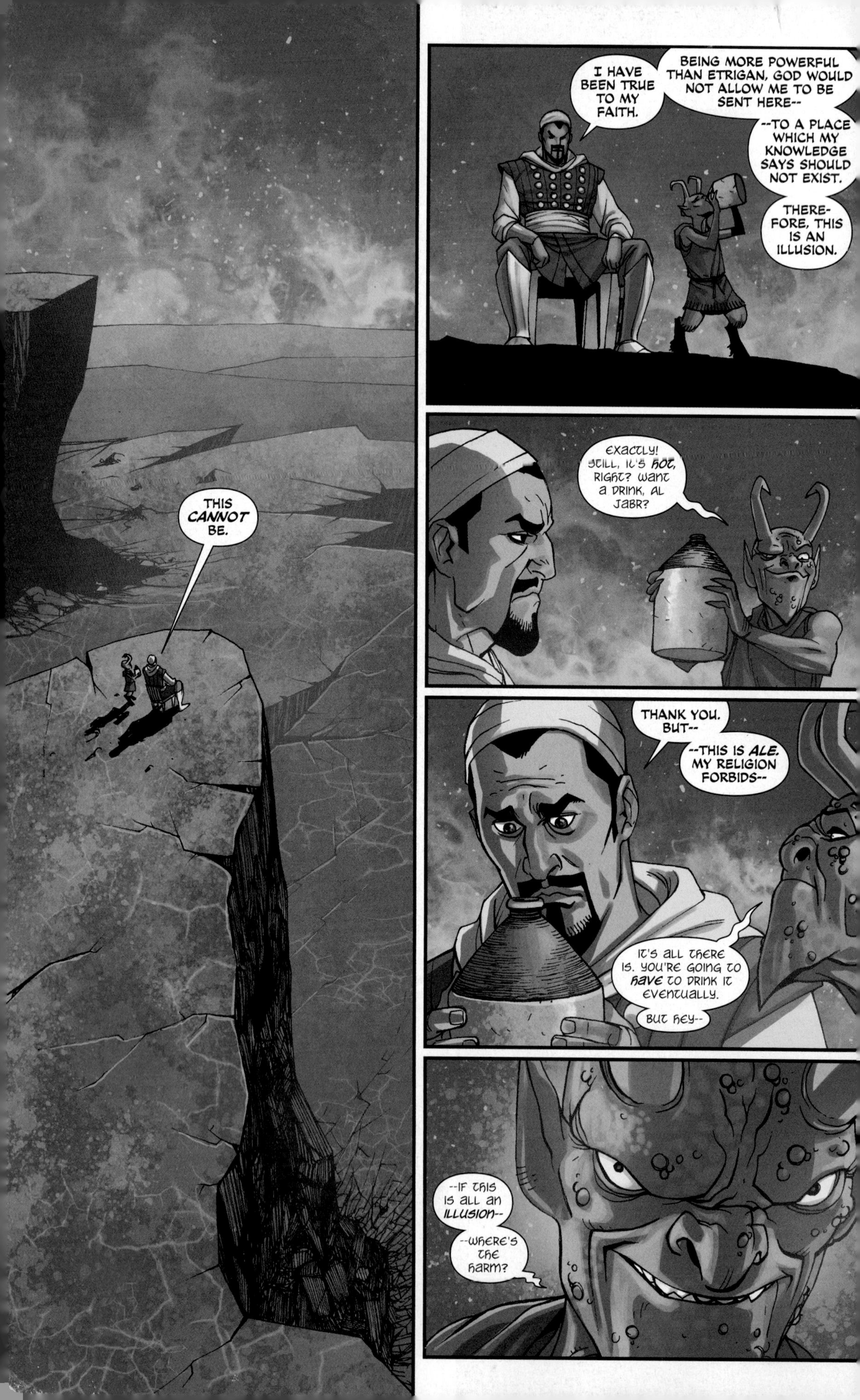
THIS CANNOT BE.
I HAVE BEEN TRUE TO MY FAITH.
BEING MORE POWERFUL THAN ETRIGAN, GOD WOULD NOT ALLOW ME TO BE SENT HERE--
--TO A PLACE WHICH MY KNOWLEDGE SAYS SHOULD NOT EXIST.
THEREFORE, THIS IS AN ILLUSION.
EXACTLY! STILL, IT'S HOT, RIGHT? WANT A DRINK, AL JABR?
THANK YOU. BUT--
--THIS IS ALE. MY RELIGION FORBIDS--
IT'S ALL THERE IS. YOU'RE GOING TO HAVE TO DRINK IT EVENTUALLY.
BUT HEY--
--IF THIS IS ALL AN ILLUSION--
--WHERE'S THE HARM?

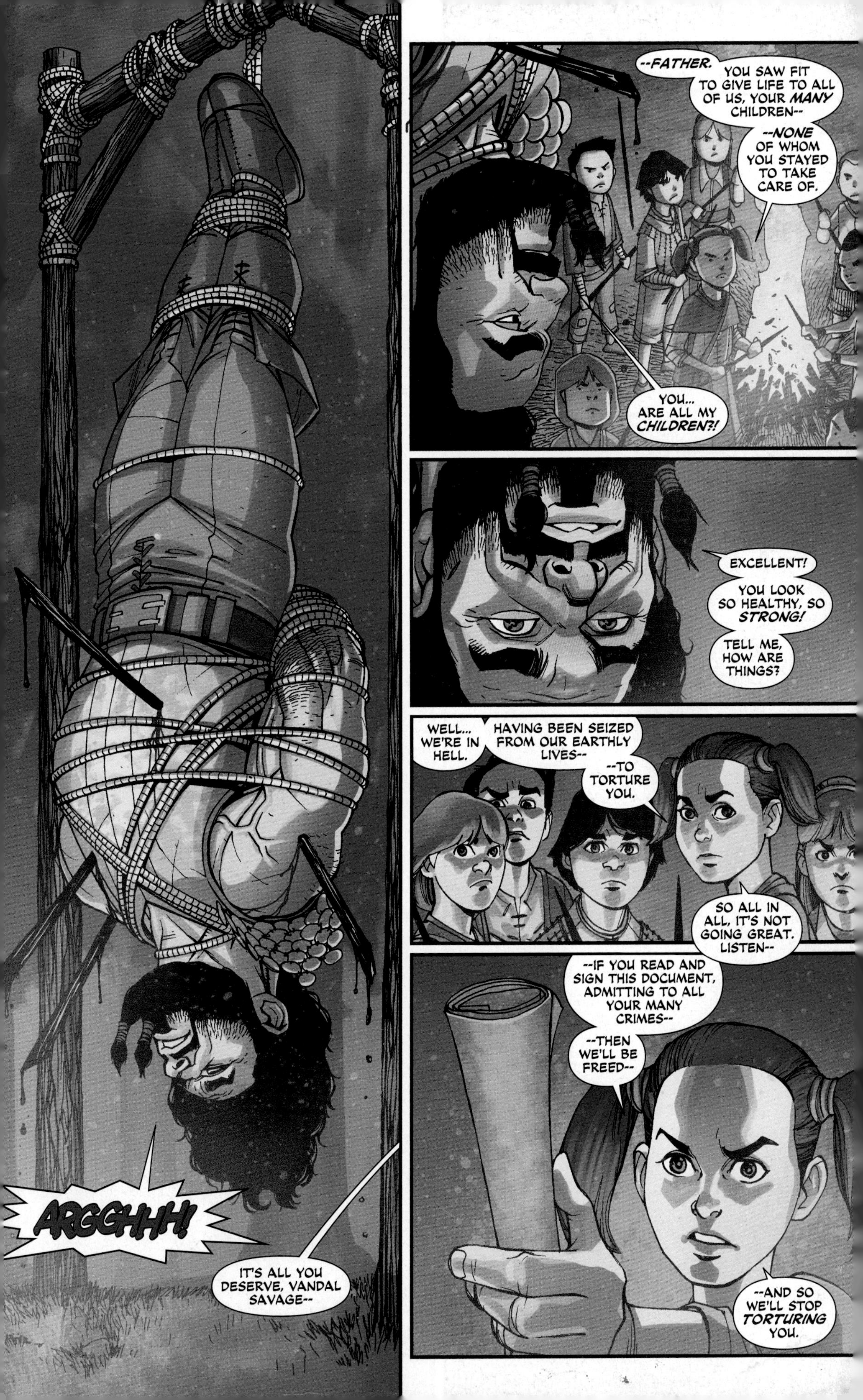
ARGGHHH!
IT'S ALL YOU DESERVE, VANDAL SAVAGE--
--FATHER.
YOU SAW FIT TO GIVE LIFE TO ALL OF US, YOUR MANY CHILDREN--
--NONE OF WHOM YOU STAYED TO TAKE CARE OF.
YOU... ARE ALL MY CHILDREN?!
EXCELLENT!
YOU LOOK SO HEALTHY, SO STRONG!
TELL ME, HOW ARE THINGS?
WELL... WE'RE IN HELL.
HAVING BEEN SEIZED FROM OUR EARTHLY LIVES--
--TO TORTURE YOU.
SO ALL IN ALL, IT'S NOT GOING GREAT. LISTEN--
--IF YOU READ AND SIGN THIS DOCUMENT, ADMITTING TO ALL YOUR MANY CRIMES--
--THEN WE'LL BE FREED--
--AND SO WE'LL STOP TORTURING YOU.

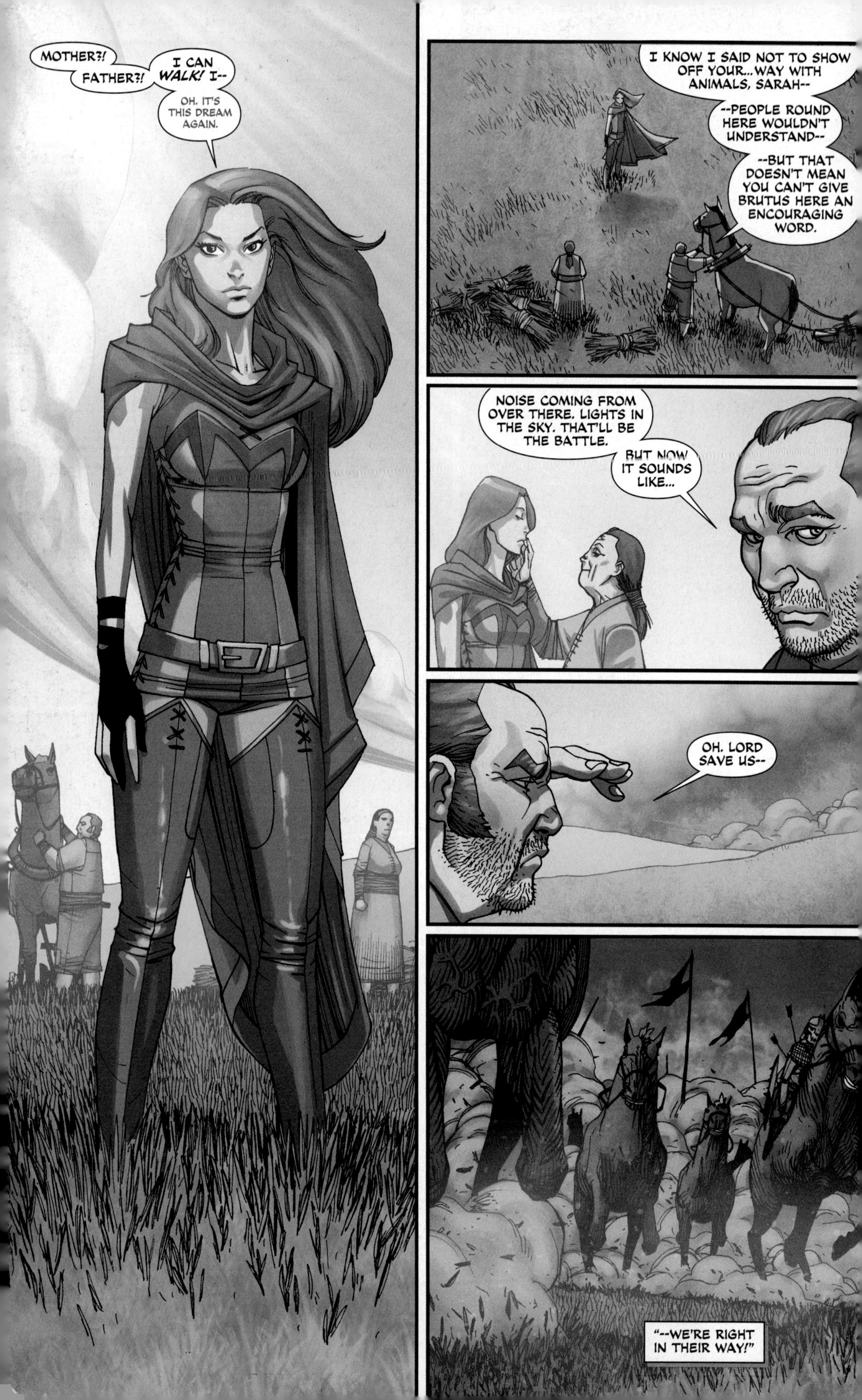
MOTHER?!
FATHER?!
I CAN WALK! I--
OH. IT'S THIS DREAM AGAIN.
I KNOW I SAID NOT TO SHOW OFF YOUR...WAY WITH ANIMALS, SARAH--
--PEOPLE ROUND HERE WOULDN'T UNDERSTAND--
--BUT THAT DOESN'T MEAN YOU CAN'T GIVE BRUTUS HERE AN ENCOURAGING WORD.
NOISE COMING FROM OVER THERE. LIGHTS IN THE SKY. THAT'LL BE THE BATTLE.
BUT NOW IT SOUNDS LIKE...
OH. LORD SAVE US--
"--WE'RE RIGHT IN THEIR WAY!"

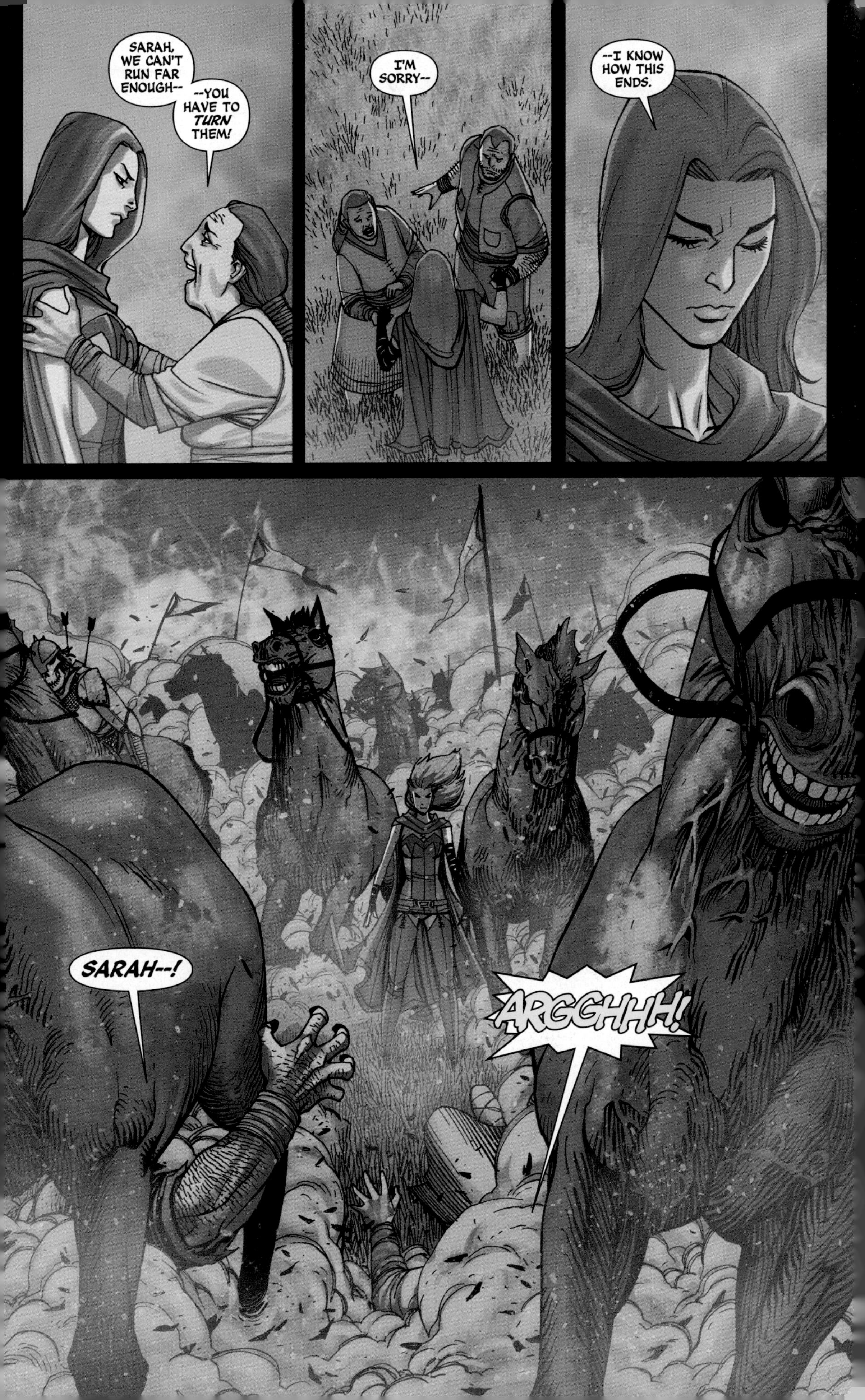

SARAH, WE CAN'T RUN FAR ENOUGH--
--YOU HAVE TO *TURN* THEM!
I'M SORRY--
--I KNOW HOW THIS ENDS.
SARAH--!
ARGGHHH!

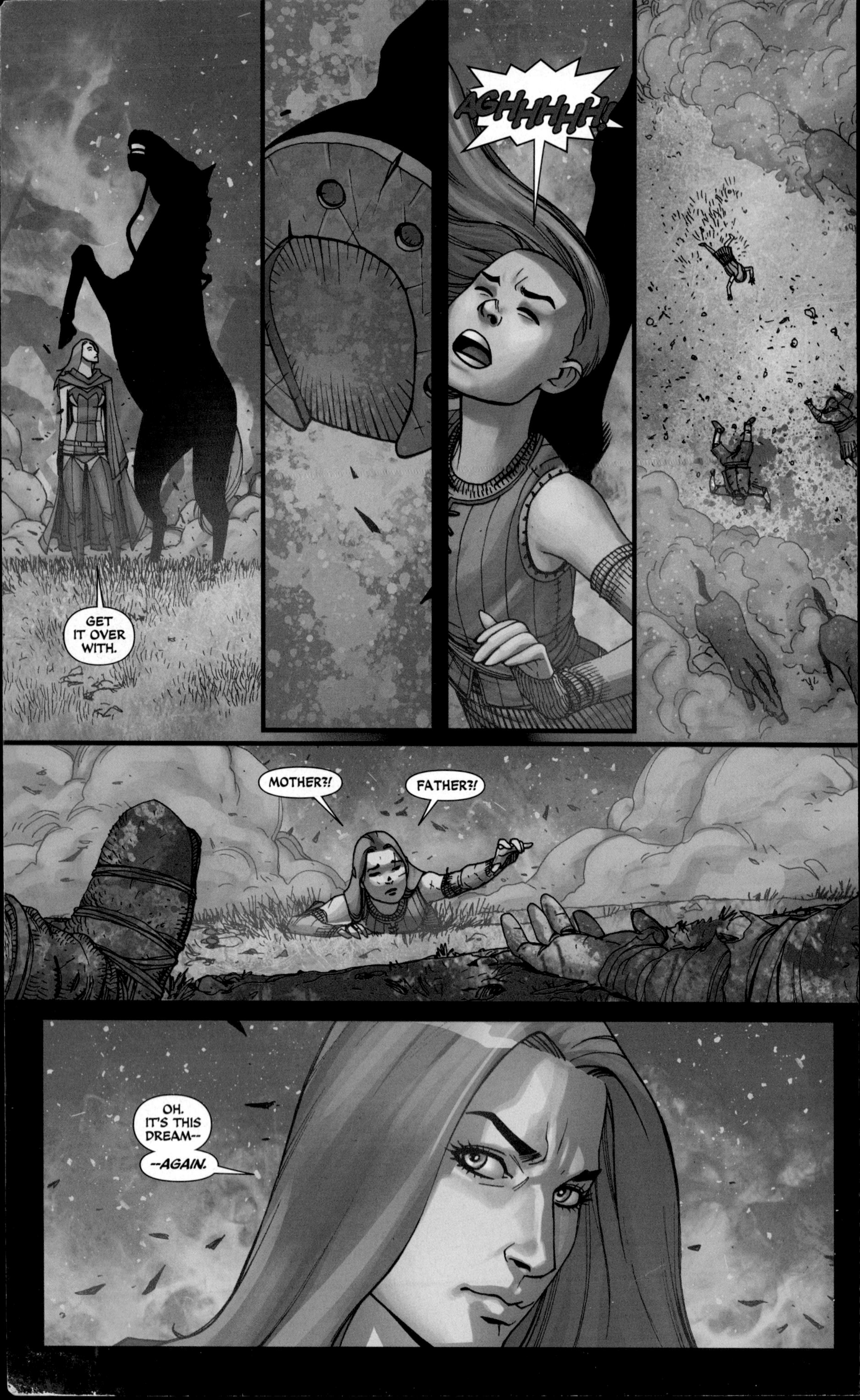
GET IT OVER WITH.
AGHHHHH!
MOTHER?!
FATHER?!
OH. IT'S THIS DREAM--
--AGAIN.

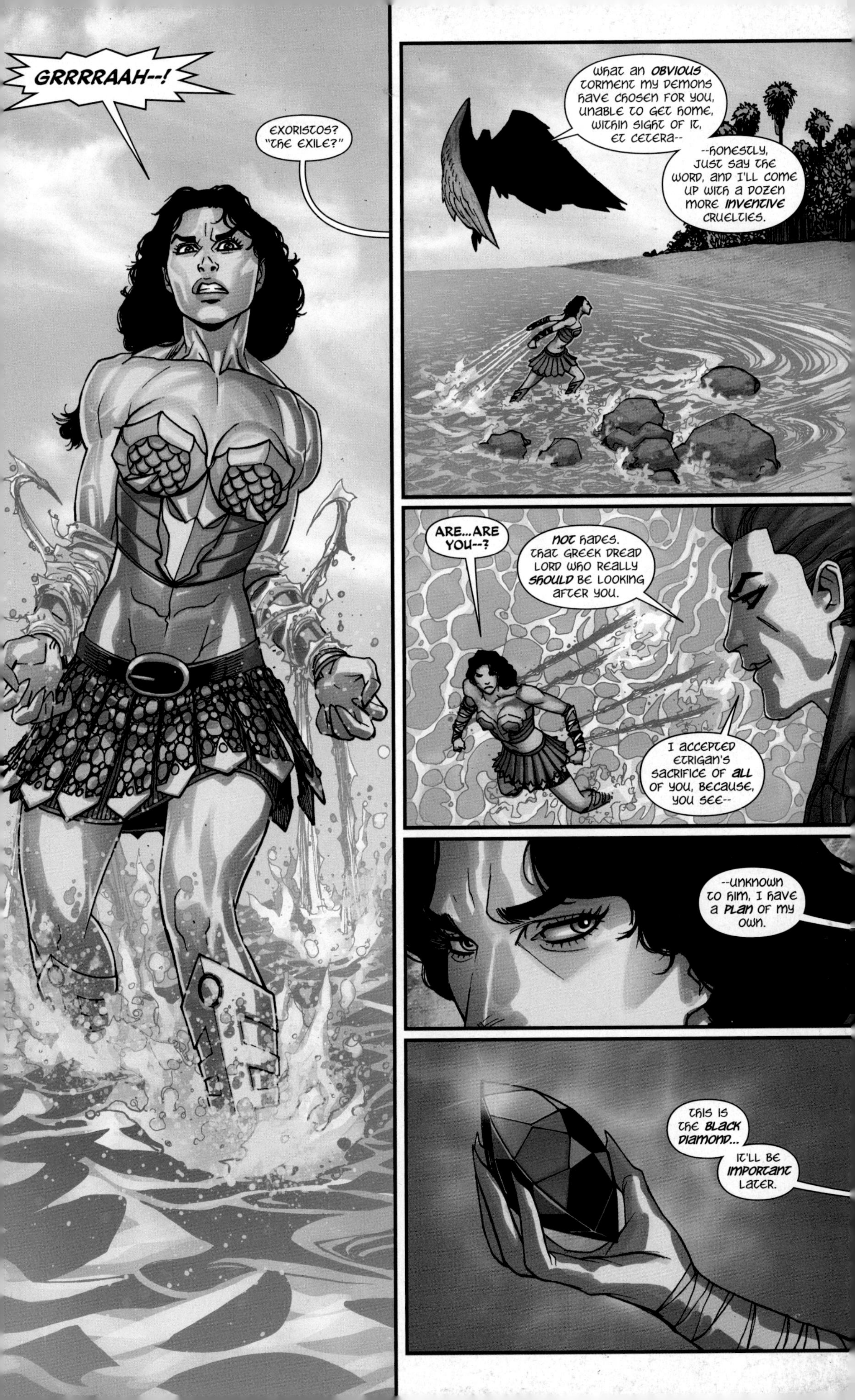
GRRRRAAH--!
EXORISTOS? "THE EXILE?"
WHAT AN OBVIOUS TORMENT MY DEMONS HAVE CHOSEN FOR YOU, UNABLE TO GET HOME, WITHIN SIGHT OF IT, ET CETERA--
--HONESTLY, JUST SAY THE WORD, AND I'LL COME UP WITH A DOZEN MORE INVENTIVE CRUELTIES.
ARE...ARE YOU--?
NOT HADES. THAT GREEK DREAD LORD WHO REALLY SHOULD BE LOOKING AFTER YOU.
I ACCEPTED ETRIGAN'S SACRIFICE OF ALL OF YOU, BECAUSE, YOU SEE--
--UNKNOWN TO HIM, I HAVE A PLAN OF MY OWN.
THIS IS THE BLACK DIAMOND...
IT'LL BE IMPORTANT LATER.

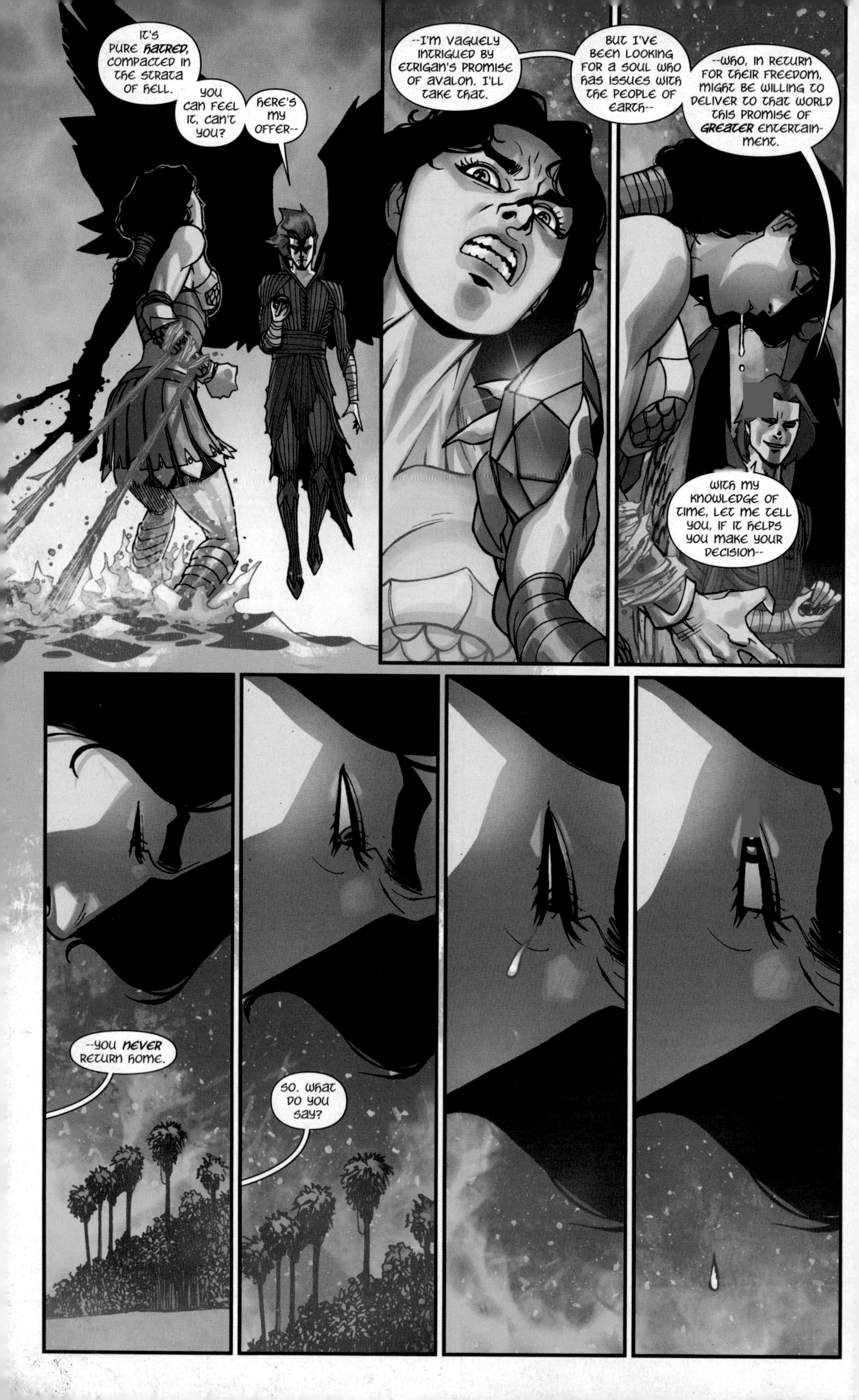
IT'S PURE HATRED, COMPACTED IN THE STRATA OF HELL.
YOU CAN FEEL IT, CAN'T YOU?
HERE'S MY OFFER--
--I'M VAGUELY INTRIGUED BY ETRIGAN'S PROMISE OF AVALON. I'LL TAKE THAT.
BUT I'VE BEEN LOOKING FOR A SOUL WHO HAS ISSUES WITH THE PEOPLE OF EARTH--
--WHO, IN RETURN FOR THEIR FREEDOM, MIGHT BE WILLING TO DELIVER TO THAT WORLD THIS PROMISE OF GREATER ENTERTAINMENT.
WITH MY KNOWLEDGE OF TIME, LET ME TELL YOU, IF IT HELPS YOU MAKE YOUR DECISION--
--YOU NEVER RETURN HOME.
SO. WHAT DO YOU SAY?

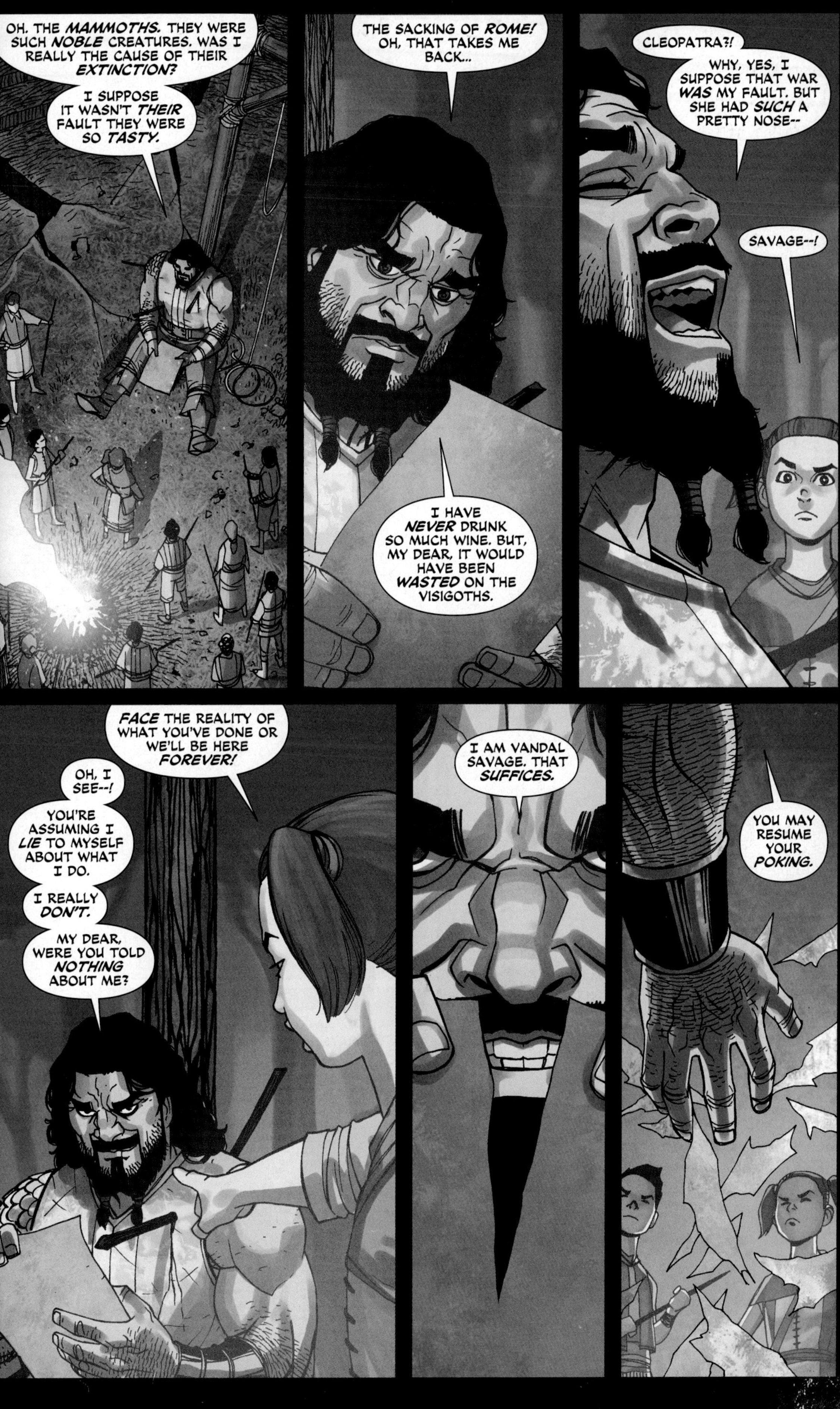
OH. THE *MAMMOTHS.* THEY WERE SUCH *NOBLE* CREATURES. WAS I REALLY THE CAUSE OF THEIR *EXTINCTION?*
I SUPPOSE IT WASN'T *THEIR* FAULT THEY WERE SO *TASTY.*
THE SACKING OF *ROME!* OH, THAT TAKES ME BACK...
I HAVE *NEVER* DRUNK SO MUCH WINE. BUT, MY DEAR, IT WOULD HAVE BEEN *WASTED* ON THE VISIGOTHS.
CLEOPATRA?!
WHY, YES, I SUPPOSE THAT WAR *WAS* MY FAULT. BUT SHE HAD *SUCH* A PRETTY NOSE--
SAVAGE--!
FACE THE REALITY OF WHAT YOU'VE DONE OR WE'LL BE HERE *FOREVER!*
OH, I SEE--!
YOU'RE ASSUMING I *LIE* TO MYSELF ABOUT WHAT I DO.
I REALLY *DON'T.*
MY DEAR, WERE YOU TOLD *NOTHING* ABOUT ME?
I AM VANDAL SAVAGE. THAT *SUFFICES.*
YOU MAY RESUME YOUR *POKING.*

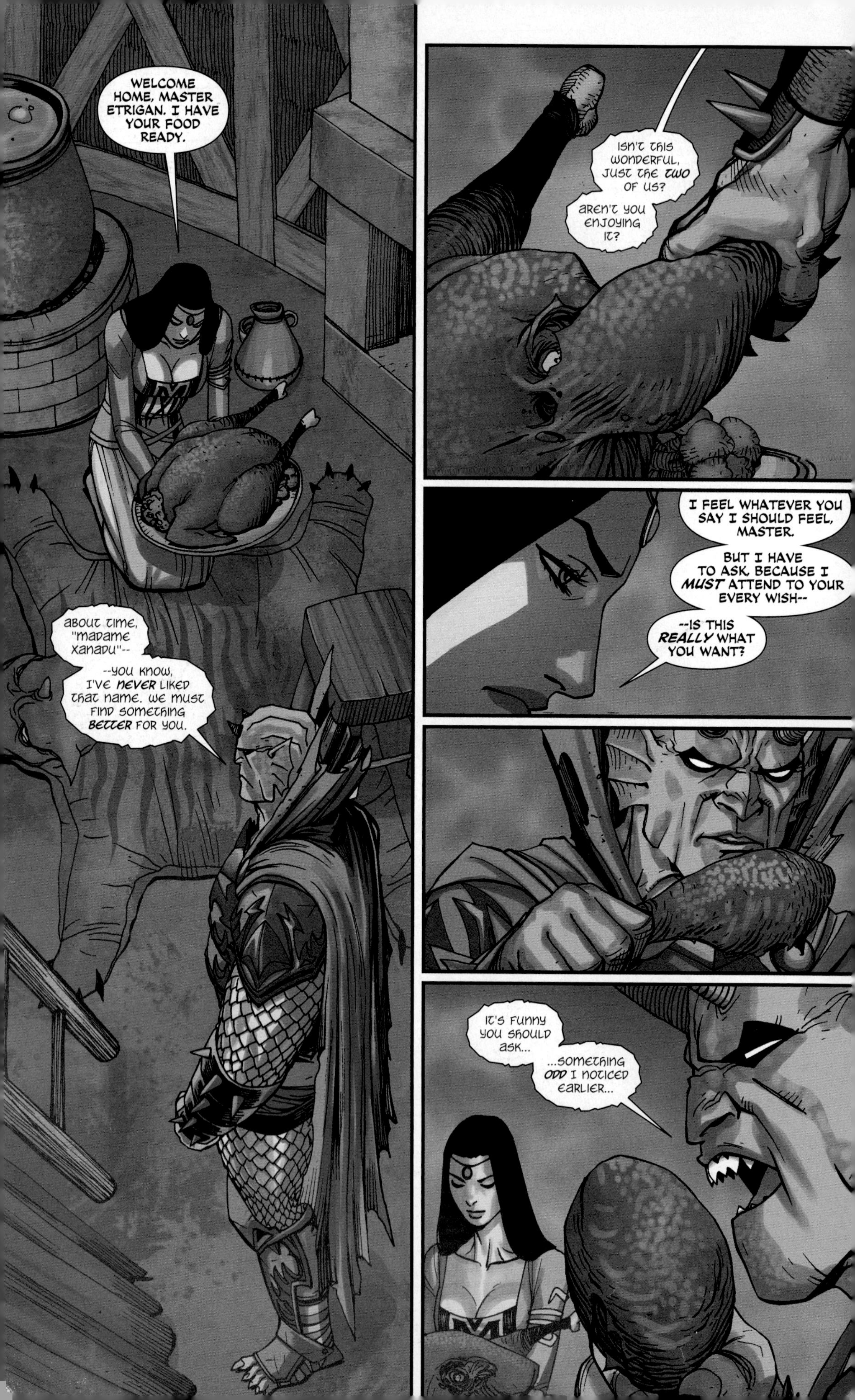
WELCOME HOME, MASTER ETRIGAN. I HAVE YOUR FOOD READY.
ABOUT TIME, "MADAME XANADU"--
--YOU KNOW, I'VE NEVER LIKED THAT NAME. WE MUST FIND SOMETHING BETTER FOR YOU.
ISN'T THIS WONDERFUL, JUST THE TWO OF US?
AREN'T YOU ENJOYING IT?
I FEEL WHATEVER YOU SAY I SHOULD FEEL, MASTER.
BUT I HAVE TO ASK, BECAUSE I MUST ATTEND TO YOUR EVERY WISH--
--IS THIS REALLY WHAT YOU WANT?
IT'S FUNNY YOU SHOULD ASK...
...SOMETHING ODD I NOTICED EARLIER...

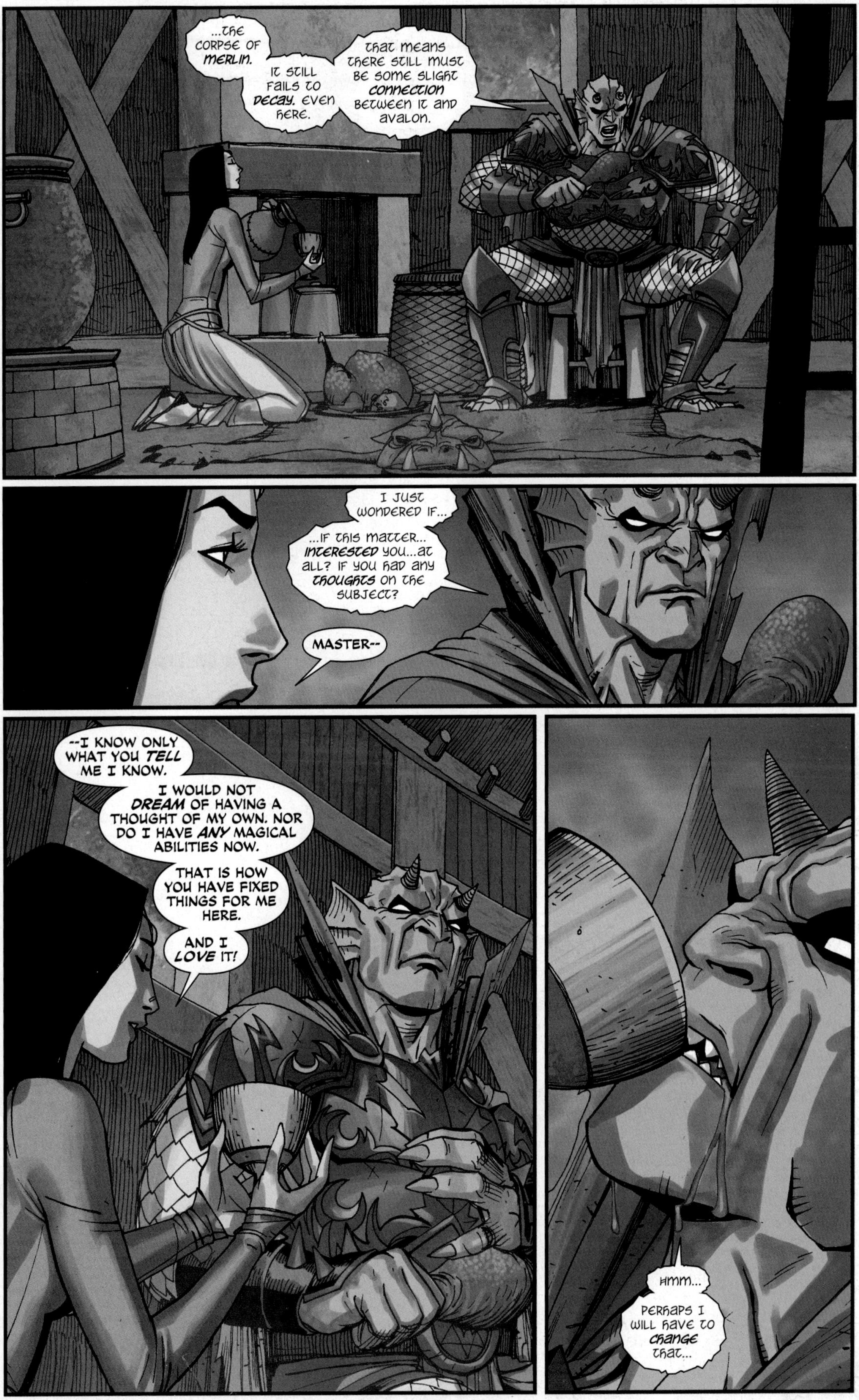
...THE CORPSE OF MERLIN.
IT STILL FAILS TO DECAY. EVEN HERE.
THAT MEANS THERE STILL MUST BE SOME SLIGHT CONNECTION BETWEEN IT AND AVALON.
I JUST WONDERED IF...
...IF THIS MATTER... INTERESTED YOU...AT ALL? IF YOU HAD ANY THOUGHTS ON THE SUBJECT?
MASTER--
--I KNOW ONLY WHAT YOU TELL ME I KNOW.
I WOULD NOT DREAM OF HAVING A THOUGHT OF MY OWN. NOR DO I HAVE ANY MAGICAL ABILITIES NOW.
THAT IS HOW YOU HAVE FIXED THINGS FOR ME HERE.
AND I LOVE IT!
HMM...
PERHAPS I WILL HAVE TO CHANGE THAT...

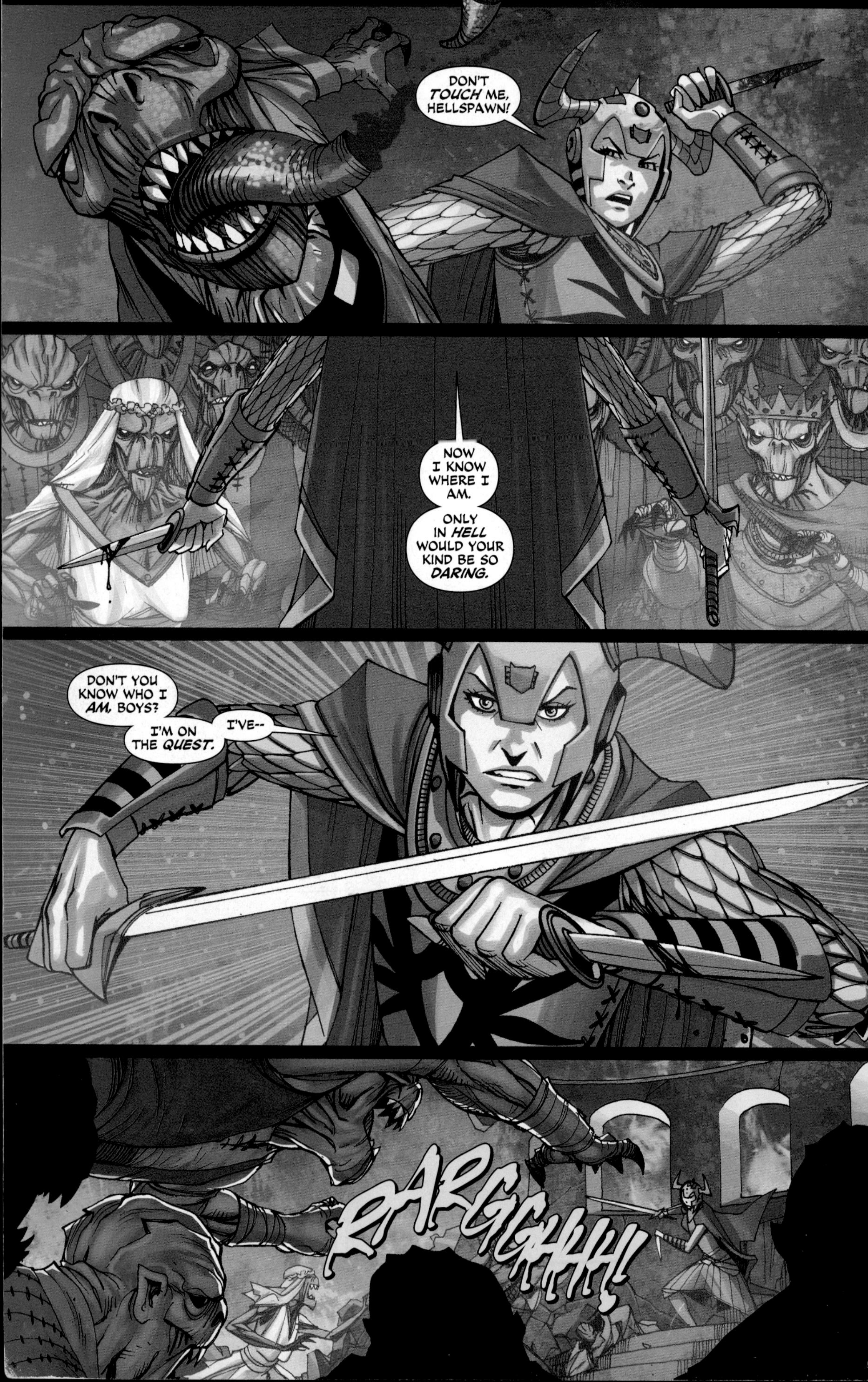
DON'T *TOUCH* ME, HELLSPAWN!
NOW I KNOW WHERE I AM.
ONLY IN *HELL* WOULD YOUR KIND BE SO *DARING.*
DON'T YOU KNOW WHO I *AM,* BOYS?
I'M ON THE *QUEST.*
I'VE--
RARGGHHH!

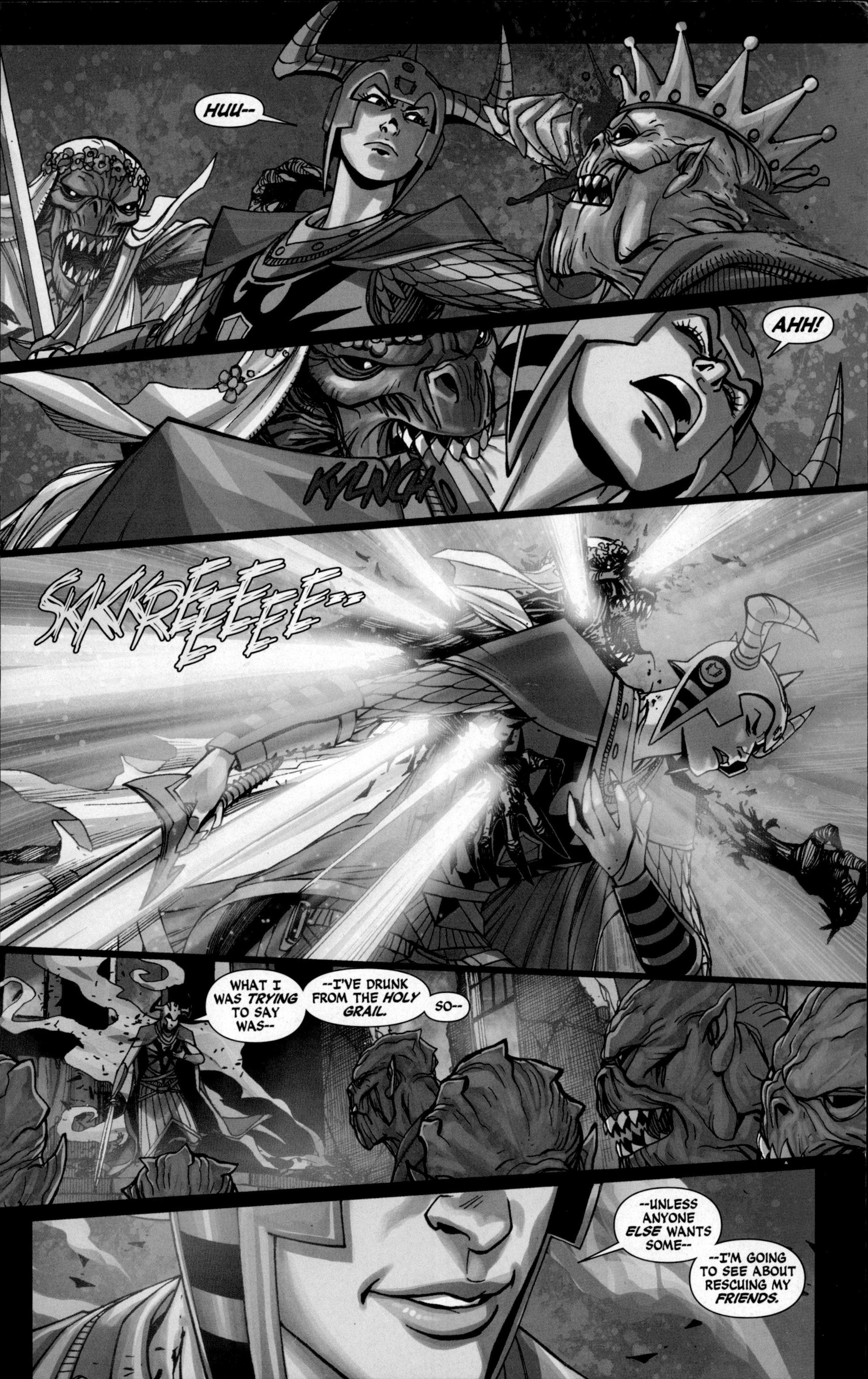
HUU--
AHH!
KYLNCH
SKKKREEEEEE--
WHAT I WAS TRYING TO SAY WAS--
--I'VE DRUNK FROM THE HOLY GRAIL.
SO--
--UNLESS ANYONE ELSE WANTS SOME--
--I'M GOING TO SEE ABOUT RESCUING MY FRIENDS.

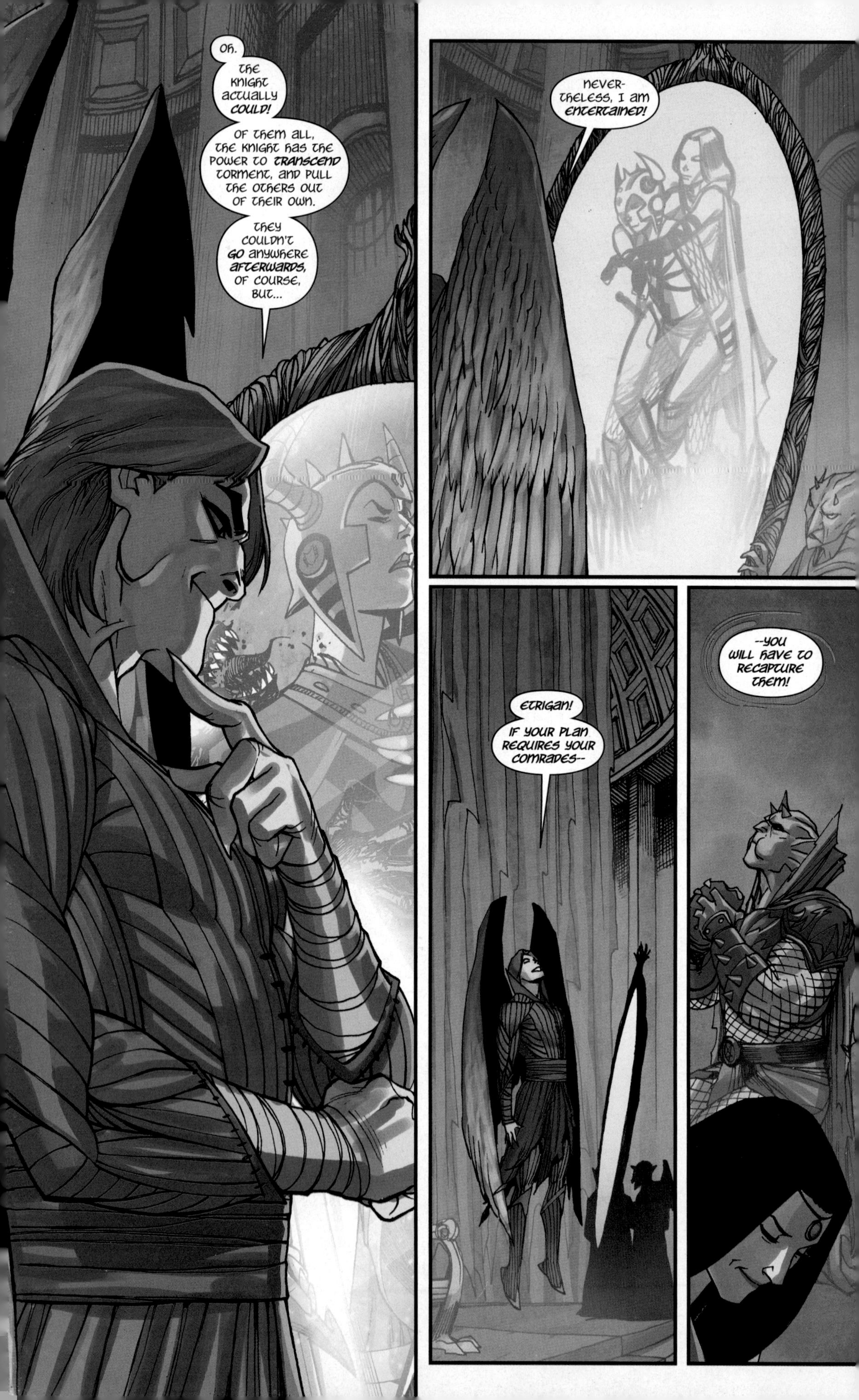
OH.
THE KNIGHT ACTUALLY COULD!
OF THEM ALL, THE KNIGHT HAS THE POWER TO TRANSCEND TORMENT, AND PULL THE OTHERS OUT OF THEIR OWN.
THEY COULDN'T GO ANYWHERE AFTERWARDS, OF COURSE, BUT...
NEVER-THELESS, I AM ENTERTAINED!
ETRIGAN!
IF YOUR PLAN REQUIRES YOUR COMRADES--
--YOU WILL HAVE TO RECAPTURE THEM!

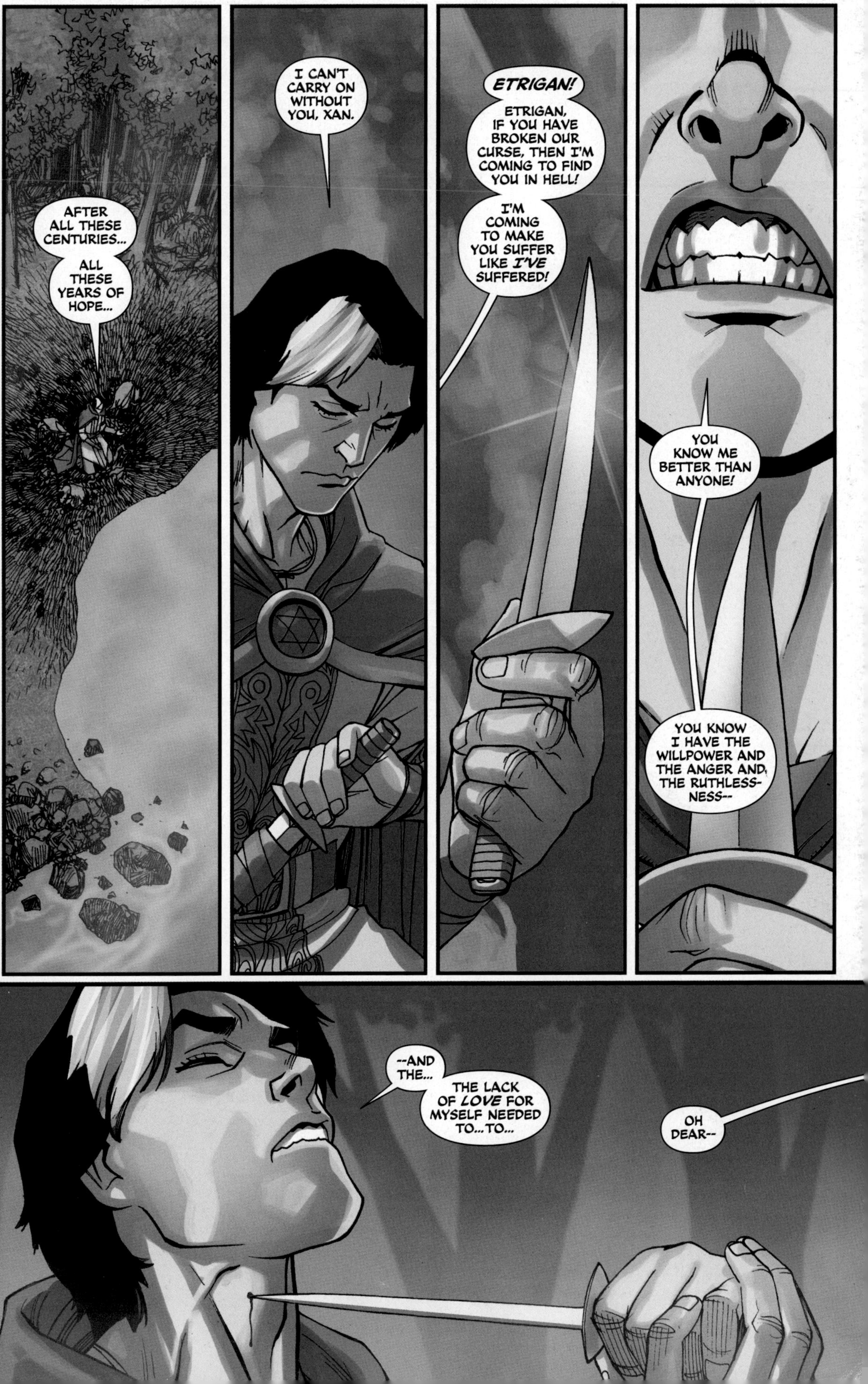
AFTER ALL THESE CENTURIES...
ALL THESE YEARS OF HOPE...
I CAN'T CARRY ON WITHOUT YOU, XAN.
ETRIGAN!
ETRIGAN, IF YOU HAVE BROKEN OUR CURSE, THEN I'M COMING TO FIND YOU IN HELL!
I'M COMING TO MAKE YOU SUFFER LIKE I'VE SUFFERED!
YOU KNOW ME BETTER THAN ANYONE!
YOU KNOW I HAVE THE WILLPOWER AND THE ANGER AND THE RUTHLESS-NESS--
--AND THE...
THE LACK OF LOVE FOR MYSELF NEEDED TO...TO...
OH DEAR--

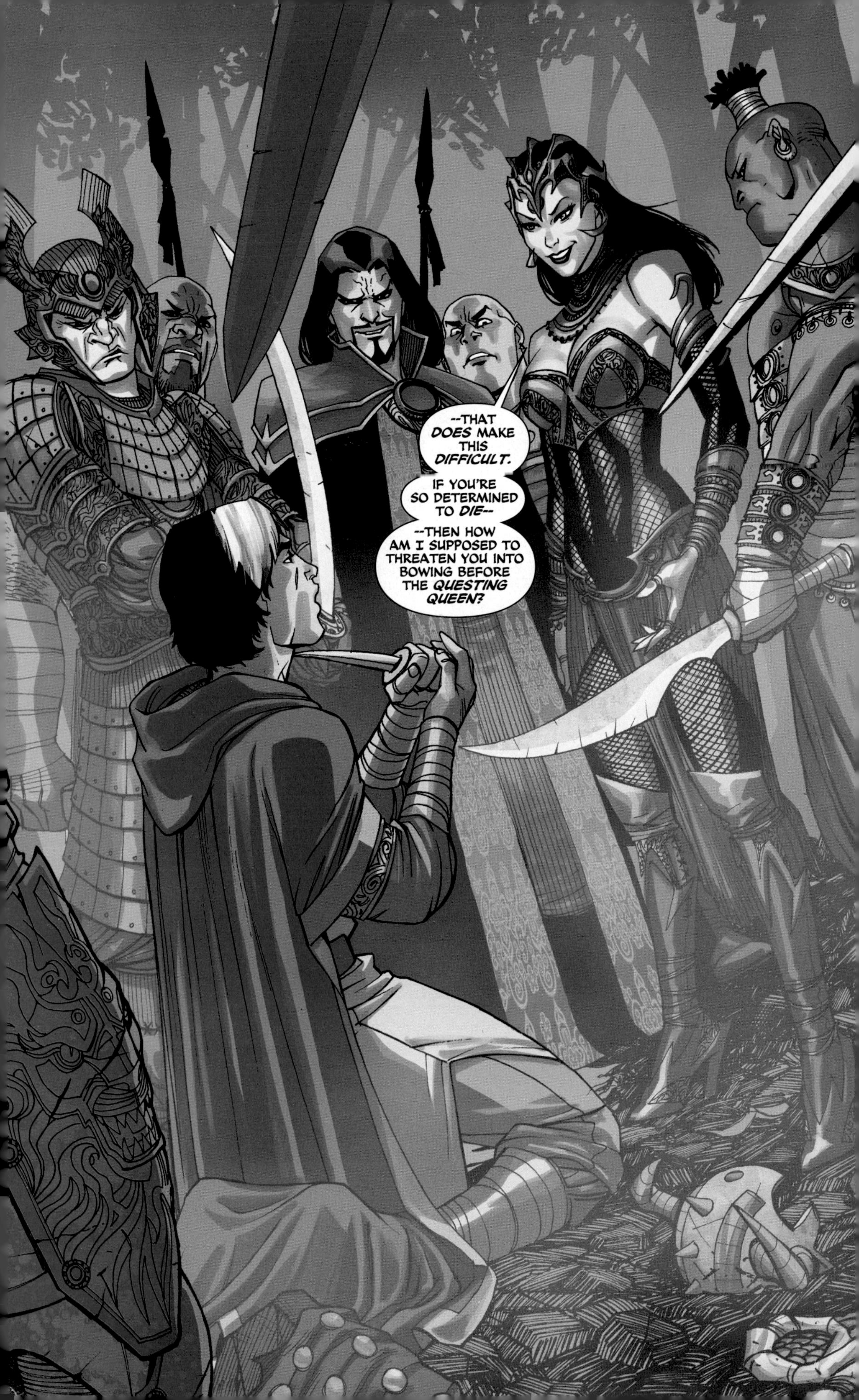
--THAT DOES MAKE THIS DIFFICULT.
IF YOU'RE SO DETERMINED TO DIE--
--THEN HOW AM I SUPPOSED TO THREATEN YOU INTO BOWING BEFORE THE QUESTING QUEEN?

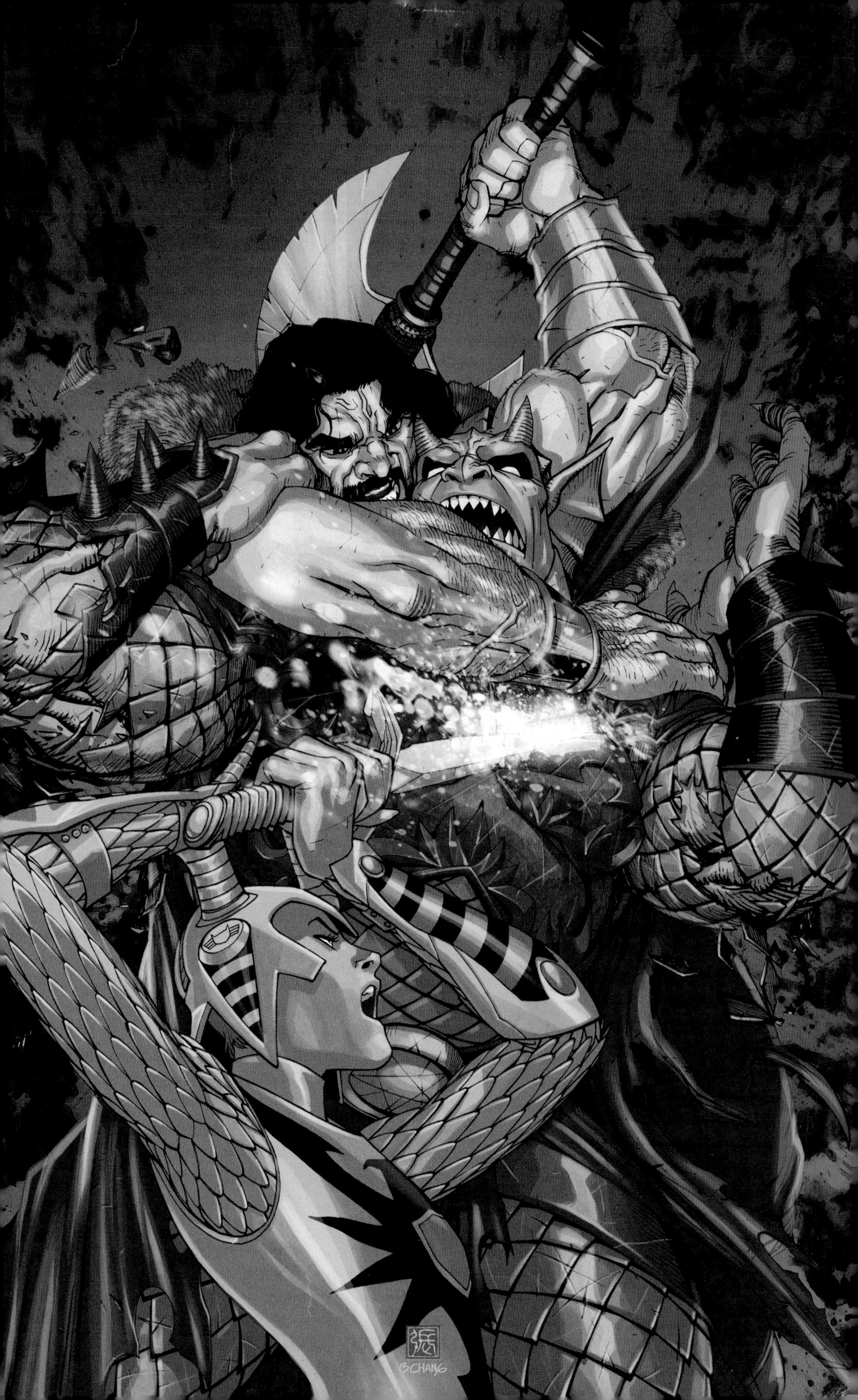
B.CHANG

PAUL CORNELL
writer

BERNARD CHANG
artist

BERNARD CHANG
cover artist

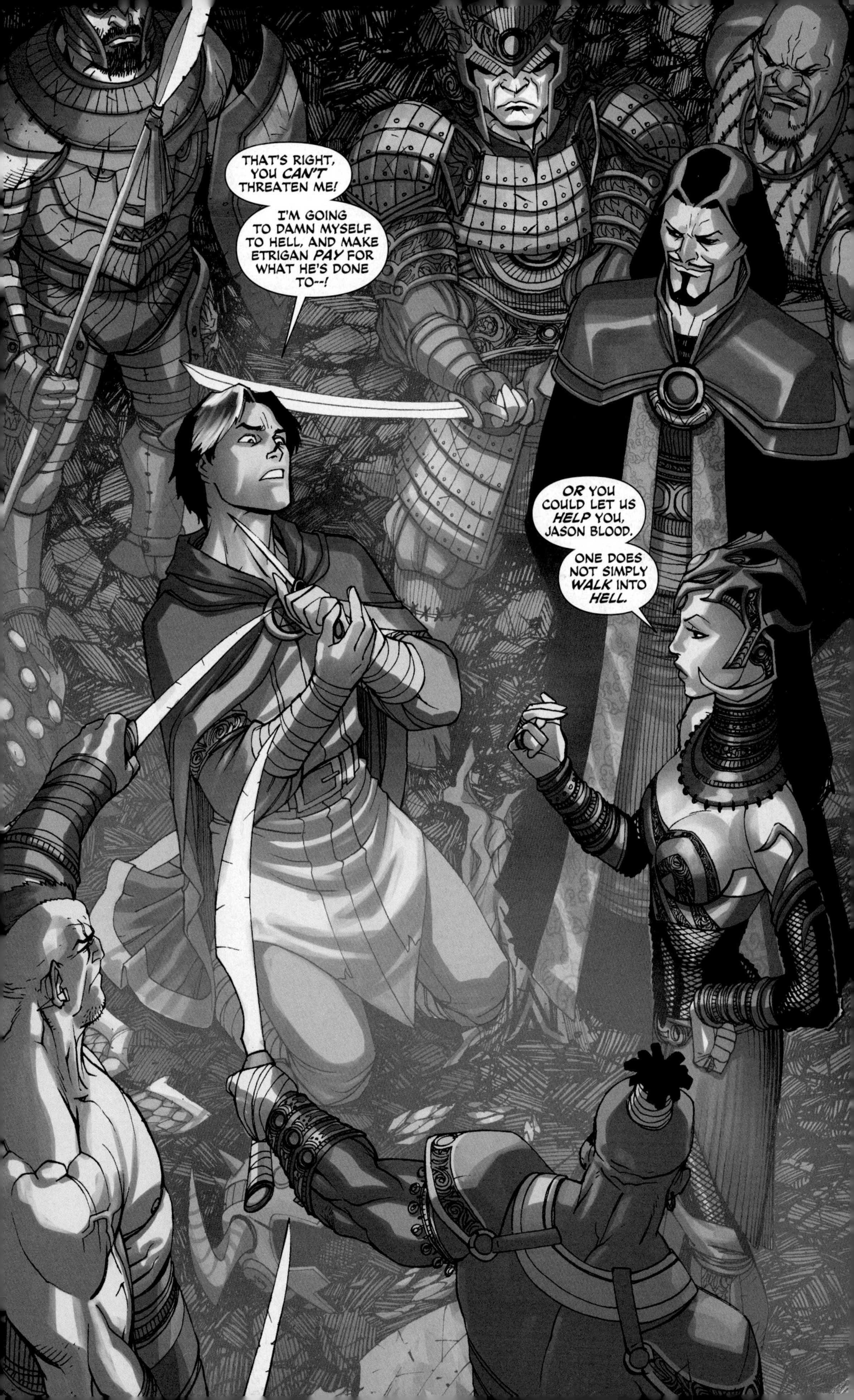
THAT'S RIGHT, YOU *CAN'T* THREATEN ME!
I'M GOING TO DAMN MYSELF TO HELL, AND MAKE ETRIGAN *PAY* FOR WHAT HE'S DONE TO--!
OR YOU COULD LET US *HELP* YOU, JASON BLOOD.
ONE DOES NOT SIMPLY *WALK* INTO *HELL.*

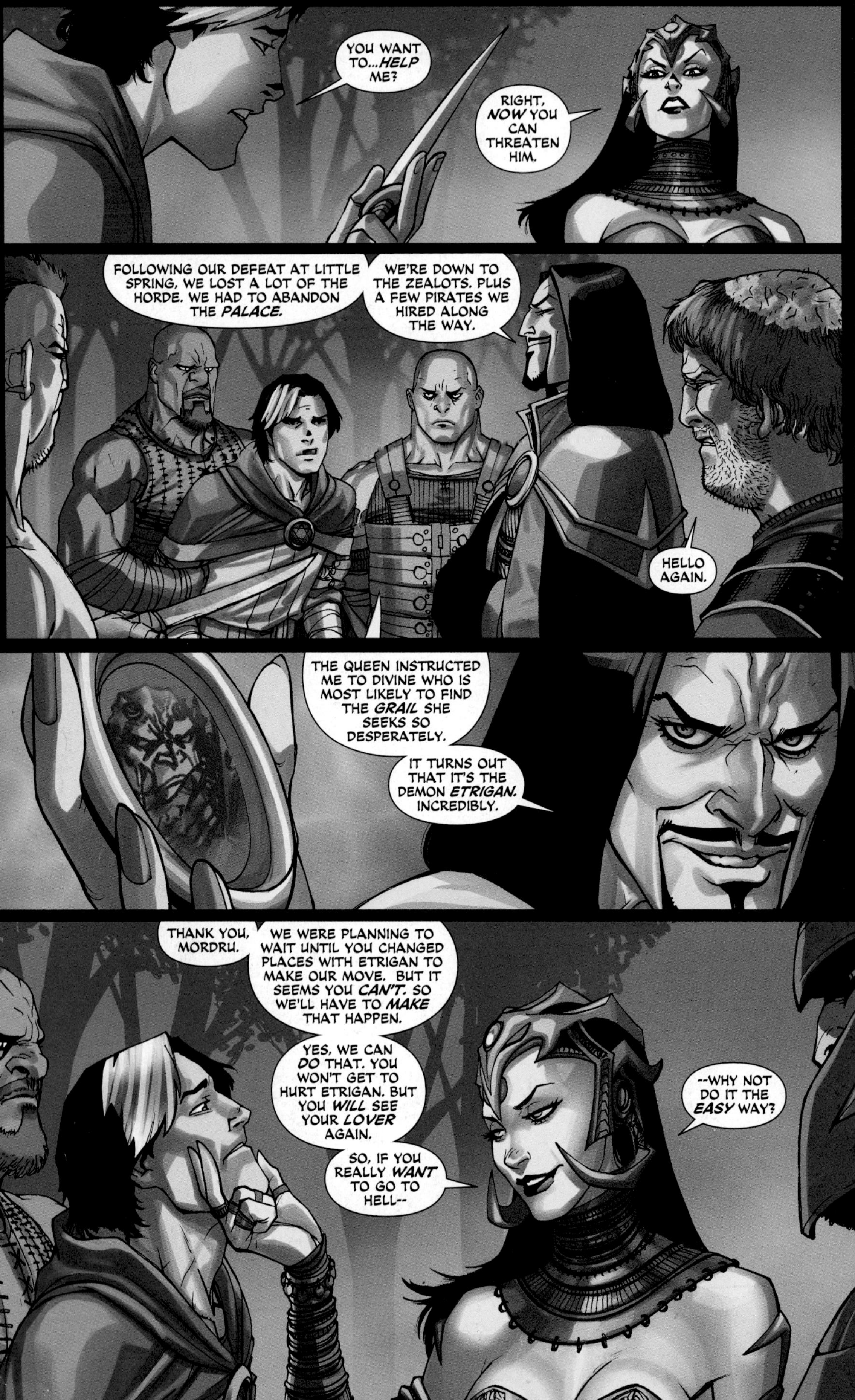

YOU WANT TO...HELP ME?
RIGHT, NOW YOU CAN THREATEN HIM.
FOLLOWING OUR DEFEAT AT LITTLE SPRING, WE LOST A LOT OF THE HORDE. WE HAD TO ABANDON THE PALACE.
WE'RE DOWN TO THE ZEALOTS. PLUS A FEW PIRATES WE HIRED ALONG THE WAY.
HELLO AGAIN.
THE QUEEN INSTRUCTED ME TO DIVINE WHO IS MOST LIKELY TO FIND THE GRAIL SHE SEEKS SO DESPERATELY.
IT TURNS OUT THAT IT'S THE DEMON ETRIGAN. INCREDIBLY.
THANK YOU, MORDRU.
WE WERE PLANNING TO WAIT UNTIL YOU CHANGED PLACES WITH ETRIGAN TO MAKE OUR MOVE. BUT IT SEEMS YOU CAN'T. SO WE'LL HAVE TO MAKE THAT HAPPEN.
YES, WE CAN DO THAT. YOU WON'T GET TO HURT ETRIGAN. BUT YOU WILL SEE YOUR LOVER AGAIN.
SO, IF YOU REALLY WANT TO GO TO HELL--
--WHY NOT DO IT THE EASY WAY?

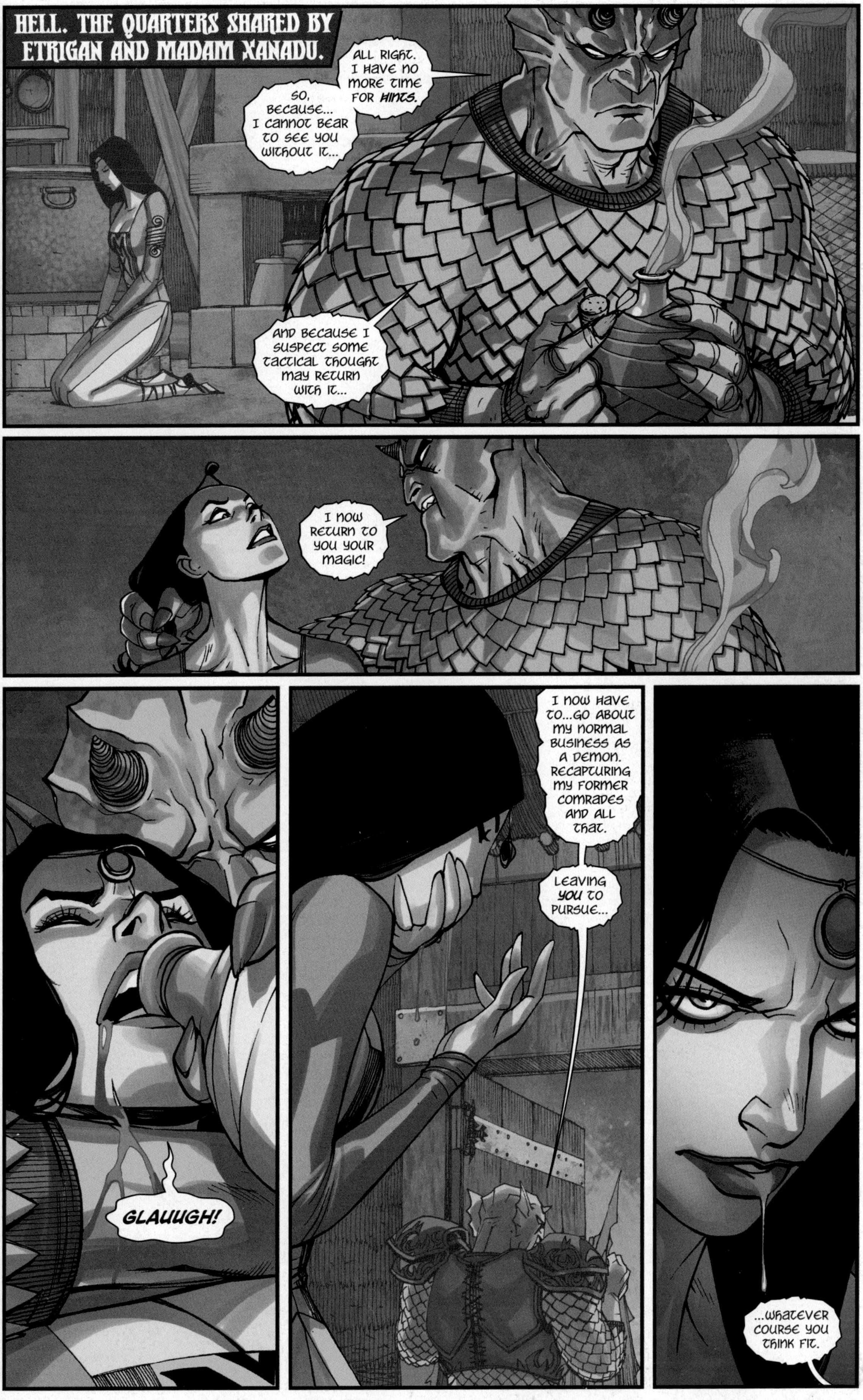
HELL. THE QUARTERS SHARED BY ETRIGAN AND MADAM XANADU.
ALL RIGHT. I HAVE NO MORE TIME FOR HINTS.
SO, BECAUSE... I CANNOT BEAR TO SEE YOU WITHOUT IT...
AND BECAUSE I SUSPECT SOME TACTICAL THOUGHT MAY RETURN WITH IT...
I NOW RETURN TO YOU YOUR MAGIC!
GLAUUGH!
I NOW HAVE TO...GO ABOUT MY NORMAL BUSINESS AS A DEMON. RECAPTURING MY FORMER COMRADES AND ALL THAT.
LEAVING YOU TO PURSUE...
...WHATEVER COURSE YOU THINK FIT.

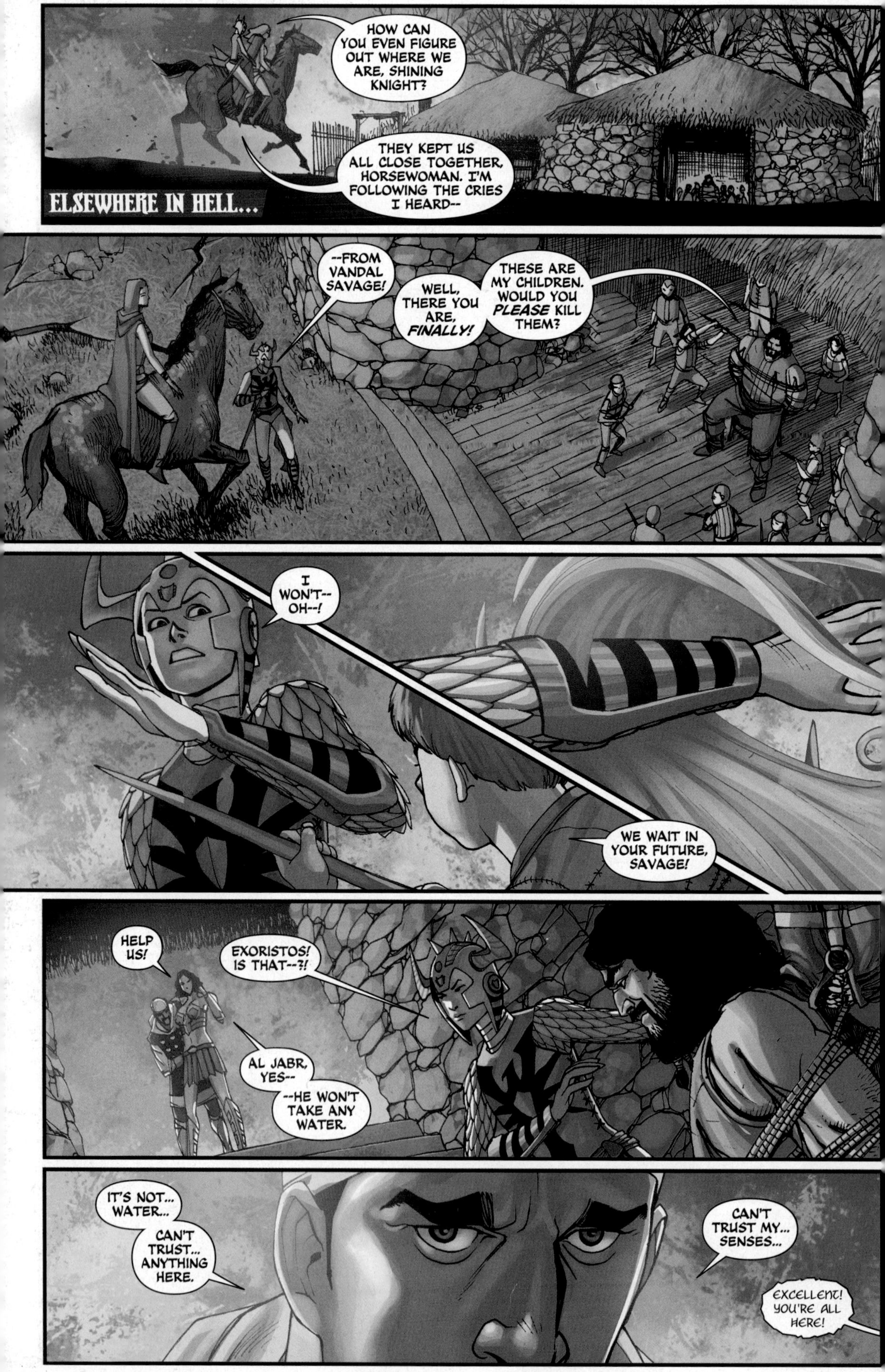
HOW CAN YOU EVEN FIGURE OUT WHERE WE ARE, SHINING KNIGHT?
THEY KEPT US ALL CLOSE TOGETHER, HORSEWOMAN. I'M FOLLOWING THE CRIES I HEARD--
ELSEWHERE IN HELL...
--FROM VANDAL SAVAGE!
WELL, THERE YOU ARE, FINALLY!
THESE ARE MY CHILDREN. WOULD YOU PLEASE KILL THEM?
I WON'T-- OH--!
WE WAIT IN YOUR FUTURE, SAVAGE!
HELP US!
EXORISTOS! IS THAT--?!
AL JABR, YES--
--HE WON'T TAKE ANY WATER.
IT'S NOT... WATER...
CAN'T TRUST... ANYTHING HERE.
CAN'T TRUST MY... SENSES...
EXCELLENT! YOU'RE ALL HERE!

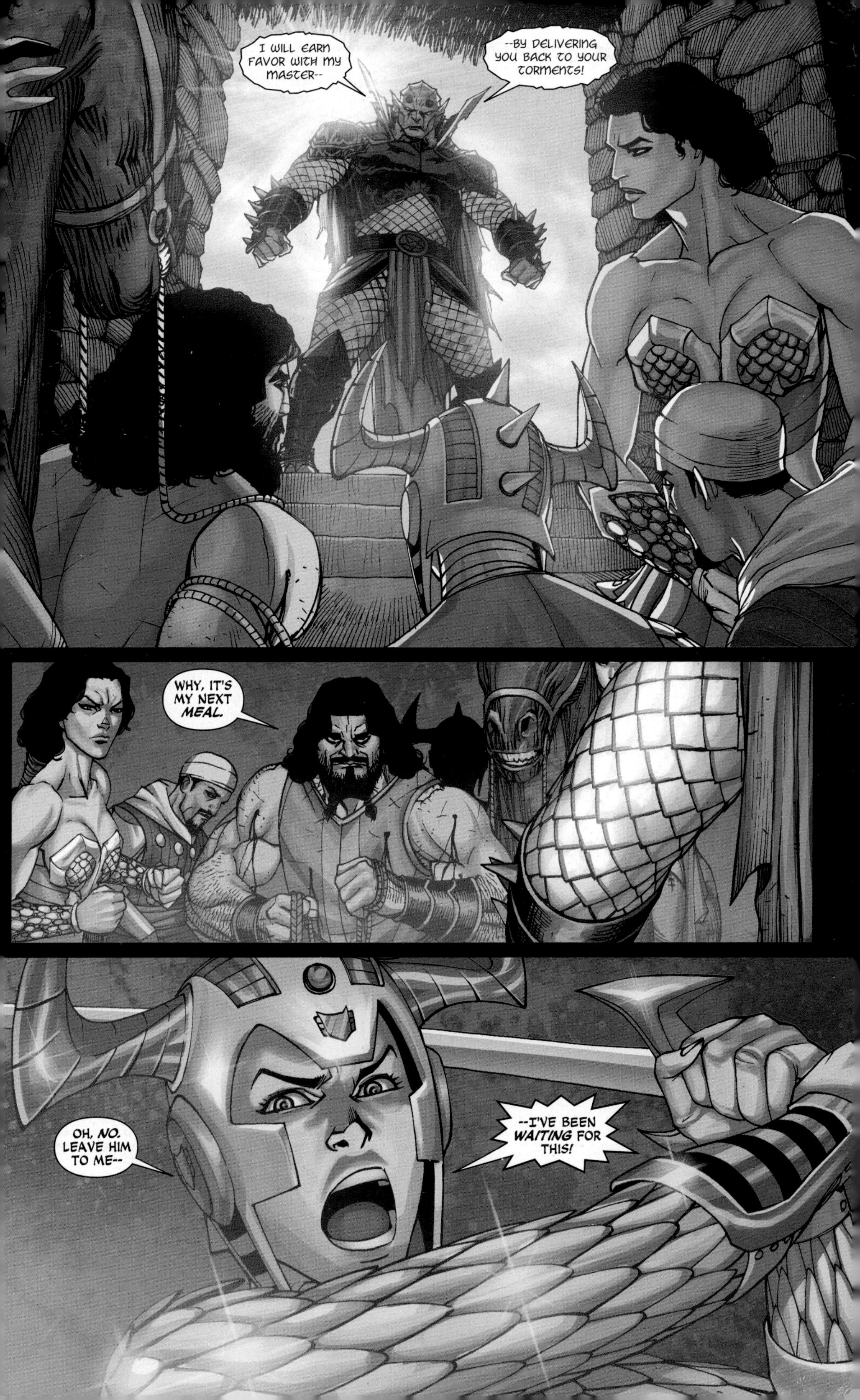
I WILL EARN FAVOR WITH MY MASTER--
--BY DELIVERING YOU BACK TO YOUR TORMENTS!
WHY, IT'S MY NEXT *MEAL.*
OH, *NO.* LEAVE HIM TO ME--
--I'VE BEEN *WAITING* FOR THIS!

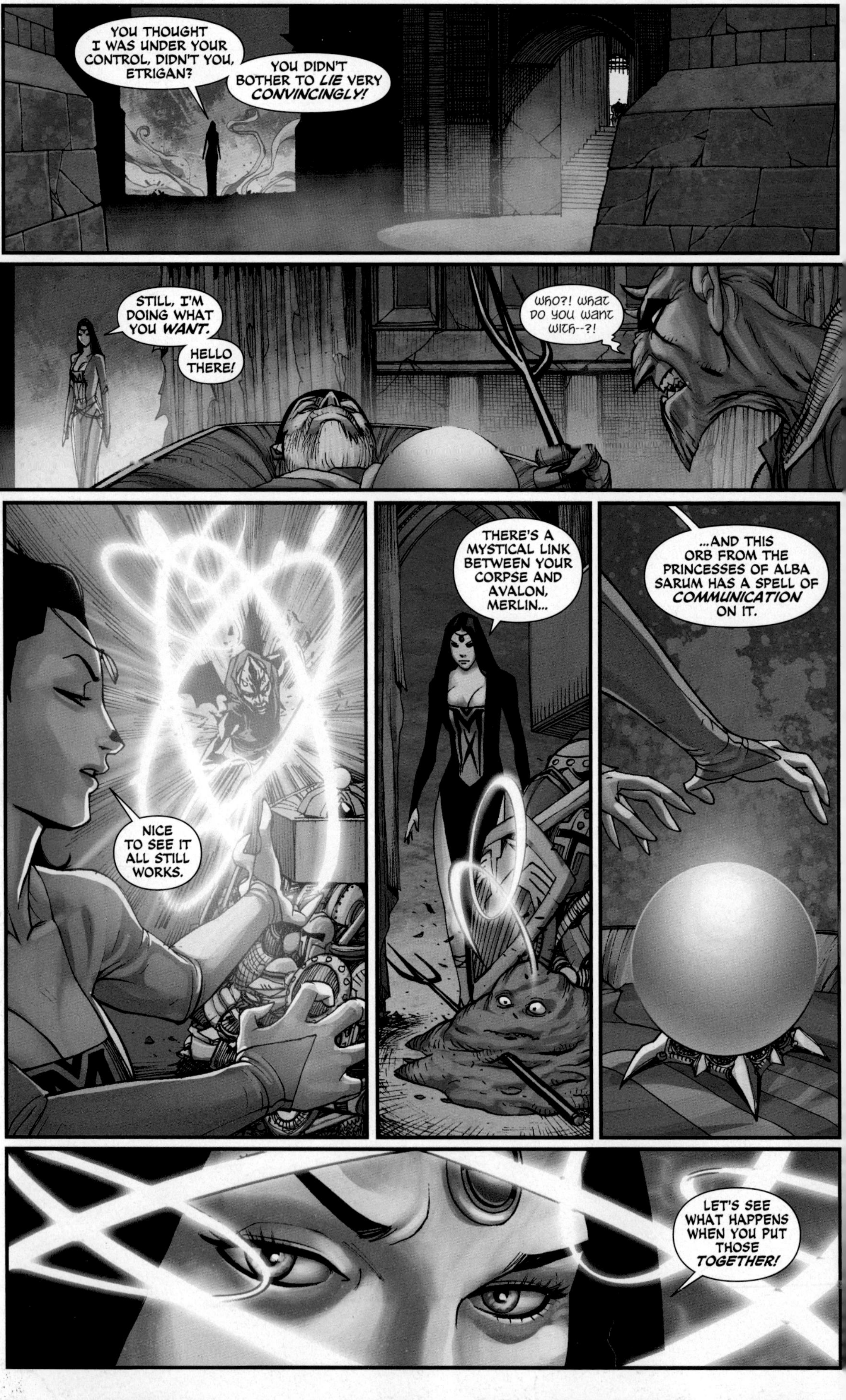
YOU THOUGHT I WAS UNDER YOUR CONTROL, DIDN'T YOU, ETRIGAN?
YOU DIDN'T BOTHER TO *LIE* VERY *CONVINCINGLY!*
STILL, I'M DOING WHAT YOU *WANT.*
HELLO THERE!
WHO?! WHAT DO YOU WANT WITH--?!
NICE TO SEE IT ALL STILL WORKS.
THERE'S A MYSTICAL LINK BETWEEN YOUR CORPSE AND AVALON, MERLIN...
...AND THIS ORB FROM THE PRINCESSES OF ALBA SARUM HAS A SPELL OF *COMMUNICATION* ON IT.
LET'S SEE WHAT HAPPENS WHEN YOU PUT THOSE *TOGETHER!*

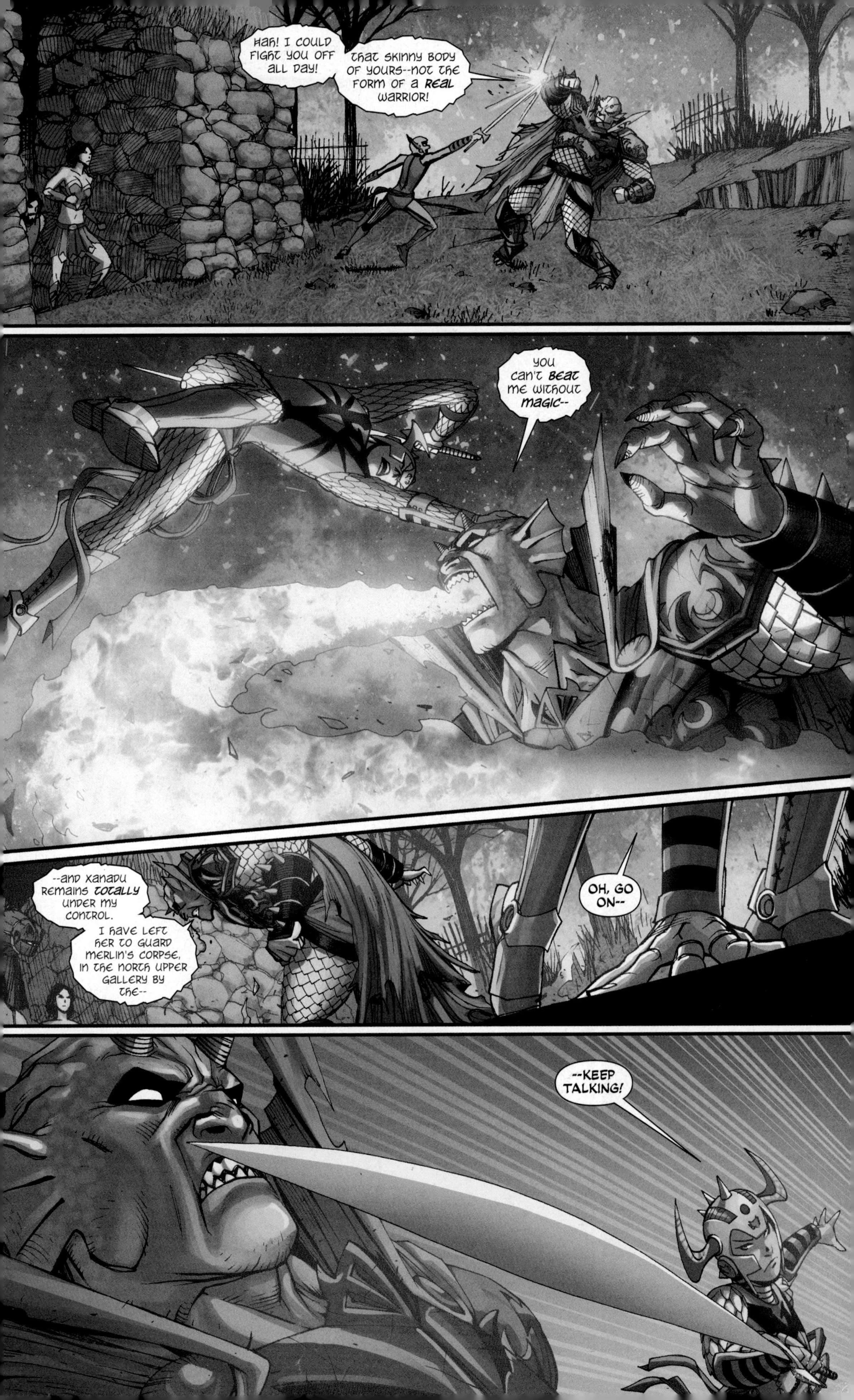
HAH! I COULD FIGHT YOU OFF ALL DAY!
THAT SKINNY BODY OF YOURS--NOT THE FORM OF A REAL WARRIOR!
YOU CAN'T BEAT ME WITHOUT MAGIC--
--AND XANADU REMAINS TOTALLY UNDER MY CONTROL.
I HAVE LEFT HER TO GUARD MERLIN'S CORPSE, IN THE NORTH UPPER GALLERY BY THE--
OH, GO ON--
--KEEP TALKING!

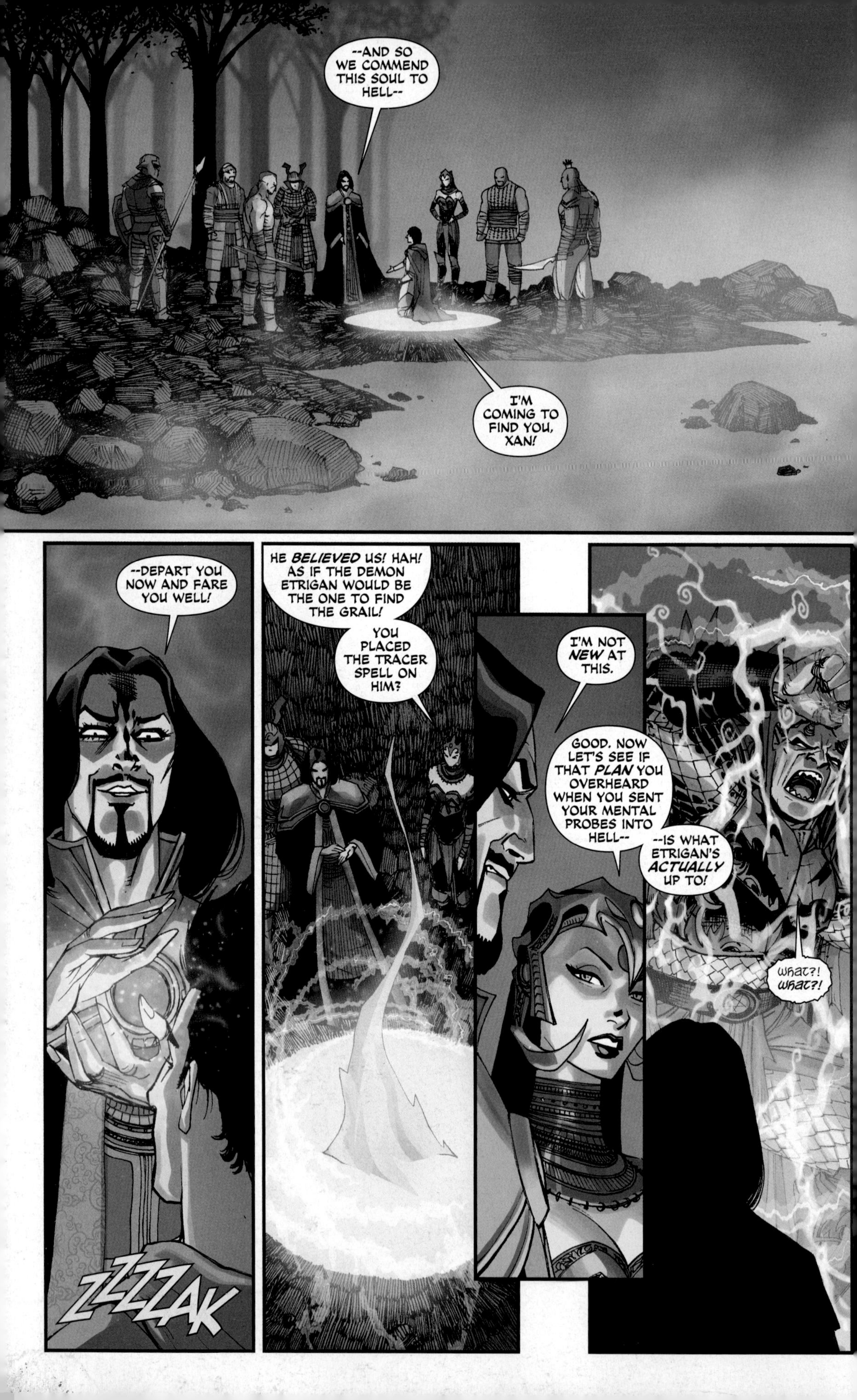
--AND SO WE COMMEND THIS SOUL TO HELL--
I'M COMING TO FIND YOU, XAN!
--DEPART YOU NOW AND FARE YOU WELL!
ZZZZAK
HE BELIEVED US! HAH! AS IF THE DEMON ETRIGAN WOULD BE THE ONE TO FIND THE GRAIL!
YOU PLACED THE TRACER SPELL ON HIM?
I'M NOT NEW AT THIS.
GOOD. NOW LET'S SEE IF THAT PLAN YOU OVERHEARD WHEN YOU SENT YOUR MENTAL PROBES INTO HELL--
--IS WHAT ETRIGAN'S ACTUALLY UP TO!
WHAT?! WHAT?!

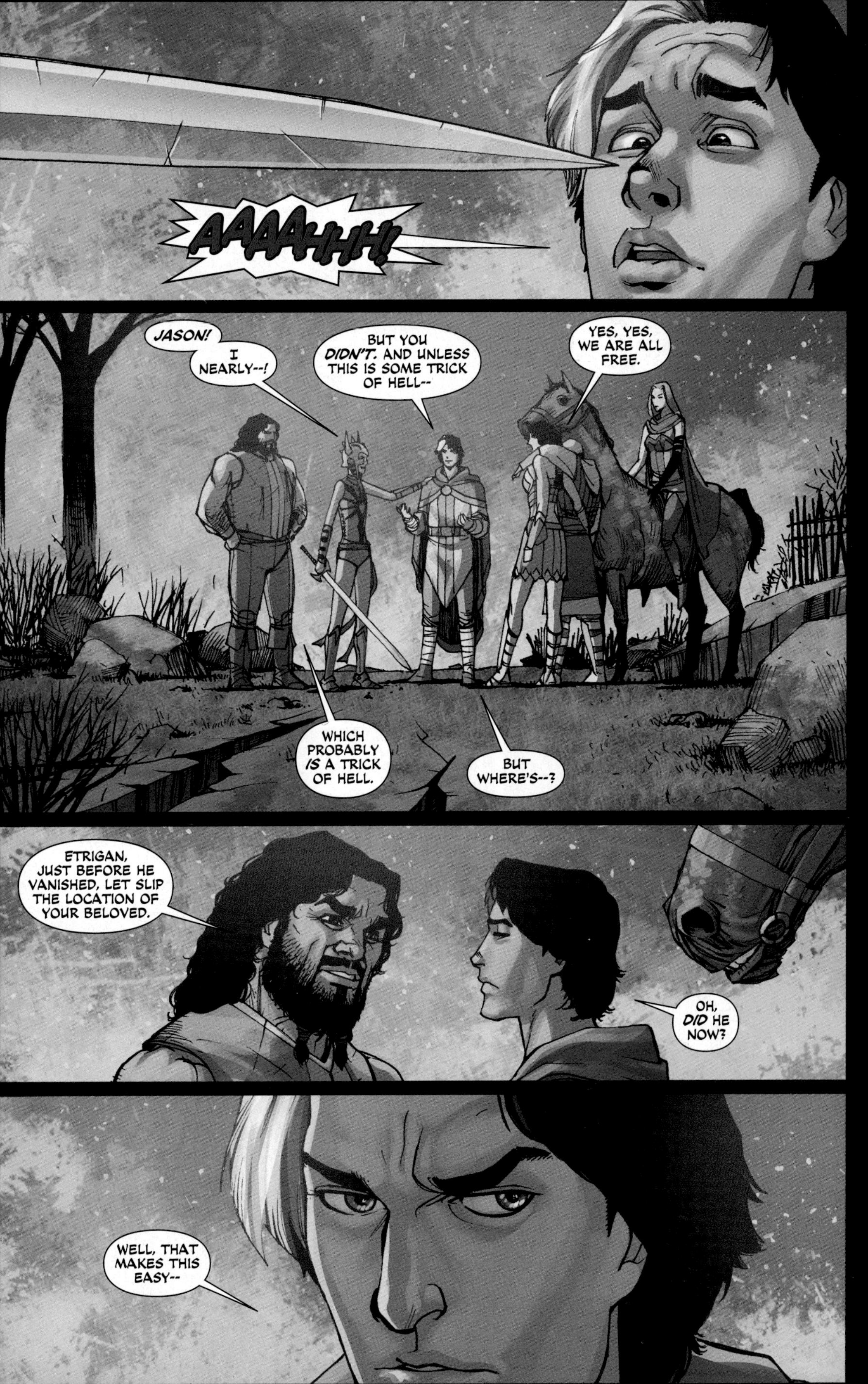
AAAAHHH!
JASON! I NEARLY--!
BUT YOU DIDN'T. AND UNLESS THIS IS SOME TRICK OF HELL--
YES, YES, WE ARE ALL FREE.
WHICH PROBABLY IS A TRICK OF HELL.
BUT WHERE'S--?
ETRIGAN, JUST BEFORE HE VANISHED, LET SLIP THE LOCATION OF YOUR BELOVED.
OH, DID HE NOW?
WELL, THAT MAKES THIS EASY--

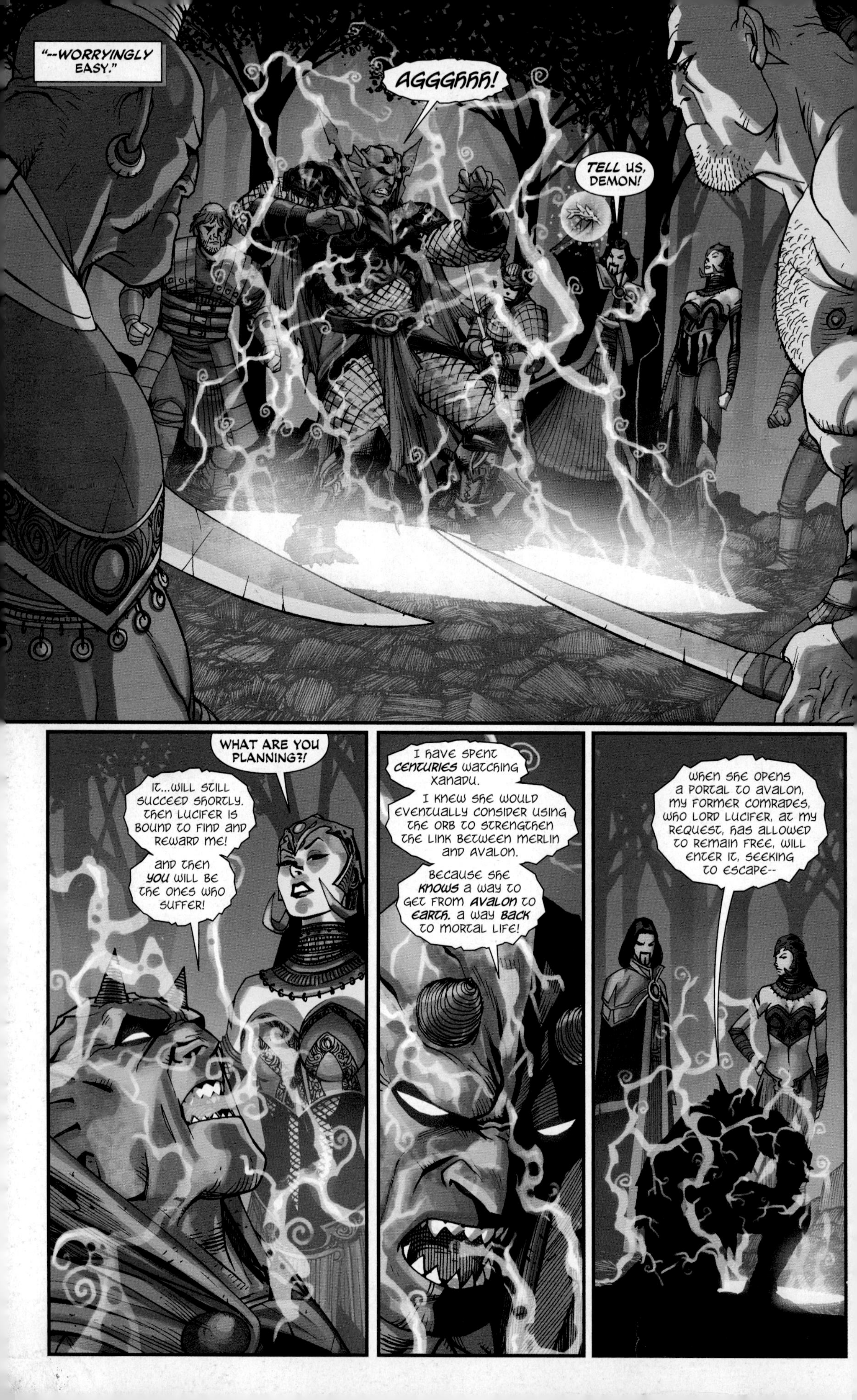
"--WORRYINGLY EASY."
AGGGHHH!
TELL US, DEMON!
WHAT ARE YOU PLANNING?!
IT...WILL STILL SUCCEED SHORTLY. THEN LUCIFER IS BOUND TO FIND AND REWARD ME!
AND THEN YOU WILL BE THE ONES WHO SUFFER!
I HAVE SPENT CENTURIES WATCHING XANADU.
I KNEW SHE WOULD EVENTUALLY CONSIDER USING THE ORB TO STRENGTHEN THE LINK BETWEEN MERLIN AND AVALON.
BECAUSE SHE KNOWS A WAY TO GET FROM AVALON TO EARTH. A WAY BACK TO MORTAL LIFE!
WHEN SHE OPENS A PORTAL TO AVALON, MY FORMER COMRADES, WHO LORD LUCIFER, AT MY REQUEST, HAS ALLOWED TO REMAIN FREE, WILL ENTER IT, SEEKING TO ESCAPE--

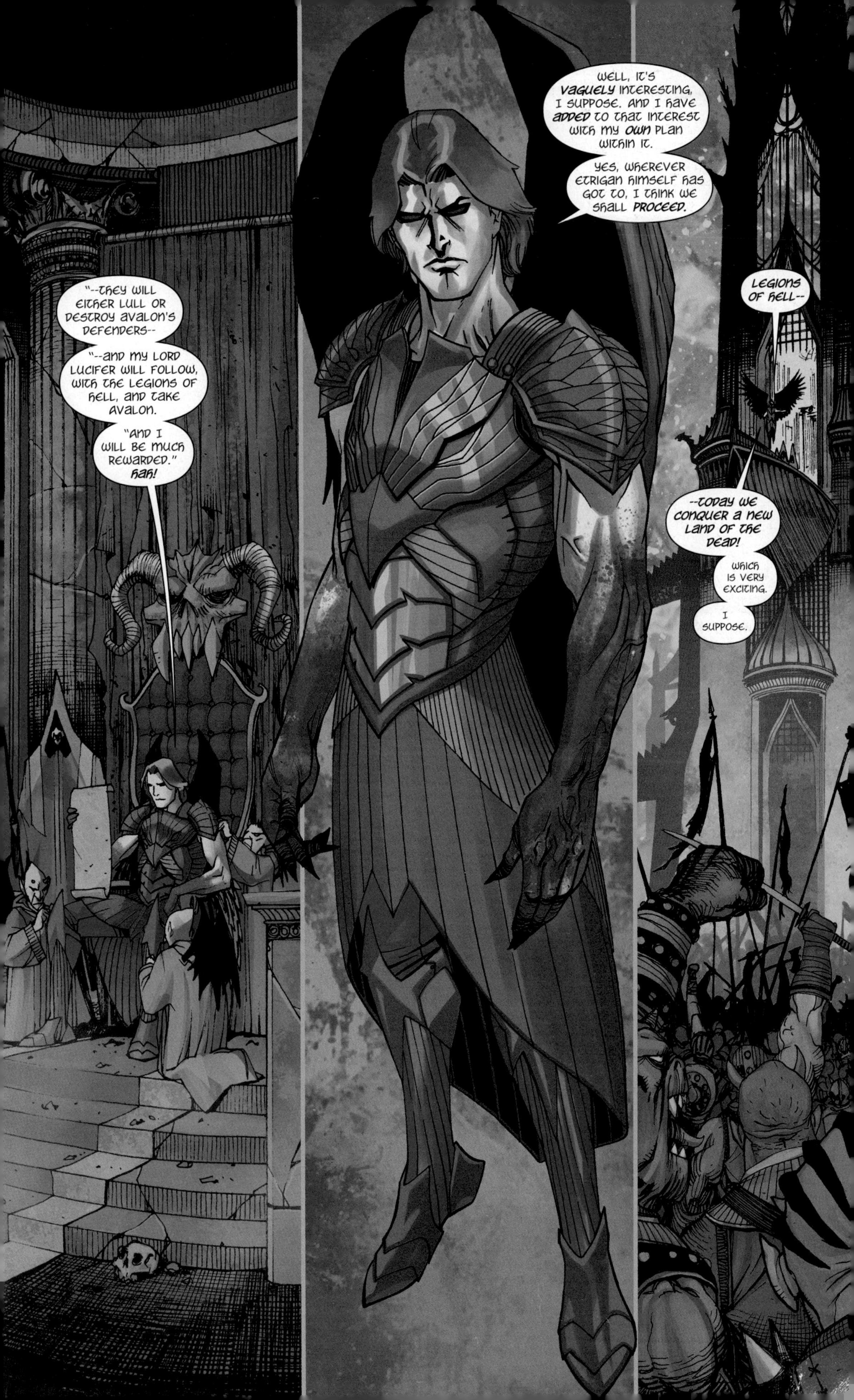
"--THEY WILL EITHER LULL OR DESTROY AVALON'S DEFENDERS--
"--AND MY LORD LUCIFER WILL FOLLOW, WITH THE LEGIONS OF HELL, AND TAKE AVALON.
"AND I WILL BE MUCH REWARDED." HAH!
WELL, IT'S VAGUELY INTERESTING, I SUPPOSE. AND I HAVE ADDED TO THAT INTEREST WITH MY OWN PLAN WITHIN IT.
YES, WHEREVER ETRIGAN HIMSELF HAS GOT TO, I THINK WE SHALL PROCEED.
LEGIONS OF HELL--
--TODAY WE CONQUER A NEW LAND OF THE DEAD!
WHICH IS VERY EXCITING.
I SUPPOSE.

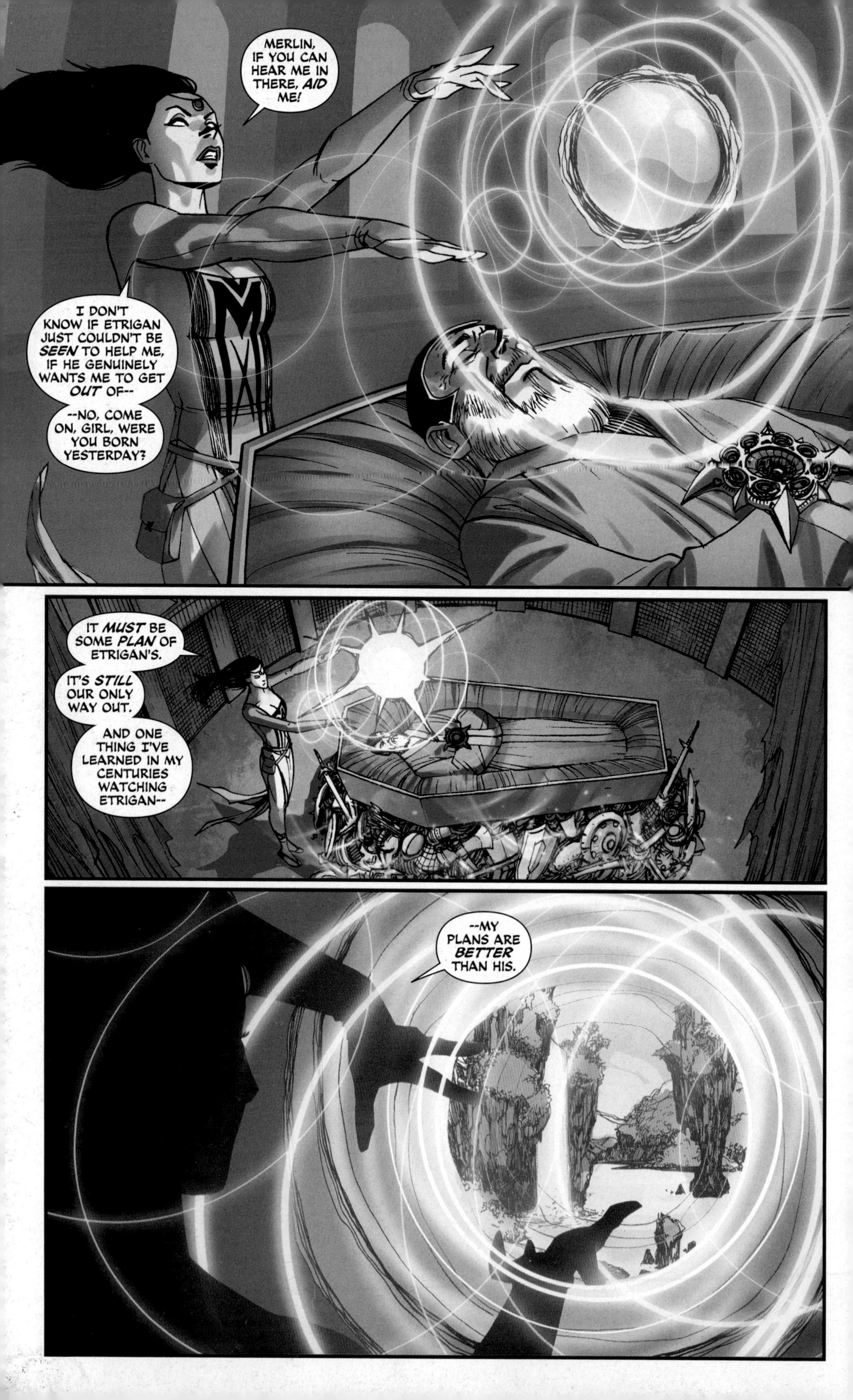
MERLIN, IF YOU CAN HEAR ME IN THERE, AID ME!
I DON'T KNOW IF ETRIGAN JUST COULDN'T BE SEEN TO HELP ME, IF HE GENUINELY WANTS ME TO GET OUT OF--
--NO, COME ON, GIRL, WERE YOU BORN YESTERDAY?
IT MUST BE SOME PLAN OF ETRIGAN'S.
IT'S STILL OUR ONLY WAY OUT.
AND ONE THING I'VE LEARNED IN MY CENTURIES WATCHING ETRIGAN--
--MY PLANS ARE BETTER THAN HIS.

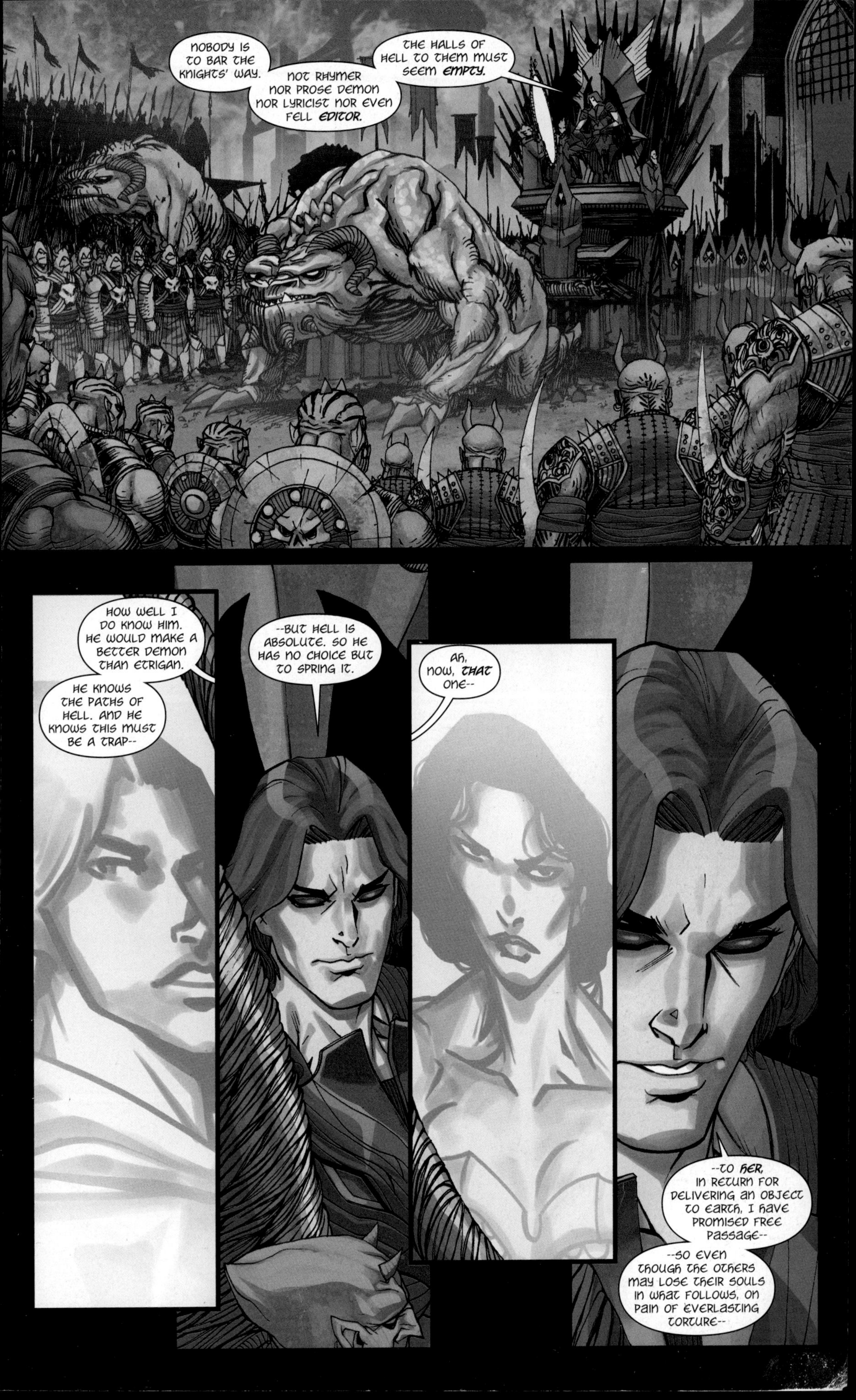
NOBODY IS TO BAR THE KNIGHTS' WAY.
NOT RHYMER NOR PROSE DEMON NOR LYRICIST NOR EVEN FELL EDITOR.
THE HALLS OF HELL TO THEM MUST SEEM EMPTY.
HOW WELL I DO KNOW HIM. HE WOULD MAKE A BETTER DEMON THAN ETRIGAN.
HE KNOWS THE PATHS OF HELL. AND HE KNOWS THIS MUST BE A TRAP--
--BUT HELL IS ABSOLUTE. SO HE HAS NO CHOICE BUT TO SPRING IT.
AH, NOW, THAT ONE--
--TO HER, IN RETURN FOR DELIVERING AN OBJECT TO EARTH, I HAVE PROMISED FREE PASSAGE--
--SO EVEN THOUGH THE OTHERS MAY LOSE THEIR SOULS IN WHAT FOLLOWS, ON PAIN OF EVERLASTING TORTURE--

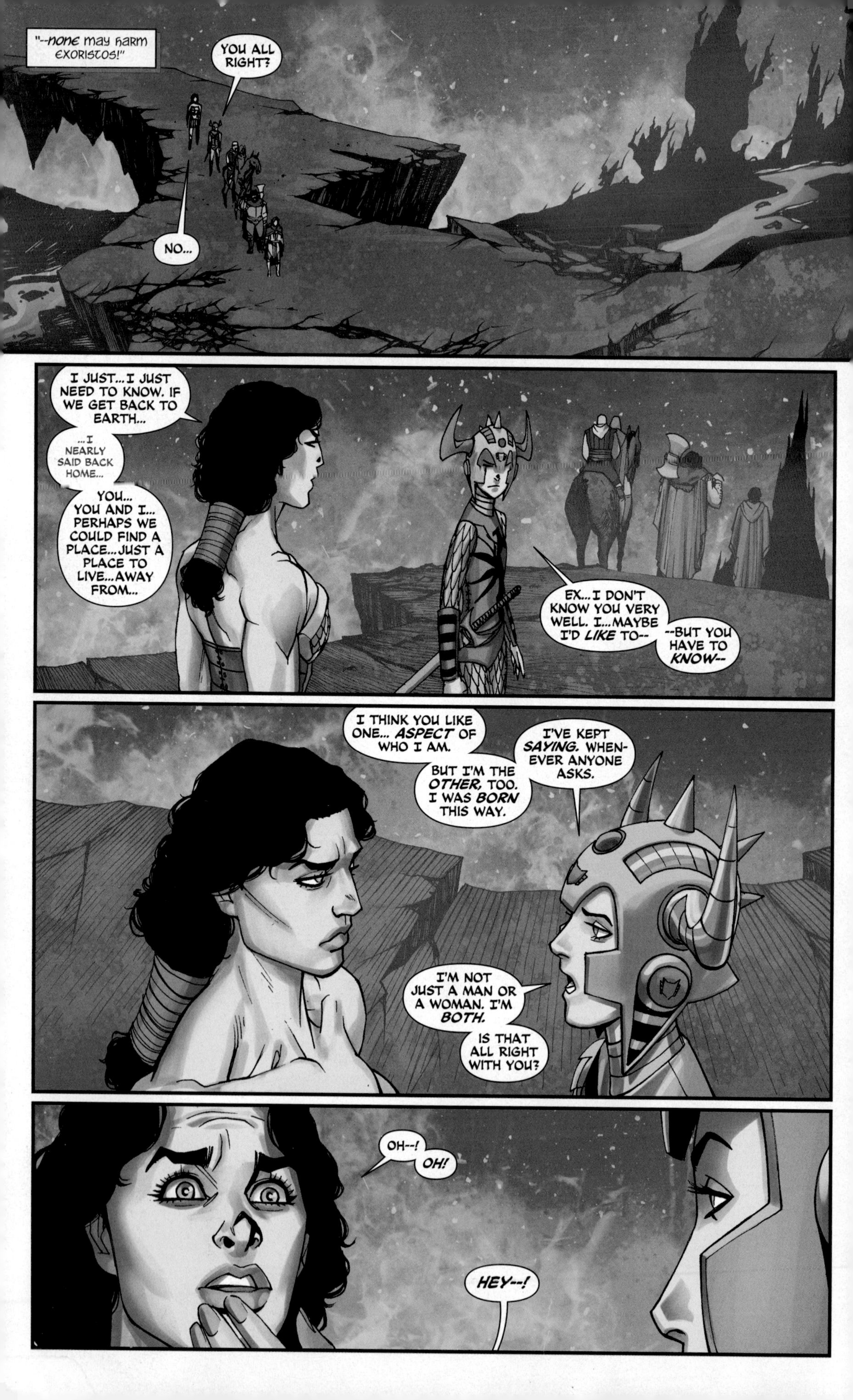
"--none may harm EXORISTOS!"
YOU ALL RIGHT?
NO...
I JUST... I JUST NEED TO KNOW. IF WE GET BACK TO EARTH...
...I NEARLY SAID BACK HOME...
YOU... YOU AND I... PERHAPS WE COULD FIND A PLACE... JUST A PLACE TO LIVE... AWAY FROM...
EX... I DON'T KNOW YOU VERY WELL. I... MAYBE I'D LIKE TO--
--BUT YOU HAVE TO KNOW--
I THINK YOU LIKE ONE... ASPECT OF WHO I AM.
BUT I'M THE OTHER, TOO. I WAS BORN THIS WAY.
I'VE KEPT SAYING. WHENEVER ANYONE ASKS.
I'M NOT JUST A MAN OR A WOMAN. I'M BOTH.
IS THAT ALL RIGHT WITH YOU?
OH--! OH!
HEY--!

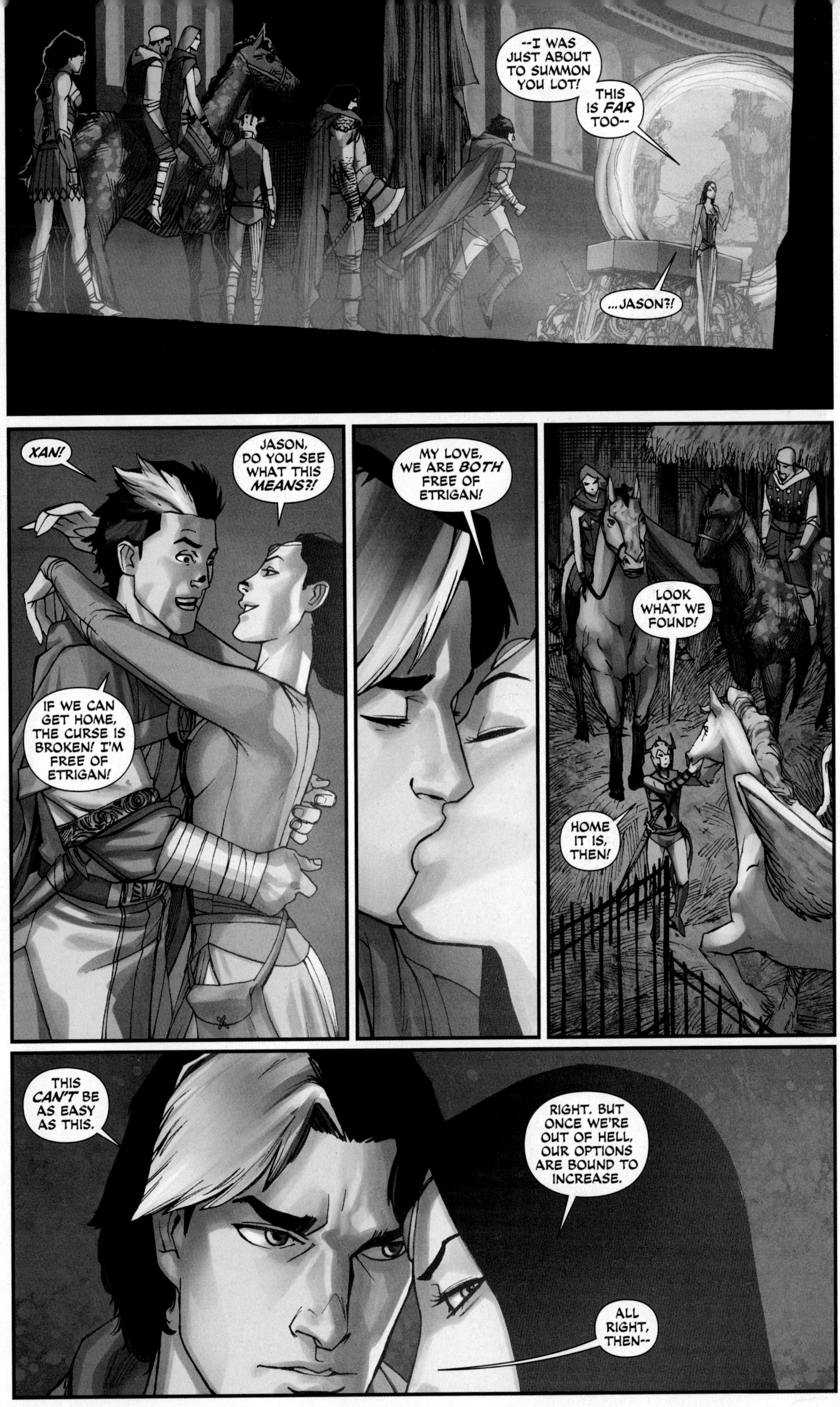
--I WAS JUST ABOUT TO SUMMON YOU LOT!
THIS IS FAR TOO--
...JASON?!
XAN!
JASON, DO YOU SEE WHAT THIS MEANS?!
IF WE CAN GET HOME, THE CURSE IS BROKEN! I'M FREE OF ETRIGAN!
MY LOVE, WE ARE BOTH FREE OF ETRIGAN!
LOOK WHAT WE FOUND!
HOME IT IS, THEN!
THIS CAN'T BE AS EASY AS THIS.
RIGHT. BUT ONCE WE'RE OUT OF HELL, OUR OPTIONS ARE BOUND TO INCREASE.
ALL RIGHT, THEN--

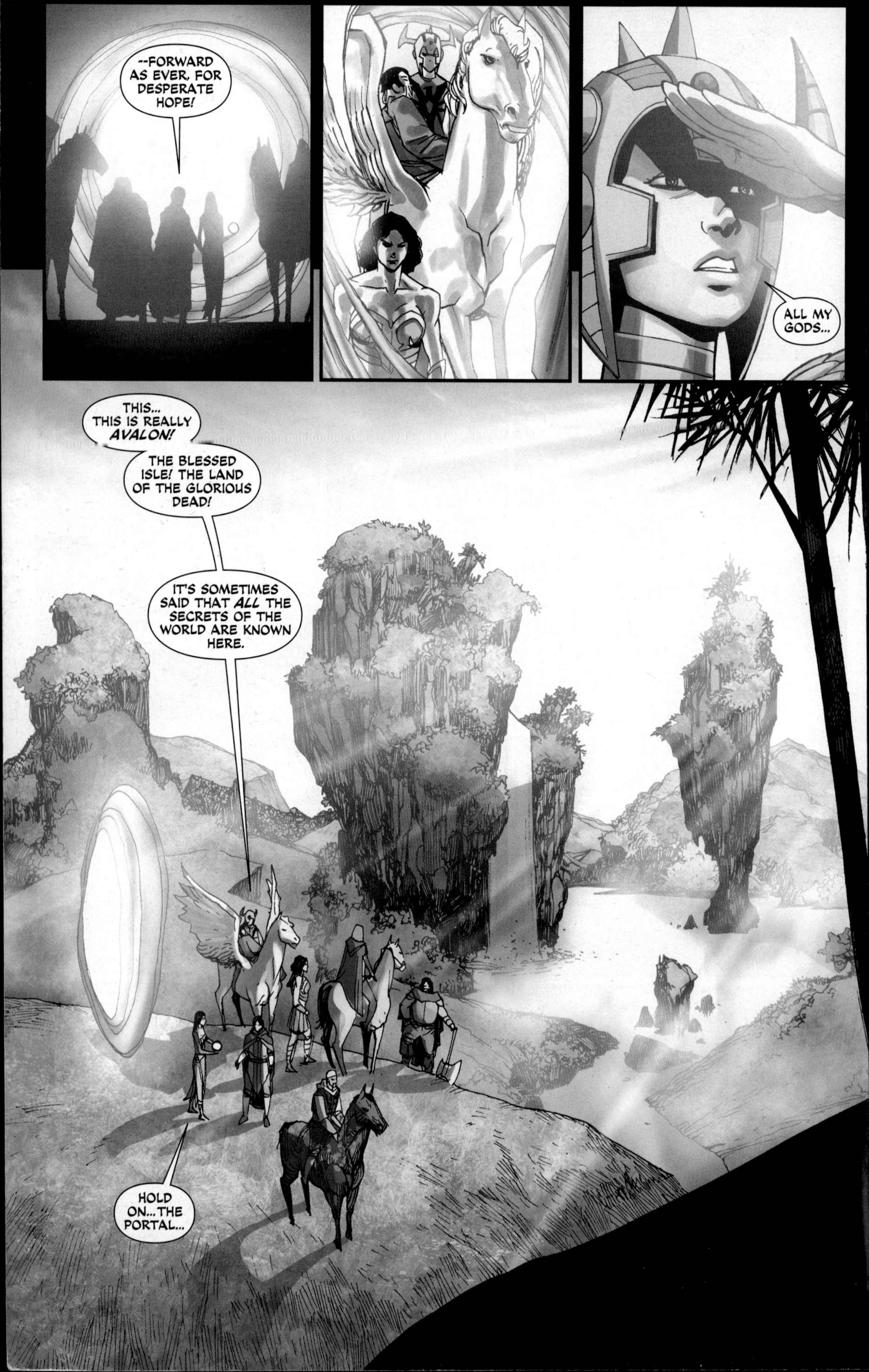
--FORWARD AS EVER, FOR DESPERATE HOPE!
ALL MY GODS...
THIS... THIS IS REALLY AVALON!
THE BLESSED ISLE! THE LAND OF THE GLORIOUS DEAD!
IT'S SOMETIMES SAID THAT ALL THE SECRETS OF THE WORLD ARE KNOWN HERE.
HOLD ON... THE PORTAL...

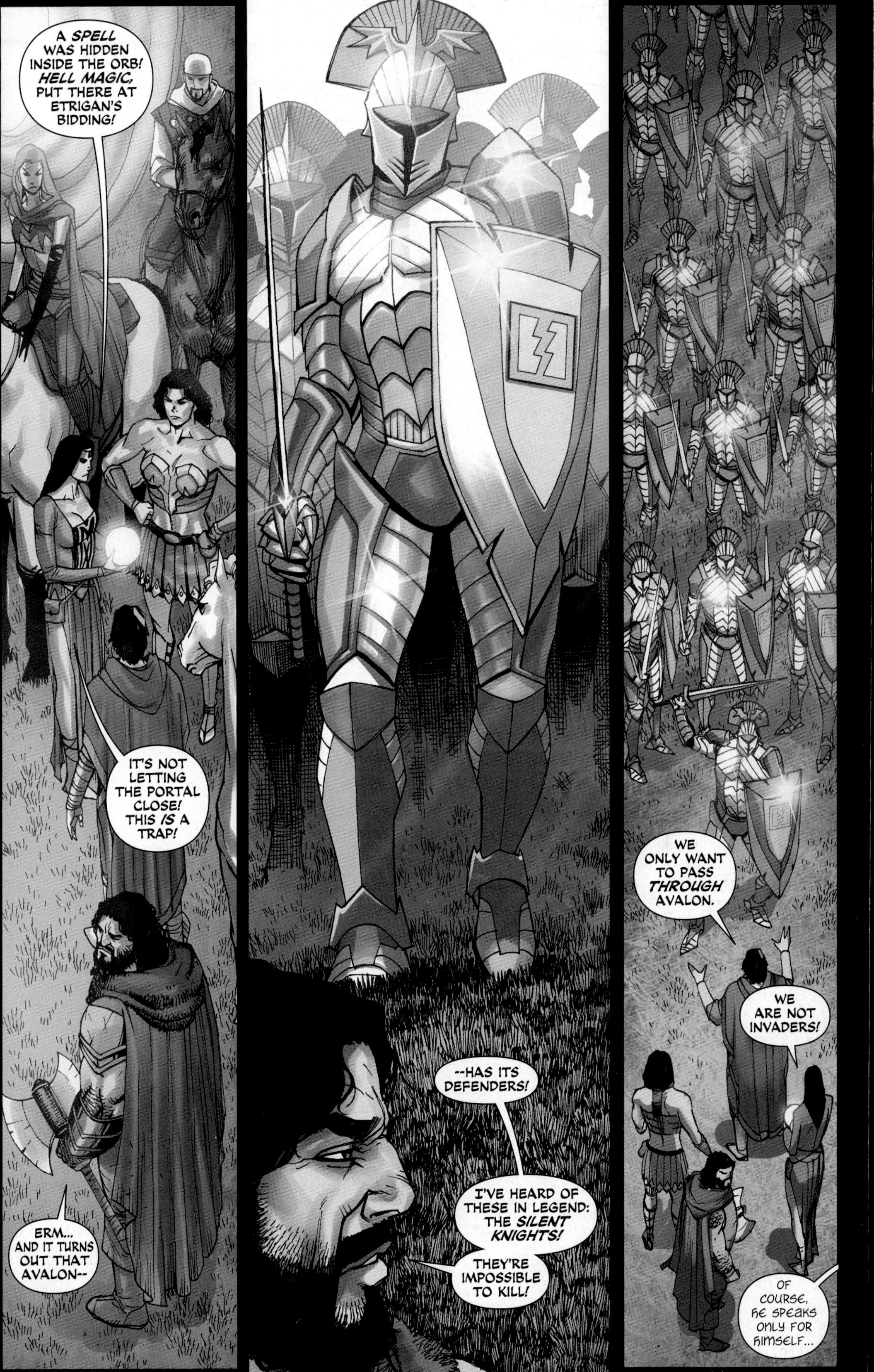
A *SPELL* WAS HIDDEN INSIDE THE ORB! *HELL MAGIC,* PUT THERE AT ETRIGAN'S BIDDING!
IT'S NOT LETTING THE PORTAL CLOSE! THIS *IS* A TRAP!
ERM... AND IT TURNS OUT THAT AVALON--
--HAS ITS DEFENDERS!
I'VE HEARD OF THESE IN LEGEND: THE *SILENT KNIGHTS!*
THEY'RE IMPOSSIBLE TO KILL!
WE ONLY WANT TO PASS *THROUGH* AVALON.
WE ARE NOT INVADERS!
OF COURSE, HE SPEAKS ONLY FOR HIMSELF...

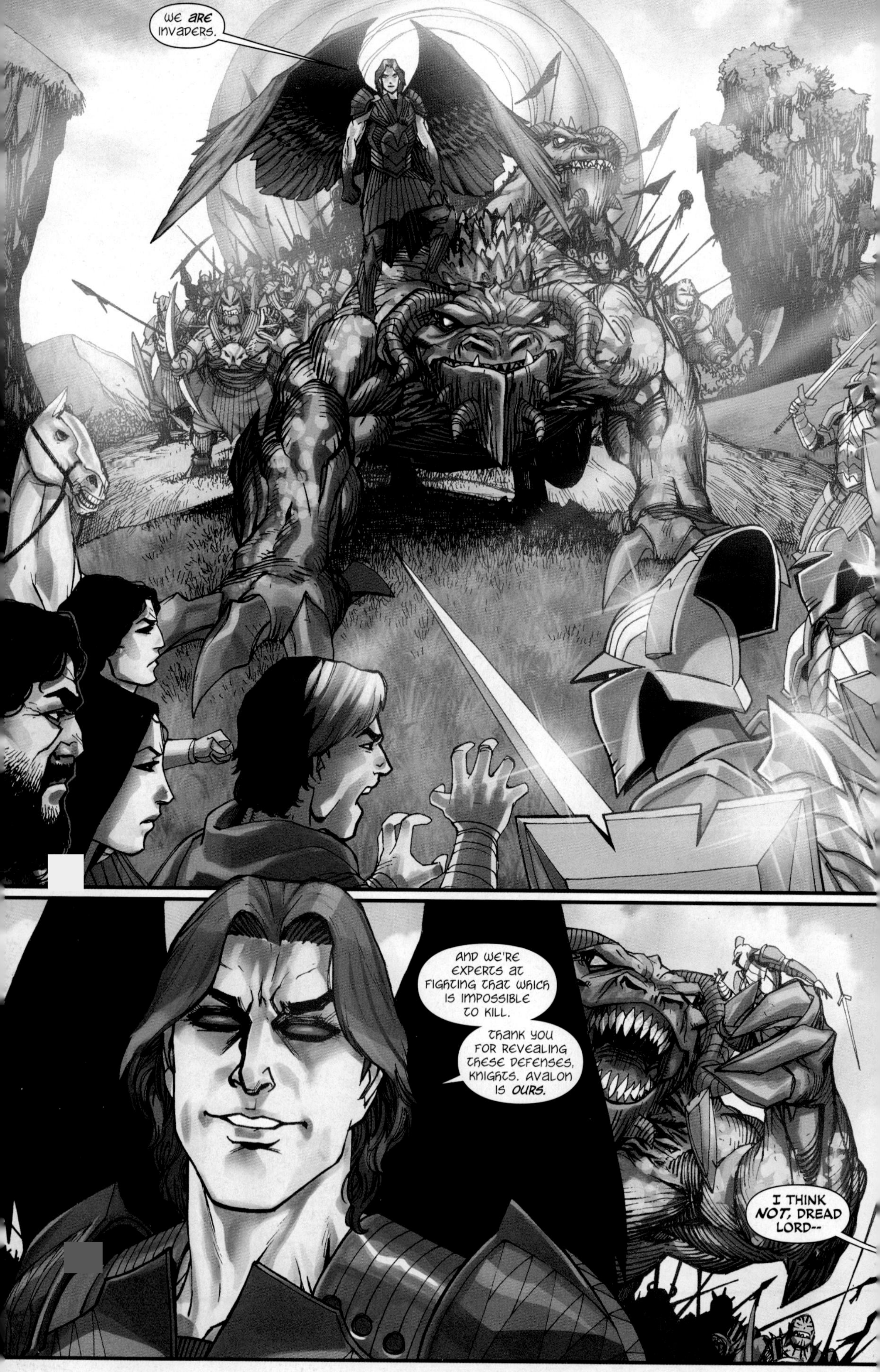
WE ARE INVADERS.
AND WE'RE EXPERTS AT FIGHTING THAT WHICH IS IMPOSSIBLE TO KILL.
THANK YOU FOR REVEALING THESE DEFENSES, KNIGHTS. AVALON IS OURS.
I THINK NOT, DREAD LORD--

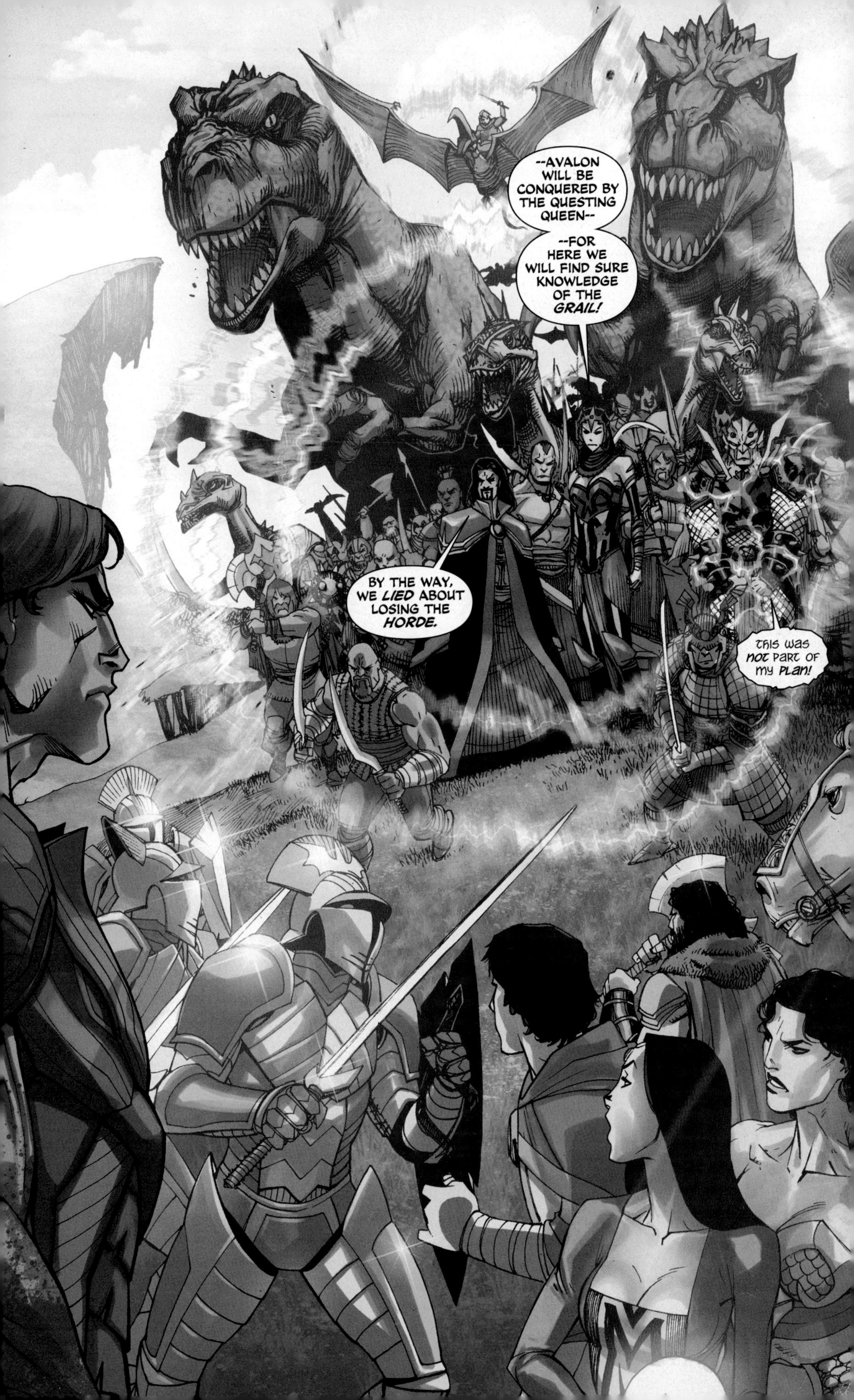
--AVALON WILL BE CONQUERED BY THE QUESTING QUEEN--
--FOR HERE WE WILL FIND SURE KNOWLEDGE OF THE GRAIL!
BY THE WAY, WE LIED ABOUT LOSING THE HORDE.
THIS WAS NOT PART OF MY PLAN!

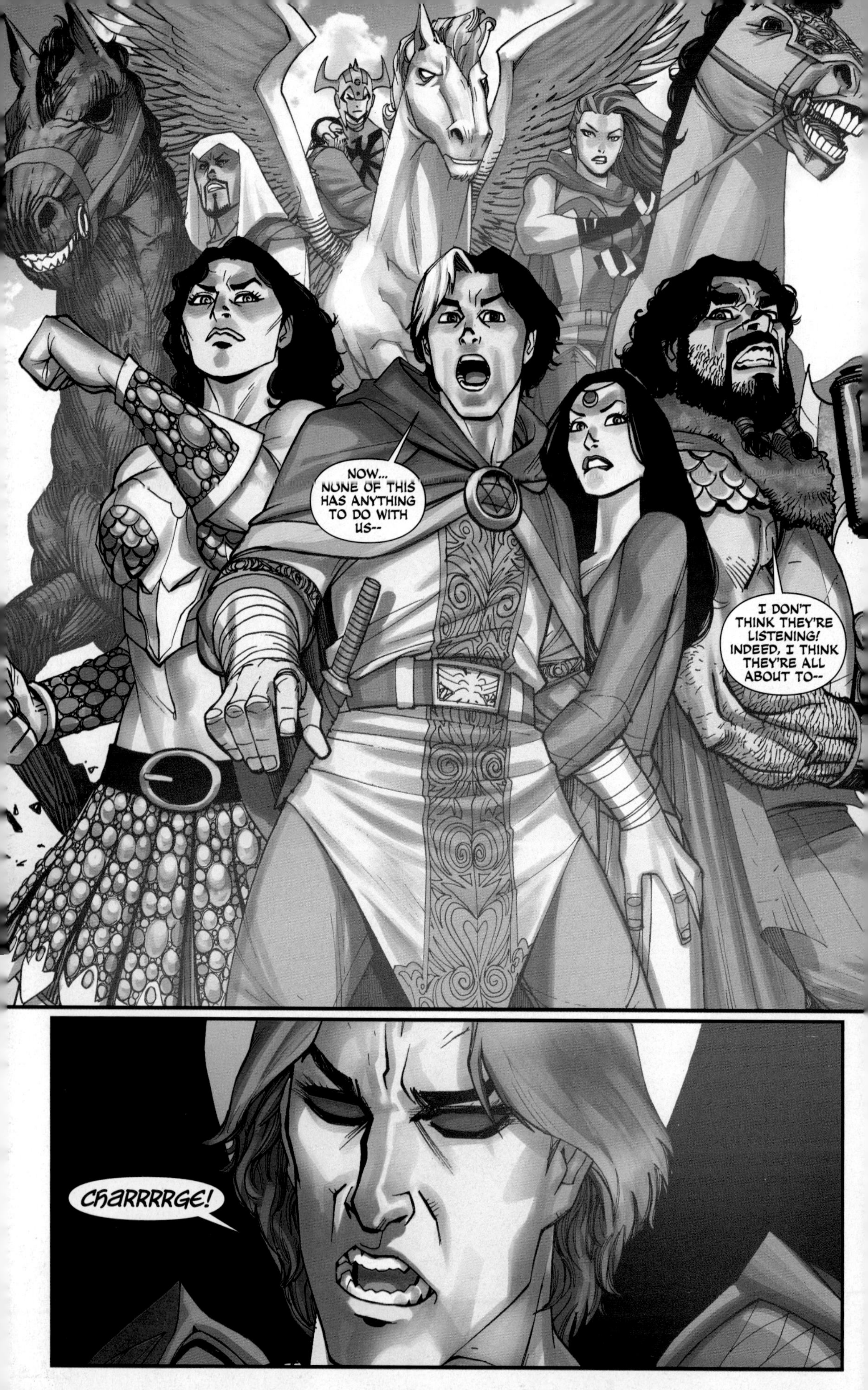
NOW... NONE OF THIS HAS ANYTHING TO DO WITH US--
I DON'T THINK THEY'RE LISTENING! INDEED, I THINK THEY'RE ALL ABOUT TO--
CHARRRRGE!

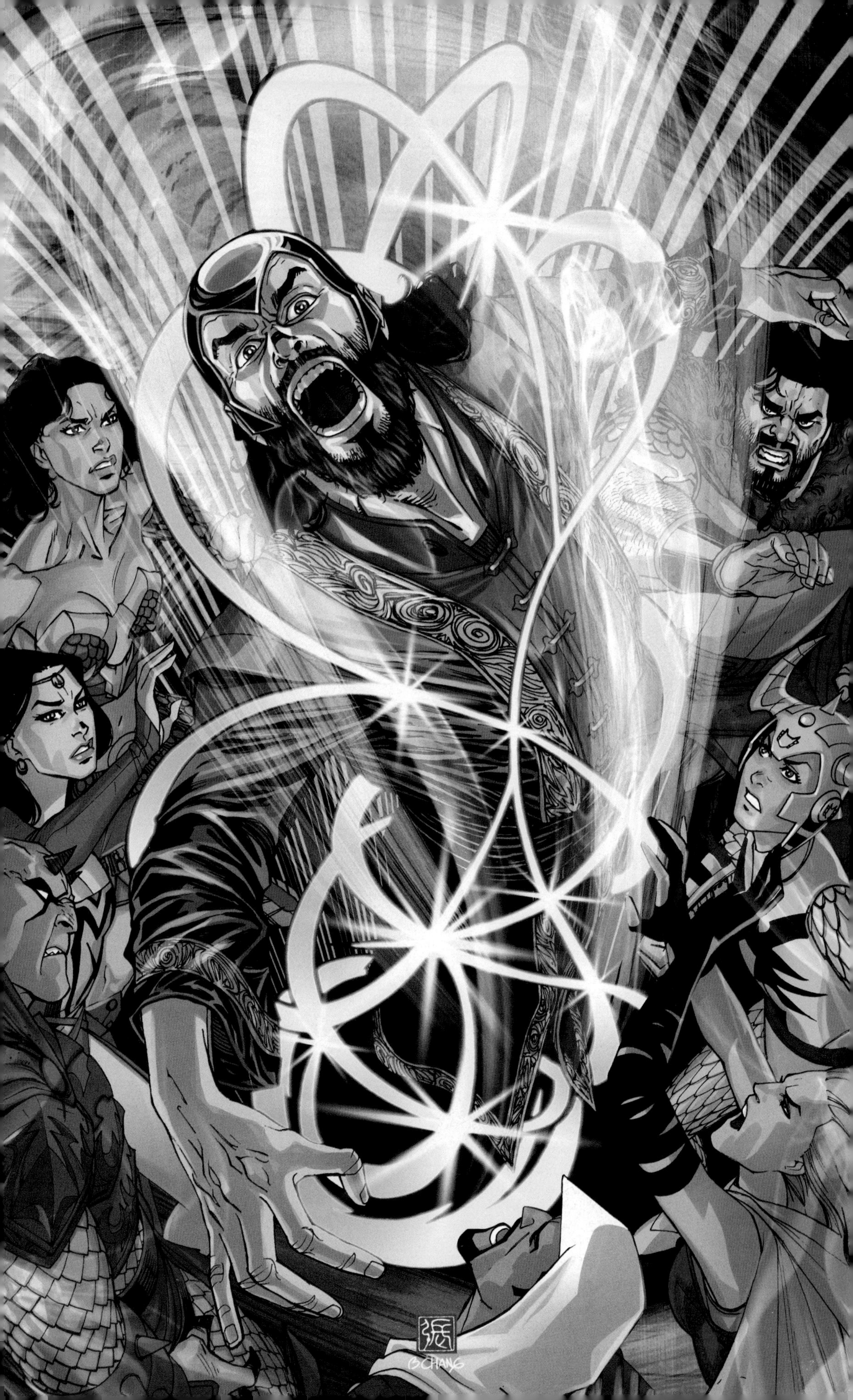
張
B CHANG

PAUL CORNELL
writer

BERNARD CHANG
artist

BERNARD CHANG
cover artist

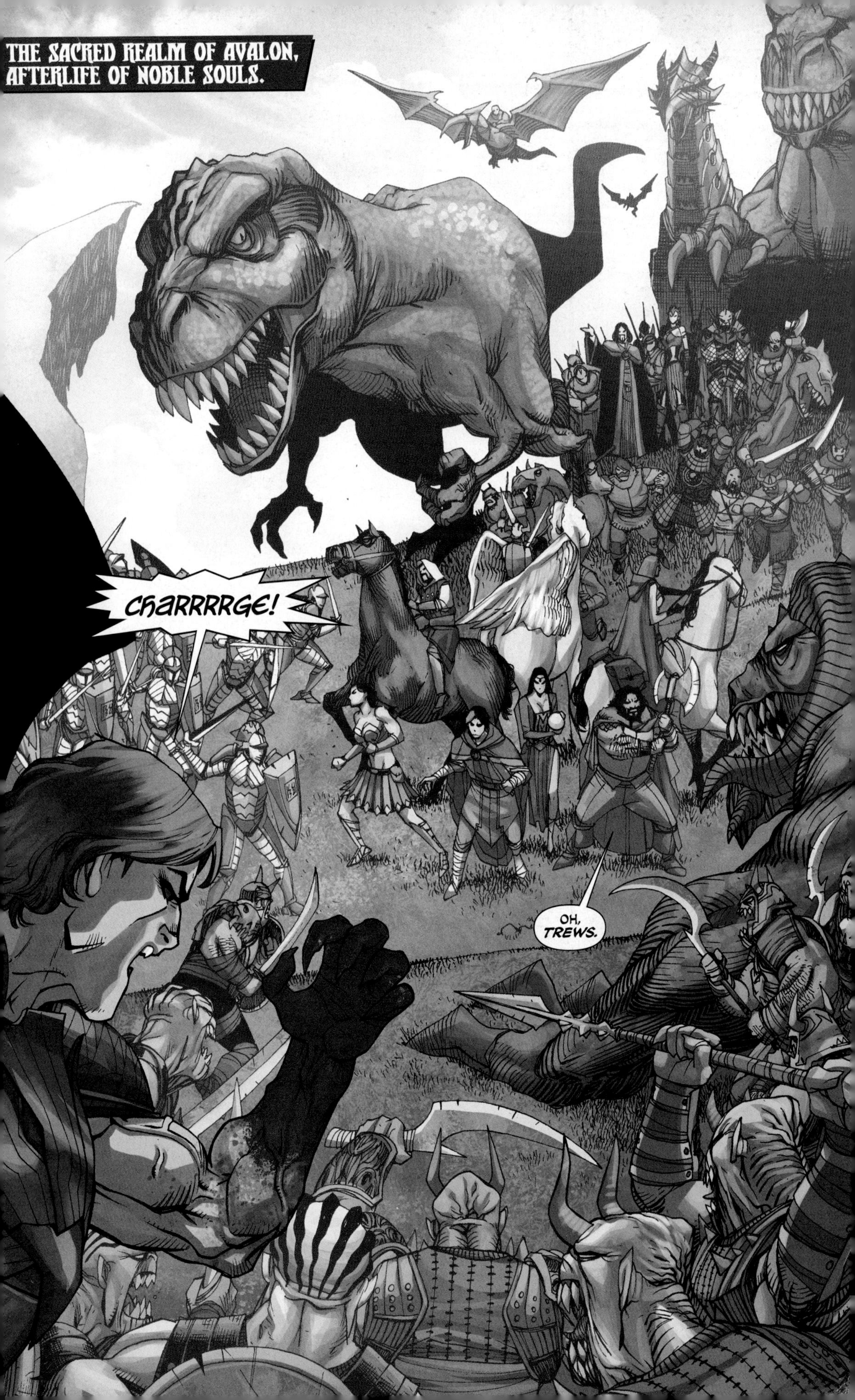
THE SACRED REALM OF AVALON, AFTERLIFE OF NOBLE SOULS.
CHARRRRGE!
OH, TREWS.

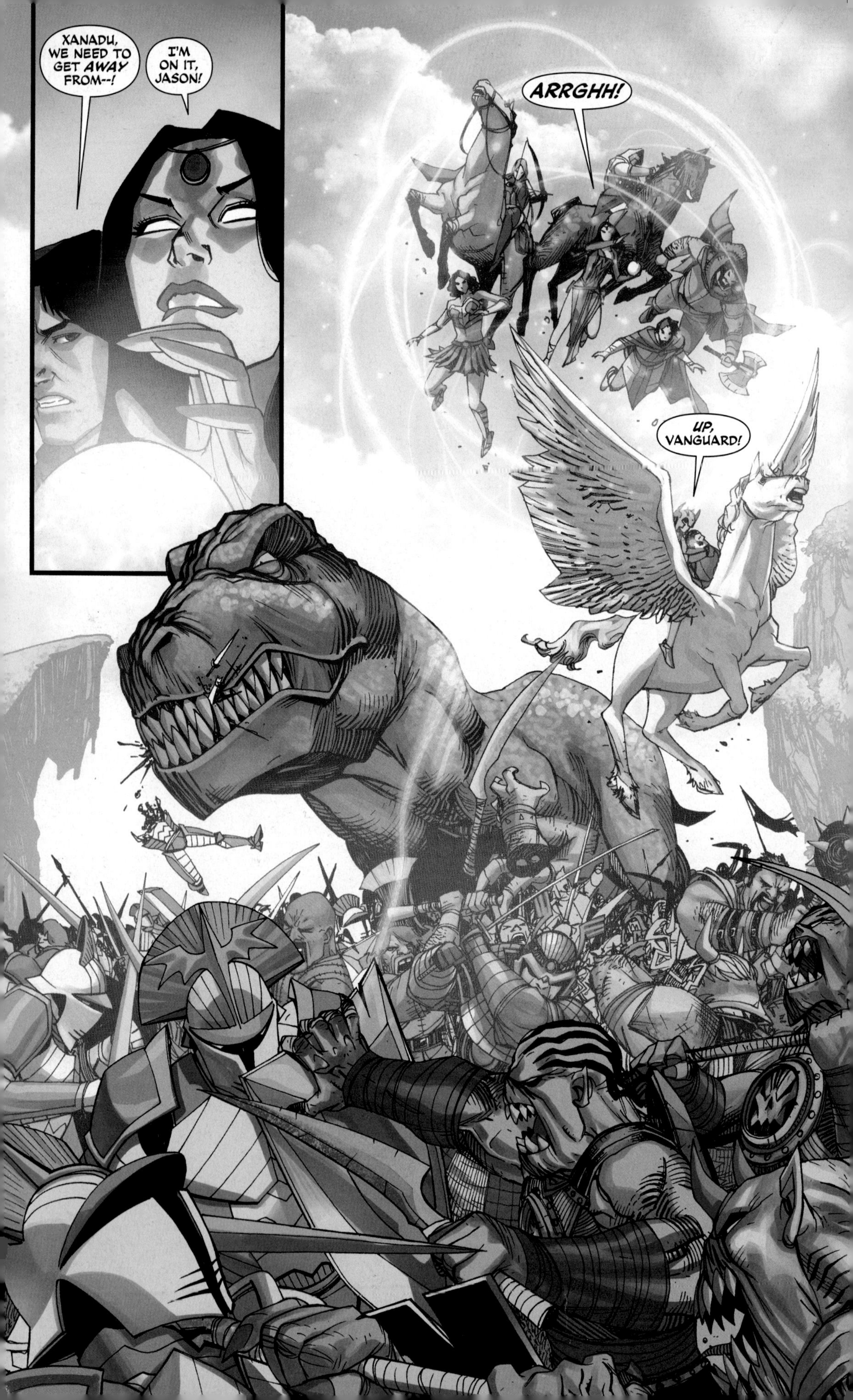

XANADU, WE NEED TO GET AWAY FROM--!
I'M ON IT, JASON!
ARRGHH!
UP, VANGUARD!

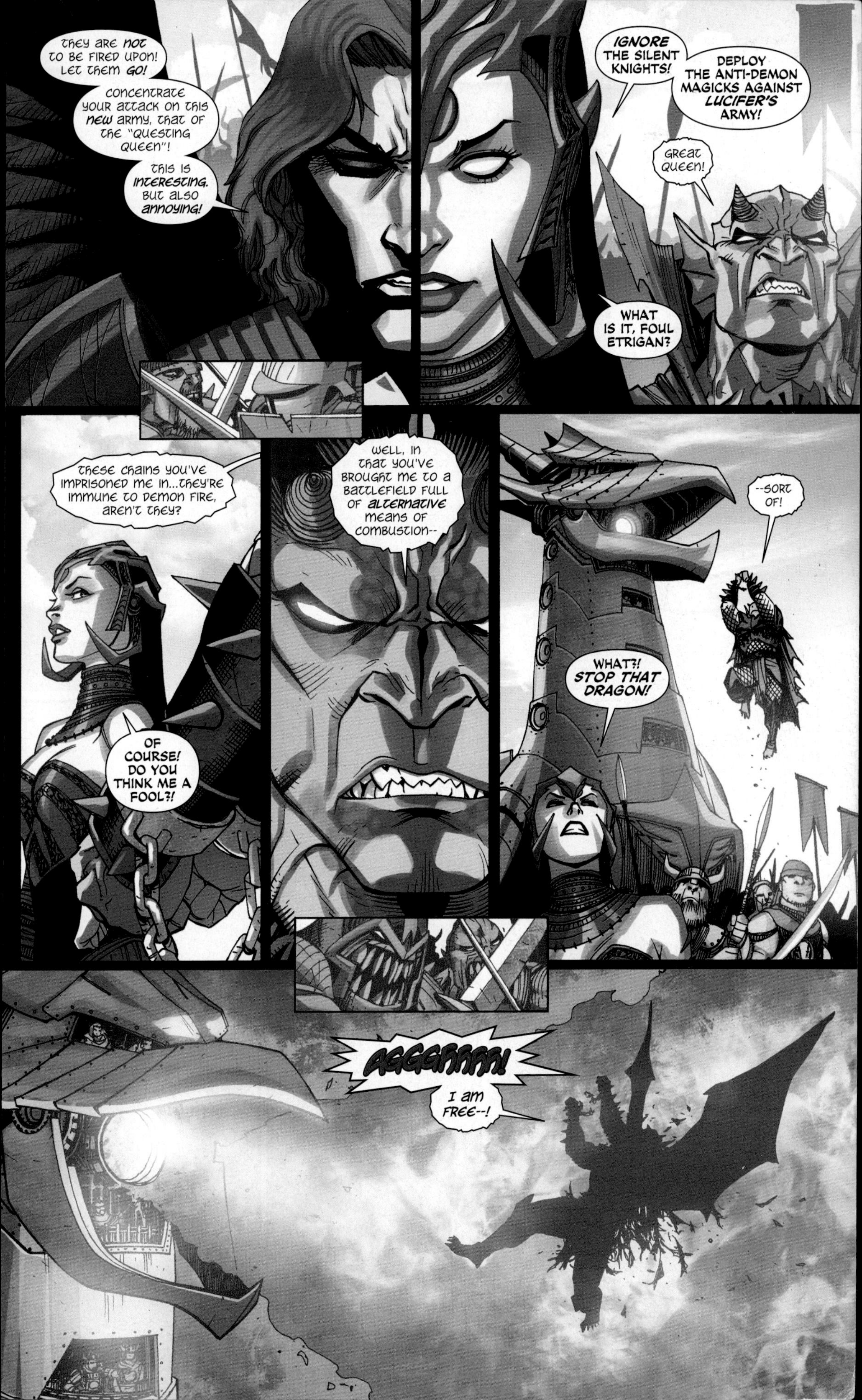
THEY ARE NOT TO BE FIRED UPON! LET THEM GO!
CONCENTRATE YOUR ATTACK ON THIS NEW ARMY, THAT OF THE "QUESTING QUEEN"!
THIS IS INTERESTING. BUT ALSO ANNOYING!
IGNORE THE SILENT KNIGHTS!
DEPLOY THE ANTI-DEMON MAGICKS AGAINST LUCIFER'S ARMY!
GREAT QUEEN!
WHAT IS IT, FOUL ETRIGAN?
THESE CHAINS YOU'VE IMPRISONED ME IN...THEY'RE IMMUNE TO DEMON FIRE, AREN'T THEY?
OF COURSE! DO YOU THINK ME A FOOL?!
WELL, IN THAT YOU'VE BROUGHT ME TO A BATTLEFIELD FULL OF ALTERNATIVE MEANS OF COMBUSTION--
--SORT OF!
WHAT?! STOP THAT DRAGON!
AGGGRRRR!
I AM FREE--!

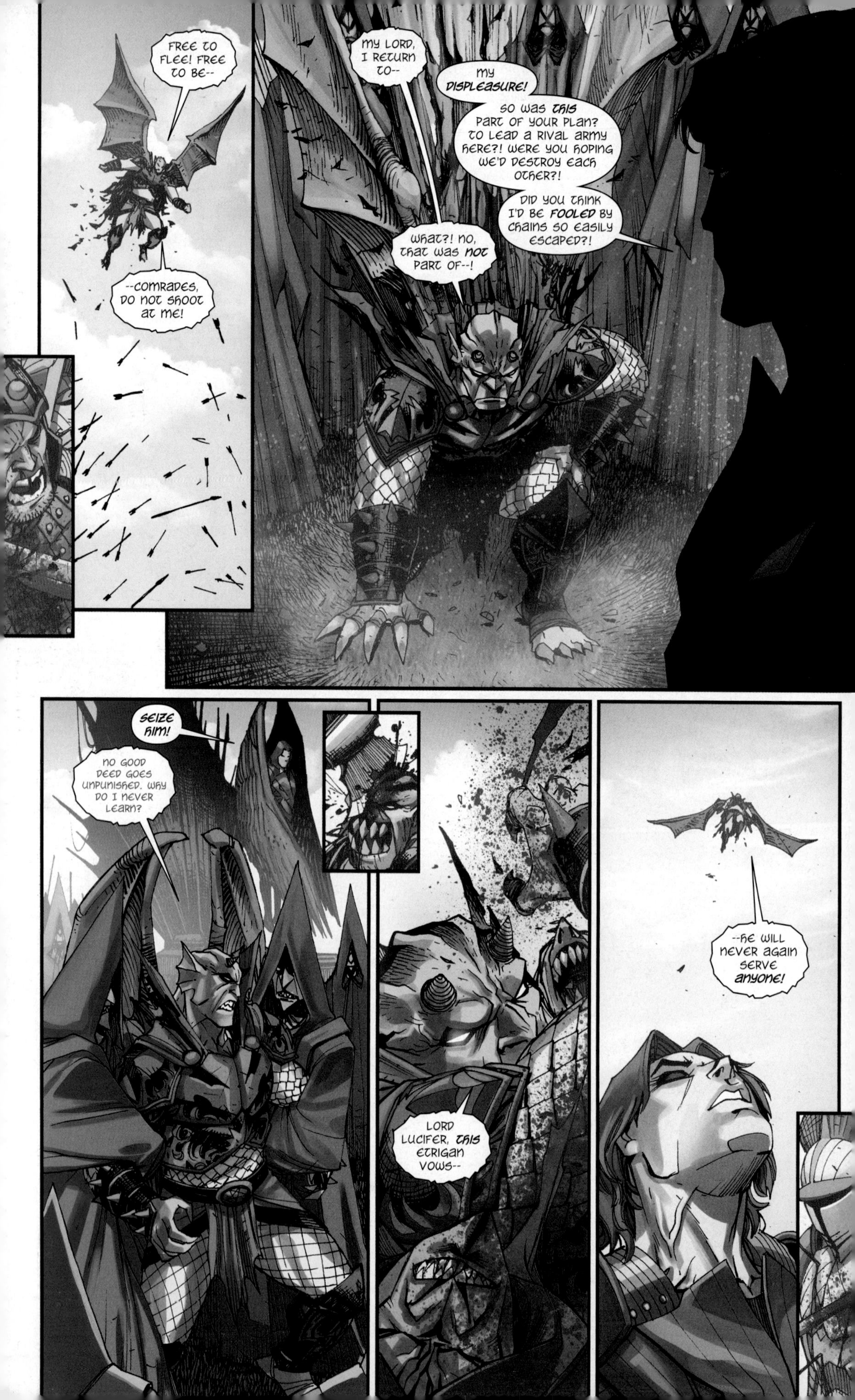
FREE TO FLEE! FREE TO BE--
--COMRADES, DO NOT SHOOT AT ME!
MY LORD, I RETURN TO--
MY DISPLEASURE!
SO WAS THIS PART OF YOUR PLAN? TO LEAD A RIVAL ARMY HERE?! WERE YOU HOPING WE'D DESTROY EACH OTHER?!
DID YOU THINK I'D BE FOOLED BY CHAINS SO EASILY ESCAPED?!
WHAT?! NO, THAT WAS NOT PART OF--!
SEIZE HIM!
NO GOOD DEED GOES UNPUNISHED. WHY DO I NEVER LEARN?
LORD LUCIFER, THIS ETRIGAN VOWS--
--HE WILL NEVER AGAIN SERVE ANYONE!

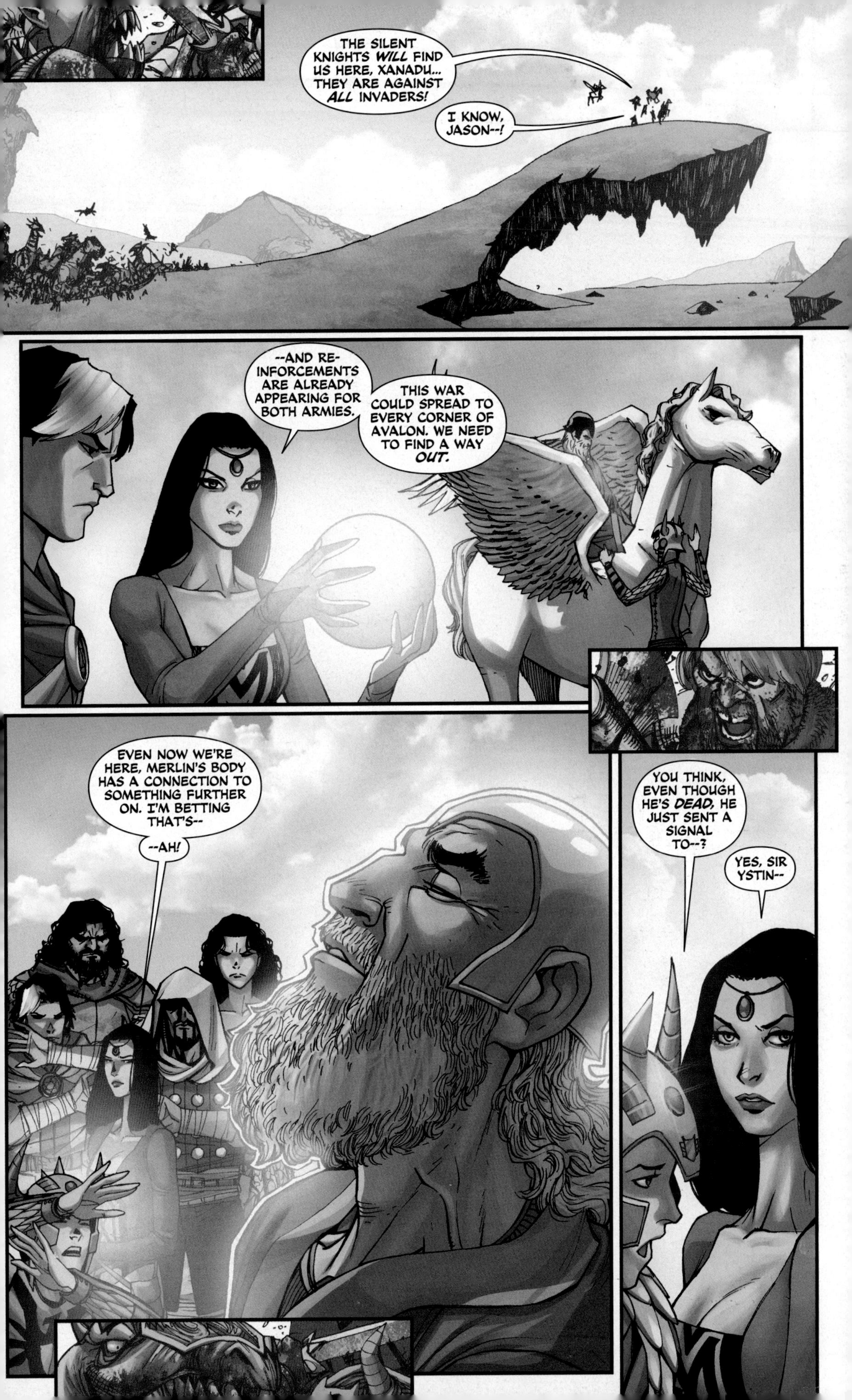
THE SILENT KNIGHTS *WILL* FIND US HERE, XANADU... THEY ARE AGAINST *ALL* INVADERS!
I KNOW, JASON--!
--AND RE-INFORCEMENTS ARE ALREADY APPEARING FOR BOTH ARMIES.
THIS WAR COULD SPREAD TO EVERY CORNER OF AVALON. WE NEED TO FIND A WAY *OUT*.
EVEN NOW WE'RE HERE, MERLIN'S BODY HAS A CONNECTION TO SOMETHING FURTHER ON. I'M BETTING THAT'S--
--AH!
YOU THINK, EVEN THOUGH HE'S *DEAD*, HE JUST SENT A SIGNAL TO--?
YES, SIR YSTIN--

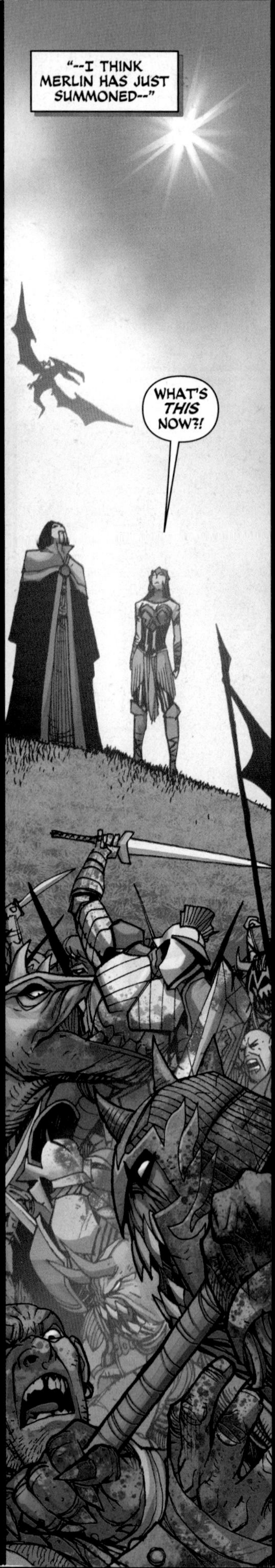
"--I THINK MERLIN HAS JUST SUMMONED--"
WHAT'S THIS NOW?!

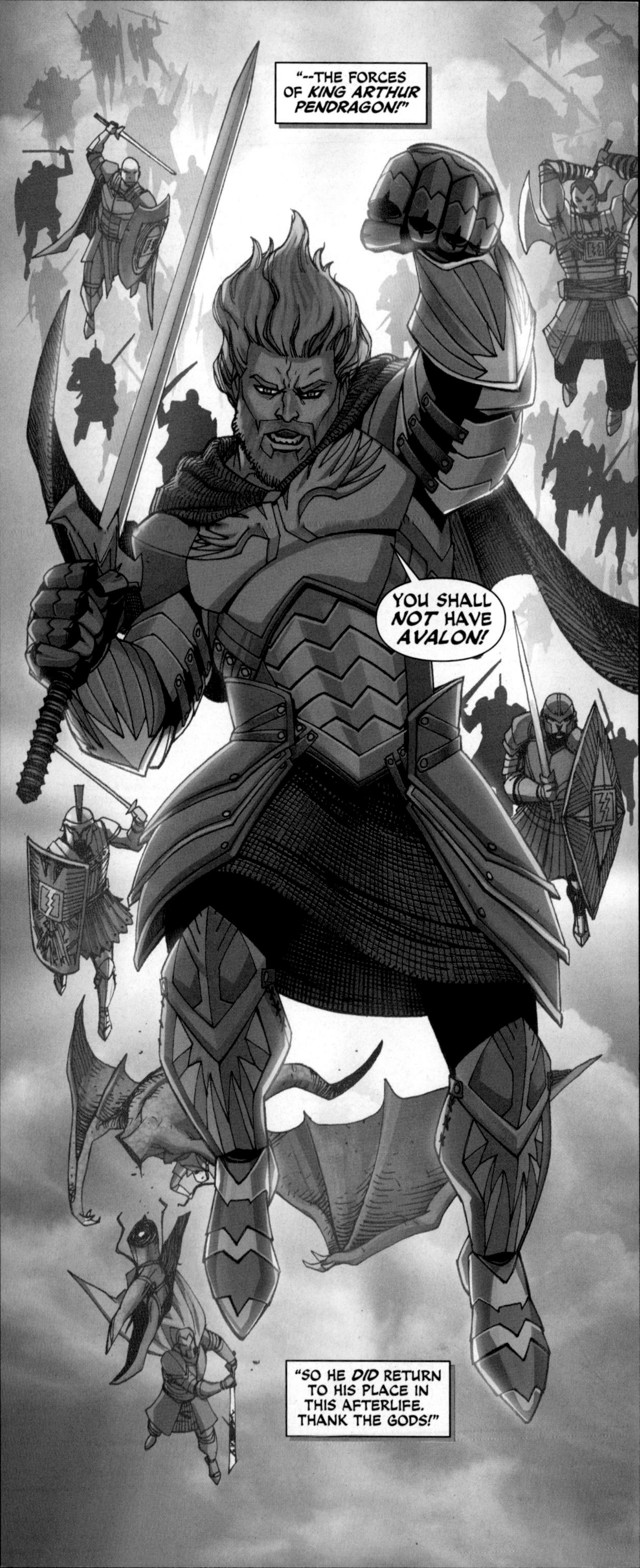
"--THE FORCES OF KING ARTHUR PENDRAGON!"
YOU SHALL NOT HAVE AVALON!
"SO HE DID RETURN TO HIS PLACE IN THIS AFTERLIFE. THANK THE GODS!"

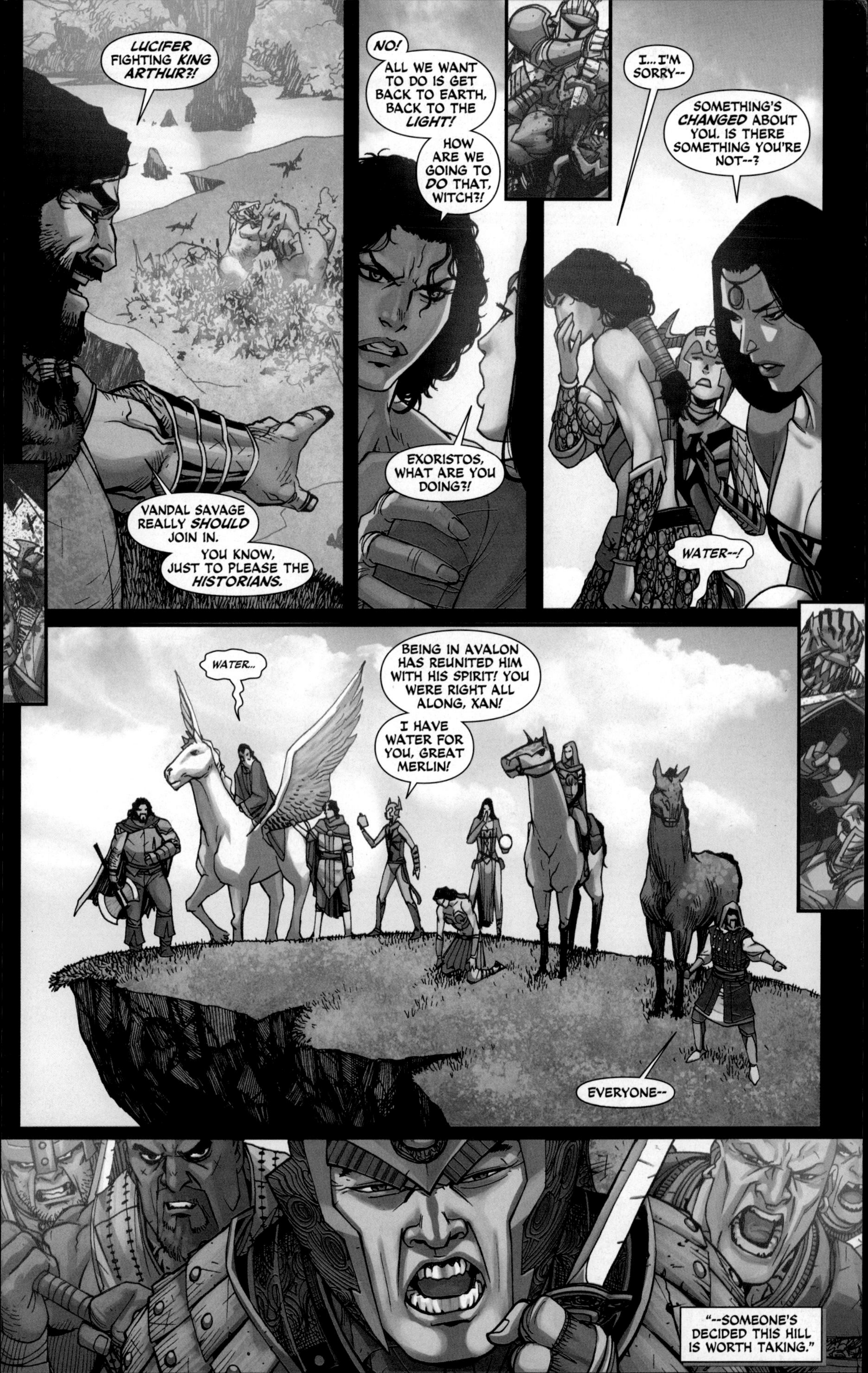
LUCIFER FIGHTING KING ARTHUR?!
VANDAL SAVAGE REALLY SHOULD JOIN IN.
YOU KNOW, JUST TO PLEASE THE HISTORIANS.
NO!
ALL WE WANT TO DO IS GET BACK TO EARTH, BACK TO THE LIGHT!
HOW ARE WE GOING TO DO THAT, WITCH?!
EXORISTOS, WHAT ARE YOU DOING?!
I...I'M SORRY--
SOMETHING'S CHANGED ABOUT YOU. IS THERE SOMETHING YOU'RE NOT--?
WATER--!
WATER...
BEING IN AVALON HAS REUNITED HIM WITH HIS SPIRIT! YOU WERE RIGHT ALL ALONG, XAN!
I HAVE WATER FOR YOU, GREAT MERLIN!
EVERYONE--
"--SOMEONE'S DECIDED THIS HILL IS WORTH TAKING."

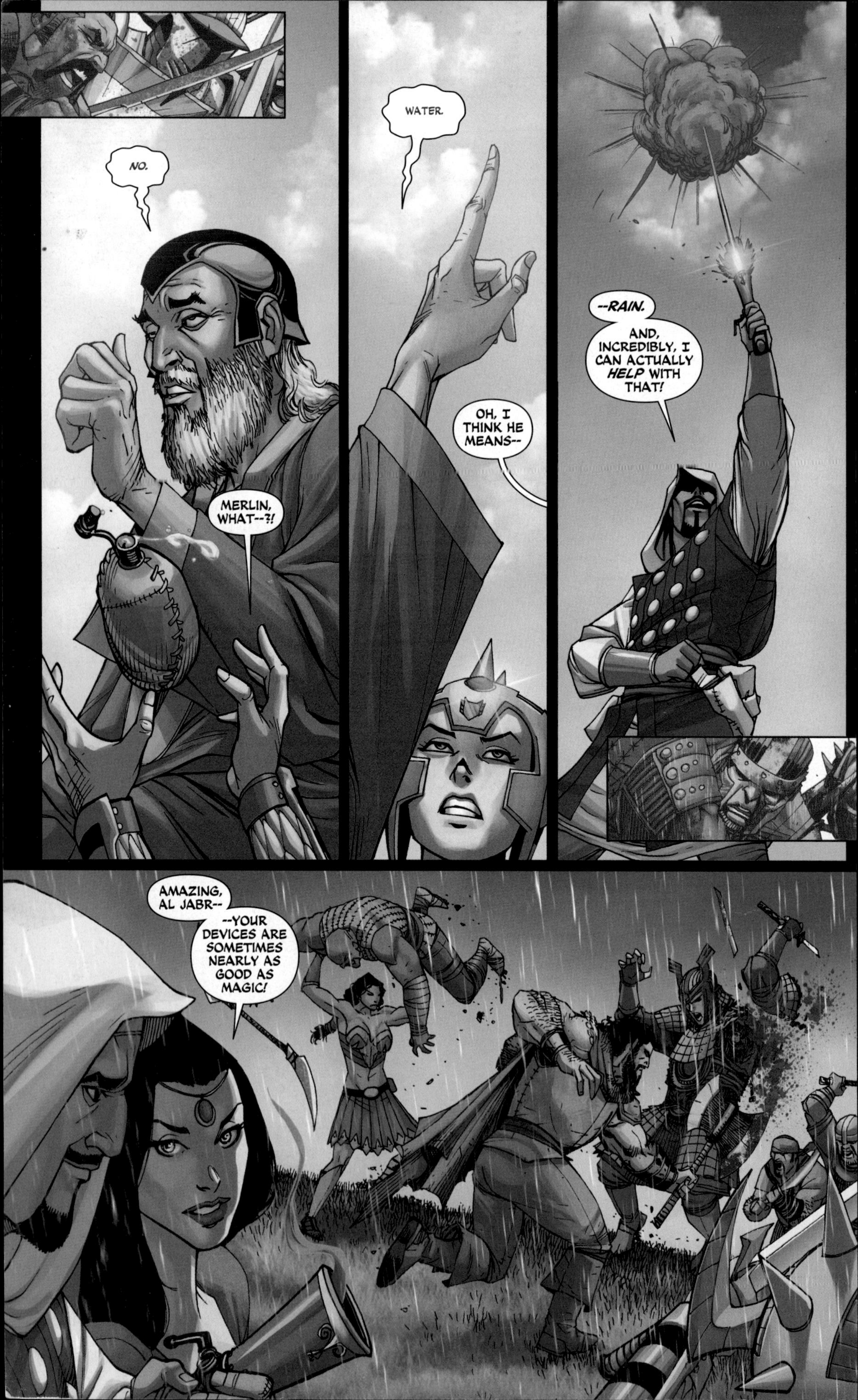

NO.
MERLIN, WHAT--?!
WATER.
OH, I THINK HE MEANS--
--RAIN.
AND, INCREDIBLY, I CAN ACTUALLY *HELP* WITH THAT!
AMAZING, AL JABR--
--YOUR DEVICES ARE SOMETIMES NEARLY AS GOOD AS MAGIC!

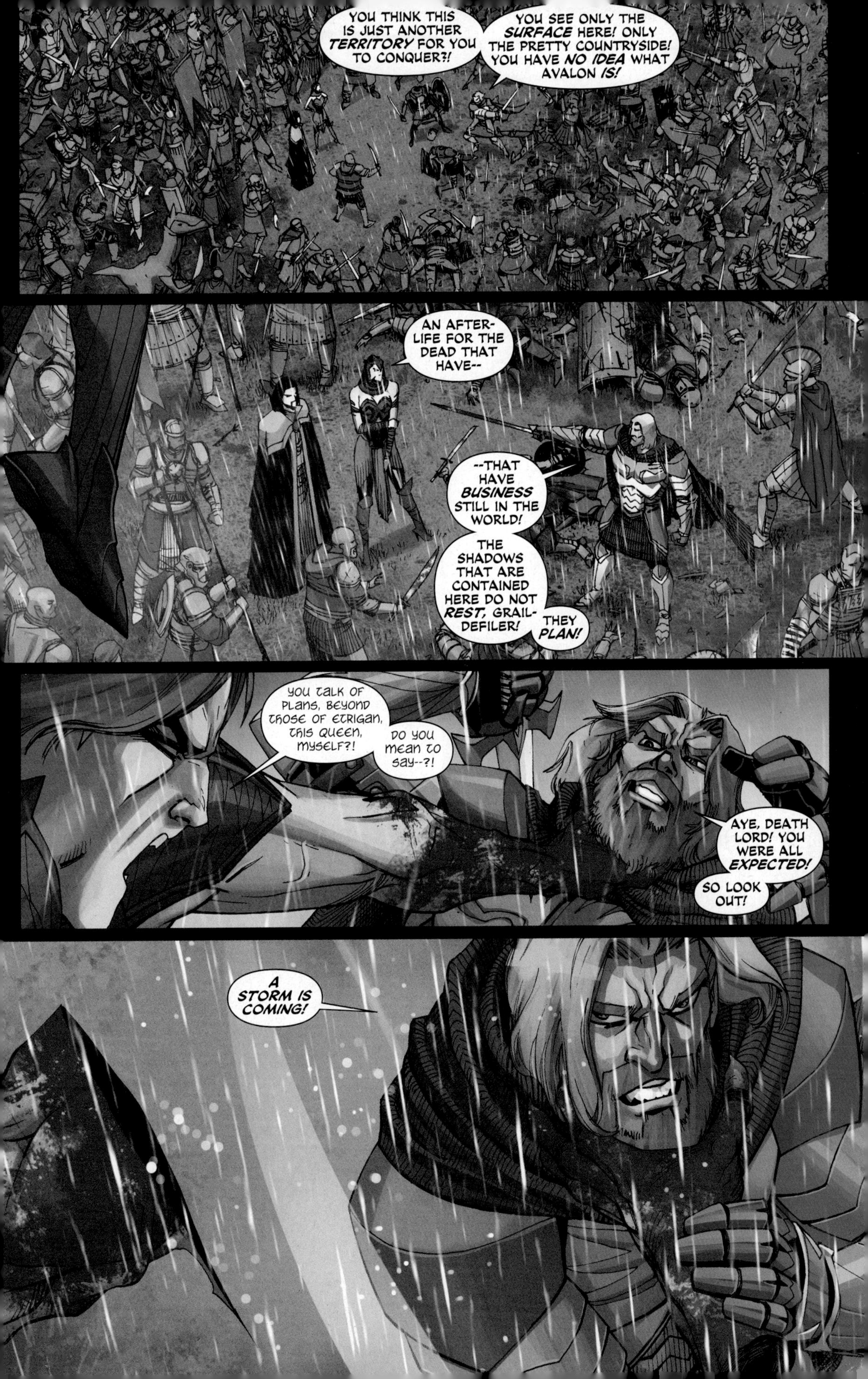
YOU THINK THIS IS JUST ANOTHER TERRITORY FOR YOU TO CONQUER?!
YOU SEE ONLY THE SURFACE HERE! ONLY THE PRETTY COUNTRYSIDE! YOU HAVE NO IDEA WHAT AVALON IS!
AN AFTER-LIFE FOR THE DEAD THAT HAVE--
--THAT HAVE BUSINESS STILL IN THE WORLD!
THE SHADOWS THAT ARE CONTAINED HERE DO NOT REST, GRAIL-DEFILER!
THEY PLAN!
YOU TALK OF PLANS, BEYOND THOSE OF ETRIGAN, THIS QUEEN, MYSELF?!
DO YOU MEAN TO SAY--?!
AYE, DEATH LORD! YOU WERE ALL EXPECTED!
SO LOOK OUT!
A STORM IS COMING!

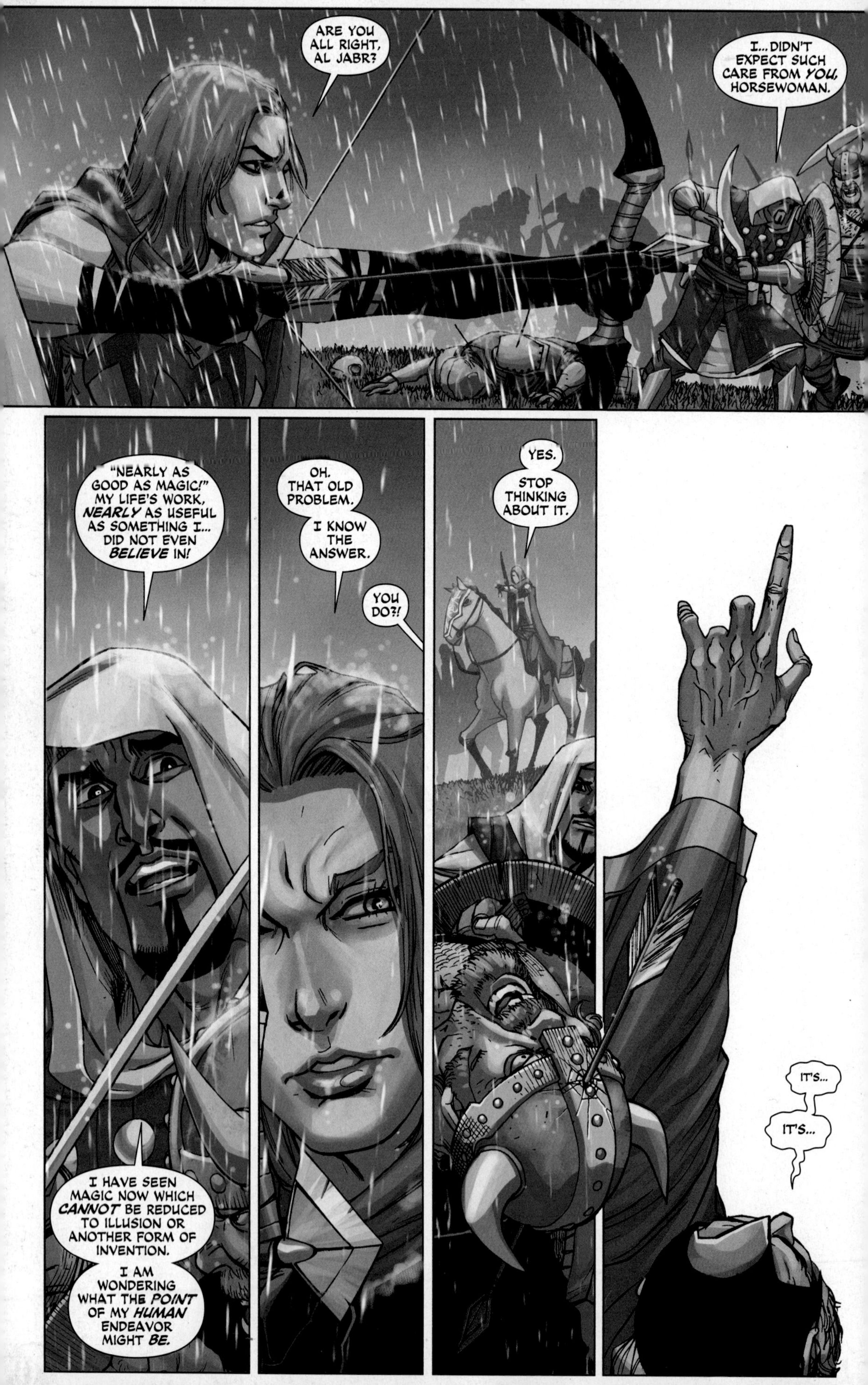
ARE YOU ALL RIGHT, AL JABR?
I...DIDN'T EXPECT SUCH CARE FROM *YOU,* HORSEWOMAN.
"NEARLY AS GOOD AS MAGIC!" MY LIFE'S WORK, *NEARLY* AS USEFUL AS SOMETHING I... DID NOT EVEN *BELIEVE* IN!
I HAVE SEEN MAGIC NOW WHICH *CANNOT* BE REDUCED TO ILLUSION OR ANOTHER FORM OF INVENTION.
I AM WONDERING WHAT THE *POINT* OF MY *HUMAN* ENDEAVOR MIGHT *BE.*
OH. THAT OLD PROBLEM.
I KNOW THE ANSWER.
YOU DO?!
YES.
STOP THINKING ABOUT IT.
IT'S...
IT'S...

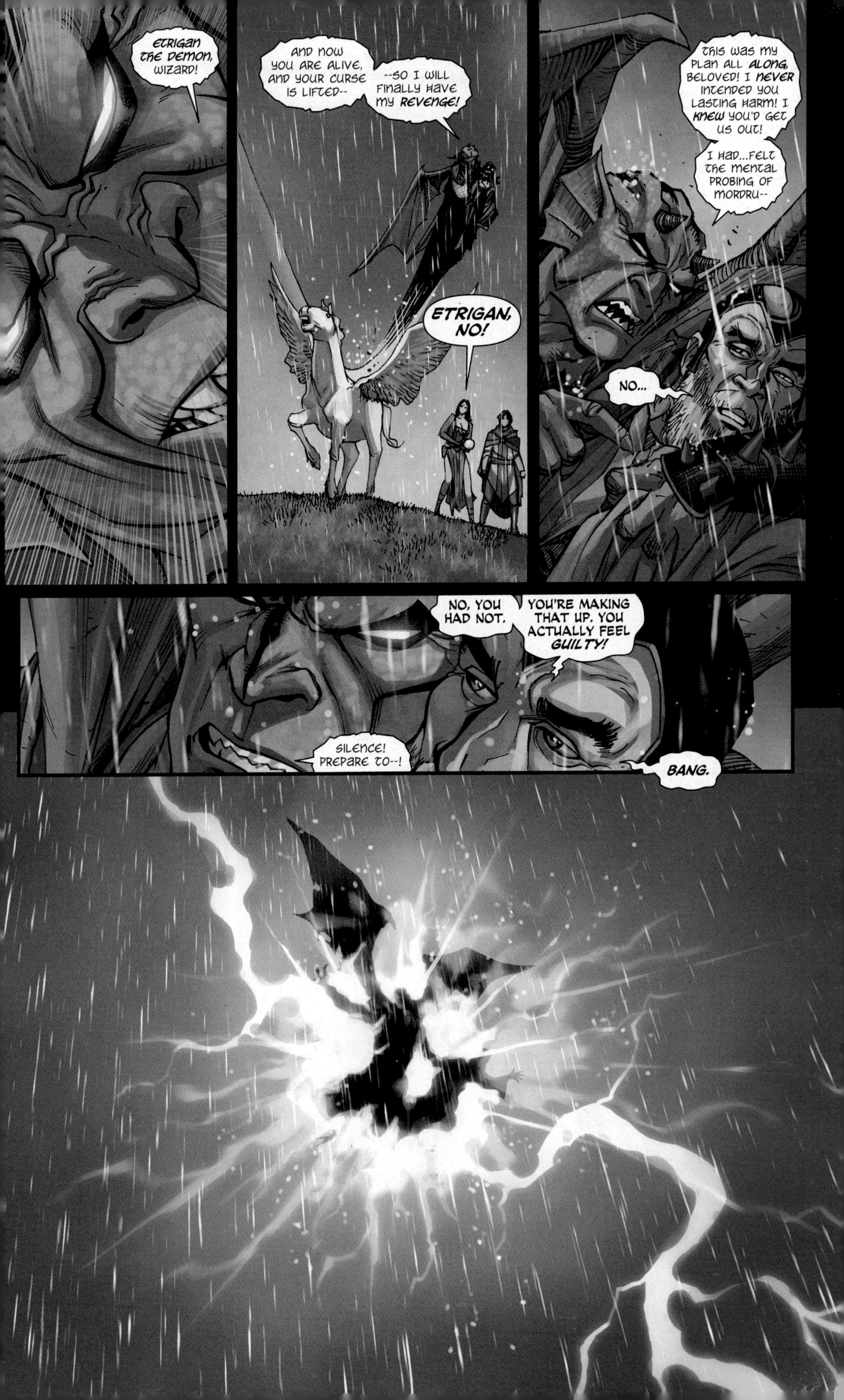
ETRIGAN THE DEMON, WIZARD!
AND NOW YOU ARE ALIVE, AND YOUR CURSE IS LIFTED--
--SO I WILL FINALLY HAVE MY REVENGE!
ETRIGAN, NO!
THIS WAS MY PLAN ALL ALONG, BELOVED! I NEVER INTENDED YOU LASTING HARM! I KNEW YOU'D GET US OUT!
I HAD...FELT THE MENTAL PROBING OF MORDRU--
NO...
NO, YOU HAD NOT.
YOU'RE MAKING THAT UP. YOU ACTUALLY FEEL GUILTY!
SILENCE! PREPARE TO--!
BANG.

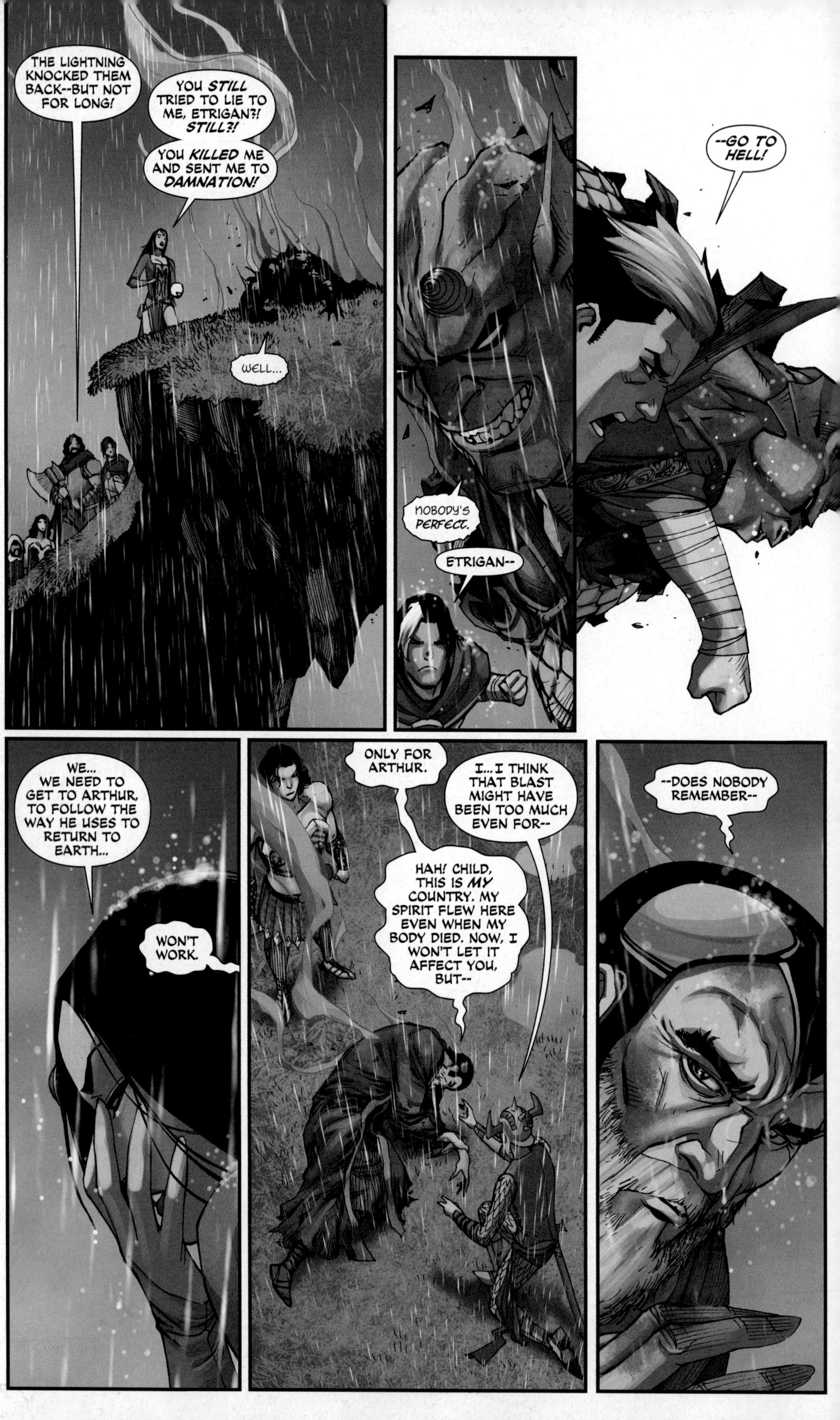
THE LIGHTNING KNOCKED THEM BACK--BUT NOT FOR LONG!
YOU STILL TRIED TO LIE TO ME, ETRIGAN?! STILL?!
YOU KILLED ME AND SENT ME TO DAMNATION!
WELL...
NOBODY'S PERFECT.
ETRIGAN--
--GO TO HELL!
WE... WE NEED TO GET TO ARTHUR, TO FOLLOW THE WAY HE USES TO RETURN TO EARTH...
WON'T WORK.
ONLY FOR ARTHUR.
I...I THINK THAT BLAST MIGHT HAVE BEEN TOO MUCH EVEN FOR--
HAH! CHILD, THIS IS MY COUNTRY. MY SPIRIT FLEW HERE EVEN WHEN MY BODY DIED. NOW, I WON'T LET IT AFFECT YOU, BUT--
--DOES NOBODY REMEMBER--

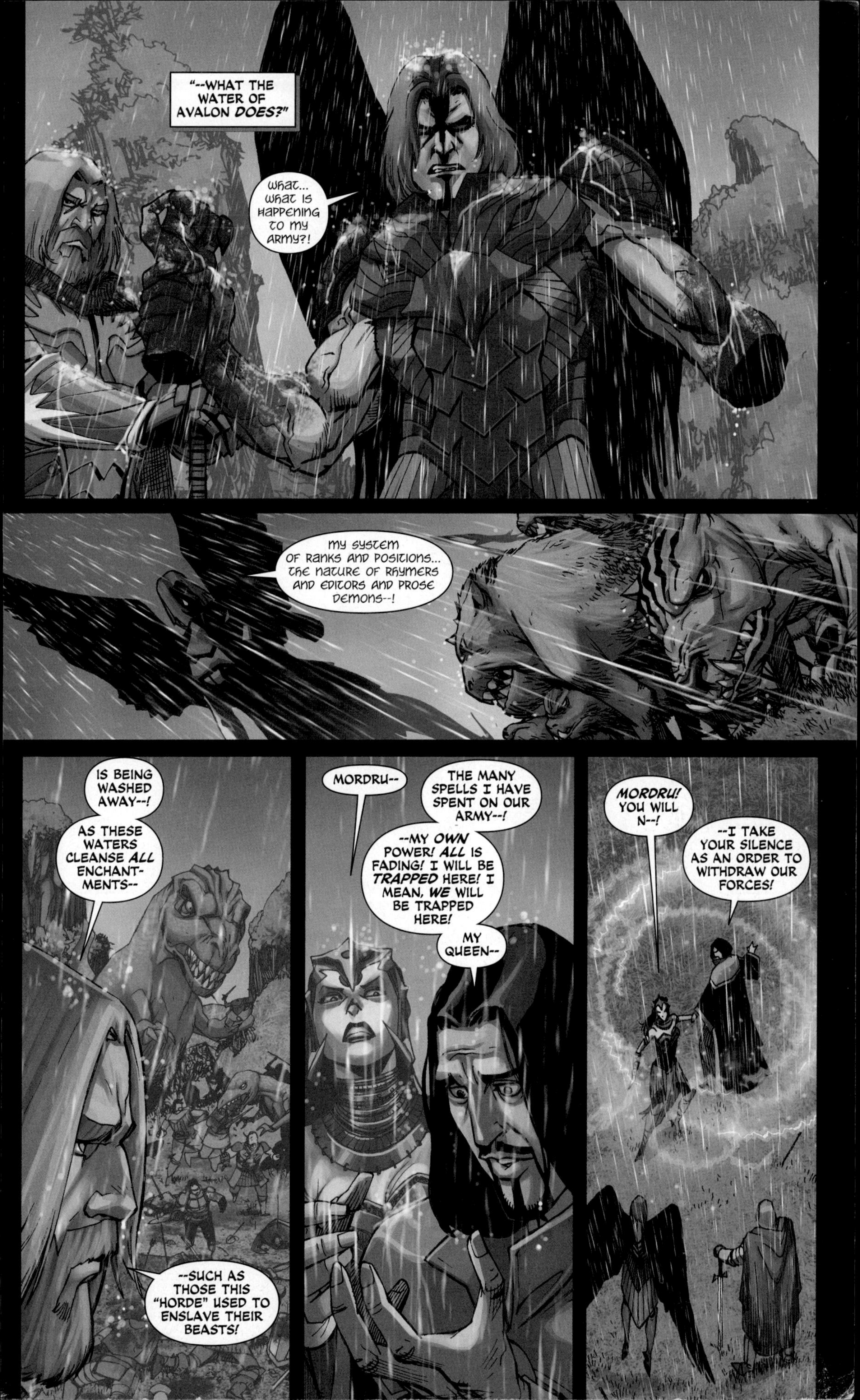
"--WHAT THE WATER OF AVALON *DOES?*"
WHAT... WHAT IS HAPPENING TO MY ARMY?!
MY SYSTEM OF RANKS AND POSITIONS... THE NATURE OF RHYMERS AND EDITORS AND PROSE DEMONS--!
IS BEING WASHED AWAY--!
AS THESE WATERS CLEANSE *ALL* ENCHANT-MENTS--
--SUCH AS THOSE THIS "HORDE" USED TO ENSLAVE THEIR BEASTS!
MORDRU--
THE MANY SPELLS I HAVE SPENT ON OUR ARMY--!
--MY *OWN* POWER! *ALL* IS FADING! I WILL BE *TRAPPED* HERE! I MEAN, *WE* WILL BE TRAPPED HERE!
MY QUEEN--
MORDRU! YOU WILL N--!
--I TAKE YOUR SILENCE AS AN ORDER TO WITHDRAW OUR FORCES!

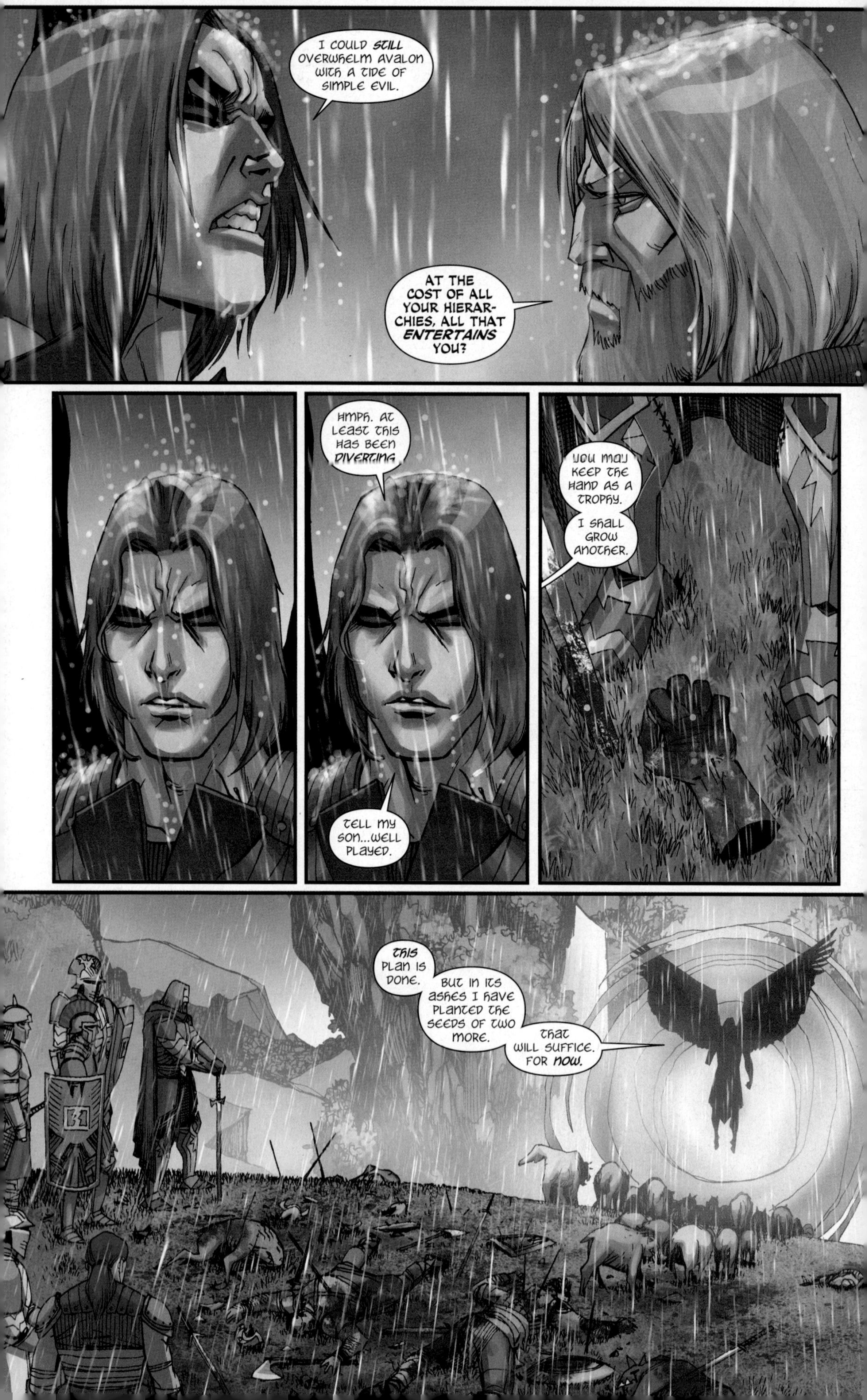
I COULD STILL OVERWHELM AVALON WITH A TIDE OF SIMPLE EVIL.
AT THE COST OF ALL YOUR HIERARCHIES, ALL THAT ENTERTAINS YOU?
HMPH. AT LEAST THIS HAS BEEN DIVERTING.
TELL MY SON...WELL PLAYED.
YOU MAY KEEP THE HAND AS A TROPHY.
I SHALL GROW ANOTHER.
THIS PLAN IS DONE.
BUT IN ITS ASHES I HAVE PLANTED THE SEEDS OF TWO MORE.
THAT WILL SUFFICE. FOR NOW.

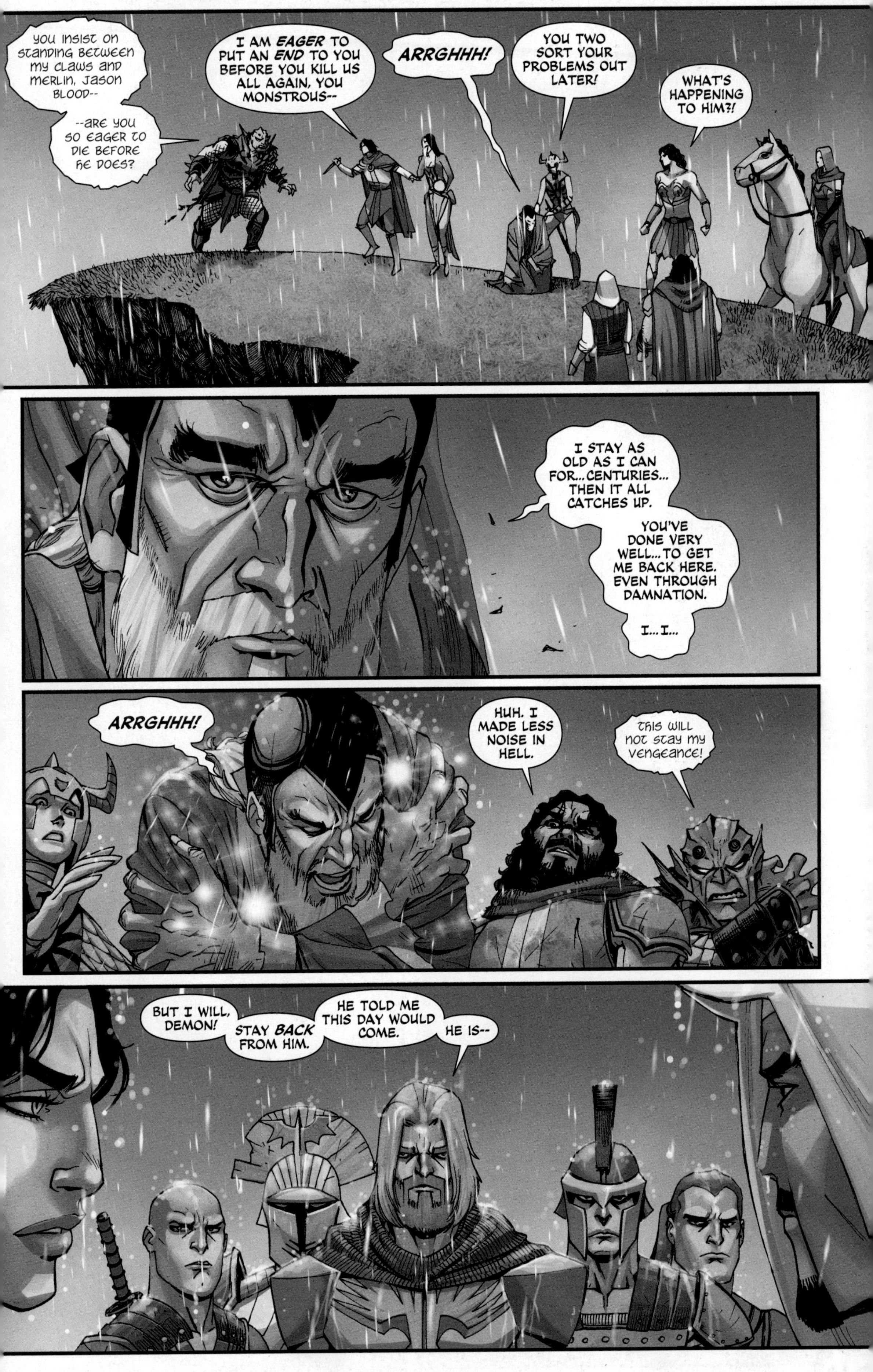

You insist on standing between my claws and Merlin, Jason Blood--
--are you so eager to die before he does?
I AM EAGER TO PUT AN END TO YOU BEFORE YOU KILL US ALL AGAIN, YOU MONSTROUS--
ARRGHHH!
YOU TWO SORT YOUR PROBLEMS OUT LATER!
WHAT'S HAPPENING TO HIM?!
I STAY AS OLD AS I CAN FOR...CENTURIES... THEN IT ALL CATCHES UP.
YOU'VE DONE VERY WELL...TO GET ME BACK HERE. EVEN THROUGH DAMNATION.
I...I...
ARRGHHH!
HUH. I MADE LESS NOISE IN HELL.
This will not stay my vengeance!
BUT I WILL, DEMON!
STAY BACK FROM HIM.
HE TOLD ME THIS DAY WOULD COME.
HE IS--

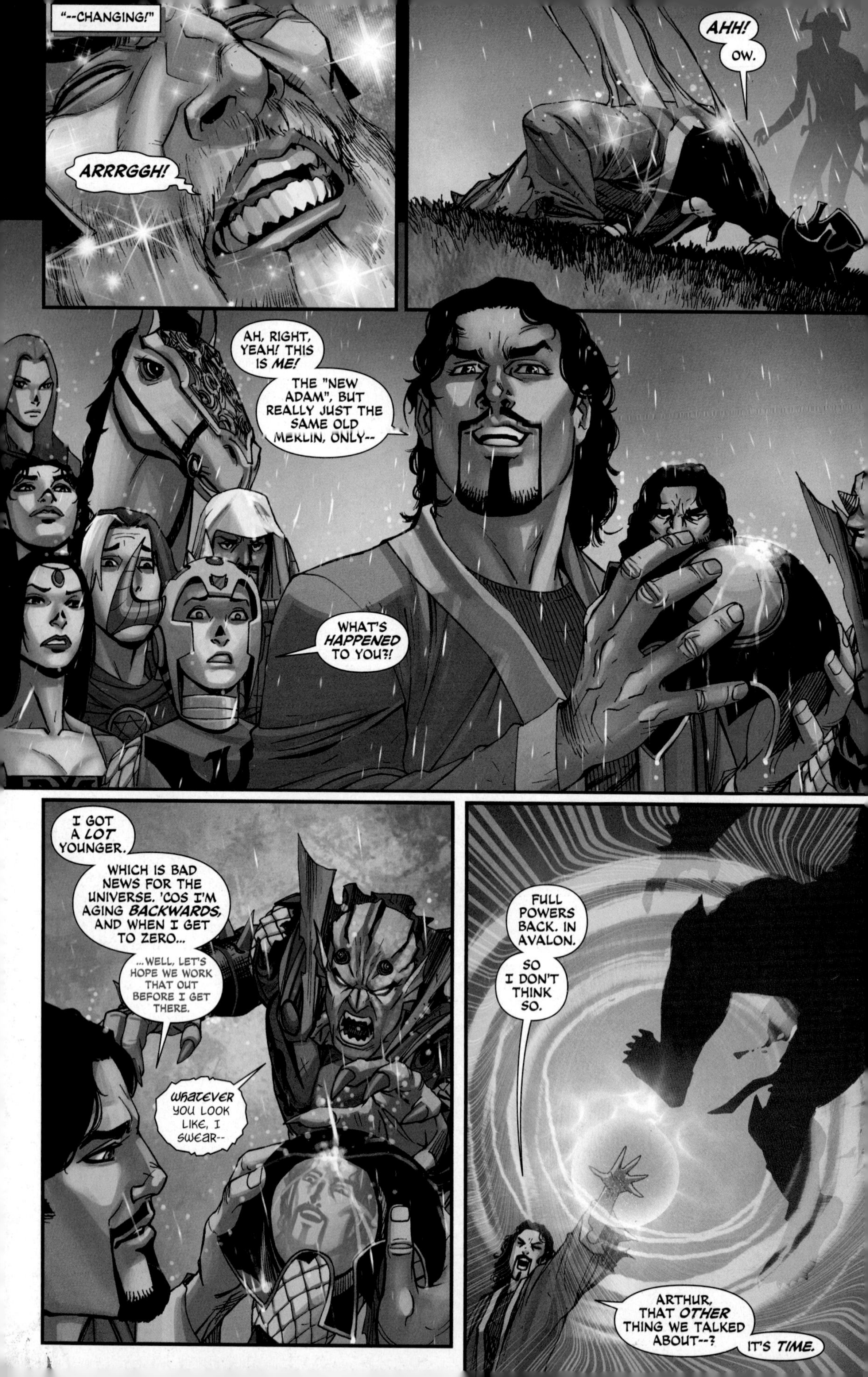
"--CHANGING!"
ARRRGGH!
AHH!
OW.
AH, RIGHT, YEAH! THIS IS ME!
THE "NEW ADAM", BUT REALLY JUST THE SAME OLD MERLIN, ONLY--
WHAT'S HAPPENED TO YOU?!
I GOT A LOT YOUNGER.
WHICH IS BAD NEWS FOR THE UNIVERSE. 'COS I'M AGING BACKWARDS, AND WHEN I GET TO ZERO...
...WELL, LET'S HOPE WE WORK THAT OUT BEFORE I GET THERE.
WHATEVER YOU LOOK LIKE, I SWEAR--
FULL POWERS BACK. IN AVALON.
SO I DON'T THINK SO.
ARTHUR, THAT OTHER THING WE TALKED ABOUT--?
IT'S TIME.

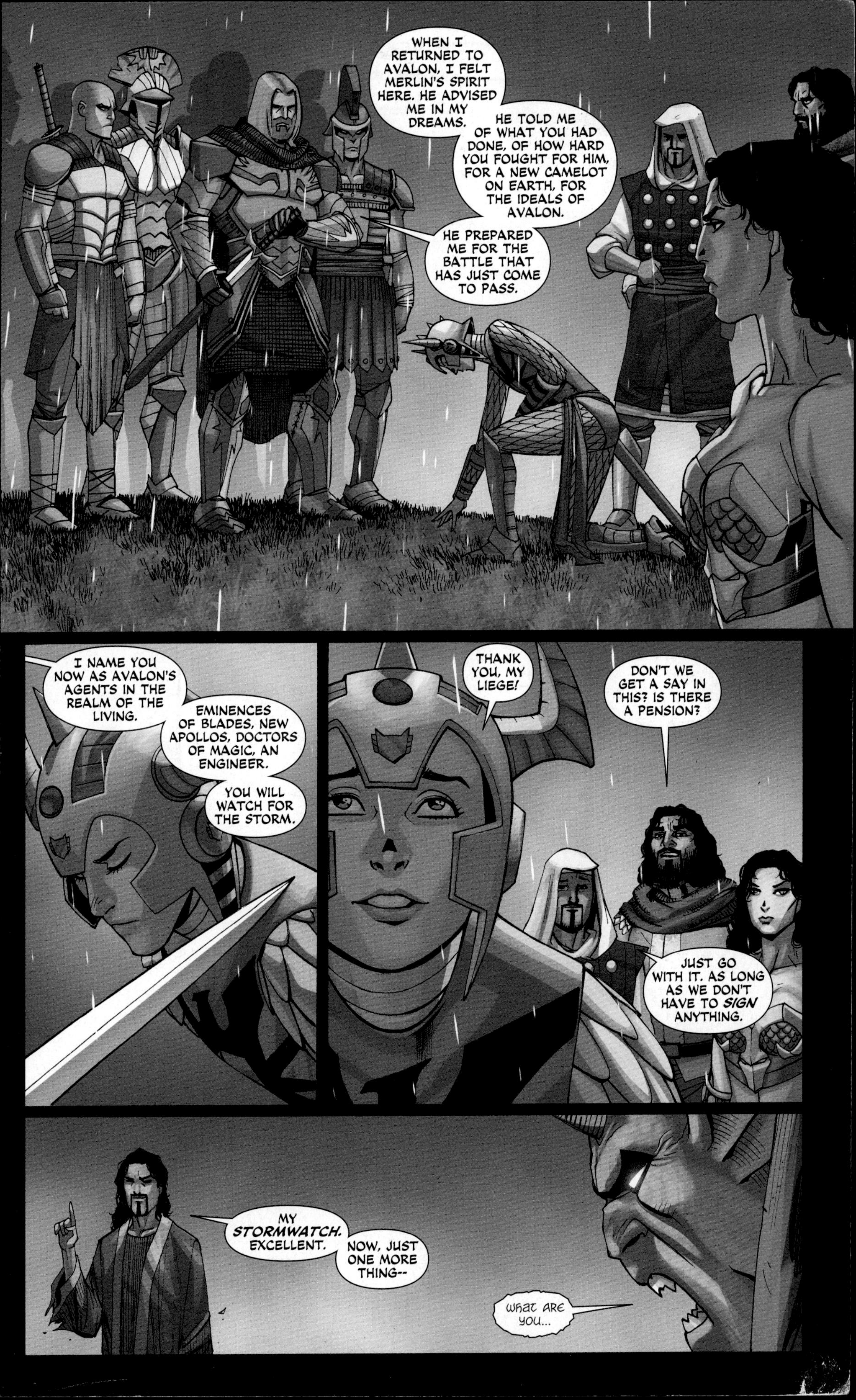
WHEN I RETURNED TO AVALON, I FELT MERLIN'S SPIRIT HERE. HE ADVISED ME IN MY DREAMS.
HE TOLD ME OF WHAT YOU HAD DONE, OF HOW HARD YOU FOUGHT FOR HIM, FOR A NEW CAMELOT ON EARTH, FOR THE IDEALS OF AVALON.
HE PREPARED ME FOR THE BATTLE THAT HAS JUST COME TO PASS.
I NAME YOU NOW AS AVALON'S AGENTS IN THE REALM OF THE LIVING.
EMINENCES OF BLADES, NEW APOLLOS, DOCTORS OF MAGIC, AN ENGINEER.
YOU WILL WATCH FOR THE STORM.
THANK YOU, MY LIEGE!
DON'T WE GET A SAY IN THIS? IS THERE A PENSION?
JUST GO WITH IT. AS LONG AS WE DON'T HAVE TO *SIGN* ANYTHING.
MY ***STORMWATCH.*** EXCELLENT.
NOW, JUST ONE MORE THING--
WHAT ARE YOU...

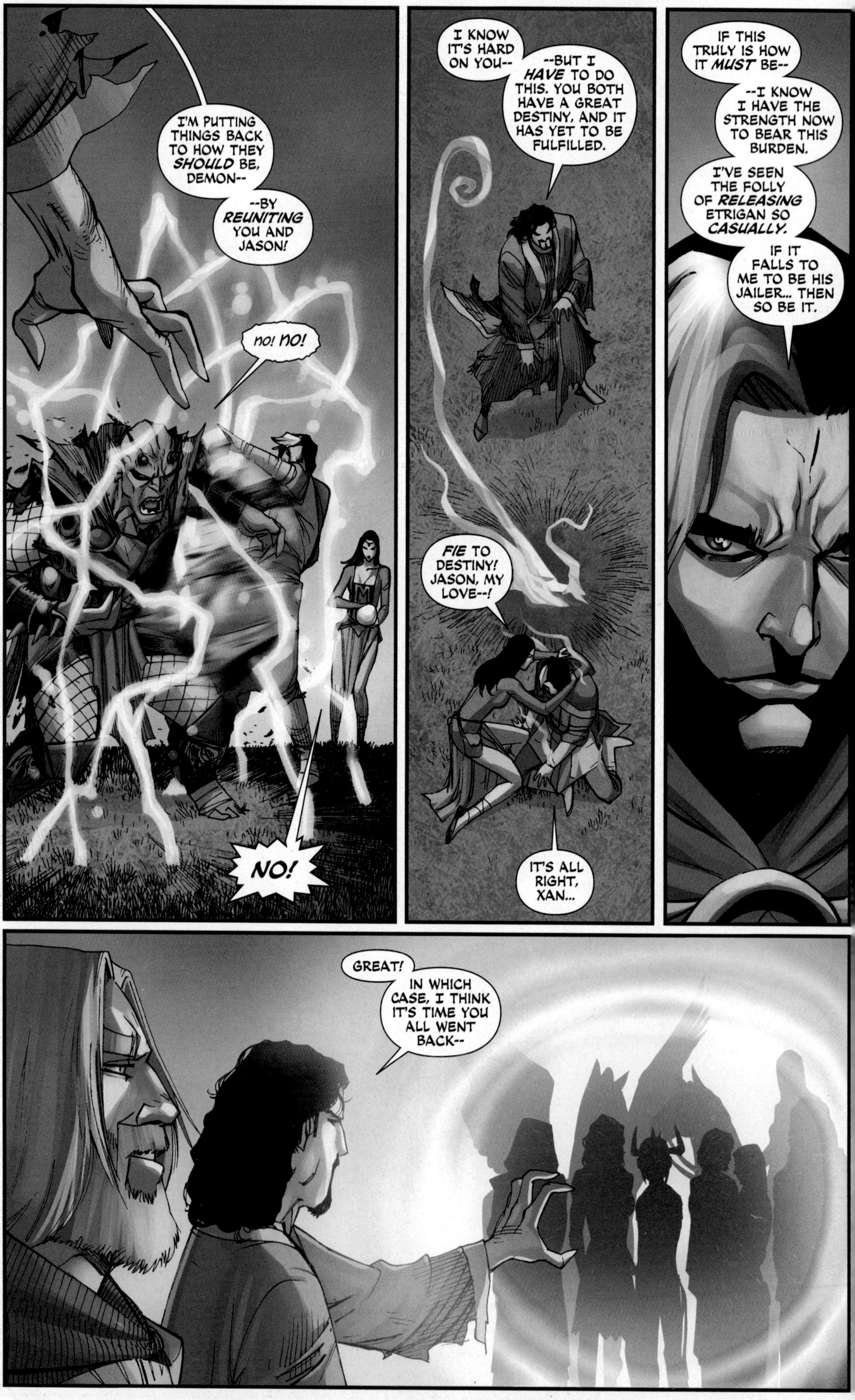
I'M PUTTING THINGS BACK TO HOW THEY *SHOULD* BE, DEMON--
--BY *REUNITING* YOU AND JASON!
no! NO!
NO!
I KNOW IT'S HARD ON YOU--
--BUT I *HAVE* TO DO THIS. YOU BOTH HAVE A GREAT DESTINY, AND IT HAS YET TO BE FULFILLED.
FIE TO DESTINY! JASON, MY LOVE--!
IT'S ALL RIGHT, XAN...
IF THIS TRULY IS HOW IT *MUST* BE--
--I KNOW I HAVE THE STRENGTH NOW TO BEAR THIS BURDEN.
I'VE SEEN THE FOLLY OF *RELEASING* ETRIGAN SO *CASUALLY*.
IF IT FALLS TO ME TO BE HIS JAILER... THEN SO BE IT.
GREAT!
IN WHICH CASE, I THINK IT'S TIME YOU ALL WENT BACK--

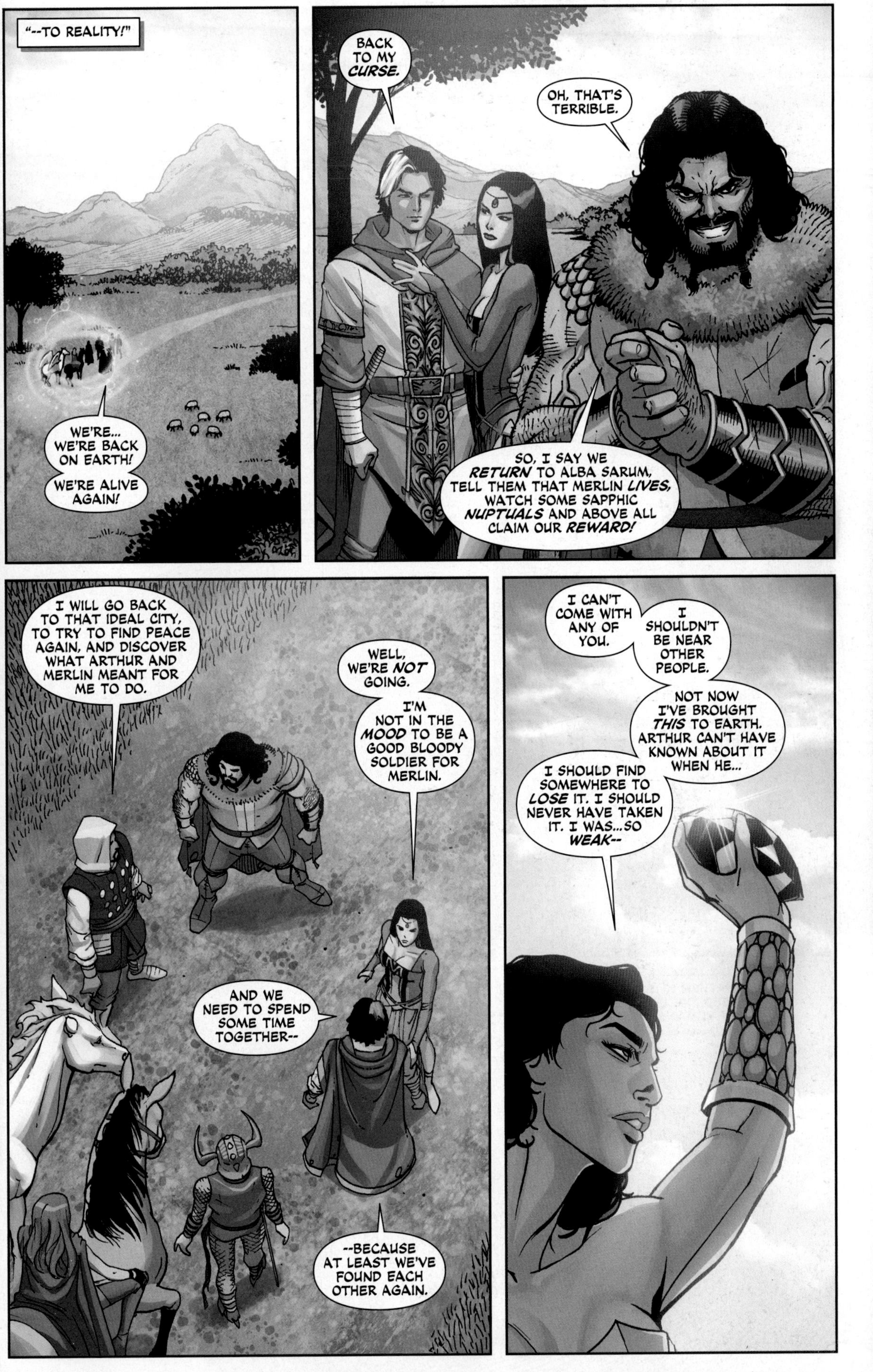
"--TO REALITY!"
WE'RE... WE'RE BACK ON EARTH!
WE'RE ALIVE AGAIN!
BACK TO MY CURSE.
OH, THAT'S TERRIBLE.
SO, I SAY WE RETURN TO ALBA SARUM, TELL THEM THAT MERLIN LIVES, WATCH SOME SAPPHIC NUPTUALS AND ABOVE ALL CLAIM OUR REWARD!
I WILL GO BACK TO THAT IDEAL CITY, TO TRY TO FIND PEACE AGAIN, AND DISCOVER WHAT ARTHUR AND MERLIN MEANT FOR ME TO DO.
WELL, WE'RE NOT GOING.
I'M NOT IN THE MOOD TO BE A GOOD BLOODY SOLDIER FOR MERLIN.
AND WE NEED TO SPEND SOME TIME TOGETHER--
--BECAUSE AT LEAST WE'VE FOUND EACH OTHER AGAIN.
I CAN'T COME WITH ANY OF YOU.
I SHOULDN'T BE NEAR OTHER PEOPLE.
NOT NOW I'VE BROUGHT THIS TO EARTH. ARTHUR CAN'T HAVE KNOWN ABOUT IT WHEN HE...
I SHOULD FIND SOMEWHERE TO LOSE IT. I SHOULD NEVER HAVE TAKEN IT. I WAS...SO WEAK--

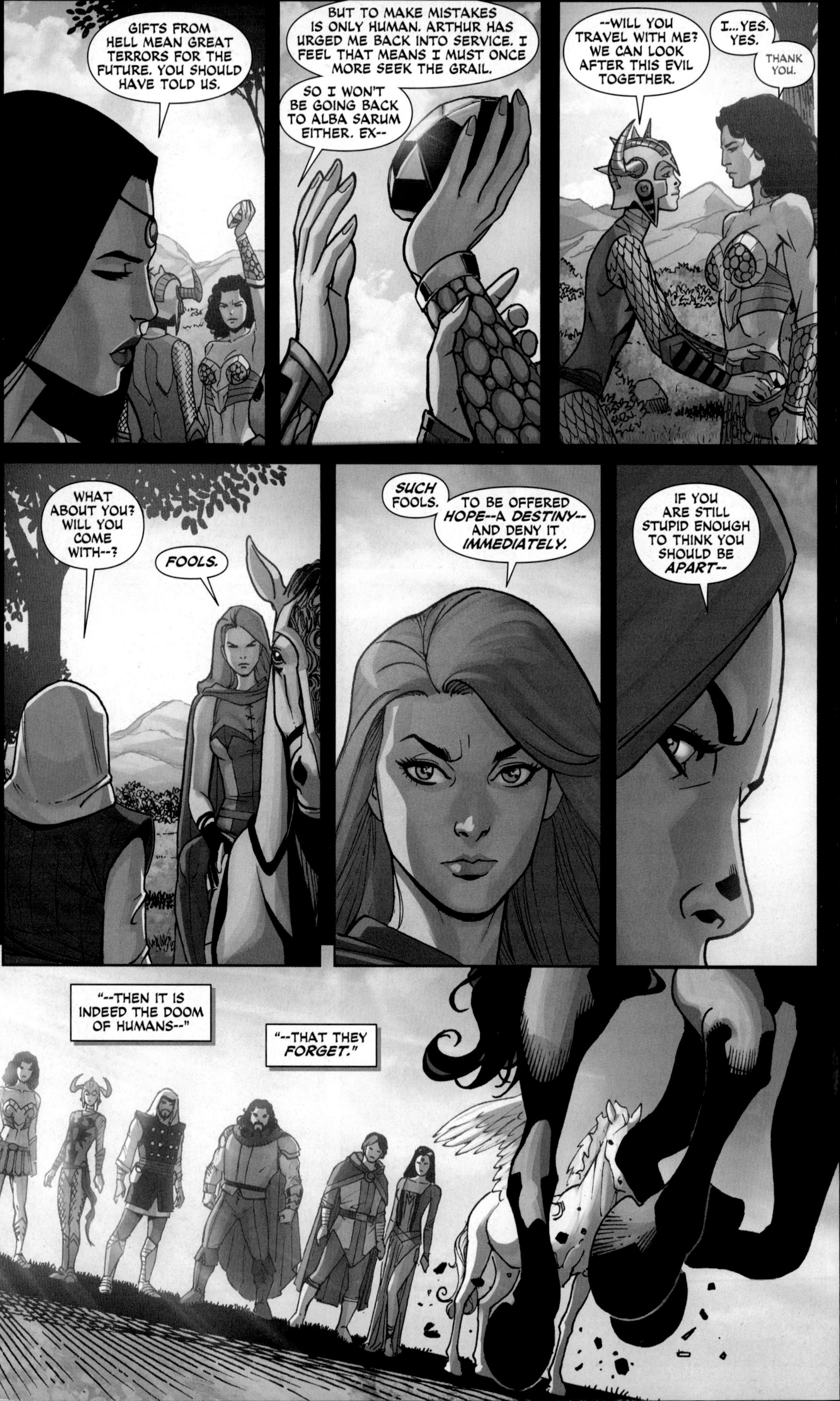
GIFTS FROM HELL MEAN GREAT TERRORS FOR THE FUTURE. YOU SHOULD HAVE TOLD US.
BUT TO MAKE MISTAKES IS ONLY HUMAN. ARTHUR HAS URGED ME BACK INTO SERVICE. I FEEL THAT MEANS I MUST ONCE MORE SEEK THE GRAIL.
SO I WON'T BE GOING BACK TO ALBA SARUM EITHER. EX--
--WILL YOU TRAVEL WITH ME? WE CAN LOOK AFTER THIS EVIL TOGETHER.
I...YES. YES.
THANK YOU.
WHAT ABOUT YOU? WILL YOU COME WITH--?
FOOLS.
SUCH FOOLS.
TO BE OFFERED HOPE--A DESTINY--AND DENY IT IMMEDIATELY.
IF YOU ARE STILL STUPID ENOUGH TO THINK YOU SHOULD BE APART--
"--THEN IT IS INDEED THE DOOM OF HUMANS--"
"--THAT THEY FORGET."

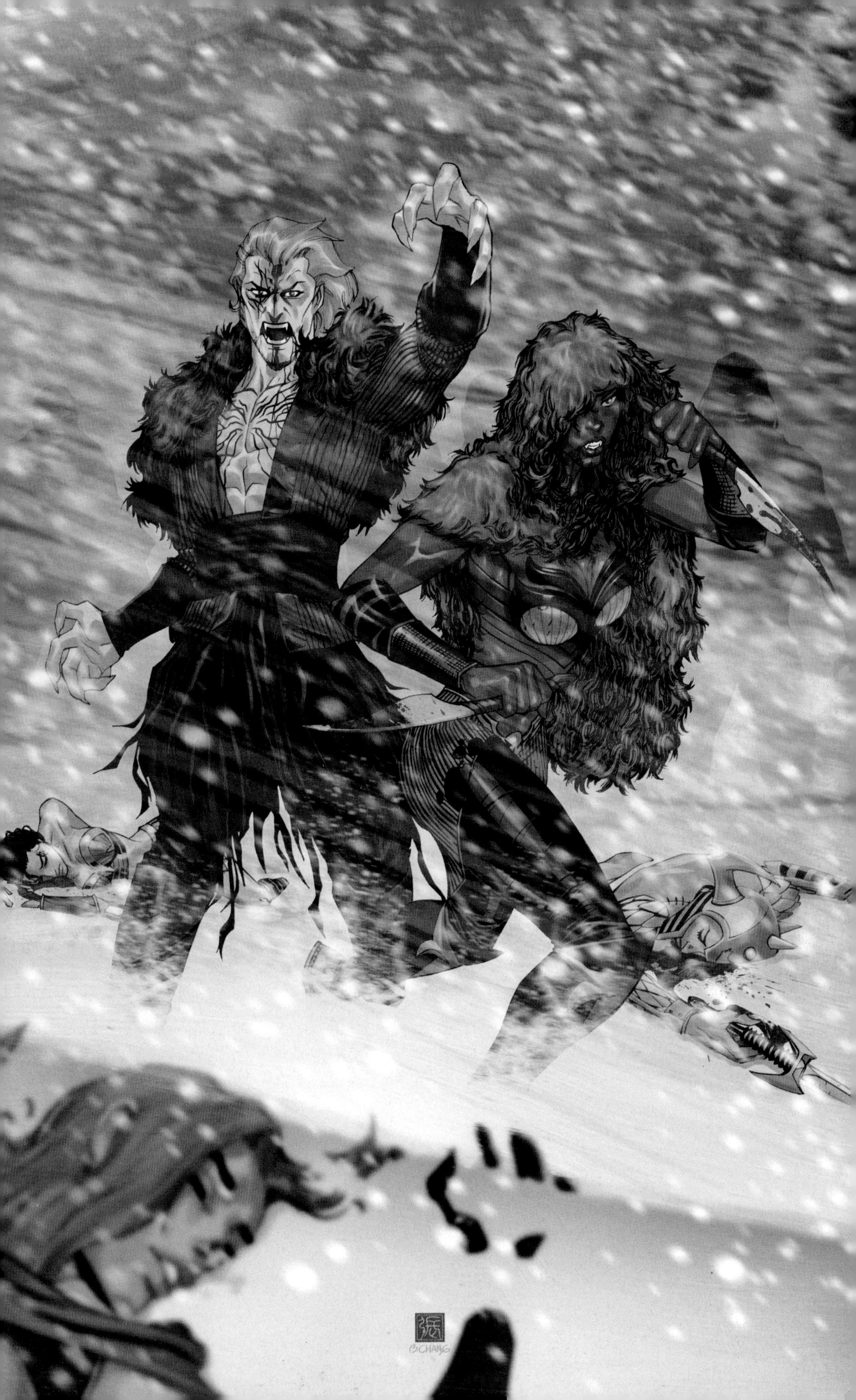
張
B.CHANG

ROBERT VENDITTI
writer

BERNARD CHANG
artist

BERNARD CHANG
cover artist

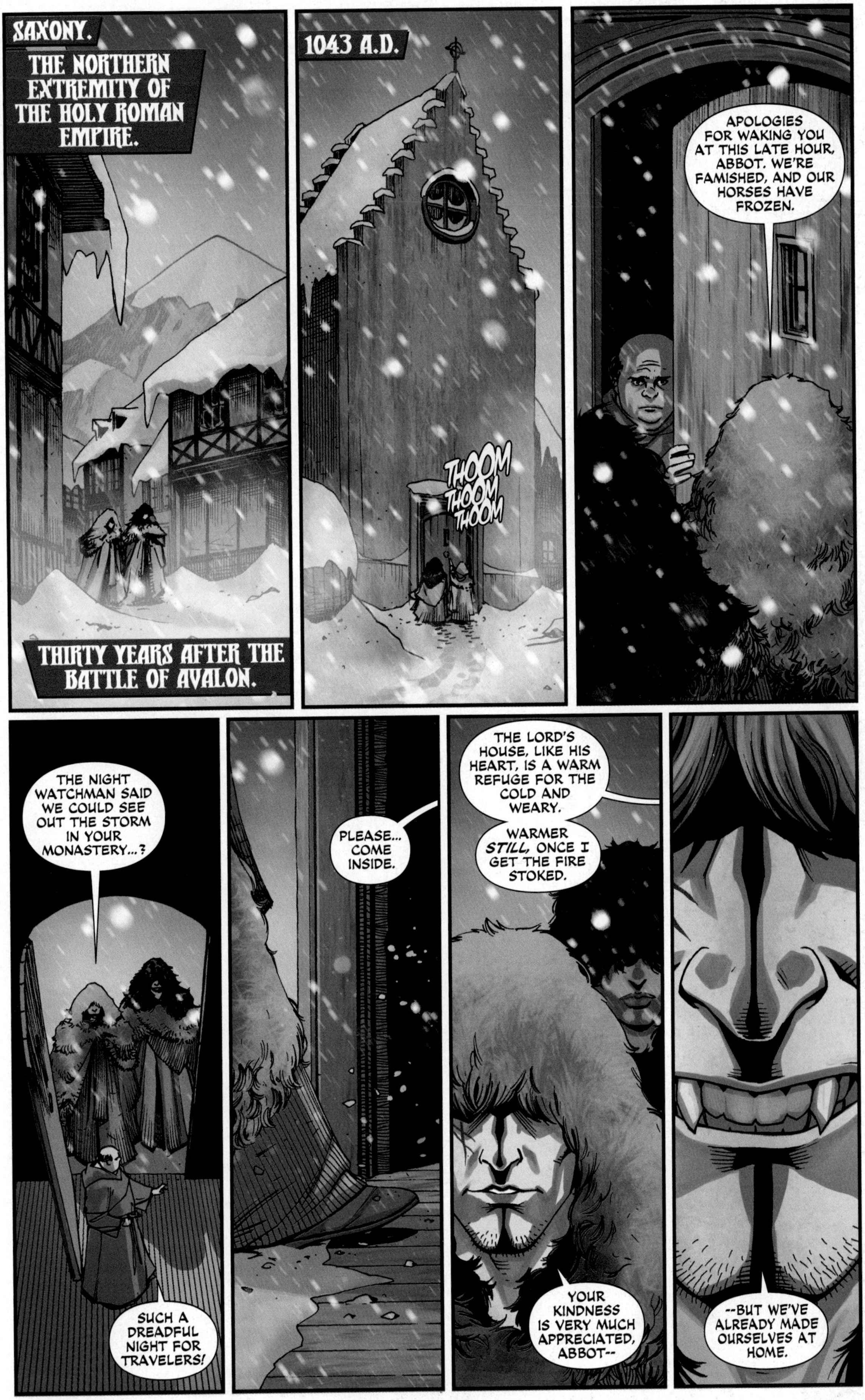
SAXONY.
THE NORTHERN EXTREMITY OF THE HOLY ROMAN EMPIRE.
THIRTY YEARS AFTER THE BATTLE OF AVALON.
1043 A.D.
THOOM THOOM THOOM
APOLOGIES FOR WAKING YOU AT THIS LATE HOUR, ABBOT. WE'RE FAMISHED, AND OUR HORSES HAVE FROZEN.
THE NIGHT WATCHMAN SAID WE COULD SEE OUT THE STORM IN YOUR MONASTERY...?
SUCH A DREADFUL NIGHT FOR TRAVELERS!
PLEASE... COME INSIDE.
THE LORD'S HOUSE, LIKE HIS HEART, IS A WARM REFUGE FOR THE COLD AND WEARY.
WARMER *STILL*, ONCE I GET THE FIRE STOKED.
YOUR KINDNESS IS VERY MUCH APPRECIATED, ABBOT--
--BUT WE'VE ALREADY MADE OURSELVES AT HOME.

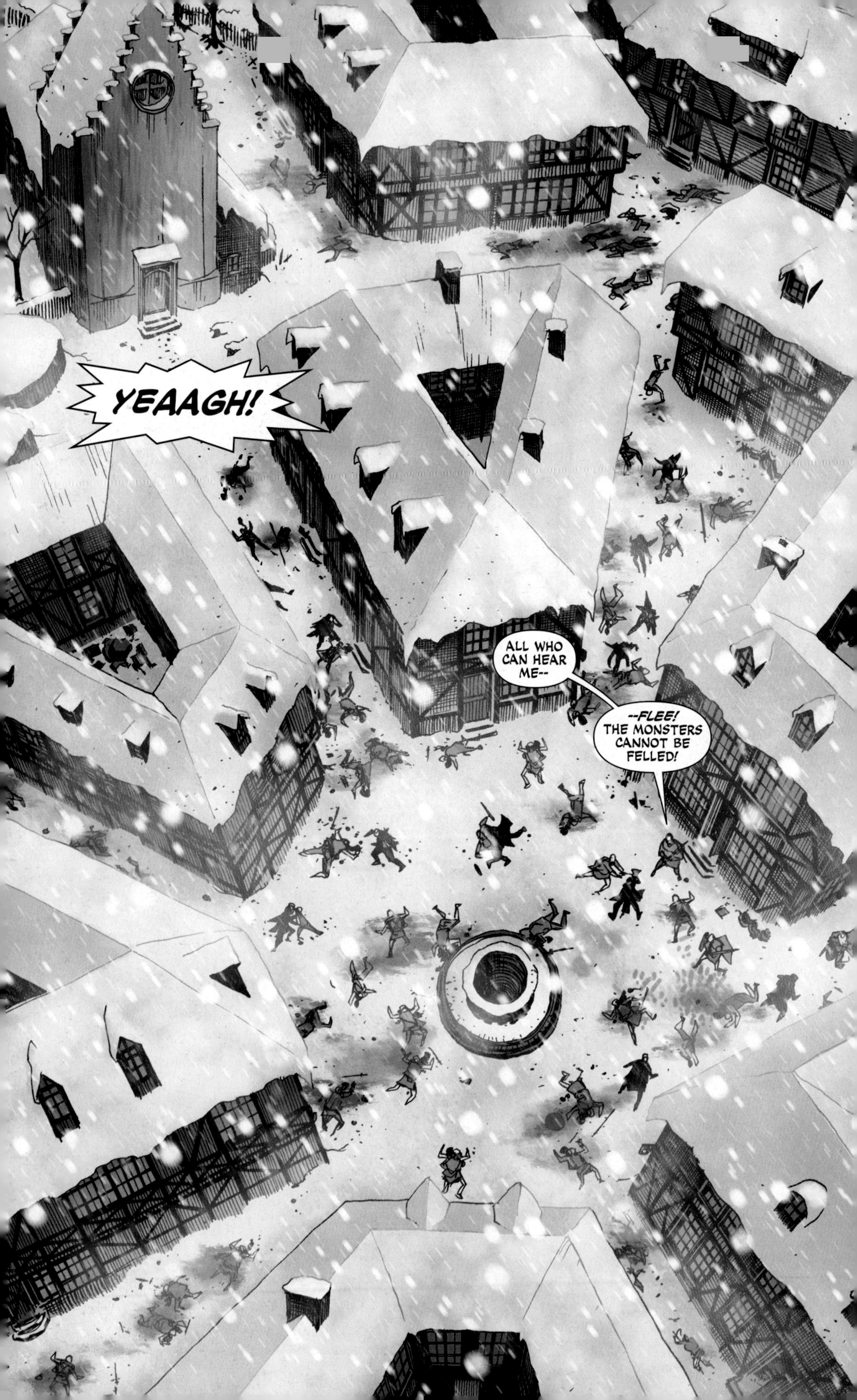
YEAAGH!
ALL WHO CAN HEAR ME--
--FLEE! THE MONSTERS CANNOT BE FELLED!

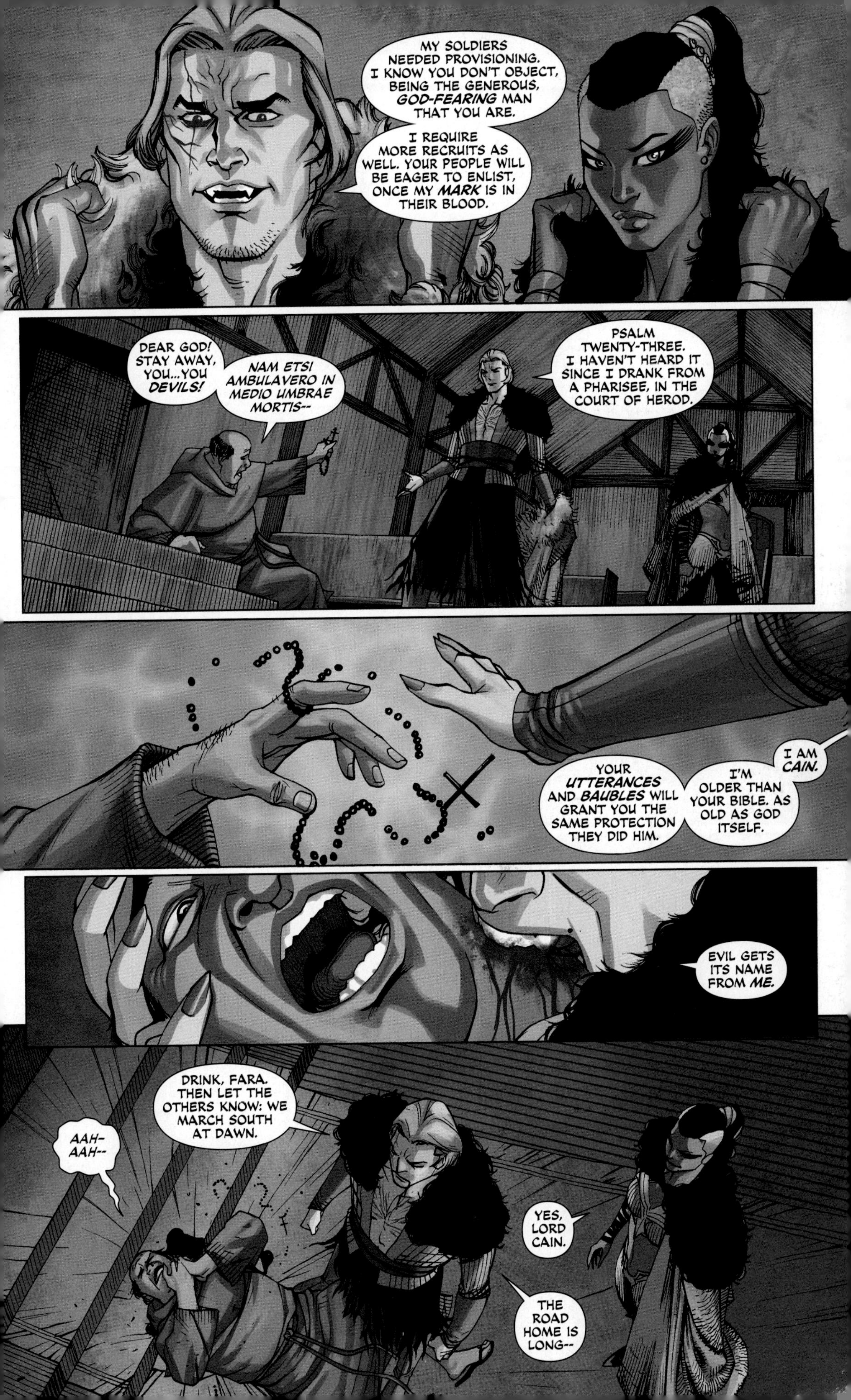
MY SOLDIERS NEEDED PROVISIONING. I KNOW YOU DON'T OBJECT, BEING THE GENEROUS, GOD-FEARING MAN THAT YOU ARE.
I REQUIRE MORE RECRUITS AS WELL. YOUR PEOPLE WILL BE EAGER TO ENLIST, ONCE MY MARK IS IN THEIR BLOOD.
DEAR GOD! STAY AWAY, YOU...YOU DEVILS!
NAM ETSI AMBULAVERO IN MEDIO UMBRAE MORTIS--
PSALM TWENTY-THREE. I HAVEN'T HEARD IT SINCE I DRANK FROM A PHARISEE, IN THE COURT OF HEROD.
YOUR UTTERANCES AND BAUBLES WILL GRANT YOU THE SAME PROTECTION THEY DID HIM.
I AM CAIN.
I'M OLDER THAN YOUR BIBLE. AS OLD AS GOD ITSELF.
EVIL GETS ITS NAME FROM ME.
DRINK, FARA. THEN LET THE OTHERS KNOW: WE MARCH SOUTH AT DAWN.
AAH-AAH--
YES, LORD CAIN.
THE ROAD HOME IS LONG--

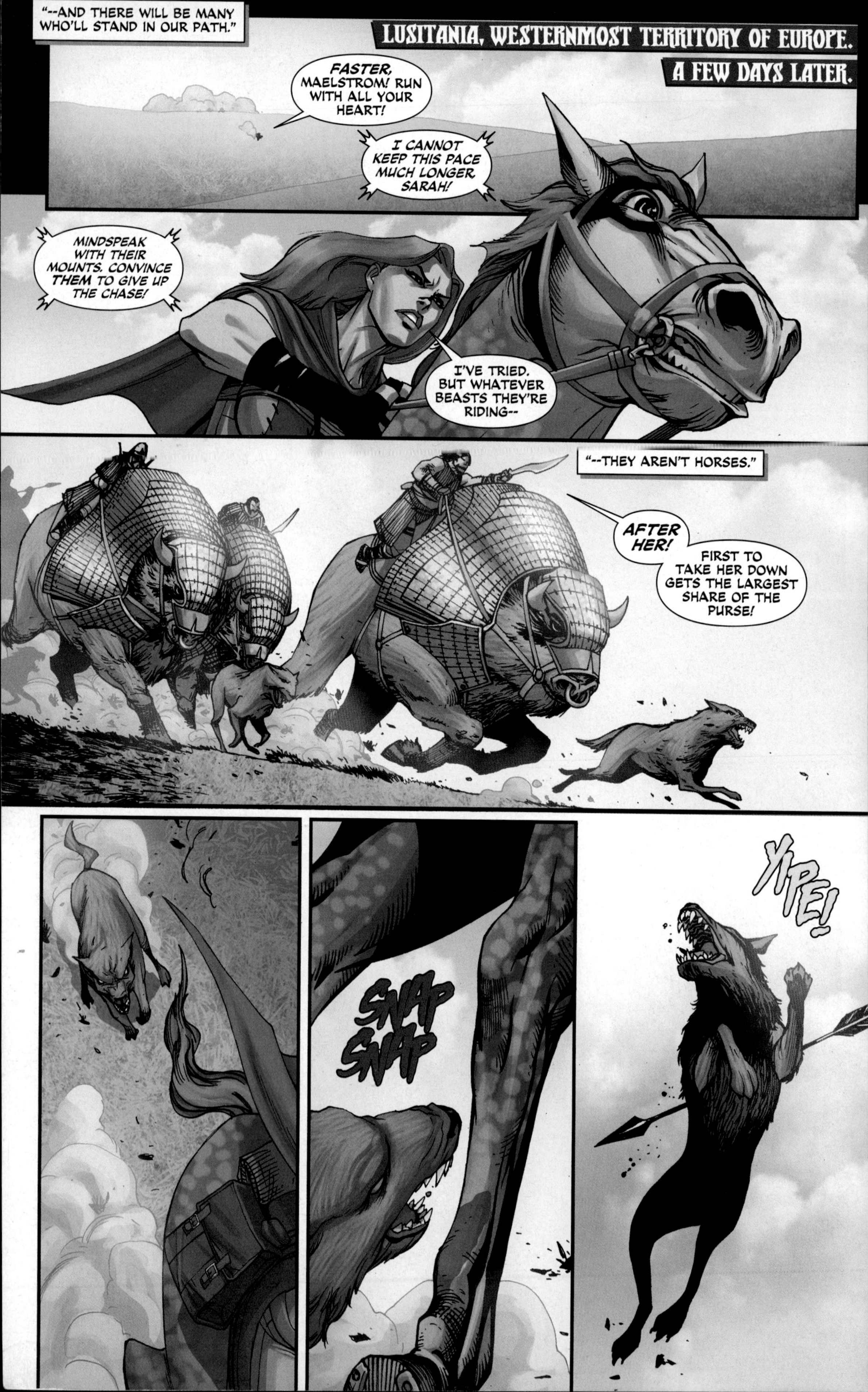
"--AND THERE WILL BE MANY WHO'LL STAND IN OUR PATH."
LUSITANIA, WESTERNMOST TERRITORY OF EUROPE.
A FEW DAYS LATER.
FASTER, MAELSTROM! RUN WITH ALL YOUR HEART!
I CANNOT KEEP THIS PACE MUCH LONGER, SARAH!
MINDSPEAK WITH THEIR MOUNTS. CONVINCE THEM TO GIVE UP THE CHASE!
I'VE TRIED. BUT WHATEVER BEASTS THEY'RE RIDING--
"--THEY AREN'T HORSES."
AFTER HER!
FIRST TO TAKE HER DOWN GETS THE LARGEST SHARE OF THE PURSE!
SNAP SNAP
YIPE!

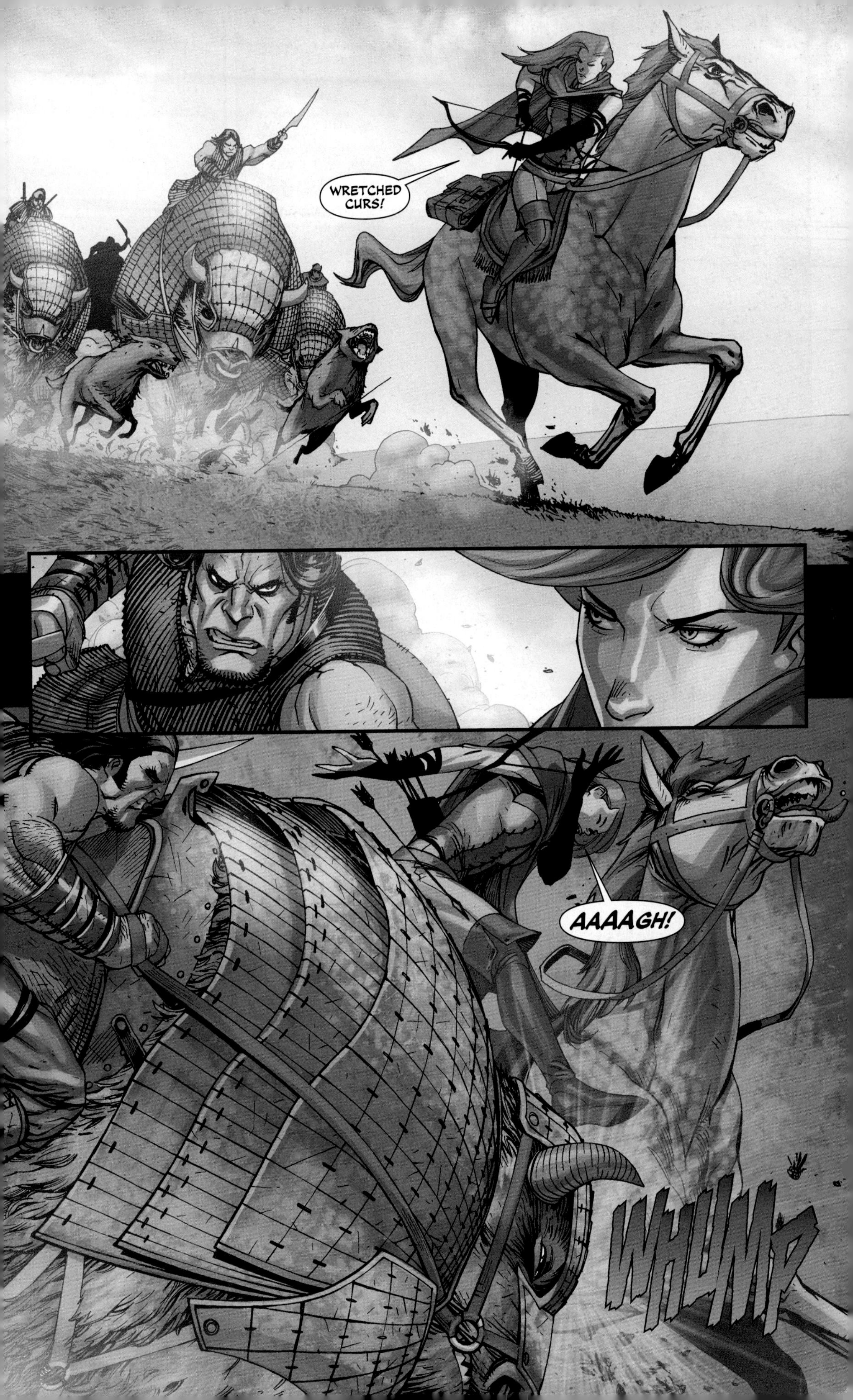
WRETCHED CURS!
AAAAGH!
WHUMP

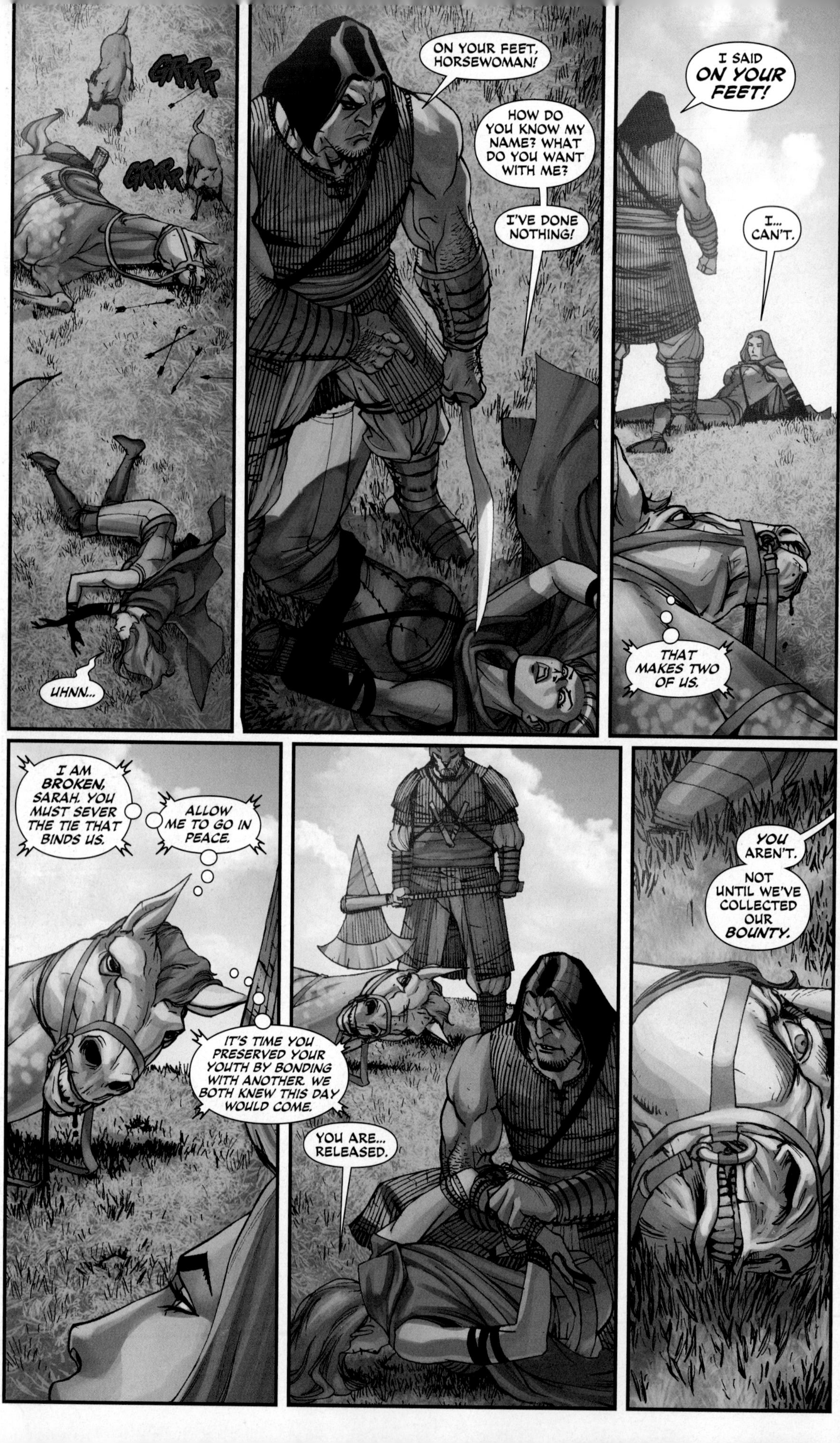
GRRRR
GRRRR
UHNN...
ON YOUR FEET, HORSEWOMAN!
HOW DO YOU KNOW MY NAME? WHAT DO YOU WANT WITH ME?
I'VE DONE NOTHING!
I SAID ON YOUR FEET!
I... CAN'T.
THAT MAKES TWO OF US.
I AM BROKEN, SARAH. YOU MUST SEVER THE TIE THAT BINDS US.
ALLOW ME TO GO IN PEACE.
IT'S TIME YOU PRESERVED YOUR YOUTH BY BONDING WITH ANOTHER. WE BOTH KNEW THIS DAY WOULD COME.
YOU ARE... RELEASED.
YOU AREN'T.
NOT UNTIL WE'VE COLLECTED OUR BOUNTY.

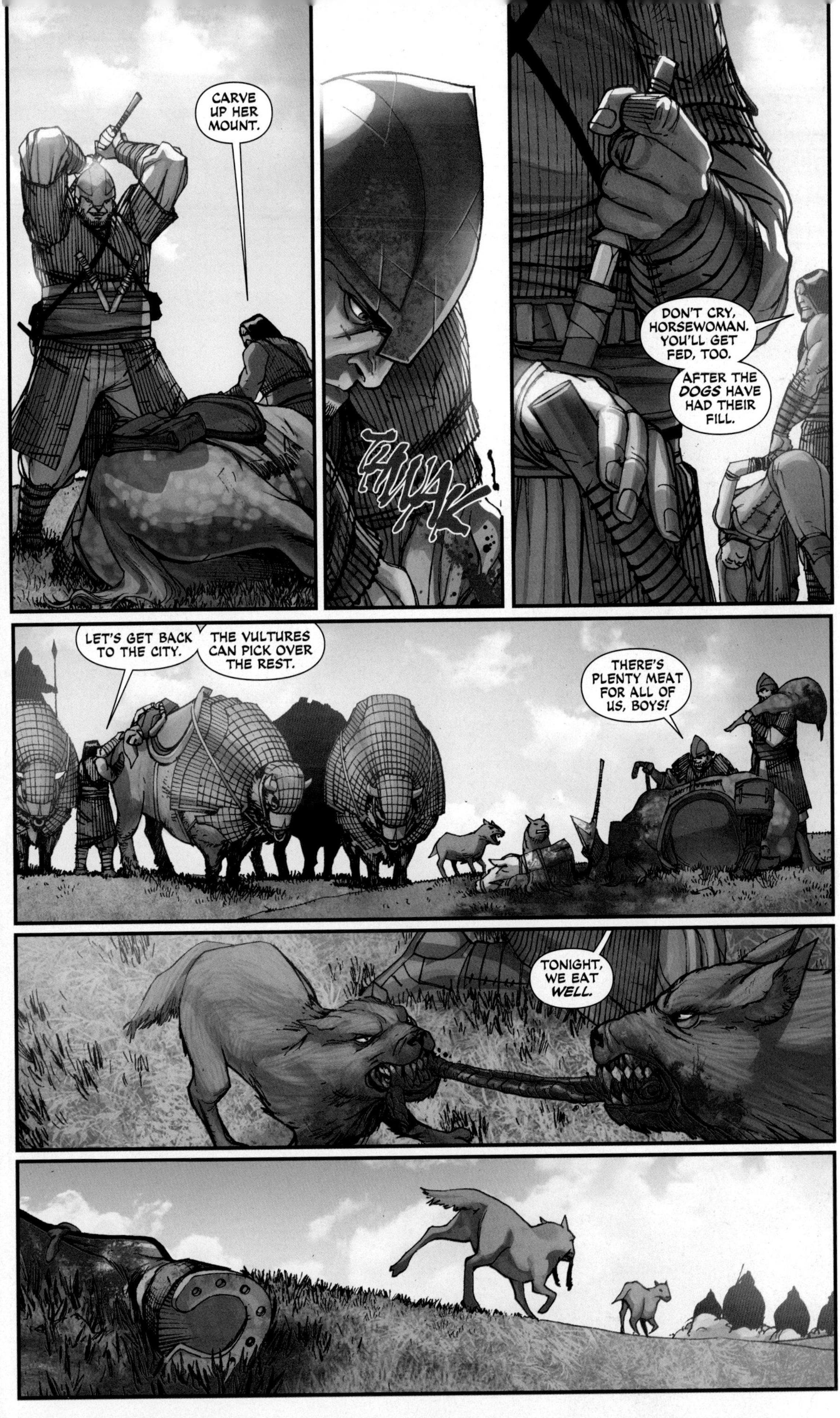
CARVE UP HER MOUNT.
THWAK
DON'T CRY, HORSEWOMAN. YOU'LL GET FED, TOO.
AFTER THE DOGS HAVE HAD THEIR FILL.
LET'S GET BACK TO THE CITY.
THE VULTURES CAN PICK OVER THE REST.
THERE'S PLENTY MEAT FOR ALL OF US, BOYS!
TONIGHT, WE EAT WELL.

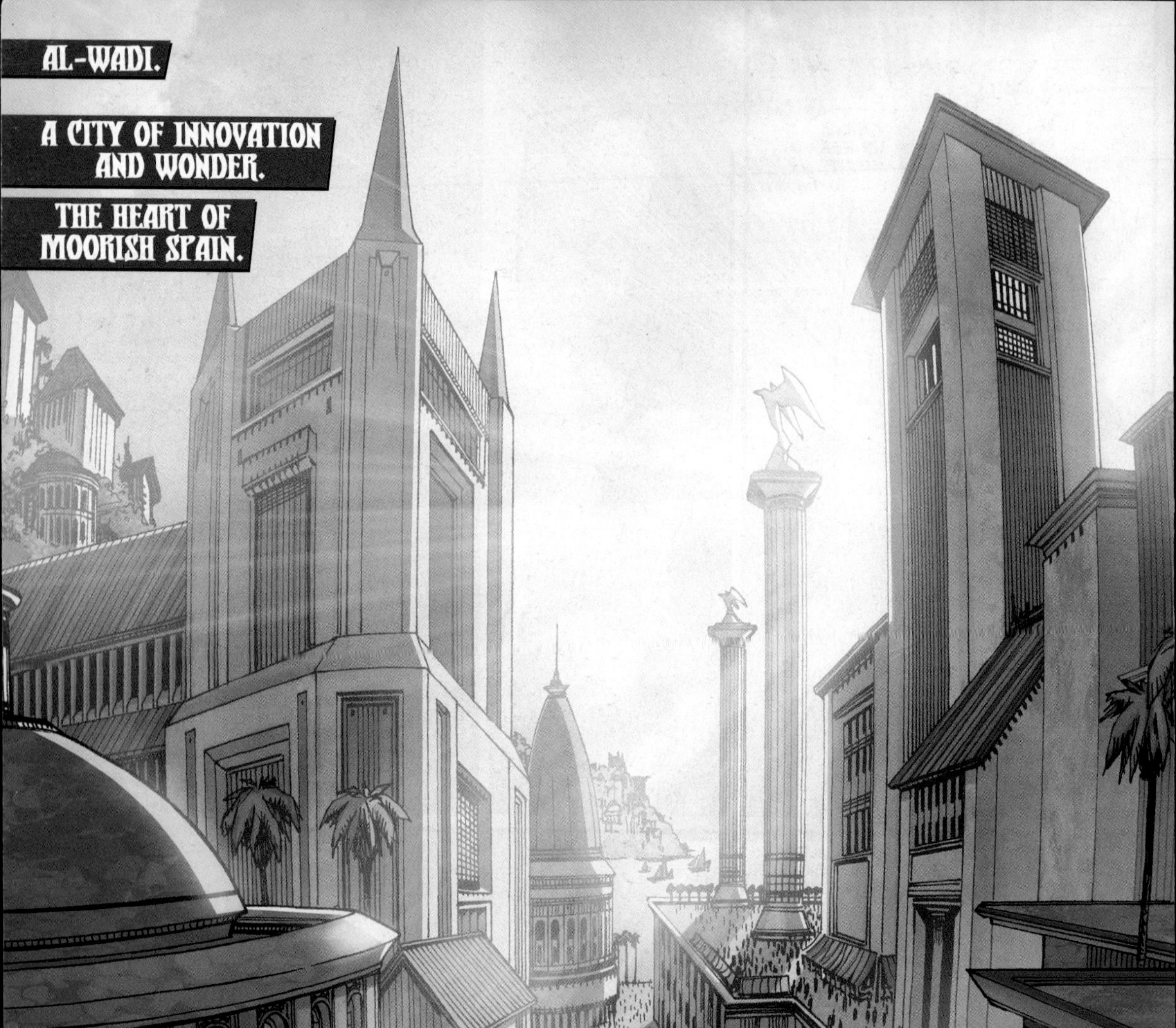
AL-WADI.
A CITY OF INNOVATION AND WONDER.
THE HEART OF MOORISH SPAIN.
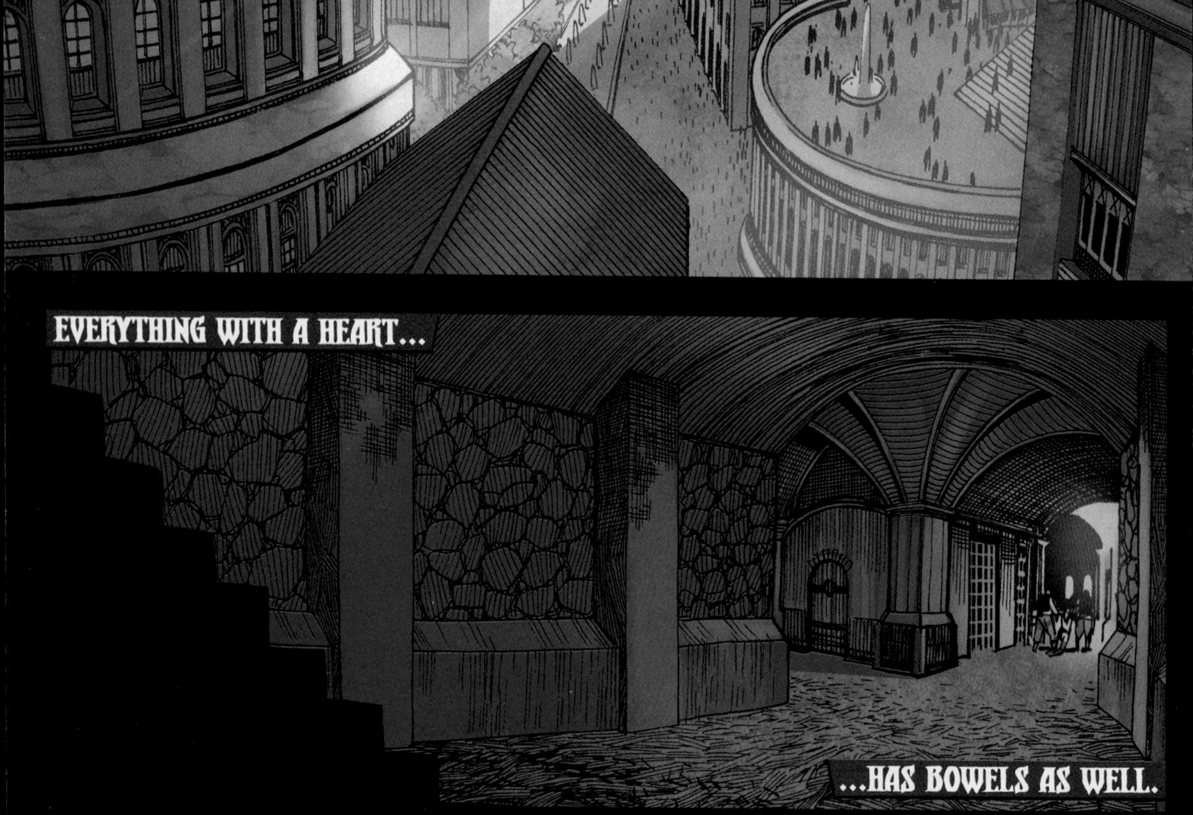
EVERYTHING WITH A HEART...
...HAS BOWELS AS WELL.

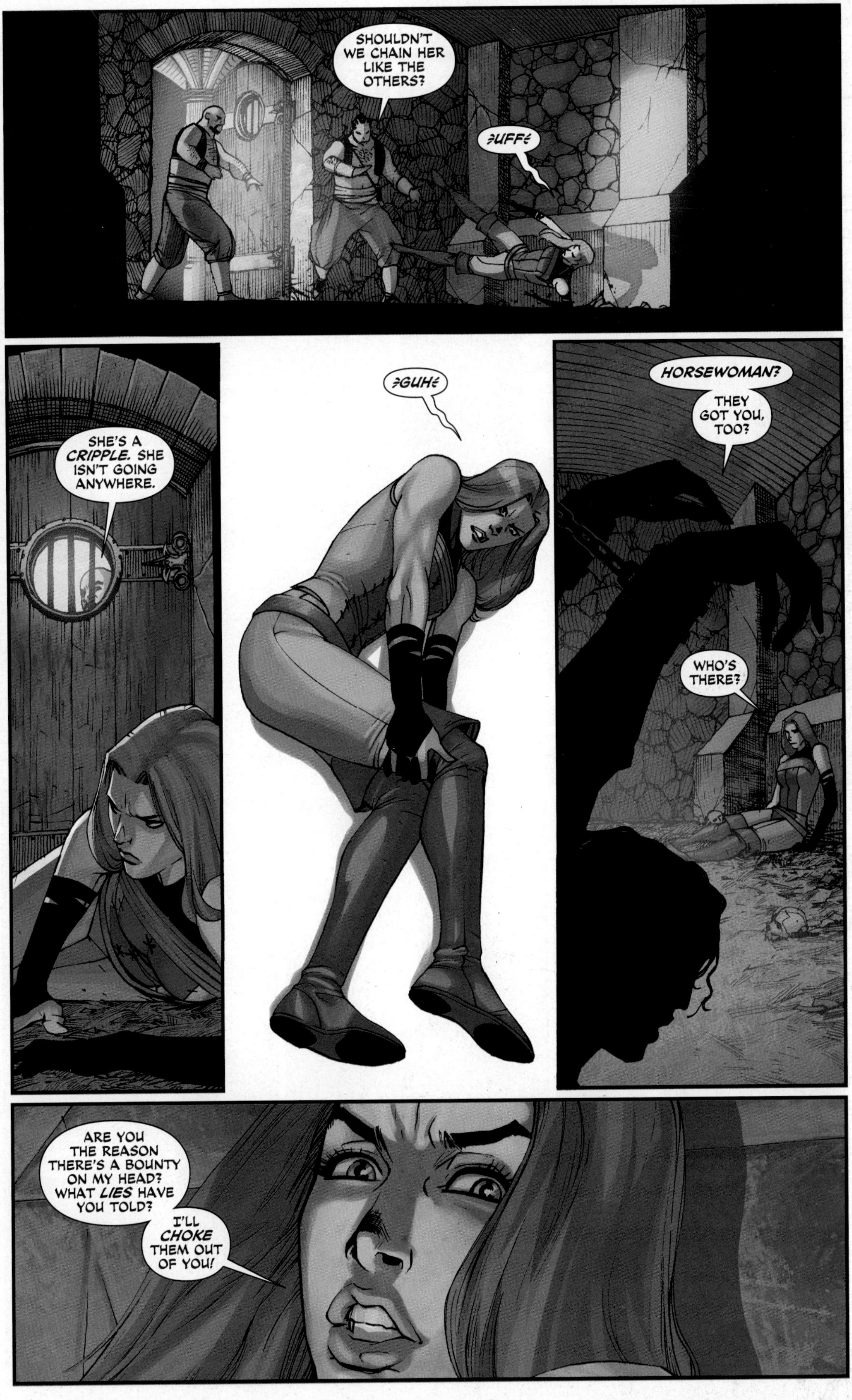
SHOULDN'T WE CHAIN HER LIKE THE OTHERS?
UFF
SHE'S A *CRIPPLE.* SHE ISN'T GOING ANYWHERE.
GUH
HORSEWOMAN?
THEY GOT YOU, TOO?
WHO'S THERE?
ARE YOU THE REASON THERE'S A BOUNTY ON MY HEAD? WHAT *LIES* HAVE YOU TOLD?
I'LL *CHOKE* THEM OUT OF YOU!

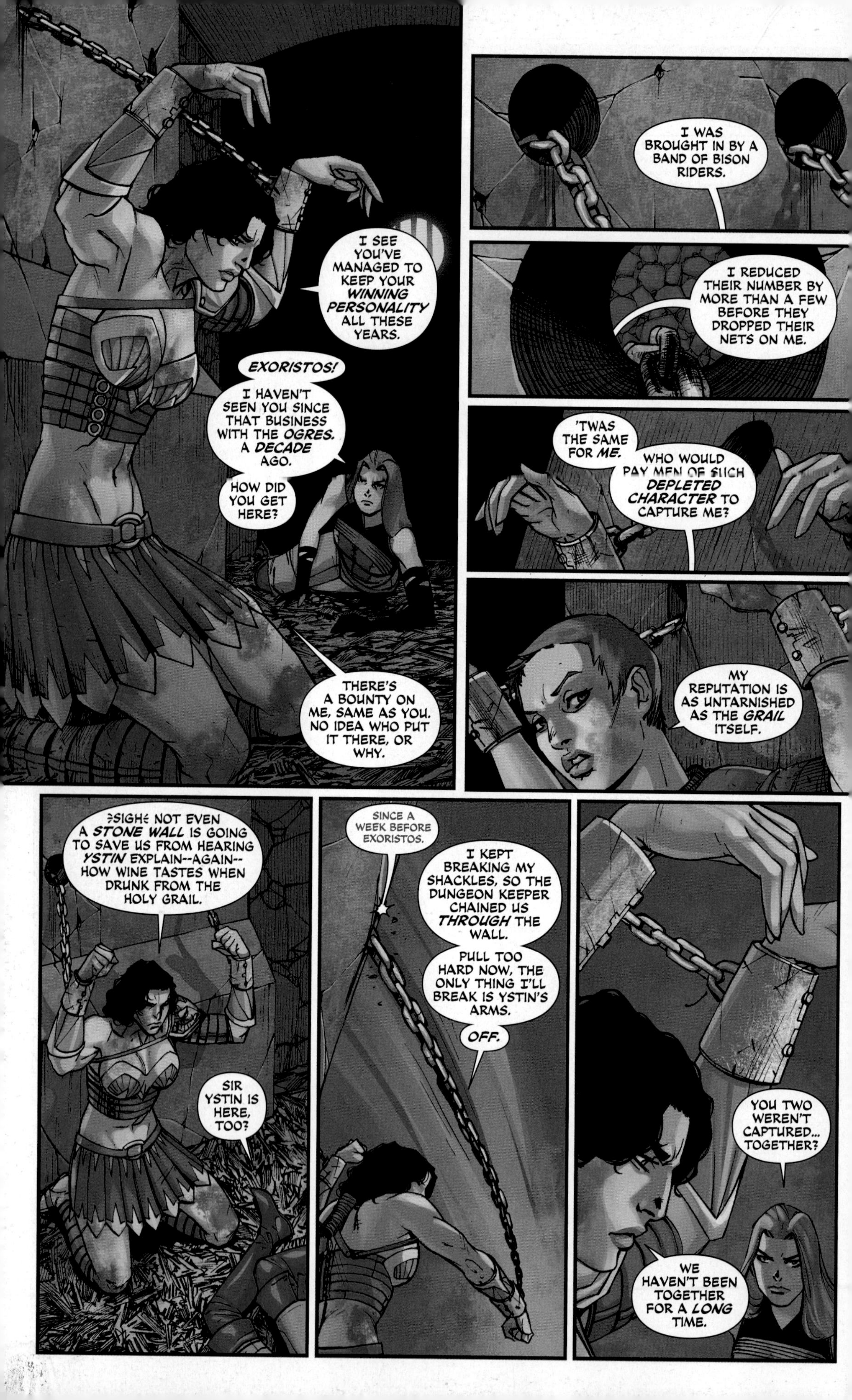
I SEE YOU'VE MANAGED TO KEEP YOUR WINNING PERSONALITY ALL THESE YEARS.
EXORISTOS!
I HAVEN'T SEEN YOU SINCE THAT BUSINESS WITH THE OGRES. A DECADE AGO.
HOW DID YOU GET HERE?
THERE'S A BOUNTY ON ME, SAME AS YOU. NO IDEA WHO PUT IT THERE, OR WHY.
I WAS BROUGHT IN BY A BAND OF BISON RIDERS.
I REDUCED THEIR NUMBER BY MORE THAN A FEW BEFORE THEY DROPPED THEIR NETS ON ME.
'TWAS THE SAME FOR ME.
WHO WOULD PAY MEN OF SUCH DEPLETED CHARACTER TO CAPTURE ME?
MY REPUTATION IS AS UNTARNISHED AS THE GRAIL ITSELF.
SIGH NOT EVEN A STONE WALL IS GOING TO SAVE US FROM HEARING YSTIN EXPLAIN--AGAIN--HOW WINE TASTES WHEN DRUNK FROM THE HOLY GRAIL.
SIR YSTIN IS HERE, TOO?
SINCE A WEEK BEFORE EXORISTOS.
I KEPT BREAKING MY SHACKLES, SO THE DUNGEON KEEPER CHAINED US THROUGH THE WALL.
PULL TOO HARD NOW, THE ONLY THING I'LL BREAK IS YSTIN'S ARMS.
OFF.
YOU TWO WEREN'T CAPTURED... TOGETHER?
WE HAVEN'T BEEN TOGETHER FOR A LONG TIME.

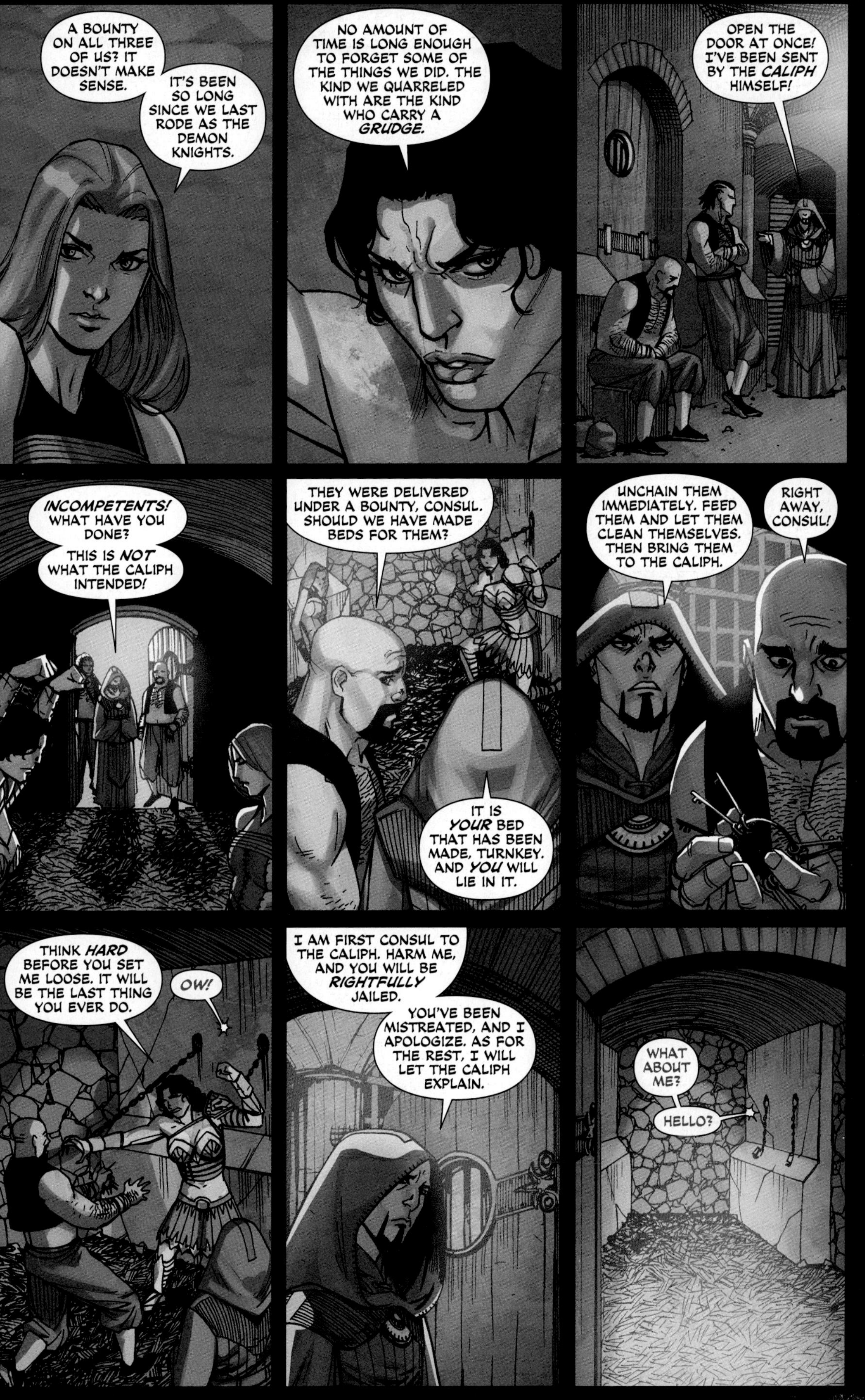

A BOUNTY ON ALL THREE OF US? IT DOESN'T MAKE SENSE.
IT'S BEEN SO LONG SINCE WE LAST RODE AS THE DEMON KNIGHTS.
NO AMOUNT OF TIME IS LONG ENOUGH TO FORGET SOME OF THE THINGS WE DID. THE KIND WE QUARRELED WITH ARE THE KIND WHO CARRY A GRUDGE.
OPEN THE DOOR AT ONCE! I'VE BEEN SENT BY THE CALIPH HIMSELF!
INCOMPETENTS! WHAT HAVE YOU DONE?
THIS IS NOT WHAT THE CALIPH INTENDED!
THEY WERE DELIVERED UNDER A BOUNTY, CONSUL. SHOULD WE HAVE MADE BEDS FOR THEM?
IT IS YOUR BED THAT HAS BEEN MADE, TURNKEY. AND YOU WILL LIE IN IT.
UNCHAIN THEM IMMEDIATELY. FEED THEM AND LET THEM CLEAN THEMSELVES. THEN BRING THEM TO THE CALIPH.
RIGHT AWAY, CONSUL!
THINK HARD BEFORE YOU SET ME LOOSE. IT WILL BE THE LAST THING YOU EVER DO.
OW!
I AM FIRST CONSUL TO THE CALIPH. HARM ME, AND YOU WILL BE RIGHTFULLY JAILED.
YOU'VE BEEN MISTREATED, AND I APOLOGIZE. AS FOR THE REST, I WILL LET THE CALIPH EXPLAIN.
WHAT ABOUT ME?
HELLO?

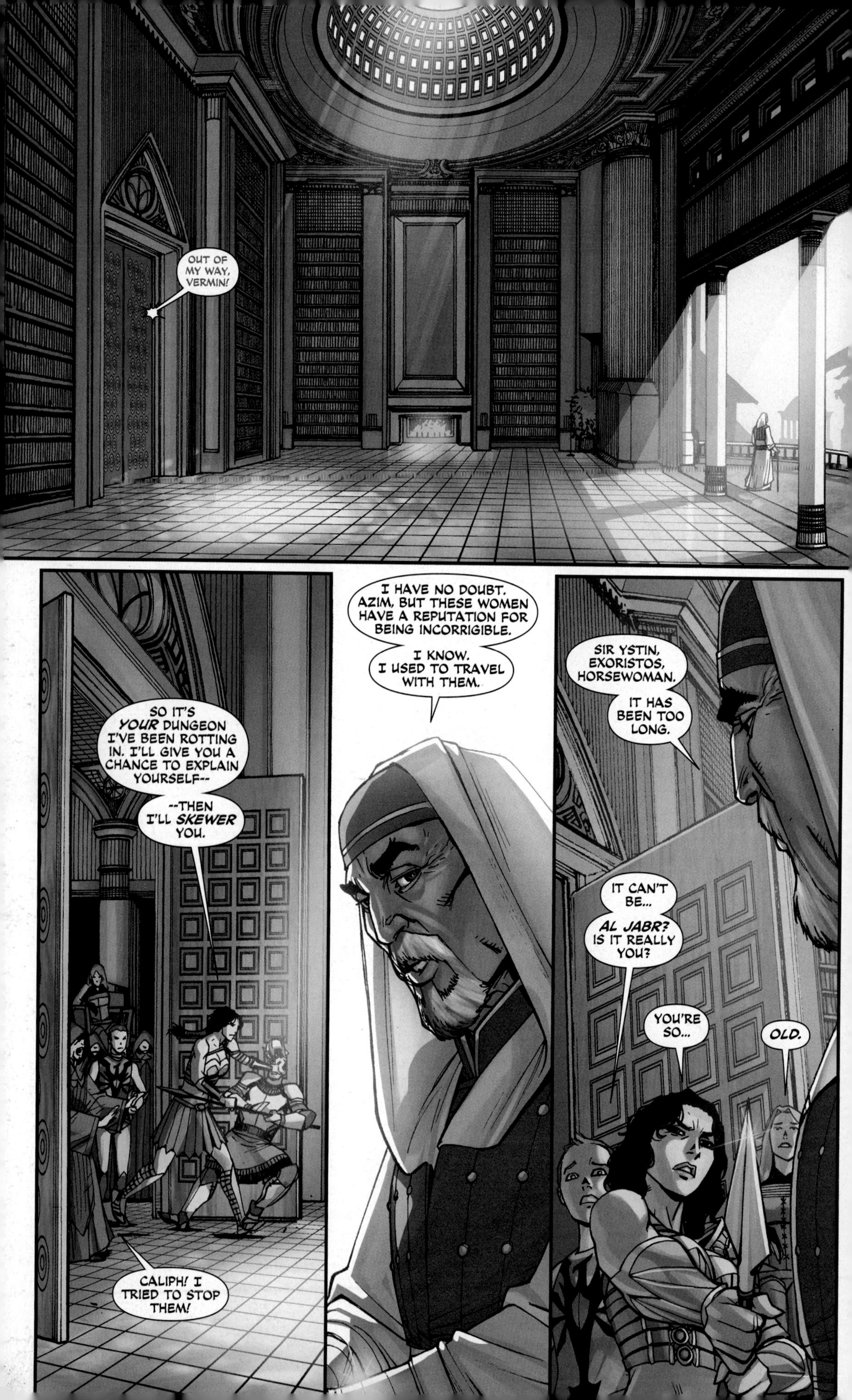
OUT OF MY WAY, VERMIN!
SO IT'S *YOUR* DUNGEON I'VE BEEN ROTTING IN. I'LL GIVE YOU A CHANCE TO EXPLAIN YOURSELF--
--THEN I'LL *SKEWER* YOU.
CALIPH! I TRIED TO STOP THEM!
I HAVE NO DOUBT. AZIM, BUT THESE WOMEN HAVE A REPUTATION FOR BEING INCORRIGIBLE.
I KNOW. I USED TO TRAVEL WITH THEM.
SIR YSTIN, EXORISTOS, HORSEWOMAN.
IT HAS BEEN TOO LONG.
IT CAN'T BE...
AL JABR? IS IT REALLY YOU?
YOU'RE SO...
OLD.

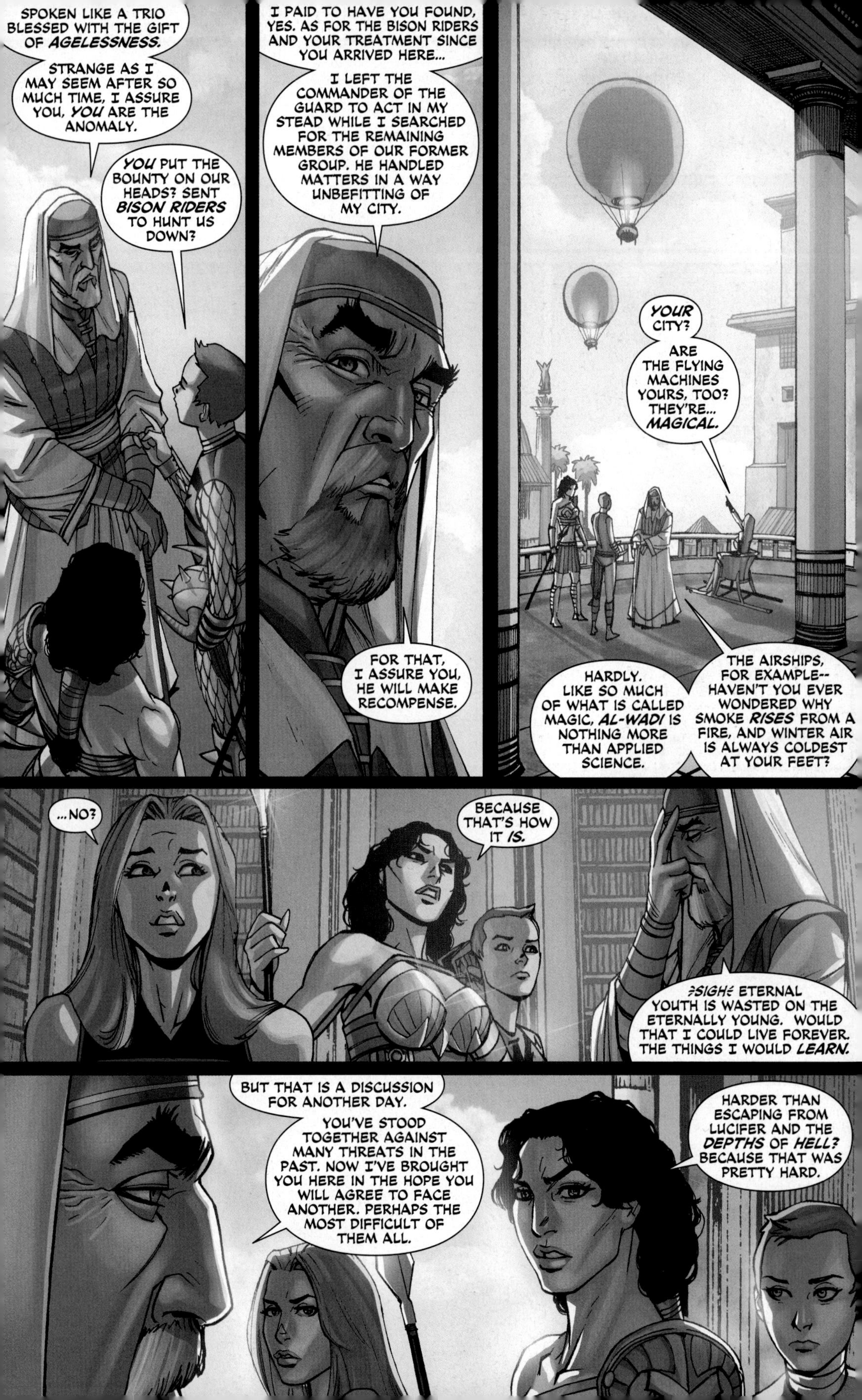
SPOKEN LIKE A TRIO BLESSED WITH THE GIFT OF AGELESSNESS.
STRANGE AS I MAY SEEM AFTER SO MUCH TIME, I ASSURE YOU, YOU ARE THE ANOMALY.
YOU PUT THE BOUNTY ON OUR HEADS? SENT BISON RIDERS TO HUNT US DOWN?
I PAID TO HAVE YOU FOUND, YES. AS FOR THE BISON RIDERS AND YOUR TREATMENT SINCE YOU ARRIVED HERE...
I LEFT THE COMMANDER OF THE GUARD TO ACT IN MY STEAD WHILE I SEARCHED FOR THE REMAINING MEMBERS OF OUR FORMER GROUP. HE HANDLED MATTERS IN A WAY UNBEFITTING OF MY CITY.
FOR THAT, I ASSURE YOU, HE WILL MAKE RECOMPENSE.
YOUR CITY?
ARE THE FLYING MACHINES YOURS, TOO? THEY'RE... MAGICAL.
HARDLY. LIKE SO MUCH OF WHAT IS CALLED MAGIC, AL-WADI IS NOTHING MORE THAN APPLIED SCIENCE.
THE AIRSHIPS, FOR EXAMPLE-- HAVEN'T YOU EVER WONDERED WHY SMOKE RISES FROM A FIRE, AND WINTER AIR IS ALWAYS COLDEST AT YOUR FEET?
...NO?
BECAUSE THAT'S HOW IT IS.
=SIGH= ETERNAL YOUTH IS WASTED ON THE ETERNALLY YOUNG. WOULD THAT I COULD LIVE FOREVER. THE THINGS I WOULD LEARN.
BUT THAT IS A DISCUSSION FOR ANOTHER DAY.
YOU'VE STOOD TOGETHER AGAINST MANY THREATS IN THE PAST. NOW I'VE BROUGHT YOU HERE IN THE HOPE YOU WILL AGREE TO FACE ANOTHER. PERHAPS THE MOST DIFFICULT OF THEM ALL.
HARDER THAN ESCAPING FROM LUCIFER AND THE DEPTHS OF HELL? BECAUSE THAT WAS PRETTY HARD.

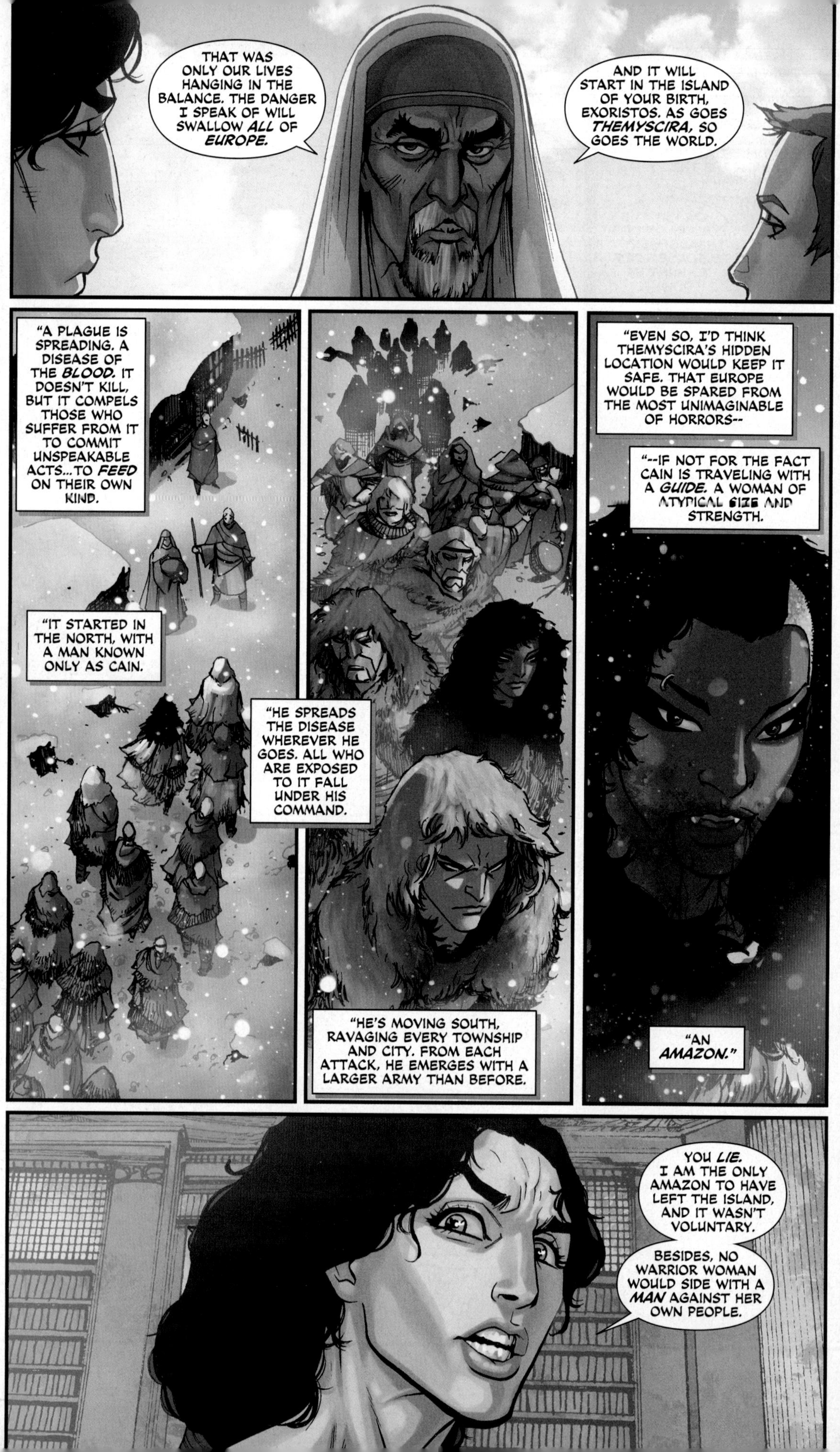
THAT WAS ONLY OUR LIVES HANGING IN THE BALANCE. THE DANGER I SPEAK OF WILL SWALLOW *ALL* OF *EUROPE.*
AND IT WILL START IN THE ISLAND OF YOUR BIRTH, EXORISTOS. AS GOES *THEMYSCIRA,* SO GOES THE WORLD.
"A PLAGUE IS SPREADING. A DISEASE OF THE *BLOOD.* IT DOESN'T KILL, BUT IT COMPELS THOSE WHO SUFFER FROM IT TO COMMIT UNSPEAKABLE ACTS...TO *FEED* ON THEIR OWN KIND.
"IT STARTED IN THE NORTH, WITH A MAN KNOWN ONLY AS CAIN.
"HE SPREADS THE DISEASE WHEREVER HE GOES. ALL WHO ARE EXPOSED TO IT FALL UNDER HIS COMMAND.
"HE'S MOVING SOUTH, RAVAGING EVERY TOWNSHIP AND CITY. FROM EACH ATTACK, HE EMERGES WITH A LARGER ARMY THAN BEFORE.
"EVEN SO, I'D THINK THEMYSCIRA'S HIDDEN LOCATION WOULD KEEP IT SAFE. THAT EUROPE WOULD BE SPARED FROM THE MOST UNIMAGINABLE OF HORRORS--
"--IF NOT FOR THE FACT CAIN IS TRAVELING WITH A *GUIDE.* A WOMAN OF ATYPICAL SIZE AND STRENGTH.
"AN *AMAZON.*"
YOU *LIE.* I AM THE ONLY AMAZON TO HAVE LEFT THE ISLAND, AND IT WASN'T VOLUNTARY.
BESIDES, NO WARRIOR WOMAN WOULD SIDE WITH A *MAN* AGAINST HER OWN PEOPLE.

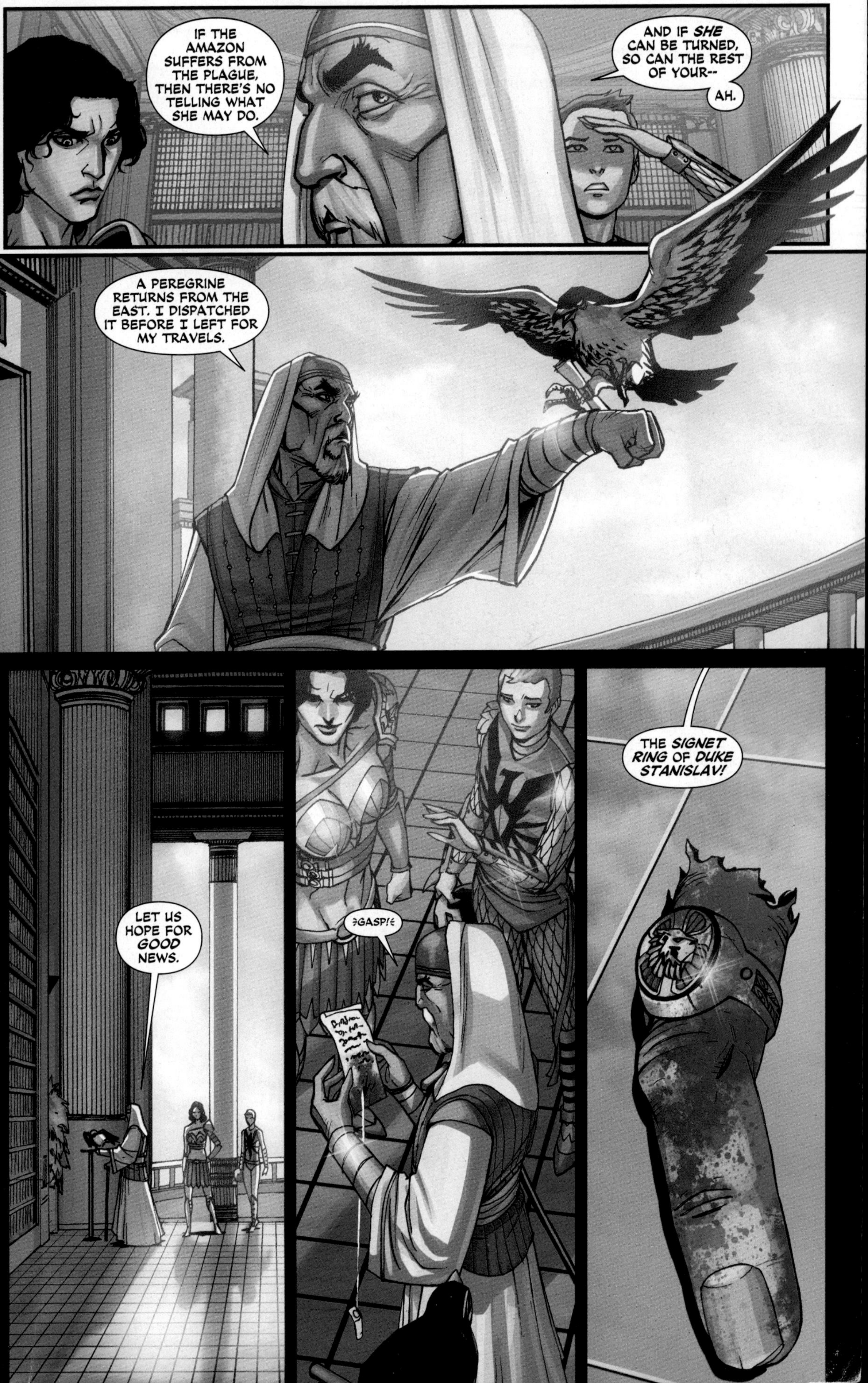
IF THE AMAZON SUFFERS FROM THE PLAGUE, THEN THERE'S NO TELLING WHAT SHE MAY DO.
AND IF SHE CAN BE TURNED, SO CAN THE REST OF YOUR--
AH.
A PEREGRINE RETURNS FROM THE EAST. I DISPATCHED IT BEFORE I LEFT FOR MY TRAVELS.
LET US HOPE FOR GOOD NEWS.
GASP!
THE SIGNET RING OF DUKE STANISLAV!

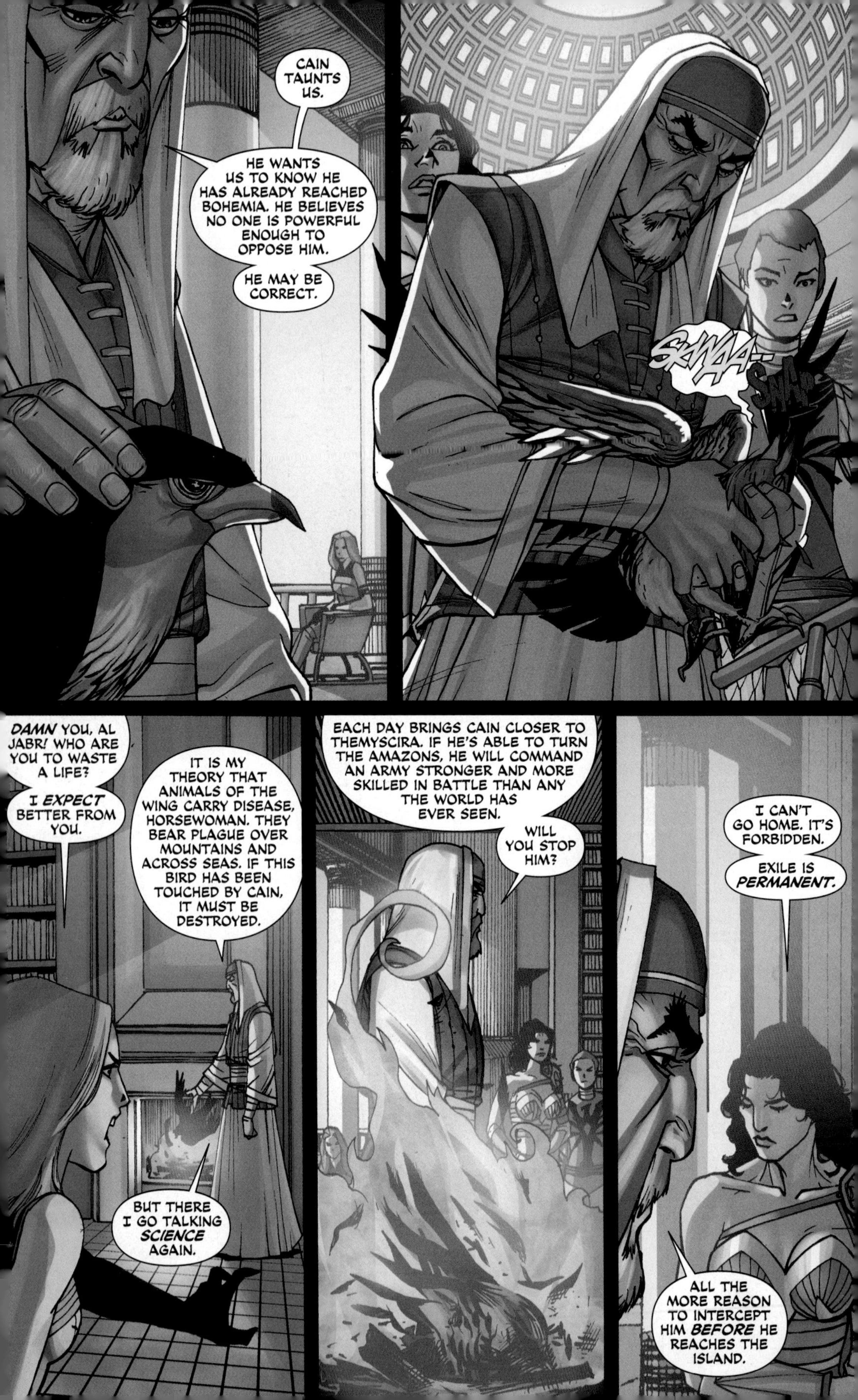
CAIN TAUNTS US.
HE WANTS US TO KNOW HE HAS ALREADY REACHED BOHEMIA. HE BELIEVES NO ONE IS POWERFUL ENOUGH TO OPPOSE HIM.
HE MAY BE CORRECT.
SKWAA--
SNAP
DAMN YOU, AL JABR! WHO ARE YOU TO WASTE A LIFE?
I EXPECT BETTER FROM YOU.
IT IS MY THEORY THAT ANIMALS OF THE WING CARRY DISEASE, HORSEWOMAN. THEY BEAR PLAGUE OVER MOUNTAINS AND ACROSS SEAS. IF THIS BIRD HAS BEEN TOUCHED BY CAIN, IT MUST BE DESTROYED.
BUT THERE I GO TALKING SCIENCE AGAIN.
EACH DAY BRINGS CAIN CLOSER TO THEMYSCIRA. IF HE'S ABLE TO TURN THE AMAZONS, HE WILL COMMAND AN ARMY STRONGER AND MORE SKILLED IN BATTLE THAN ANY THE WORLD HAS EVER SEEN.
WILL YOU STOP HIM?
I CAN'T GO HOME. IT'S FORBIDDEN.
EXILE IS PERMANENT.
ALL THE MORE REASON TO INTERCEPT HIM BEFORE HE REACHES THE ISLAND.

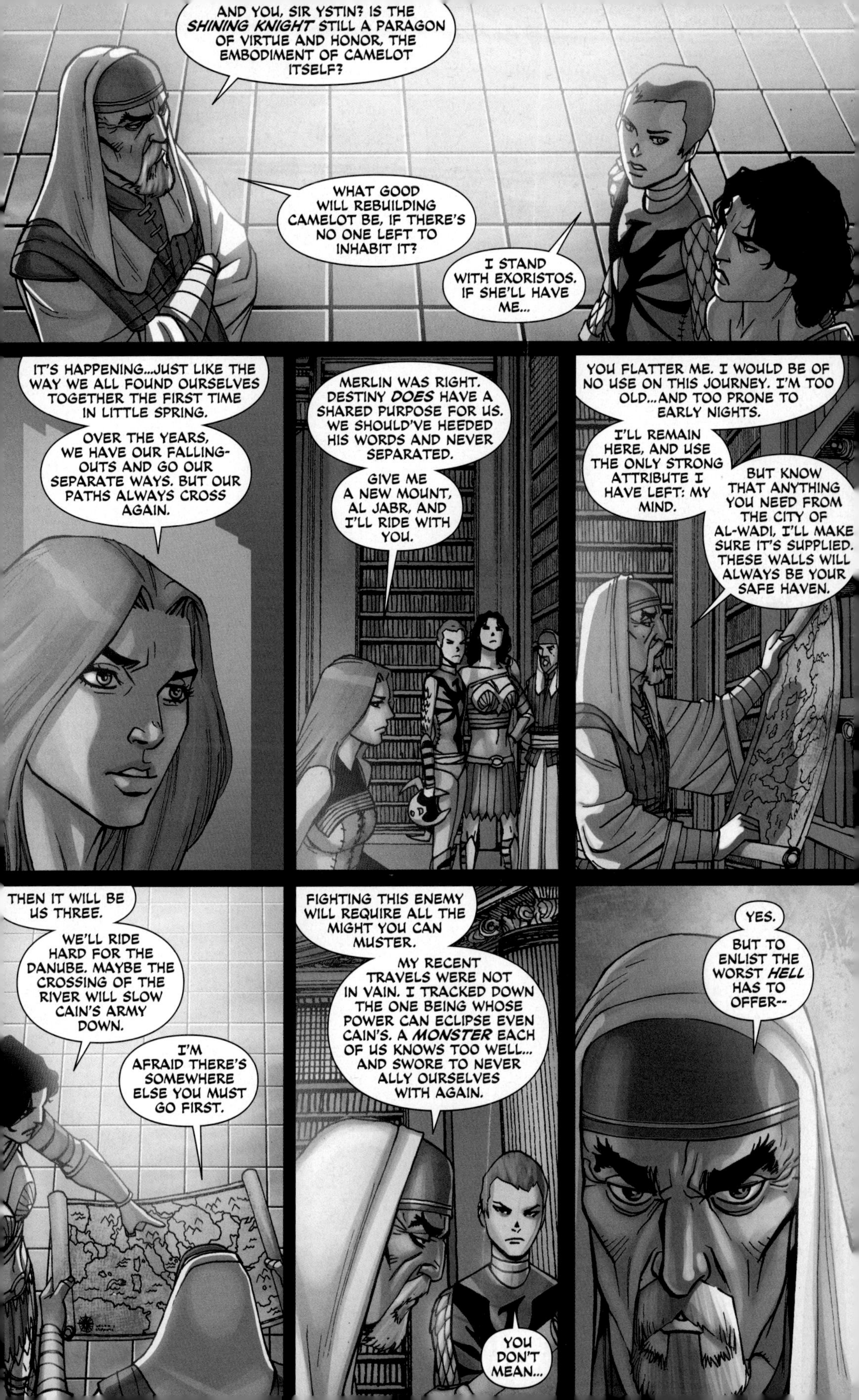
AND YOU, SIR YSTIN? IS THE SHINING KNIGHT STILL A PARAGON OF VIRTUE AND HONOR, THE EMBODIMENT OF CAMELOT ITSELF?
WHAT GOOD WILL REBUILDING CAMELOT BE, IF THERE'S NO ONE LEFT TO INHABIT IT?
I STAND WITH EXORISTOS. IF SHE'LL HAVE ME...
IT'S HAPPENING...JUST LIKE THE WAY WE ALL FOUND OURSELVES TOGETHER THE FIRST TIME IN LITTLE SPRING.
OVER THE YEARS, WE HAVE OUR FALLING-OUTS AND GO OUR SEPARATE WAYS. BUT OUR PATHS ALWAYS CROSS AGAIN.
MERLIN WAS RIGHT. DESTINY DOES HAVE A SHARED PURPOSE FOR US. WE SHOULD'VE HEEDED HIS WORDS AND NEVER SEPARATED.
GIVE ME A NEW MOUNT, AL JABR, AND I'LL RIDE WITH YOU.
YOU FLATTER ME. I WOULD BE OF NO USE ON THIS JOURNEY. I'M TOO OLD...AND TOO PRONE TO EARLY NIGHTS.
I'LL REMAIN HERE, AND USE THE ONLY STRONG ATTRIBUTE I HAVE LEFT: MY MIND.
BUT KNOW THAT ANYTHING YOU NEED FROM THE CITY OF AL-WADI, I'LL MAKE SURE IT'S SUPPLIED. THESE WALLS WILL ALWAYS BE YOUR SAFE HAVEN.
THEN IT WILL BE US THREE.
WE'LL RIDE HARD FOR THE DANUBE. MAYBE THE CROSSING OF THE RIVER WILL SLOW CAIN'S ARMY DOWN.
I'M AFRAID THERE'S SOMEWHERE ELSE YOU MUST GO FIRST.
FIGHTING THIS ENEMY WILL REQUIRE ALL THE MIGHT YOU CAN MUSTER.
MY RECENT TRAVELS WERE NOT IN VAIN. I TRACKED DOWN THE ONE BEING WHOSE POWER CAN ECLIPSE EVEN CAIN'S. A MONSTER EACH OF US KNOWS TOO WELL... AND SWORE TO NEVER ALLY OURSELVES WITH AGAIN.
YOU DON'T MEAN...
YES.
BUT TO ENLIST THE WORST HELL HAS TO OFFER--

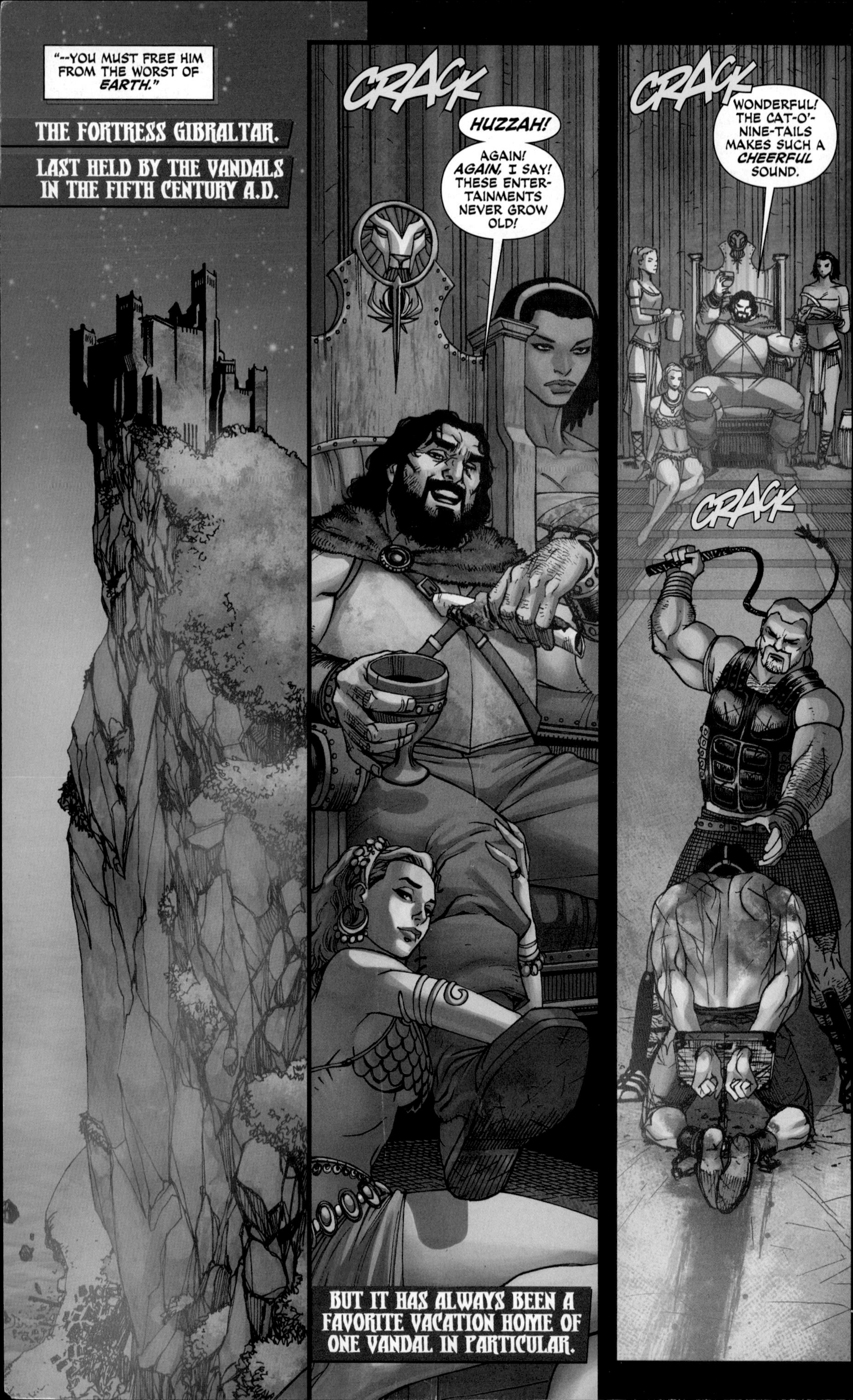
"--YOU MUST FREE HIM FROM THE WORST OF EARTH."
THE FORTRESS GIBRALTAR.
LAST HELD BY THE VANDALS IN THE FIFTH CENTURY A.D.
CRACK
HUZZAH!
AGAIN! AGAIN, I SAY! THESE ENTERTAINMENTS NEVER GROW OLD!
BUT IT HAS ALWAYS BEEN A FAVORITE VACATION HOME OF ONE VANDAL IN PARTICULAR.
CRACK
WONDERFUL! THE CAT-O'-NINE-TAILS MAKES SUCH A CHEERFUL SOUND.
CRACK

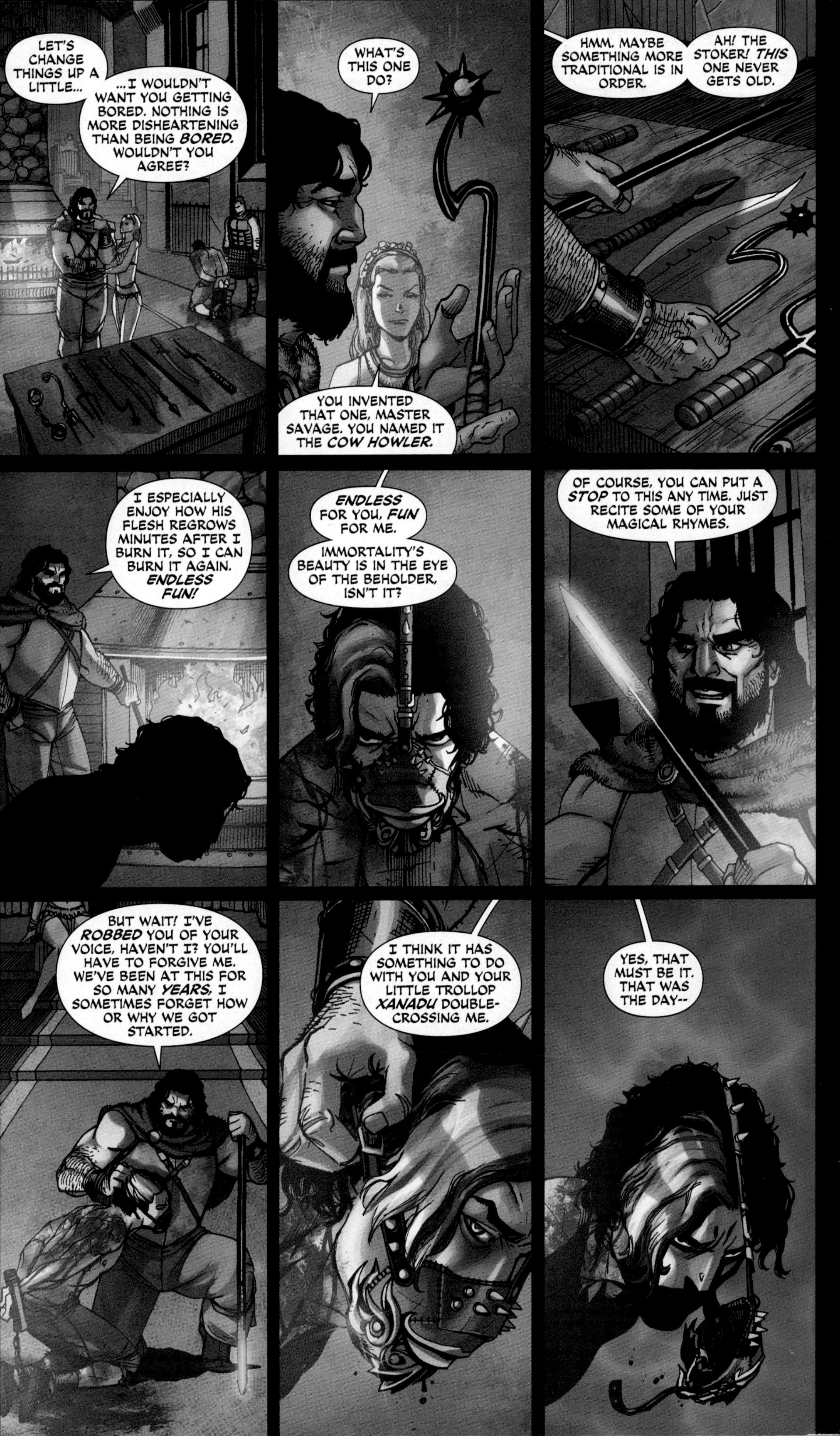
LET'S CHANGE THINGS UP A LITTLE...
...I WOULDN'T WANT YOU GETTING BORED. NOTHING IS MORE DISHEARTENING THAN BEING BORED. WOULDN'T YOU AGREE?
WHAT'S THIS ONE DO?
YOU INVENTED THAT ONE, MASTER SAVAGE. YOU NAMED IT THE COW HOWLER.
HMM. MAYBE SOMETHING MORE TRADITIONAL IS IN ORDER.
AH! THE STOKER! THIS ONE NEVER GETS OLD.
I ESPECIALLY ENJOY HOW HIS FLESH REGROWS MINUTES AFTER I BURN IT, SO I CAN BURN IT AGAIN. ENDLESS FUN!
ENDLESS FOR YOU, FUN FOR ME.
IMMORTALITY'S BEAUTY IS IN THE EYE OF THE BEHOLDER, ISN'T IT?
OF COURSE, YOU CAN PUT A STOP TO THIS ANY TIME. JUST RECITE SOME OF YOUR MAGICAL RHYMES.
BUT WAIT! I'VE ROBBED YOU OF YOUR VOICE, HAVEN'T I? YOU'LL HAVE TO FORGIVE ME. WE'VE BEEN AT THIS FOR SO MANY YEARS, I SOMETIMES FORGET HOW OR WHY WE GOT STARTED.
I THINK IT HAS SOMETHING TO DO WITH YOU AND YOUR LITTLE TROLLOP XANADU DOUBLE-CROSSING ME.
YES, THAT MUST BE IT. THAT WAS THE DAY--

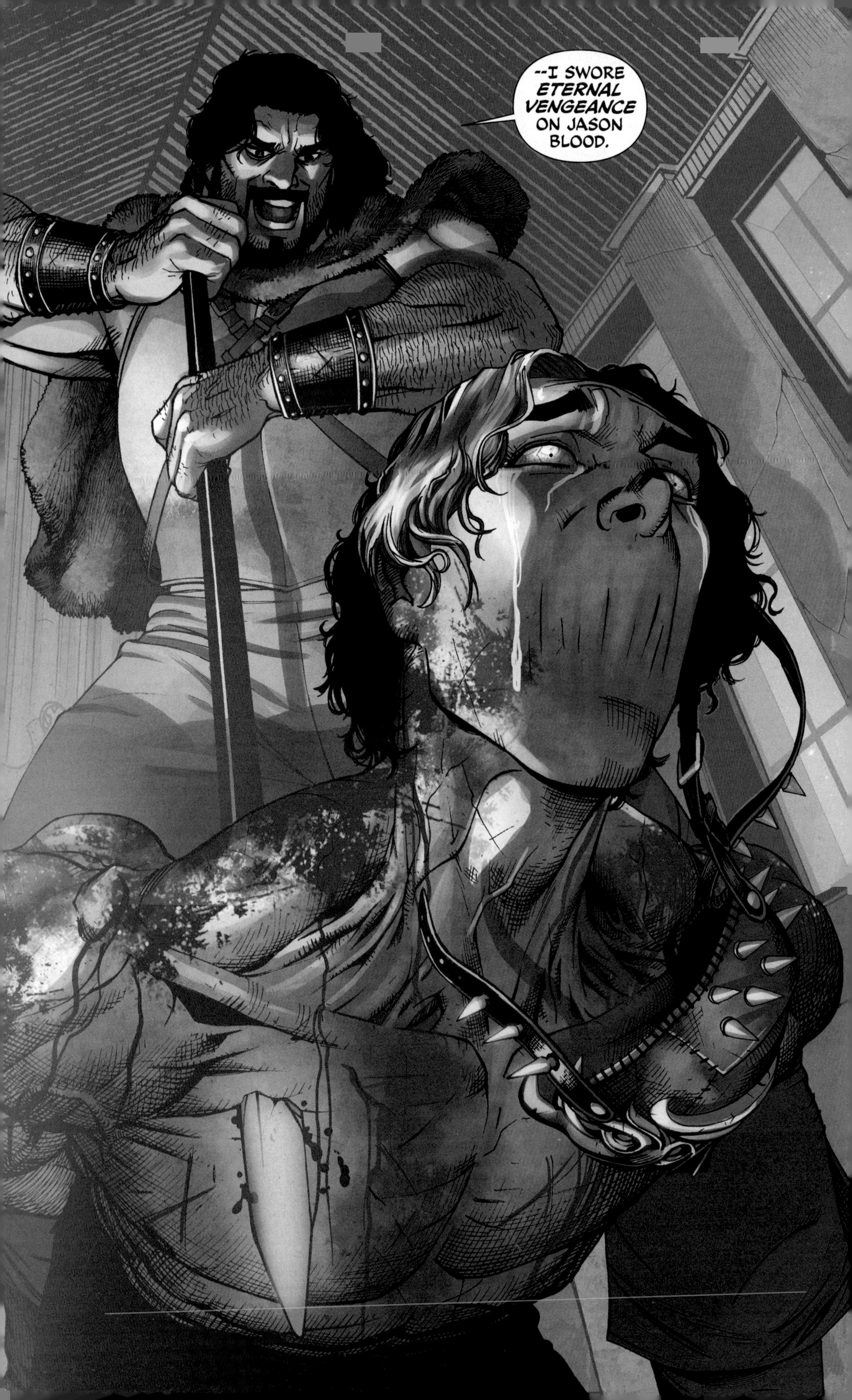
--I SWORE ETERNAL VENGEANCE ON JASON BLOOD.

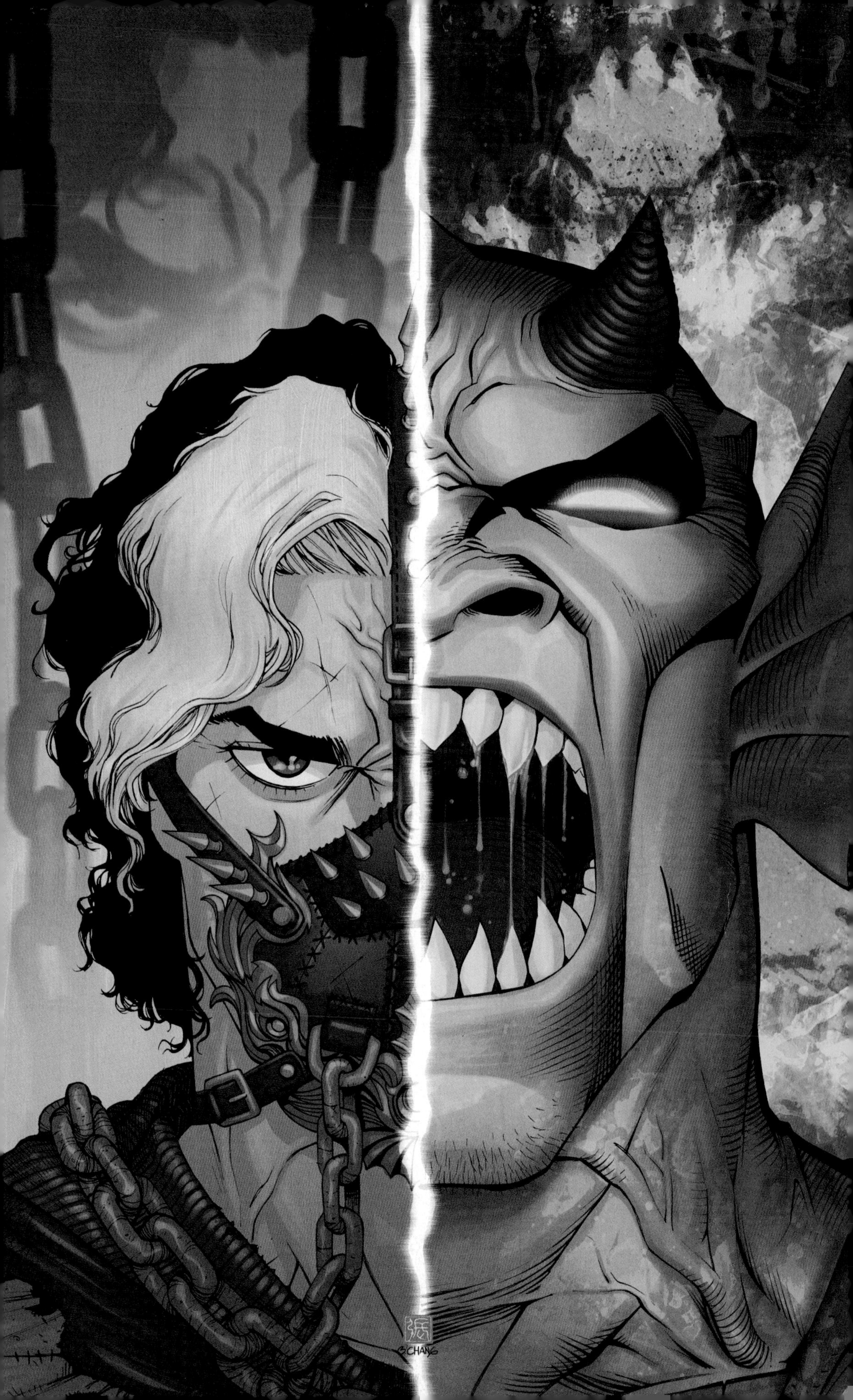
BCHANG

ROBERT VENDITTI
writer

BERNARD CHANG
artist

BERNARD CHANG
cover artist

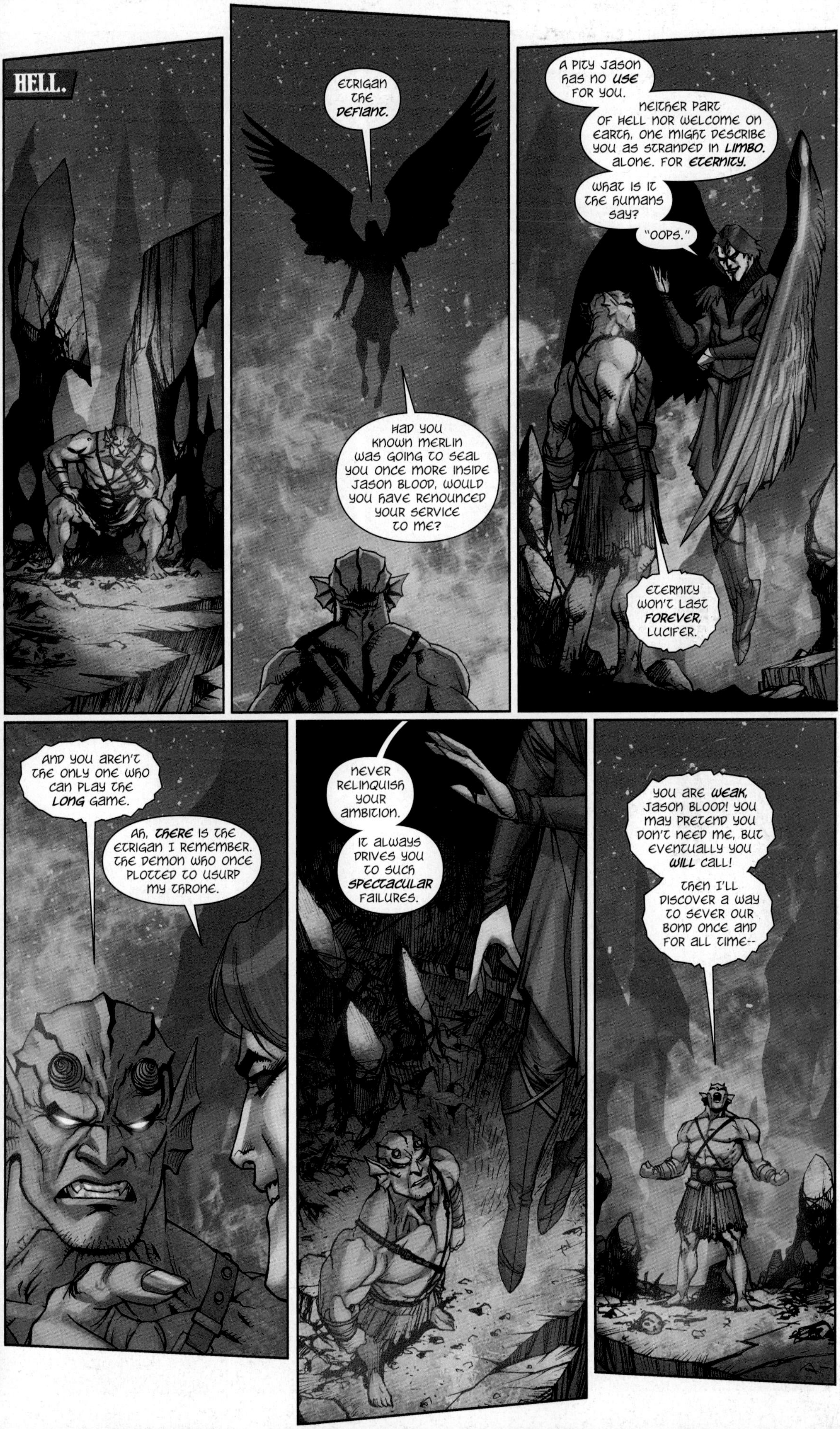
HELL.
ETRIGAN THE DEFIANT.
HAD YOU KNOWN MERLIN WAS GOING TO SEAL YOU ONCE MORE INSIDE JASON BLOOD, WOULD YOU HAVE RENOUNCED YOUR SERVICE TO ME?
A PITY JASON HAS NO USE FOR YOU.
NEITHER PART OF HELL NOR WELCOME ON EARTH, ONE MIGHT DESCRIBE YOU AS STRANDED IN LIMBO. ALONE. FOR ETERNITY.
WHAT IS IT THE HUMANS SAY?
"OOPS."
ETERNITY WON'T LAST FOREVER, LUCIFER.
AND YOU AREN'T THE ONLY ONE WHO CAN PLAY THE LONG GAME.
AH, THERE IS THE ETRIGAN I REMEMBER. THE DEMON WHO ONCE PLOTTED TO USURP MY THRONE.
NEVER RELINQUISH YOUR AMBITION.
IT ALWAYS DRIVES YOU TO SUCH SPECTACULAR FAILURES.
YOU ARE WEAK, JASON BLOOD! YOU MAY PRETEND YOU DON'T NEED ME, BUT EVENTUALLY YOU WILL CALL!
THEN I'LL DISCOVER A WAY TO SEVER OUR BOND ONCE AND FOR ALL TIME--

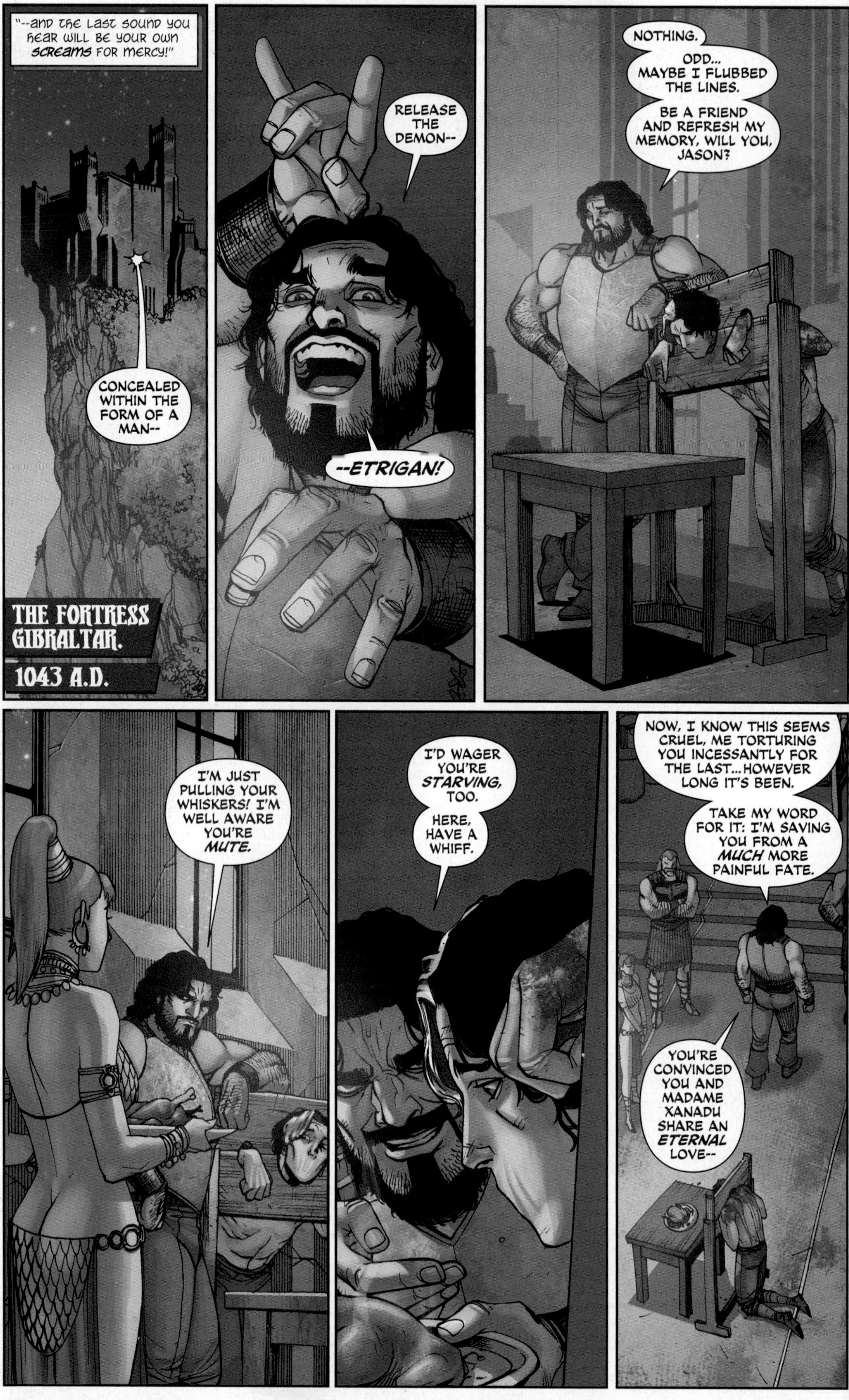
"--and the last sound you hear will be your own *screams* for mercy!"
CONCEALED WITHIN THE FORM OF A MAN--
THE FORTRESS GIBRALTAR.
1043 A.D.
RELEASE THE DEMON--
--ETRIGAN!
NOTHING.
ODD... MAYBE I FLUBBED THE LINES.
BE A FRIEND AND REFRESH MY MEMORY, WILL YOU, JASON?
I'M JUST PULLING YOUR WHISKERS! I'M WELL AWARE YOU'RE *MUTE.*
I'D WAGER YOU'RE *STARVING,* TOO.
HERE, HAVE A WHIFF.
NOW, I KNOW THIS SEEMS CRUEL, ME TORTURING YOU INCESSANTLY FOR THE LAST...HOWEVER LONG IT'S BEEN.
TAKE MY WORD FOR IT: I'M SAVING YOU FROM A *MUCH* MORE PAINFUL FATE.
YOU'RE CONVINCED YOU AND MADAME XANADU SHARE AN *ETERNAL* LOVE--

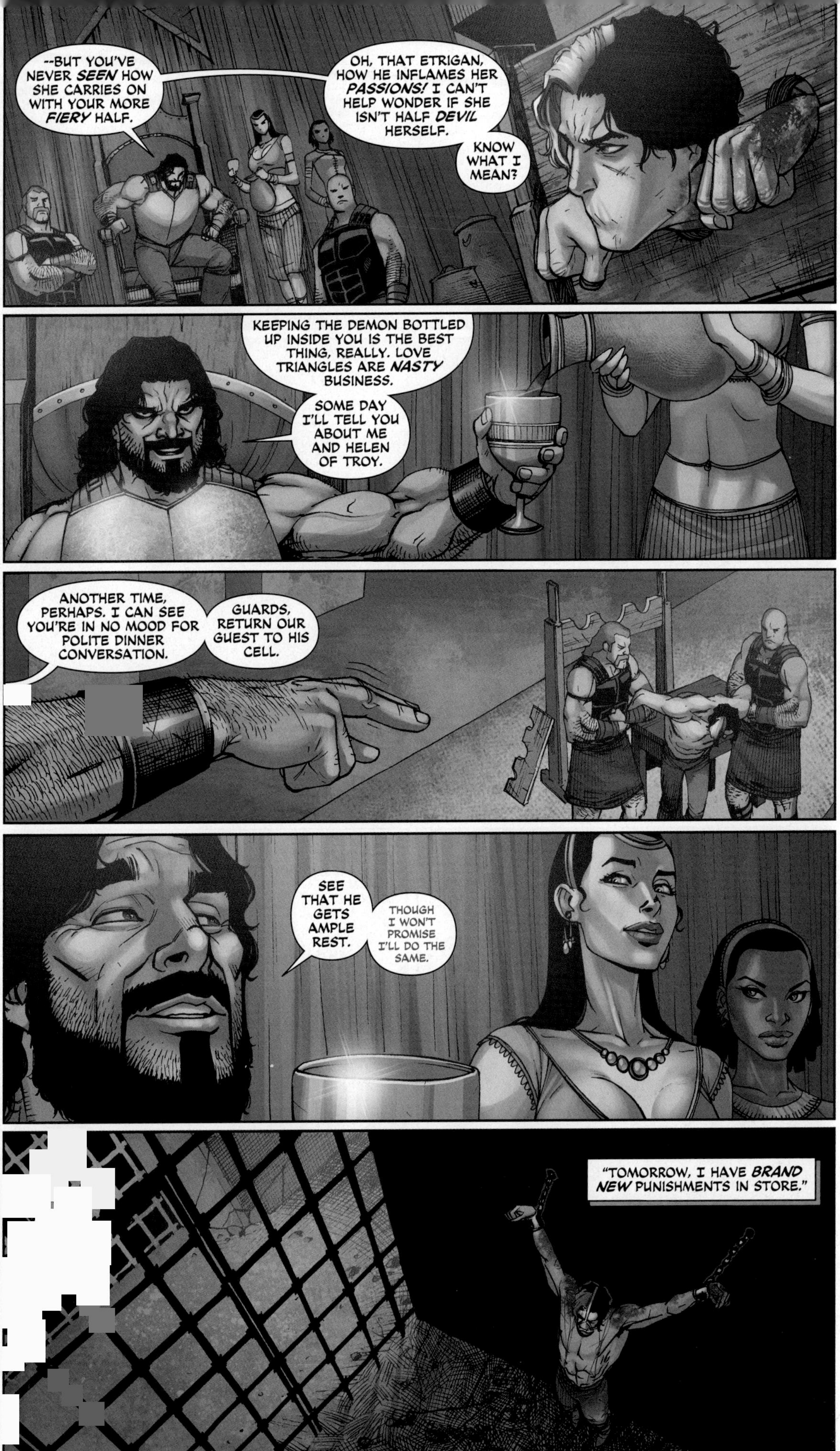
--BUT YOU'VE NEVER *SEEN* HOW SHE CARRIES ON WITH YOUR MORE *FIERY* HALF.
OH, THAT ETRIGAN, HOW HE INFLAMES HER *PASSIONS!* I CAN'T HELP WONDER IF SHE ISN'T HALF *DEVIL* HERSELF.
KNOW WHAT I MEAN?
KEEPING THE DEMON BOTTLED UP INSIDE YOU IS THE BEST THING, REALLY. LOVE TRIANGLES ARE *NASTY* BUSINESS.
SOME DAY I'LL TELL YOU ABOUT ME AND HELEN OF TROY.
ANOTHER TIME, PERHAPS. I CAN SEE YOU'RE IN NO MOOD FOR POLITE DINNER CONVERSATION.
GUARDS, RETURN OUR GUEST TO HIS CELL.
SEE THAT HE GETS AMPLE REST.
THOUGH I WON'T PROMISE I'LL DO THE SAME.
"TOMORROW, I HAVE *BRAND NEW* PUNISHMENTS IN STORE."

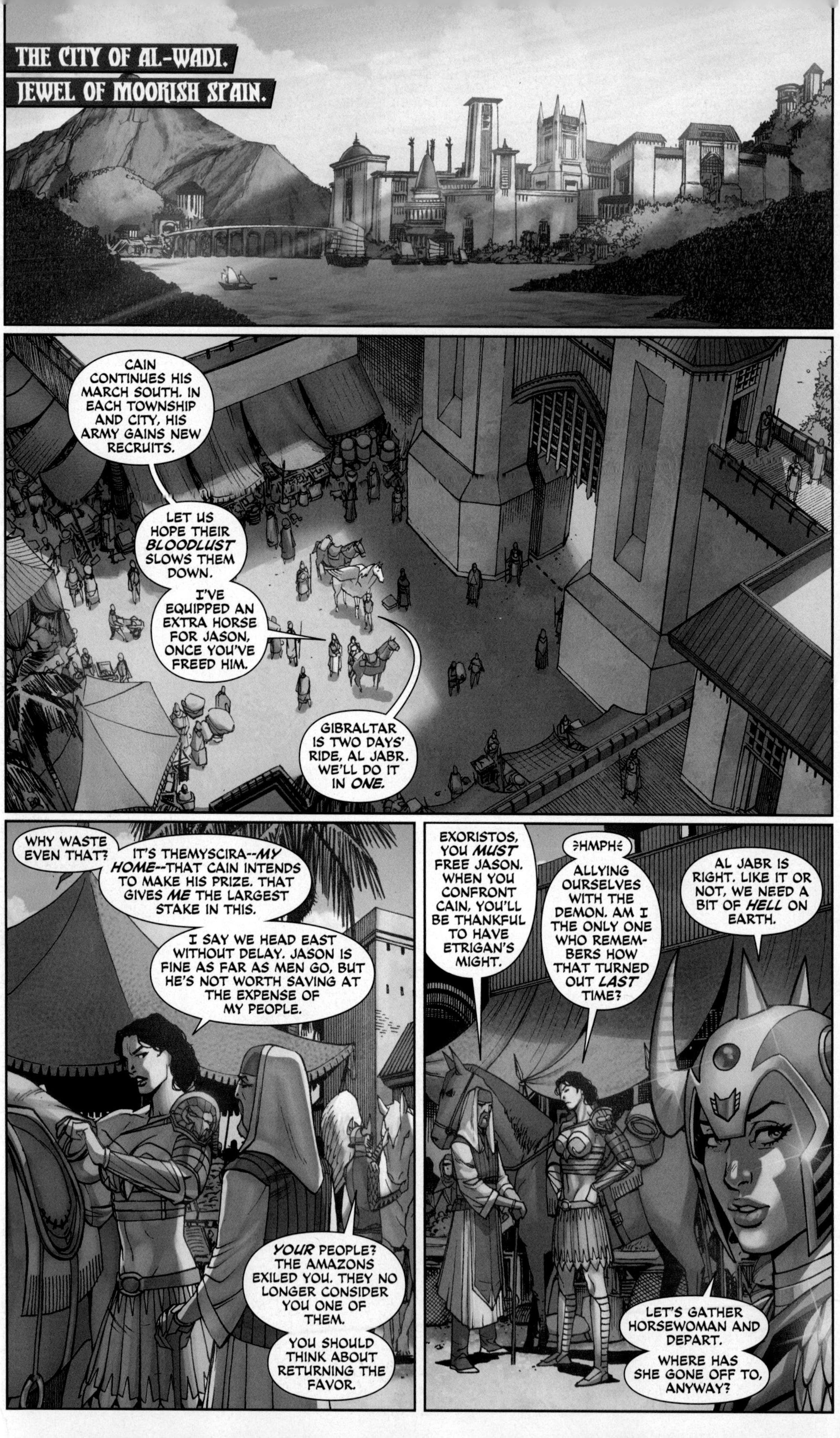
THE CITY OF AL-WADI.
JEWEL OF MOORISH SPAIN.
CAIN CONTINUES HIS MARCH SOUTH. IN EACH TOWNSHIP AND CITY, HIS ARMY GAINS NEW RECRUITS.
LET US HOPE THEIR BLOODLUST SLOWS THEM DOWN.
I'VE EQUIPPED AN EXTRA HORSE FOR JASON, ONCE YOU'VE FREED HIM.
GIBRALTAR IS TWO DAYS' RIDE, AL JABR. WE'LL DO IT IN ONE.
WHY WASTE EVEN THAT?
IT'S THEMYSCIRA--MY HOME--THAT CAIN INTENDS TO MAKE HIS PRIZE. THAT GIVES ME THE LARGEST STAKE IN THIS.
I SAY WE HEAD EAST WITHOUT DELAY. JASON IS FINE AS FAR AS MEN GO, BUT HE'S NOT WORTH SAVING AT THE EXPENSE OF MY PEOPLE.
YOUR PEOPLE? THE AMAZONS EXILED YOU. THEY NO LONGER CONSIDER YOU ONE OF THEM.
YOU SHOULD THINK ABOUT RETURNING THE FAVOR.
EXORISTOS, YOU MUST FREE JASON. WHEN YOU CONFRONT CAIN, YOU'LL BE THANKFUL TO HAVE ETRIGAN'S MIGHT.
HMPH
ALLYING OURSELVES WITH THE DEMON. AM I THE ONLY ONE WHO REMEMBERS HOW THAT TURNED OUT LAST TIME?
AL JABR IS RIGHT. LIKE IT OR NOT, WE NEED A BIT OF HELL ON EARTH.
LET'S GATHER HORSEWOMAN AND DEPART.
WHERE HAS SHE GONE OFF TO, ANYWAY?

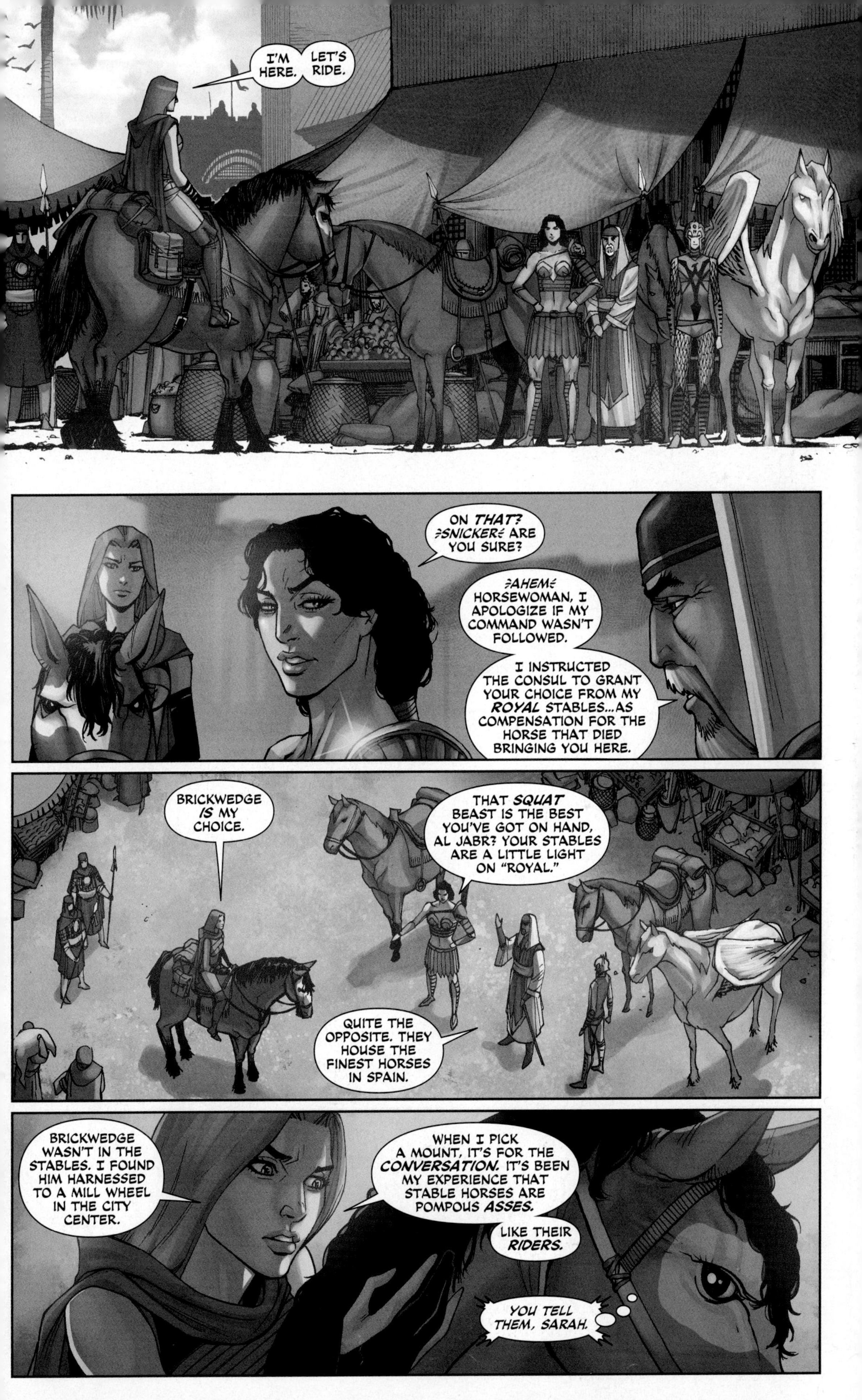
I'M HERE.
LET'S RIDE.
ON THAT? ≈SNICKER≈ ARE YOU SURE?
≈AHEM≈ HORSEWOMAN, I APOLOGIZE IF MY COMMAND WASN'T FOLLOWED.
I INSTRUCTED THE CONSUL TO GRANT YOUR CHOICE FROM MY ROYAL STABLES...AS COMPENSATION FOR THE HORSE THAT DIED BRINGING YOU HERE.
BRICKWEDGE IS MY CHOICE.
THAT SQUAT BEAST IS THE BEST YOU'VE GOT ON HAND, AL JABR? YOUR STABLES ARE A LITTLE LIGHT ON "ROYAL."
QUITE THE OPPOSITE. THEY HOUSE THE FINEST HORSES IN SPAIN.
BRICKWEDGE WASN'T IN THE STABLES. I FOUND HIM HARNESSED TO A MILL WHEEL IN THE CITY CENTER.
WHEN I PICK A MOUNT, IT'S FOR THE CONVERSATION. IT'S BEEN MY EXPERIENCE THAT STABLE HORSES ARE POMPOUS ASSES.
LIKE THEIR RIDERS.
YOU TELL THEM, SARAH.

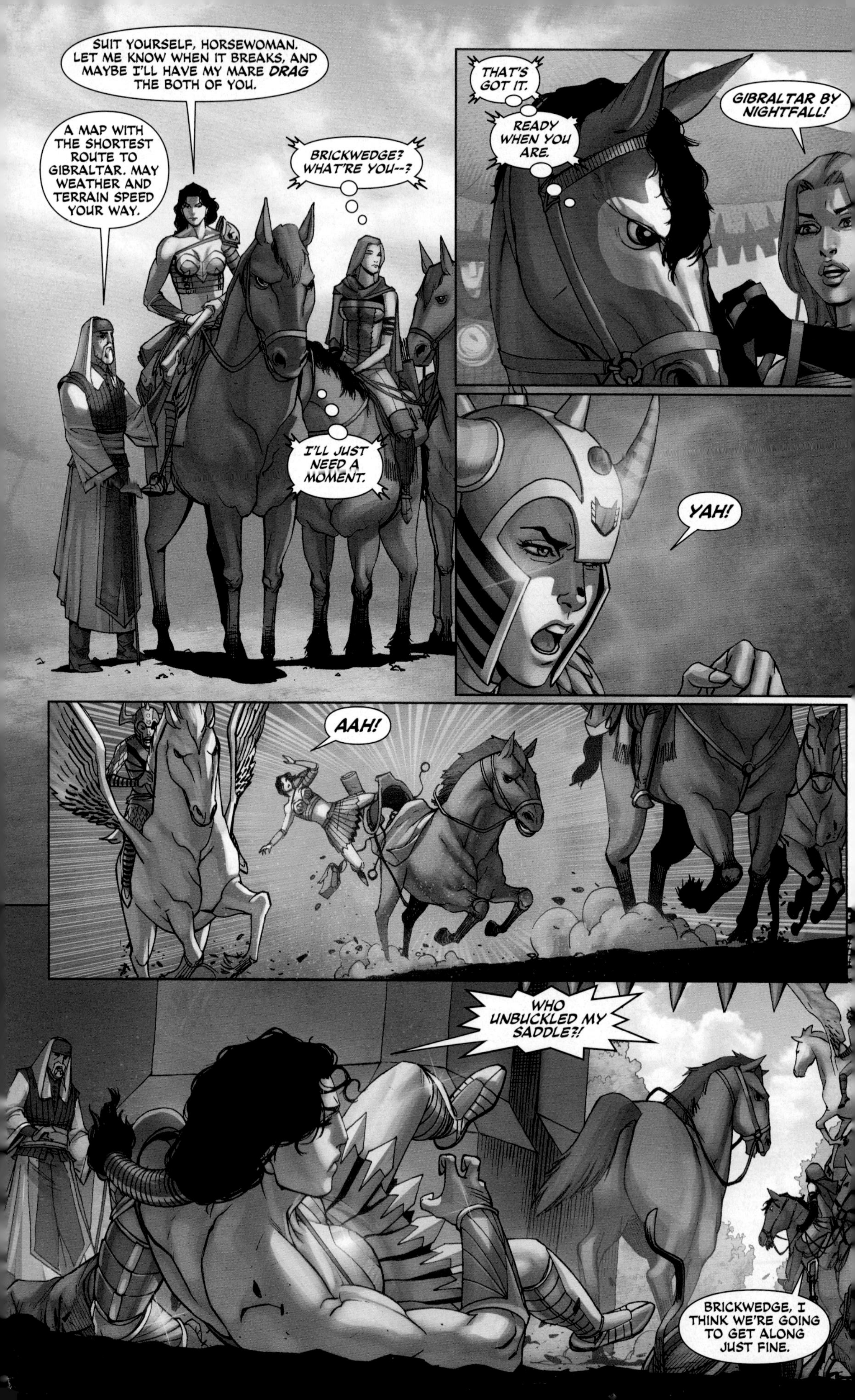
SUIT YOURSELF, HORSEWOMAN. LET ME KNOW WHEN IT BREAKS, AND MAYBE I'LL HAVE MY MARE *DRAG* THE BOTH OF YOU.
A MAP WITH THE SHORTEST ROUTE TO GIBRALTAR. MAY WEATHER AND TERRAIN SPEED YOUR WAY.
BRICKWEDGE? WHAT'RE YOU--?
I'LL JUST NEED A MOMENT.
THAT'S GOT IT.
READY WHEN YOU ARE.
GIBRALTAR BY NIGHTFALL!
YAH!
AAH!
WHO UNBUCKLED MY SADDLE?!
BRICKWEDGE, I THINK WE'RE GOING TO GET ALONG JUST FINE.

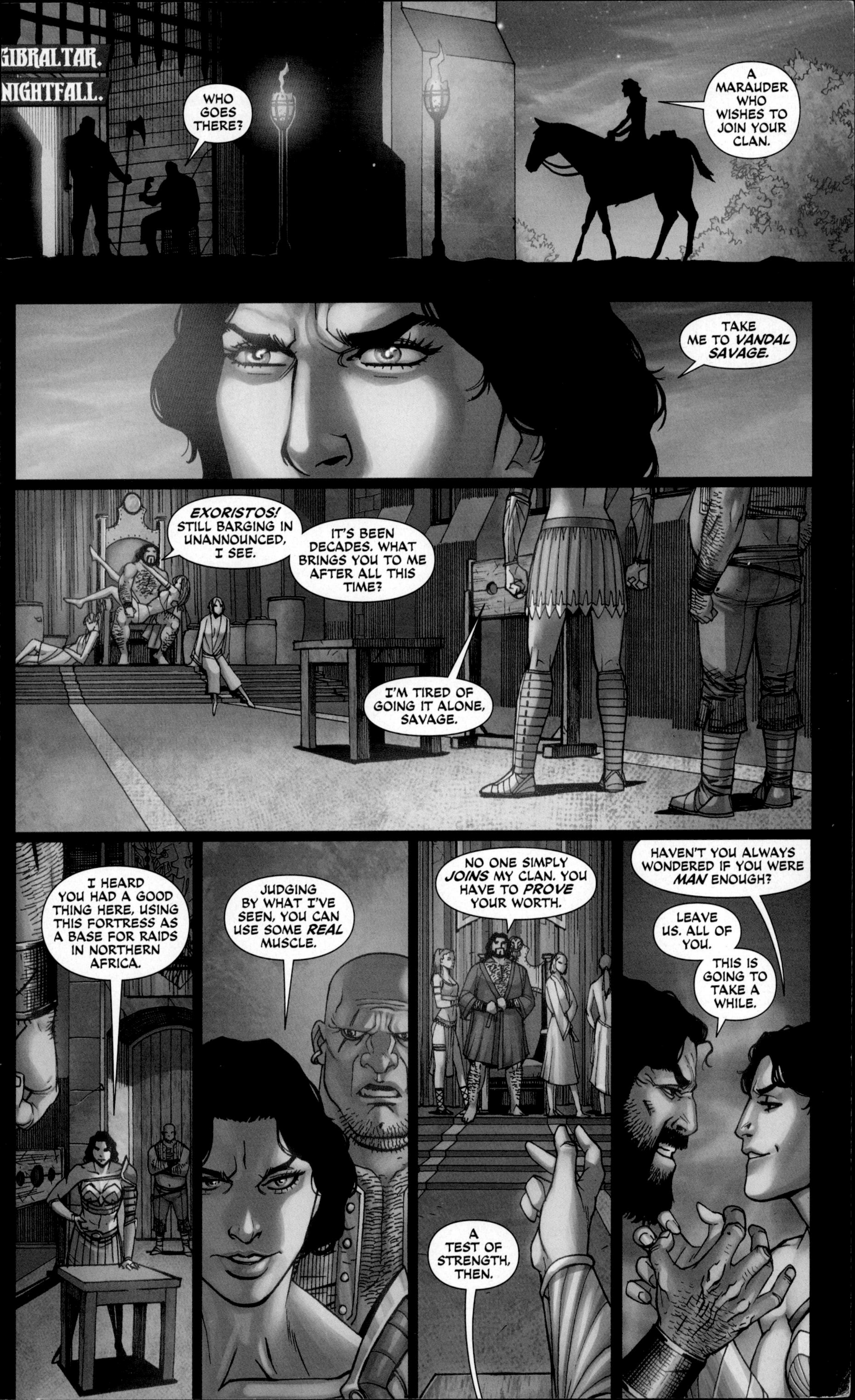
GIBRALTAR.
NIGHTFALL.
WHO GOES THERE?
A MARAUDER WHO WISHES TO JOIN YOUR CLAN.
TAKE ME TO VANDAL SAVAGE.
EXORISTOS! STILL BARGING IN UNANNOUNCED, I SEE.
IT'S BEEN DECADES. WHAT BRINGS YOU TO ME AFTER ALL THIS TIME?
I'M TIRED OF GOING IT ALONE, SAVAGE.
I HEARD YOU HAD A GOOD THING HERE, USING THIS FORTRESS AS A BASE FOR RAIDS IN NORTHERN AFRICA.
JUDGING BY WHAT I'VE SEEN, YOU CAN USE SOME REAL MUSCLE.
NO ONE SIMPLY JOINS MY CLAN. YOU HAVE TO PROVE YOUR WORTH.
A TEST OF STRENGTH, THEN.
HAVEN'T YOU ALWAYS WONDERED IF YOU WERE MAN ENOUGH?
LEAVE US. ALL OF YOU.
THIS IS GOING TO TAKE A WHILE.

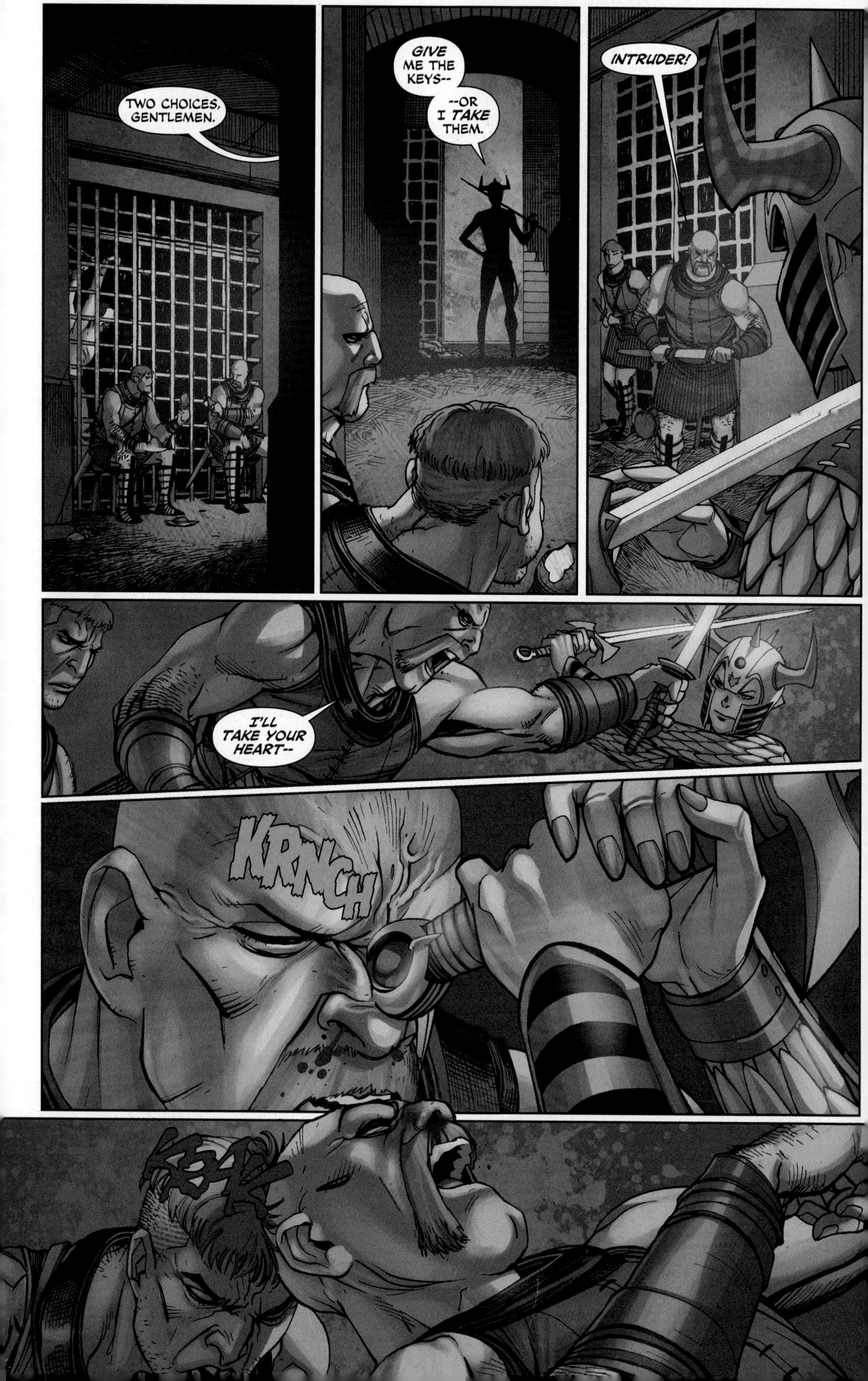
TWO CHOICES, GENTLEMEN.
GIVE ME THE KEYS--
--OR I TAKE THEM.
INTRUDER!
I'LL TAKE YOUR HEART--
KRNCH

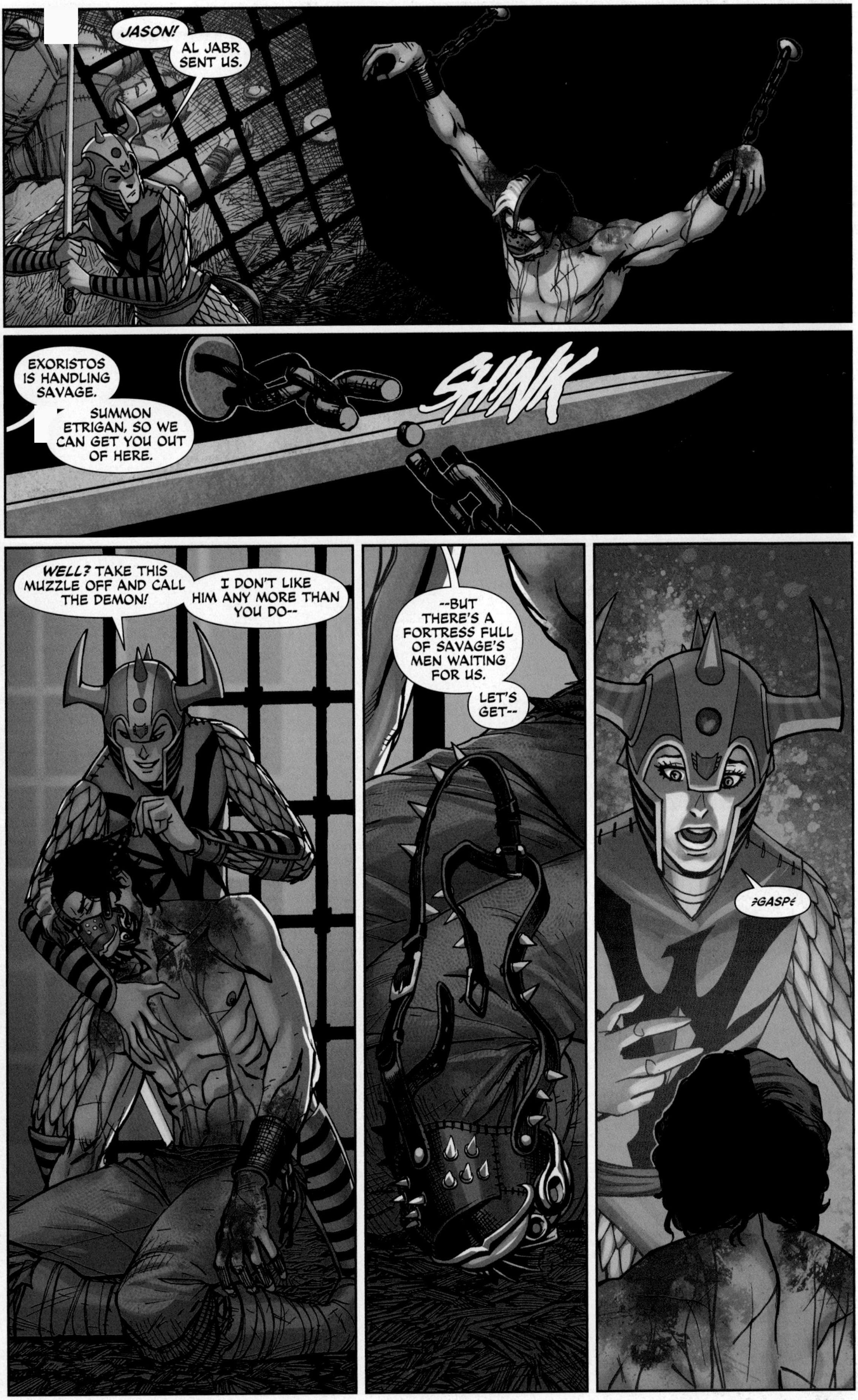

JASON!
AL JABR SENT US.
EXORISTOS IS HANDLING SAVAGE.
SUMMON ETRIGAN, SO WE CAN GET YOU OUT OF HERE.
SHINK
WELL? TAKE THIS MUZZLE OFF AND CALL THE DEMON!
I DON'T LIKE HIM ANY MORE THAN YOU DO--
--BUT THERE'S A FORTRESS FULL OF SAVAGE'S MEN WAITING FOR US.
LET'S GET--
GASP

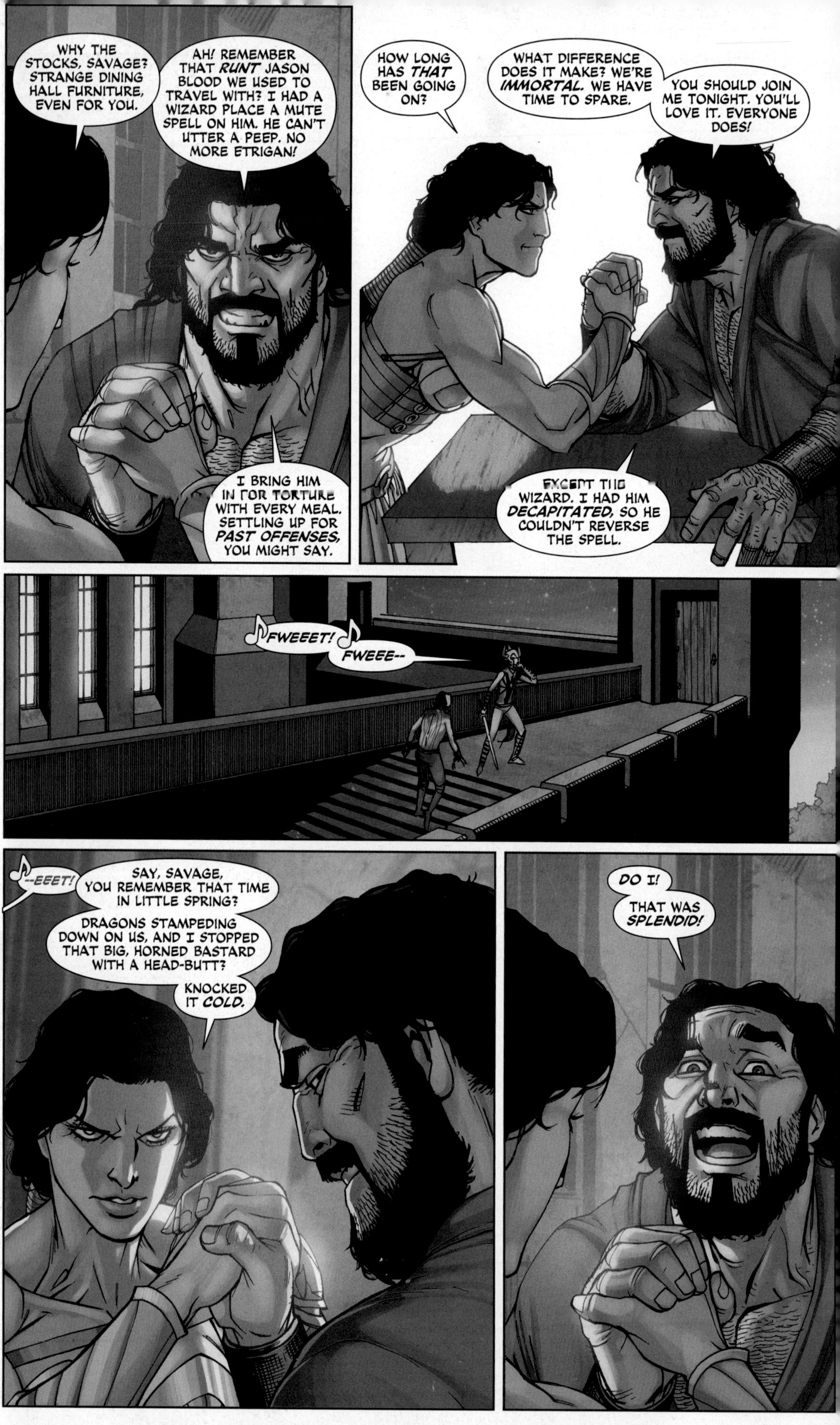
WHY THE STOCKS, SAVAGE? STRANGE DINING HALL FURNITURE, EVEN FOR YOU.
AH! REMEMBER THAT RUNT JASON BLOOD WE USED TO TRAVEL WITH? I HAD A WIZARD PLACE A MUTE SPELL ON HIM. HE CAN'T UTTER A PEEP. NO MORE ETRIGAN!
I BRING HIM IN FOR TORTURE WITH EVERY MEAL. SETTLING UP FOR PAST OFFENSES, YOU MIGHT SAY.
HOW LONG HAS THAT BEEN GOING ON?
WHAT DIFFERENCE DOES IT MAKE? WE'RE IMMORTAL. WE HAVE TIME TO SPARE.
YOU SHOULD JOIN ME TONIGHT. YOU'LL LOVE IT. EVERYONE DOES!
EXCEPT THE WIZARD. I HAD HIM DECAPITATED, SO HE COULDN'T REVERSE THE SPELL.
FWEEET!
FWEEE--
--EEET!
SAY, SAVAGE, YOU REMEMBER THAT TIME IN LITTLE SPRING?
DRAGONS STAMPEDING DOWN ON US, AND I STOPPED THAT BIG, HORNED BASTARD WITH A HEAD-BUTT?
KNOCKED IT COLD.
DO I!
THAT WAS SPLENDID!

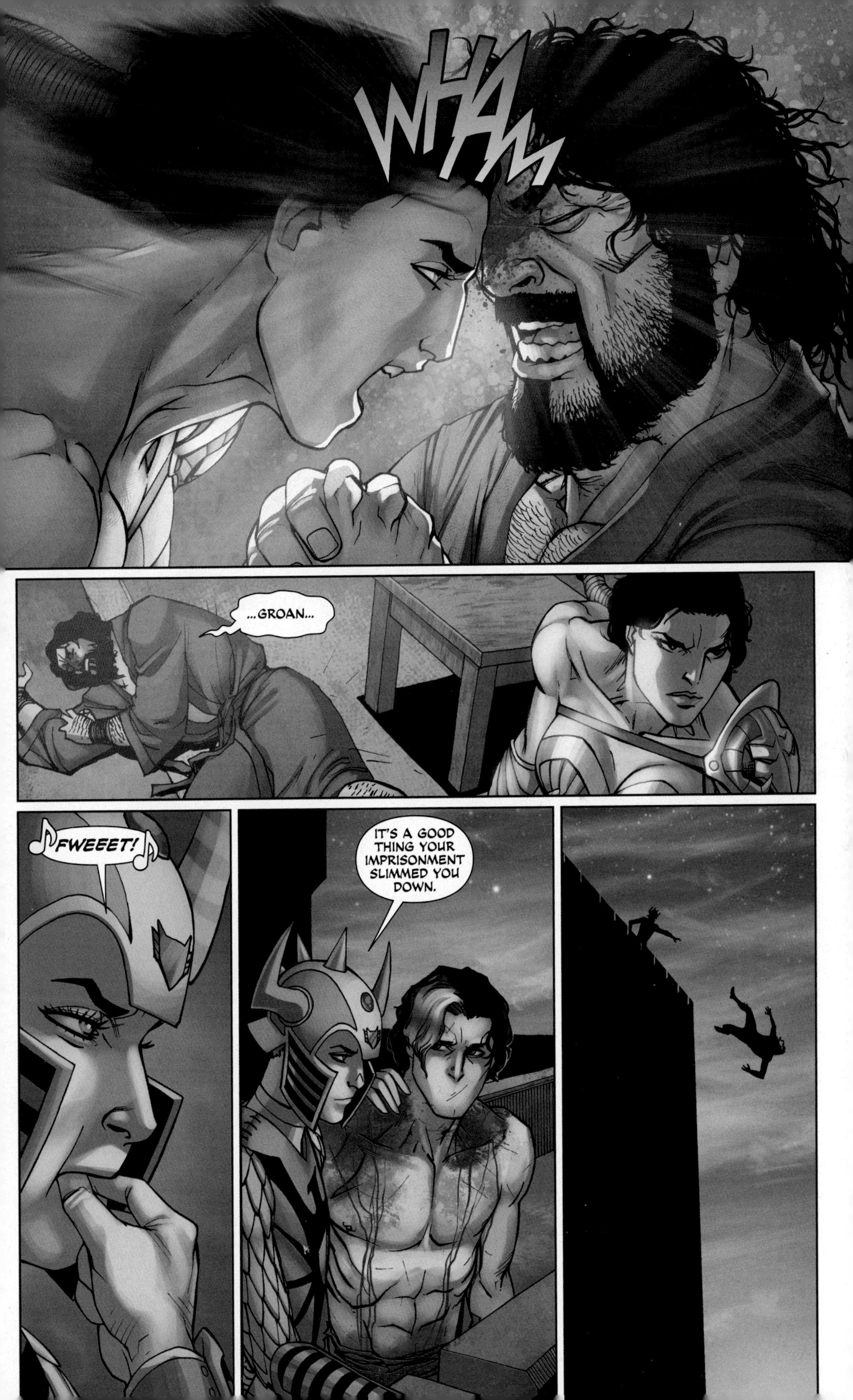
WHAM
...GROAN...
FWEEET!
IT'S A GOOD THING YOUR IMPRISONMENT SLIMMED YOU DOWN.

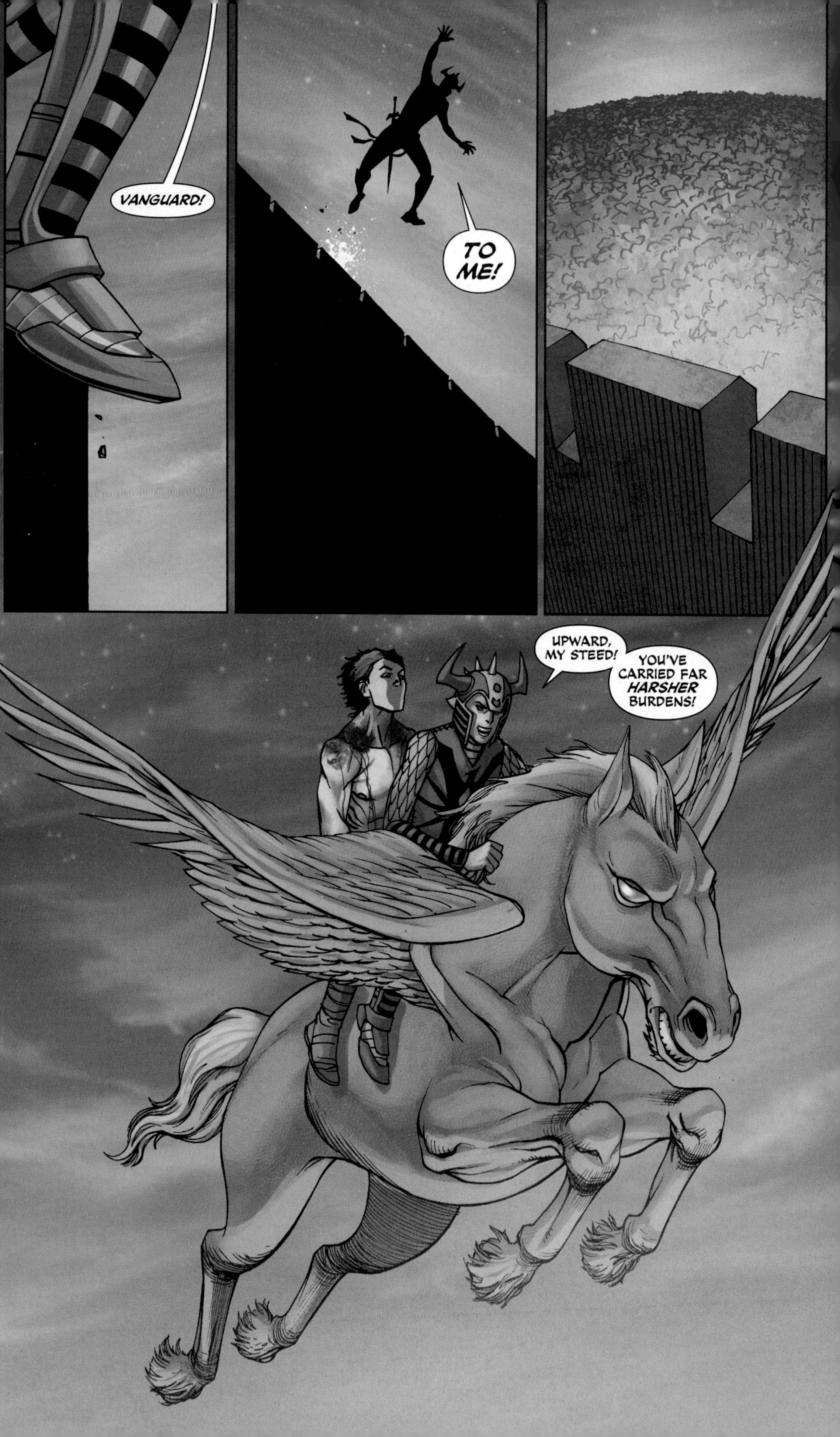
VANGUARD!
TO ME!
UPWARD, MY STEED!
YOU'VE CARRIED FAR HARSHER BURDENS!

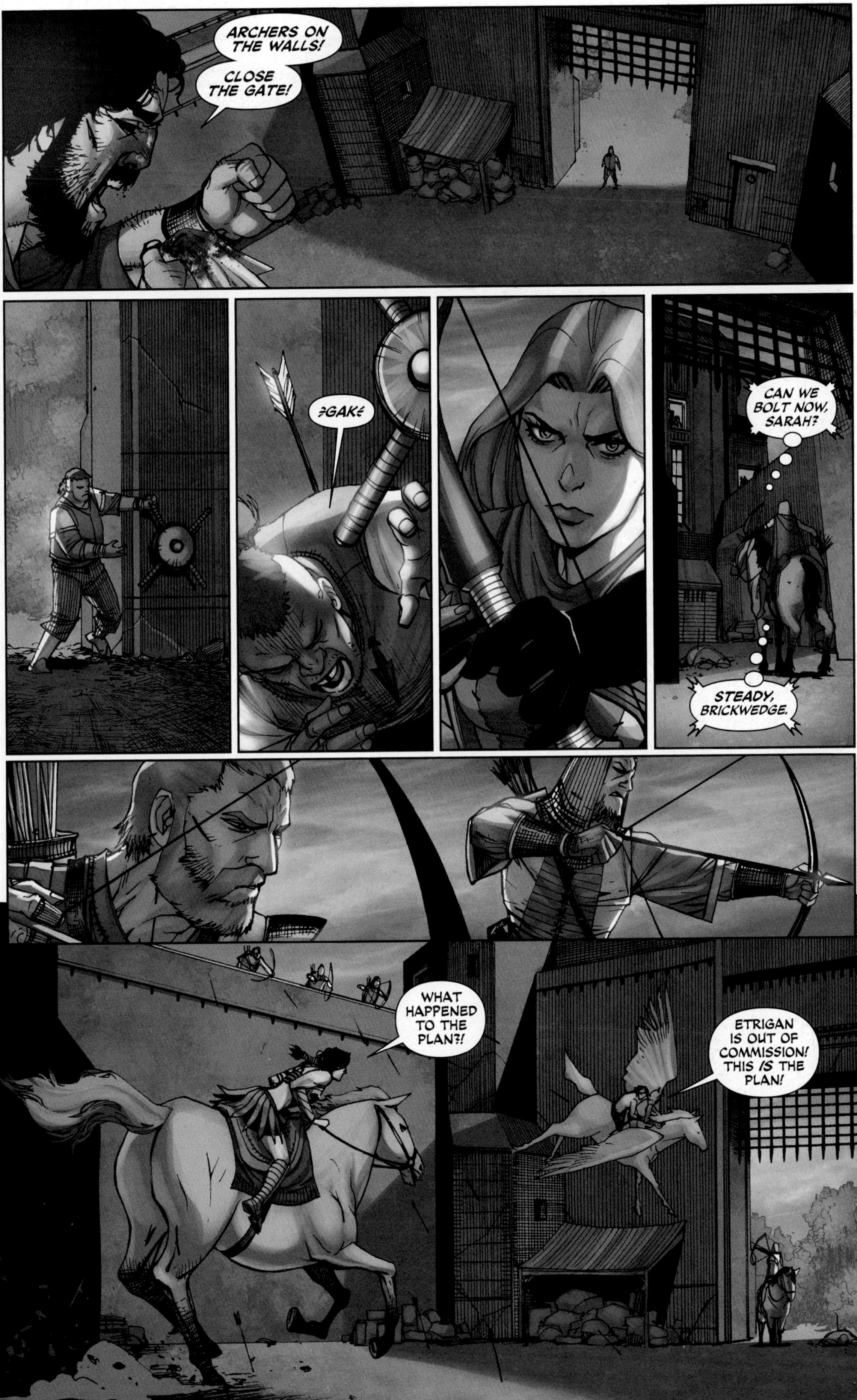
ARCHERS ON THE WALLS!
CLOSE THE GATE!
GAK
CAN WE BOLT NOW, SARAH?
STEADY, BRICKWEDGE.
WHAT HAPPENED TO THE PLAN?!
ETRIGAN IS OUT OF COMMISSION! THIS IS THE PLAN!

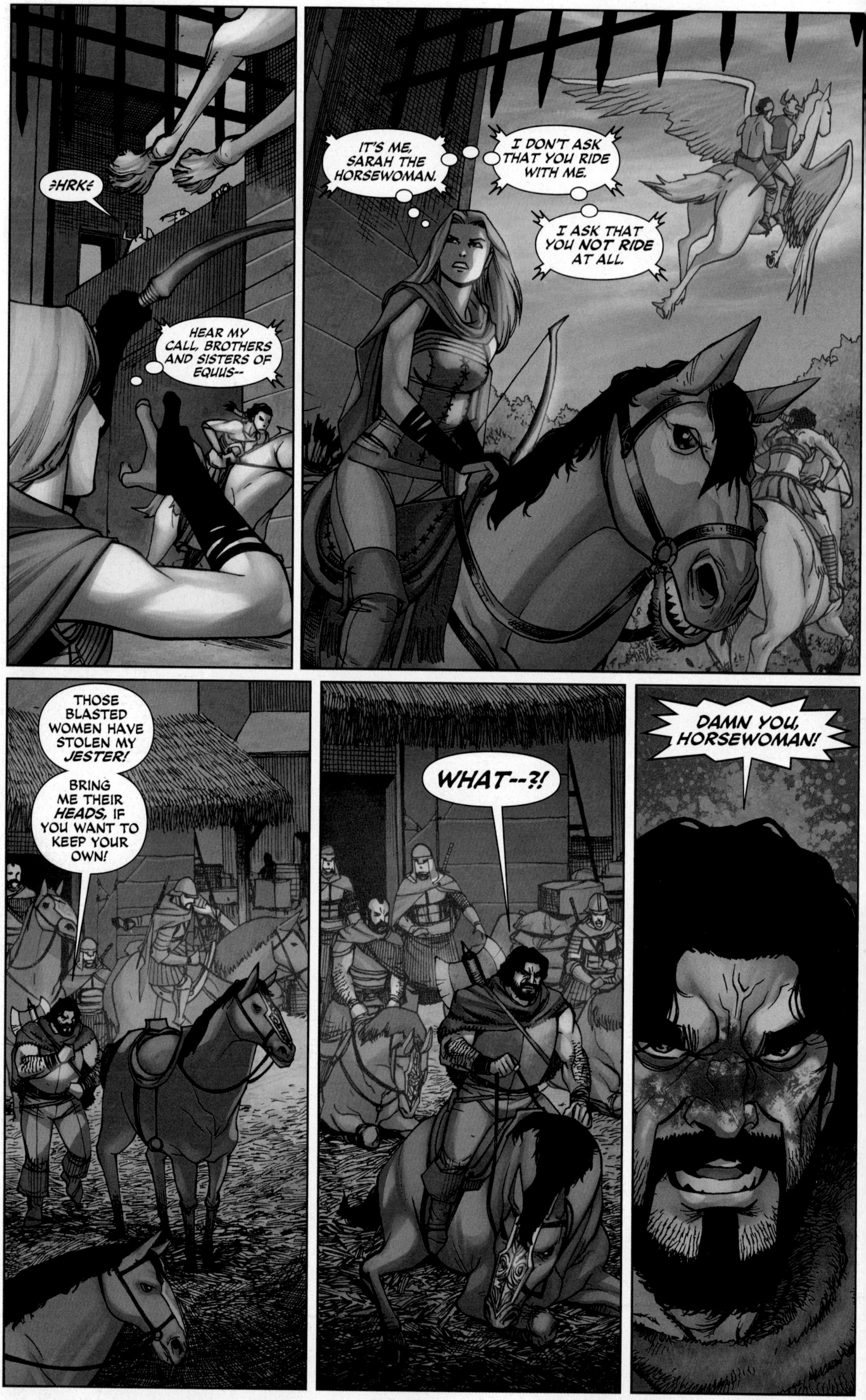

?HRK?
HEAR MY CALL, BROTHERS AND SISTERS OF EQUUS--
IT'S ME, SARAH THE HORSEWOMAN.
I DON'T ASK THAT YOU RIDE WITH ME.
I ASK THAT YOU NOT RIDE AT ALL.
THOSE BLASTED WOMEN HAVE STOLEN MY JESTER!
BRING ME THEIR HEADS, IF YOU WANT TO KEEP YOUR OWN!
WHAT--?!
DAMN YOU, HORSEWOMAN!

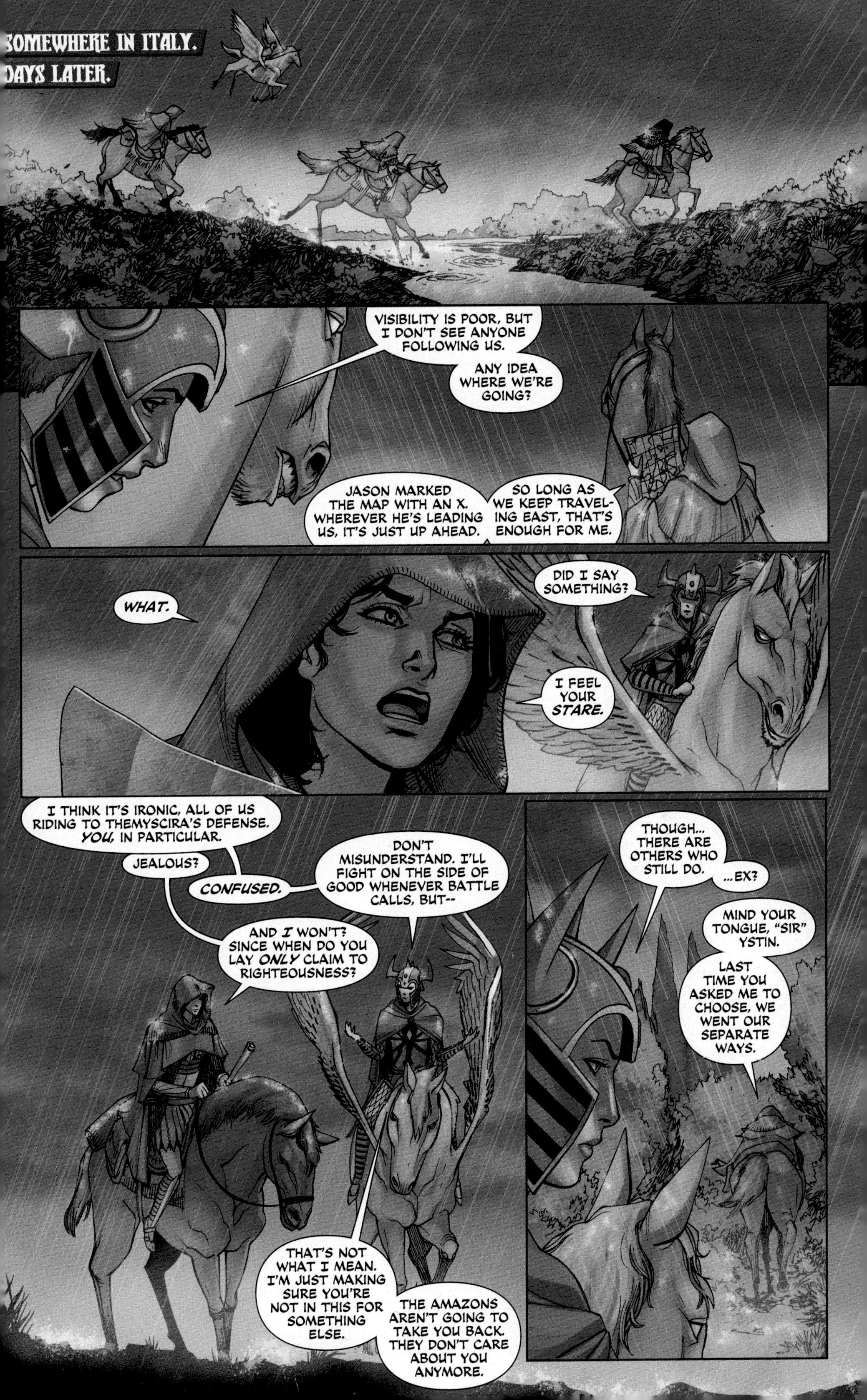
SOMEWHERE IN ITALY.
DAYS LATER.
VISIBILITY IS POOR, BUT I DON'T SEE ANYONE FOLLOWING US.
ANY IDEA WHERE WE'RE GOING?
JASON MARKED THE MAP WITH AN X. WHEREVER HE'S LEADING US, IT'S JUST UP AHEAD.
SO LONG AS WE KEEP TRAVELING EAST, THAT'S ENOUGH FOR ME.
WHAT.
DID I SAY SOMETHING?
I FEEL YOUR STARE.
I THINK IT'S IRONIC, ALL OF US RIDING TO THEMYSCIRA'S DEFENSE. YOU, IN PARTICULAR.
JEALOUS?
CONFUSED.
DON'T MISUNDERSTAND. I'LL FIGHT ON THE SIDE OF GOOD WHENEVER BATTLE CALLS, BUT--
AND I WON'T? SINCE WHEN DO YOU LAY ONLY CLAIM TO RIGHTEOUSNESS?
THAT'S NOT WHAT I MEAN. I'M JUST MAKING SURE YOU'RE NOT IN THIS FOR SOMETHING ELSE.
THE AMAZONS AREN'T GOING TO TAKE YOU BACK. THEY DON'T CARE ABOUT YOU ANYMORE.
THOUGH... THERE ARE OTHERS WHO STILL DO.
...EX?
MIND YOUR TONGUE, "SIR" YSTIN.
LAST TIME YOU ASKED ME TO CHOOSE, WE WENT OUR SEPARATE WAYS.

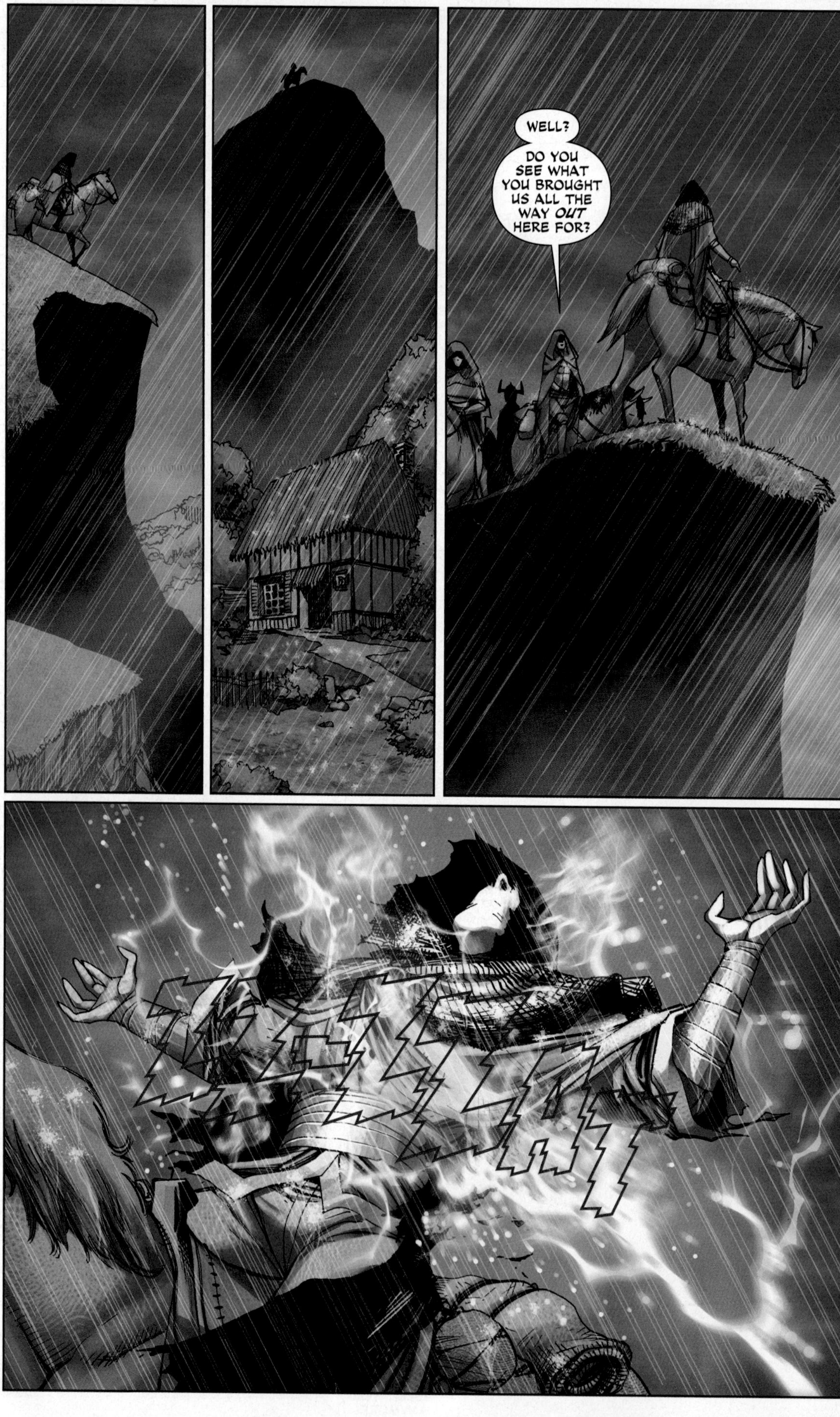
WELL?
DO YOU SEE WHAT YOU BROUGHT US ALL THE WAY *OUT* HERE FOR?

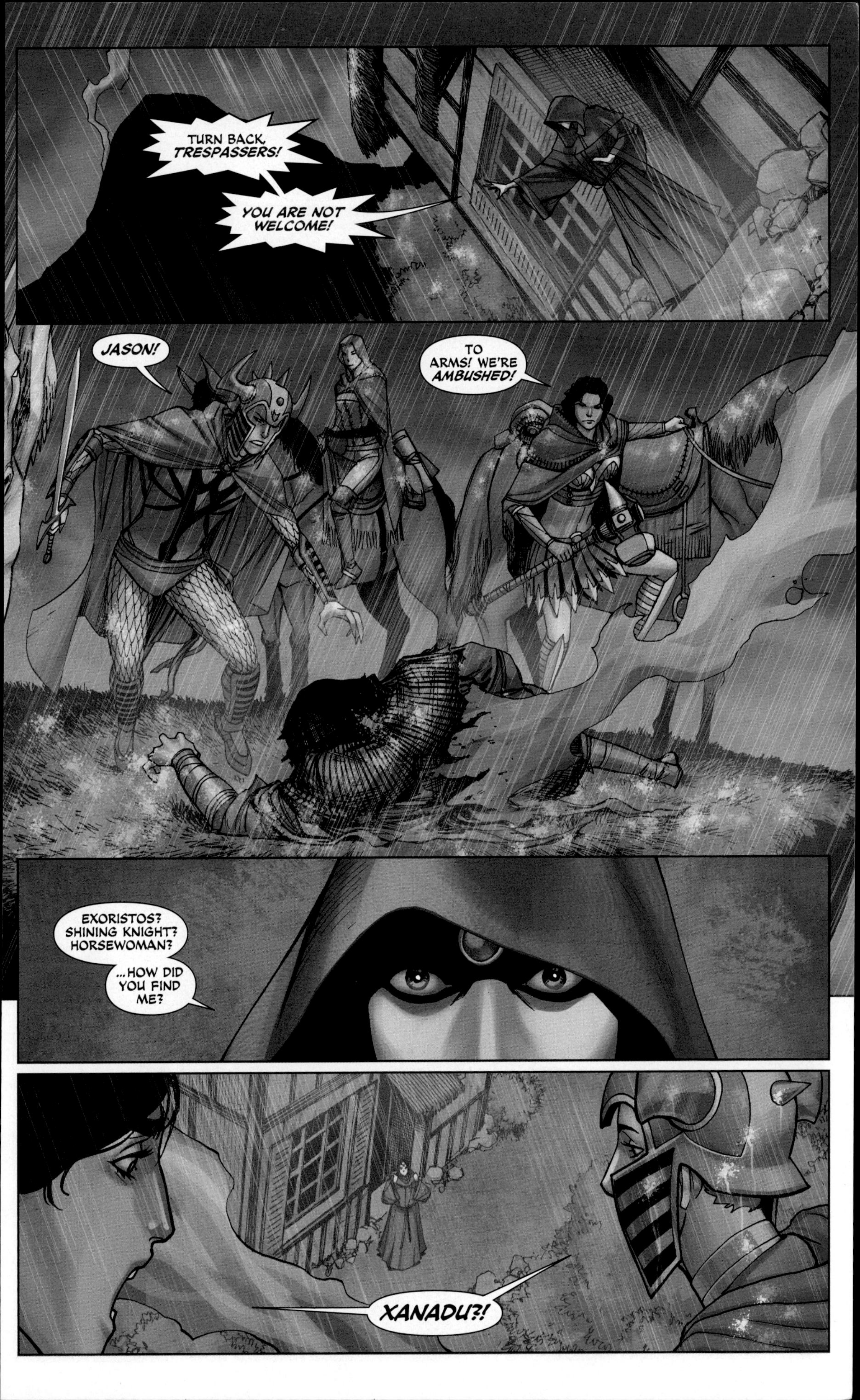
TURN BACK, TRESPASSERS!
YOU ARE NOT WELCOME!
JASON!
TO ARMS! WE'RE AMBUSHED!
EXORISTOS? SHINING KNIGHT? HORSEWOMAN?
...HOW DID YOU FIND ME?
XANADU?!

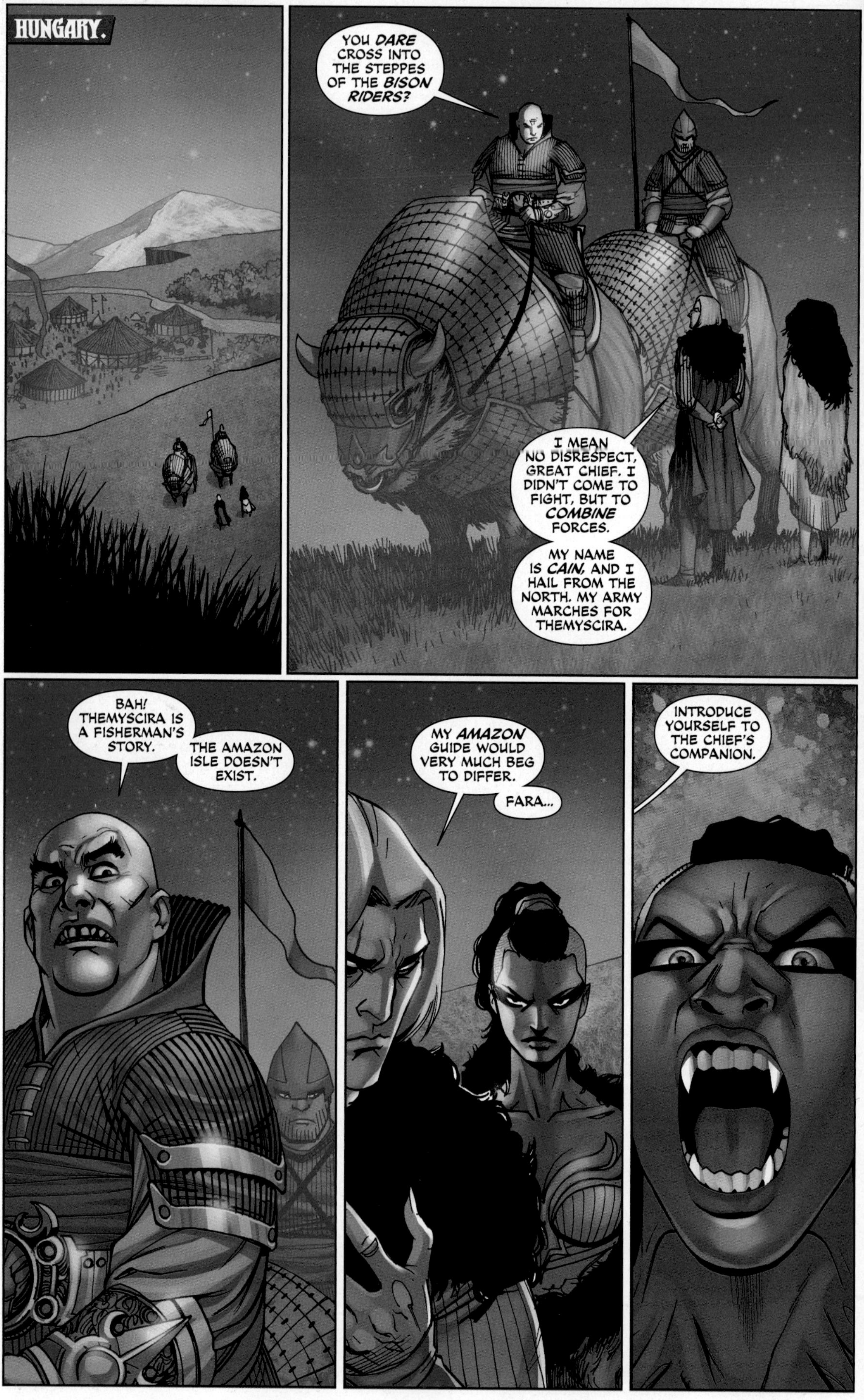
HUNGARY.
YOU DARE CROSS INTO THE STEPPES OF THE BISON RIDERS?
I MEAN NO DISRESPECT, GREAT CHIEF. I DIDN'T COME TO FIGHT, BUT TO COMBINE FORCES.
MY NAME IS CAIN, AND I HAIL FROM THE NORTH. MY ARMY MARCHES FOR THEMYSCIRA.
BAH! THEMYSCIRA IS A FISHERMAN'S STORY.
THE AMAZON ISLE DOESN'T EXIST.
MY AMAZON GUIDE WOULD VERY MUCH BEG TO DIFFER.
FARA...
INTRODUCE YOURSELF TO THE CHIEF'S COMPANION.

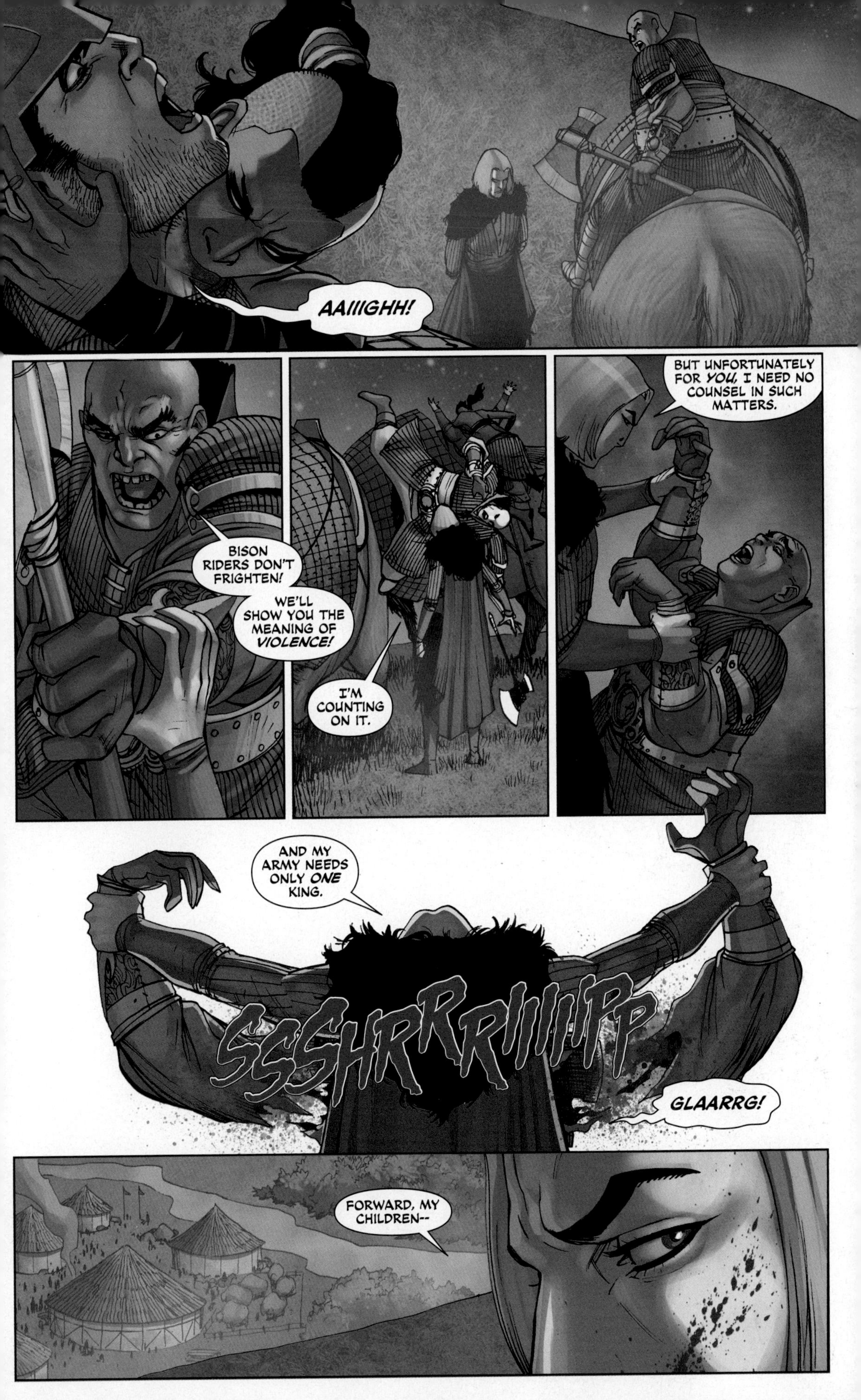
AAIIIGHH!
BISON RIDERS DON'T FRIGHTEN!
WE'LL SHOW YOU THE MEANING OF *VIOLENCE!*
I'M COUNTING ON IT.
BUT UNFORTUNATELY FOR *YOU,* I NEED NO COUNSEL IN SUCH MATTERS.
AND MY ARMY NEEDS ONLY *ONE* KING.
SSSHRRRIIIIIPP
GLAARRG!
FORWARD, MY CHILDREN--

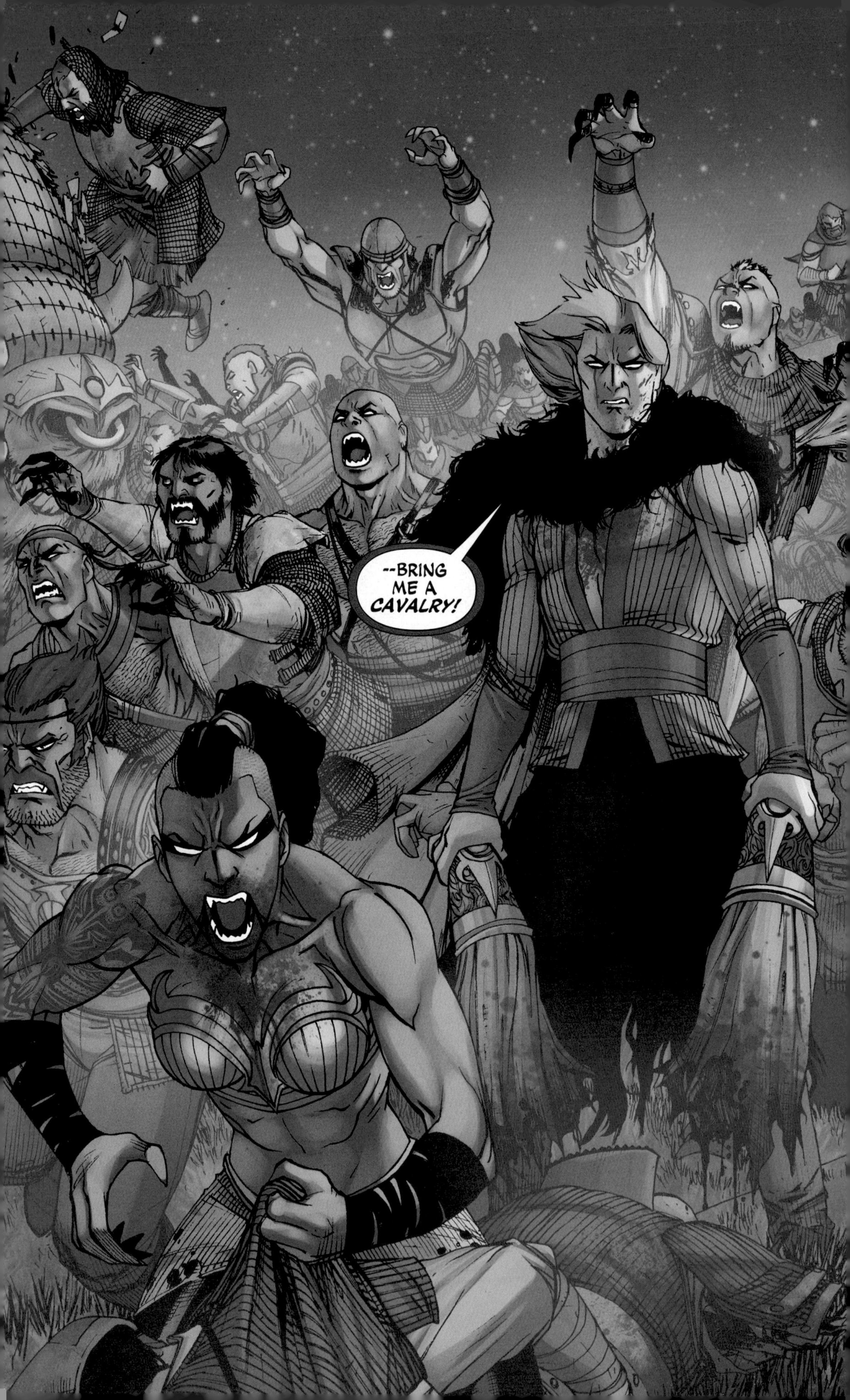
--BRING ME A CAVALRY!

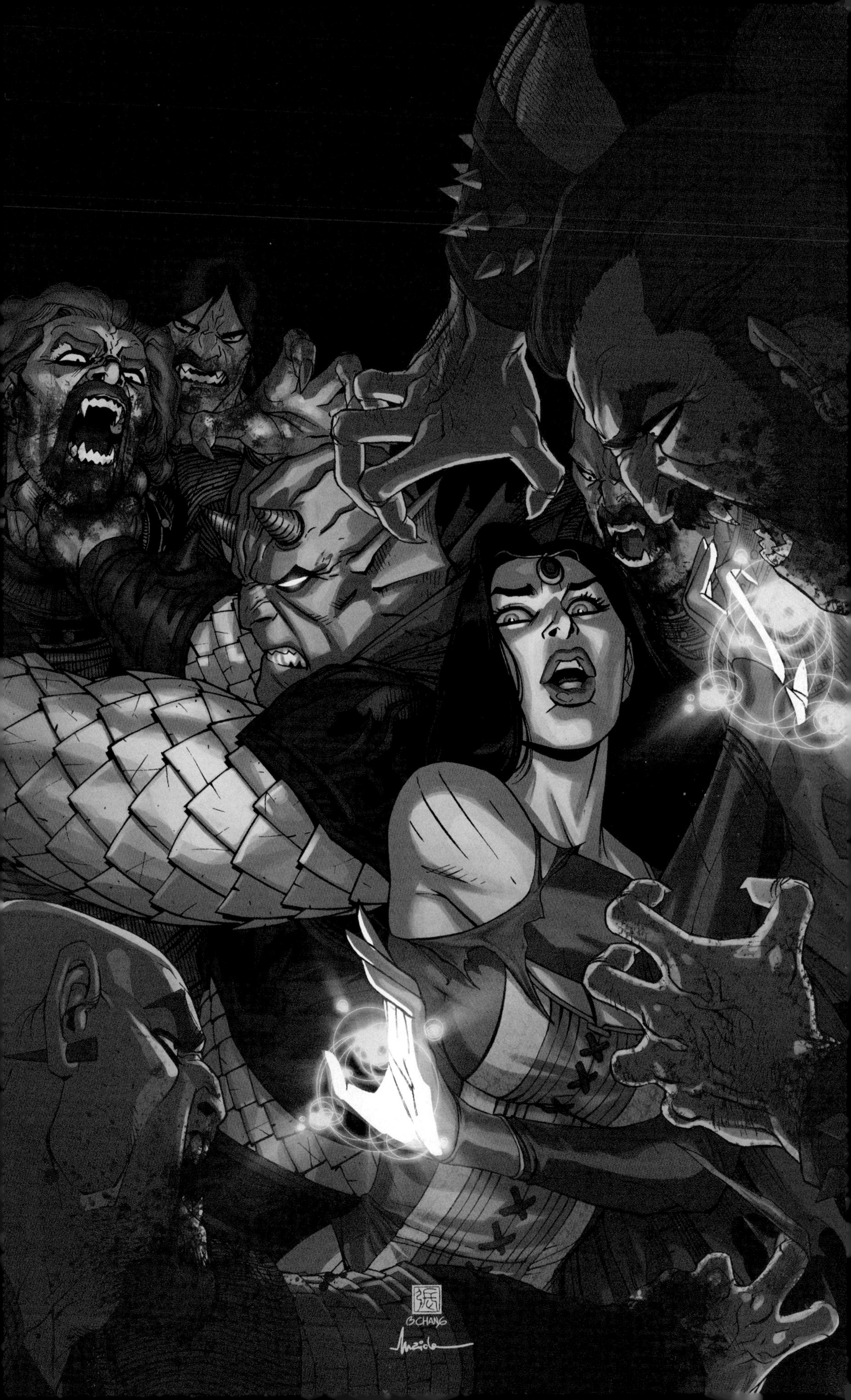
B CHANG

ROBERT VENDITTI
writer

BERNARD CHANG
artist

BERNARD CHANG
cover artist

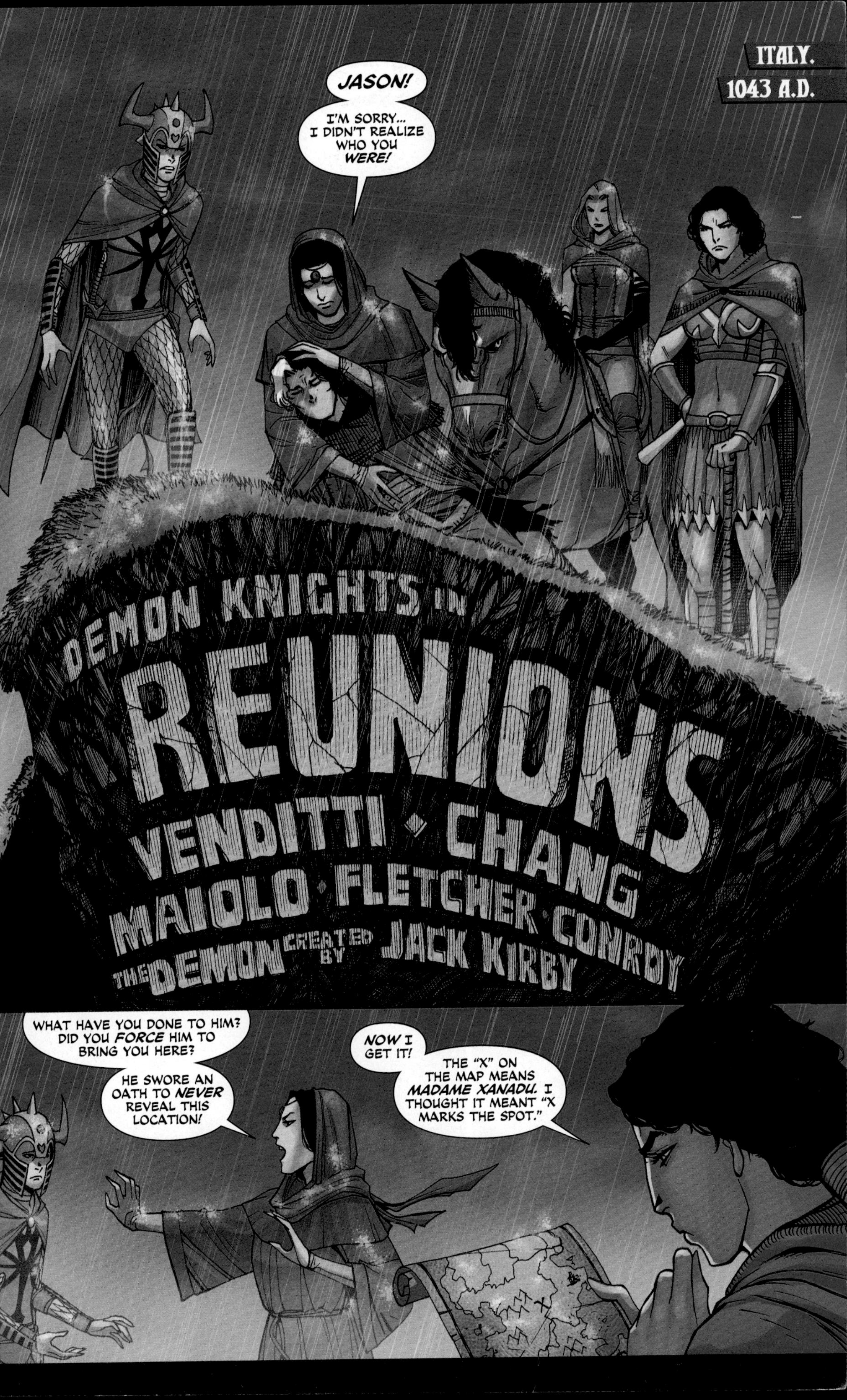
ITALY.
1043 A.D.
JASON!
I'M SORRY... I DIDN'T REALIZE WHO YOU WERE!
DEMON KNIGHTS IN
REUNIONS
VENDITTI · CHANG
MAIOLO · FLETCHER · CONROY
THE DEMON CREATED BY JACK KIRBY
WHAT HAVE YOU DONE TO HIM? DID YOU FORCE HIM TO BRING YOU HERE?
HE SWORE AN OATH TO NEVER REVEAL THIS LOCATION!
NOW I GET IT!
THE "X" ON THE MAP MEANS MADAME XANADU. I THOUGHT IT MEANT "X MARKS THE SPOT."

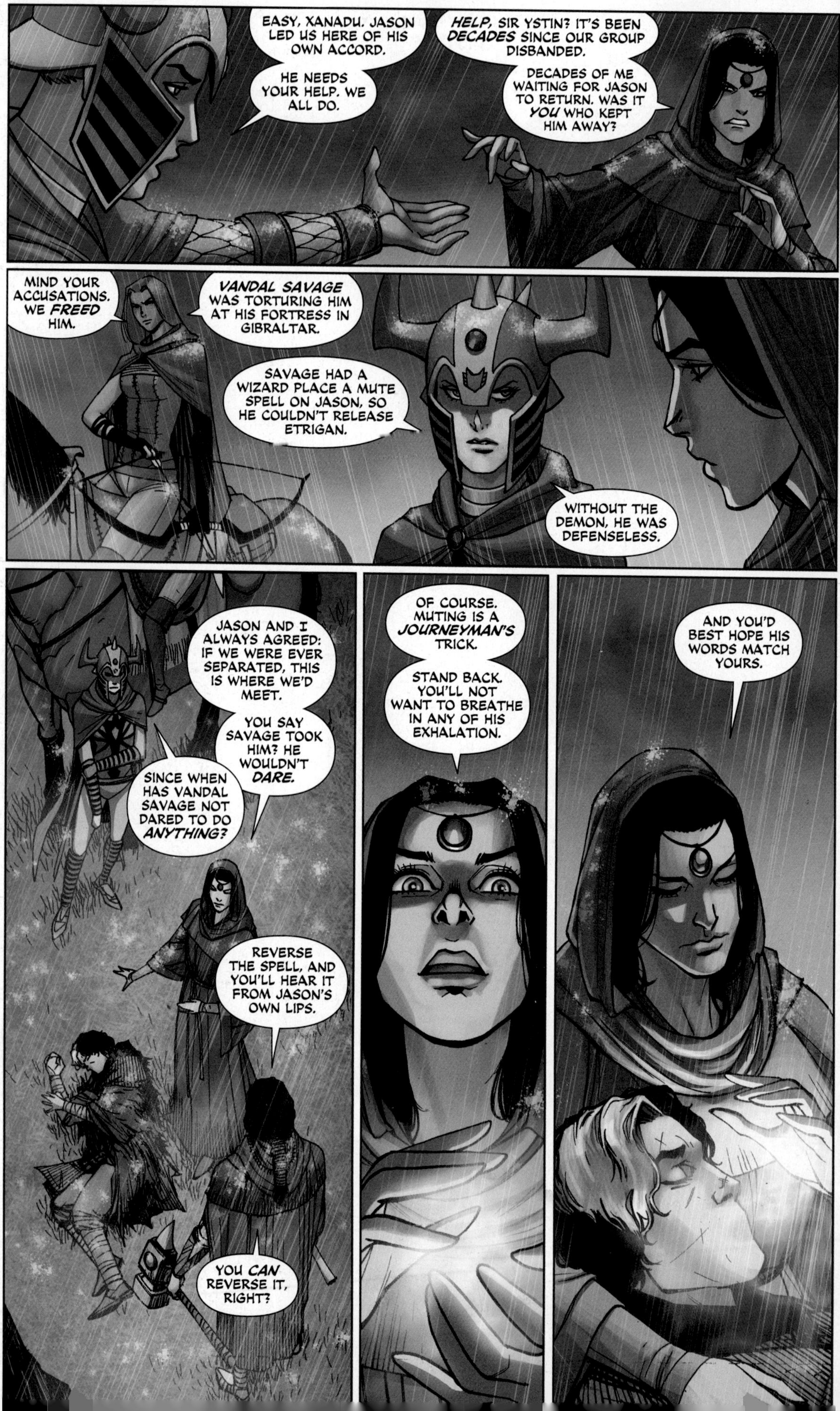
EASY, XANADU. JASON LED US HERE OF HIS OWN ACCORD.
HE NEEDS YOUR HELP. WE ALL DO.
HELP, SIR YSTIN? IT'S BEEN DECADES SINCE OUR GROUP DISBANDED.
DECADES OF ME WAITING FOR JASON TO RETURN. WAS IT YOU WHO KEPT HIM AWAY?
MIND YOUR ACCUSATIONS. WE FREED HIM.
VANDAL SAVAGE WAS TORTURING HIM AT HIS FORTRESS IN GIBRALTAR.
SAVAGE HAD A WIZARD PLACE A MUTE SPELL ON JASON, SO HE COULDN'T RELEASE ETRIGAN.
WITHOUT THE DEMON, HE WAS DEFENSELESS.
JASON AND I ALWAYS AGREED: IF WE WERE EVER SEPARATED, THIS IS WHERE WE'D MEET.
YOU SAY SAVAGE TOOK HIM? HE WOULDN'T DARE.
SINCE WHEN HAS VANDAL SAVAGE NOT DARED TO DO ANYTHING?
REVERSE THE SPELL, AND YOU'LL HEAR IT FROM JASON'S OWN LIPS.
YOU CAN REVERSE IT, RIGHT?
OF COURSE. MUTING IS A JOURNEYMAN'S TRICK.
STAND BACK. YOU'LL NOT WANT TO BREATHE IN ANY OF HIS EXHALATION.
AND YOU'D BEST HOPE HIS WORDS MATCH YOURS.

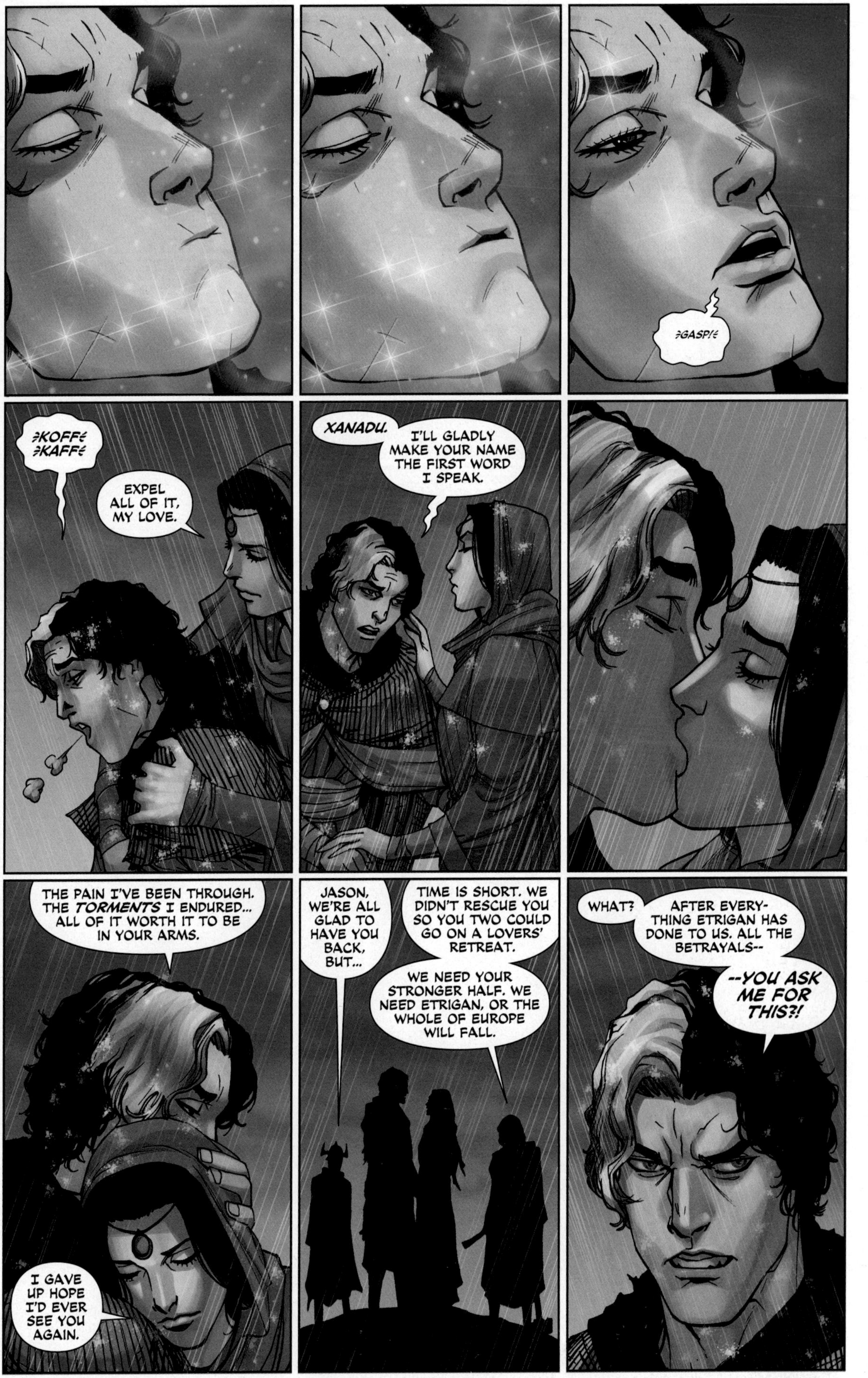

⋛GASP!⋚
⋛KOFF⋚ ⋛KAFF⋚
EXPEL ALL OF IT, MY LOVE.
XANADU.
I'LL GLADLY MAKE YOUR NAME THE FIRST WORD I SPEAK.
THE PAIN I'VE BEEN THROUGH. THE *TORMENTS* I ENDURED... ALL OF IT WORTH IT TO BE IN YOUR ARMS.
I GAVE UP HOPE I'D EVER SEE YOU AGAIN.
JASON, WE'RE ALL GLAD TO HAVE YOU BACK, BUT...
TIME IS SHORT. WE DIDN'T RESCUE YOU SO YOU TWO COULD GO ON A LOVERS' RETREAT.
WE NEED YOUR STRONGER HALF. WE NEED ETRIGAN, OR THE WHOLE OF EUROPE WILL FALL.
WHAT?
AFTER EVERYTHING ETRIGAN HAS DONE TO US. ALL THE BETRAYALS--
--YOU ASK ME FOR THIS?!

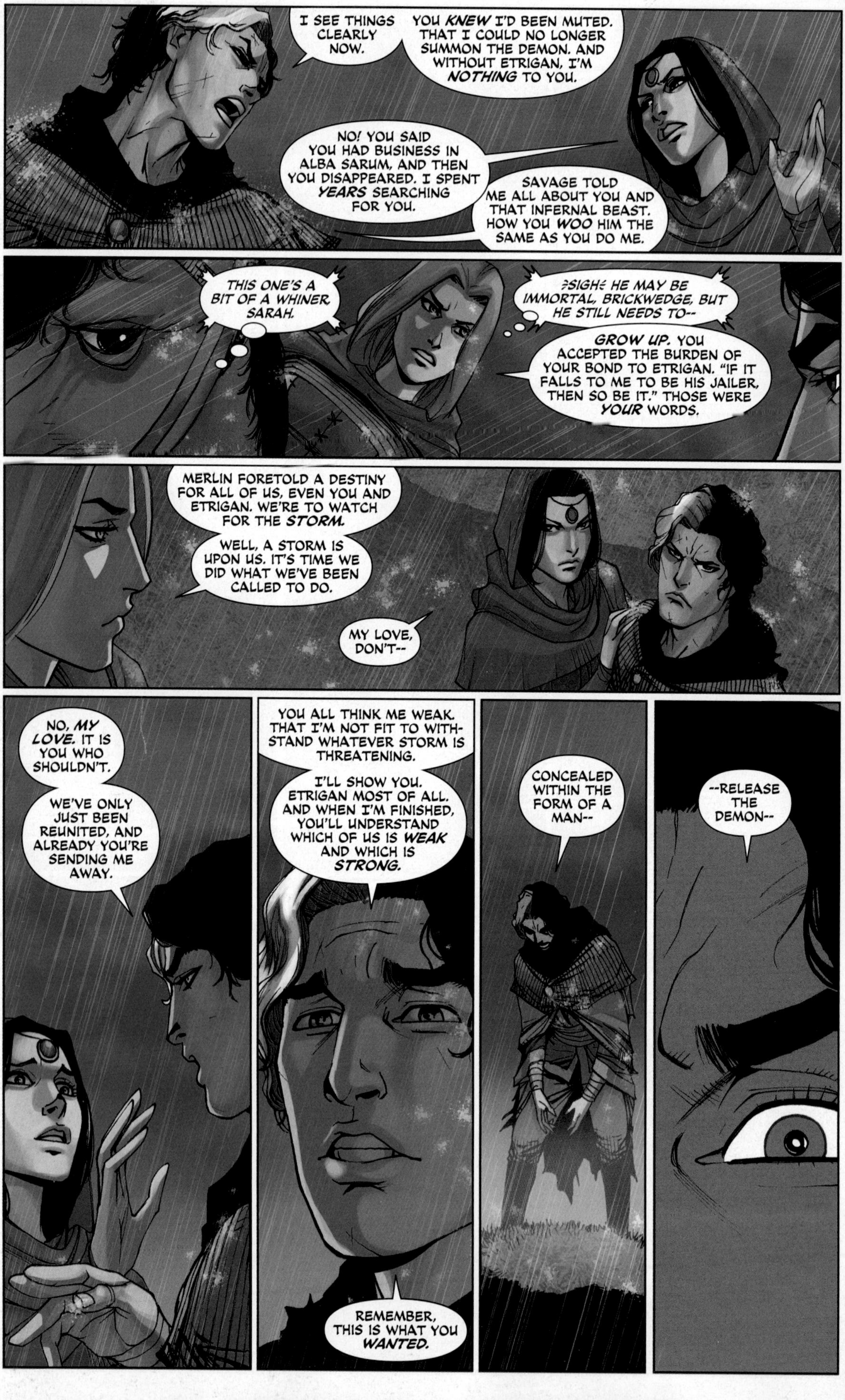
I SEE THINGS CLEARLY NOW.
YOU *KNEW* I'D BEEN MUTED. THAT I COULD NO LONGER SUMMON THE DEMON. AND WITHOUT ETRIGAN, I'M *NOTHING* TO YOU.
NO! YOU SAID YOU HAD BUSINESS IN ALBA SARUM, AND THEN YOU DISAPPEARED. I SPENT *YEARS* SEARCHING FOR YOU.
SAVAGE TOLD ME ALL ABOUT YOU AND THAT INFERNAL BEAST. HOW YOU *WOO* HIM THE SAME AS YOU DO ME.
THIS ONE'S A BIT OF A WHINER, SARAH.
SIGH HE MAY BE IMMORTAL, BRICKWEDGE, BUT HE STILL NEEDS TO--
GROW UP. YOU ACCEPTED THE BURDEN OF YOUR BOND TO ETRIGAN. "IF IT FALLS TO ME TO BE HIS JAILER, THEN SO BE IT." THOSE WERE *YOUR* WORDS.
MERLIN FORETOLD A DESTINY FOR ALL OF US, EVEN YOU AND ETRIGAN. WE'RE TO WATCH FOR THE *STORM.*
WELL, A STORM IS UPON US. IT'S TIME WE DID WHAT WE'VE BEEN CALLED TO DO.
MY LOVE, DON'T--
NO, *MY LOVE.* IT IS YOU WHO SHOULDN'T.
WE'VE ONLY JUST BEEN REUNITED, AND ALREADY YOU'RE SENDING ME AWAY.
YOU ALL THINK ME WEAK. THAT I'M NOT FIT TO WITHSTAND WHATEVER STORM IS THREATENING.
I'LL SHOW YOU. ETRIGAN MOST OF ALL. AND WHEN I'M FINISHED, YOU'LL UNDERSTAND WHICH OF US IS *WEAK* AND WHICH IS *STRONG.*
REMEMBER, THIS IS WHAT YOU *WANTED.*
CONCEALED WITHIN THE FORM OF A MAN--
--RELEASE THE DEMON--

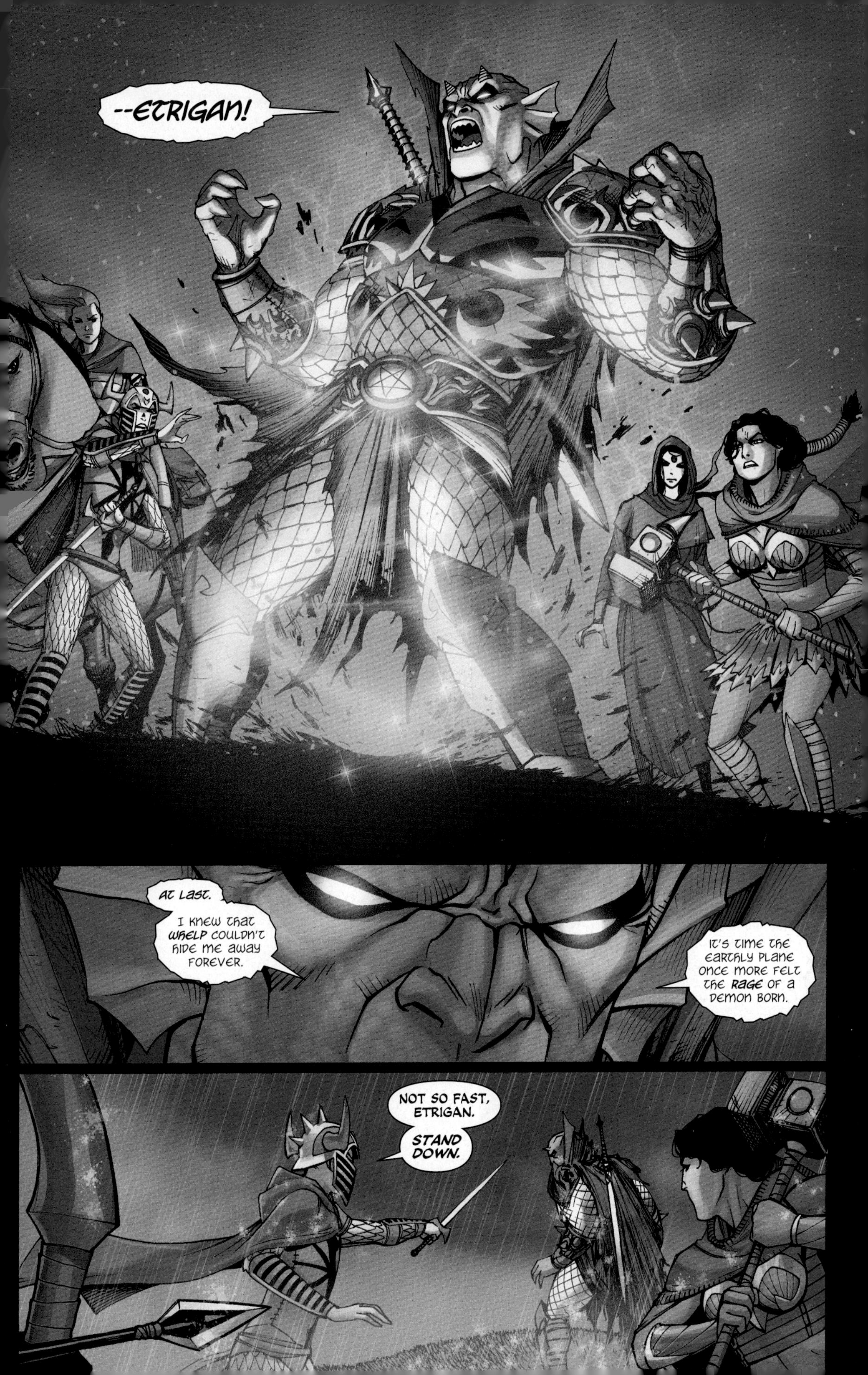
--ETRIGAN!
AT LAST.
I KNEW THAT WHELP COULDN'T HIDE ME AWAY FOREVER.
IT'S TIME THE EARTHLY PLANE ONCE MORE FELT THE RAGE OF A DEMON BORN.
NOT SO FAST, ETRIGAN.
STAND DOWN.

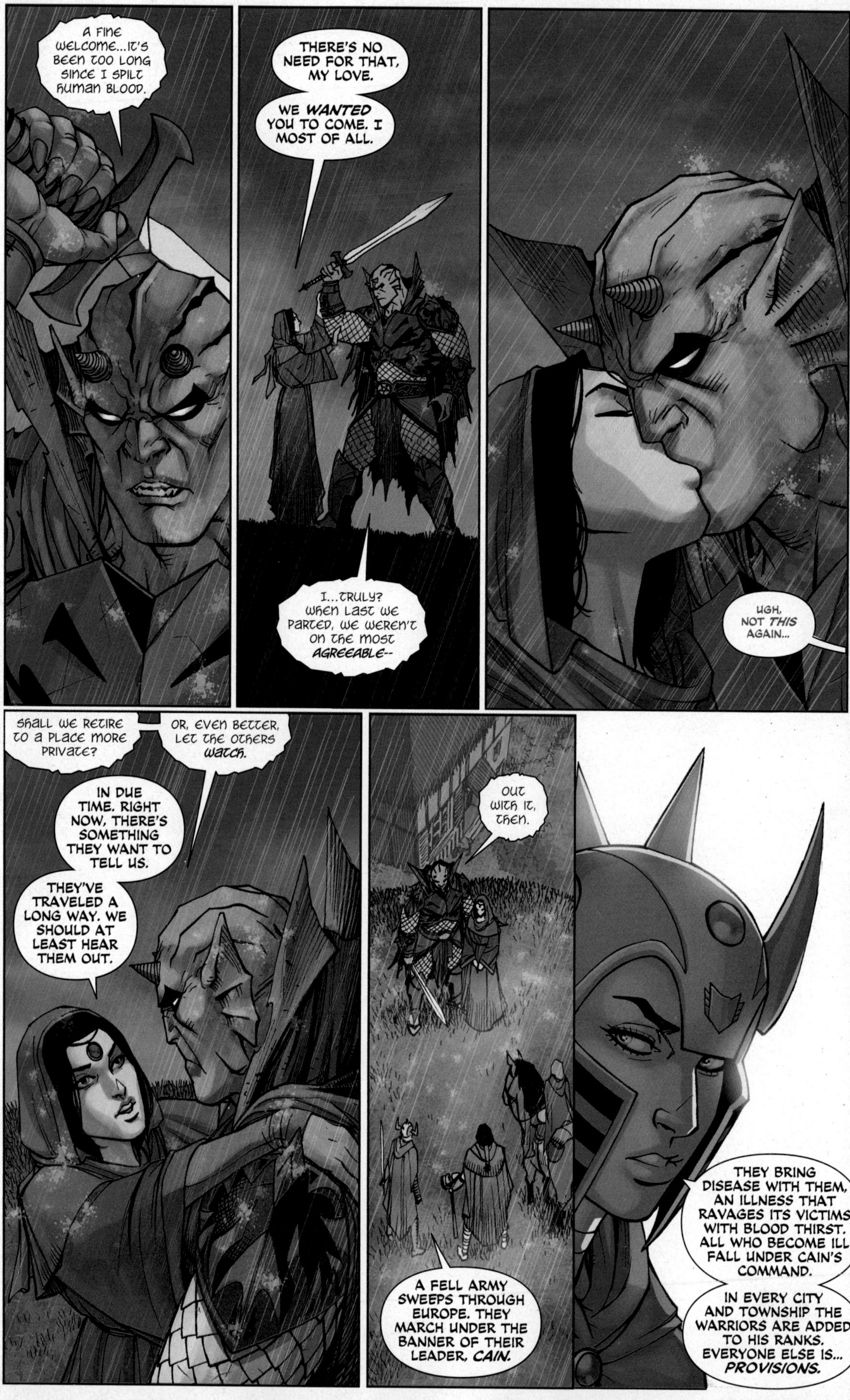

A FINE WELCOME...IT'S BEEN TOO LONG SINCE I SPILT HUMAN BLOOD.
THERE'S NO NEED FOR THAT, MY LOVE.
WE *WANTED* YOU TO COME. I MOST OF ALL.
I...TRULY? WHEN LAST WE PARTED, WE WEREN'T ON THE MOST *AGREEABLE*--
UGH, NOT *THIS* AGAIN...
SHALL WE RETIRE TO A PLACE MORE PRIVATE?
OR, EVEN BETTER, LET THE OTHERS *WATCH*.
IN DUE TIME. RIGHT NOW, THERE'S SOMETHING THEY WANT TO TELL US.
THEY'VE TRAVELED A LONG WAY. WE SHOULD AT LEAST HEAR THEM OUT.
OUT WITH IT, THEN.
A FELL ARMY SWEEPS THROUGH EUROPE. THEY MARCH UNDER THE BANNER OF THEIR LEADER, *CAIN*.
THEY BRING DISEASE WITH THEM, AN ILLNESS THAT RAVAGES ITS VICTIMS WITH BLOOD THIRST. ALL WHO BECOME ILL FALL UNDER CAIN'S COMMAND.
IN EVERY CITY AND TOWNSHIP THE WARRIORS ARE ADDED TO HIS RANKS. EVERYONE ELSE IS... *PROVISIONS*.

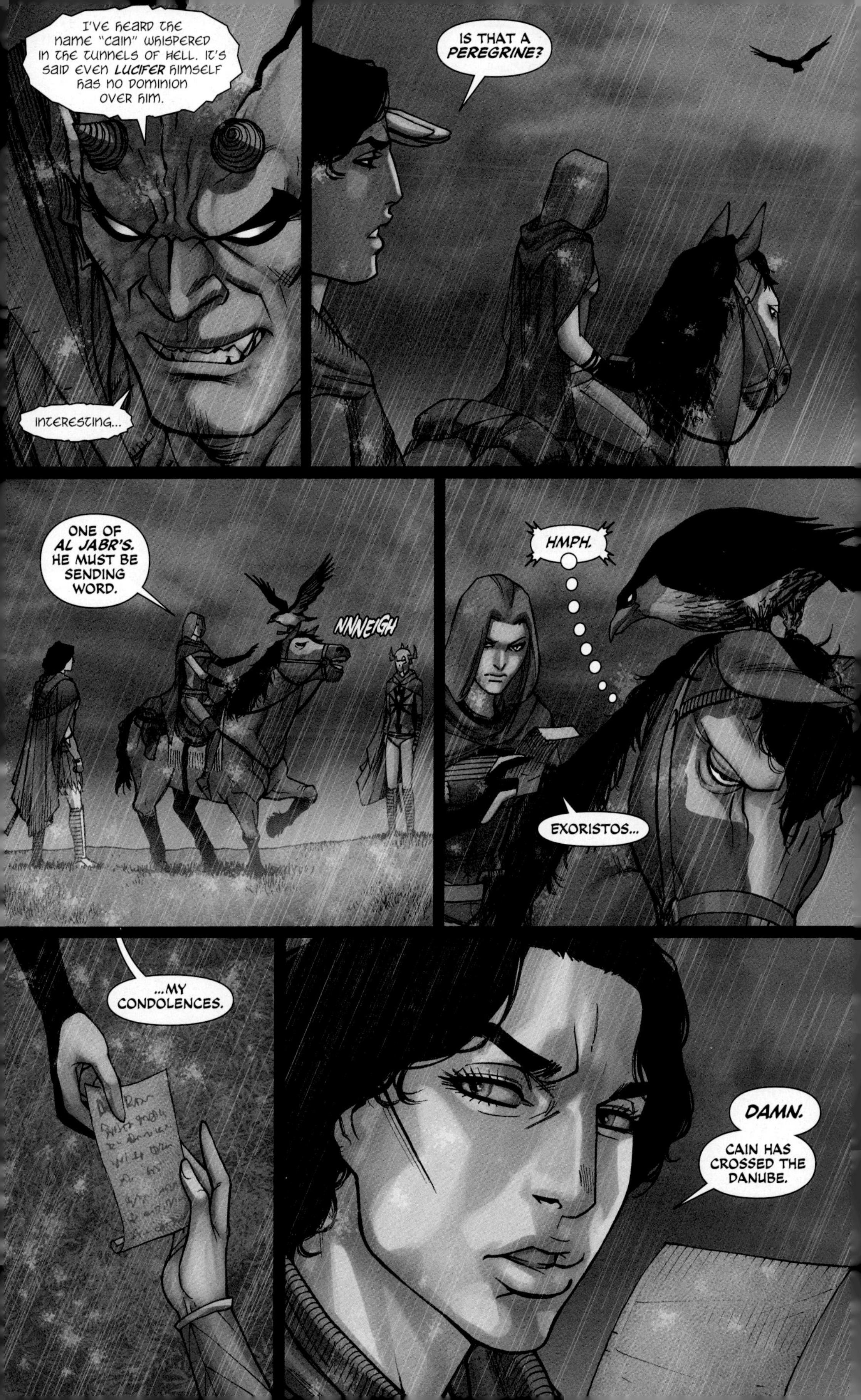
I'VE HEARD THE NAME "CAIN" WHISPERED IN THE TUNNELS OF HELL. IT'S SAID EVEN LUCIFER HIMSELF HAS NO DOMINION OVER HIM.
INTERESTING...
IS THAT A PEREGRINE?
ONE OF AL JABR'S. HE MUST BE SENDING WORD.
NNNEIGH
HMPH.
EXORISTOS...
...MY CONDOLENCES.
DAMN.
CAIN HAS CROSSED THE DANUBE.

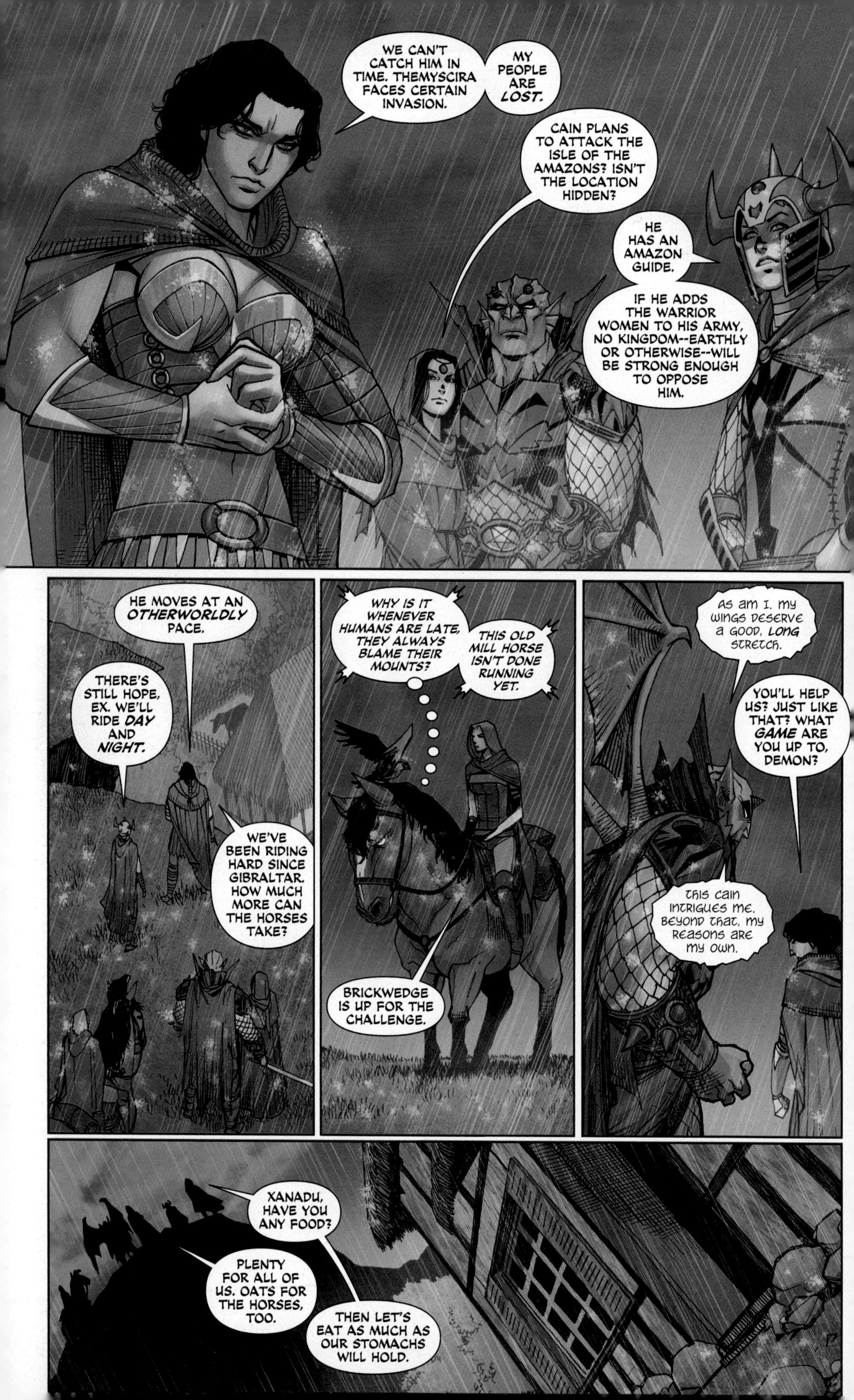

WE CAN'T CATCH HIM IN TIME. THEMYSCIRA FACES CERTAIN INVASION.
MY PEOPLE ARE LOST.
CAIN PLANS TO ATTACK THE ISLE OF THE AMAZONS? ISN'T THE LOCATION HIDDEN?
HE HAS AN AMAZON GUIDE.
IF HE ADDS THE WARRIOR WOMEN TO HIS ARMY, NO KINGDOM--EARTHLY OR OTHERWISE--WILL BE STRONG ENOUGH TO OPPOSE HIM.
HE MOVES AT AN OTHERWORLDLY PACE.
THERE'S STILL HOPE, EX. WE'LL RIDE DAY AND NIGHT.
WE'VE BEEN RIDING HARD SINCE GIBRALTAR. HOW MUCH MORE CAN THE HORSES TAKE?
WHY IS IT WHENEVER HUMANS ARE LATE, THEY ALWAYS BLAME THEIR MOUNTS?
THIS OLD MILL HORSE ISN'T DONE RUNNING YET.
BRICKWEDGE IS UP FOR THE CHALLENGE.
AS AM I. MY WINGS DESERVE A GOOD, LONG STRETCH.
YOU'LL HELP US? JUST LIKE THAT? WHAT GAME ARE YOU UP TO, DEMON?
THIS CAIN INTRIGUES ME. BEYOND THAT, MY REASONS ARE MY OWN.
XANADU, HAVE YOU ANY FOOD?
PLENTY FOR ALL OF US. OATS FOR THE HORSES, TOO.
THEN LET'S EAT AS MUCH AS OUR STOMACHS WILL HOLD.

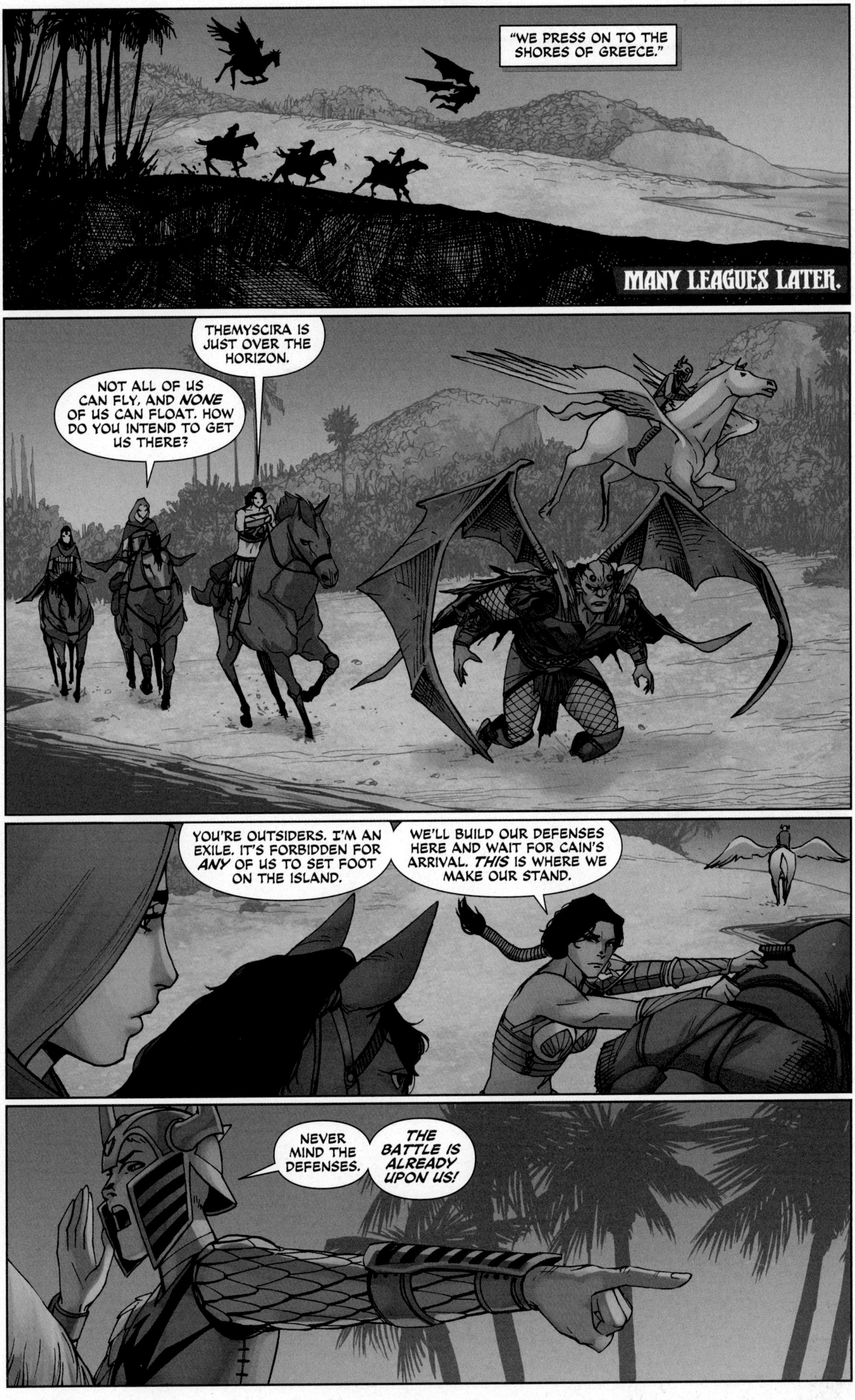
"WE PRESS ON TO THE SHORES OF GREECE."
MANY LEAGUES LATER.
THEMYSCIRA IS JUST OVER THE HORIZON.
NOT ALL OF US CAN FLY, AND *NONE* OF US CAN FLOAT. HOW DO YOU INTEND TO GET US THERE?
YOU'RE OUTSIDERS. I'M AN EXILE. IT'S FORBIDDEN FOR *ANY* OF US TO SET FOOT ON THE ISLAND.
WE'LL BUILD OUR DEFENSES HERE AND WAIT FOR CAIN'S ARRIVAL. *THIS* IS WHERE WE MAKE OUR STAND.
NEVER MIND THE DEFENSES.
THE BATTLE IS ALREADY UPON US!

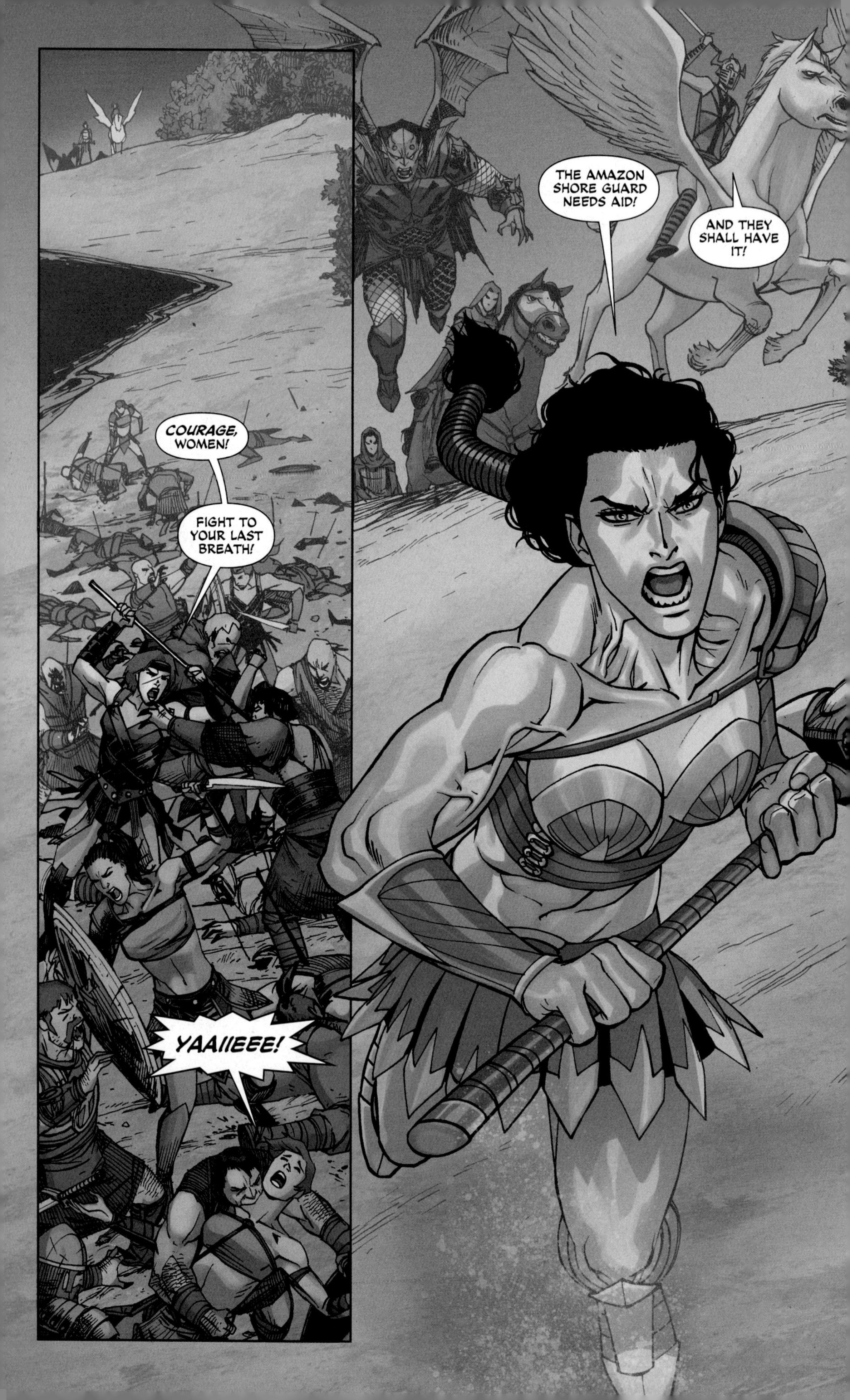
COURAGE, WOMEN!
FIGHT TO YOUR LAST BREATH!
YAAIIEEE!
THE AMAZON SHORE GUARD NEEDS AID!
AND THEY SHALL HAVE IT!

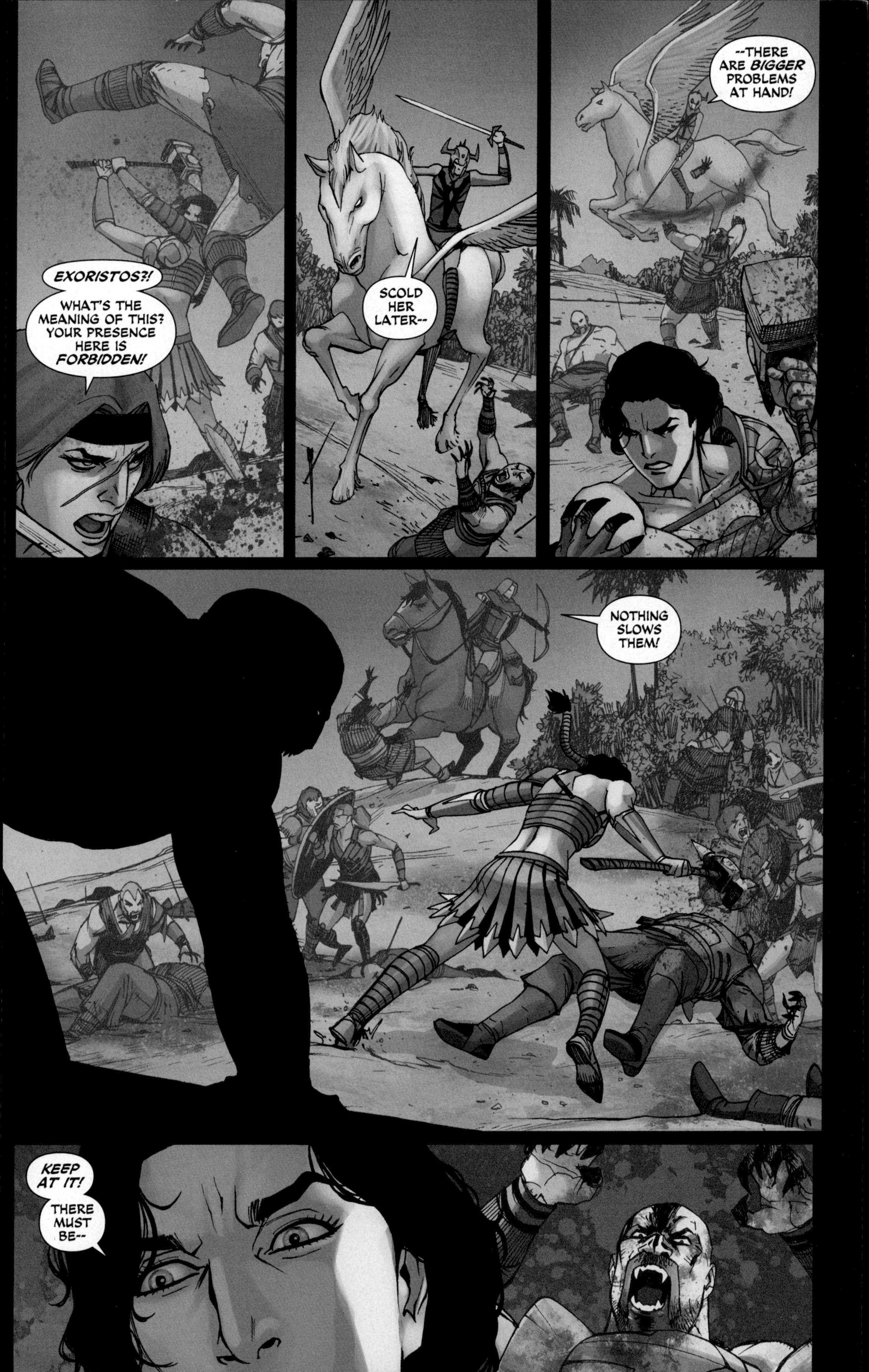
EXORISTOS?!
WHAT'S THE MEANING OF THIS? YOUR PRESENCE HERE IS FORBIDDEN!
SCOLD HER LATER--
--THERE ARE BIGGER PROBLEMS AT HAND!
NOTHING SLOWS THEM!
KEEP AT IT!
THERE MUST BE--

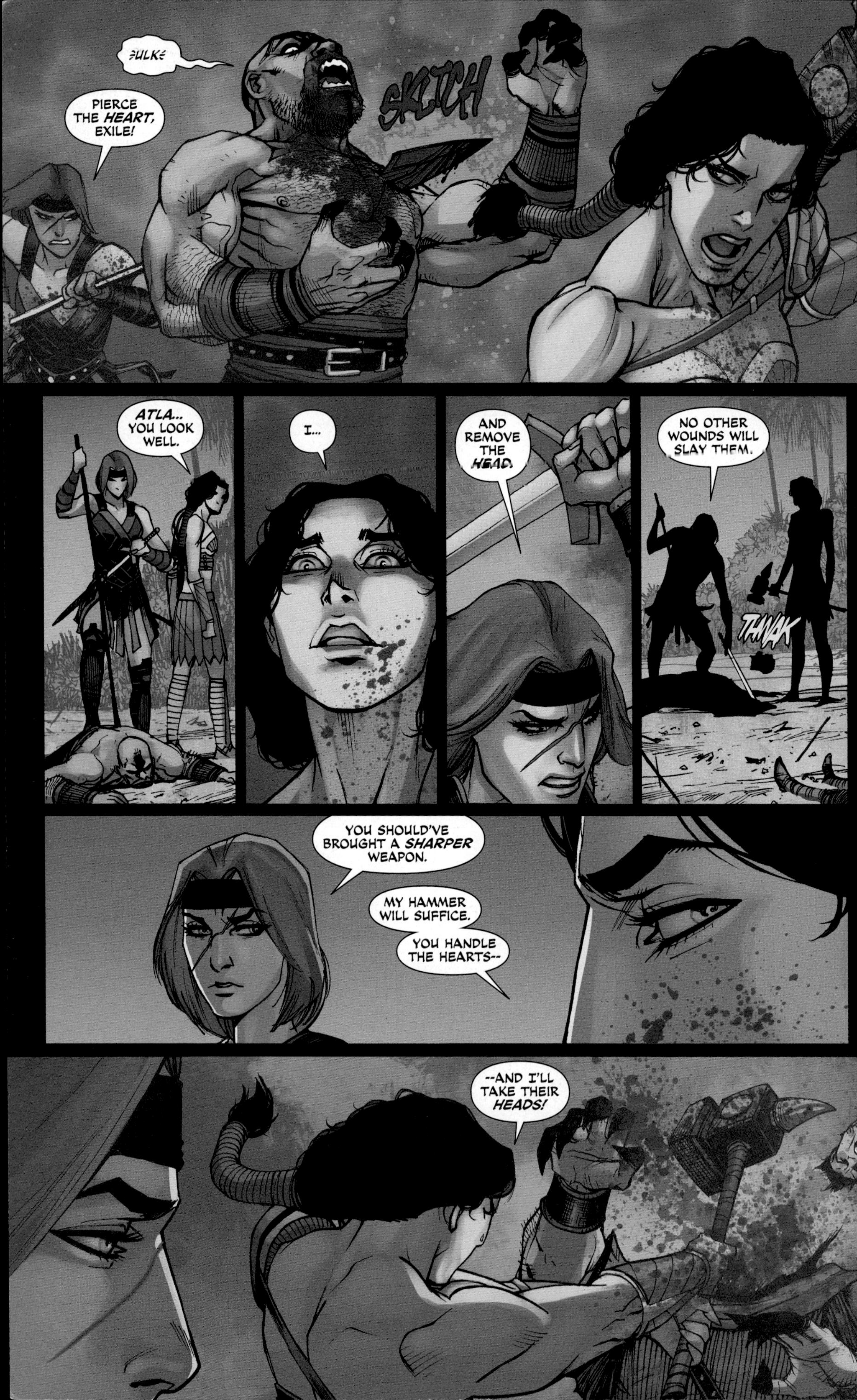

ƎULK
PIERCE THE *HEART*, EXILE!
SKLTCH
ATLA... YOU LOOK WELL.
I...
AND REMOVE THE *HEAD*.
NO OTHER WOUNDS WILL SLAY THEM.
THWAK
YOU SHOULD'VE BROUGHT A *SHARPER* WEAPON.
MY HAMMER WILL SUFFICE.
YOU HANDLE THE HEARTS--
--AND I'LL TAKE THEIR *HEADS*!

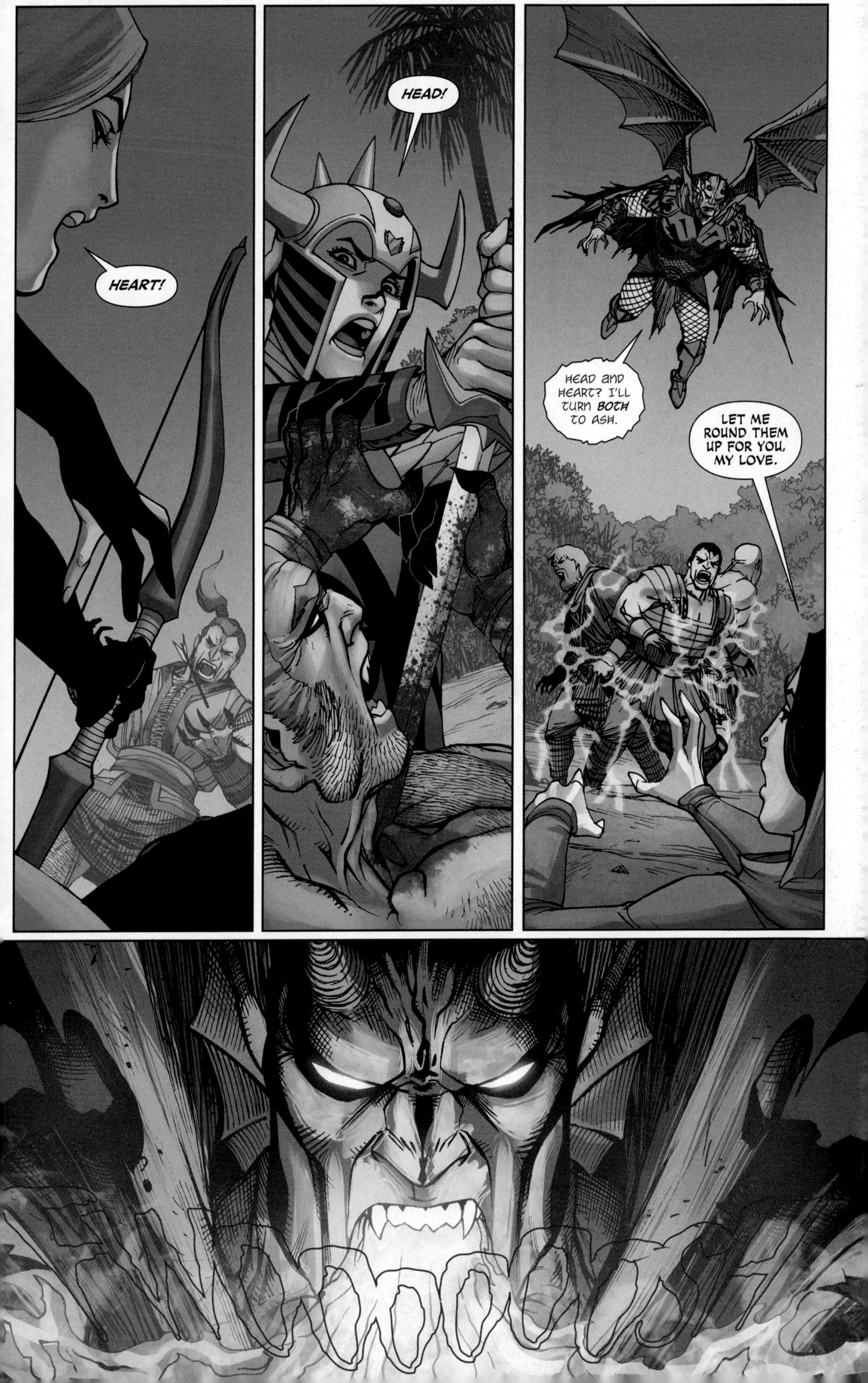
HEART!
HEAD!
HEAD AND HEART? I'LL TURN BOTH TO ASH.
LET ME ROUND THEM UP FOR YOU, MY LOVE.

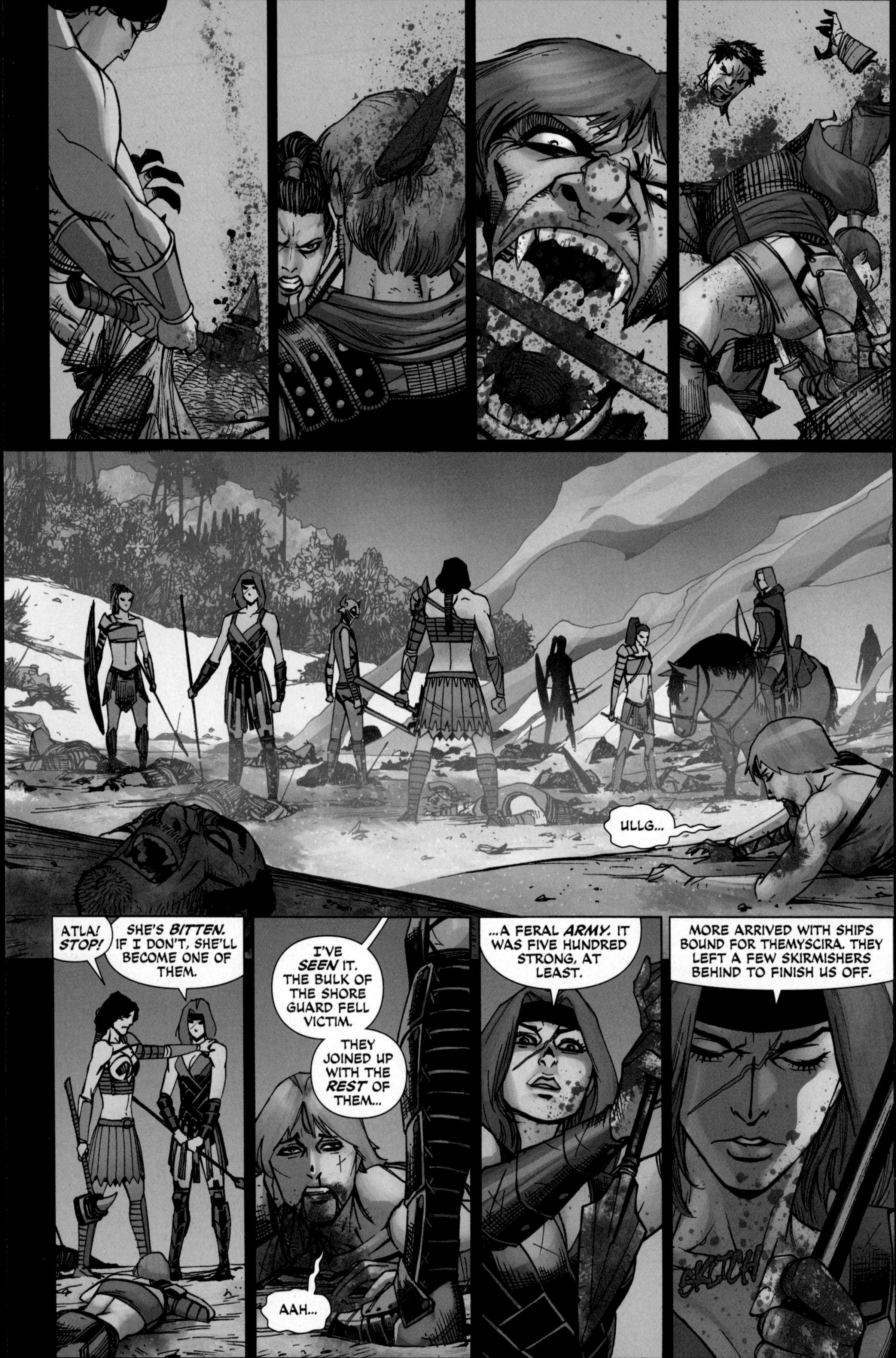
ULLG...
ATLA! STOP!
SHE'S BITTEN. IF I DON'T, SHE'LL BECOME ONE OF THEM.
I'VE SEEN IT. THE BULK OF THE SHORE GUARD FELL VICTIM.
THEY JOINED UP WITH THE REST OF THEM...
AAH...
...A FERAL ARMY. IT WAS FIVE HUNDRED STRONG, AT LEAST.
MORE ARRIVED WITH SHIPS BOUND FOR THEMYSCIRA. THEY LEFT A FEW SKIRMISHERS BEHIND TO FINISH US OFF.

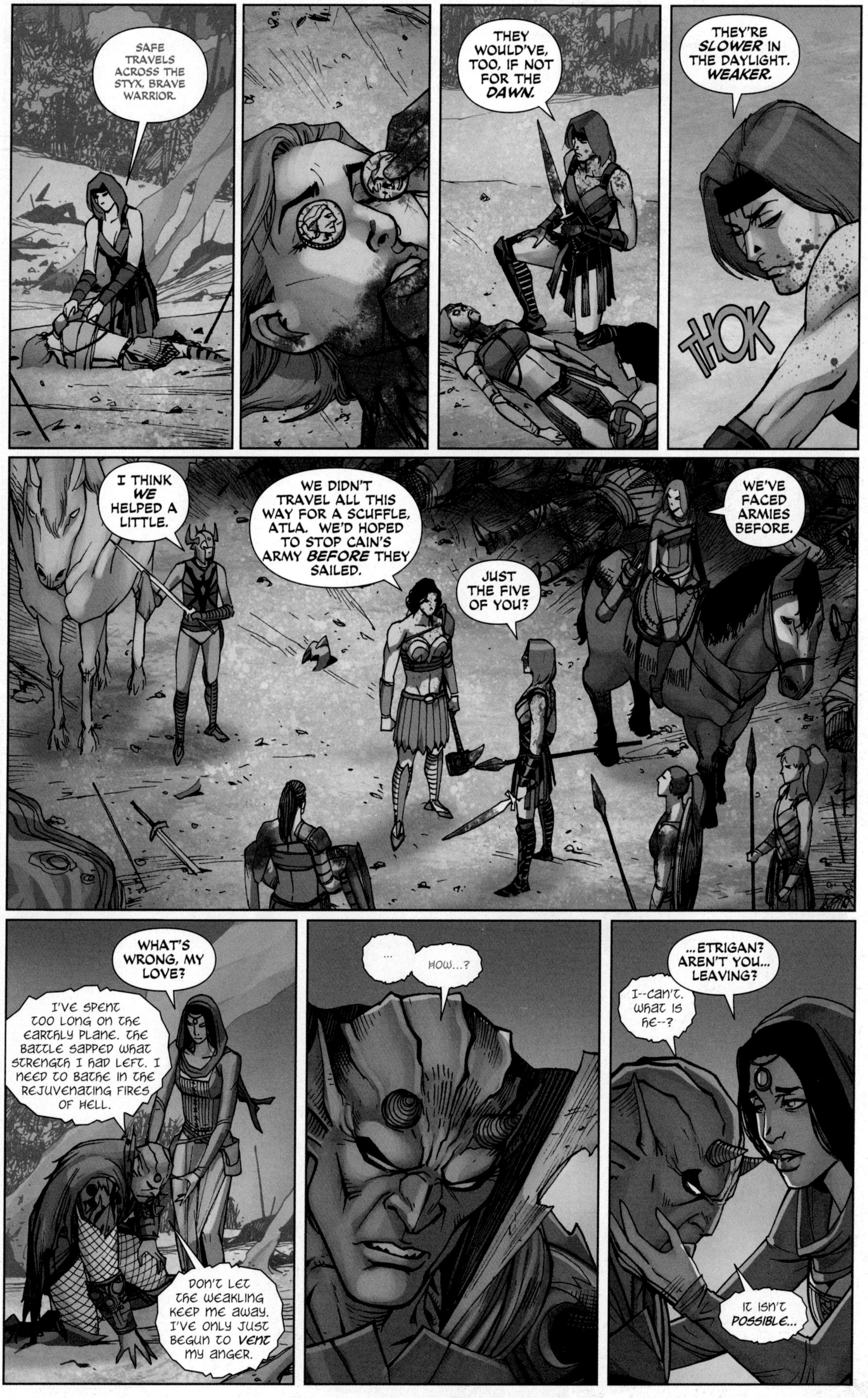
SAFE TRAVELS ACROSS THE STYX, BRAVE WARRIOR.
THEY WOULD'VE, TOO, IF NOT FOR THE DAWN.
THEY'RE SLOWER IN THE DAYLIGHT. WEAKER.
THOK
I THINK WE HELPED A LITTLE.
WE DIDN'T TRAVEL ALL THIS WAY FOR A SCUFFLE, ATLA. WE'D HOPED TO STOP CAIN'S ARMY BEFORE THEY SAILED.
JUST THE FIVE OF YOU?
WE'VE FACED ARMIES BEFORE.
WHAT'S WRONG, MY LOVE?
I'VE SPENT TOO LONG ON THE EARTHLY PLANE. THE BATTLE SAPPED WHAT STRENGTH I HAD LEFT. I NEED TO BATHE IN THE REJUVENATING FIRES OF HELL.
DON'T LET THE WEAKLING KEEP ME AWAY. I'VE ONLY JUST BEGUN TO VENT MY ANGER.
...
HOW...?
...ETRIGAN? AREN'T YOU... LEAVING?
I--CAN'T. WHAT IS HE--?
IT ISN'T POSSIBLE...

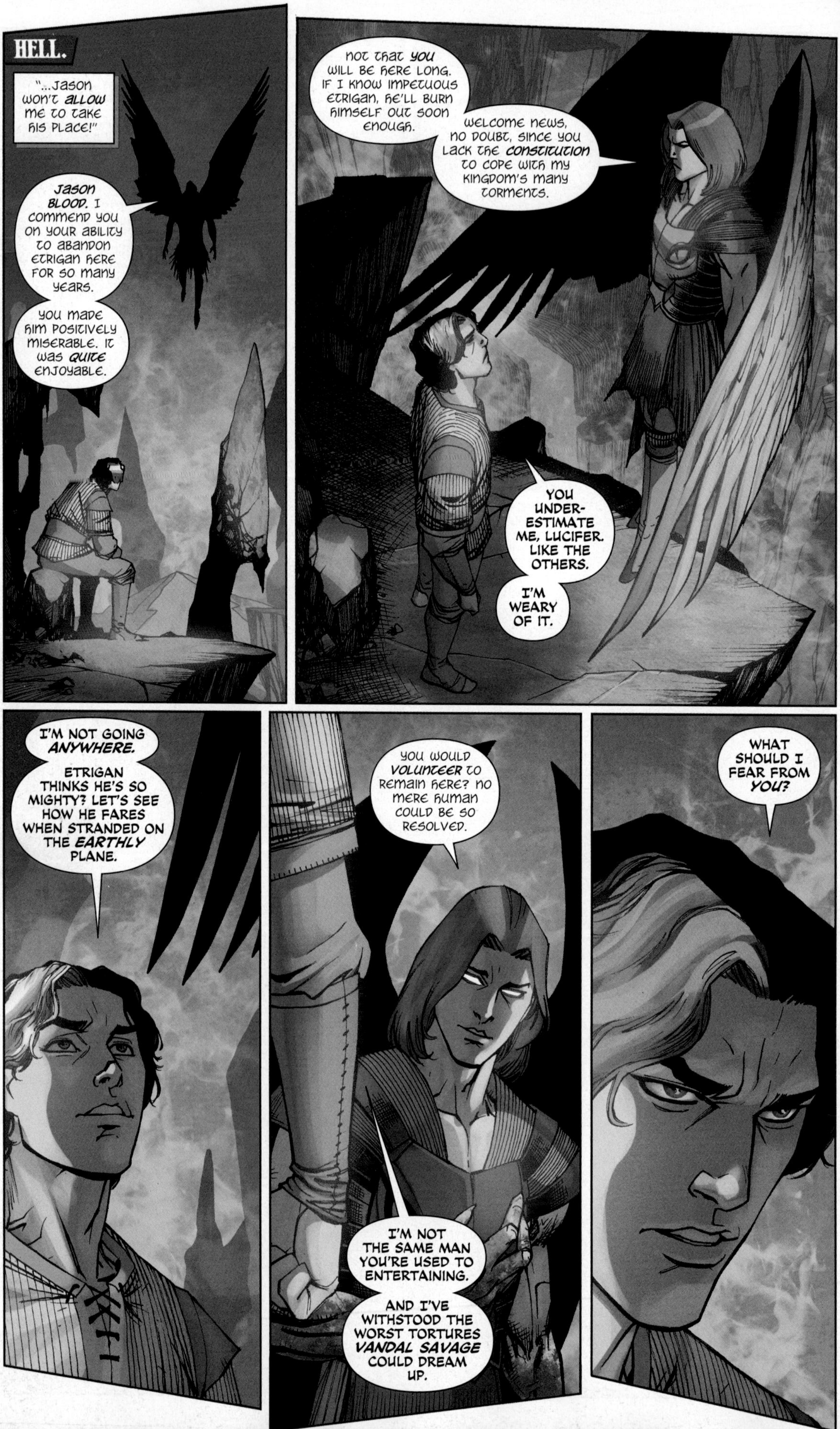
HELL.
"...Jason won't ALLOW me to take his place!"
Jason BLOOD. I commend you on your ability to abandon Etrigan here for so many years.
You made him positively miserable. It was QUITE enjoyable.
Not that YOU will be here long. If I know impetuous Etrigan, he'll burn himself out soon enough.
Welcome news, no doubt, since you lack the CONSTITUTION to cope with my kingdom's many torments.
YOU UNDER-ESTIMATE ME, LUCIFER. LIKE THE OTHERS.
I'M WEARY OF IT.
I'M NOT GOING ANYWHERE.
ETRIGAN THINKS HE'S SO MIGHTY? LET'S SEE HOW HE FARES WHEN STRANDED ON THE EARTHLY PLANE.
You would VOLUNTEER to remain here? No mere human could be so resolved.
I'M NOT THE SAME MAN YOU'RE USED TO ENTERTAINING.
AND I'VE WITHSTOOD THE WORST TORTURES VANDAL SAVAGE COULD DREAM UP.
WHAT SHOULD I FEAR FROM YOU?

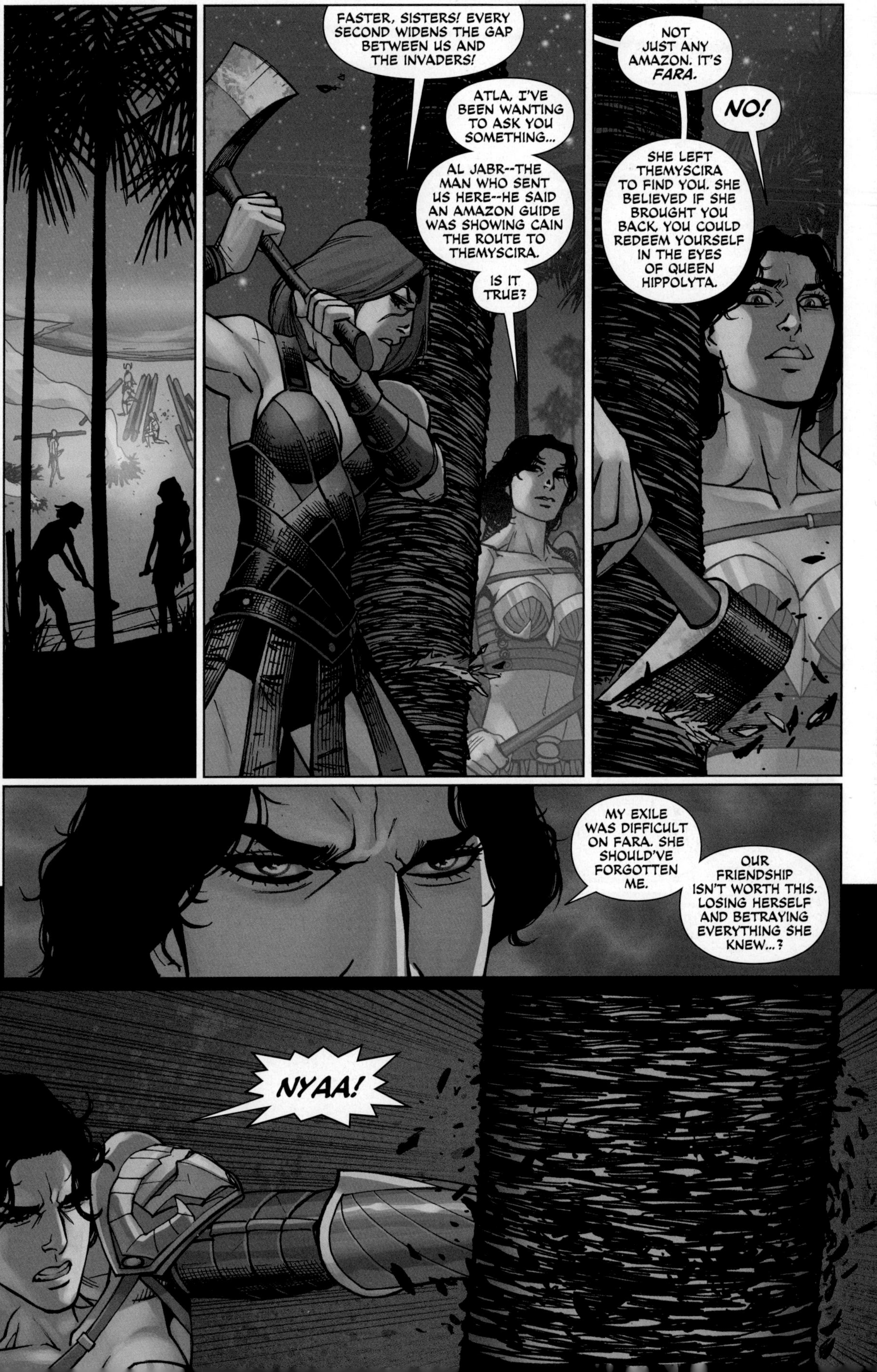
FASTER, SISTERS! EVERY SECOND WIDENS THE GAP BETWEEN US AND THE INVADERS!
ATLA, I'VE BEEN WANTING TO ASK YOU SOMETHING...
AL JABR--THE MAN WHO SENT US HERE--HE SAID AN AMAZON GUIDE WAS SHOWING CAIN THE ROUTE TO THEMYSCIRA.
IS IT TRUE?
NOT JUST ANY AMAZON. IT'S *FARA.*
NO!
SHE LEFT THEMYSCIRA TO FIND YOU. SHE BELIEVED IF SHE BROUGHT YOU BACK, YOU COULD REDEEM YOURSELF IN THE EYES OF QUEEN HIPPOLYTA.
MY EXILE WAS DIFFICULT ON FARA. SHE SHOULD'VE FORGOTTEN ME.
OUR FRIENDSHIP ISN'T WORTH THIS. LOSING HERSELF AND BETRAYING EVERYTHING SHE KNEW...?
NYAA!

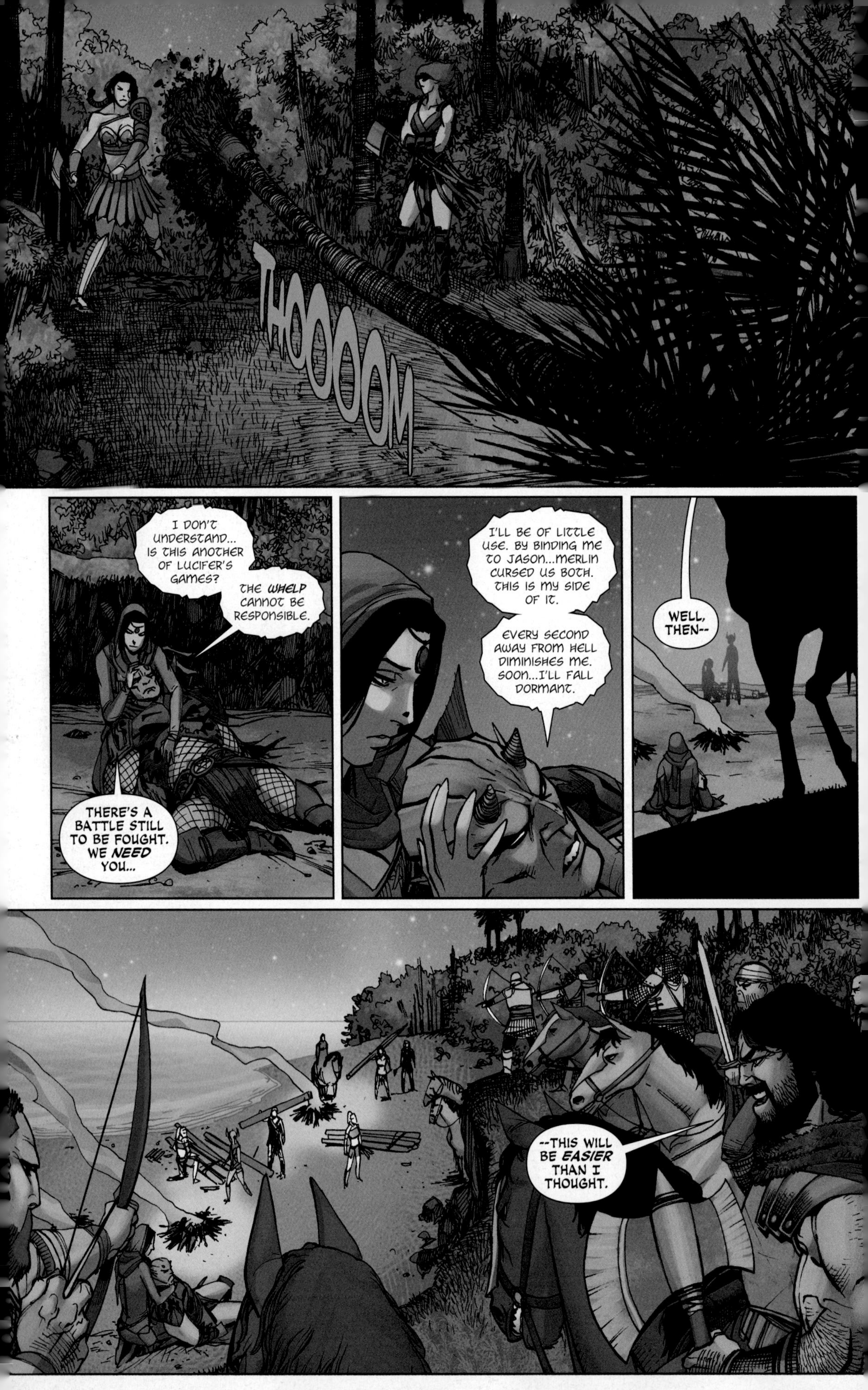
THOOOOM
I DON'T UNDERSTAND... IS THIS ANOTHER OF LUCIFER'S GAMES?
THE WHELP CANNOT BE RESPONSIBLE.
THERE'S A BATTLE STILL TO BE FOUGHT. WE NEED YOU...
I'LL BE OF LITTLE USE. BY BINDING ME TO JASON...MERLIN CURSED US BOTH. THIS IS MY SIDE OF IT.
EVERY SECOND AWAY FROM HELL DIMINISHES ME. SOON...I'LL FALL DORMANT.
WELL, THEN--
--THIS WILL BE EASIER THAN I THOUGHT.

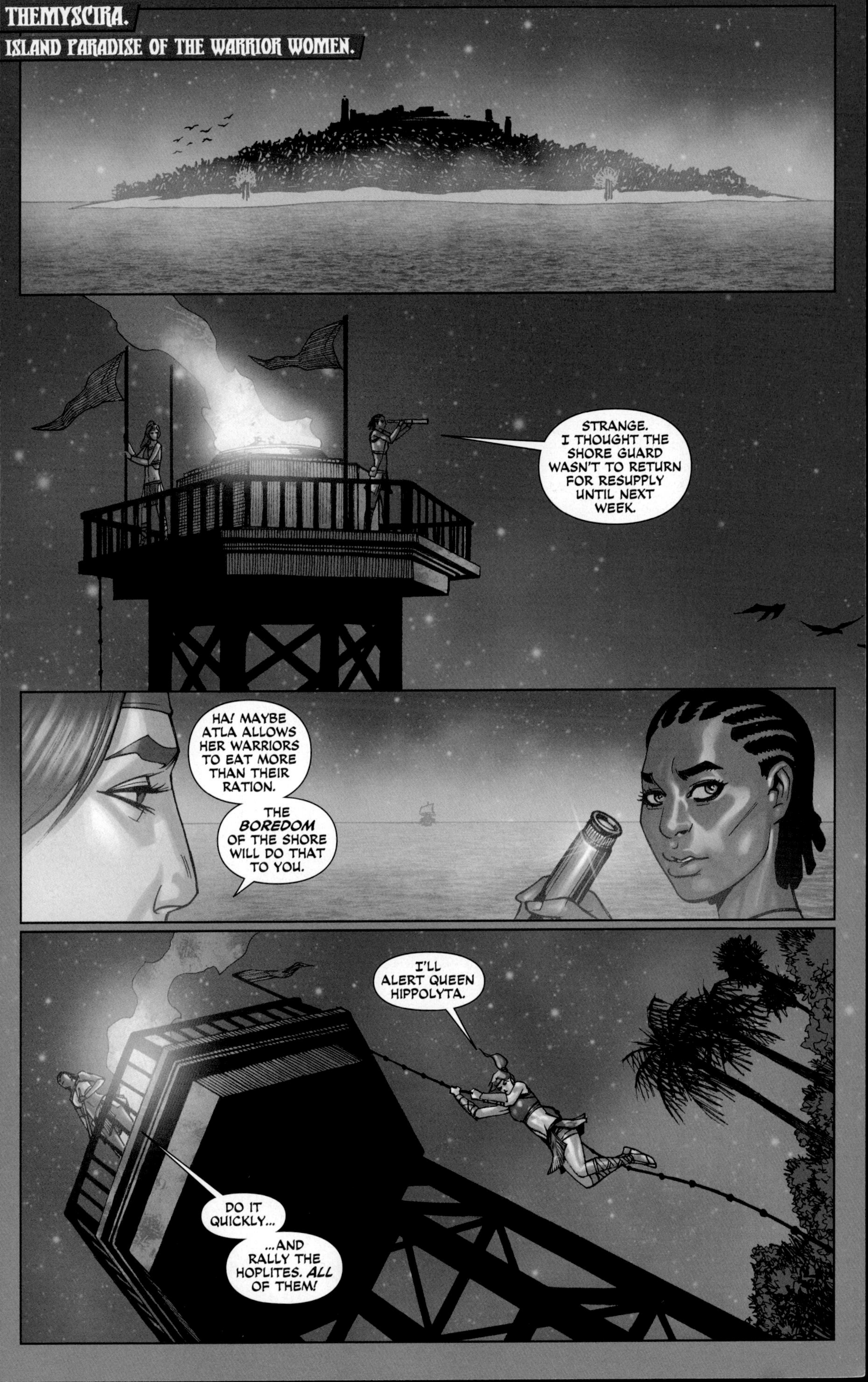
THEMYSCIRA.
ISLAND PARADISE OF THE WARRIOR WOMEN.
STRANGE. I THOUGHT THE SHORE GUARD WASN'T TO RETURN FOR RESUPPLY UNTIL NEXT WEEK.
HA! MAYBE ATLA ALLOWS HER WARRIORS TO EAT MORE THAN THEIR RATION.
THE *BOREDOM* OF THE SHORE WILL DO THAT TO YOU.
I'LL ALERT QUEEN HIPPOLYTA.
DO IT QUICKLY...
...AND RALLY THE HOPLITES. *ALL* OF THEM!

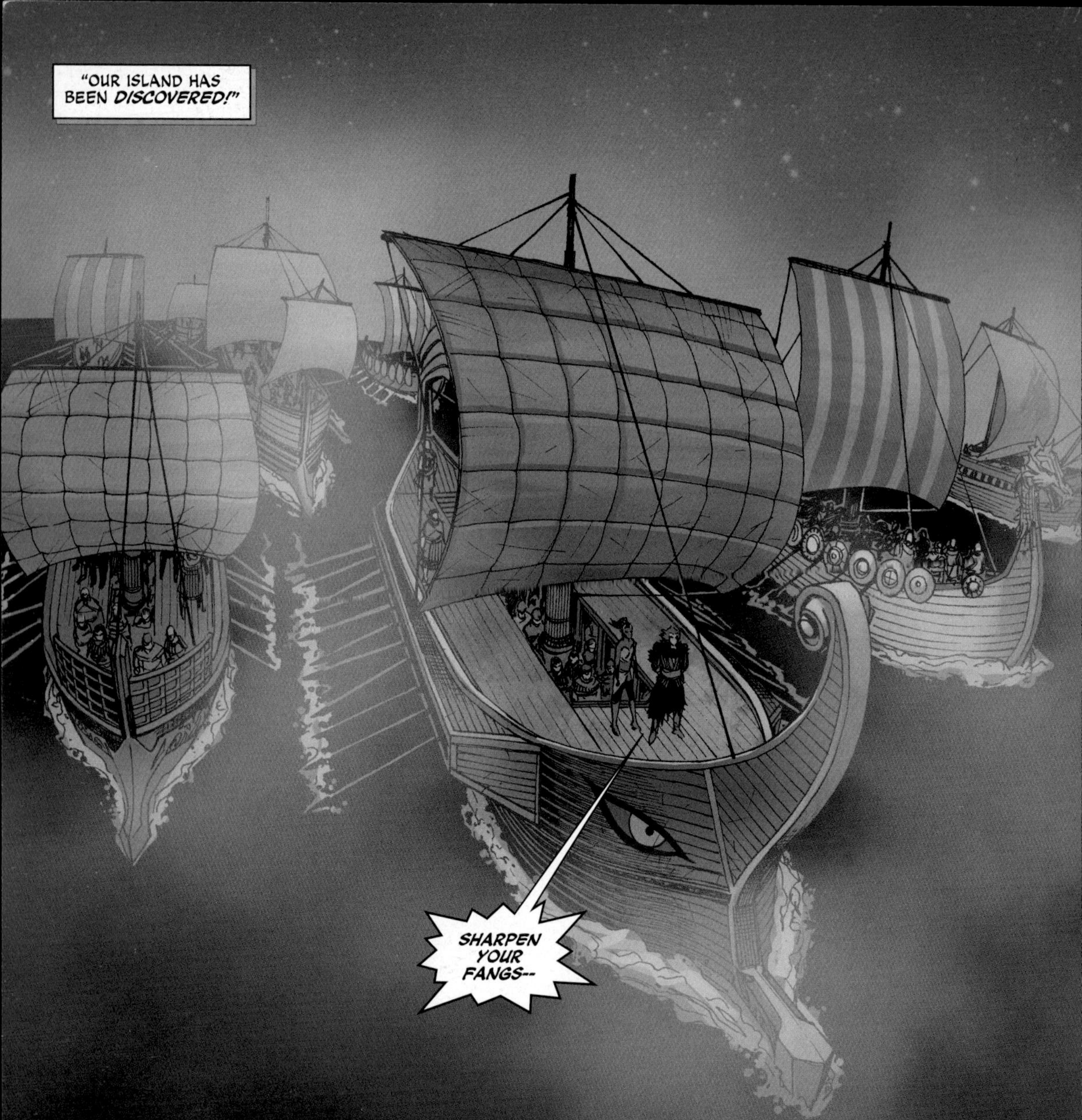
"OUR ISLAND HAS BEEN DISCOVERED!"
SHARPEN YOUR FANGS--

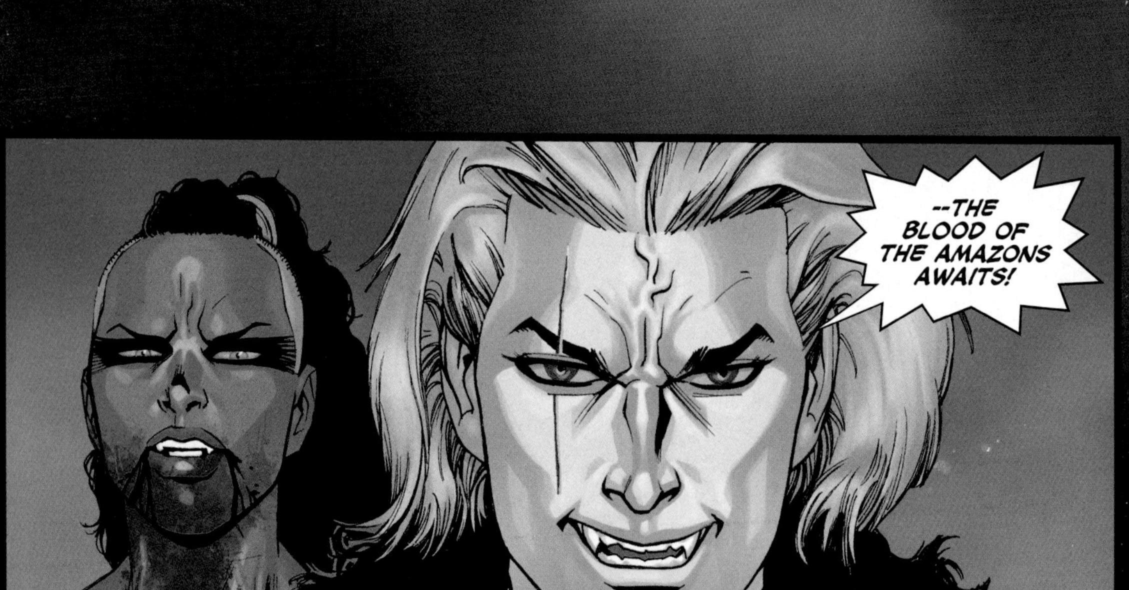
--THE BLOOD OF THE AMAZONS AWAITS!

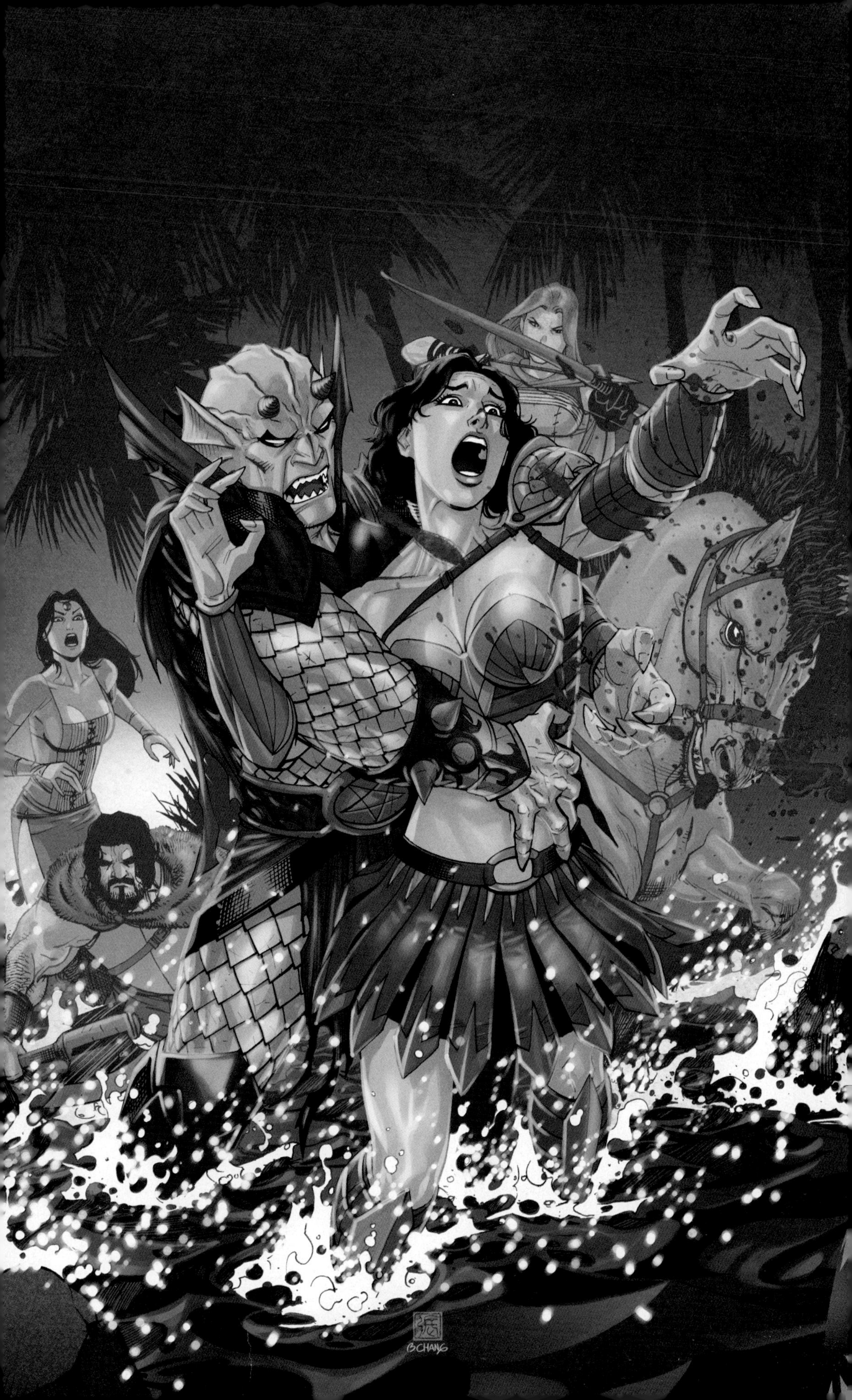
BCHANG

ROBERT VENDITTI
writer

BERNARD CHANG
artist

BERNARD CHANG
cover artist

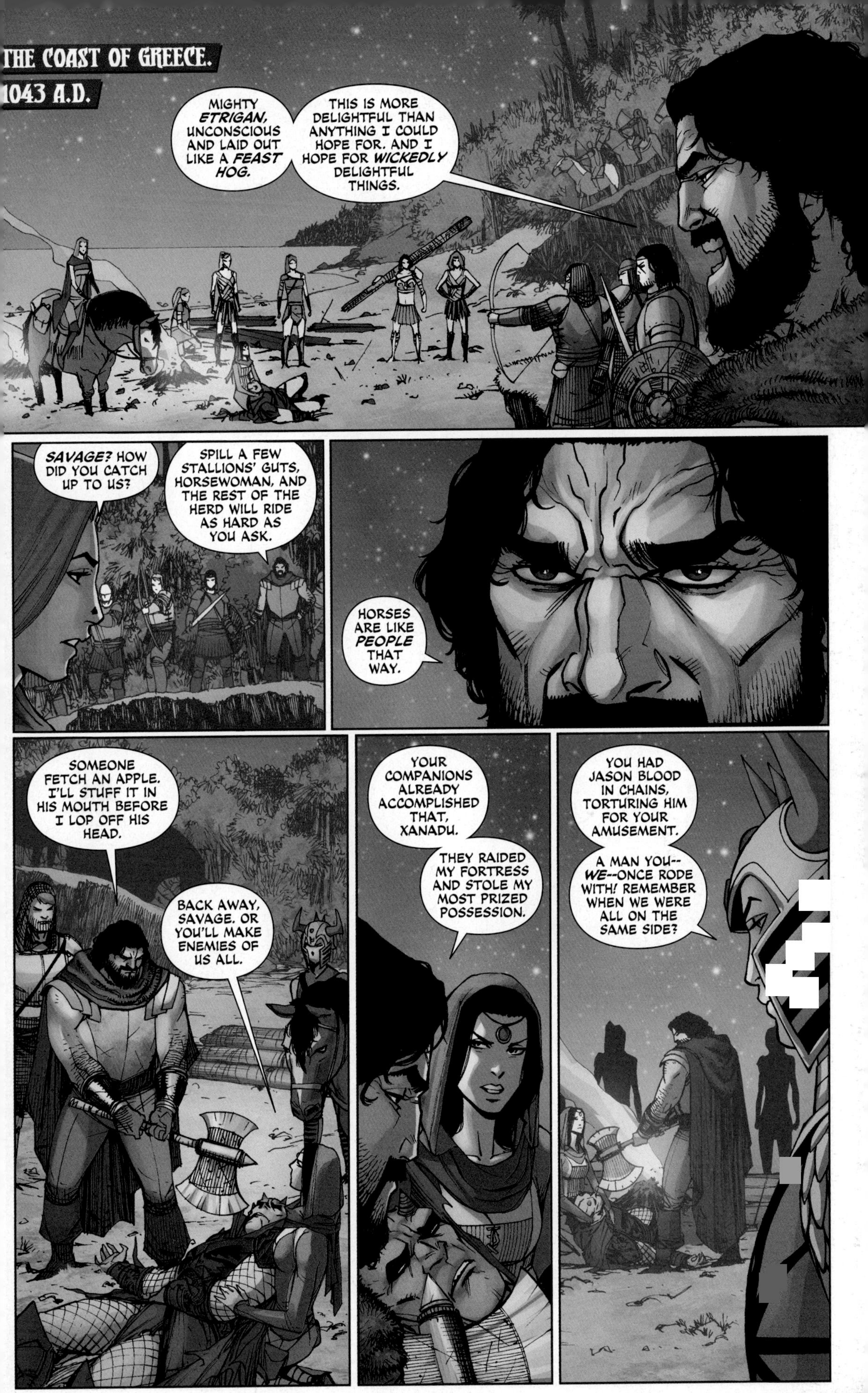

THE COAST OF GREECE.
1043 A.D.
MIGHTY ETRIGAN, UNCONSCIOUS AND LAID OUT LIKE A FEAST HOG.
THIS IS MORE DELIGHTFUL THAN ANYTHING I COULD HOPE FOR. AND I HOPE FOR WICKEDLY DELIGHTFUL THINGS.
SAVAGE? HOW DID YOU CATCH UP TO US?
SPILL A FEW STALLIONS' GUTS, HORSEWOMAN, AND THE REST OF THE HERD WILL RIDE AS HARD AS YOU ASK.
HORSES ARE LIKE PEOPLE THAT WAY.
SOMEONE FETCH AN APPLE. I'LL STUFF IT IN HIS MOUTH BEFORE I LOP OFF HIS HEAD.
BACK AWAY, SAVAGE. OR YOU'LL MAKE ENEMIES OF US ALL.
YOUR COMPANIONS ALREADY ACCOMPLISHED THAT, XANADU.
THEY RAIDED MY FORTRESS AND STOLE MY MOST PRIZED POSSESSION.
YOU HAD JASON BLOOD IN CHAINS, TORTURING HIM FOR YOUR AMUSEMENT.
A MAN YOU--WE--ONCE RODE WITH! REMEMBER WHEN WE WERE ALL ON THE SAME SIDE?

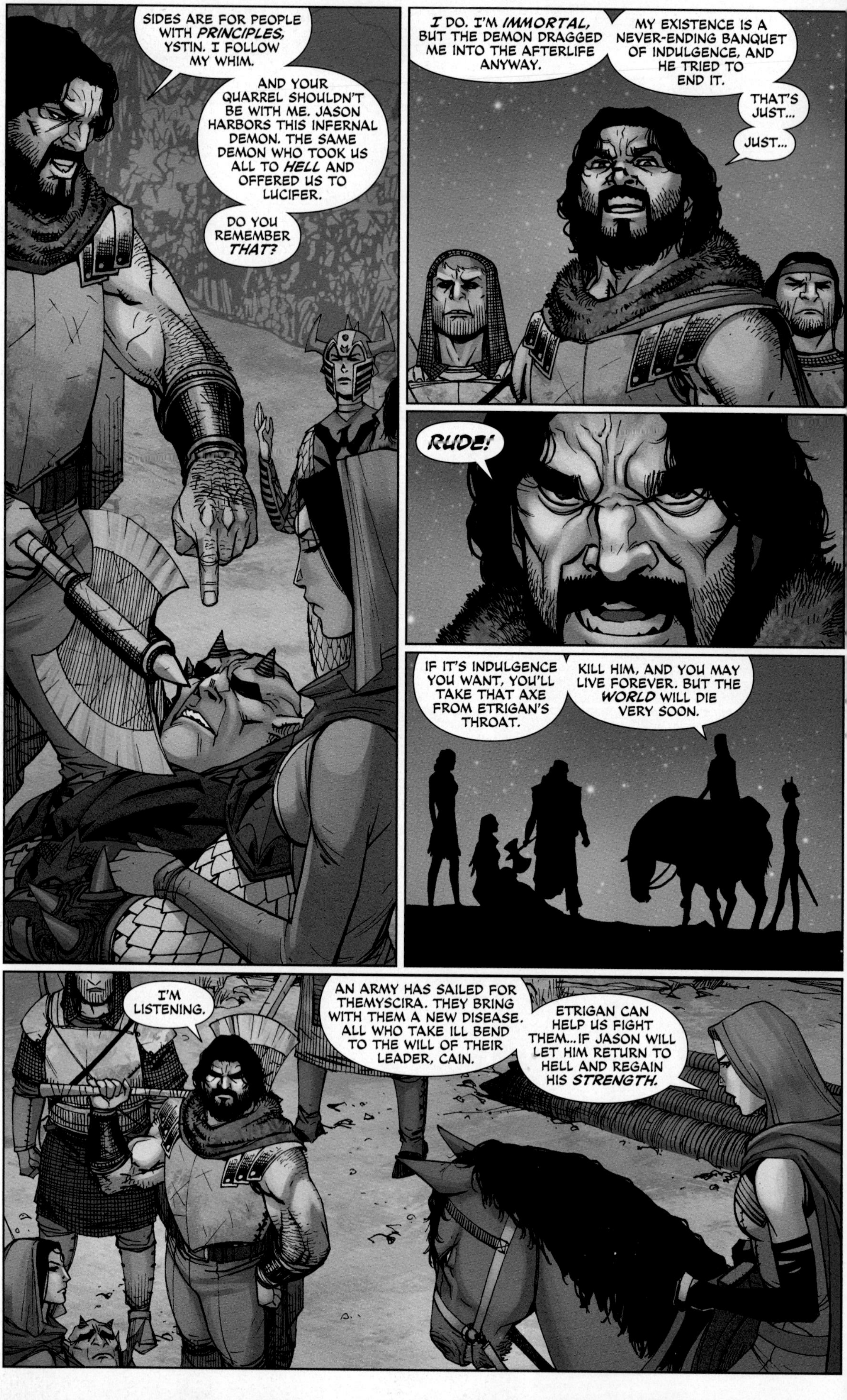

SIDES ARE FOR PEOPLE WITH PRINCIPLES, YSTIN. I FOLLOW MY WHIM.
AND YOUR QUARREL SHOULDN'T BE WITH ME. JASON HARBORS THIS INFERNAL DEMON. THE SAME DEMON WHO TOOK US ALL TO HELL AND OFFERED US TO LUCIFER.
DO YOU REMEMBER THAT?
I DO. I'M IMMORTAL, BUT THE DEMON DRAGGED ME INTO THE AFTERLIFE ANYWAY.
MY EXISTENCE IS A NEVER-ENDING BANQUET OF INDULGENCE, AND HE TRIED TO END IT.
THAT'S JUST...
JUST...
RUDE!
IF IT'S INDULGENCE YOU WANT, YOU'LL TAKE THAT AXE FROM ETRIGAN'S THROAT.
KILL HIM, AND YOU MAY LIVE FOREVER. BUT THE WORLD WILL DIE VERY SOON.
I'M LISTENING.
AN ARMY HAS SAILED FOR THEMYSCIRA. THEY BRING WITH THEM A NEW DISEASE. ALL WHO TAKE ILL BEND TO THE WILL OF THEIR LEADER, CAIN.
ETRIGAN CAN HELP US FIGHT THEM...IF JASON WILL LET HIM RETURN TO HELL AND REGAIN HIS STRENGTH.

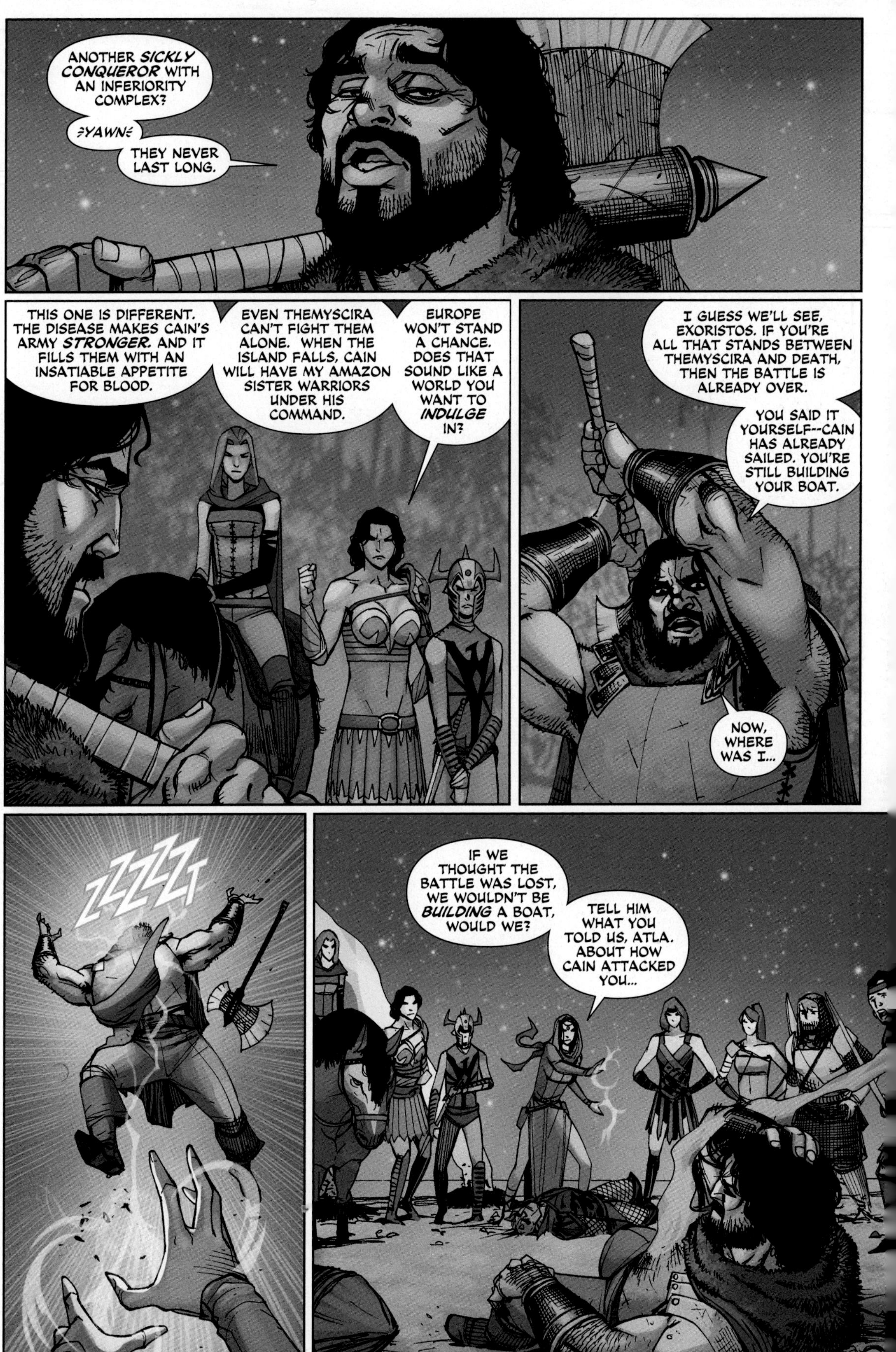
ANOTHER SICKLY CONQUEROR WITH AN INFERIORITY COMPLEX?
YAWN
THEY NEVER LAST LONG.
THIS ONE IS DIFFERENT. THE DISEASE MAKES CAIN'S ARMY STRONGER. AND IT FILLS THEM WITH AN INSATIABLE APPETITE FOR BLOOD.
EVEN THEMYSCIRA CAN'T FIGHT THEM ALONE. WHEN THE ISLAND FALLS, CAIN WILL HAVE MY AMAZON SISTER WARRIORS UNDER HIS COMMAND.
EUROPE WON'T STAND A CHANCE. DOES THAT SOUND LIKE A WORLD YOU WANT TO INDULGE IN?
I GUESS WE'LL SEE, EXORISTOS. IF YOU'RE ALL THAT STANDS BETWEEN THEMYSCIRA AND DEATH, THEN THE BATTLE IS ALREADY OVER.
YOU SAID IT YOURSELF--CAIN HAS ALREADY SAILED. YOU'RE STILL BUILDING YOUR BOAT.
NOW, WHERE WAS I...
ZZZZZT
IF WE THOUGHT THE BATTLE WAS LOST, WE WOULDN'T BE BUILDING A BOAT, WOULD WE?
TELL HIM WHAT YOU TOLD US, ATLA. ABOUT HOW CAIN ATTACKED YOU...

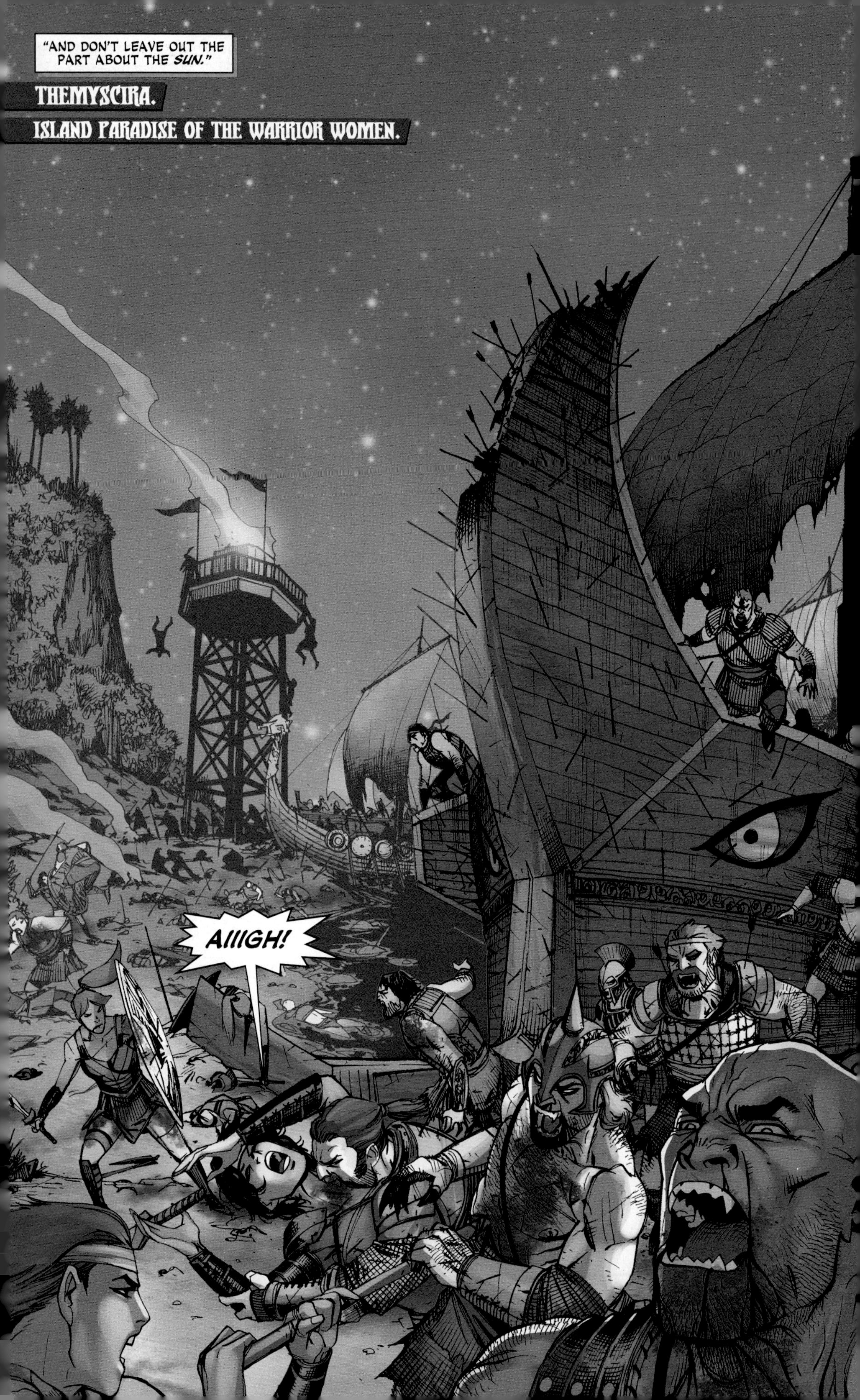
"AND DON'T LEAVE OUT THE PART ABOUT THE SUN."
THEMYSCIRA.
ISLAND PARADISE OF THE WARRIOR WOMEN.
AIIIGH!

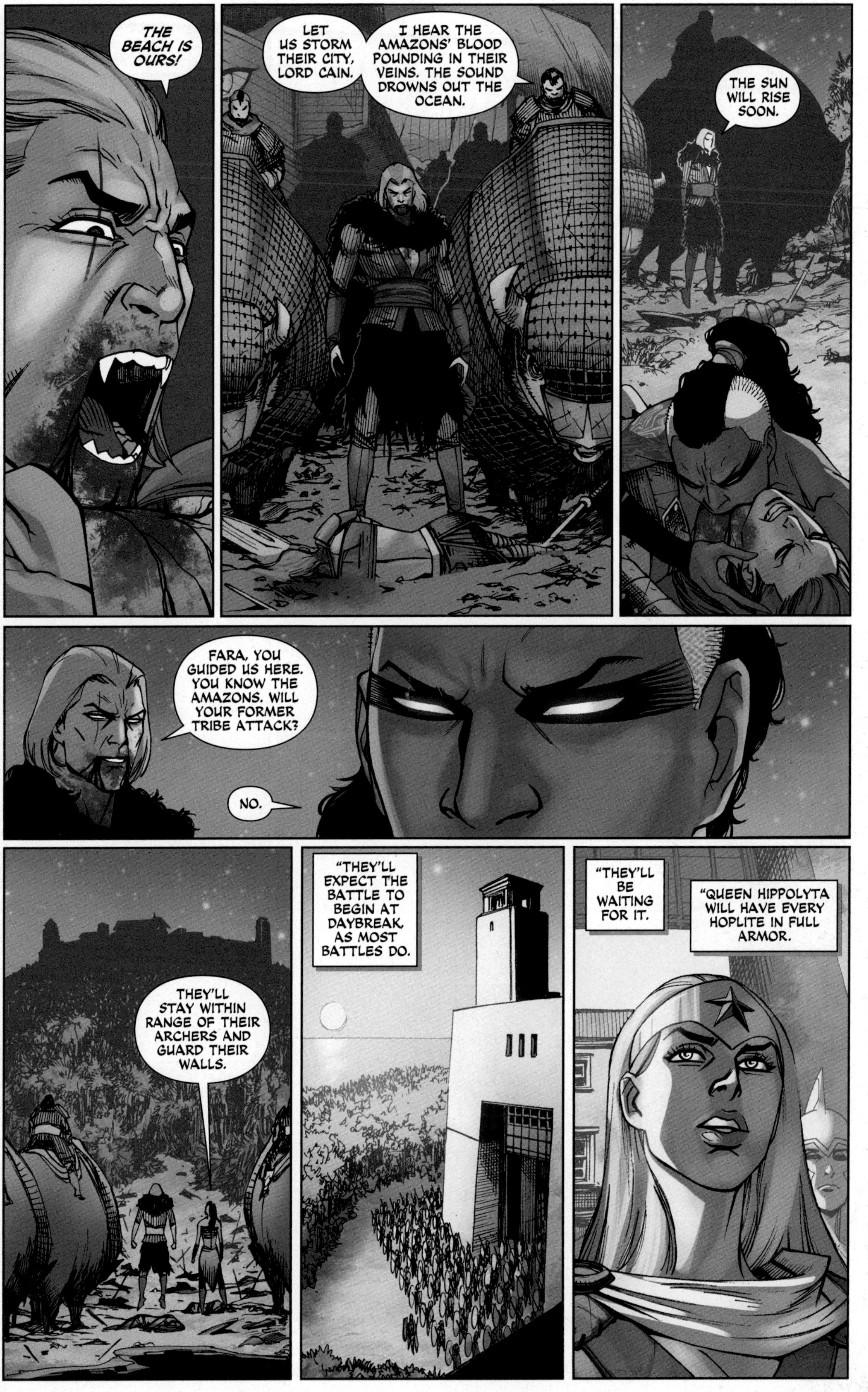
THE BEACH IS OURS!
LET US STORM THEIR CITY, LORD CAIN.
I HEAR THE AMAZONS' BLOOD POUNDING IN THEIR VEINS. THE SOUND DROWNS OUT THE OCEAN.
THE SUN WILL RISE SOON.
FARA, YOU GUIDED US HERE. YOU KNOW THE AMAZONS. WILL YOUR FORMER TRIBE ATTACK?
NO.
THEY'LL STAY WITHIN RANGE OF THEIR ARCHERS AND GUARD THEIR WALLS.
"THEY'LL EXPECT THE BATTLE TO BEGIN AT DAYBREAK, AS MOST BATTLES DO.
"THEY'LL BE WAITING FOR IT.
"QUEEN HIPPOLYTA WILL HAVE EVERY HOPLITE IN FULL ARMOR.

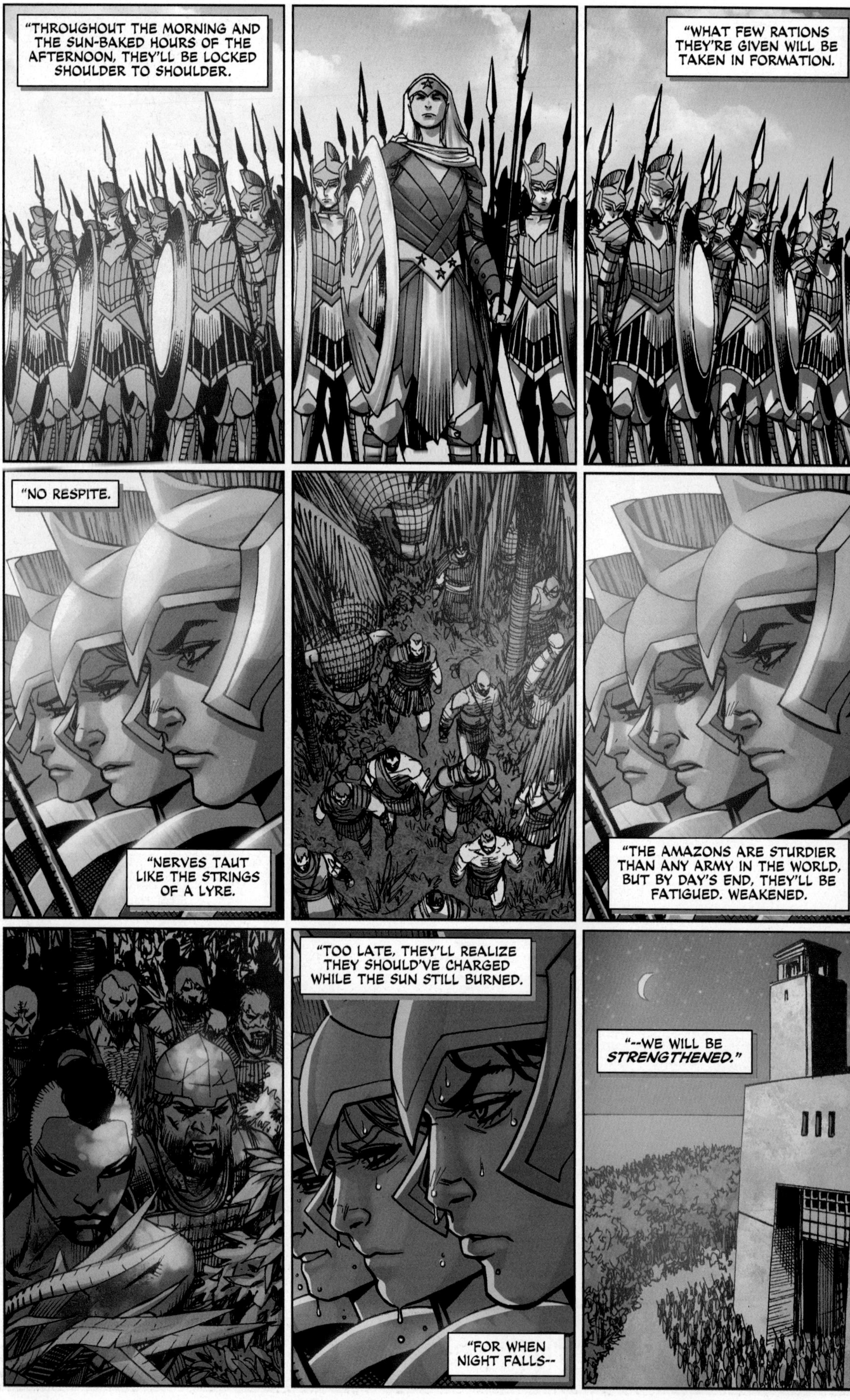
"THROUGHOUT THE MORNING AND THE SUN-BAKED HOURS OF THE AFTERNOON, THEY'LL BE LOCKED SHOULDER TO SHOULDER.
"WHAT FEW RATIONS THEY'RE GIVEN WILL BE TAKEN IN FORMATION.
"NO RESPITE.
"NERVES TAUT LIKE THE STRINGS OF A LYRE.
"THE AMAZONS ARE STURDIER THAN ANY ARMY IN THE WORLD, BUT BY DAY'S END, THEY'LL BE FATIGUED. WEAKENED.
"TOO LATE, THEY'LL REALIZE THEY SHOULD'VE CHARGED WHILE THE SUN STILL BURNED.
"FOR WHEN NIGHT FALLS--
"--WE WILL BE *STRENGTHENED.*"

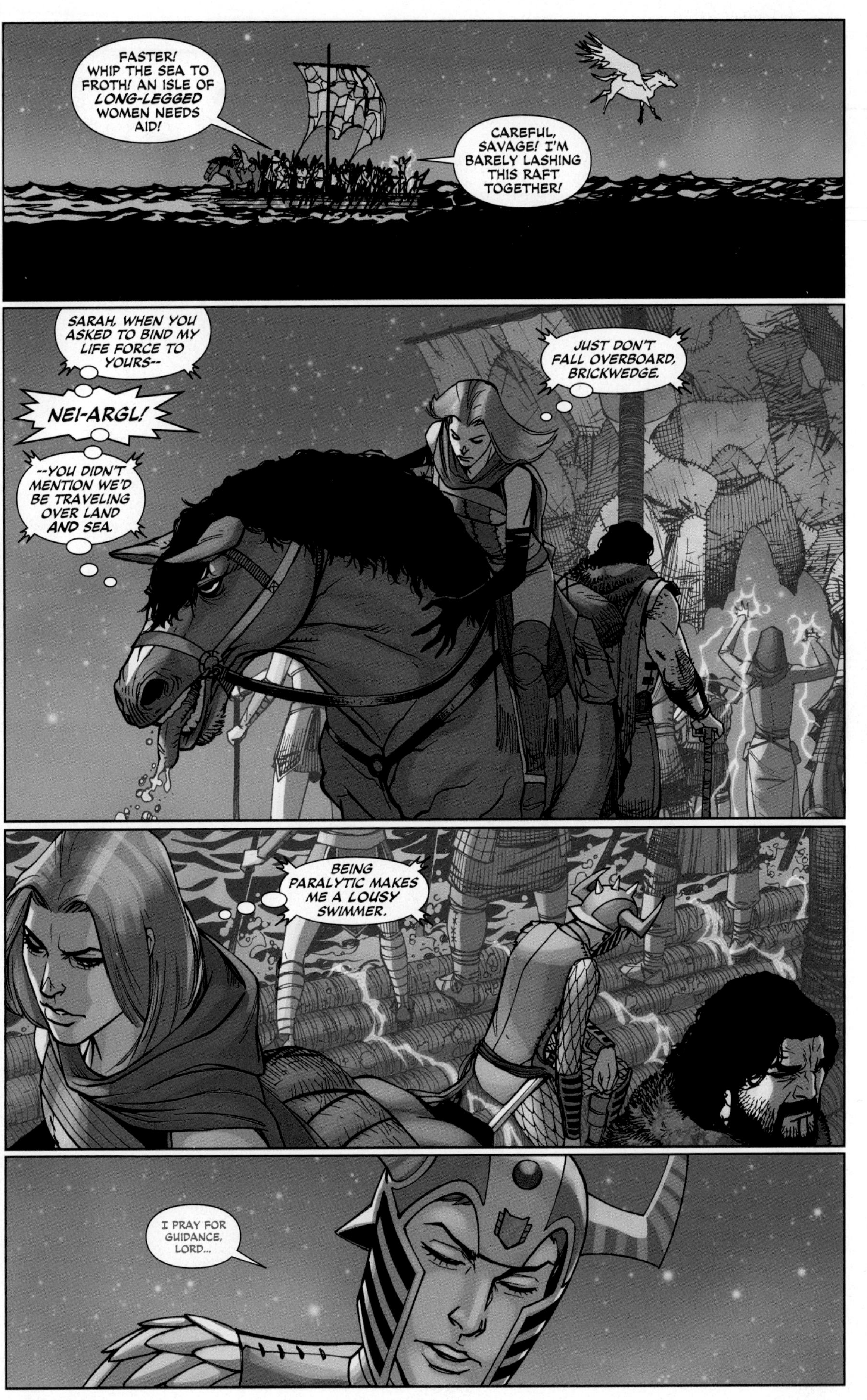
FASTER! WHIP THE SEA TO FROTH! AN ISLE OF LONG-LEGGED WOMEN NEEDS AID!
CAREFUL, SAVAGE! I'M BARELY LASHING THIS RAFT TOGETHER!
SARAH, WHEN YOU ASKED TO BIND MY LIFE FORCE TO YOURS--
NEI-ARGL!
--YOU DIDN'T MENTION WE'D BE TRAVELING OVER LAND AND SEA.
JUST DON'T FALL OVERBOARD, BRICKWEDGE.
BEING PARALYTIC MAKES ME A LOUSY SWIMMER.
I PRAY FOR GUIDANCE, LORD...

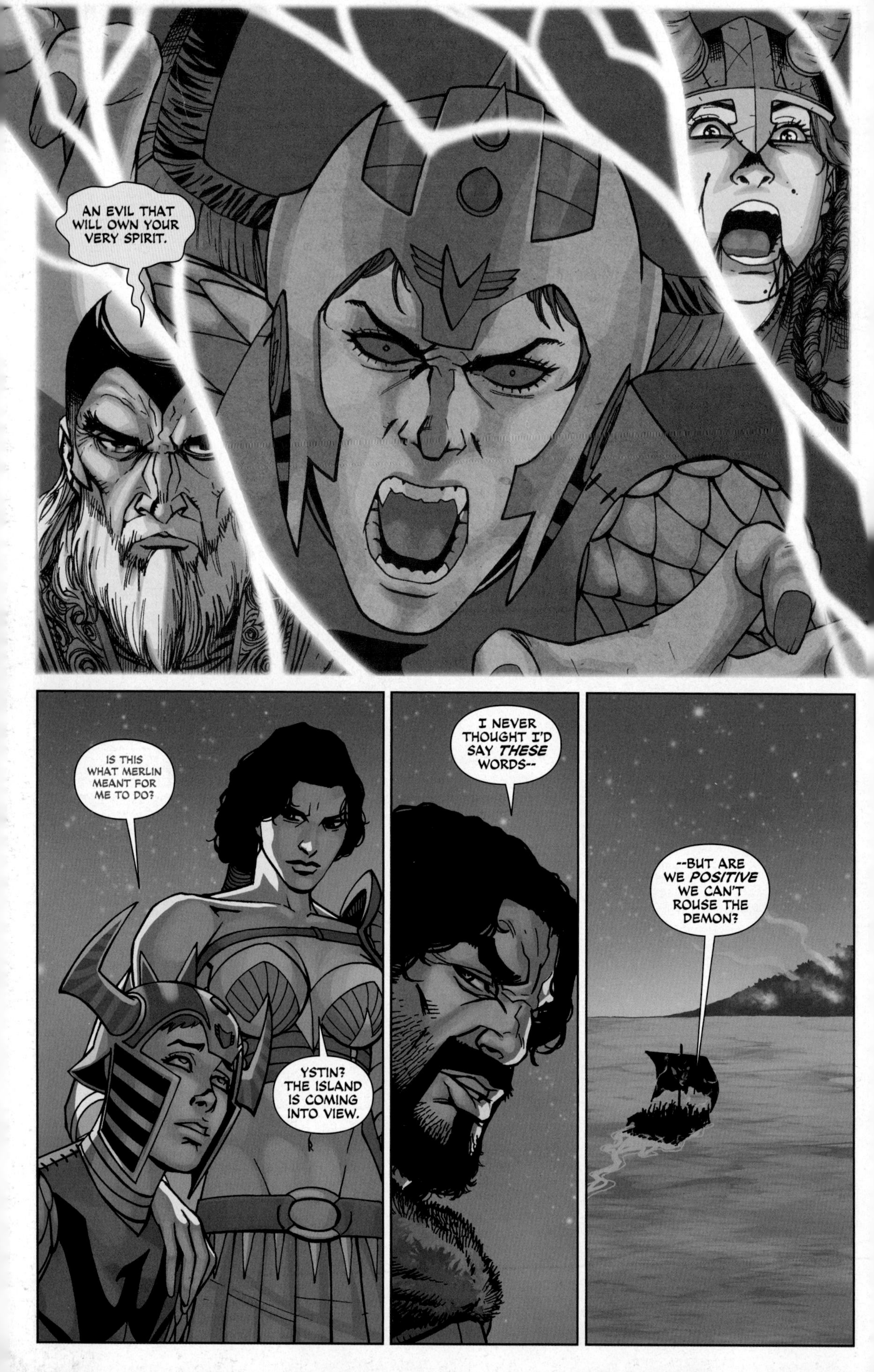
AN EVIL THAT WILL OWN YOUR VERY SPIRIT.
IS THIS WHAT MERLIN MEANT FOR ME TO DO?
YSTIN? THE ISLAND IS COMING INTO VIEW.
I NEVER THOUGHT I'D SAY THESE WORDS--
--BUT ARE WE POSITIVE WE CAN'T ROUSE THE DEMON?

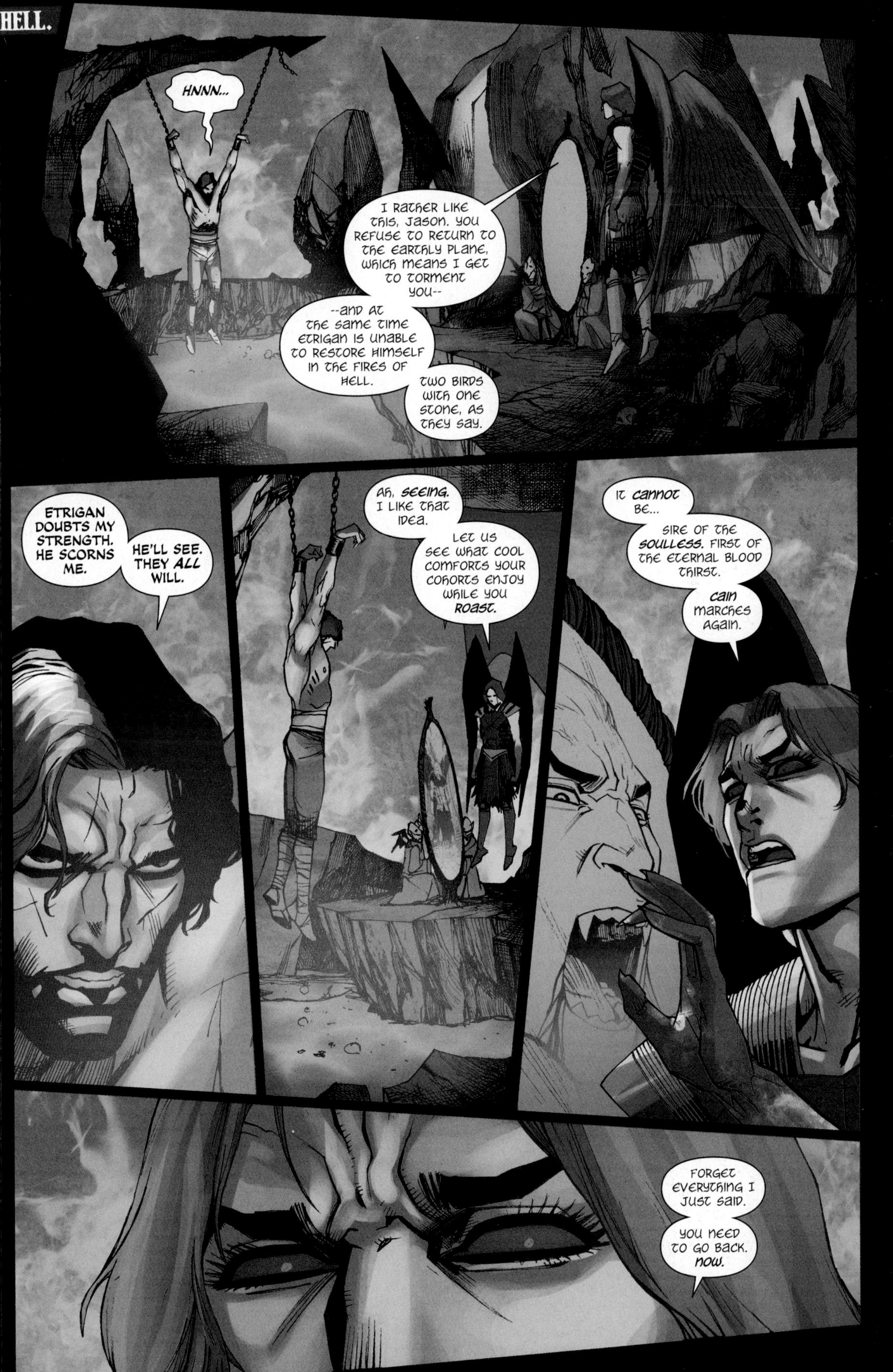
HELL.
HNNN...
I RATHER LIKE THIS, JASON. YOU REFUSE TO RETURN TO THE EARTHLY PLANE, WHICH MEANS I GET TO TORMENT YOU--
--AND AT THE SAME TIME ETRIGAN IS UNABLE TO RESTORE HIMSELF IN THE FIRES OF HELL.
TWO BIRDS WITH ONE STONE, AS THEY SAY.
ETRIGAN DOUBTS MY STRENGTH. HE SCORNS ME.
HE'LL SEE. THEY ALL WILL.
AH, SEEING. I LIKE THAT IDEA.
LET US SEE WHAT COOL COMFORTS YOUR COHORTS ENJOY WHILE YOU ROAST.
IT CANNOT BE...
SIRE OF THE SOULLESS. FIRST OF THE ETERNAL BLOOD THIRST.
CAIN MARCHES AGAIN.
FORGET EVERYTHING I JUST SAID.
YOU NEED TO GO BACK. NOW.

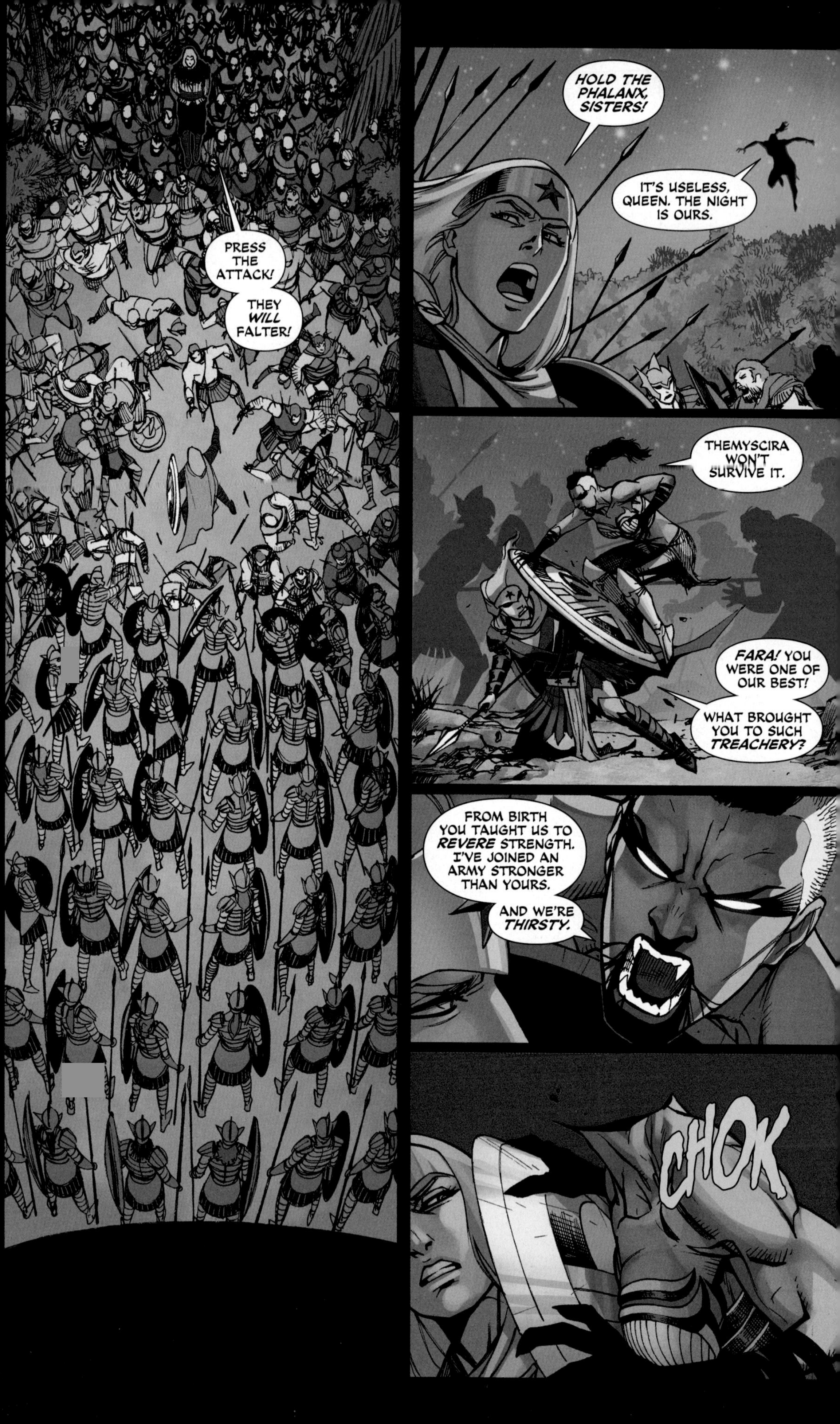
PRESS THE ATTACK!
THEY WILL FALTER!
HOLD THE PHALANX, SISTERS!
IT'S USELESS, QUEEN. THE NIGHT IS OURS.
THEMYSCIRA WON'T SURVIVE IT.
FARA! YOU WERE ONE OF OUR BEST!
WHAT BROUGHT YOU TO SUCH TREACHERY?
FROM BIRTH YOU TAUGHT US TO REVERE STRENGTH. I'VE JOINED AN ARMY STRONGER THAN YOURS.
AND WE'RE THIRSTY.
CHOK

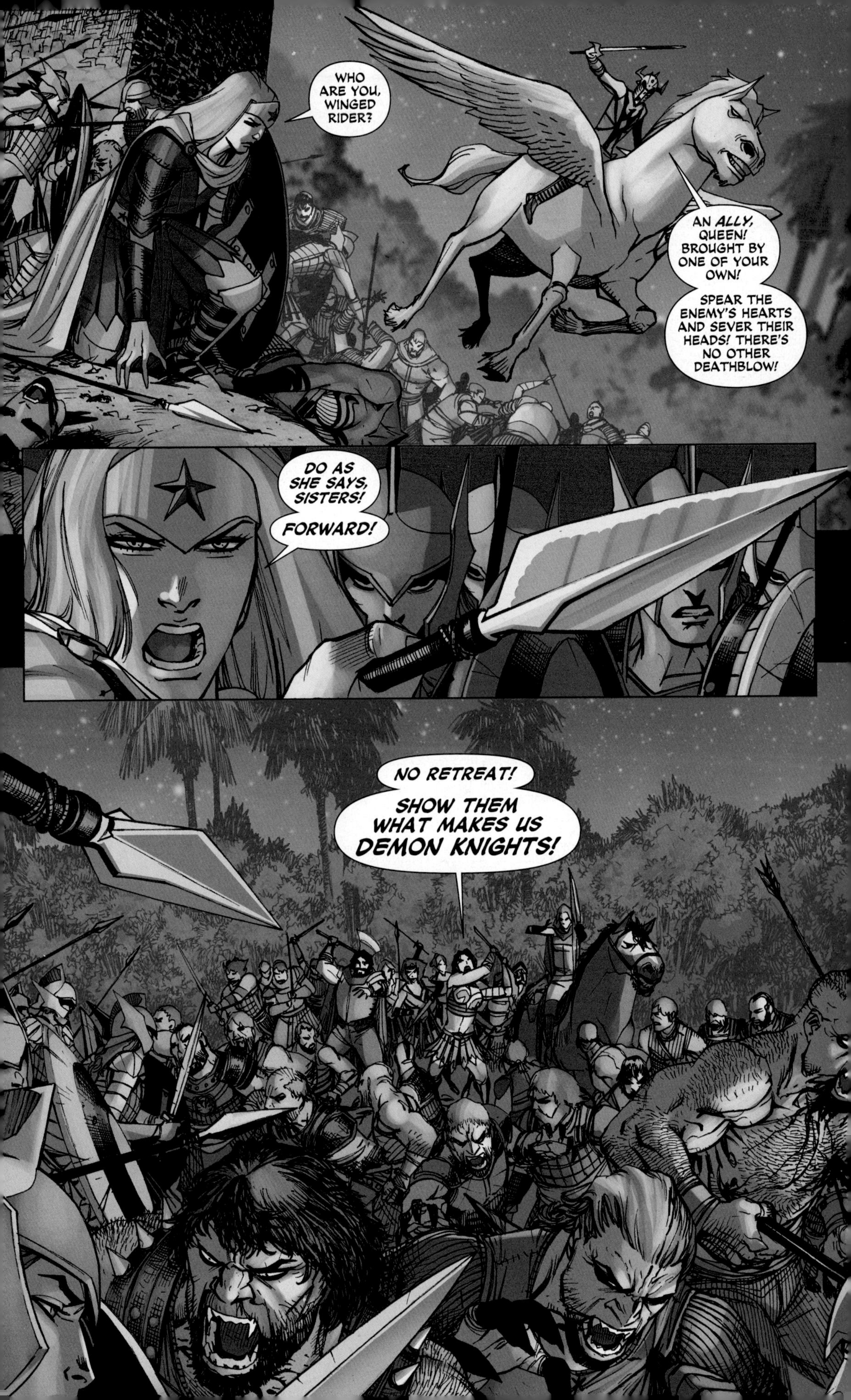
WHO ARE YOU, WINGED RIDER?
AN ALLY, QUEEN! BROUGHT BY ONE OF YOUR OWN!
SPEAR THE ENEMY'S HEARTS AND SEVER THEIR HEADS! THERE'S NO OTHER DEATHBLOW!
DO AS SHE SAYS, SISTERS!
FORWARD!
NO RETREAT!
SHOW THEM WHAT MAKES US DEMON KNIGHTS!

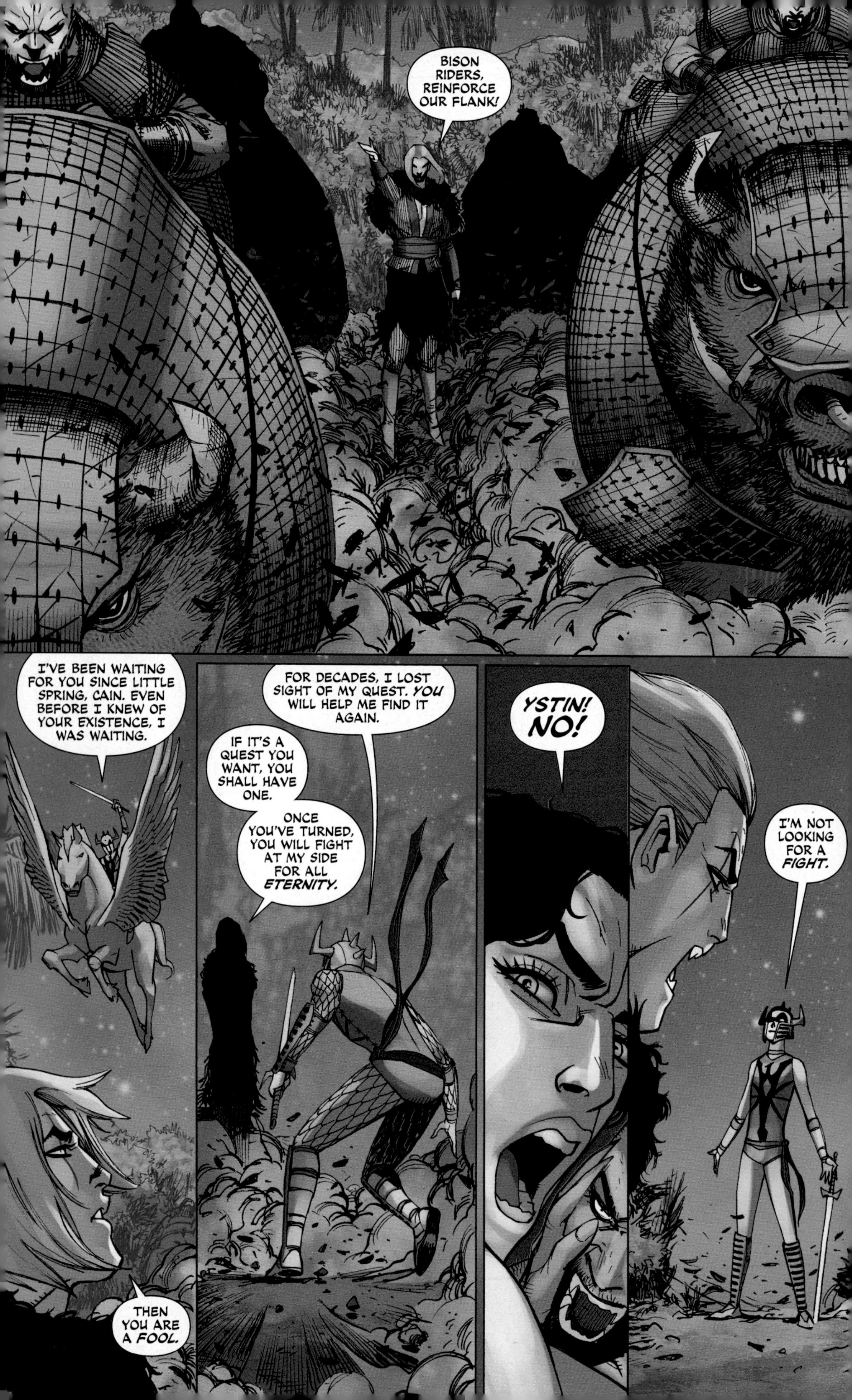
BISON RIDERS, REINFORCE OUR FLANK!
I'VE BEEN WAITING FOR YOU SINCE LITTLE SPRING, CAIN. EVEN BEFORE I KNEW OF YOUR EXISTENCE, I WAS WAITING.
THEN YOU ARE A *FOOL.*
FOR DECADES, I LOST SIGHT OF MY QUEST. *YOU* WILL HELP ME FIND IT AGAIN.
IF IT'S A QUEST YOU WANT, YOU SHALL HAVE ONE.
ONCE YOU'VE TURNED, YOU WILL FIGHT AT MY SIDE FOR ALL *ETERNITY.*
YSTIN! NO!
I'M NOT LOOKING FOR A *FIGHT.*

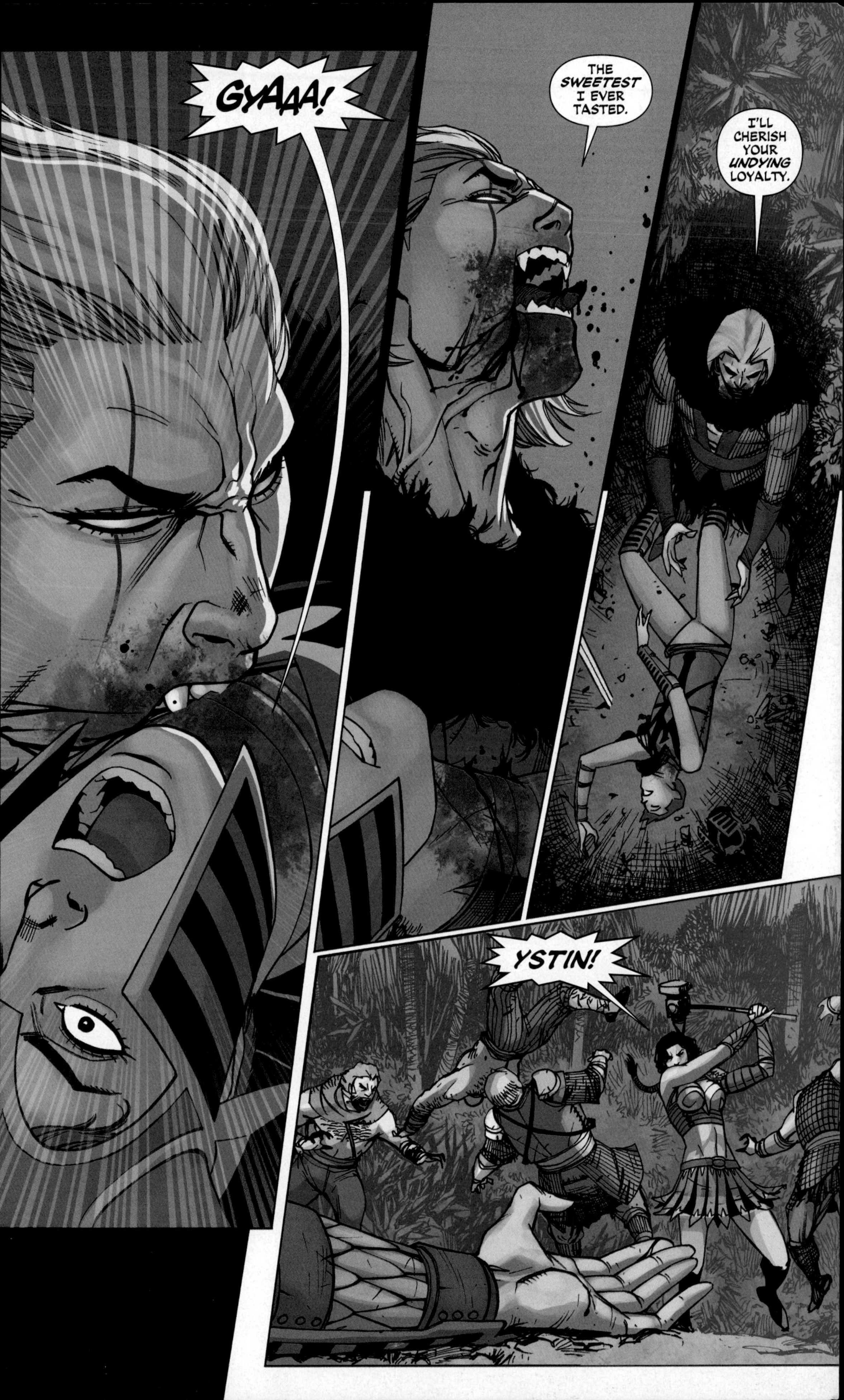
GYAAA!
THE SWEETEST I EVER TASTED.
I'LL CHERISH YOUR UNDYING LOYALTY.
YSTIN!

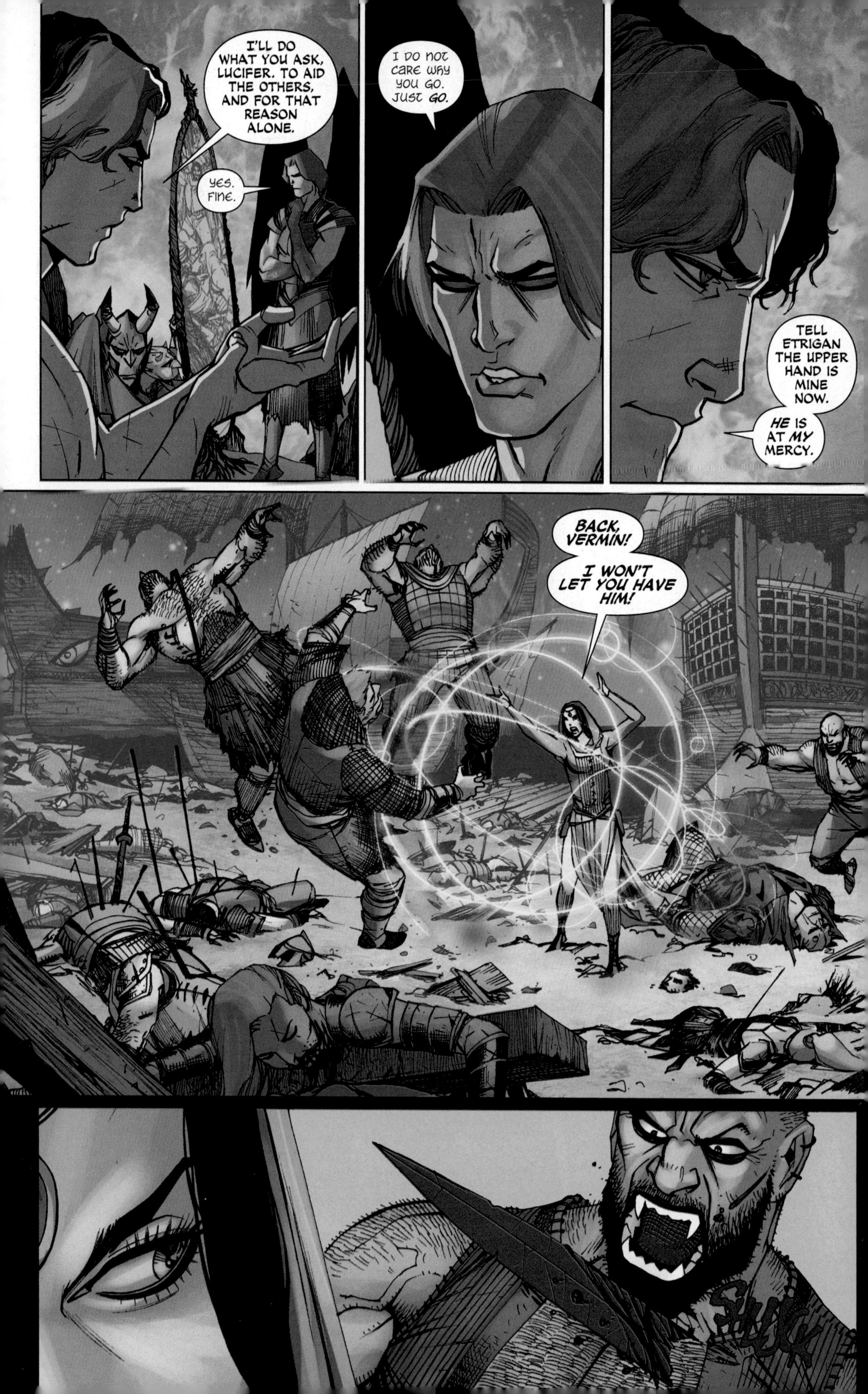
I'LL DO WHAT YOU ASK, LUCIFER. TO AID THE OTHERS, AND FOR THAT REASON ALONE.
YES. FINE.
I DO NOT CARE WHY YOU GO. JUST GO.
TELL ETRIGAN THE UPPER HAND IS MINE NOW.
HE IS AT MY MERCY.
BACK, VERMIN!
I WON'T LET YOU HAVE HIM!

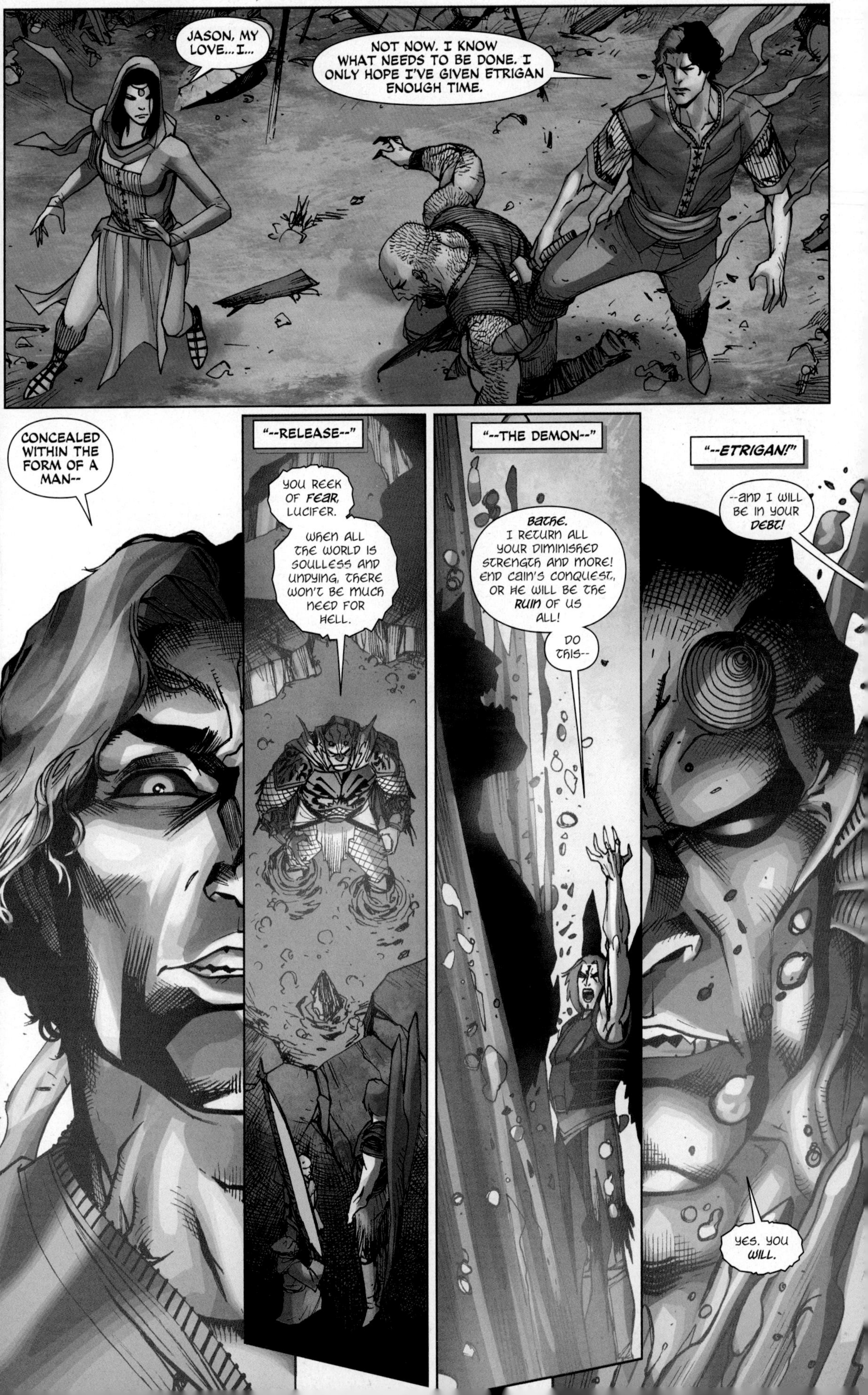
JASON, MY LOVE... I...
NOT NOW. I KNOW WHAT NEEDS TO BE DONE. I ONLY HOPE I'VE GIVEN ETRIGAN ENOUGH TIME.
CONCEALED WITHIN THE FORM OF A MAN--
"--RELEASE--"
YOU REEK OF FEAR, LUCIFER.
WHEN ALL THE WORLD IS SOULLESS AND UNDYING, THERE WON'T BE MUCH NEED FOR HELL.
"--THE DEMON--"
BATHE. I RETURN ALL YOUR DIMINISHED STRENGTH AND MORE! END CAIN'S CONQUEST, OR HE WILL BE THE RUIN OF US ALL!
DO THIS--
"--ETRIGAN!"
--AND I WILL BE IN YOUR DEBT!
YES. YOU WILL.

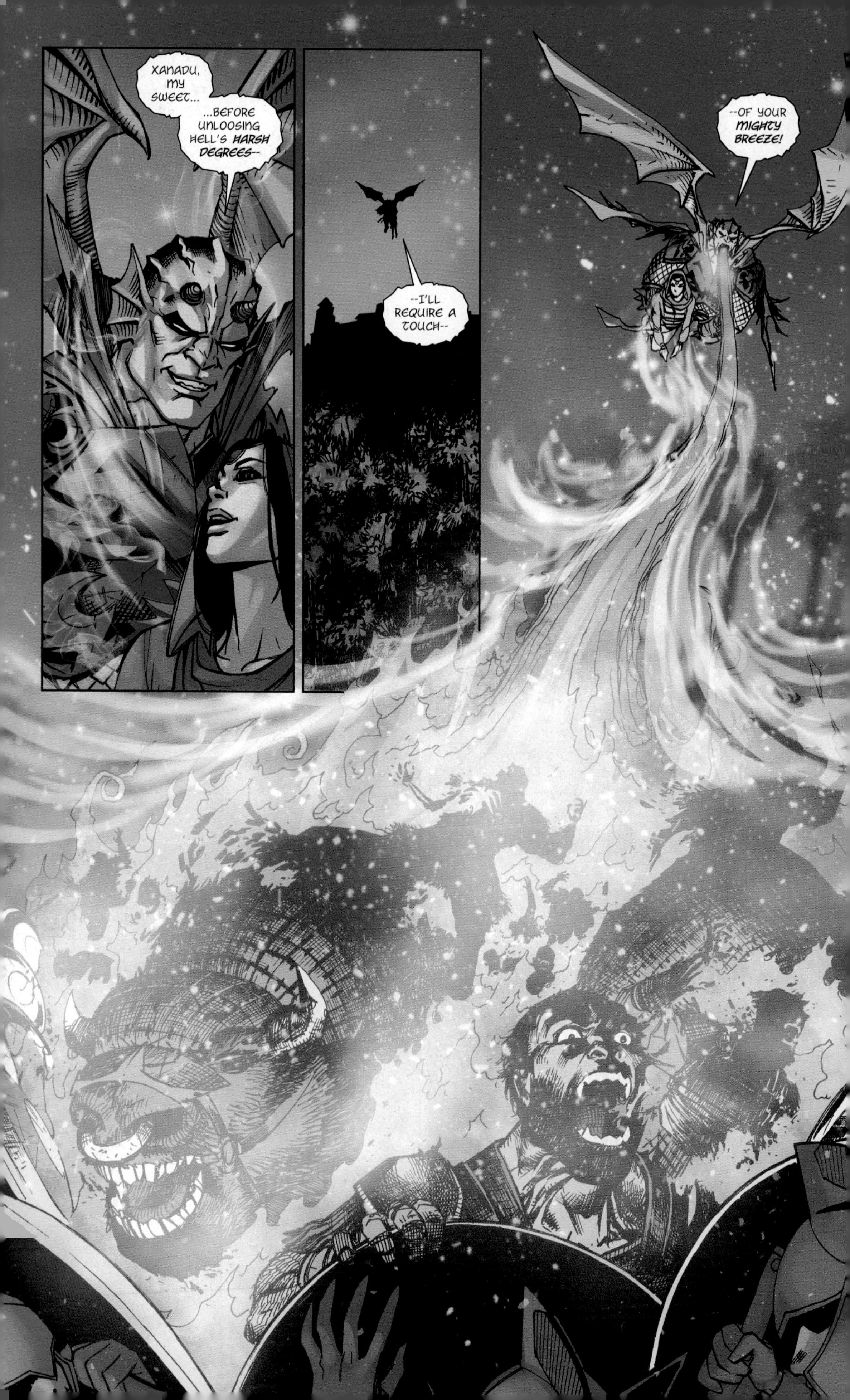
XANADU, MY SWEET...
...BEFORE UNLOOSING HELL'S HARSH DEGREES--
--I'LL REQUIRE A TOUCH--
--OF YOUR MIGHTY BREEZE!

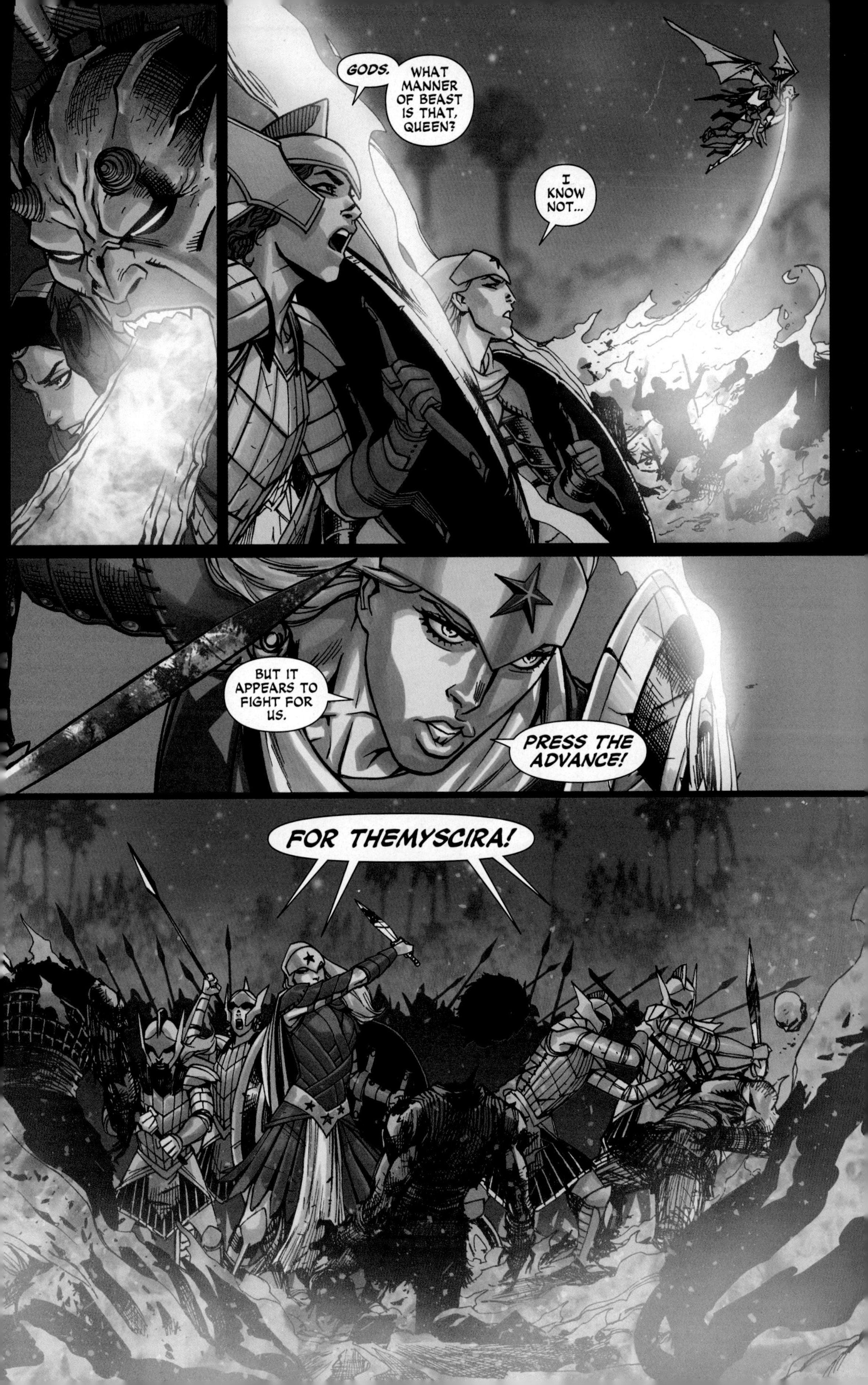
GODS.
WHAT MANNER OF BEAST IS THAT, QUEEN?
I KNOW NOT...
BUT IT APPEARS TO FIGHT FOR US.
PRESS THE ADVANCE!
FOR THEMYSCIRA!

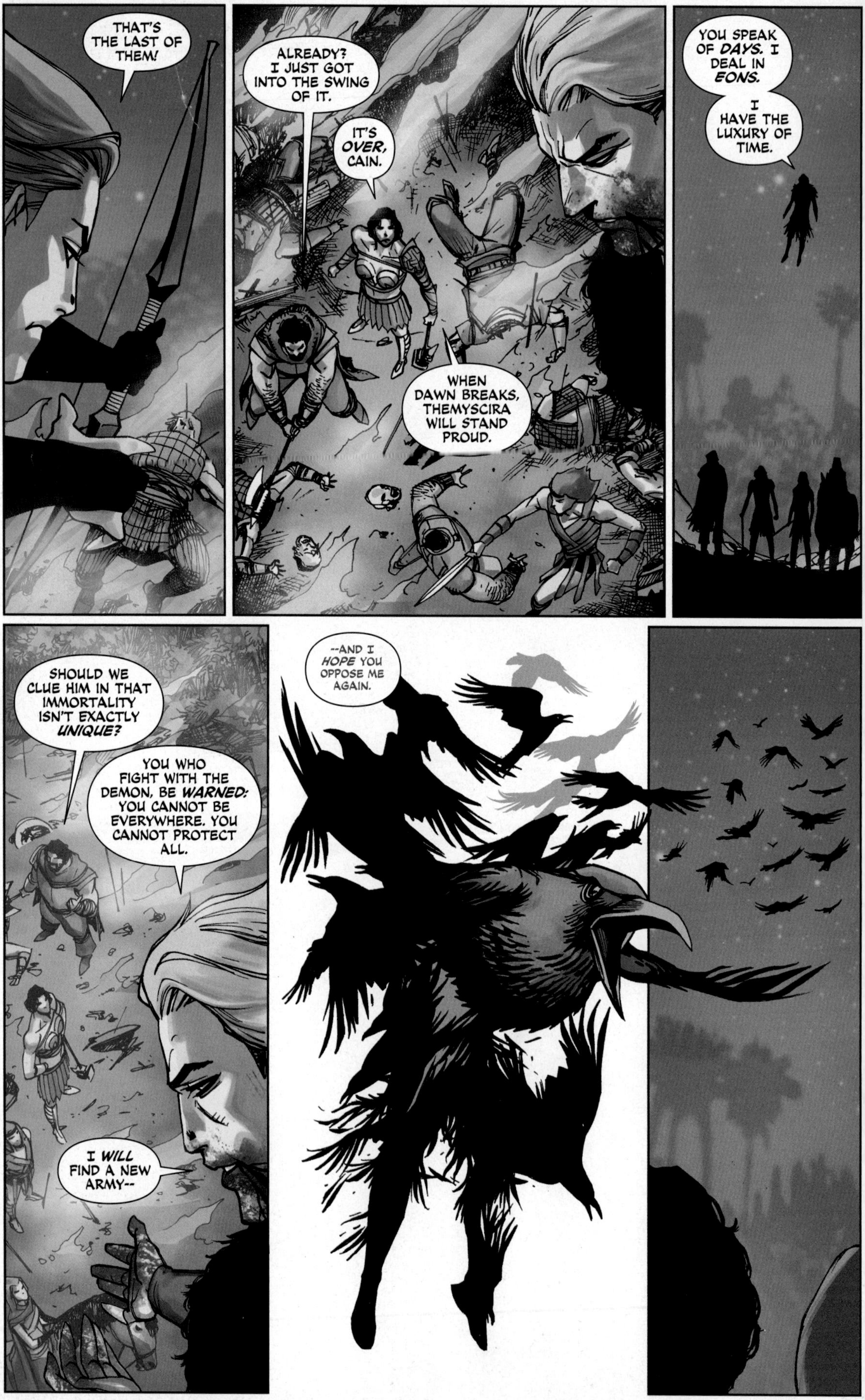
THAT'S THE LAST OF THEM!
ALREADY? I JUST GOT INTO THE SWING OF IT.
IT'S *OVER,* CAIN.
WHEN DAWN BREAKS, THEMYSCIRA WILL STAND PROUD.
YOU SPEAK OF *DAYS.* I DEAL IN *EONS.*
I HAVE THE LUXURY OF TIME.
SHOULD WE CLUE HIM IN THAT IMMORTALITY ISN'T EXACTLY *UNIQUE?*
YOU WHO FIGHT WITH THE DEMON, BE *WARNED:* YOU CANNOT BE EVERYWHERE. YOU CANNOT PROTECT ALL.
I *WILL* FIND A NEW ARMY--
--AND I *HOPE* YOU OPPOSE ME AGAIN.

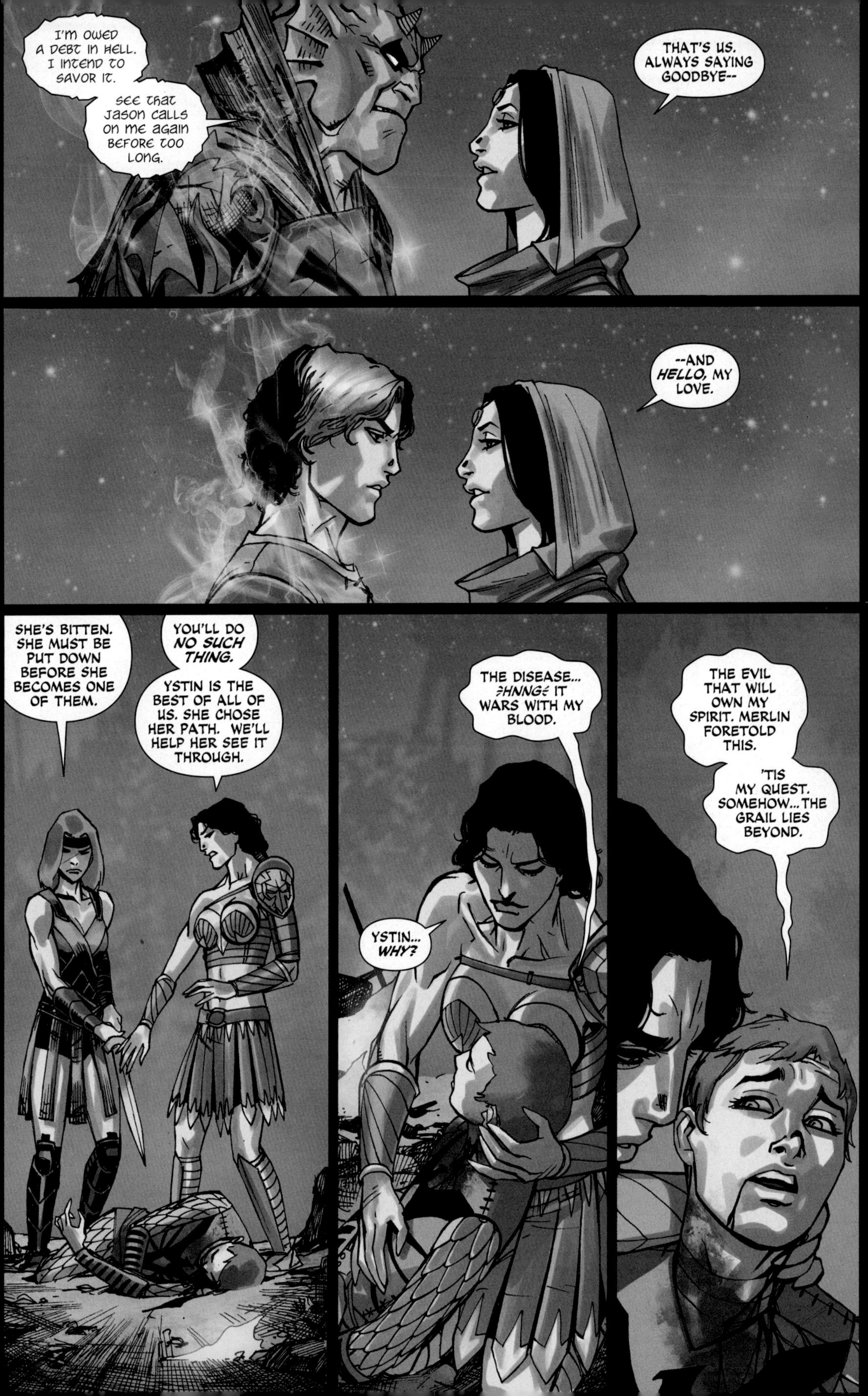
I'M OWED A DEBT IN HELL. I INTEND TO SAVOR IT.
SEE THAT JASON CALLS ON ME AGAIN BEFORE TOO LONG.
THAT'S US. ALWAYS SAYING GOODBYE--
--AND *HELLO,* MY LOVE.
SHE'S BITTEN. SHE MUST BE PUT DOWN BEFORE SHE BECOMES ONE OF THEM.
YOU'LL DO *NO SUCH THING.*
YSTIN IS THE BEST OF ALL OF US. SHE CHOSE HER PATH. WE'LL HELP HER SEE IT THROUGH.
THE DISEASE... HHNNG IT WARS WITH MY BLOOD.
YSTIN... *WHY?*
THE EVIL THAT WILL OWN MY SPIRIT. MERLIN FORETOLD THIS.
'TIS MY QUEST. SOMEHOW... THE GRAIL LIES BEYOND.

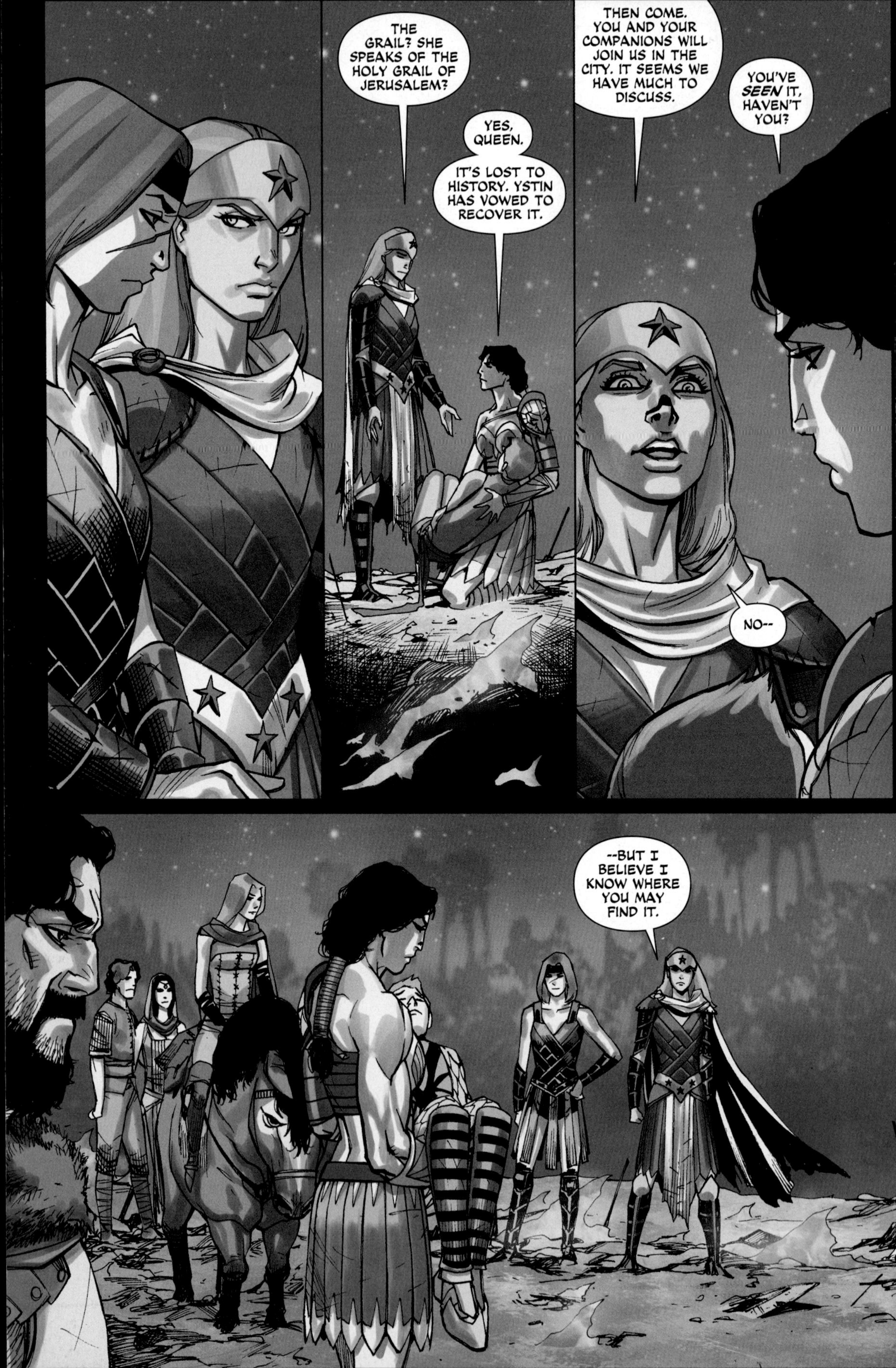
THE GRAIL? SHE SPEAKS OF THE HOLY GRAIL OF JERUSALEM?
YES, QUEEN.
IT'S LOST TO HISTORY. YSTIN HAS VOWED TO RECOVER IT.
THEN COME. YOU AND YOUR COMPANIONS WILL JOIN US IN THE CITY. IT SEEMS WE HAVE MUCH TO DISCUSS.
YOU'VE *SEEN* IT, HAVEN'T YOU?
NO--
--BUT I BELIEVE I KNOW WHERE YOU MAY FIND IT.

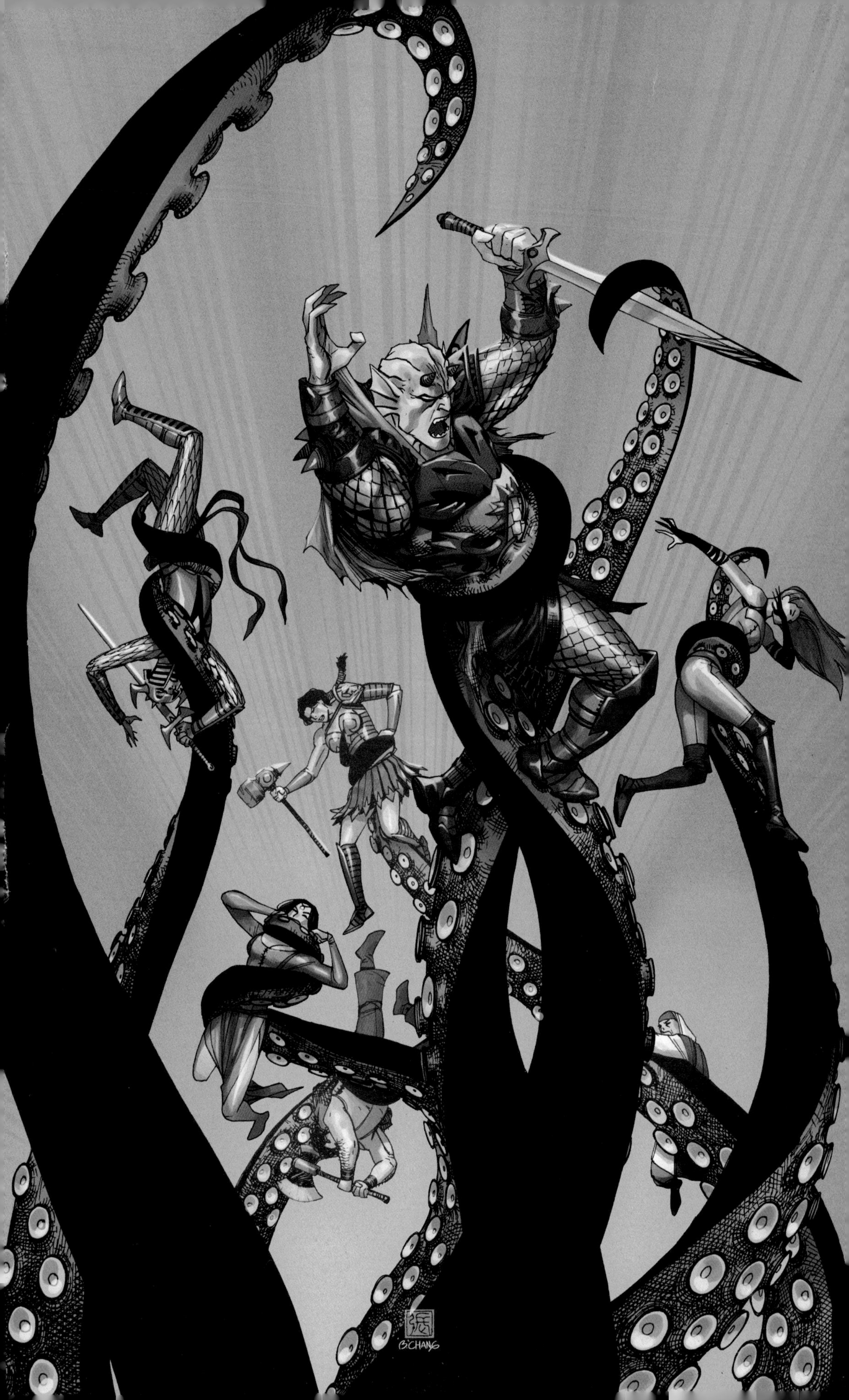

ROBERT VENDITTI
writer

CHAD HARDIN
penciller

WAYNE FAUCHER
inker

BERNARD CHANG
cover artist

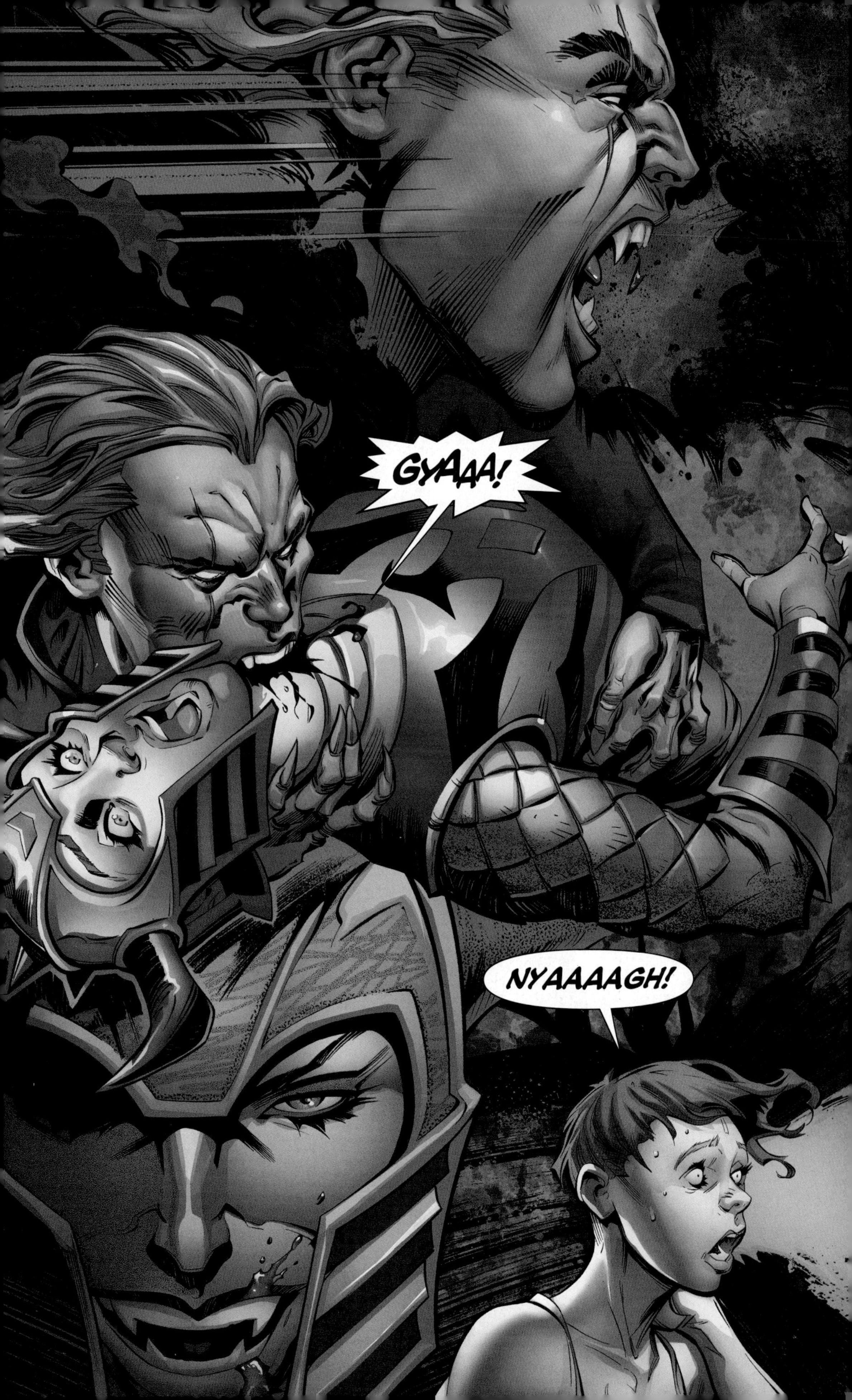
GYAAA!
NYAAAAGH!

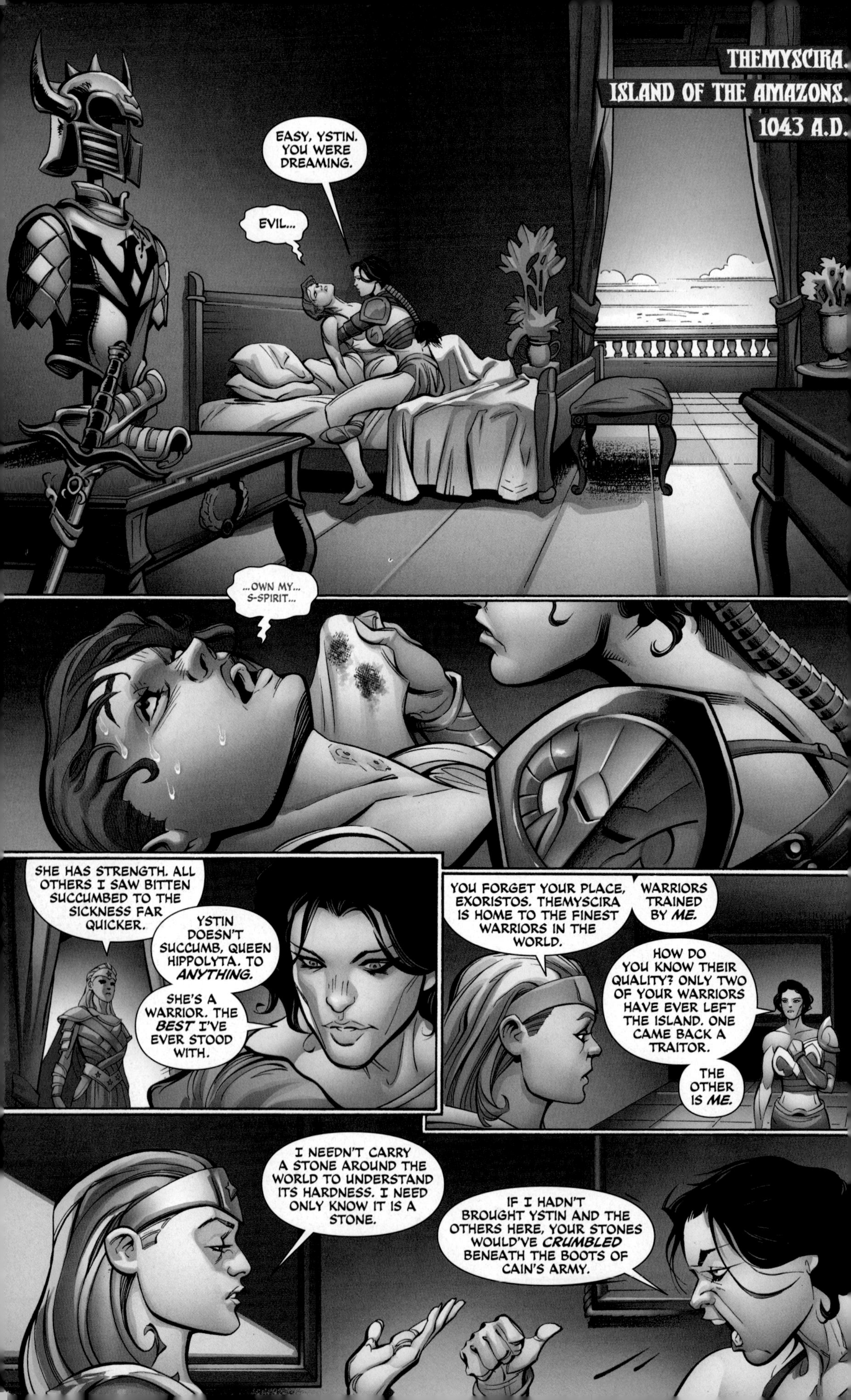
THEMYSCIRA.
ISLAND OF THE AMAZONS.
1043 A.D.
EASY, YSTIN. YOU WERE DREAMING.
EVIL...
...OWN MY... S-SPIRIT...
SHE HAS STRENGTH. ALL OTHERS I SAW BITTEN SUCCUMBED TO THE SICKNESS FAR QUICKER.
YSTIN DOESN'T SUCCUMB, QUEEN HIPPOLYTA. TO ANYTHING.
SHE'S A WARRIOR. THE BEST I'VE EVER STOOD WITH.
YOU FORGET YOUR PLACE, EXORISTOS. THEMYSCIRA IS HOME TO THE FINEST WARRIORS IN THE WORLD.
WARRIORS TRAINED BY ME.
HOW DO YOU KNOW THEIR QUALITY? ONLY TWO OF YOUR WARRIORS HAVE EVER LEFT THE ISLAND. ONE CAME BACK A TRAITOR.
THE OTHER IS ME.
I NEEDN'T CARRY A STONE AROUND THE WORLD TO UNDERSTAND ITS HARDNESS. I NEED ONLY KNOW IT IS A STONE.
IF I HADN'T BROUGHT YSTIN AND THE OTHERS HERE, YOUR STONES WOULD'VE CRUMBLED BENEATH THE BOOTS OF CAIN'S ARMY.

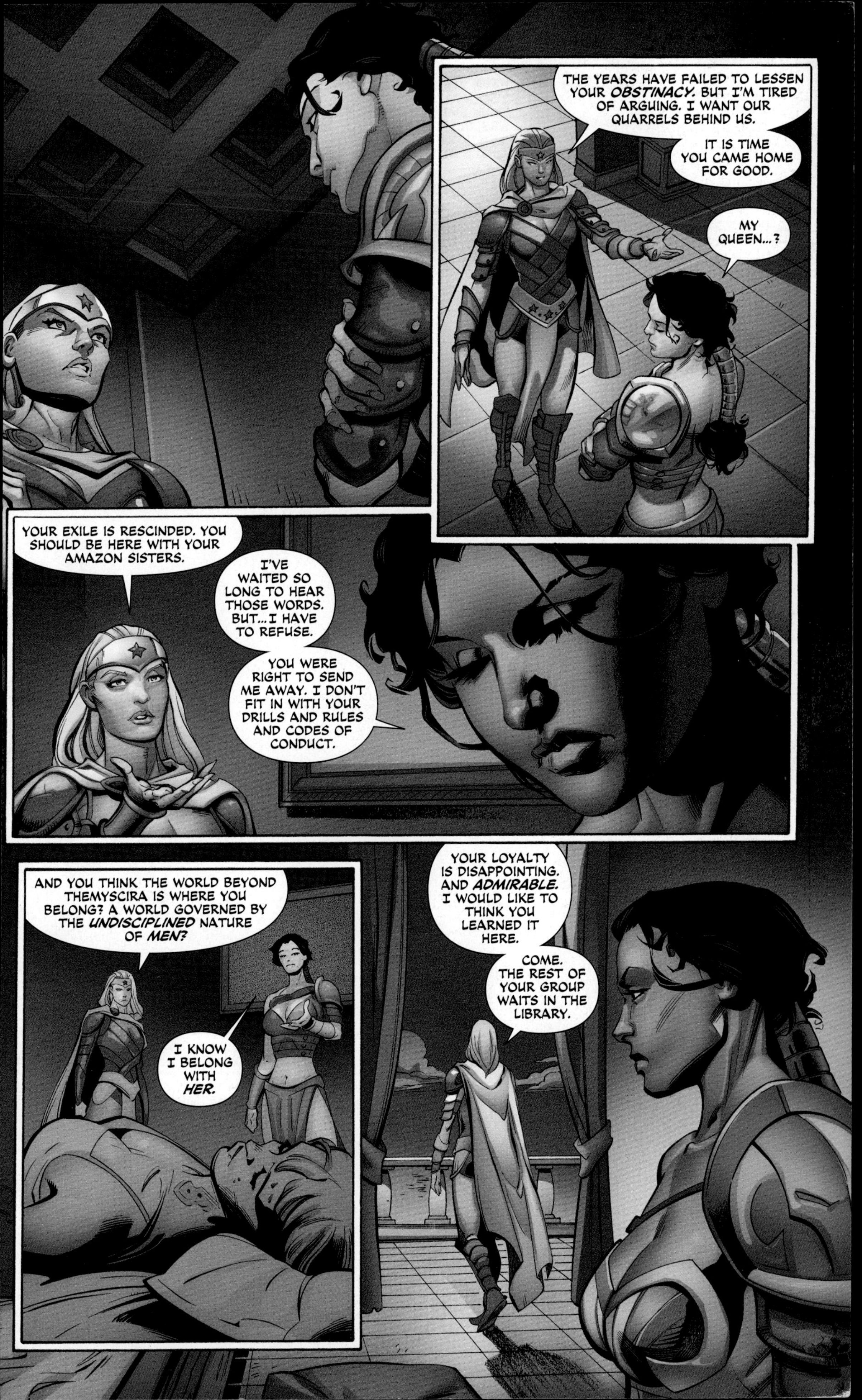
THE YEARS HAVE FAILED TO LESSEN YOUR *OBSTINACY.* BUT I'M TIRED OF ARGUING. I WANT OUR QUARRELS BEHIND US.
IT IS TIME YOU CAME HOME FOR GOOD.
MY QUEEN...?
YOUR EXILE IS RESCINDED. YOU SHOULD BE HERE WITH YOUR AMAZON SISTERS.
I'VE WAITED SO LONG TO HEAR THOSE WORDS. BUT...I HAVE TO REFUSE.
YOU WERE RIGHT TO SEND ME AWAY. I DON'T FIT IN WITH YOUR DRILLS AND RULES AND CODES OF CONDUCT.
AND YOU THINK THE WORLD BEYOND THEMYSCIRA IS WHERE YOU BELONG? A WORLD GOVERNED BY THE *UNDISCIPLINED* NATURE OF *MEN?*
I KNOW I BELONG WITH *HER.*
YOUR LOYALTY IS DISAPPOINTING. AND *ADMIRABLE.* I WOULD LIKE TO THINK YOU LEARNED IT HERE.
COME. THE REST OF YOUR GROUP WAITS IN THE LIBRARY.

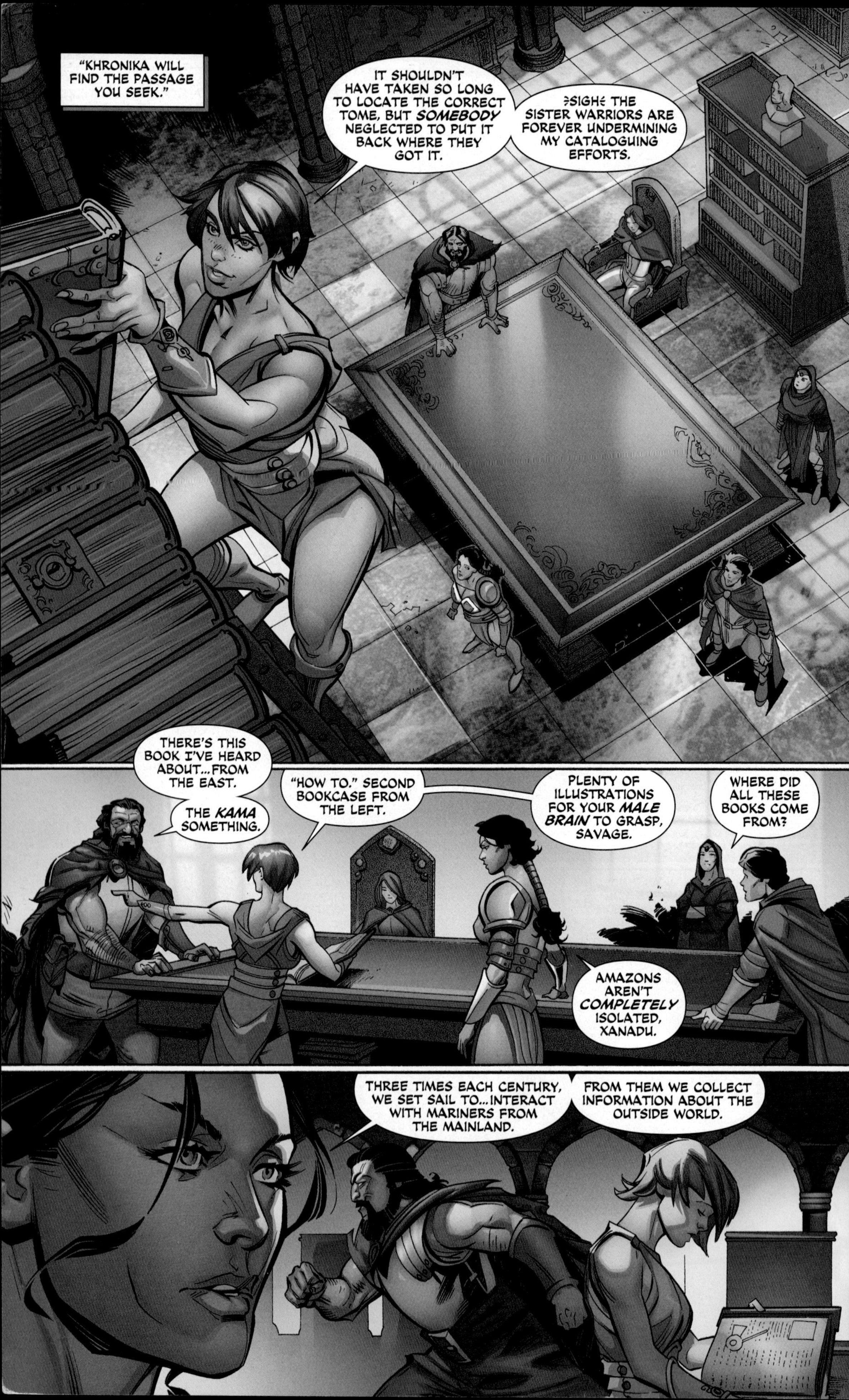
"KHRONIKA WILL FIND THE PASSAGE YOU SEEK."
IT SHOULDN'T HAVE TAKEN SO LONG TO LOCATE THE CORRECT TOME, BUT *SOMEBODY* NEGLECTED TO PUT IT BACK WHERE THEY GOT IT.
SIGH THE SISTER WARRIORS ARE FOREVER UNDERMINING MY CATALOGUING EFFORTS.
THERE'S THIS BOOK I'VE HEARD ABOUT...FROM THE EAST.
THE *KAMA* SOMETHING.
"HOW TO." SECOND BOOKCASE FROM THE LEFT.
PLENTY OF ILLUSTRATIONS FOR YOUR *MALE BRAIN* TO GRASP, SAVAGE.
WHERE DID ALL THESE BOOKS COME FROM?
AMAZONS AREN'T *COMPLETELY* ISOLATED, XANADU.
THREE TIMES EACH CENTURY, WE SET SAIL TO...INTERACT WITH MARINERS FROM THE MAINLAND.
FROM THEM WE COLLECT INFORMATION ABOUT THE OUTSIDE WORLD.

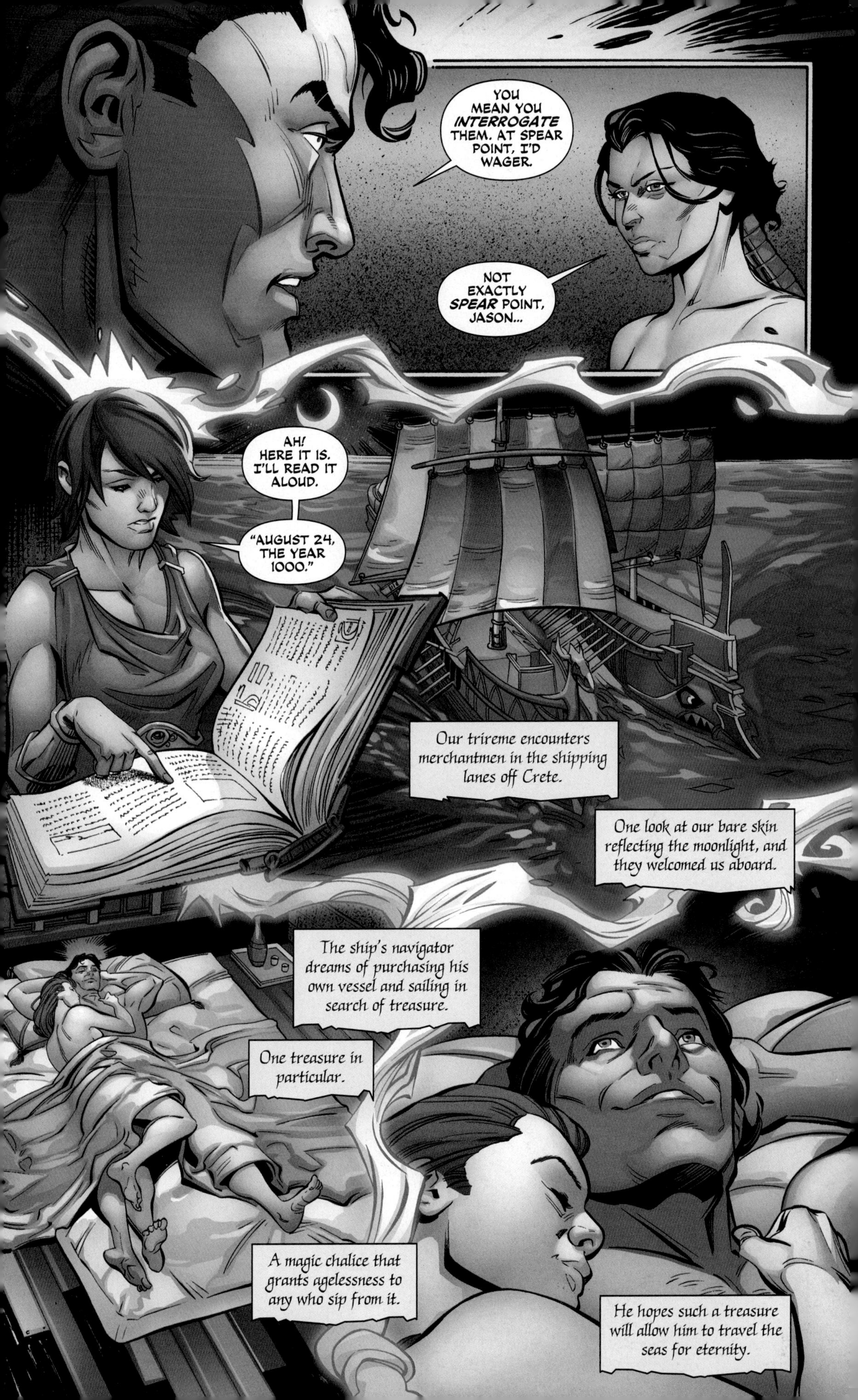
YOU MEAN YOU *INTERROGATE* THEM. AT SPEAR POINT, I'D WAGER.
NOT EXACTLY *SPEAR* POINT, JASON...
AH! HERE IT IS. I'LL READ IT ALOUD.
"AUGUST 24, THE YEAR 1000."
Our trireme encounters merchantmen in the shipping lanes off Crete.
One look at our bare skin reflecting the moonlight, and they welcomed us aboard.
The ship's navigator dreams of purchasing his own vessel and sailing in search of treasure.
One treasure in particular.
A magic chalice that grants agelessness to any who sip from it.
He hopes such a treasure will allow him to travel the seas for eternity.

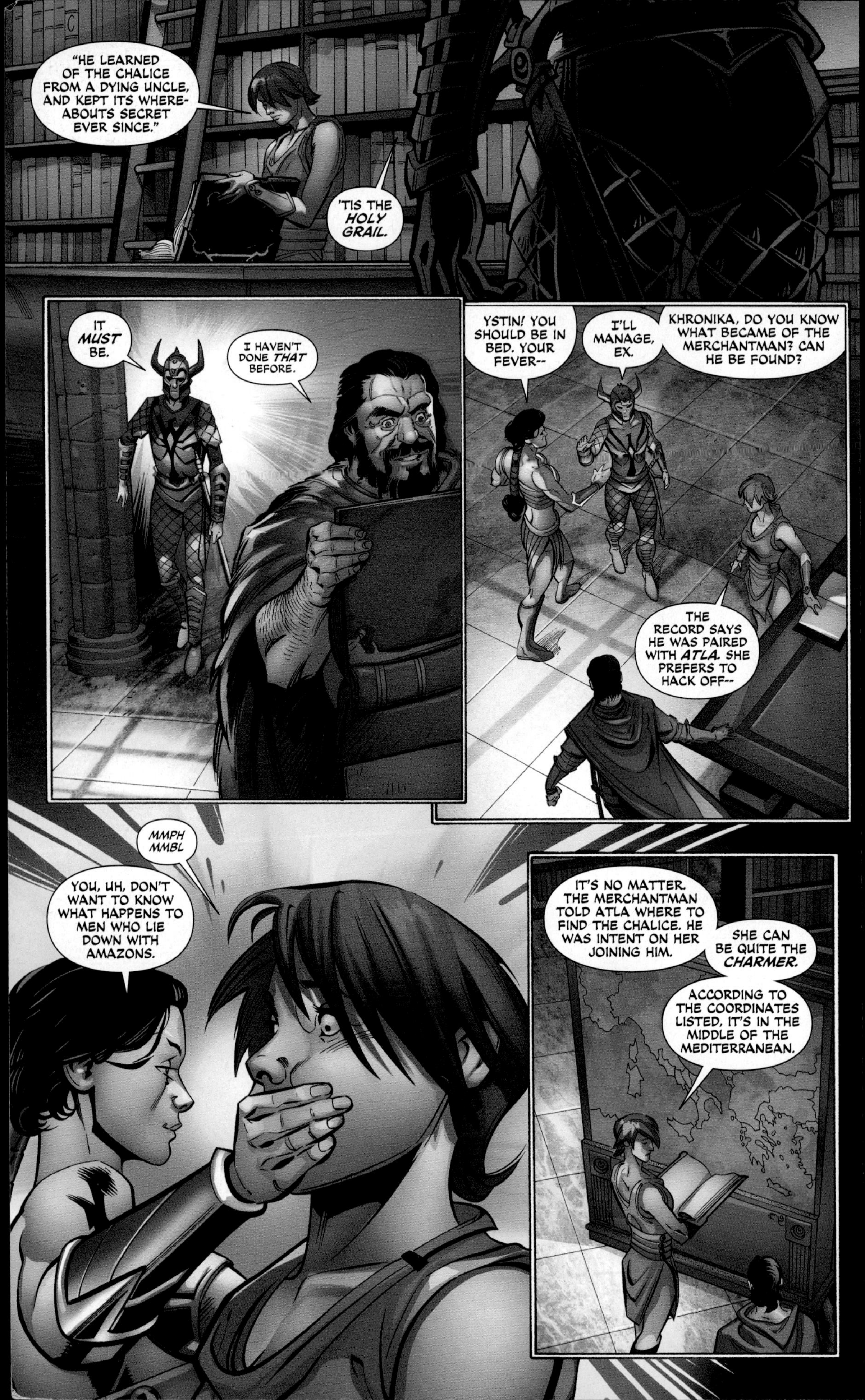
"HE LEARNED OF THE CHALICE FROM A DYING UNCLE, AND KEPT ITS WHERE-ABOUTS SECRET EVER SINCE."
'TIS THE HOLY GRAIL.
IT MUST BE.
I HAVEN'T DONE THAT BEFORE.
YSTIN! YOU SHOULD BE IN BED. YOUR FEVER--
I'LL MANAGE, EX.
KHRONIKA, DO YOU KNOW WHAT BECAME OF THE MERCHANTMAN? CAN HE BE FOUND?
THE RECORD SAYS HE WAS PAIRED WITH ATLA. SHE PREFERS TO HACK OFF--
MMPH MMBL
YOU, UH, DON'T WANT TO KNOW WHAT HAPPENS TO MEN WHO LIE DOWN WITH AMAZONS.
IT'S NO MATTER. THE MERCHANTMAN TOLD ATLA WHERE TO FIND THE CHALICE. HE WAS INTENT ON HER JOINING HIM.
SHE CAN BE QUITE THE CHARMER.
ACCORDING TO THE COORDINATES LISTED, IT'S IN THE MIDDLE OF THE MEDITERRANEAN.

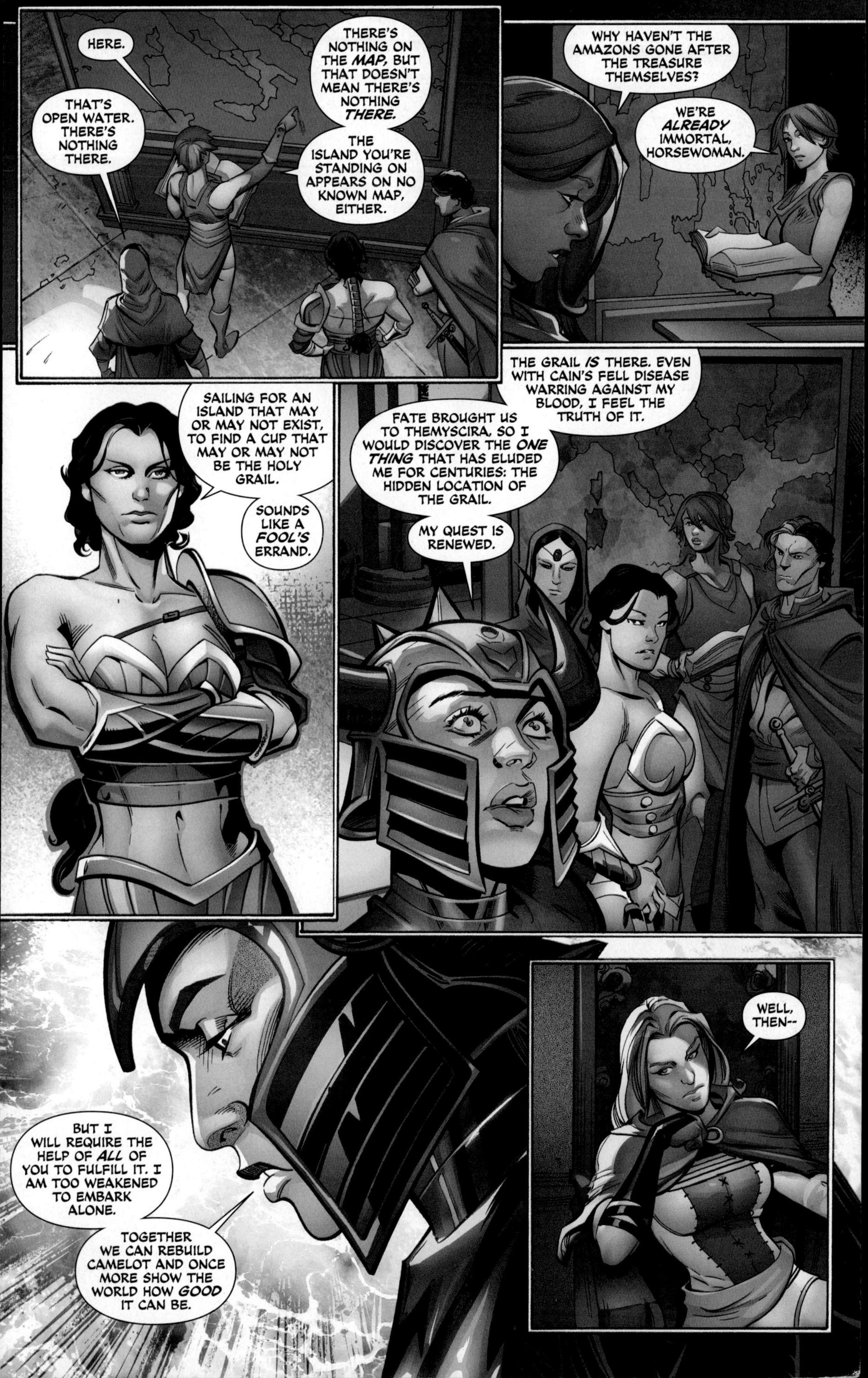
HERE.
THAT'S OPEN WATER. THERE'S NOTHING THERE.
THERE'S NOTHING ON THE *MAP*, BUT THAT DOESN'T MEAN THERE'S NOTHING *THERE.*
THE ISLAND YOU'RE STANDING ON APPEARS ON NO KNOWN MAP, EITHER.
WHY HAVEN'T THE AMAZONS GONE AFTER THE TREASURE THEMSELVES?
WE'RE *ALREADY* IMMORTAL, HORSEWOMAN.
SAILING FOR AN ISLAND THAT MAY OR MAY NOT EXIST, TO FIND A CUP THAT MAY OR MAY NOT BE THE HOLY GRAIL.
SOUNDS LIKE A *FOOL'S* ERRAND.
THE GRAIL *IS* THERE. EVEN WITH CAIN'S FELL DISEASE WARRING AGAINST MY BLOOD, I FEEL THE TRUTH OF IT.
FATE BROUGHT US TO THEMYSCIRA, SO I WOULD DISCOVER THE *ONE THING* THAT HAS ELUDED ME FOR CENTURIES: THE HIDDEN LOCATION OF THE GRAIL.
MY QUEST IS RENEWED.
BUT I WILL REQUIRE THE HELP OF *ALL* OF YOU TO FULFILL IT. I AM TOO WEAKENED TO EMBARK ALONE.
TOGETHER WE CAN REBUILD CAMELOT AND ONCE MORE SHOW THE WORLD HOW *GOOD* IT CAN BE.
WELL, THEN--

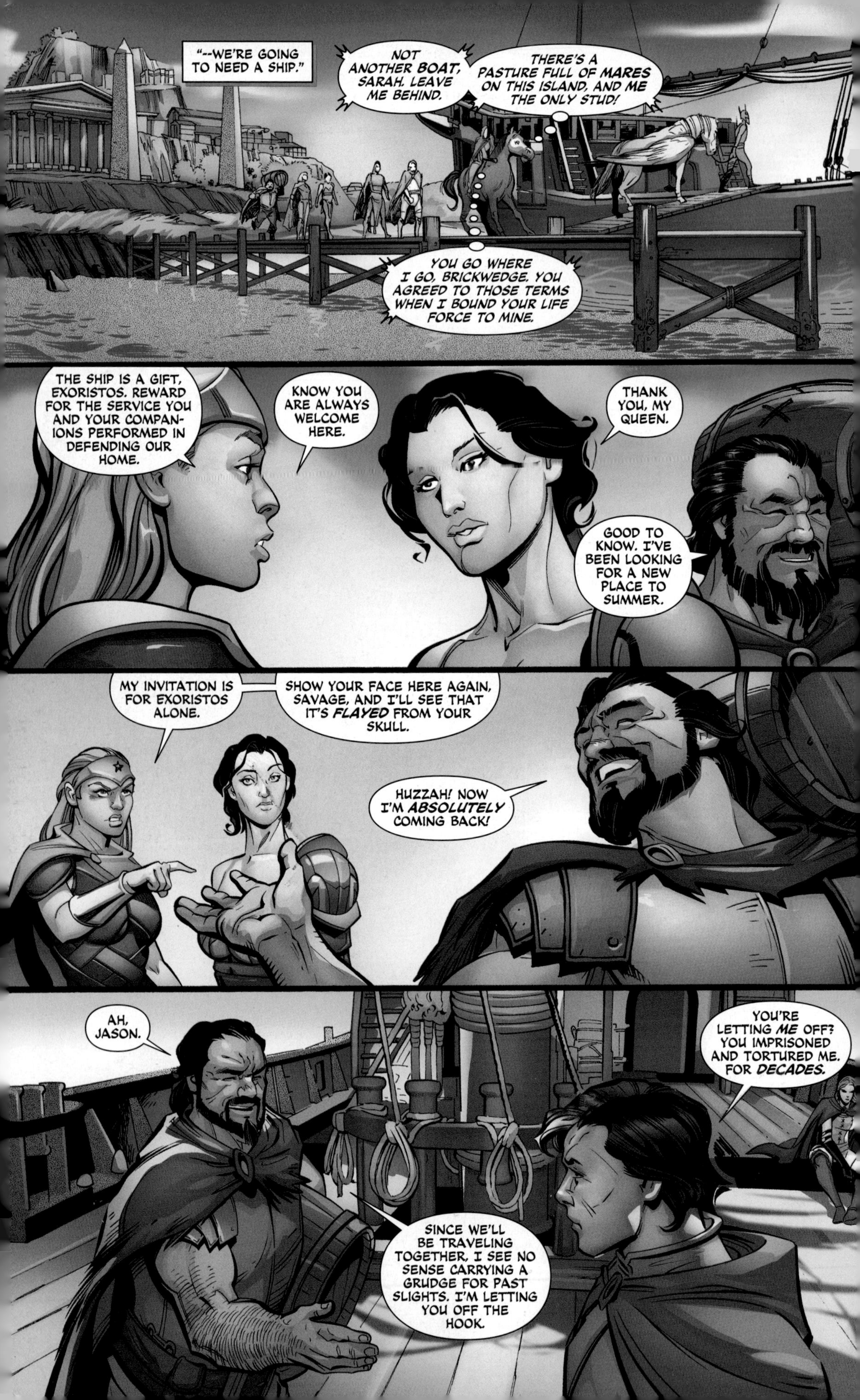
"--WE'RE GOING TO NEED A SHIP."
NOT ANOTHER BOAT, SARAH. LEAVE ME BEHIND.
THERE'S A PASTURE FULL OF MARES ON THIS ISLAND, AND ME THE ONLY STUD!
YOU GO WHERE I GO, BRICKWEDGE. YOU AGREED TO THOSE TERMS WHEN I BOUND YOUR LIFE FORCE TO MINE.
THE SHIP IS A GIFT, EXORISTOS. REWARD FOR THE SERVICE YOU AND YOUR COMPANIONS PERFORMED IN DEFENDING OUR HOME.
KNOW YOU ARE ALWAYS WELCOME HERE.
THANK YOU, MY QUEEN.
GOOD TO KNOW. I'VE BEEN LOOKING FOR A NEW PLACE TO SUMMER.
MY INVITATION IS FOR EXORISTOS ALONE.
SHOW YOUR FACE HERE AGAIN, SAVAGE, AND I'LL SEE THAT IT'S FLAYED FROM YOUR SKULL.
HUZZAH! NOW I'M ABSOLUTELY COMING BACK!
AH, JASON.
SINCE WE'LL BE TRAVELING TOGETHER, I SEE NO SENSE CARRYING A GRUDGE FOR PAST SLIGHTS. I'M LETTING YOU OFF THE HOOK.
YOU'RE LETTING ME OFF? YOU IMPRISONED AND TORTURED ME. FOR DECADES.

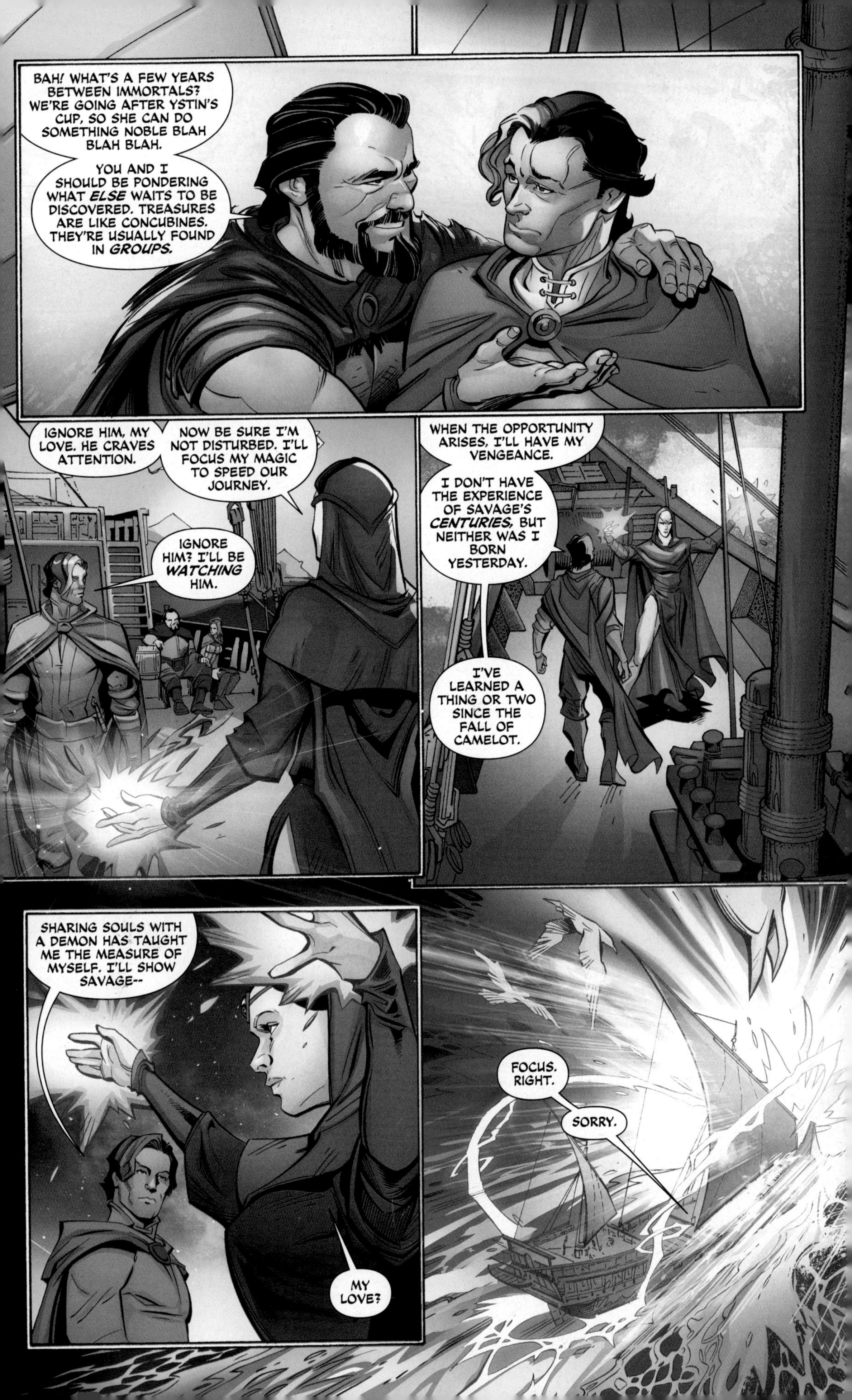
BAH! WHAT'S A FEW YEARS BETWEEN IMMORTALS? WE'RE GOING AFTER YSTIN'S CUP, SO SHE CAN DO SOMETHING NOBLE BLAH BLAH BLAH.
YOU AND I SHOULD BE PONDERING WHAT *ELSE* WAITS TO BE DISCOVERED. TREASURES ARE LIKE CONCUBINES. THEY'RE USUALLY FOUND IN *GROUPS.*
IGNORE HIM, MY LOVE. HE CRAVES ATTENTION.
NOW BE SURE I'M NOT DISTURBED. I'LL FOCUS MY MAGIC TO SPEED OUR JOURNEY.
IGNORE HIM? I'LL BE *WATCHING* HIM.
WHEN THE OPPORTUNITY ARISES, I'LL HAVE MY VENGEANCE.
I DON'T HAVE THE EXPERIENCE OF SAVAGE'S *CENTURIES,* BUT NEITHER WAS I BORN YESTERDAY.
I'VE LEARNED A THING OR TWO SINCE THE FALL OF CAMELOT.
SHARING SOULS WITH A DEMON HAS TAUGHT ME THE MEASURE OF MYSELF. I'LL SHOW SAVAGE--
MY LOVE?
FOCUS. RIGHT.
SORRY.

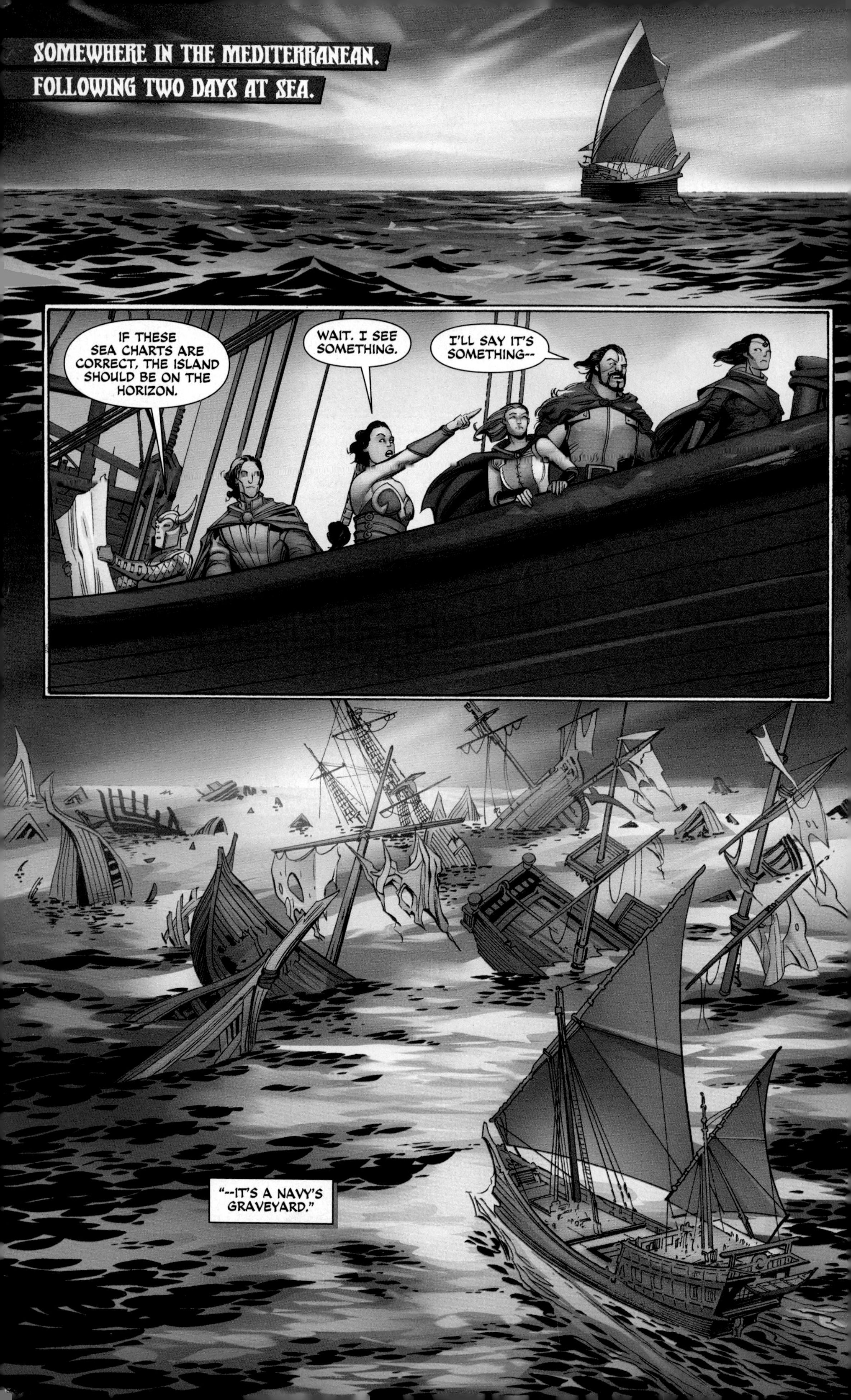
SOMEWHERE IN THE MEDITERRANEAN.
FOLLOWING TWO DAYS AT SEA.
IF THESE SEA CHARTS ARE CORRECT, THE ISLAND SHOULD BE ON THE HORIZON.
WAIT. I SEE SOMETHING.
I'LL SAY IT'S SOMETHING--
"--IT'S A NAVY'S GRAVEYARD."

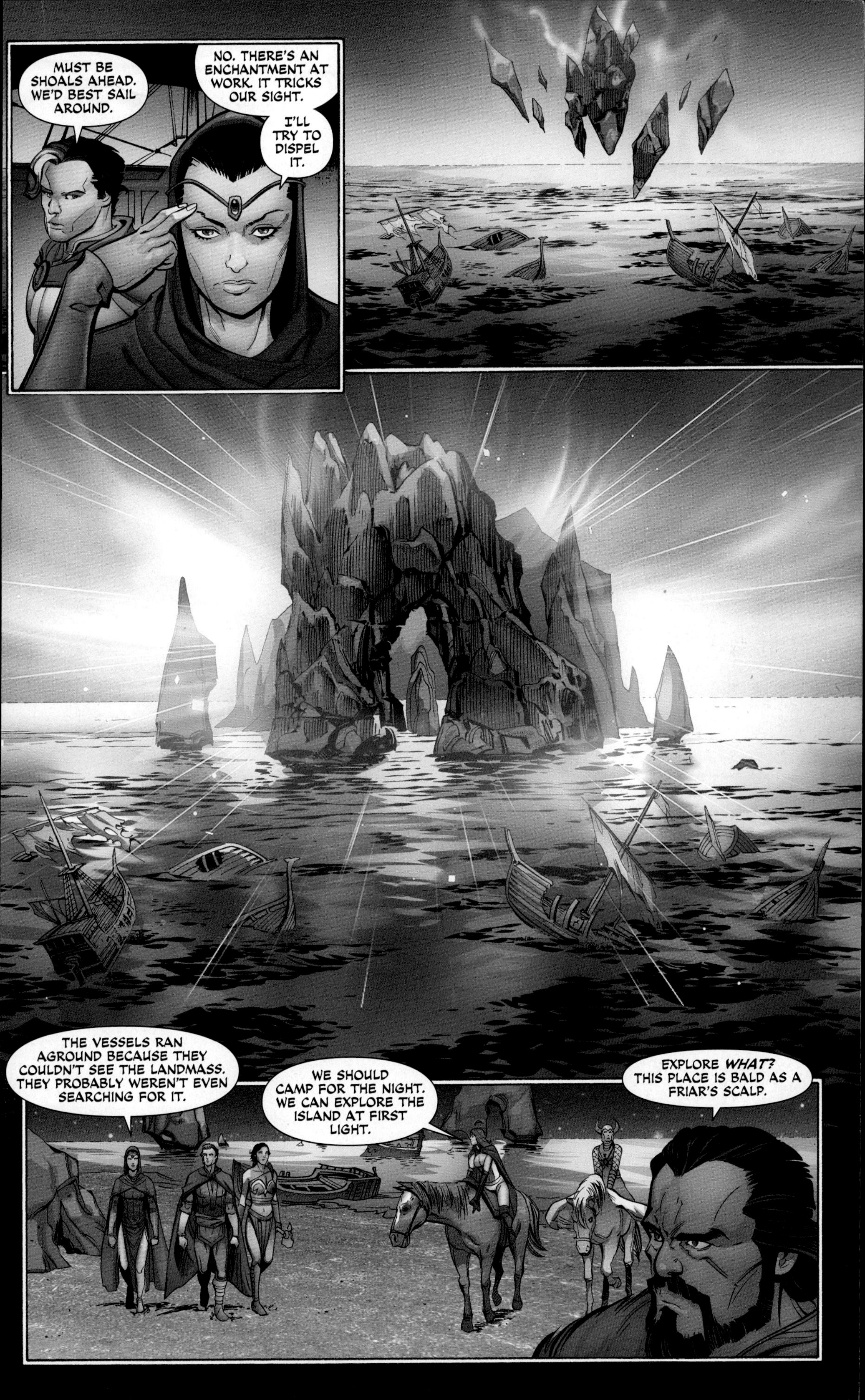
MUST BE SHOALS AHEAD. WE'D BEST SAIL AROUND.
NO. THERE'S AN ENCHANTMENT AT WORK. IT TRICKS OUR SIGHT.
I'LL TRY TO DISPEL IT.
THE VESSELS RAN AGROUND BECAUSE THEY COULDN'T SEE THE LANDMASS. THEY PROBABLY WEREN'T EVEN SEARCHING FOR IT.
WE SHOULD CAMP FOR THE NIGHT. WE CAN EXPLORE THE ISLAND AT FIRST LIGHT.
EXPLORE *WHAT?* THIS PLACE IS BALD AS A FRIAR'S SCALP.

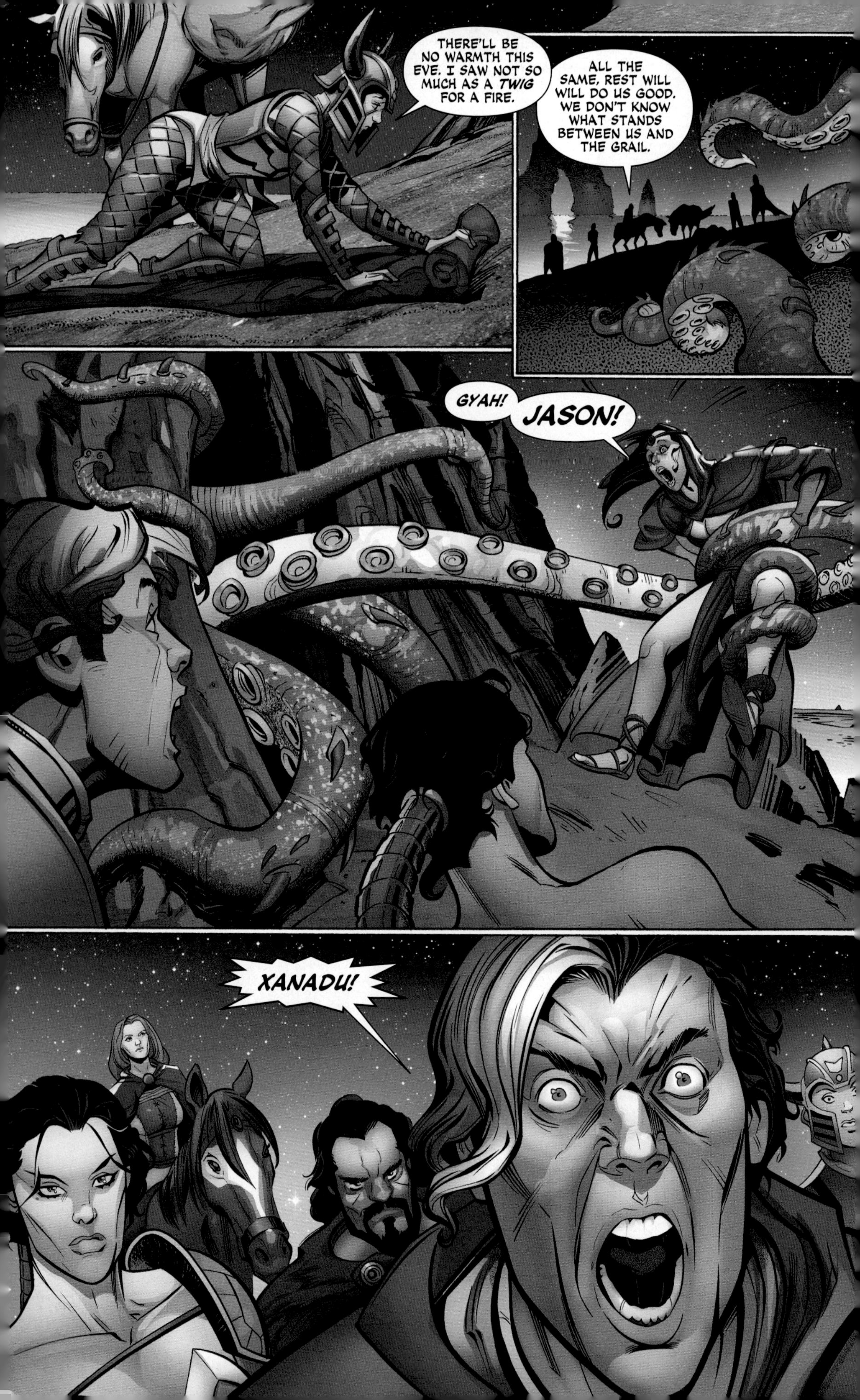
THERE'LL BE NO WARMTH THIS EVE. I SAW NOT SO MUCH AS A *TWIG* FOR A FIRE.
ALL THE SAME, REST WILL WILL DO US GOOD. WE DON'T KNOW WHAT STANDS BETWEEN US AND THE GRAIL.
GYAH!
JASON!
XANADU!

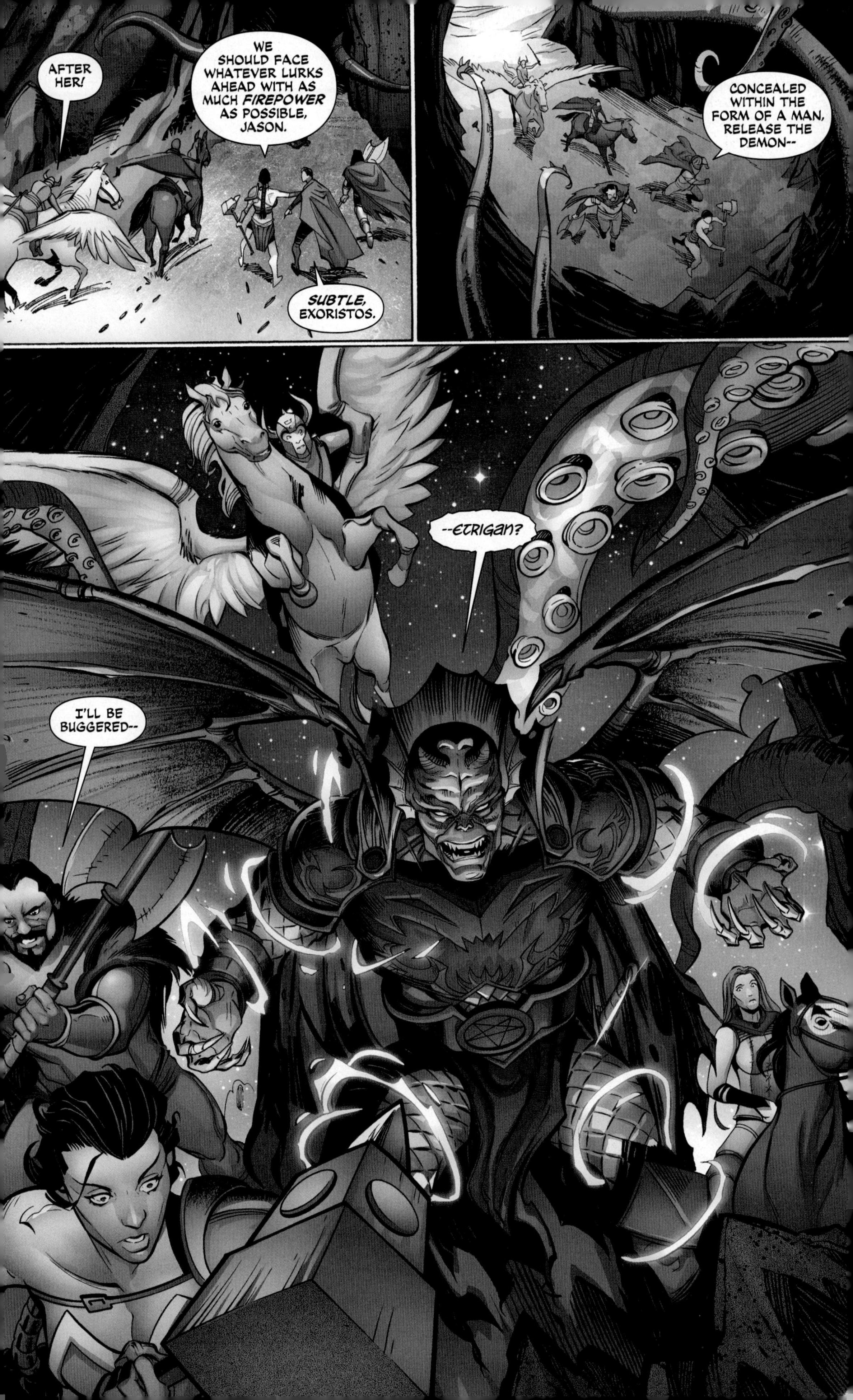
AFTER HER!
WE SHOULD FACE WHATEVER LURKS AHEAD WITH AS MUCH *FIREPOWER* AS POSSIBLE, JASON.
SUBTLE, EXORISTOS.
CONCEALED WITHIN THE FORM OF A MAN, RELEASE THE DEMON--
--ETRIGAN?
I'LL BE BUGGERED--

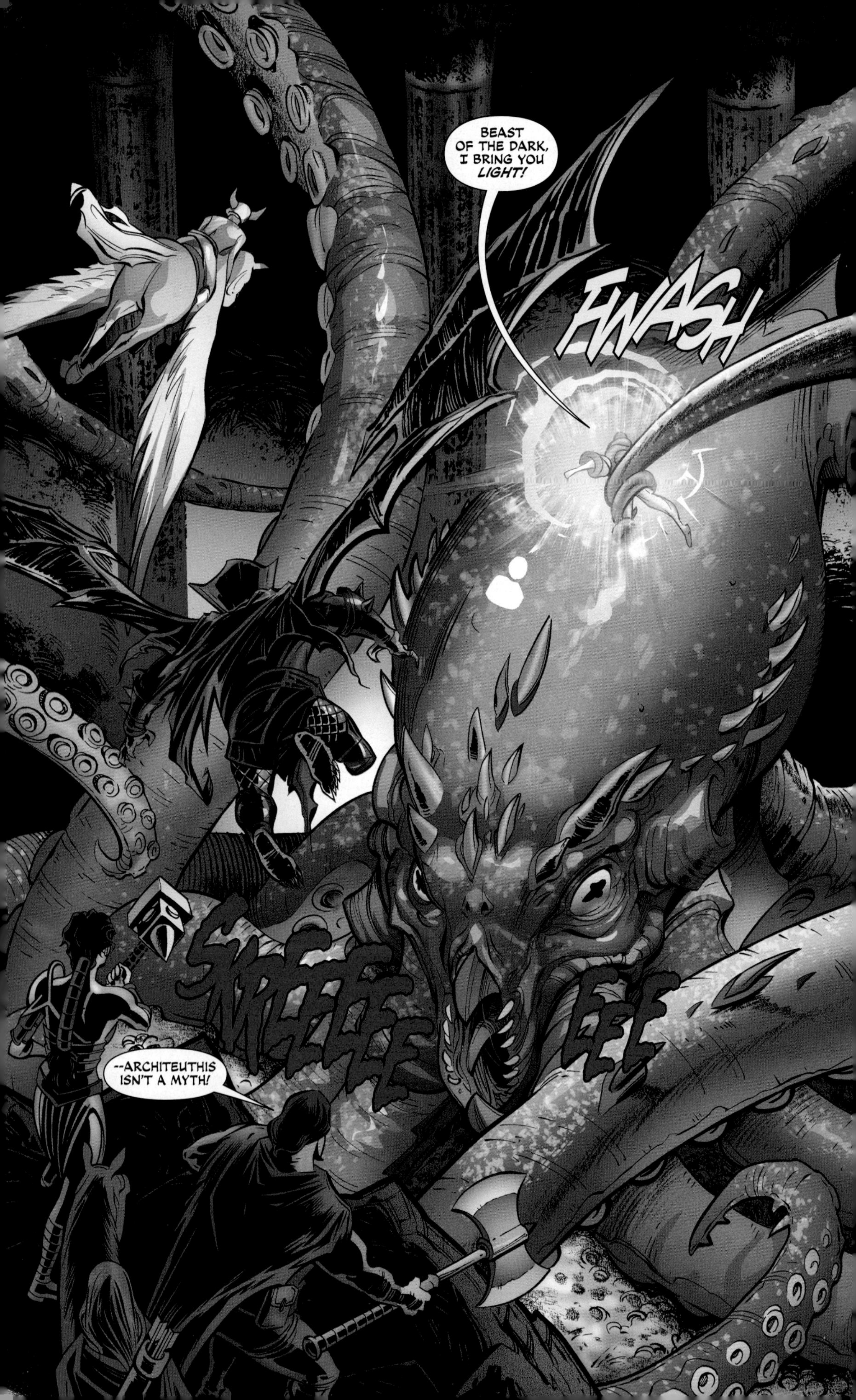
BEAST OF THE DARK, I BRING YOU *LIGHT!*
FWASH
SKREEEEEEE
--ARCHITEUTHIS ISN'T A MYTH!

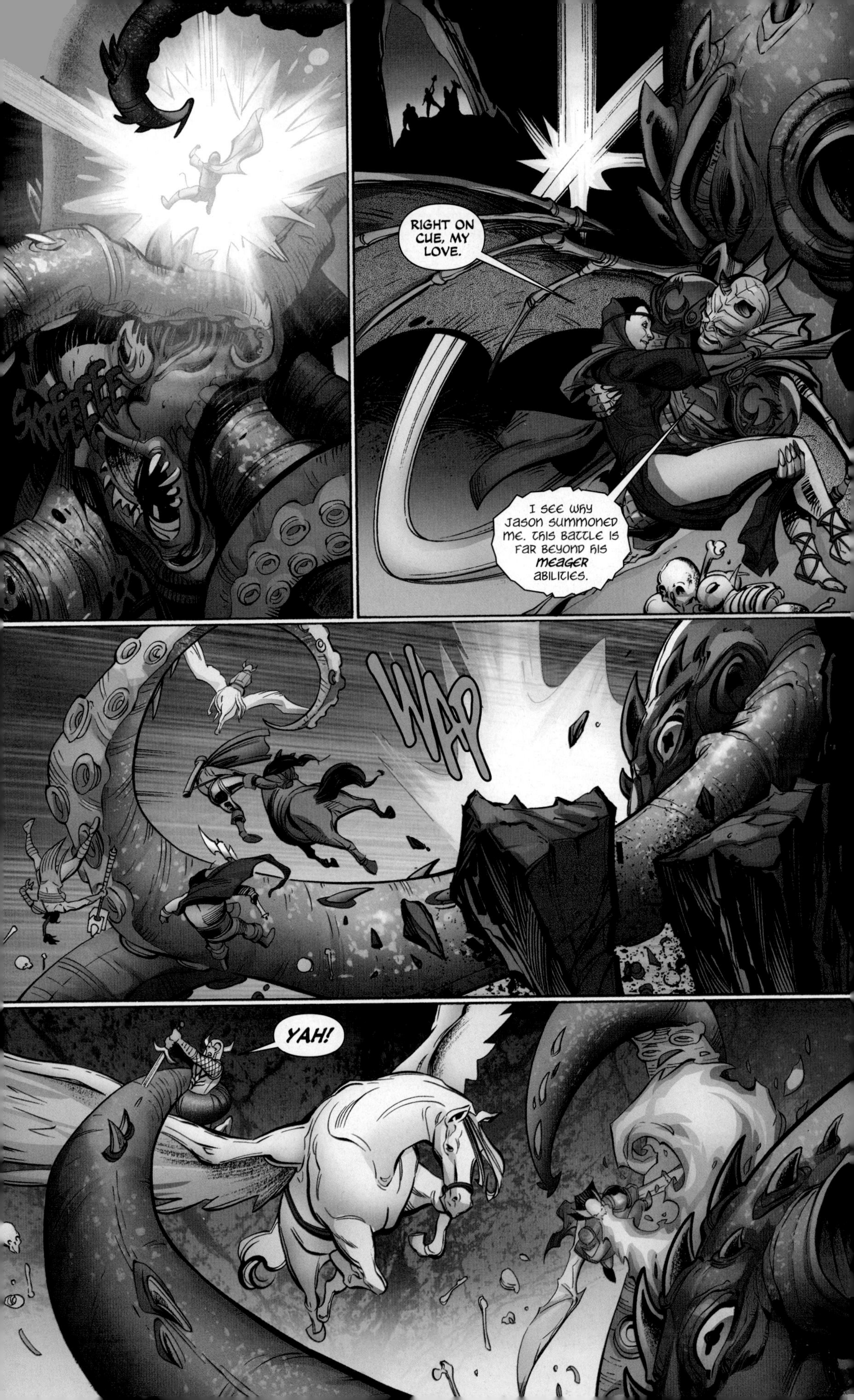
SKREEEE
RIGHT ON CUE, MY LOVE.
I SEE WHY JASON SUMMONED ME. THIS BATTLE IS FAR BEYOND HIS MEAGER ABILITIES.
WAP
YAH!

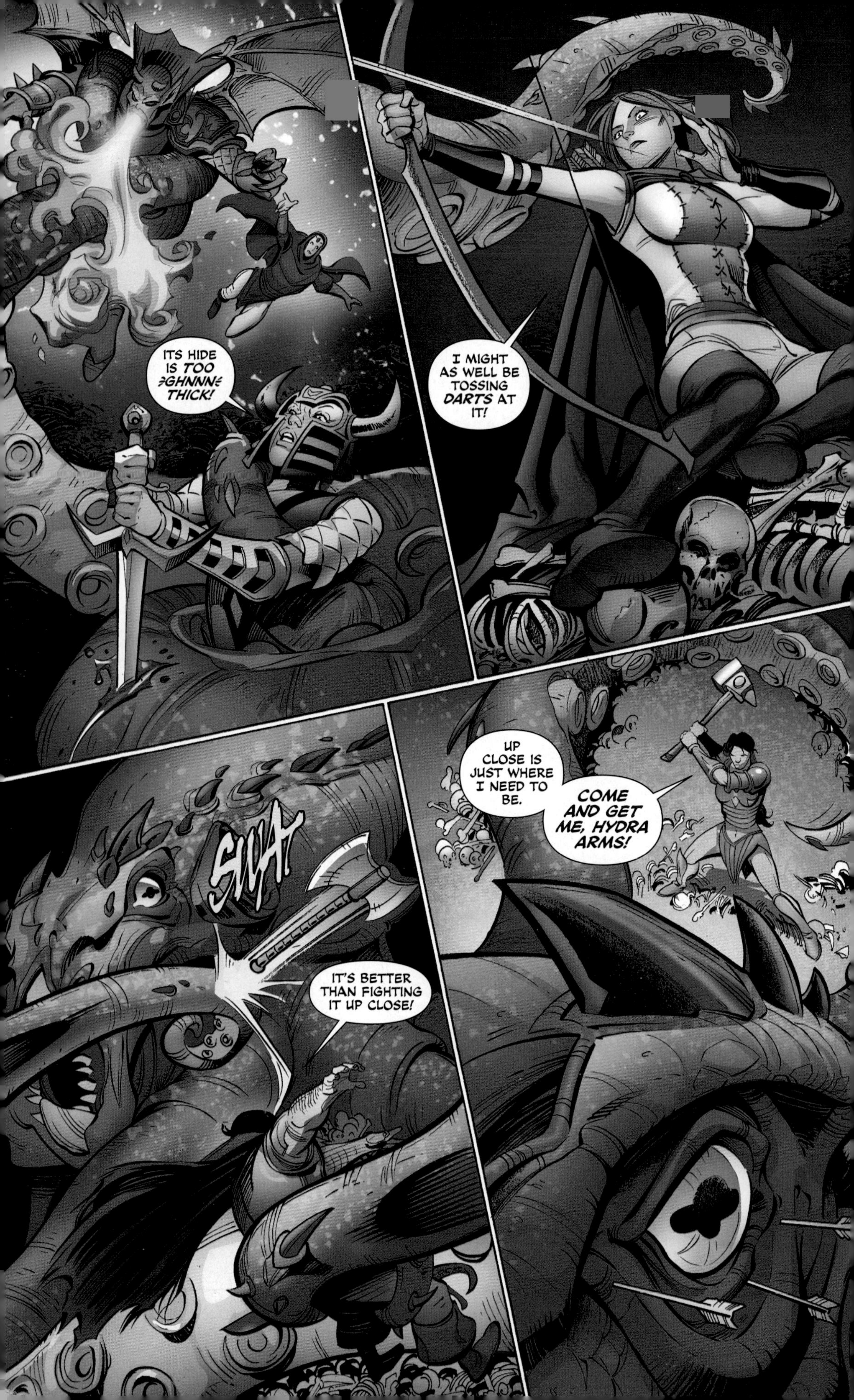
ITS HIDE IS TOO GHNNN THICK!
I MIGHT AS WELL BE TOSSING DARTS AT IT!
IT'S BETTER THAN FIGHTING IT UP CLOSE!
UP CLOSE IS JUST WHERE I NEED TO BE.
COME AND GET ME, HYDRA ARMS!

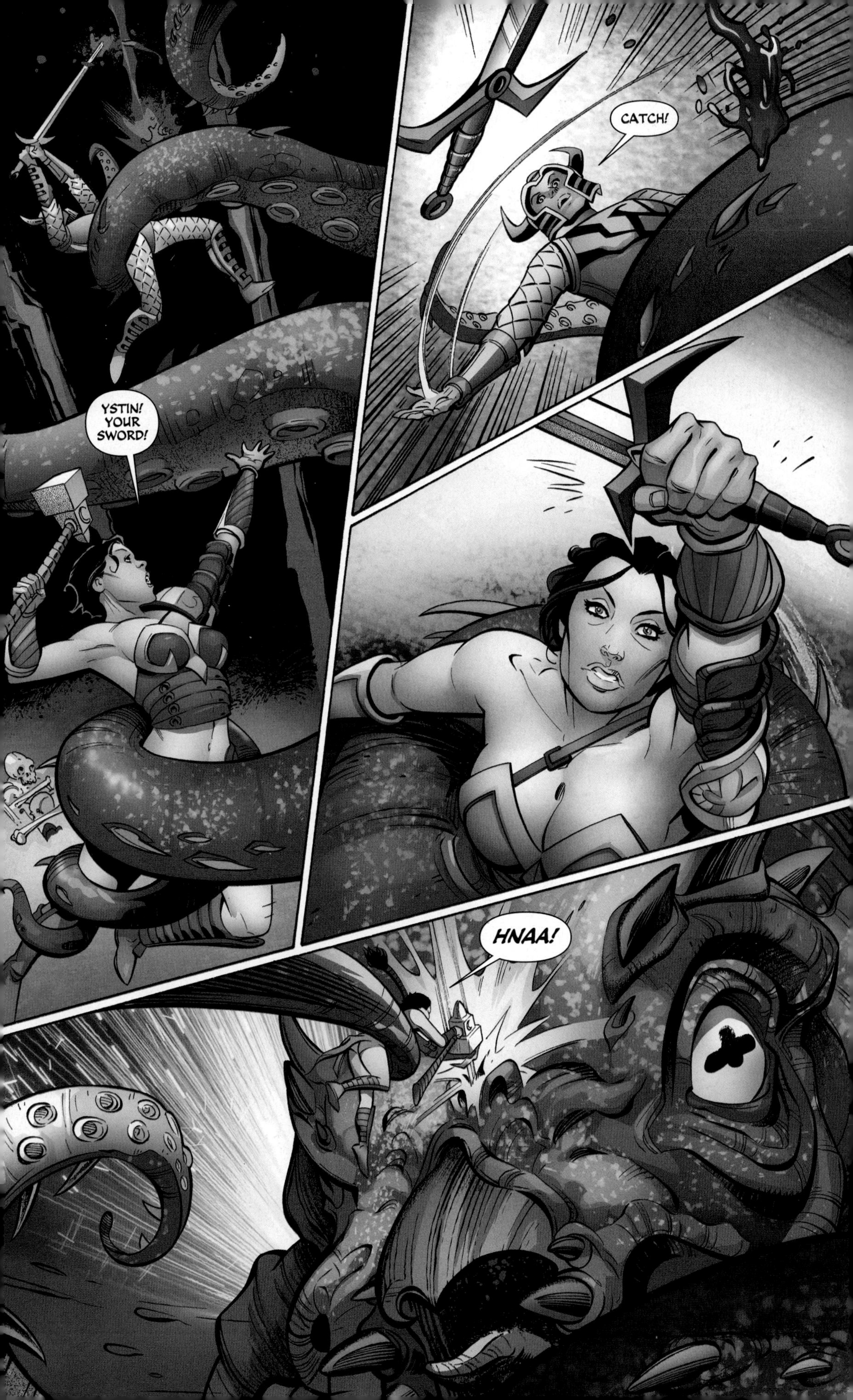
CATCH!
YSTIN! YOUR SWORD!
HNAA!

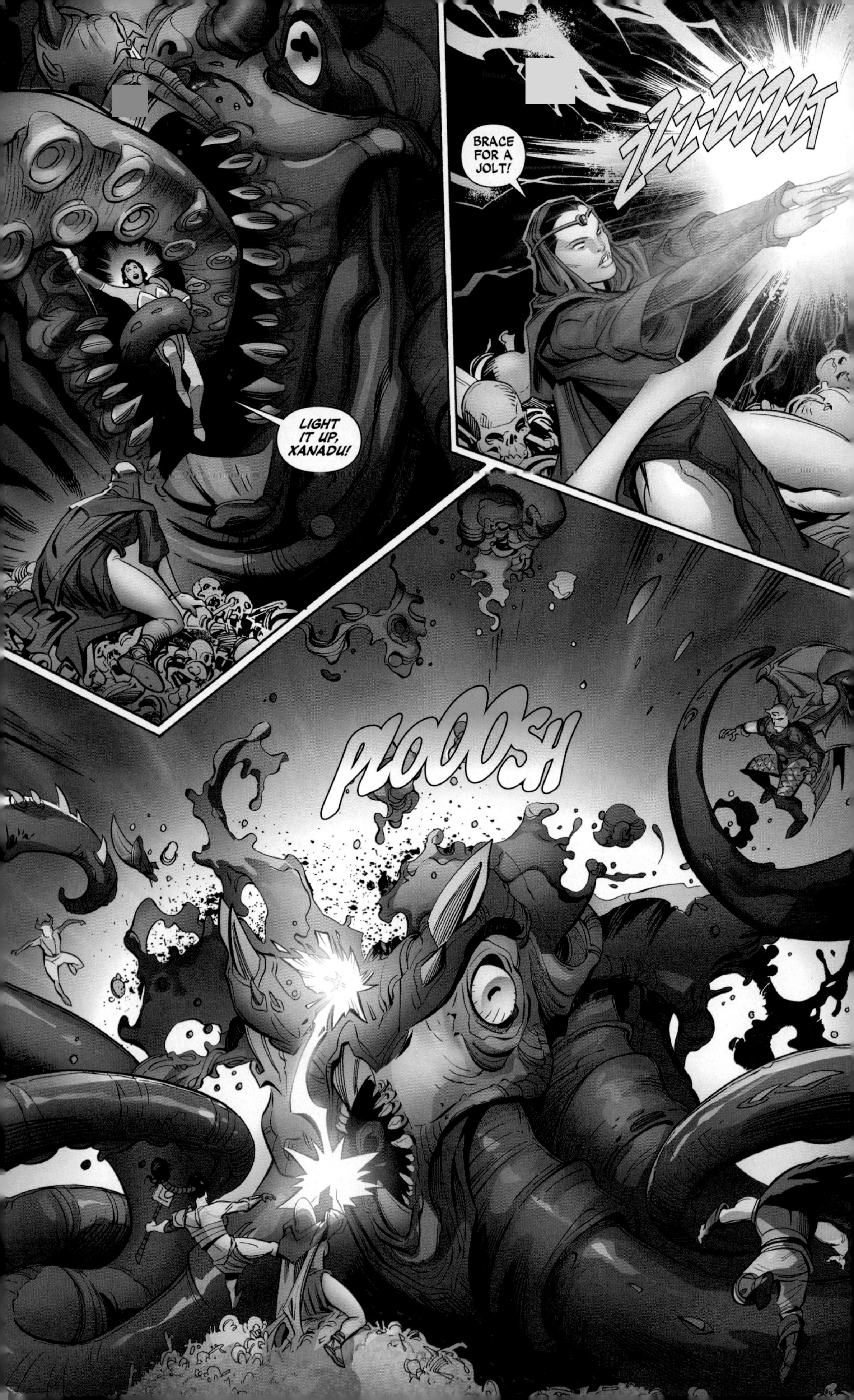
LIGHT IT UP, XANADU!
BRACE FOR A JOLT!
ZZ-ZZZZT

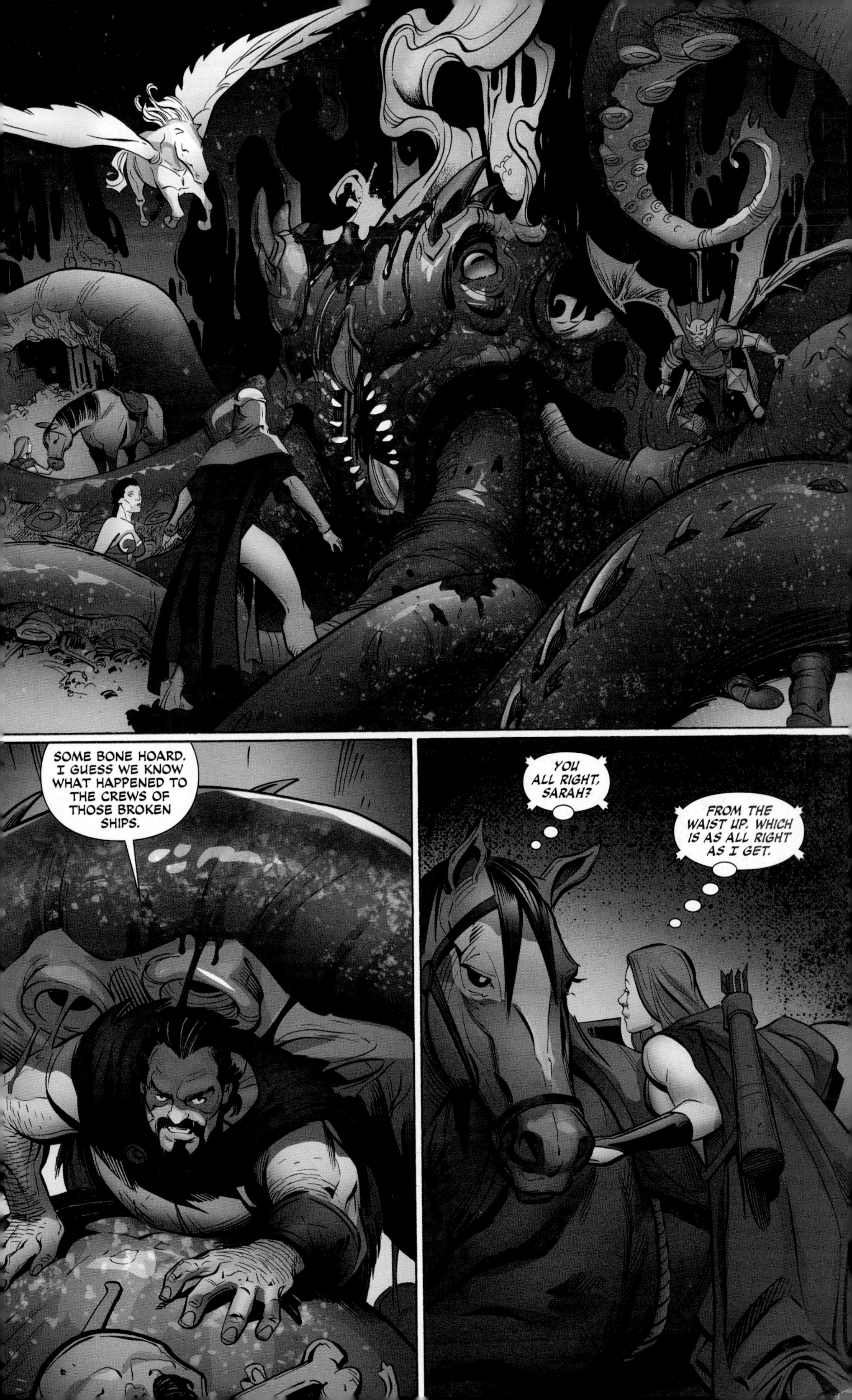
SOME BONE HOARD. I GUESS WE KNOW WHAT HAPPENED TO THE CREWS OF THOSE BROKEN SHIPS.
YOU ALL RIGHT, SARAH?
FROM THE WAIST UP. WHICH IS AS ALL RIGHT AS I GET.

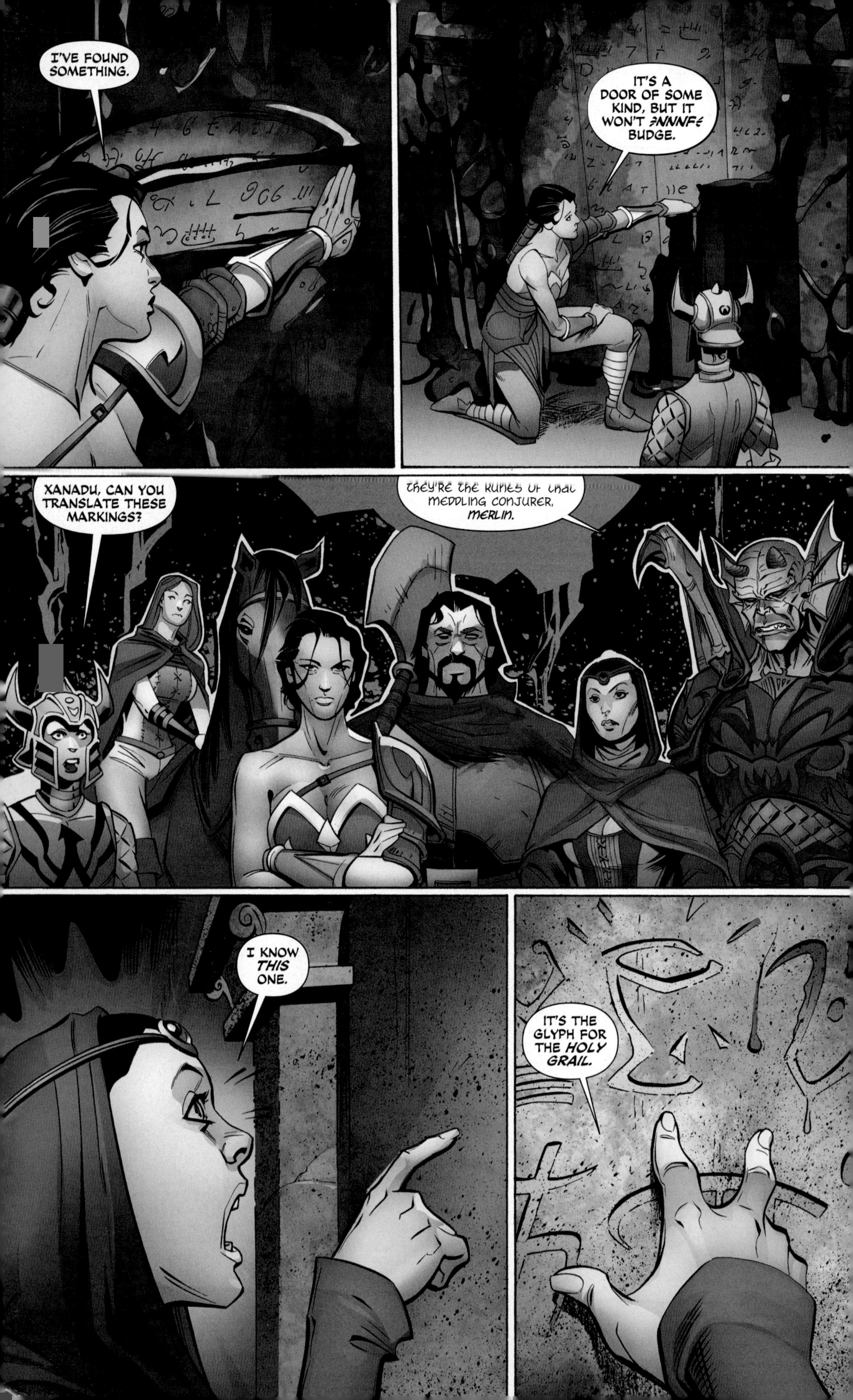
I'VE FOUND SOMETHING.
IT'S A DOOR OF SOME KIND, BUT IT WON'T ƎNNNF€ BUDGE.
XANADU, CAN YOU TRANSLATE THESE MARKINGS?
THEY'RE THE RUNES OF THAT MEDDLING CONJURER, *MERLIN.*
I KNOW *THIS* ONE.
IT'S THE GLYPH FOR THE *HOLY GRAIL.*

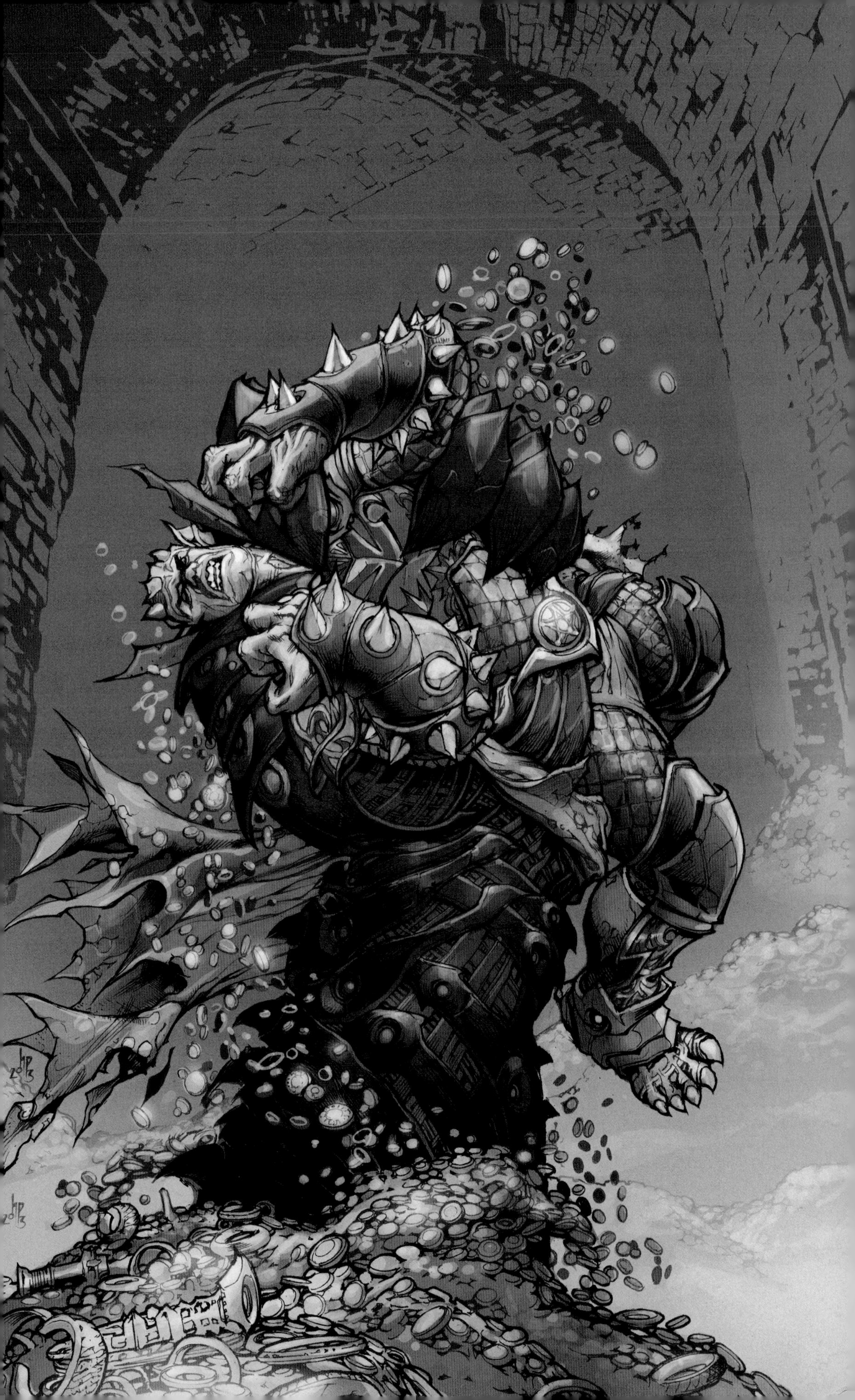

ROBERT VENDITTI
writer

CHAD HARDIN
penciller

CHAD HARDIN
WAYNE FAUCHER
inkers

HOWARD PORTER
cover artist

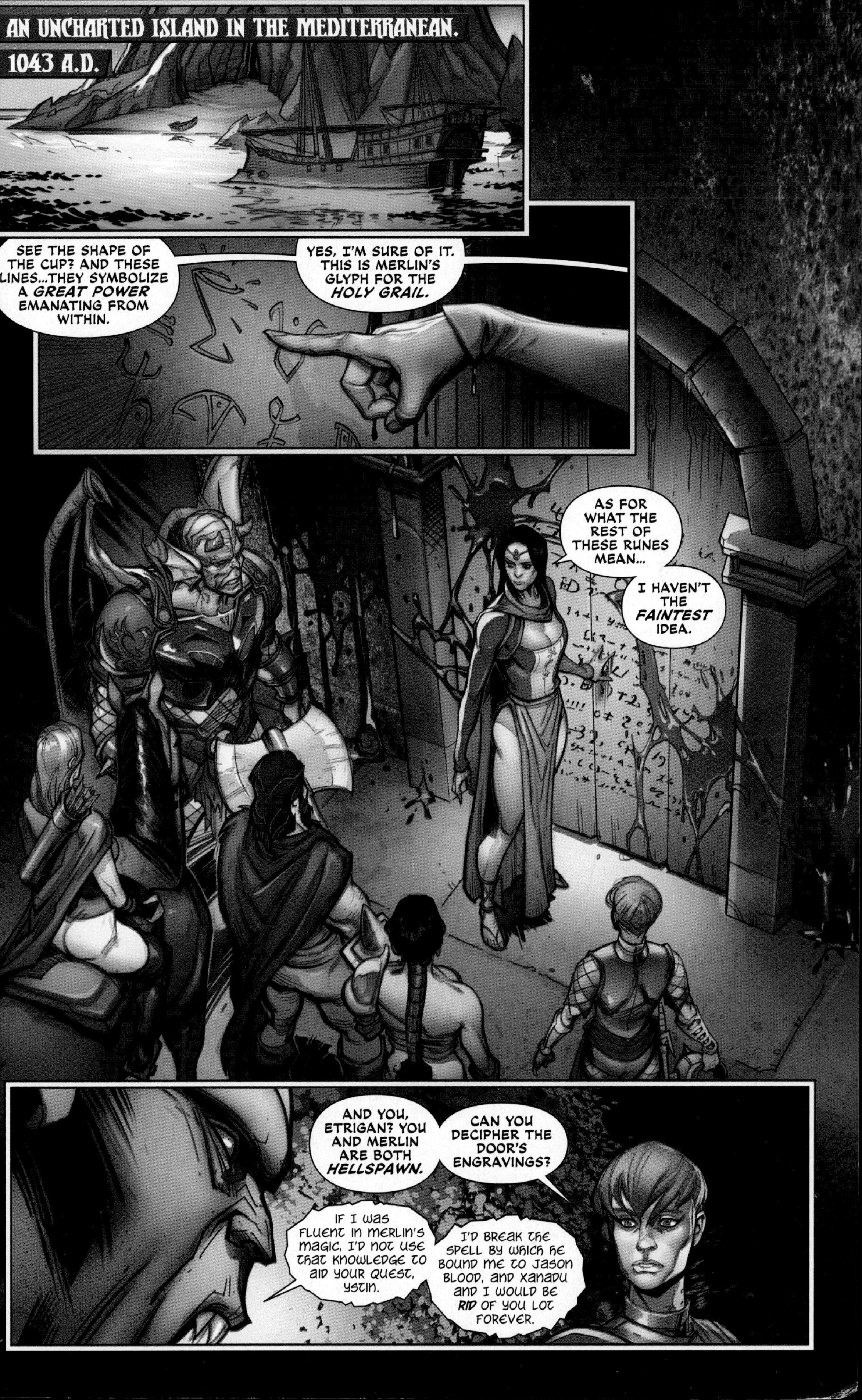
AN UNCHARTED ISLAND IN THE MEDITERRANEAN.
1043 A.D.
SEE THE SHAPE OF THE CUP? AND THESE LINES...THEY SYMBOLIZE A GREAT POWER EMANATING FROM WITHIN.
YES, I'M SURE OF IT. THIS IS MERLIN'S GLYPH FOR THE HOLY GRAIL.
AS FOR WHAT THE REST OF THESE RUNES MEAN...
I HAVEN'T THE FAINTEST IDEA.
AND YOU, ETRIGAN? YOU AND MERLIN ARE BOTH HELLSPAWN.
CAN YOU DECIPHER THE DOOR'S ENGRAVINGS?
IF I WAS FLUENT IN MERLIN'S MAGIC, I'D NOT USE THAT KNOWLEDGE TO AID YOUR QUEST, YSTIN.
I'D BREAK THE SPELL BY WHICH HE BOUND ME TO JASON BLOOD, AND XANADU AND I WOULD BE RID OF YOU LOT FOREVER.

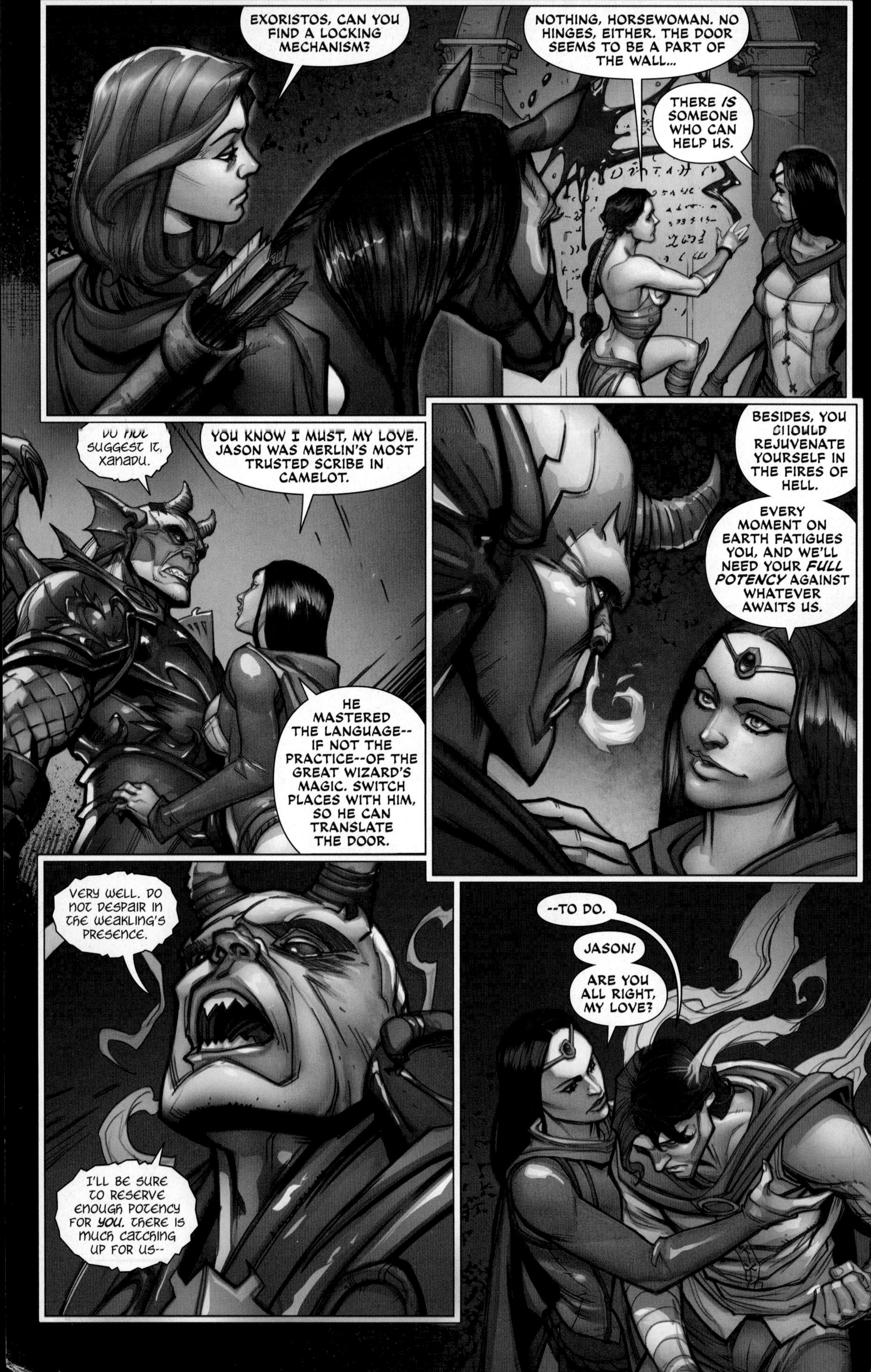
EXORISTOS, CAN YOU FIND A LOCKING MECHANISM?
NOTHING, HORSEWOMAN. NO HINGES, EITHER. THE DOOR SEEMS TO BE A PART OF THE WALL...
THERE *IS* SOMEONE WHO CAN HELP US.
SUGGEST IT, XANADU.
YOU KNOW I MUST, MY LOVE. JASON WAS MERLIN'S MOST TRUSTED SCRIBE IN CAMELOT.
HE MASTERED THE LANGUAGE--IF NOT THE PRACTICE--OF THE GREAT WIZARD'S MAGIC. SWITCH PLACES WITH HIM, SO HE CAN TRANSLATE THE DOOR.
BESIDES, YOU SHOULD REJUVENATE YOURSELF IN THE FIRES OF HELL.
EVERY MOMENT ON EARTH FATIGUES YOU, AND WE'LL NEED YOUR ***FULL POTENCY*** AGAINST WHATEVER AWAITS US.
VERY WELL. DO NOT DESPAIR IN THE WEAKLING'S PRESENCE.
I'LL BE SURE TO RESERVE ENOUGH POTENCY FOR ***YOU.*** THERE IS MUCH CATCHING UP FOR US--
--TO DO.
JASON!
ARE YOU ALL RIGHT, MY LOVE?

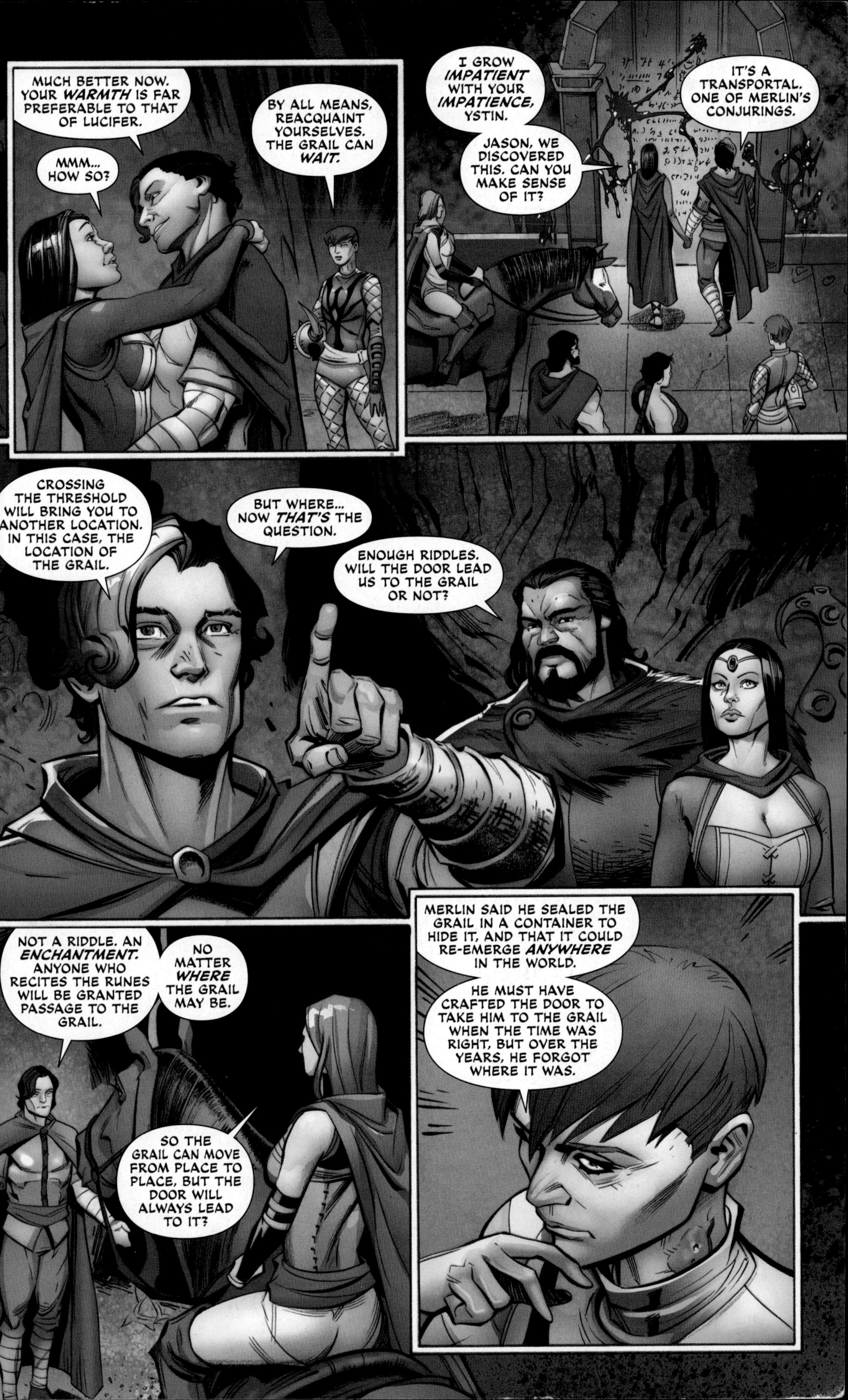
MUCH BETTER NOW. YOUR *WARMTH* IS FAR PREFERABLE TO THAT OF LUCIFER.
MMM... HOW SO?
BY ALL MEANS, REACQUAINT YOURSELVES. THE GRAIL CAN *WAIT.*
I GROW *IMPATIENT* WITH YOUR *IMPATIENCE,* YSTIN.
JASON, WE DISCOVERED THIS. CAN YOU MAKE SENSE OF IT?
IT'S A TRANSPORTAL. ONE OF MERLIN'S CONJURINGS.
CROSSING THE THRESHOLD WILL BRING YOU TO ANOTHER LOCATION. IN THIS CASE, THE LOCATION OF THE GRAIL.
BUT WHERE... NOW *THAT'S* THE QUESTION.
ENOUGH RIDDLES. WILL THE DOOR LEAD US TO THE GRAIL OR NOT?
NOT A RIDDLE. AN *ENCHANTMENT.* ANYONE WHO RECITES THE RUNES WILL BE GRANTED PASSAGE TO THE GRAIL.
NO MATTER *WHERE* THE GRAIL MAY BE.
SO THE GRAIL CAN MOVE FROM PLACE TO PLACE, BUT THE DOOR WILL ALWAYS LEAD TO IT?
MERLIN SAID HE SEALED THE GRAIL IN A CONTAINER TO HIDE IT, AND THAT IT COULD RE-EMERGE *ANYWHERE* IN THE WORLD.
HE MUST HAVE CRAFTED THE DOOR TO TAKE HIM TO THE GRAIL WHEN THE TIME WAS RIGHT, BUT OVER THE YEARS, HE FORGOT WHERE IT WAS.

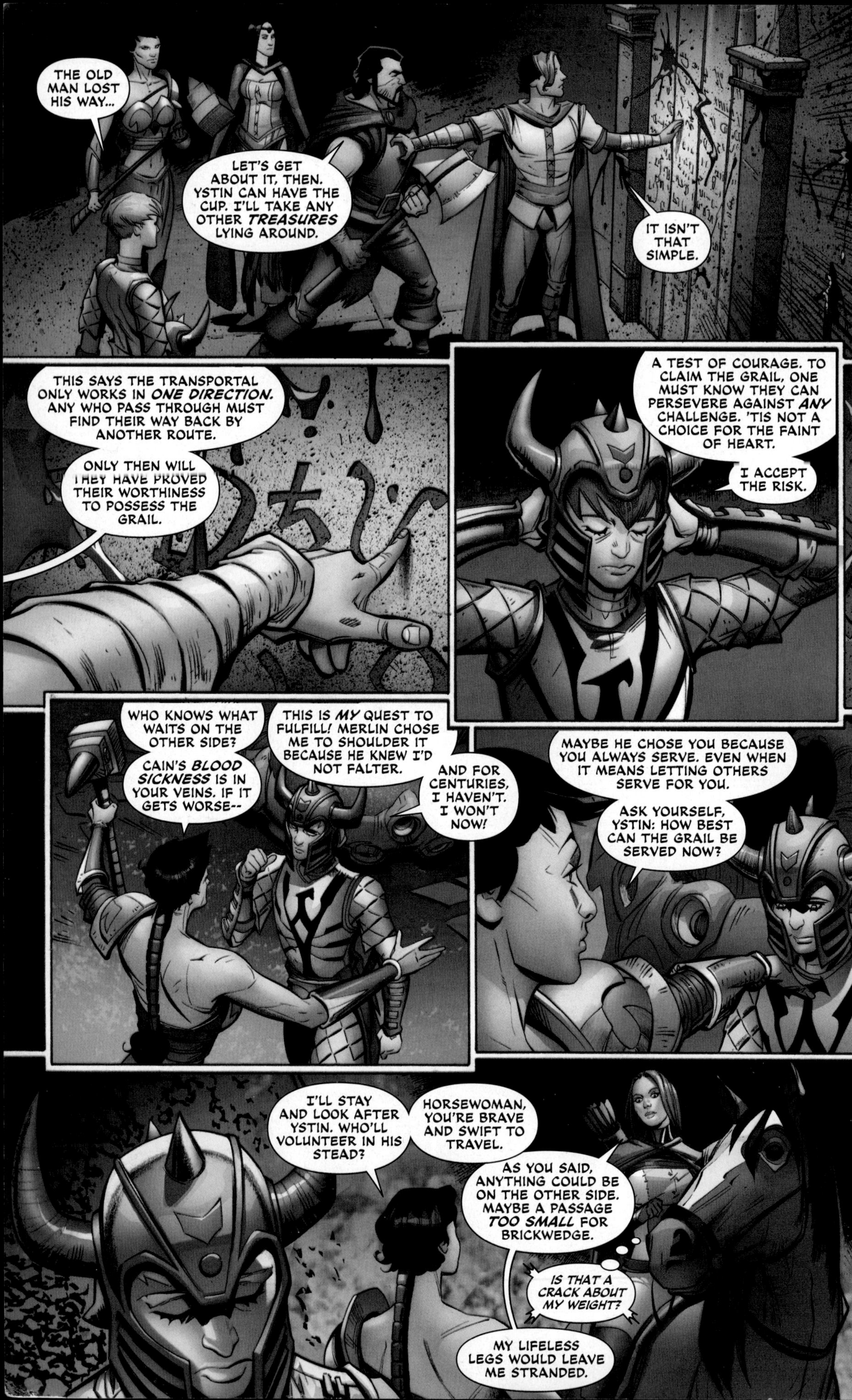
THE OLD MAN LOST HIS WAY...
LET'S GET ABOUT IT, THEN. YSTIN CAN HAVE THE CUP. I'LL TAKE ANY OTHER *TREASURES* LYING AROUND.
IT ISN'T THAT SIMPLE.
THIS SAYS THE TRANSPORTAL ONLY WORKS IN *ONE DIRECTION*. ANY WHO PASS THROUGH MUST FIND THEIR WAY BACK BY ANOTHER ROUTE.
ONLY THEN WILL THEY HAVE PROVED THEIR WORTHINESS TO POSSESS THE GRAIL.
A TEST OF COURAGE. TO CLAIM THE GRAIL, ONE MUST KNOW THEY CAN PERSEVERE AGAINST *ANY* CHALLENGE. 'TIS NOT A CHOICE FOR THE FAINT OF HEART.
I ACCEPT THE RISK.
WHO KNOWS WHAT WAITS ON THE OTHER SIDE?
CAIN'S *BLOOD SICKNESS* IS IN YOUR VEINS. IF IT GETS WORSE--
THIS IS *MY* QUEST TO FULFILL! MERLIN CHOSE ME TO SHOULDER IT BECAUSE HE KNEW I'D NOT FALTER.
AND FOR CENTURIES, I HAVEN'T. I WON'T NOW!
MAYBE HE CHOSE YOU BECAUSE YOU ALWAYS SERVE. EVEN WHEN IT MEANS LETTING OTHERS SERVE FOR YOU.
ASK YOURSELF, YSTIN: HOW BEST CAN THE GRAIL BE SERVED NOW?
I'LL STAY AND LOOK AFTER YSTIN. WHO'LL VOLUNTEER IN HIS STEAD?
HORSEWOMAN, YOU'RE BRAVE AND SWIFT TO TRAVEL.
AS YOU SAID, ANYTHING COULD BE ON THE OTHER SIDE. MAYBE A PASSAGE *TOO SMALL* FOR BRICKWEDGE.
IS THAT A CRACK ABOUT MY WEIGHT?
MY LIFELESS LEGS WOULD LEAVE ME STRANDED.

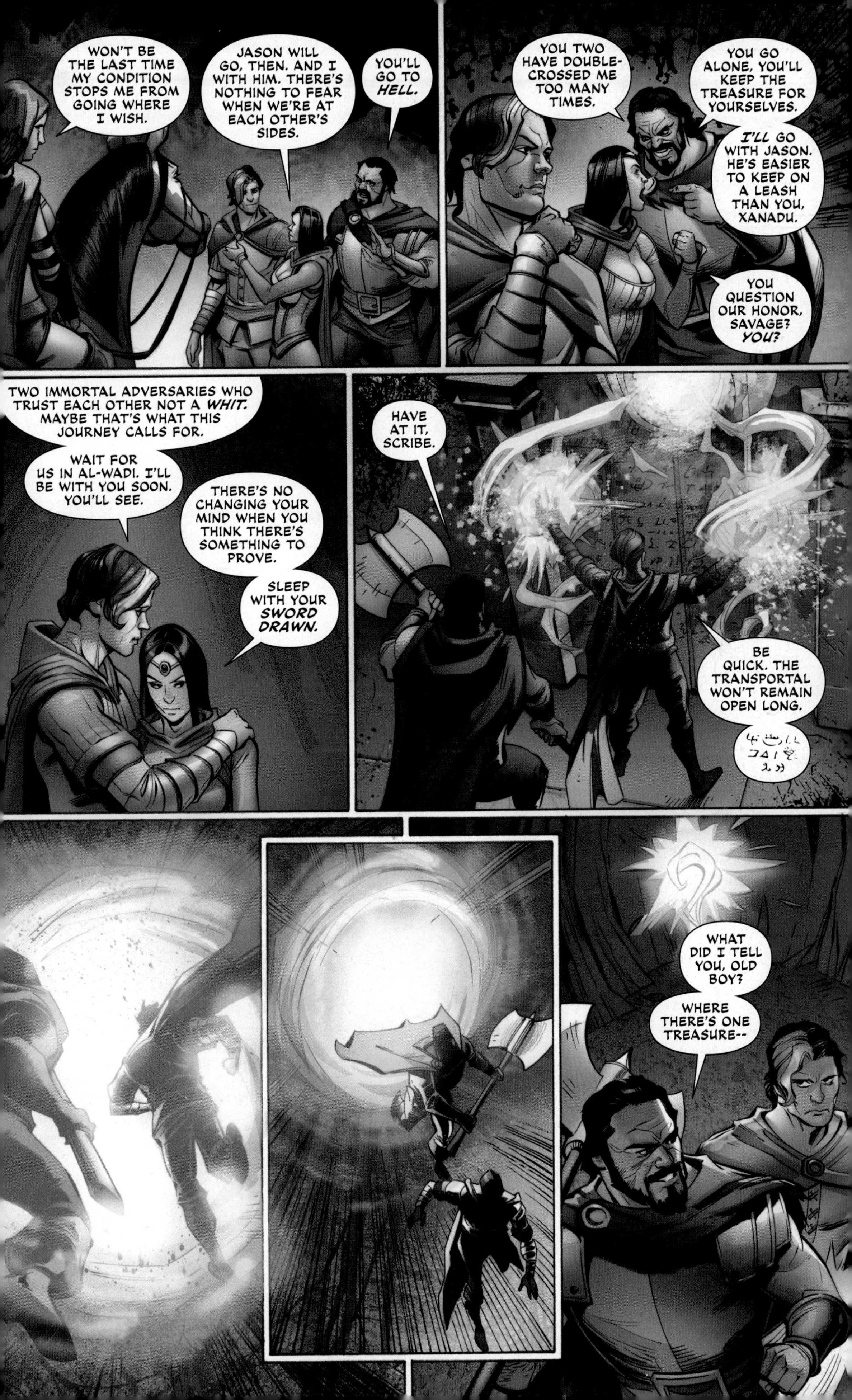
WON'T BE THE LAST TIME MY CONDITION STOPS ME FROM GOING WHERE I WISH.
JASON WILL GO, THEN. AND I WITH HIM. THERE'S NOTHING TO FEAR WHEN WE'RE AT EACH OTHER'S SIDES.
YOU'LL GO TO HELL.
YOU TWO HAVE DOUBLE-CROSSED ME TOO MANY TIMES.
YOU GO ALONE, YOU'LL KEEP THE TREASURE FOR YOURSELVES.
I'LL GO WITH JASON. HE'S EASIER TO KEEP ON A LEASH THAN YOU, XANADU.
YOU QUESTION OUR HONOR, SAVAGE? YOU?
TWO IMMORTAL ADVERSARIES WHO TRUST EACH OTHER NOT A WHIT. MAYBE THAT'S WHAT THIS JOURNEY CALLS FOR.
WAIT FOR US IN AL-WADI. I'LL BE WITH YOU SOON. YOU'LL SEE.
THERE'S NO CHANGING YOUR MIND WHEN YOU THINK THERE'S SOMETHING TO PROVE.
SLEEP WITH YOUR SWORD DRAWN.
HAVE AT IT, SCRIBE.
BE QUICK. THE TRANSPORTAL WON'T REMAIN OPEN LONG.
WHAT DID I TELL YOU, OLD BOY?
WHERE THERE'S ONE TREASURE--

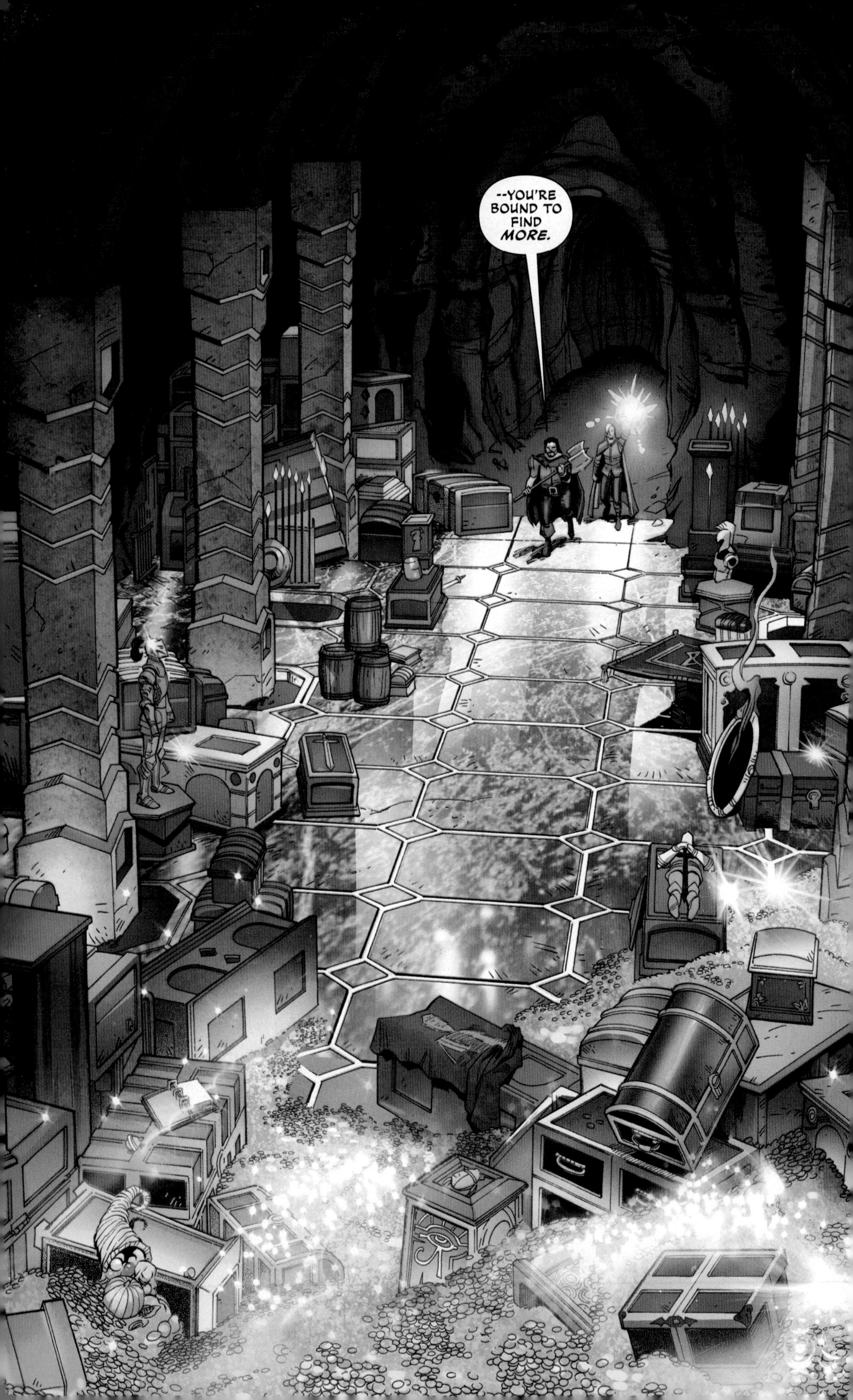
--YOU'RE BOUND TO FIND *MORE.*

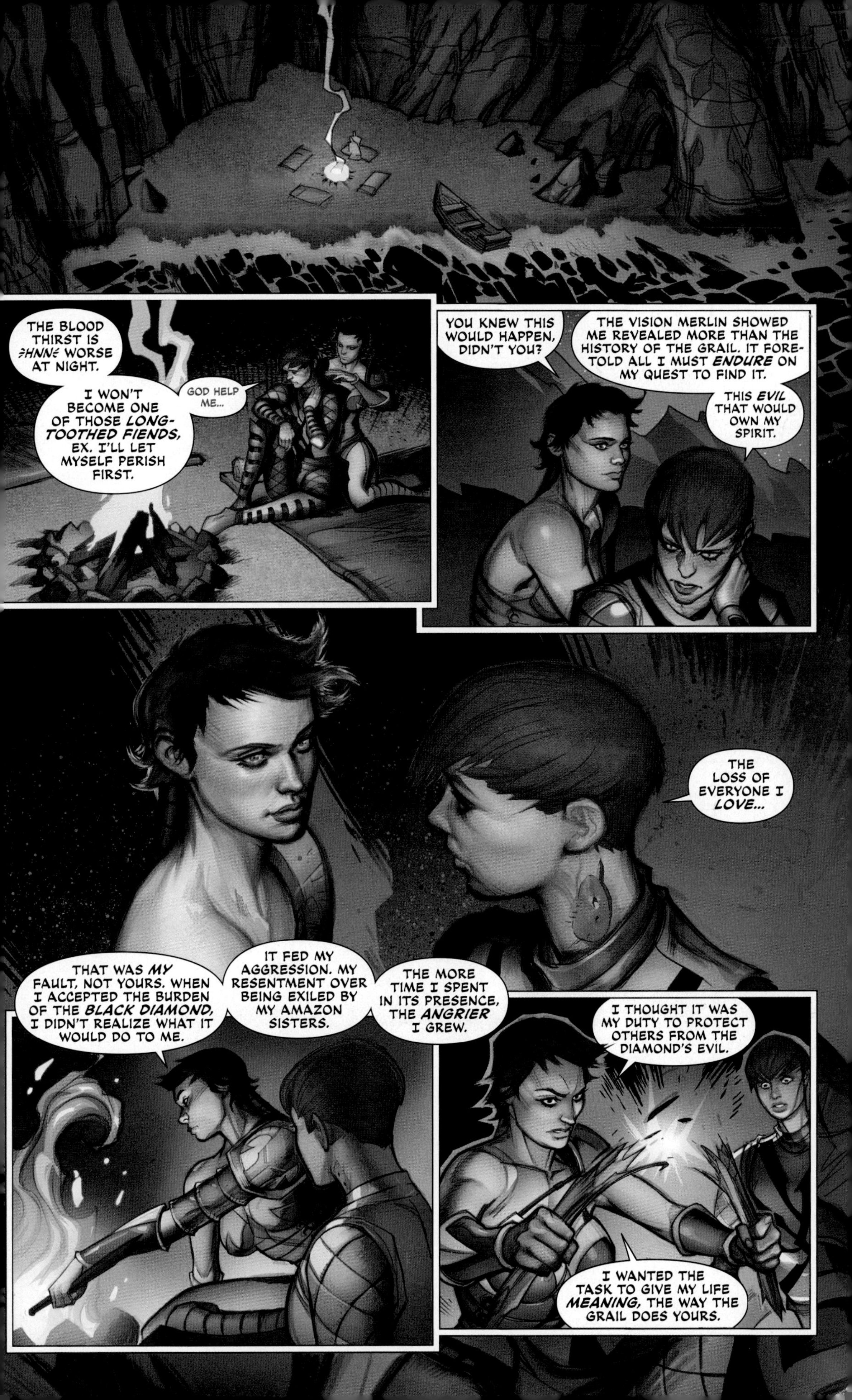

THE BLOOD THIRST IS *HNN* WORSE AT NIGHT.
I WON'T BECOME ONE OF THOSE *LONG-TOOTHED FIENDS,* EX. I'LL LET MYSELF PERISH FIRST.
GOD HELP ME...
YOU KNEW THIS WOULD HAPPEN, DIDN'T YOU?
THE VISION MERLIN SHOWED ME REVEALED MORE THAN THE HISTORY OF THE GRAIL. IT FORETOLD ALL I MUST *ENDURE* ON MY QUEST TO FIND IT.
THIS *EVIL* THAT WOULD OWN MY SPIRIT.
THE LOSS OF EVERYONE I *LOVE...*
THAT WAS *MY* FAULT, NOT YOURS. WHEN I ACCEPTED THE BURDEN OF THE *BLACK DIAMOND,* I DIDN'T REALIZE WHAT IT WOULD DO TO ME.
IT FED MY AGGRESSION. MY RESENTMENT OVER BEING EXILED BY MY AMAZON SISTERS.
THE MORE TIME I SPENT IN ITS PRESENCE, THE *ANGRIER* I GREW.
I THOUGHT IT WAS MY DUTY TO PROTECT OTHERS FROM THE DIAMOND'S EVIL.
I WANTED THE TASK TO GIVE MY LIFE *MEANING,* THE WAY THE GRAIL DOES YOURS.

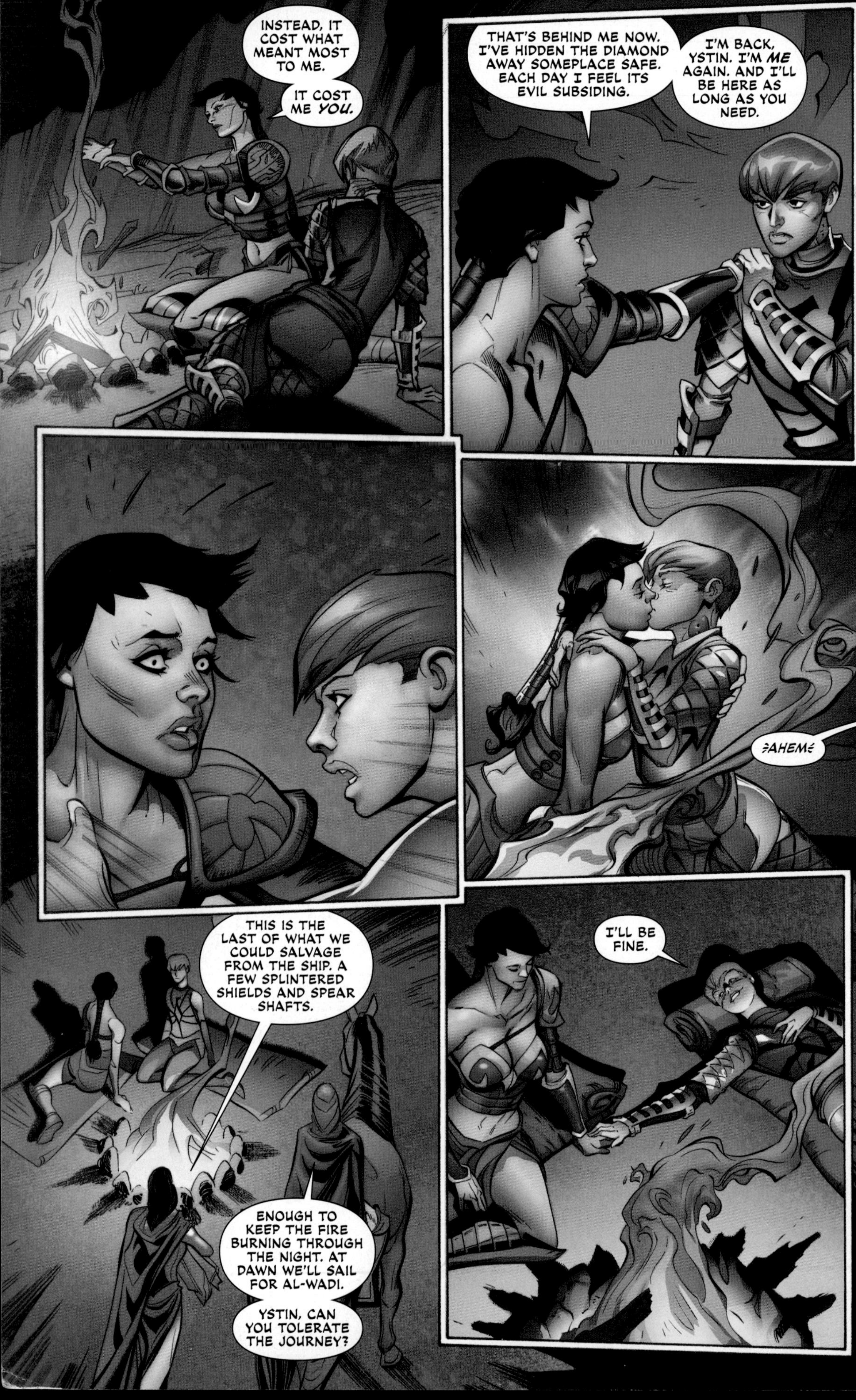
INSTEAD, IT COST WHAT MEANT MOST TO ME.
IT COST ME *YOU.*
THAT'S BEHIND ME NOW. I'VE HIDDEN THE DIAMOND AWAY SOMEPLACE SAFE. EACH DAY I FEEL ITS EVIL SUBSIDING.
I'M BACK, YSTIN. I'M *ME* AGAIN. AND I'LL BE HERE AS LONG AS YOU NEED.
AHEM
THIS IS THE LAST OF WHAT WE COULD SALVAGE FROM THE SHIP. A FEW SPLINTERED SHIELDS AND SPEAR SHAFTS.
ENOUGH TO KEEP THE FIRE BURNING THROUGH THE NIGHT. AT DAWN WE'LL SAIL FOR AL-WADI.
YSTIN, CAN YOU TOLERATE THE JOURNEY?
I'LL BE FINE.

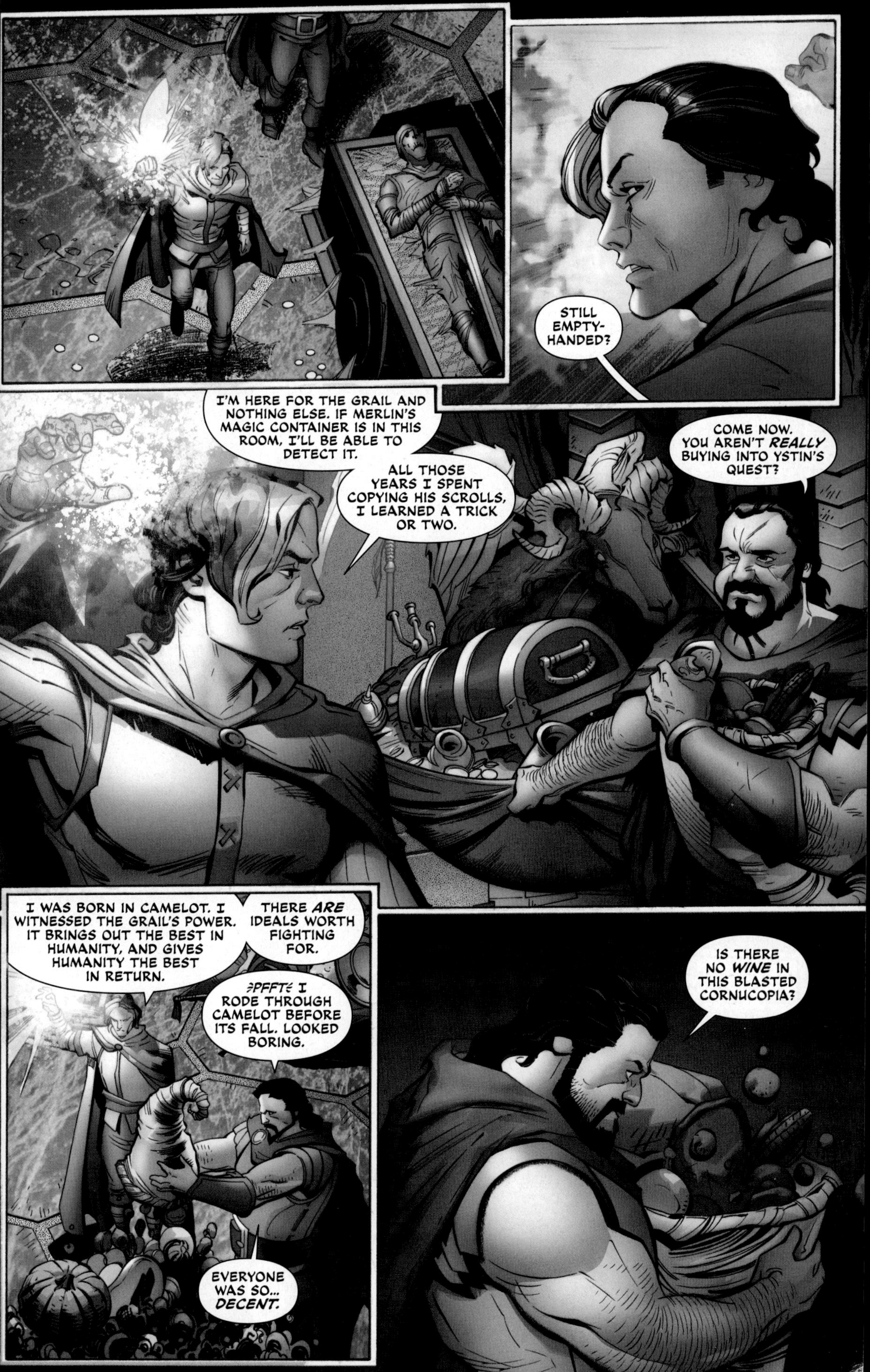
STILL EMPTY-HANDED?
I'M HERE FOR THE GRAIL AND NOTHING ELSE. IF MERLIN'S MAGIC CONTAINER IS IN THIS ROOM, I'LL BE ABLE TO DETECT IT.
ALL THOSE YEARS I SPENT COPYING HIS SCROLLS, I LEARNED A TRICK OR TWO.
COME NOW. YOU AREN'T *REALLY* BUYING INTO YSTIN'S QUEST?
I WAS BORN IN CAMELOT. I WITNESSED THE GRAIL'S POWER. IT BRINGS OUT THE BEST IN HUMANITY, AND GIVES HUMANITY THE BEST IN RETURN.
THERE *ARE* IDEALS WORTH FIGHTING FOR.
PFFT I RODE THROUGH CAMELOT BEFORE ITS FALL. LOOKED BORING.
EVERYONE WAS SO... *DECENT.*
IS THERE NO *WINE* IN THIS BLASTED CORNUCOPIA?

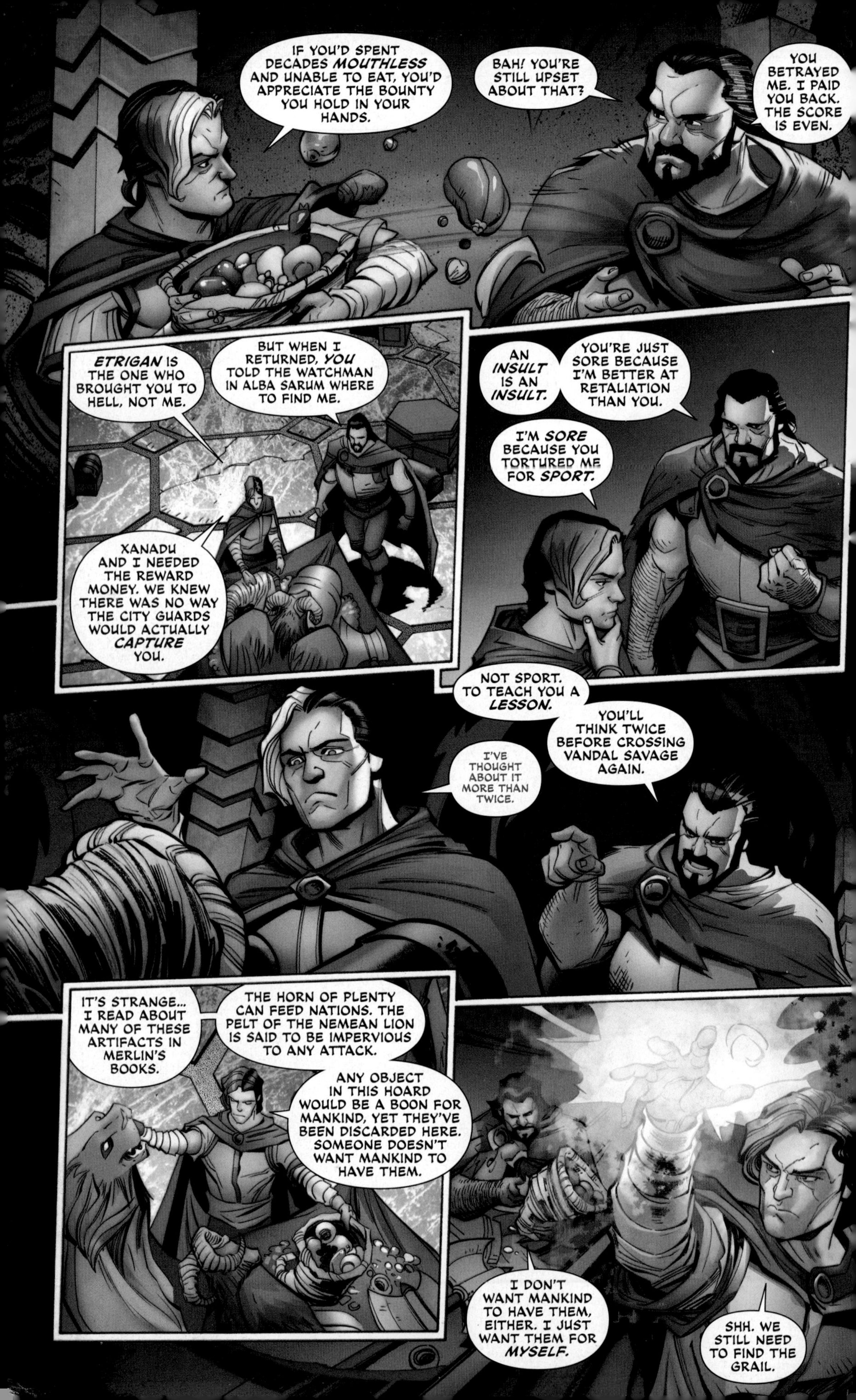
IF YOU'D SPENT DECADES *MOUTHLESS* AND UNABLE TO EAT, YOU'D APPRECIATE THE BOUNTY YOU HOLD IN YOUR HANDS.
BAH! YOU'RE STILL UPSET ABOUT THAT?
YOU BETRAYED ME. I PAID YOU BACK. THE SCORE IS EVEN.
ETRIGAN IS THE ONE WHO BROUGHT YOU TO HELL, NOT ME.
BUT WHEN I RETURNED, *YOU* TOLD THE WATCHMAN IN ALBA SARUM WHERE TO FIND ME.
XANADU AND I NEEDED THE REWARD MONEY. WE KNEW THERE WAS NO WAY THE CITY GUARDS WOULD ACTUALLY *CAPTURE* YOU.
AN *INSULT* IS AN *INSULT.*
YOU'RE JUST SORE BECAUSE I'M BETTER AT RETALIATION THAN YOU.
I'M *SORE* BECAUSE YOU TORTURED ME FOR *SPORT.*
NOT SPORT. TO TEACH YOU A *LESSON.*
YOU'LL THINK TWICE BEFORE CROSSING VANDAL SAVAGE AGAIN.
I'VE THOUGHT ABOUT IT MORE THAN TWICE.
IT'S STRANGE... I READ ABOUT MANY OF THESE ARTIFACTS IN MERLIN'S BOOKS.
THE HORN OF PLENTY CAN FEED NATIONS. THE PELT OF THE NEMEAN LION IS SAID TO BE IMPERVIOUS TO ANY ATTACK.
ANY OBJECT IN THIS HOARD WOULD BE A BOON FOR MANKIND, YET THEY'VE BEEN DISCARDED HERE. SOMEONE DOESN'T WANT MANKIND TO HAVE THEM.
I DON'T WANT MANKIND TO HAVE THEM, EITHER. I JUST WANT THEM FOR *MYSELF.*
SHH. WE STILL NEED TO FIND THE GRAIL.

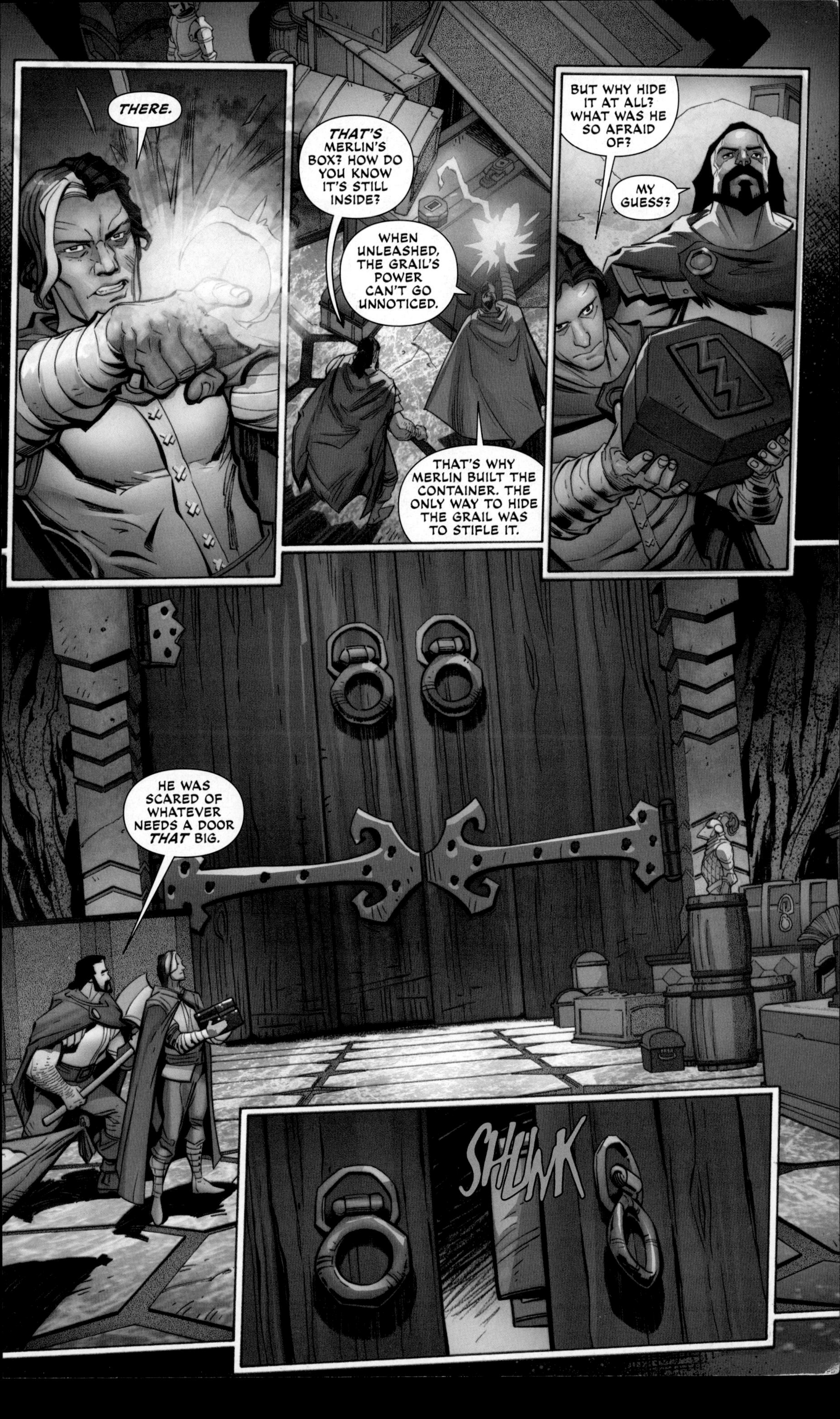
THERE.
THAT'S MERLIN'S BOX? HOW DO YOU KNOW IT'S STILL INSIDE?
WHEN UNLEASHED, THE GRAIL'S POWER CAN'T GO UNNOTICED.
THAT'S WHY MERLIN BUILT THE CONTAINER. THE ONLY WAY TO HIDE THE GRAIL WAS TO STIFLE IT.
BUT WHY HIDE IT AT ALL? WHAT WAS HE SO AFRAID OF?
MY GUESS?
HE WAS SCARED OF WHATEVER NEEDS A DOOR THAT BIG.
SHLUNK

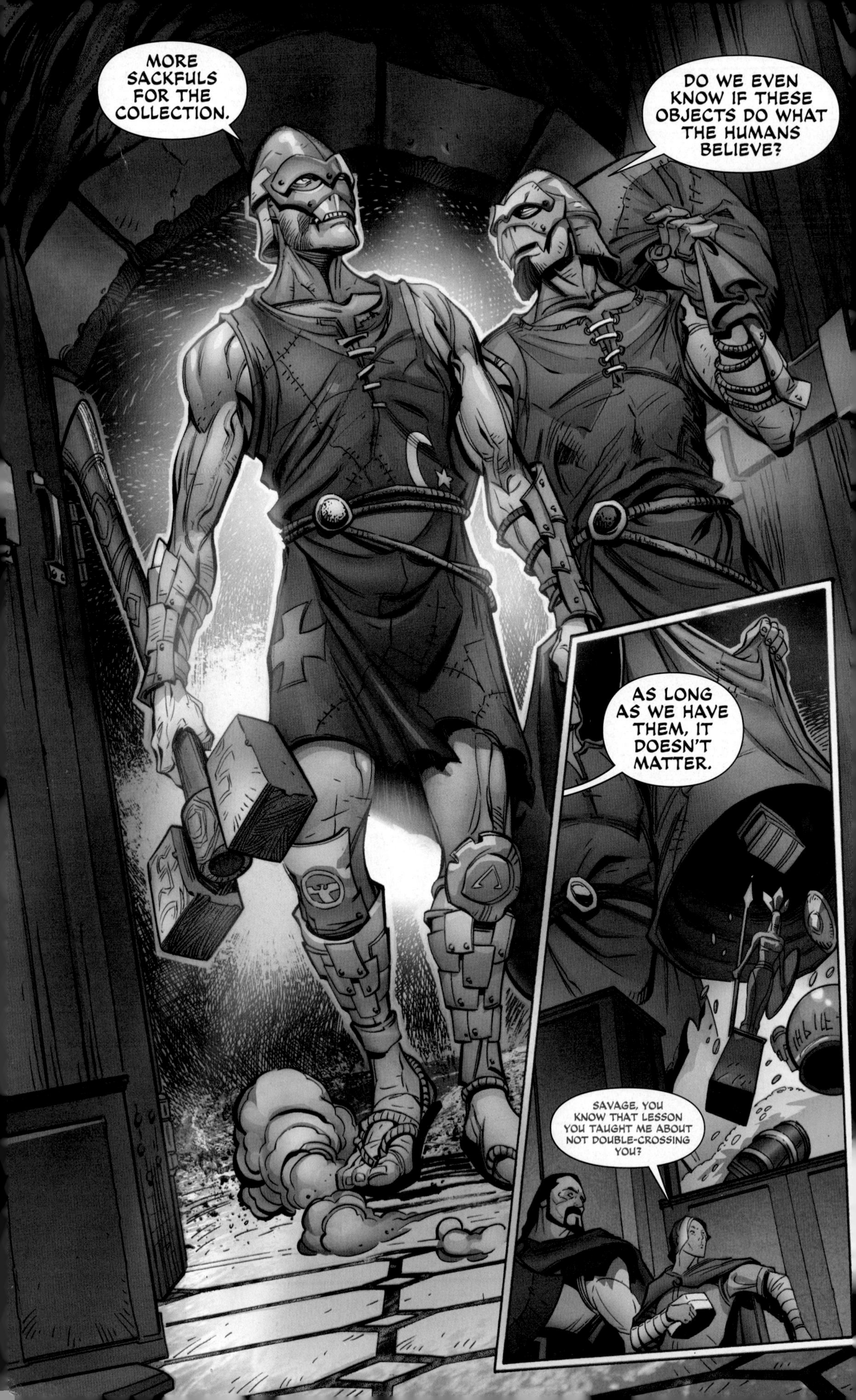
MORE SACKFULS FOR THE COLLECTION.
DO WE EVEN KNOW IF THESE OBJECTS DO WHAT THE HUMANS BELIEVE?
AS LONG AS WE HAVE THEM, IT DOESN'T MATTER.
SAVAGE, YOU KNOW THAT LESSON YOU TAUGHT ME ABOUT NOT DOUBLE-CROSSING YOU?

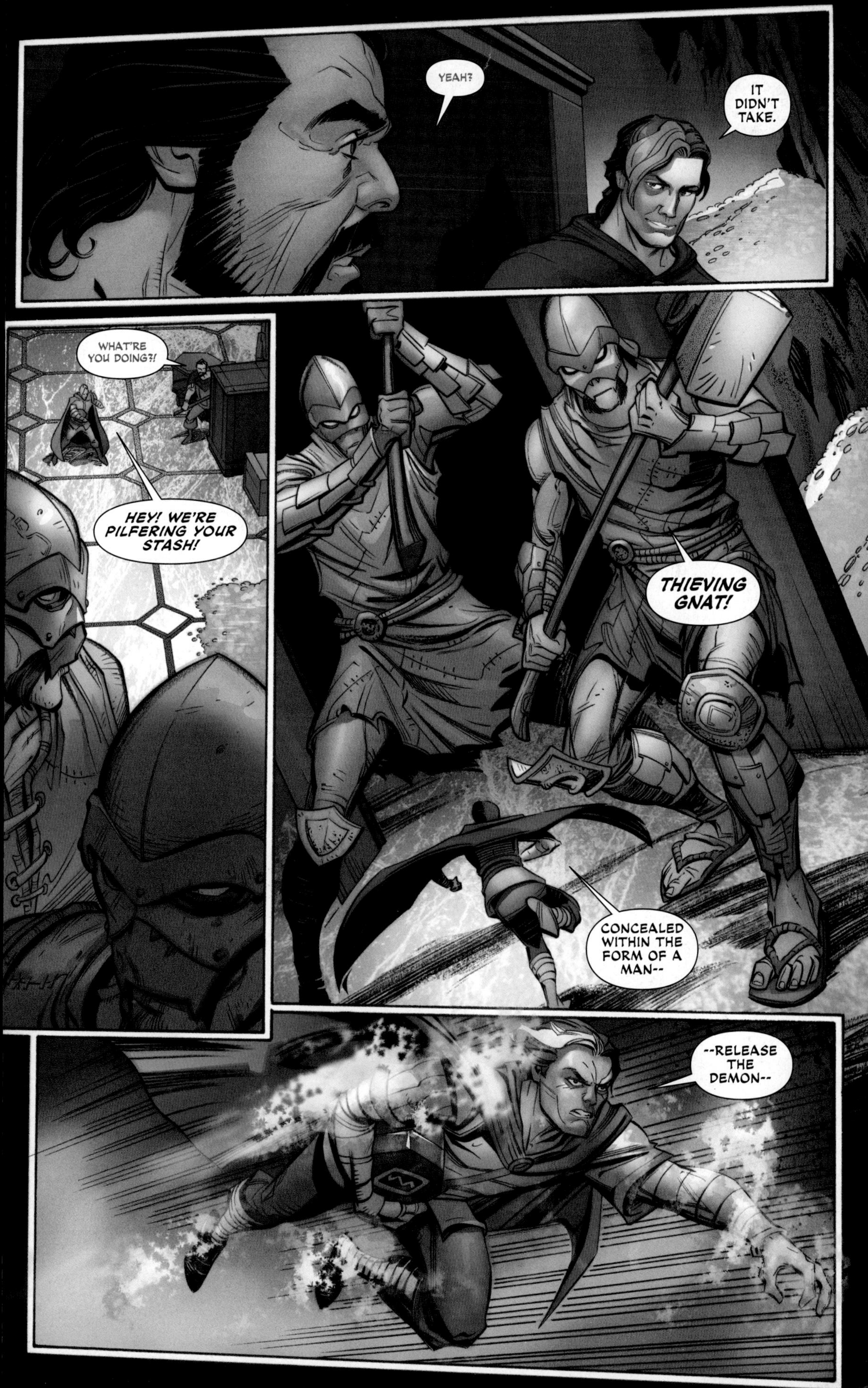
YEAH?
IT DIDN'T TAKE.
WHAT'RE YOU DOING?!
HEY! WE'RE PILFERING YOUR STASH!
THIEVING GNAT!
CONCEALED WITHIN THE FORM OF A MAN--
--RELEASE THE DEMON--

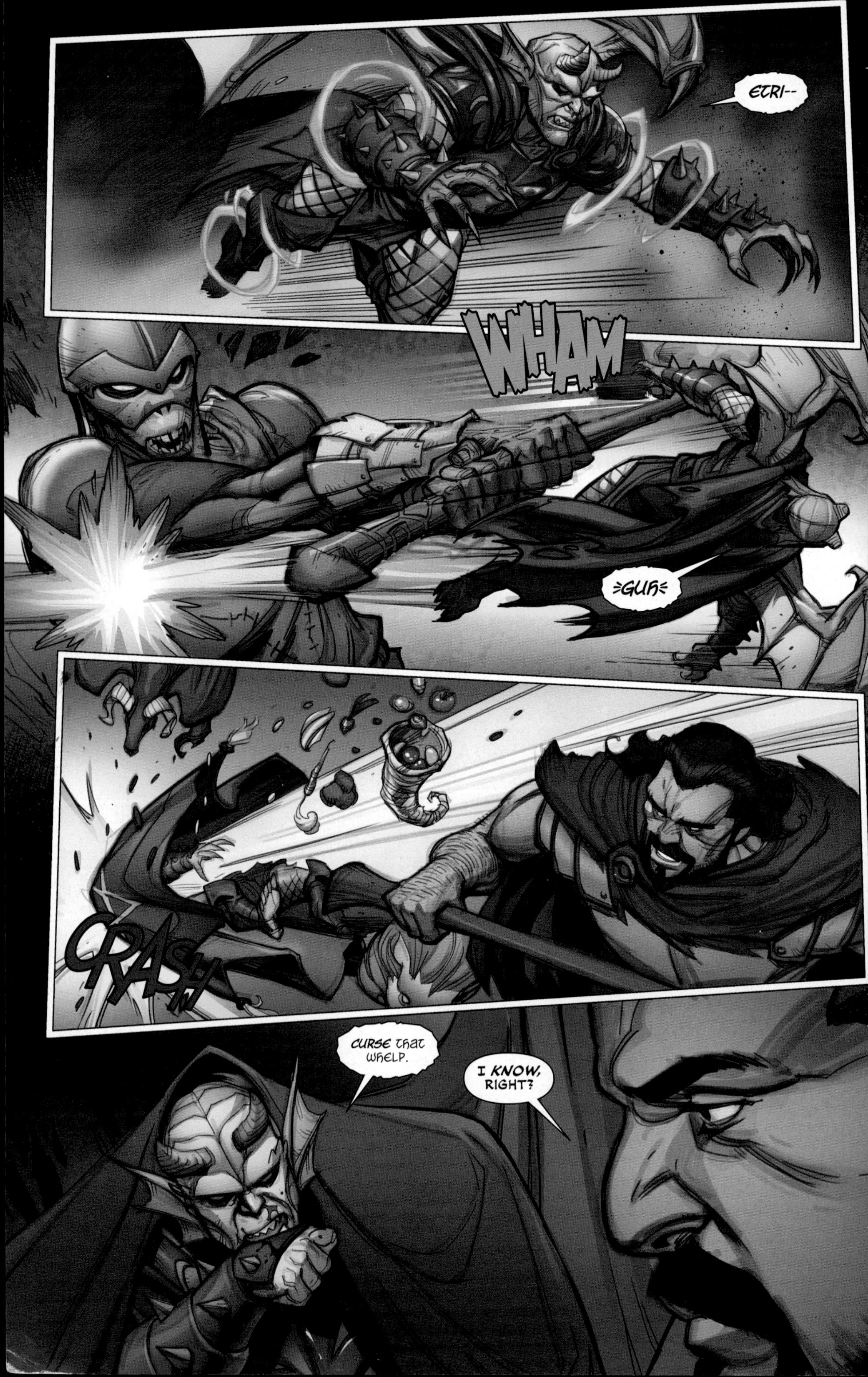
ETRI--
WHAM
GUH
CRASH
CURSE THAT WHELP.
I KNOW, RIGHT?

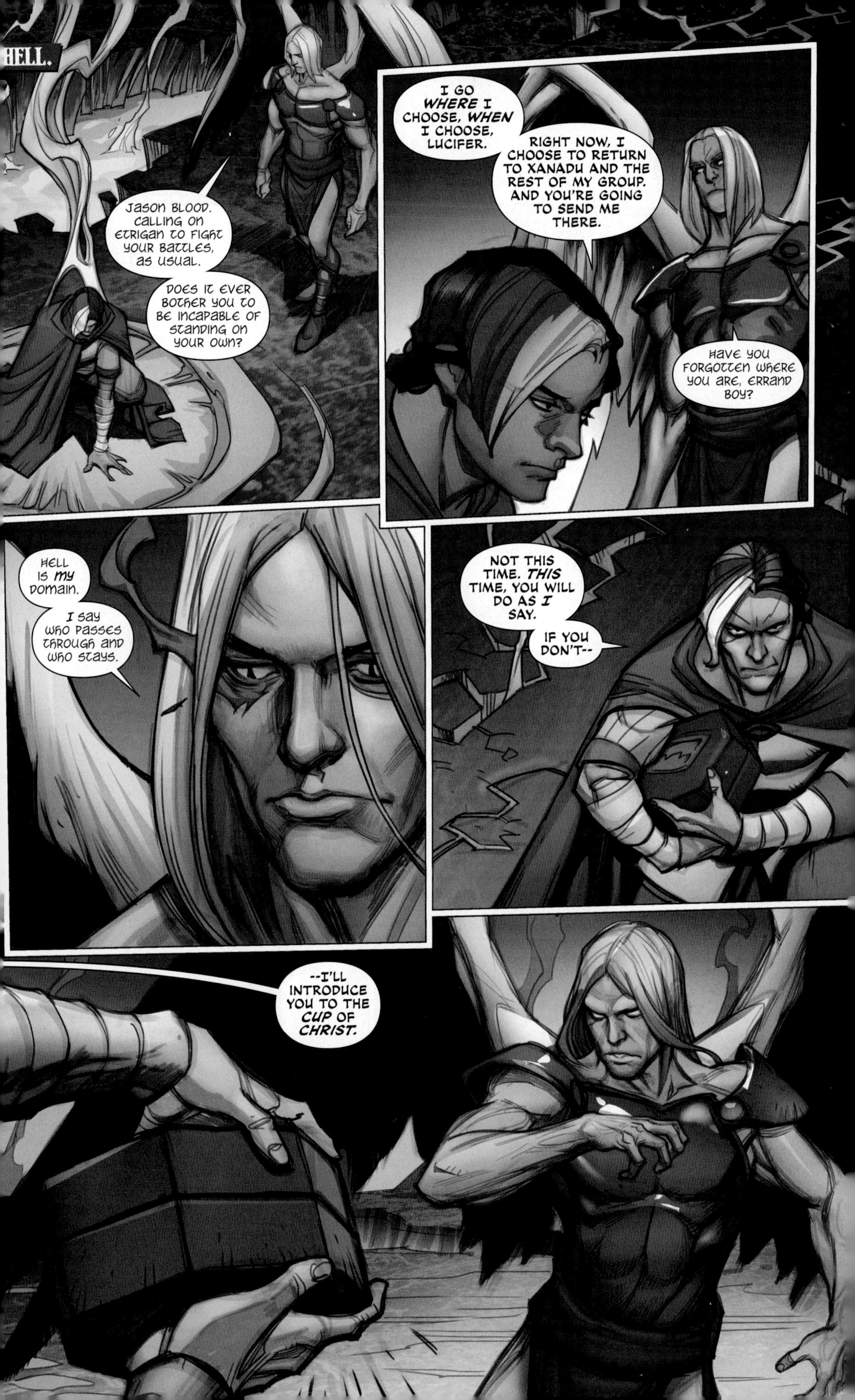
HELL.
JASON BLOOD. CALLING ON ETRIGAN TO FIGHT YOUR BATTLES, AS USUAL.
DOES IT EVER BOTHER YOU TO BE INCAPABLE OF STANDING ON YOUR OWN?
I GO *WHERE* I CHOOSE, *WHEN* I CHOOSE, LUCIFER.
RIGHT NOW, I CHOOSE TO RETURN TO XANADU AND THE REST OF MY GROUP. AND YOU'RE GOING TO SEND ME THERE.
HAVE YOU FORGOTTEN WHERE YOU ARE, ERRAND BOY?
HELL IS *MY* DOMAIN.
I SAY WHO PASSES THROUGH AND WHO STAYS.
NOT THIS TIME. *THIS* TIME, YOU WILL DO AS *I* SAY.
IF YOU DON'T--
--I'LL INTRODUCE YOU TO THE *CUP* OF *CHRIST.*

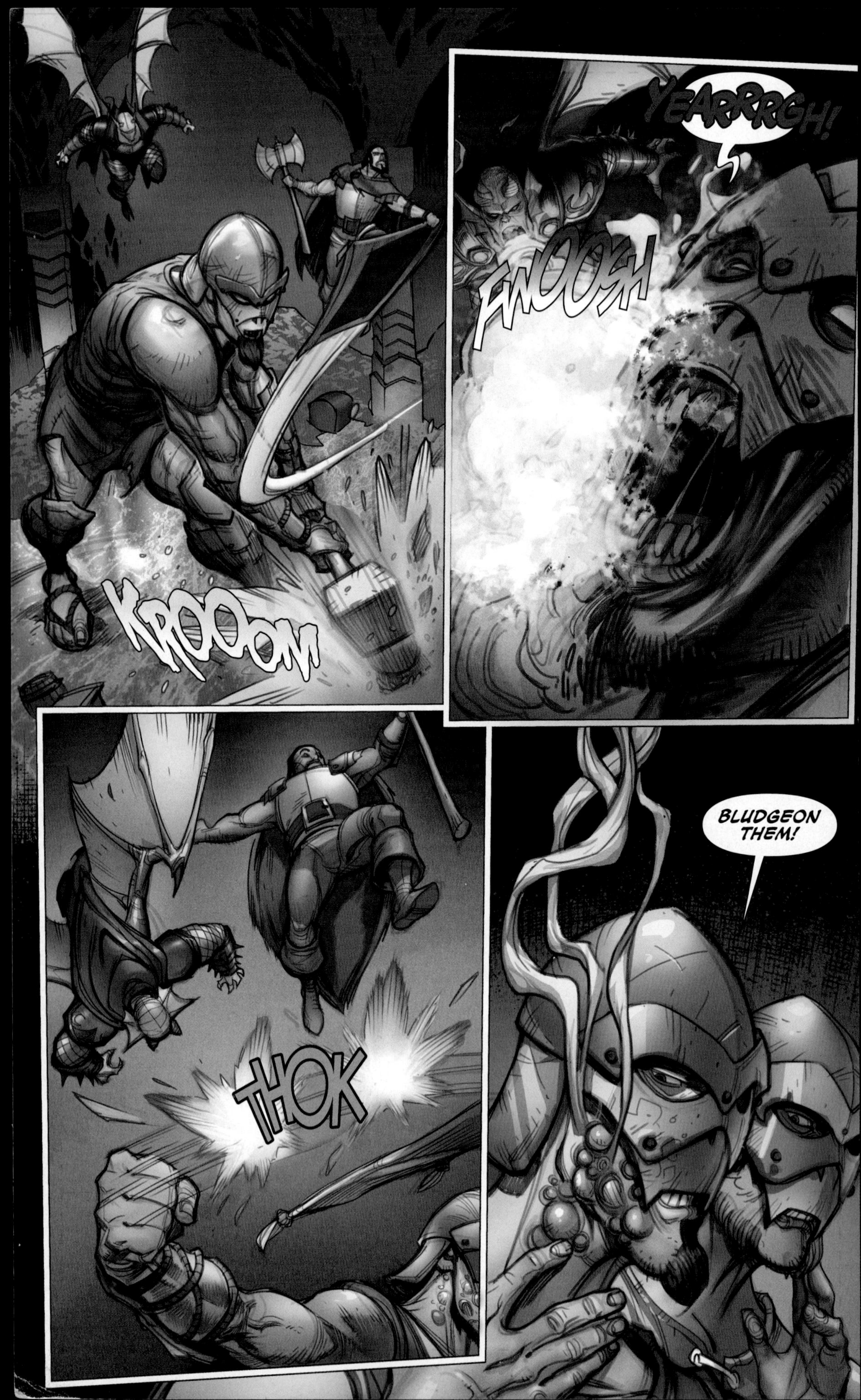
KROOOM!
YEARRRGH!
FWOOSH
THOK
BLUDGEON THEM!

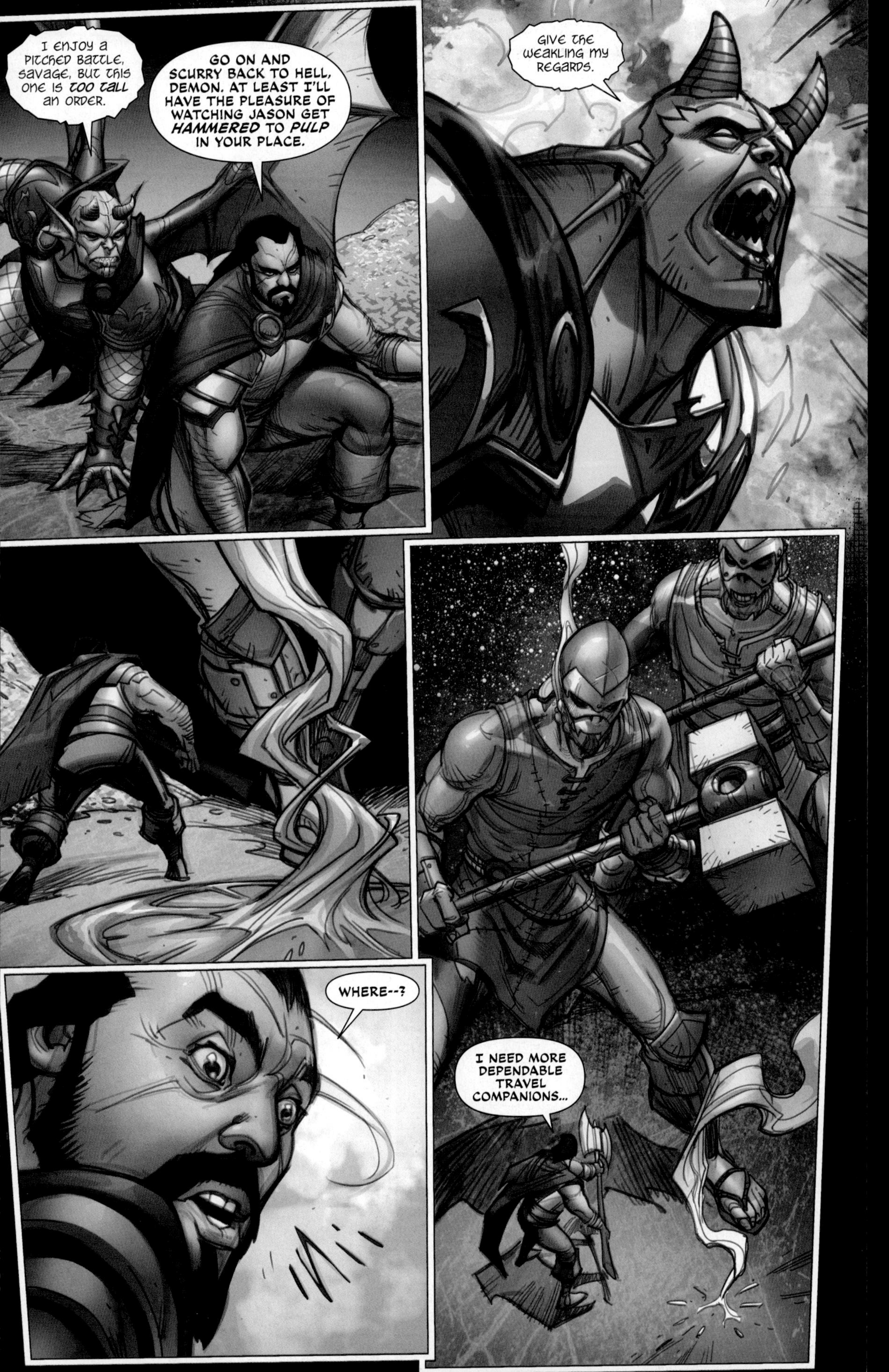
I ENJOY A PITCHED BATTLE, SAVAGE, BUT THIS ONE IS TOO TALL AN ORDER.
GO ON AND SCURRY BACK TO HELL, DEMON. AT LEAST I'LL HAVE THE PLEASURE OF WATCHING JASON GET HAMMERED TO PULP IN YOUR PLACE.
GIVE THE WEAKLING MY REGARDS.
WHERE--?
I NEED MORE DEPENDABLE TRAVEL COMPANIONS...

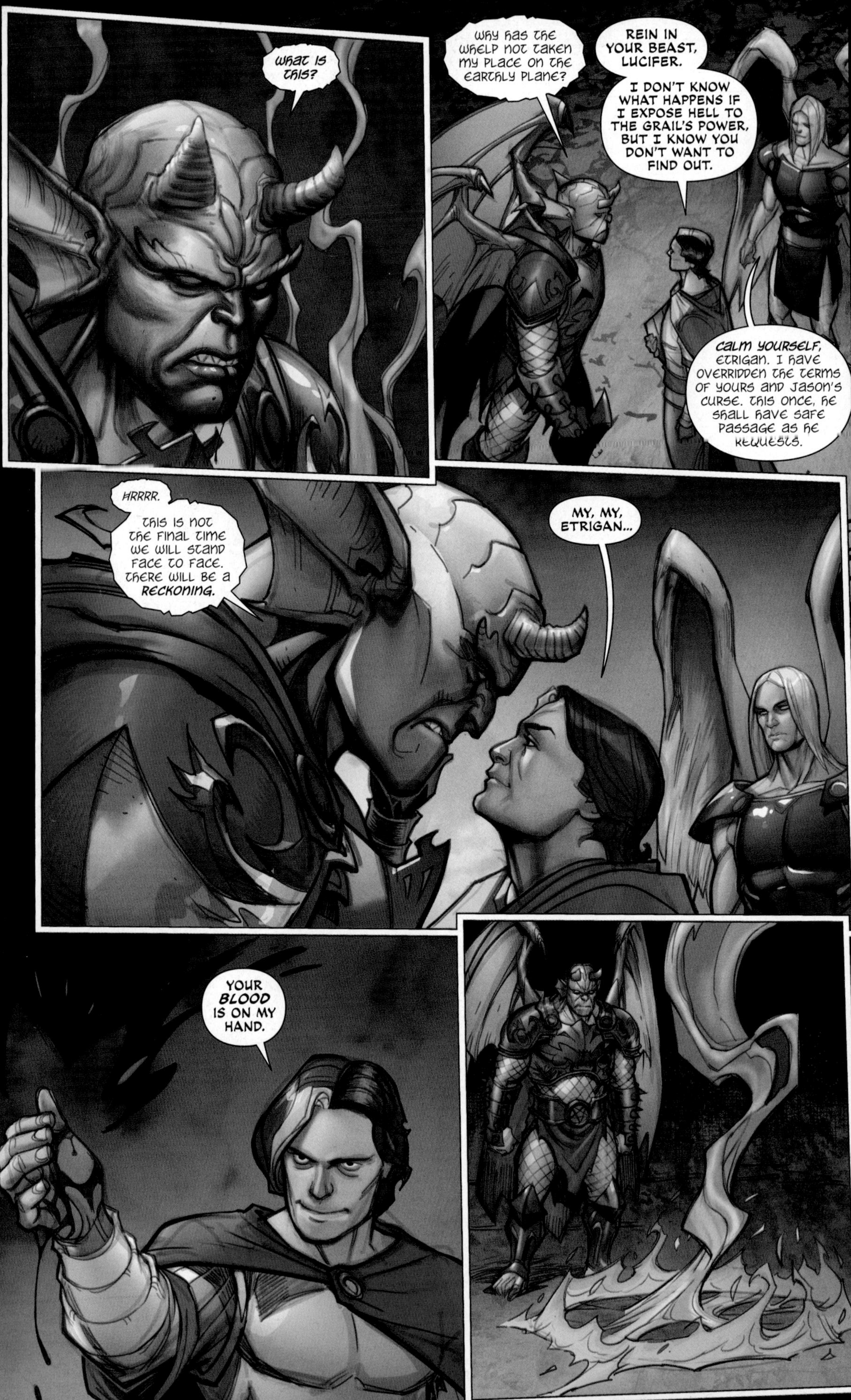
WHAT IS THIS?
WHY HAS THE WHELP NOT TAKEN MY PLACE ON THE EARTHLY PLANE?
REIN IN YOUR BEAST, LUCIFER.
I DON'T KNOW WHAT HAPPENS IF I EXPOSE HELL TO THE GRAIL'S POWER, BUT I KNOW YOU DON'T WANT TO FIND OUT.
CALM YOURSELF, ETRIGAN. I HAVE OVERRIDDEN THE TERMS OF YOURS AND JASON'S CURSE. THIS ONCE, HE SHALL HAVE SAFE PASSAGE AS HE REQUESTS.
HRRRR.
THIS IS NOT THE FINAL TIME WE WILL STAND FACE TO FACE. THERE WILL BE A RECKONING.
MY, MY, ETRIGAN...
YOUR BLOOD IS ON MY HAND.

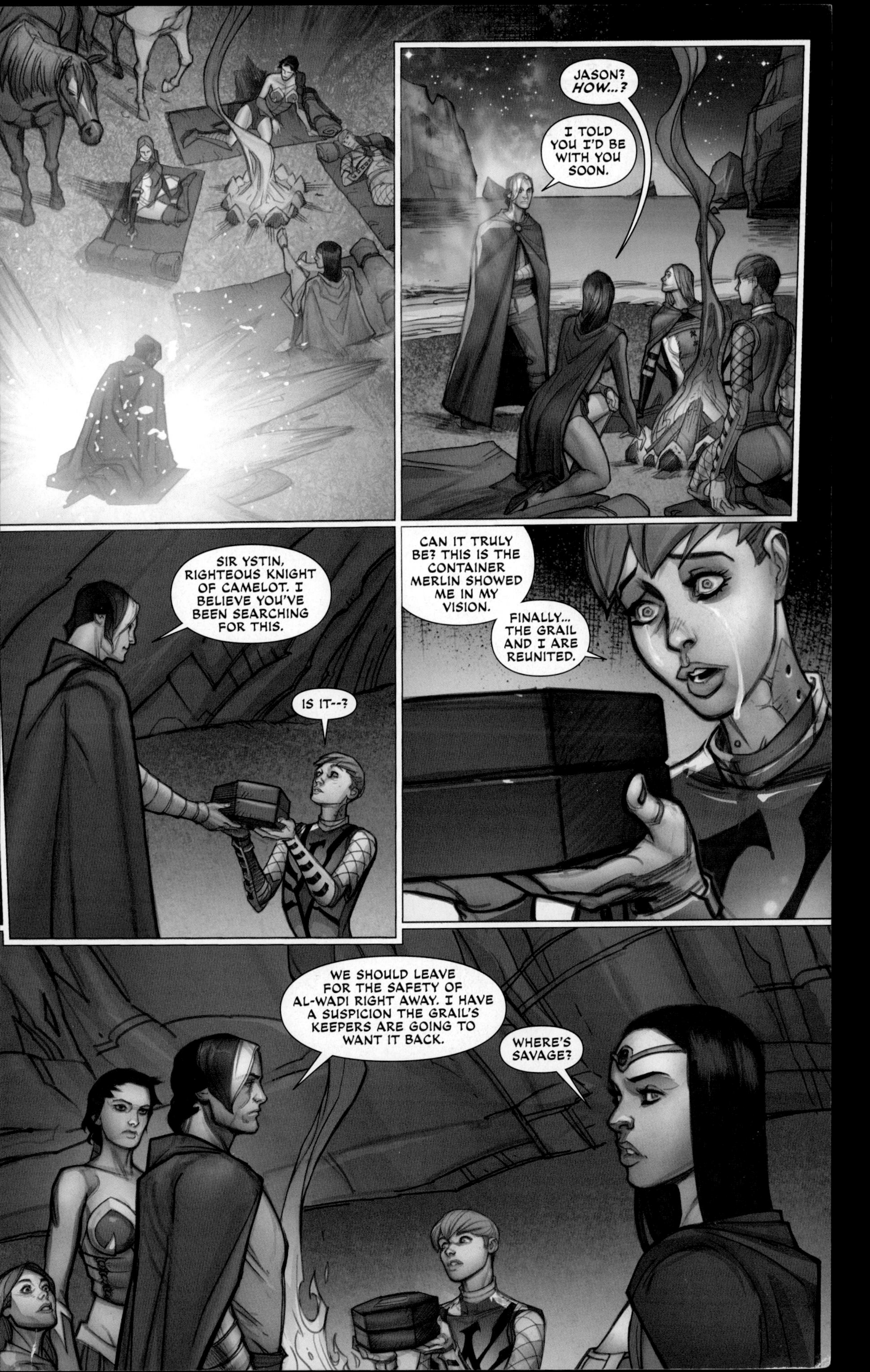
JASON? HOW...?
I TOLD YOU I'D BE WITH YOU SOON.
SIR YSTIN, RIGHTEOUS KNIGHT OF CAMELOT. I BELIEVE YOU'VE BEEN SEARCHING FOR THIS.
IS IT--?
CAN IT TRULY BE? THIS IS THE CONTAINER MERLIN SHOWED ME IN MY VISION.
FINALLY... THE GRAIL AND I ARE REUNITED.
WE SHOULD LEAVE FOR THE SAFETY OF AL-WADI RIGHT AWAY. I HAVE A SUSPICION THE GRAIL'S KEEPERS ARE GOING TO WANT IT BACK.
WHERE'S SAVAGE?

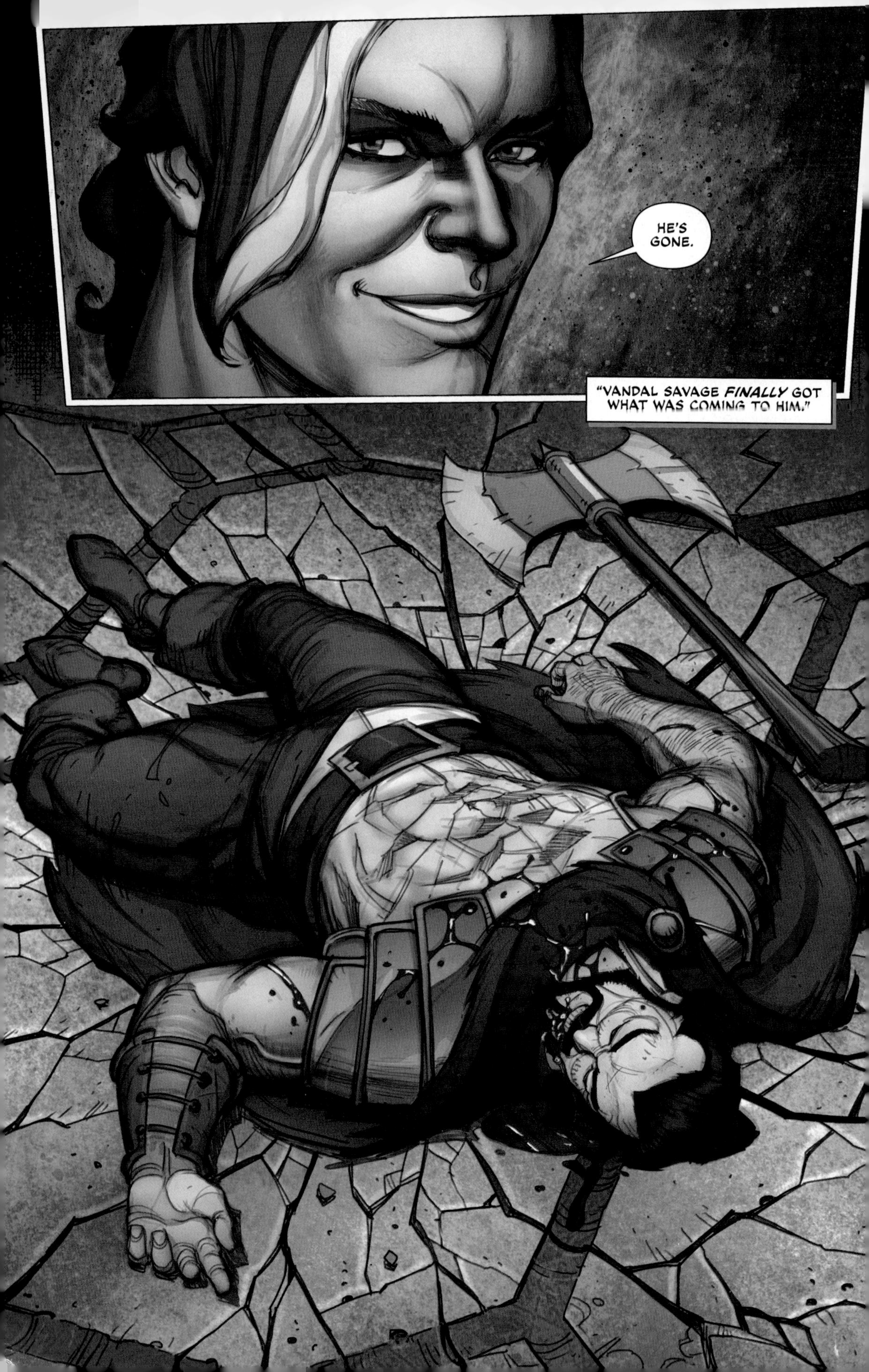
HE'S GONE.
"VANDAL SAVAGE *FINALLY* GOT WHAT WAS COMING TO HIM."

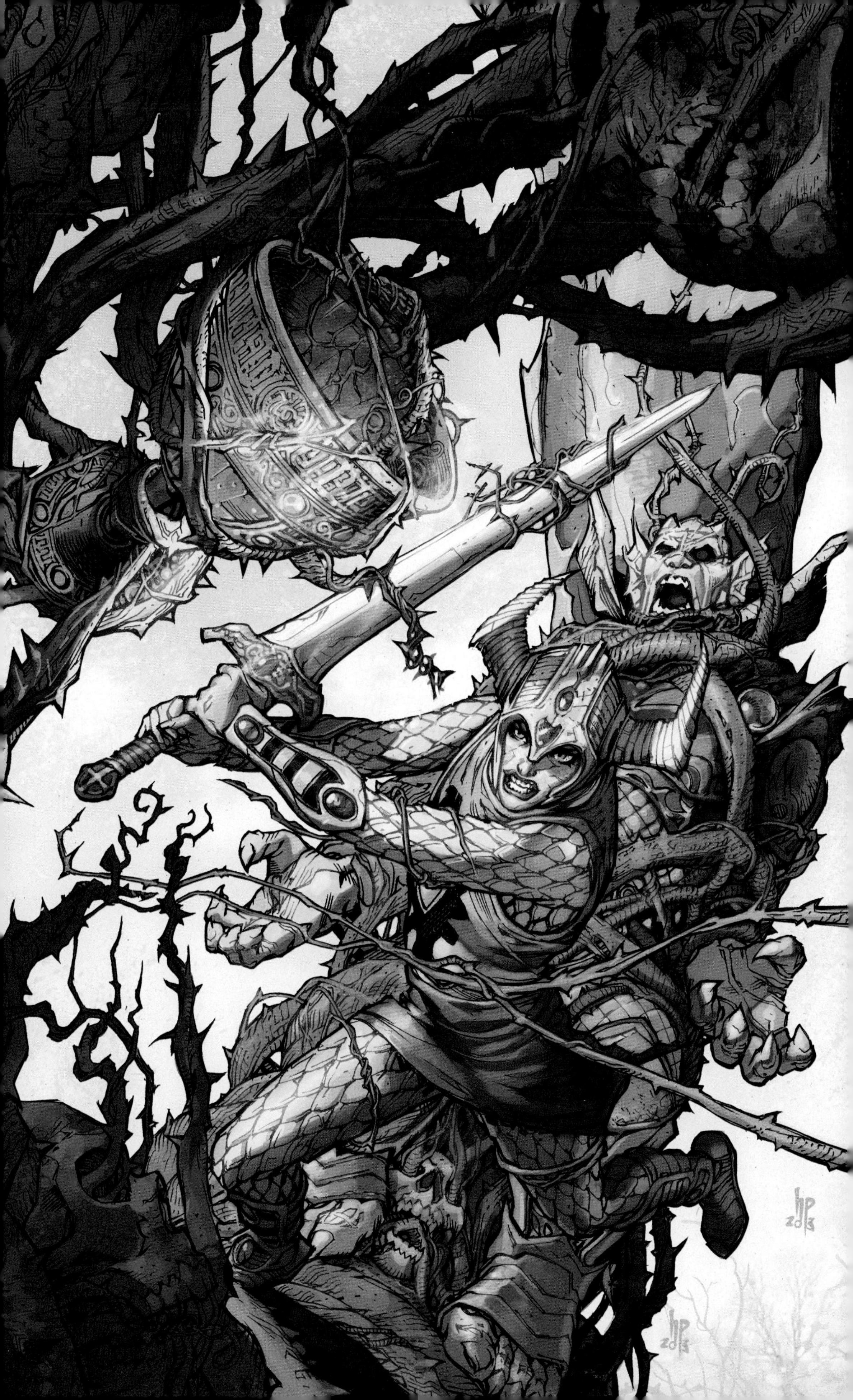

ROBERT VENDITTI
writer

CHAD HARDIN
artist

HOWARD PORTER
cover artist

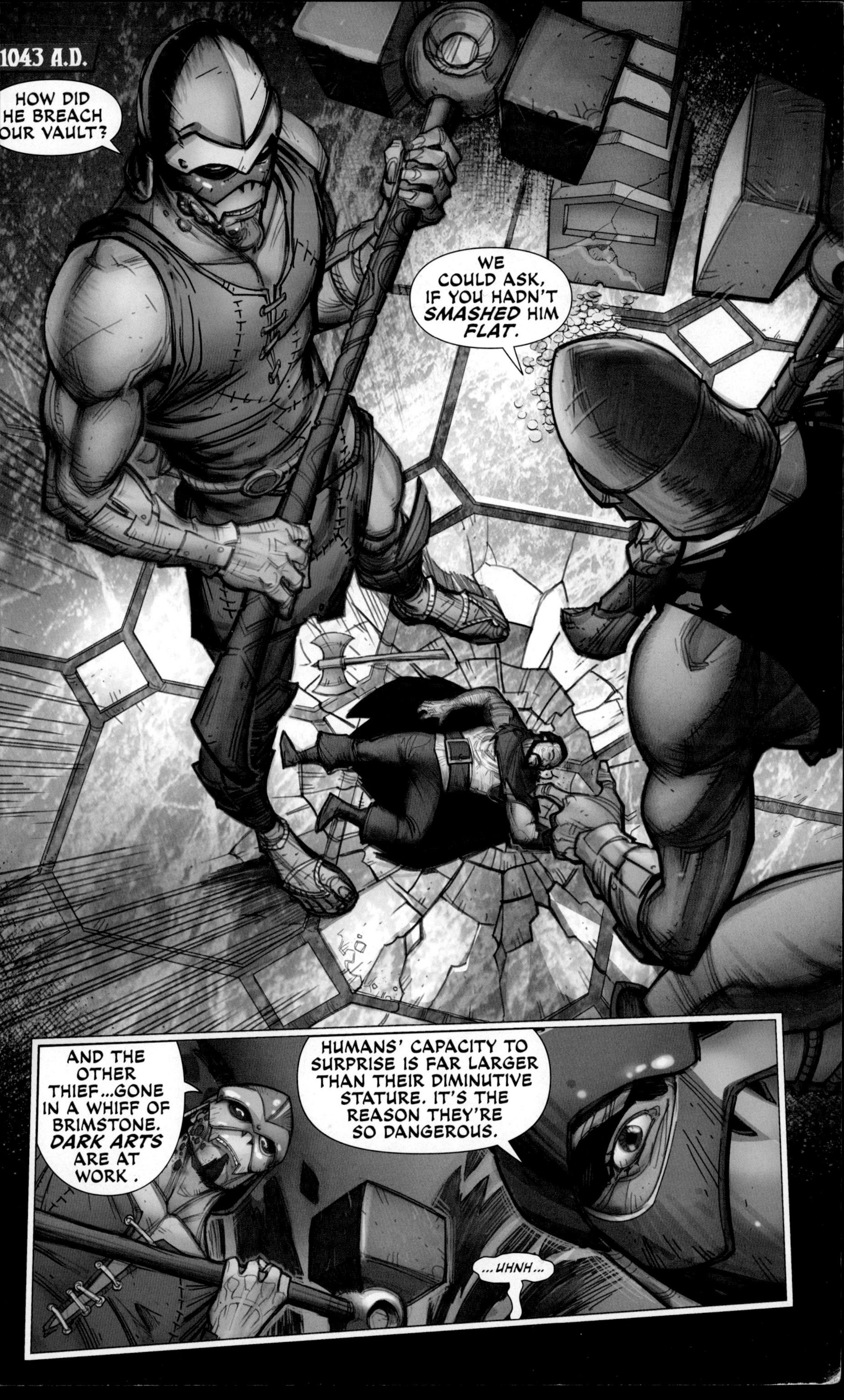
1043 A.D.
HOW DID HE BREACH OUR VAULT?
WE COULD ASK, IF YOU HADN'T SMASHED HIM FLAT.
AND THE OTHER THIEF...GONE IN A WHIFF OF BRIMSTONE. DARK ARTS ARE AT WORK.
HUMANS' CAPACITY TO SURPRISE IS FAR LARGER THAN THEIR DIMINUTIVE STATURE. IT'S THE REASON THEY'RE SO DANGEROUS.
...UHNH...

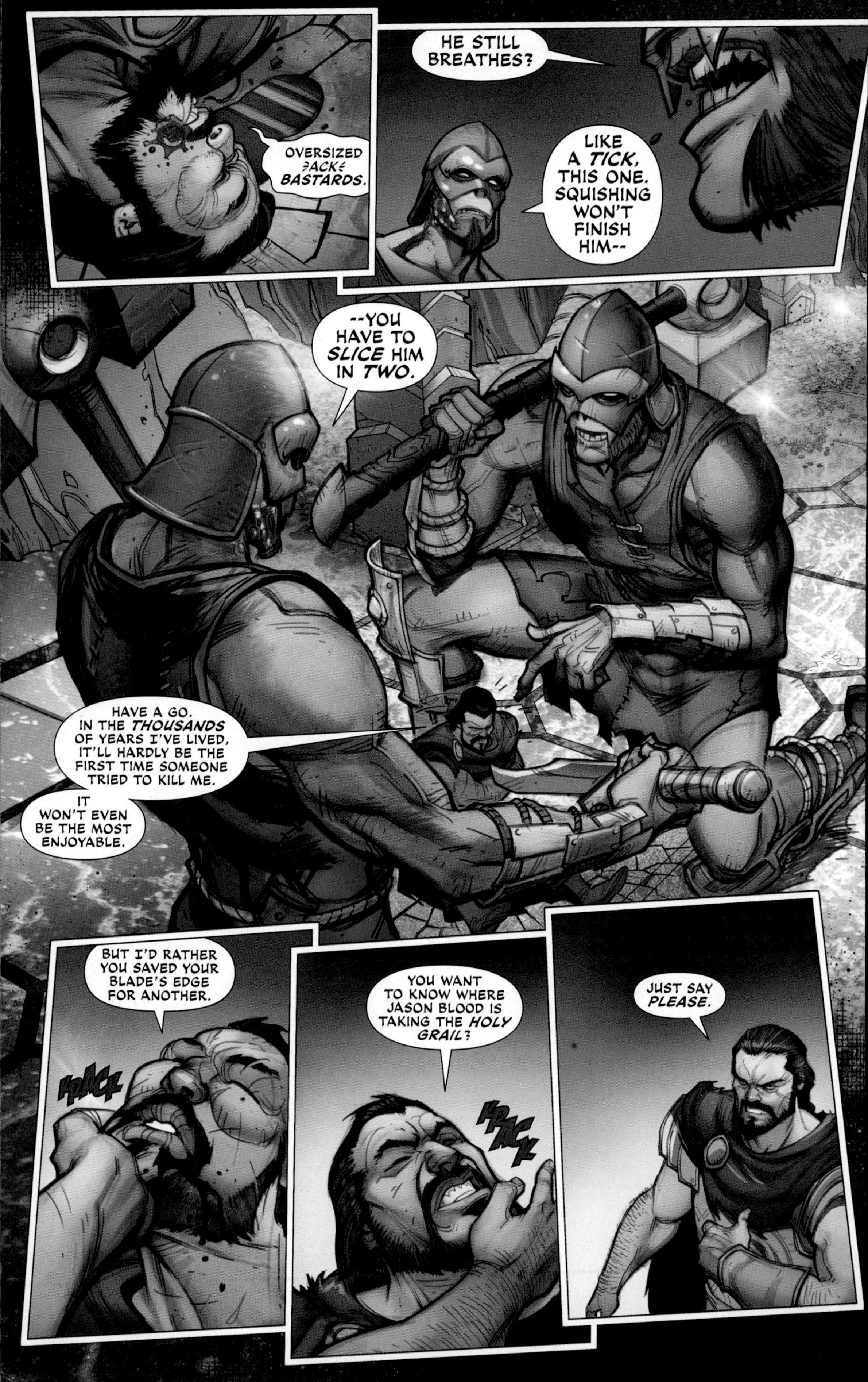
OVERSIZED ≥ACK≤ BASTARDS.
HE STILL BREATHES?
LIKE A TICK, THIS ONE. SQUISHING WON'T FINISH HIM--
--YOU HAVE TO SLICE HIM IN TWO.
HAVE A GO. IN THE THOUSANDS OF YEARS I'VE LIVED, IT'LL HARDLY BE THE FIRST TIME SOMEONE TRIED TO KILL ME.
IT WON'T EVEN BE THE MOST ENJOYABLE.
BUT I'D RATHER YOU SAVED YOUR BLADE'S EDGE FOR ANOTHER.
KRACK
YOU WANT TO KNOW WHERE JASON BLOOD IS TAKING THE HOLY GRAIL?
KRACK
JUST SAY PLEASE.

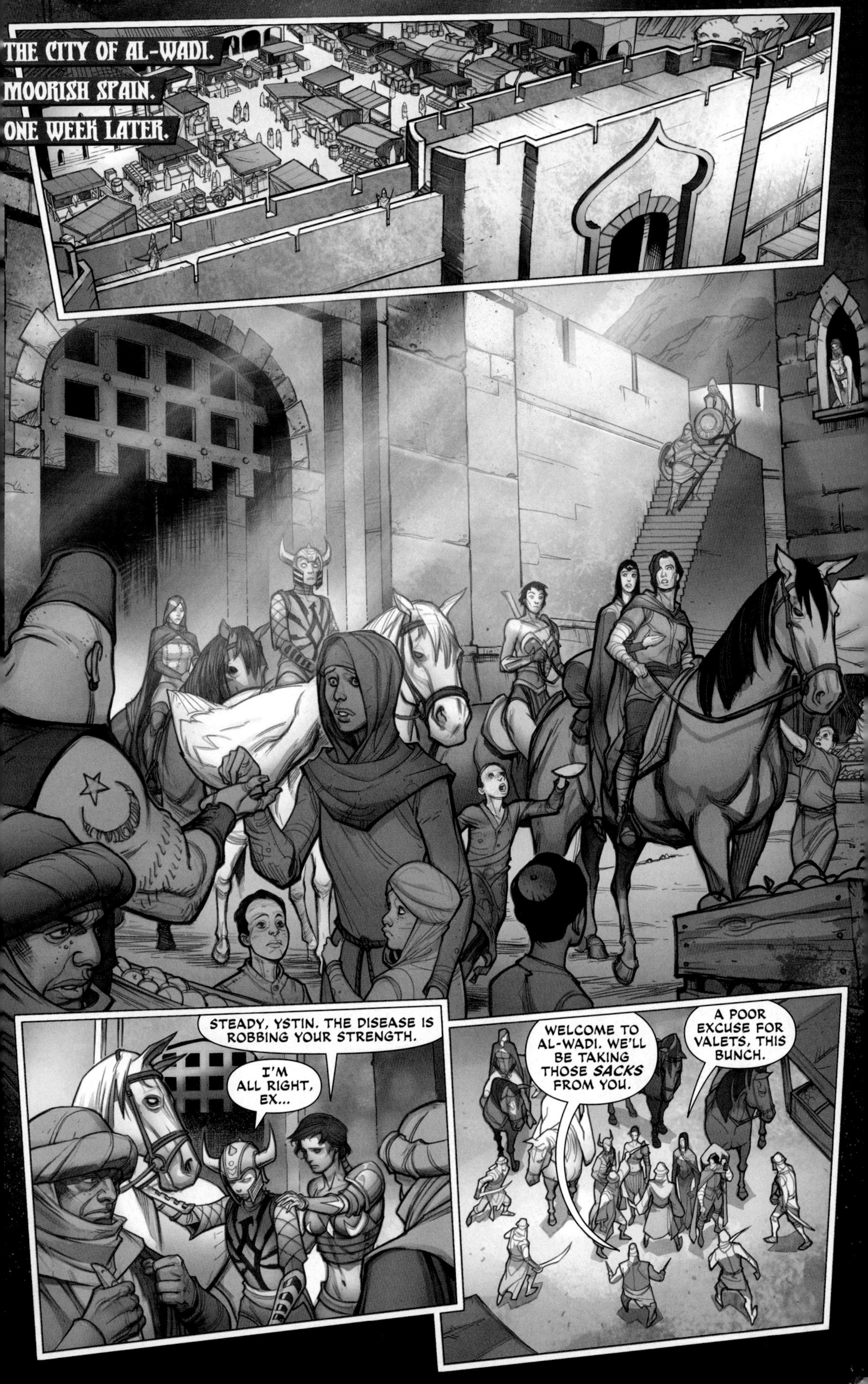
THE CITY OF AL-WADI.
MOORISH SPAIN.
ONE WEEK LATER.
STEADY, YSTIN. THE DISEASE IS ROBBING YOUR STRENGTH.
I'M ALL RIGHT, EX...
WELCOME TO AL-WADI. WE'LL BE TAKING THOSE *SACKS* FROM YOU.
A POOR EXCUSE FOR VALETS, THIS BUNCH.

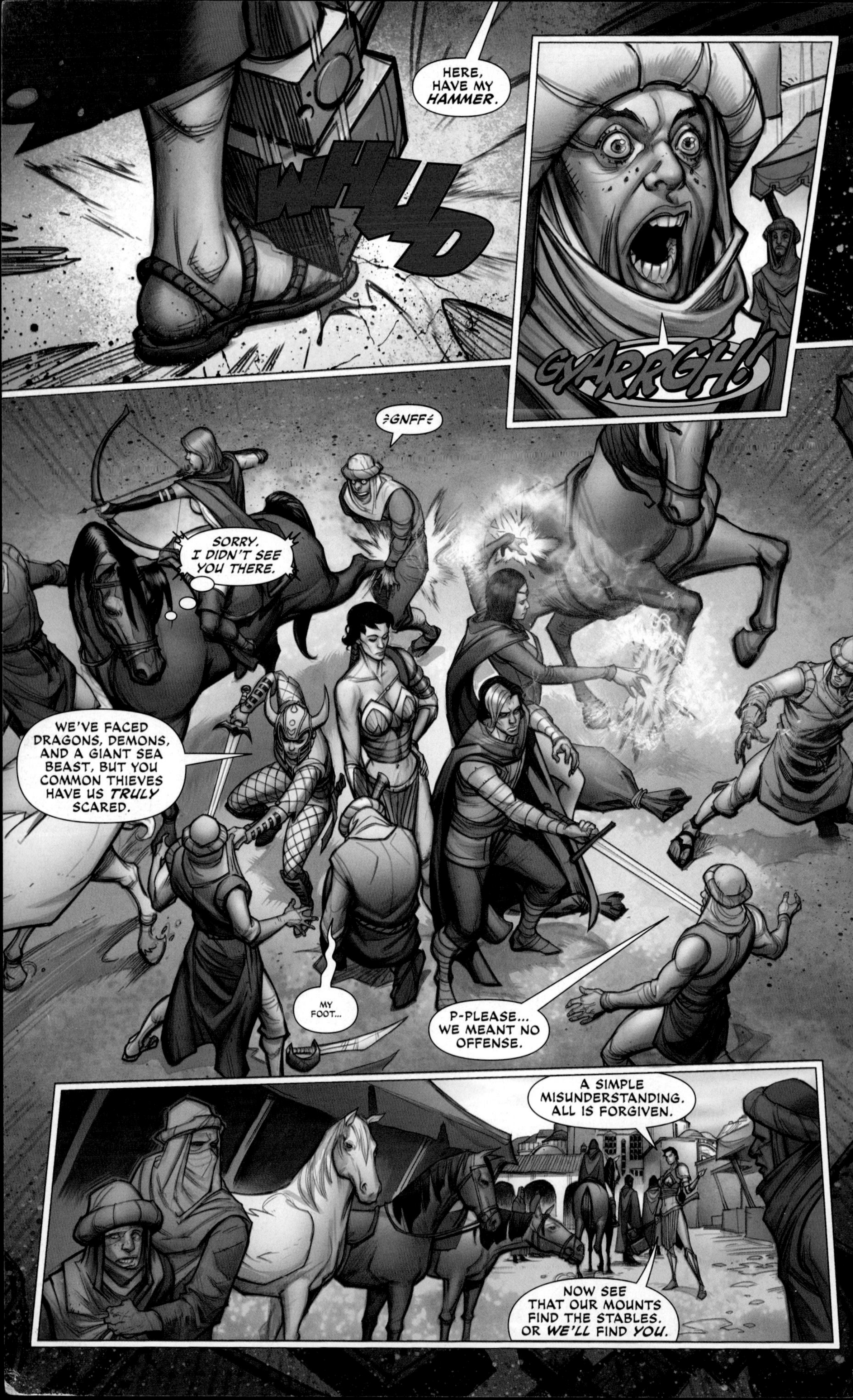
HERE, HAVE MY *HAMMER*.
WHUD
GYARRGH!
GNFF
SORRY. I DIDN'T SEE YOU THERE.
WE'VE FACED DRAGONS, DEMONS, AND A GIANT SEA BEAST, BUT YOU COMMON THIEVES HAVE US *TRULY* SCARED.
MY FOOT...
P-PLEASE... WE MEANT NO OFFENSE.
A SIMPLE MISUNDERSTANDING. ALL IS FORGIVEN.
NOW SEE THAT OUR MOUNTS FIND THE STABLES. OR *WE'LL* FIND *YOU*.

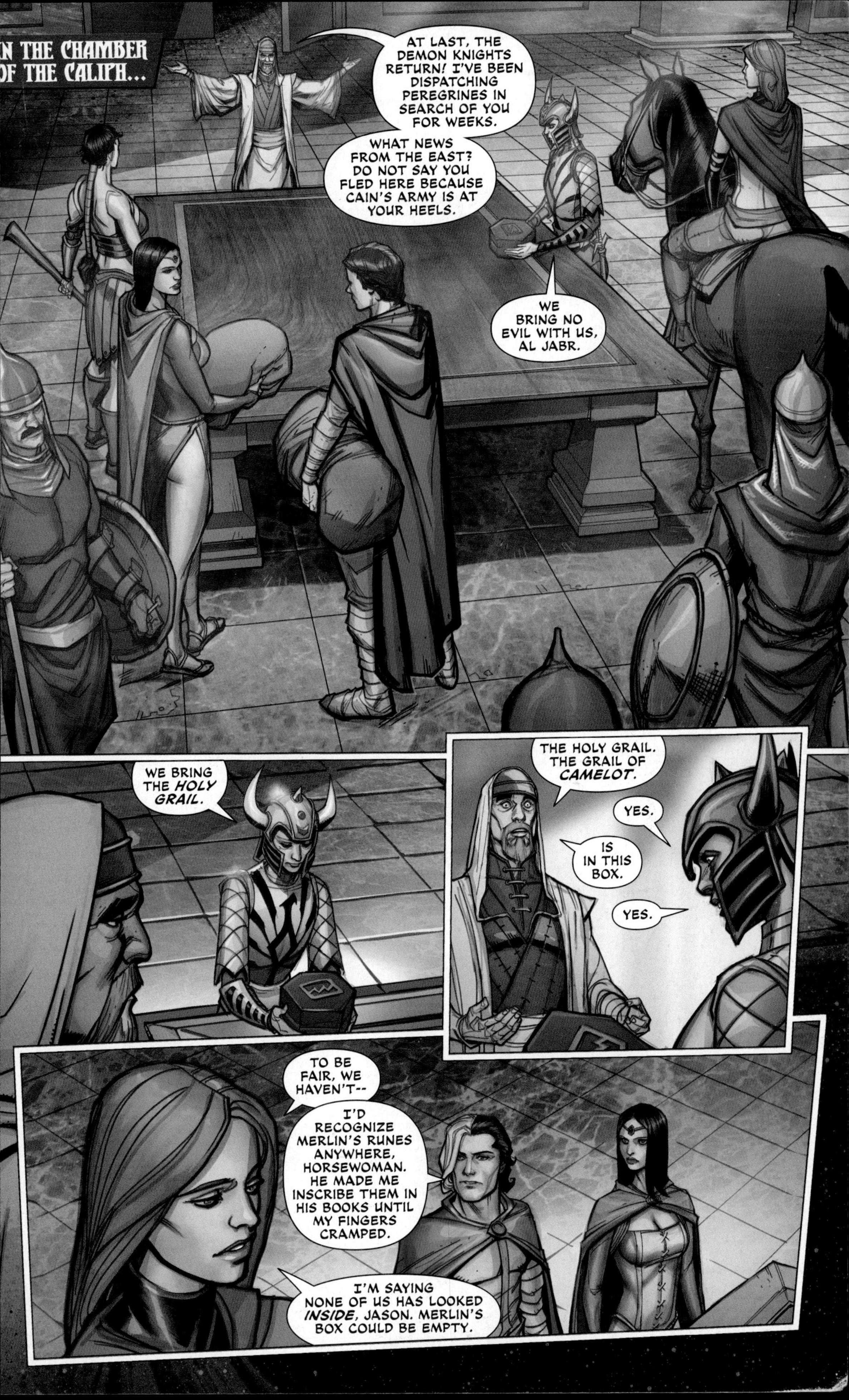
IN THE CHAMBER OF THE CALIPH...
AT LAST, THE DEMON KNIGHTS RETURN! I'VE BEEN DISPATCHING PEREGRINES IN SEARCH OF YOU FOR WEEKS.
WHAT NEWS FROM THE EAST? DO NOT SAY YOU FLED HERE BECAUSE CAIN'S ARMY IS AT YOUR HEELS.
WE BRING NO EVIL WITH US, AL JABR.
WE BRING THE HOLY GRAIL.
THE HOLY GRAIL. THE GRAIL OF CAMELOT.
YES.
IS IN THIS BOX.
YES.
TO BE FAIR, WE HAVEN'T--
I'D RECOGNIZE MERLIN'S RUNES ANYWHERE, HORSEWOMAN. HE MADE ME INSCRIBE THEM IN HIS BOOKS UNTIL MY FINGERS CRAMPED.
I'M SAYING NONE OF US HAS LOOKED INSIDE, JASON. MERLIN'S BOX COULD BE EMPTY.

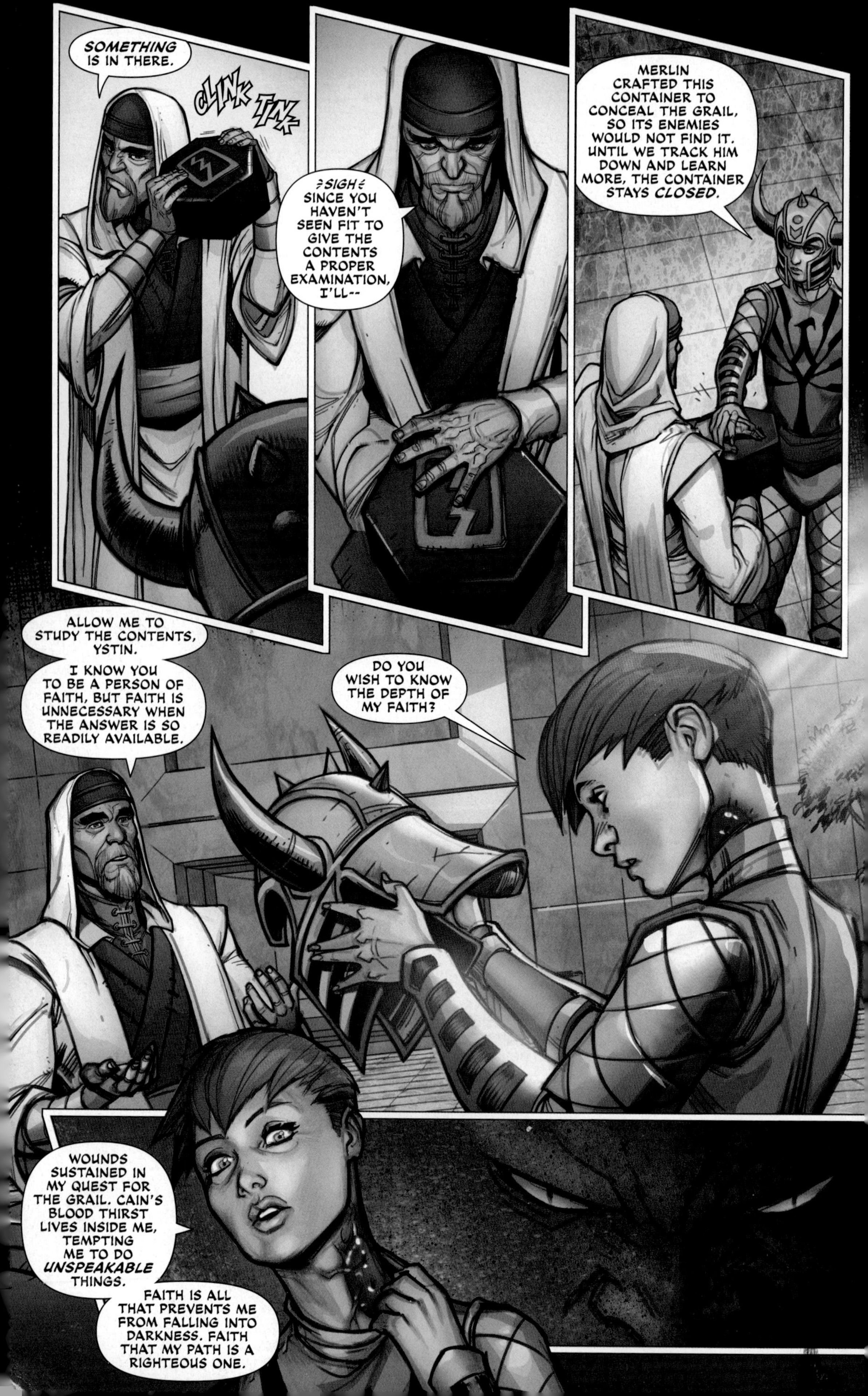
SOMETHING IS IN THERE.
CLINK TINK
⩶SIGH⩶ SINCE YOU HAVEN'T SEEN FIT TO GIVE THE CONTENTS A PROPER EXAMINATION, I'LL--
MERLIN CRAFTED THIS CONTAINER TO CONCEAL THE GRAIL, SO ITS ENEMIES WOULD NOT FIND IT. UNTIL WE TRACK HIM DOWN AND LEARN MORE, THE CONTAINER STAYS CLOSED.
ALLOW ME TO STUDY THE CONTENTS, YSTIN.
I KNOW YOU TO BE A PERSON OF FAITH, BUT FAITH IS UNNECESSARY WHEN THE ANSWER IS SO READILY AVAILABLE.
DO YOU WISH TO KNOW THE DEPTH OF MY FAITH?
WOUNDS SUSTAINED IN MY QUEST FOR THE GRAIL. CAIN'S BLOOD THIRST LIVES INSIDE ME, TEMPTING ME TO DO UNSPEAKABLE THINGS.
FAITH IS ALL THAT PREVENTS ME FROM FALLING INTO DARKNESS. FAITH THAT MY PATH IS A RIGHTEOUS ONE.

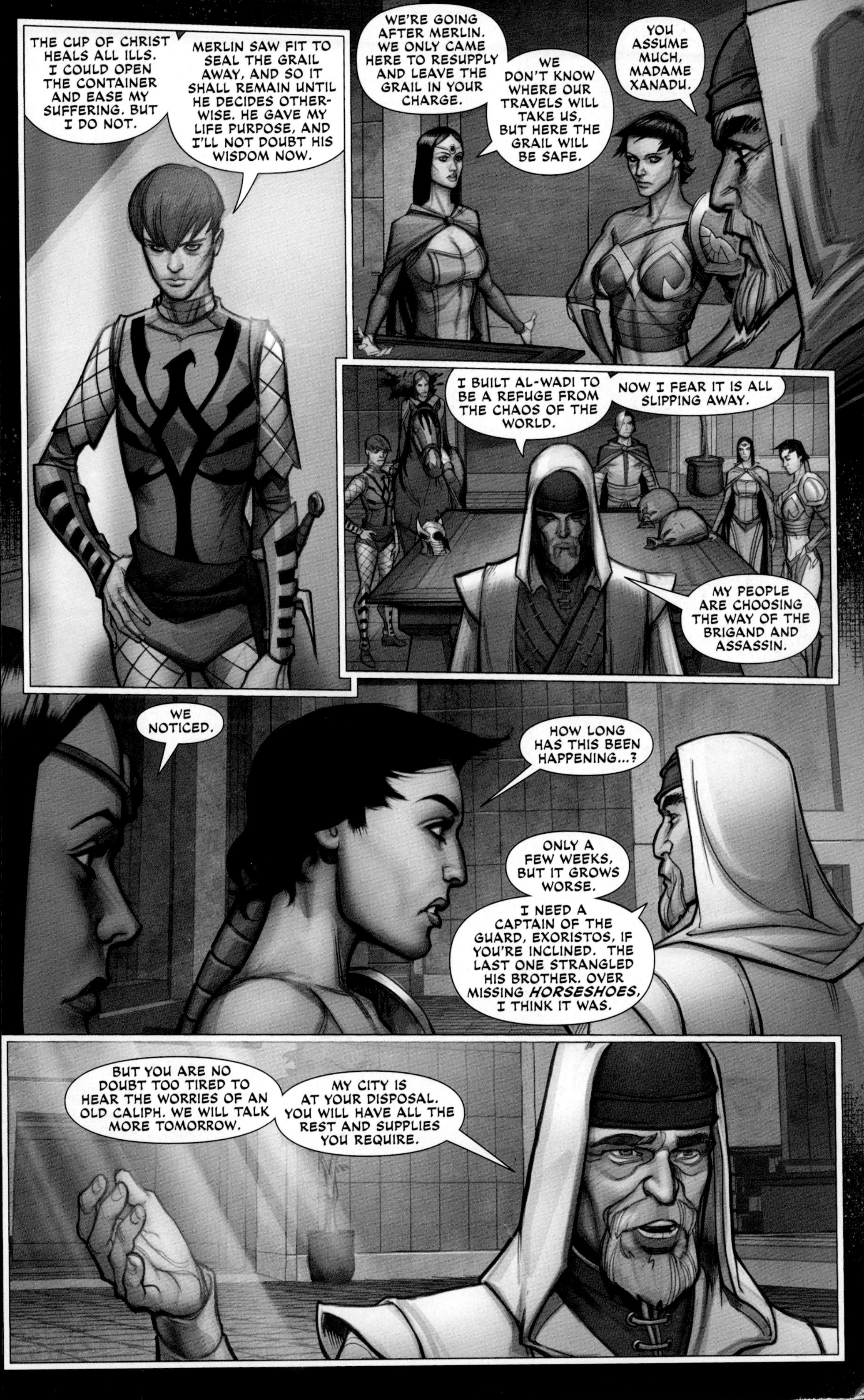
THE CUP OF CHRIST HEALS ALL ILLS. I COULD OPEN THE CONTAINER AND EASE MY SUFFERING. BUT I DO NOT.
MERLIN SAW FIT TO SEAL THE GRAIL AWAY, AND SO IT SHALL REMAIN UNTIL HE DECIDES OTHER-WISE. HE GAVE MY LIFE PURPOSE, AND I'LL NOT DOUBT HIS WISDOM NOW.
WE'RE GOING AFTER MERLIN. WE ONLY CAME HERE TO RESUPPLY AND LEAVE THE GRAIL IN YOUR CHARGE.
WE DON'T KNOW WHERE OUR TRAVELS WILL TAKE US, BUT HERE THE GRAIL WILL BE SAFE.
YOU ASSUME MUCH, MADAME XANADU.
I BUILT AL-WADI TO BE A REFUGE FROM THE CHAOS OF THE WORLD.
NOW I FEAR IT IS ALL SLIPPING AWAY.
MY PEOPLE ARE CHOOSING THE WAY OF THE BRIGAND AND ASSASSIN.
WE NOTICED.
HOW LONG HAS THIS BEEN HAPPENING...?
ONLY A FEW WEEKS, BUT IT GROWS WORSE.
I NEED A CAPTAIN OF THE GUARD, EXORISTOS, IF YOU'RE INCLINED. THE LAST ONE STRANGLED HIS BROTHER. OVER MISSING *HORSESHOES*, I THINK IT WAS.
BUT YOU ARE NO DOUBT TOO TIRED TO HEAR THE WORRIES OF AN OLD CALIPH. WE WILL TALK MORE TOMORROW.
MY CITY IS AT YOUR DISPOSAL. YOU WILL HAVE ALL THE REST AND SUPPLIES YOU REQUIRE.

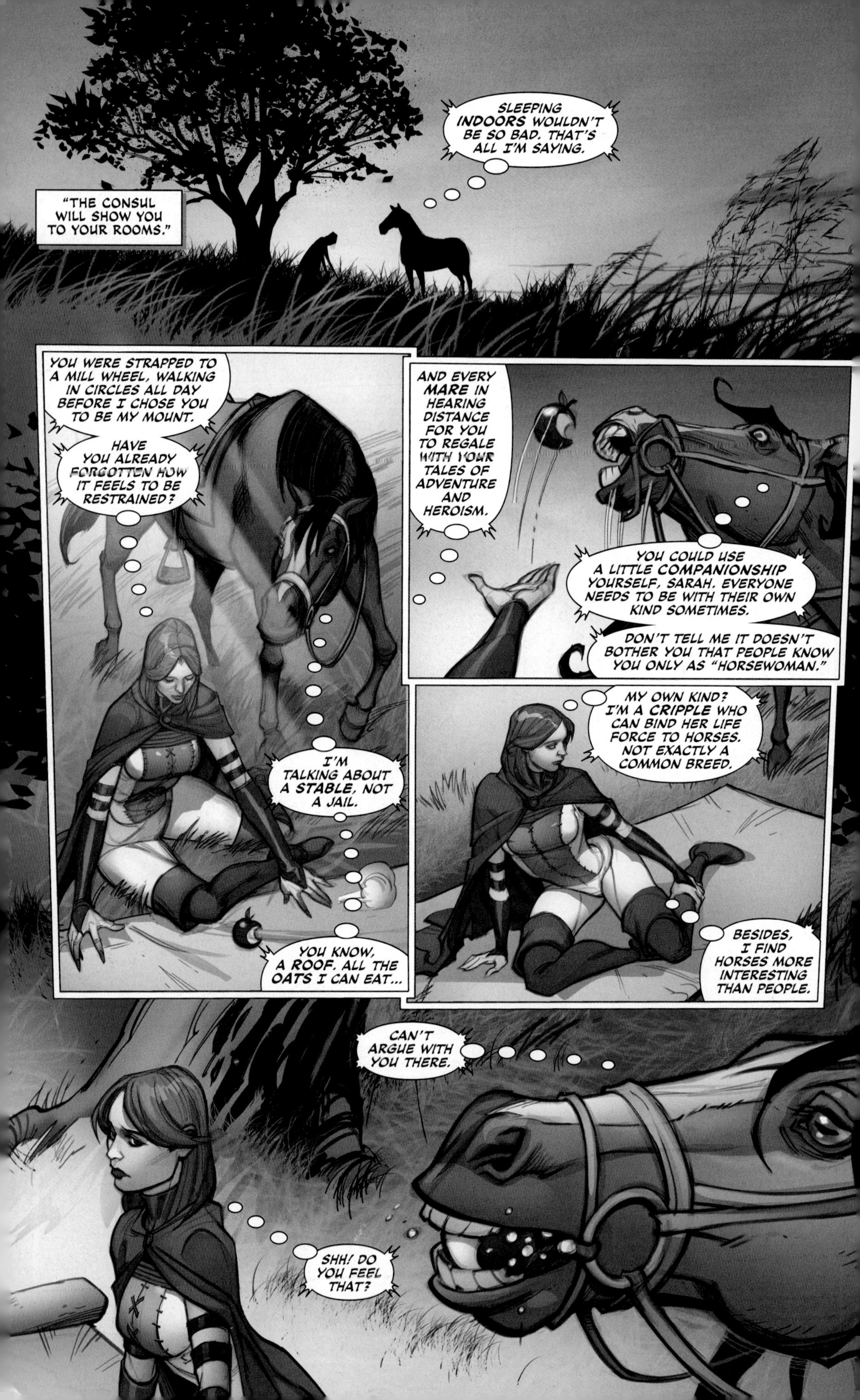

"THE CONSUL WILL SHOW YOU TO YOUR ROOMS."
SLEEPING INDOORS WOULDN'T BE SO BAD. THAT'S ALL I'M SAYING.
YOU WERE STRAPPED TO A MILL WHEEL, WALKING IN CIRCLES ALL DAY BEFORE I CHOSE YOU TO BE MY MOUNT.
HAVE YOU ALREADY FORGOTTEN HOW IT FEELS TO BE RESTRAINED?
I'M TALKING ABOUT A STABLE, NOT A JAIL.
YOU KNOW, A ROOF. ALL THE OATS I CAN EAT...
AND EVERY MARE IN HEARING DISTANCE FOR YOU TO REGALE WITH YOUR TALES OF ADVENTURE AND HEROISM.
YOU COULD USE A LITTLE COMPANIONSHIP YOURSELF, SARAH. EVERYONE NEEDS TO BE WITH THEIR OWN KIND SOMETIMES.
DON'T TELL ME IT DOESN'T BOTHER YOU THAT PEOPLE KNOW YOU ONLY AS "HORSEWOMAN."
MY OWN KIND? I'M A CRIPPLE WHO CAN BIND HER LIFE FORCE TO HORSES. NOT EXACTLY A COMMON BREED.
BESIDES, I FIND HORSES MORE INTERESTING THAN PEOPLE.
CAN'T ARGUE WITH YOU THERE.
SHH! DO YOU FEEL THAT?

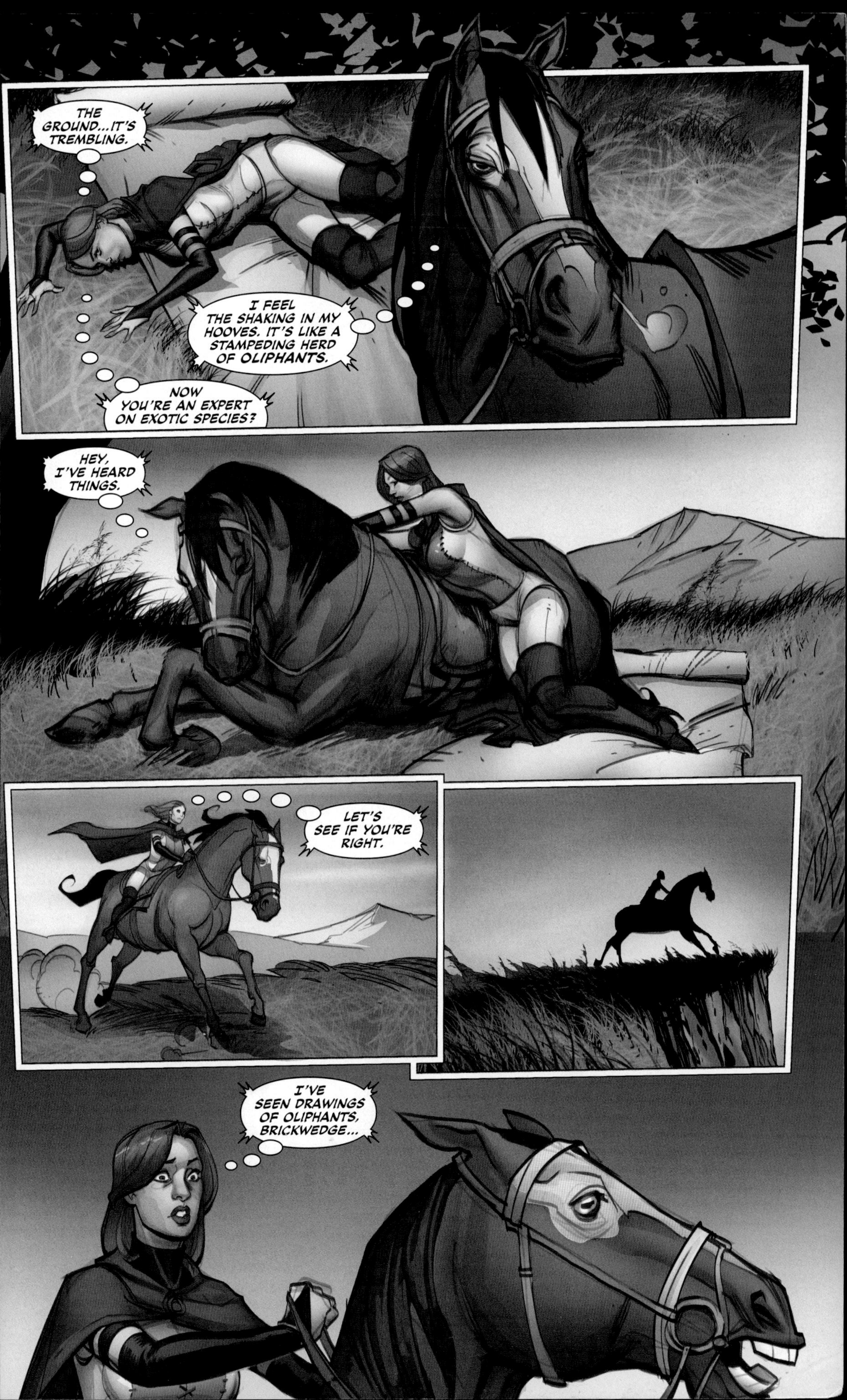
THE GROUND...IT'S TREMBLING.
I FEEL THE SHAKING IN MY HOOVES. IT'S LIKE A STAMPEDING HERD OF OLIPHANTS.
NOW YOU'RE AN EXPERT ON EXOTIC SPECIES?
HEY, I'VE HEARD THINGS.
LET'S SEE IF YOU'RE RIGHT.
I'VE SEEN DRAWINGS OF OLIPHANTS, BRICKWEDGE...

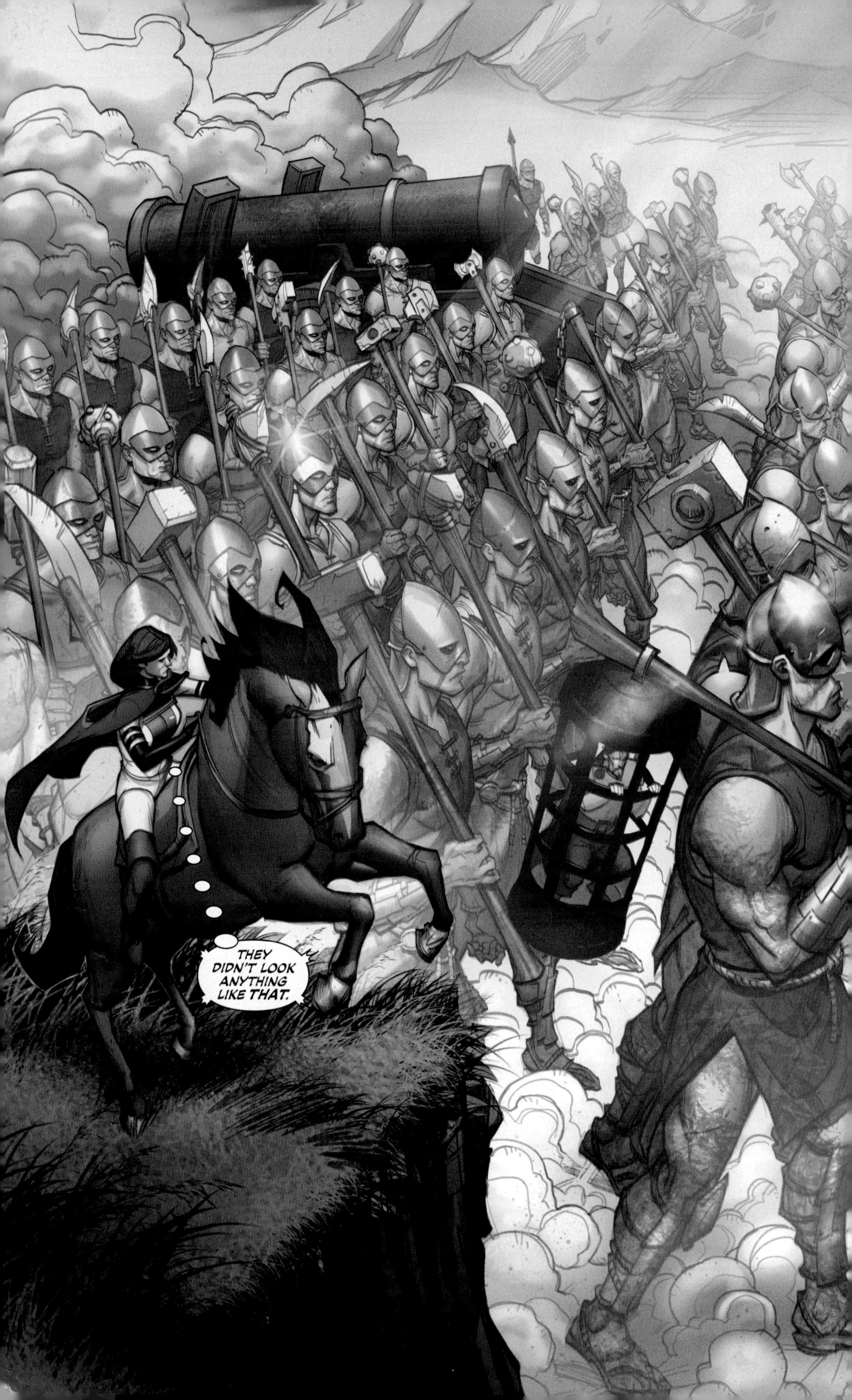
THEY DIDN'T LOOK ANYTHING LIKE THAT.

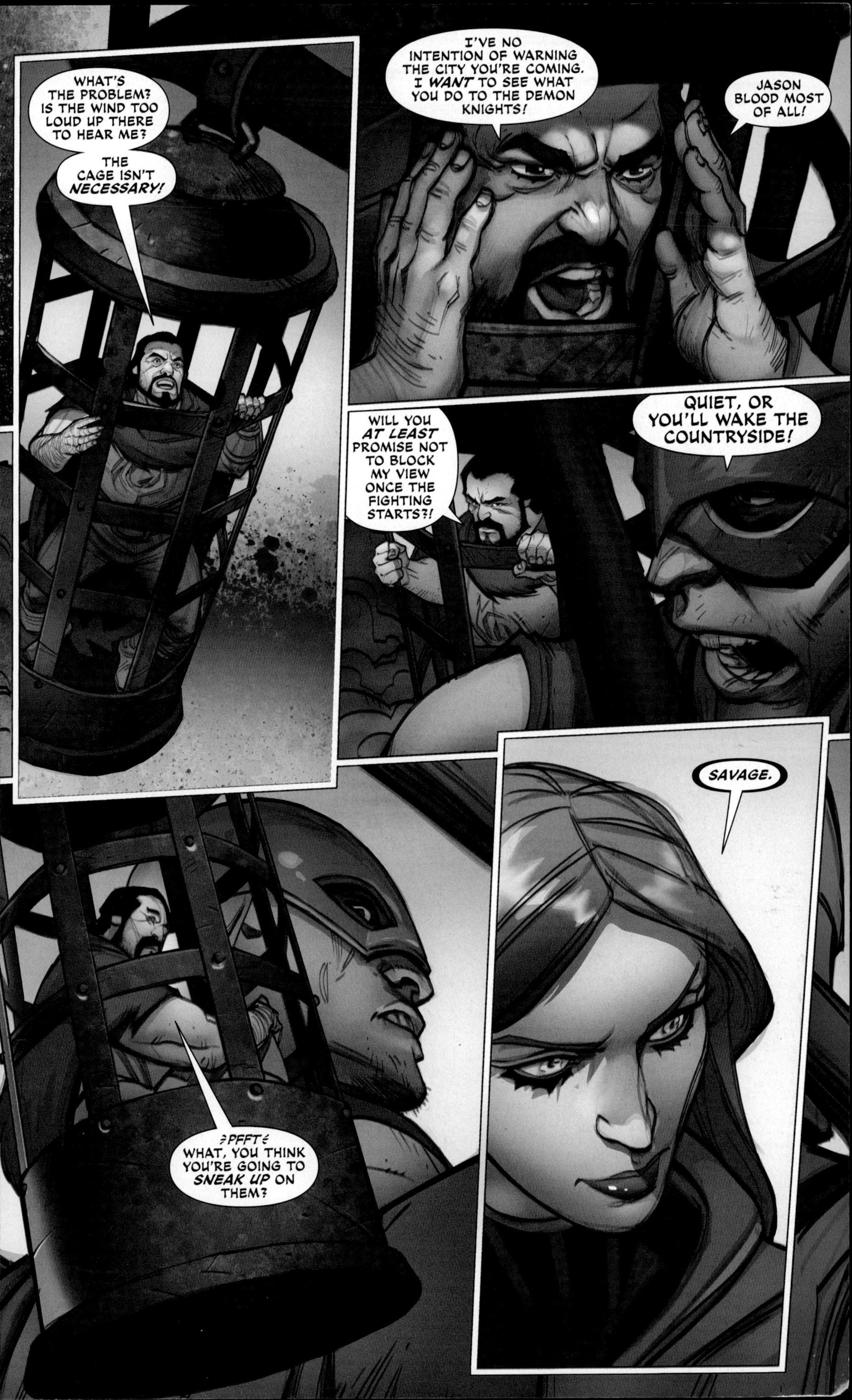
WHAT'S THE PROBLEM? IS THE WIND TOO LOUD UP THERE TO HEAR ME?
THE CAGE ISN'T *NECESSARY!*
I'VE NO INTENTION OF WARNING THE CITY YOU'RE COMING. I *WANT* TO SEE WHAT YOU DO TO THE DEMON KNIGHTS!
JASON BLOOD MOST OF ALL!
WILL YOU *AT LEAST* PROMISE NOT TO BLOCK MY VIEW ONCE THE FIGHTING STARTS?!
QUIET, OR YOU'LL WAKE THE COUNTRYSIDE!
PFFT
WHAT, YOU THINK YOU'RE GOING TO *SNEAK UP* ON THEM?
SAVAGE.

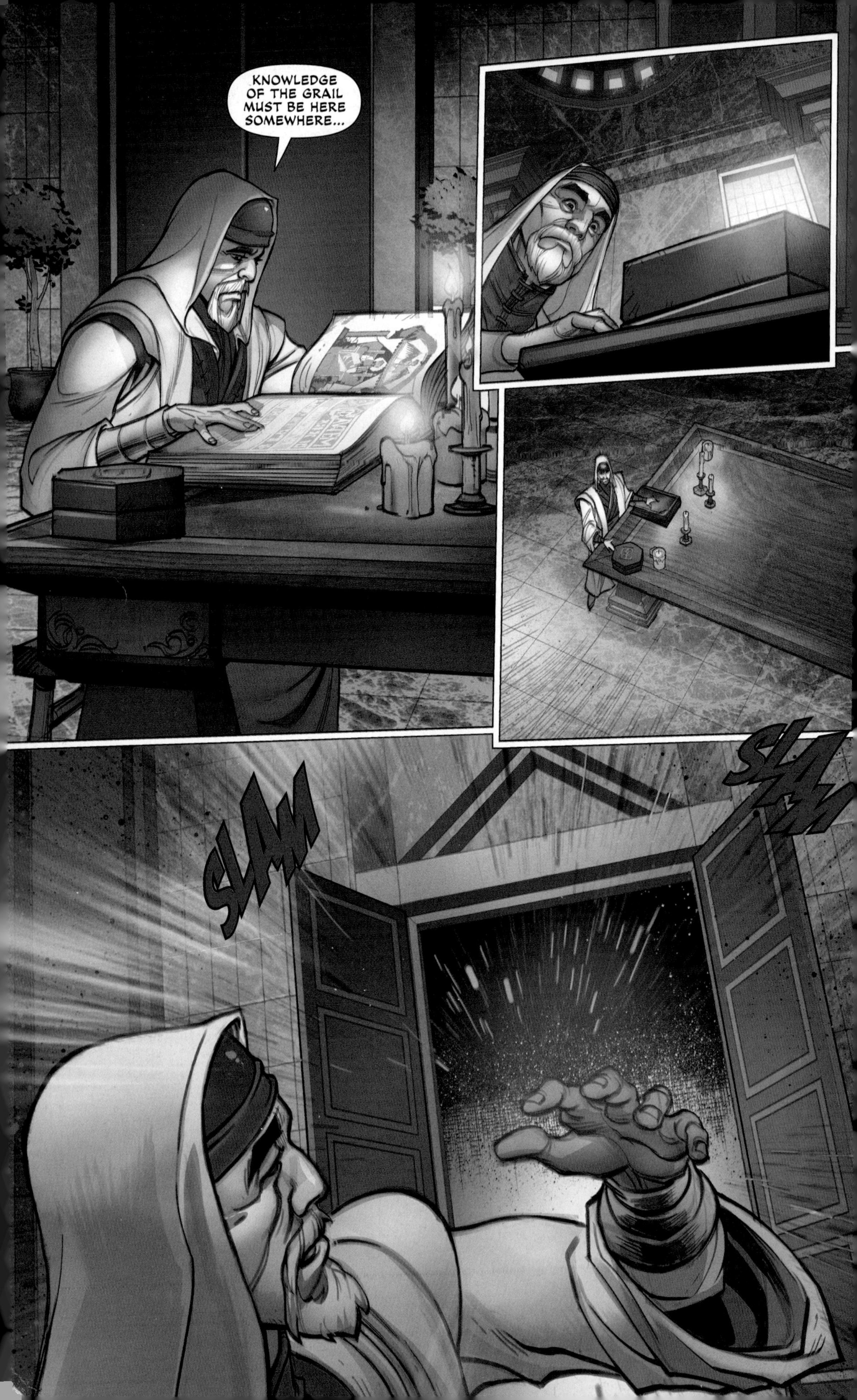
KNOWLEDGE OF THE GRAIL MUST BE HERE SOMEWHERE...
SLAM
SLAM

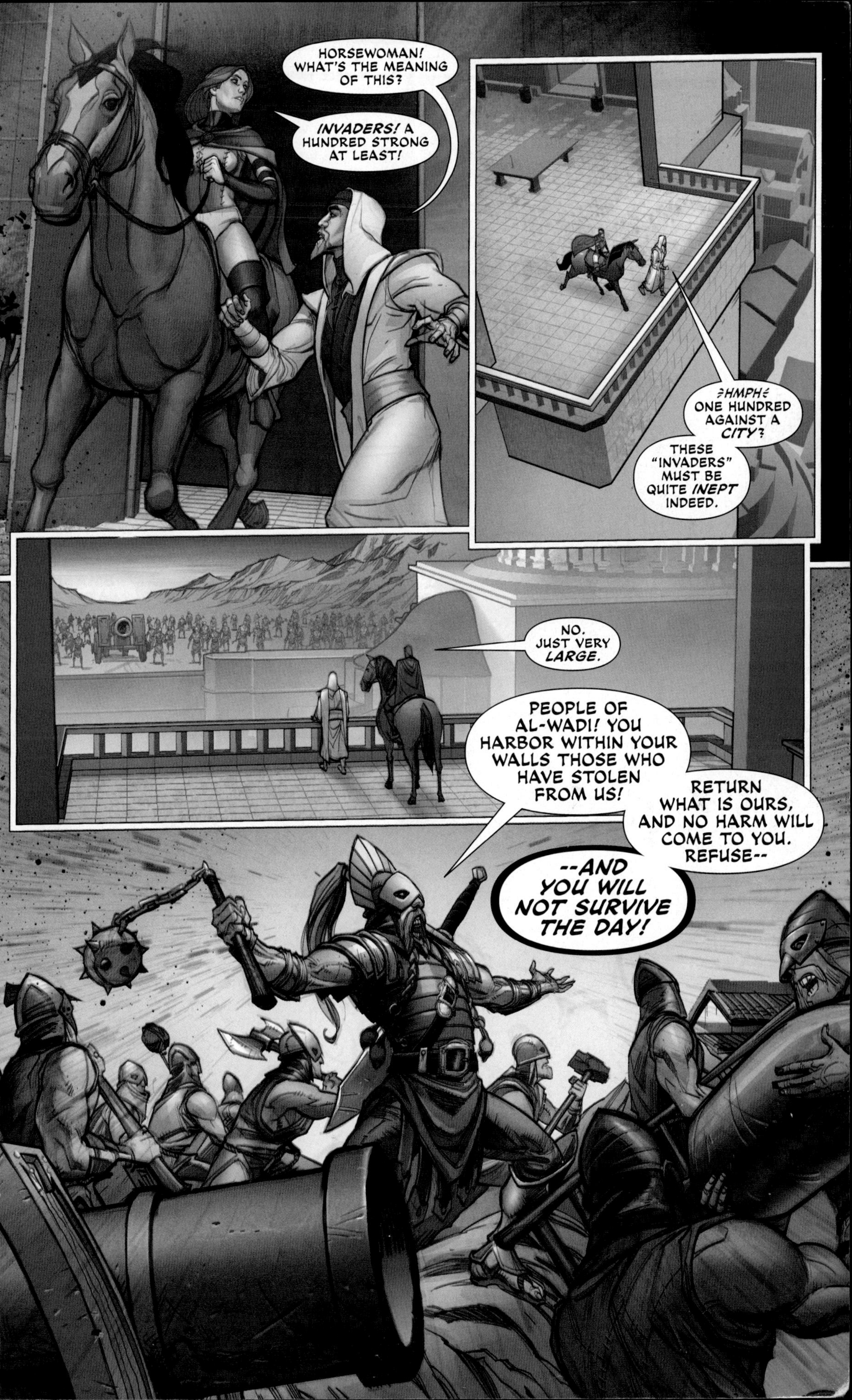
HORSEWOMAN! WHAT'S THE MEANING OF THIS?
INVADERS! A HUNDRED STRONG AT LEAST!
≈HMPH≈ ONE HUNDRED AGAINST A CITY?
THESE "INVADERS" MUST BE QUITE INEPT INDEED.
NO. JUST VERY LARGE.
PEOPLE OF AL-WADI! YOU HARBOR WITHIN YOUR WALLS THOSE WHO HAVE STOLEN FROM US!
RETURN WHAT IS OURS, AND NO HARM WILL COME TO YOU. REFUSE--
--AND YOU WILL NOT SURVIVE THE DAY!

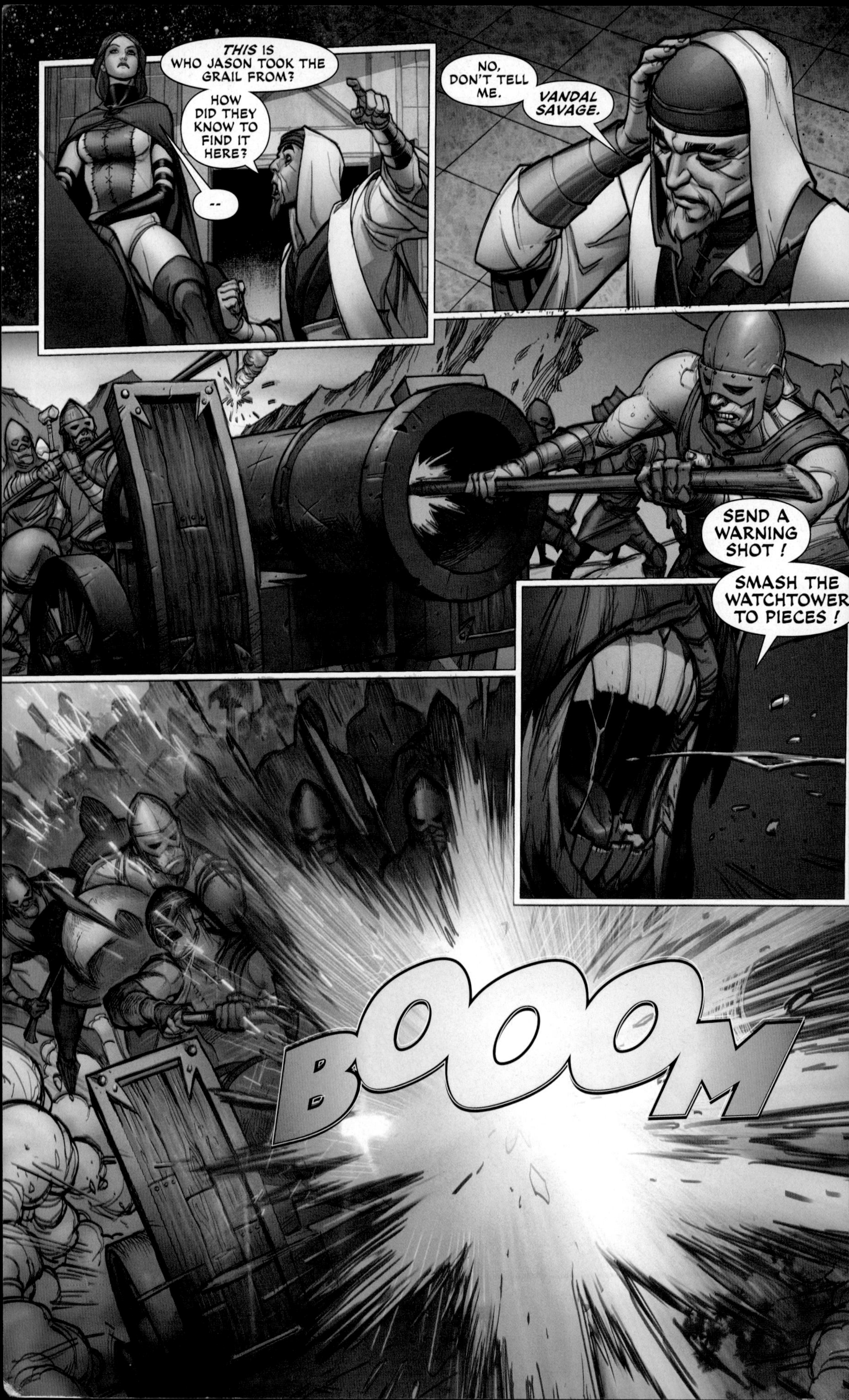
THIS IS WHO JASON TOOK THE GRAIL FROM?
HOW DID THEY KNOW TO FIND IT HERE?
--
NO, DON'T TELL ME.
VANDAL SAVAGE.
SEND A WARNING SHOT !
SMASH THE WATCHTOWER TO PIECES !
BOOOM

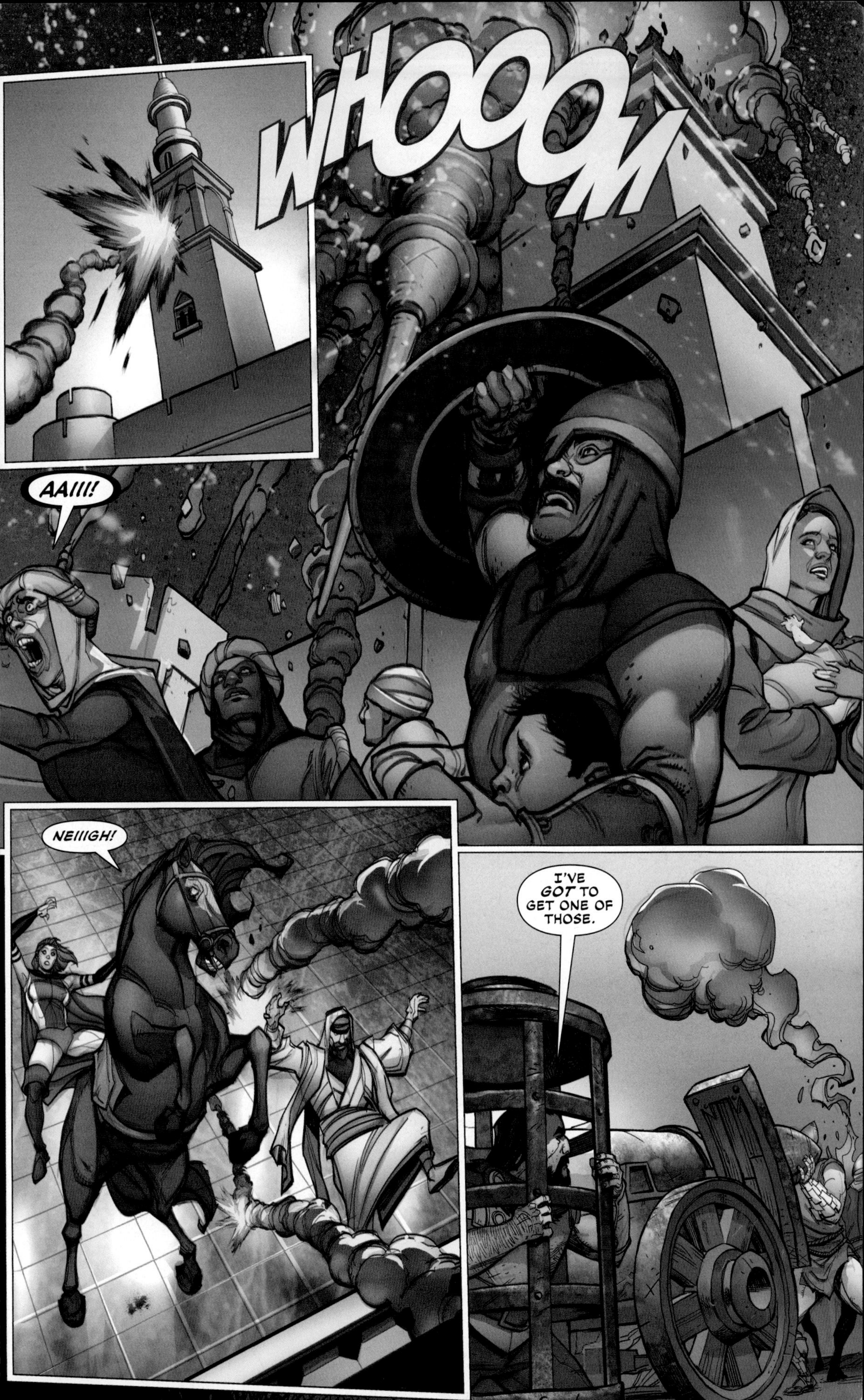
WHOOOM
AAIII!
NEIIIGH!
I'VE GOT TO GET ONE OF THOSE.

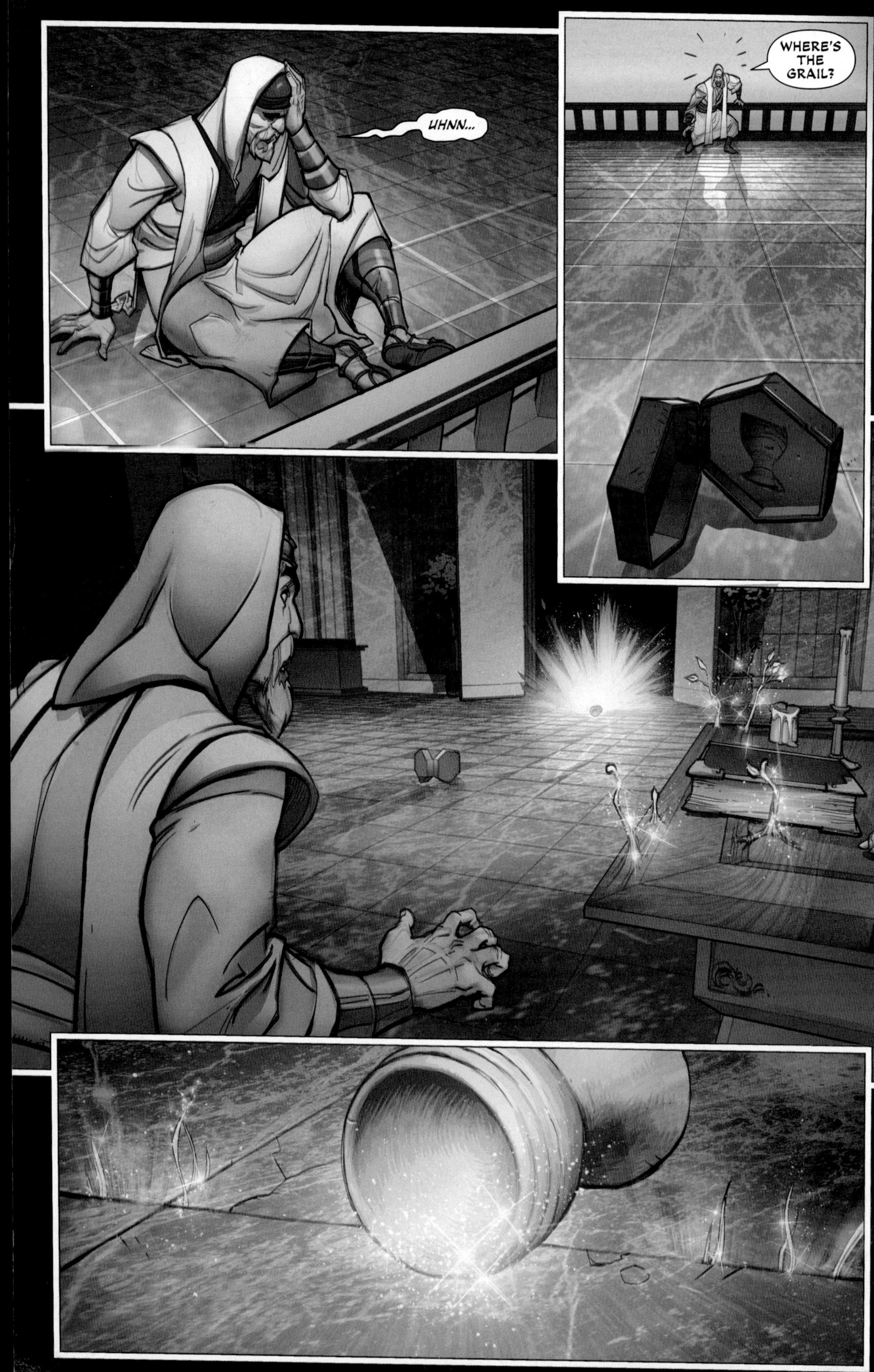
UHNN...
WHERE'S THE GRAIL?

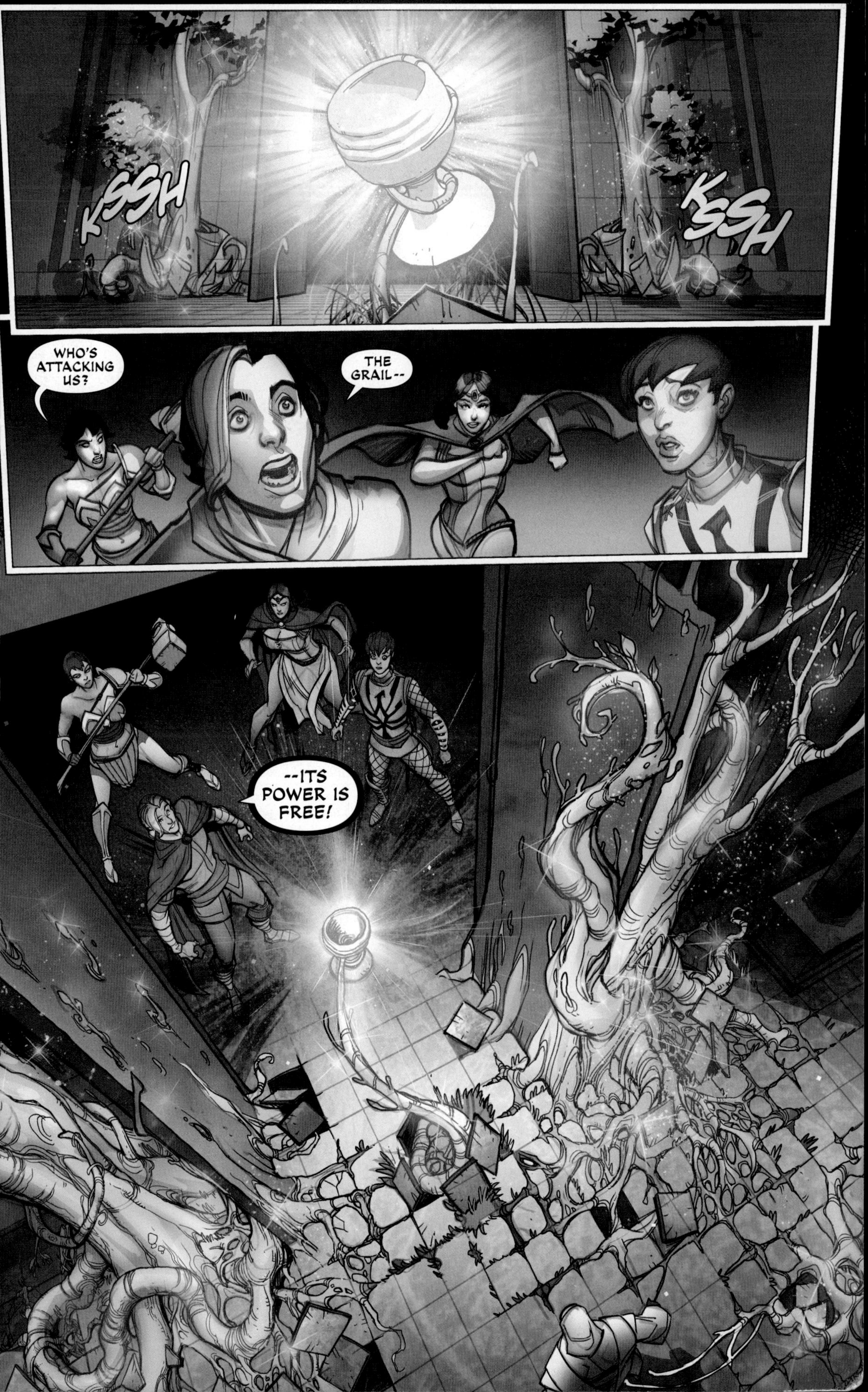
KSSH
KSSH
WHO'S ATTACKING US?
THE GRAIL--
--ITS POWER IS FREE!

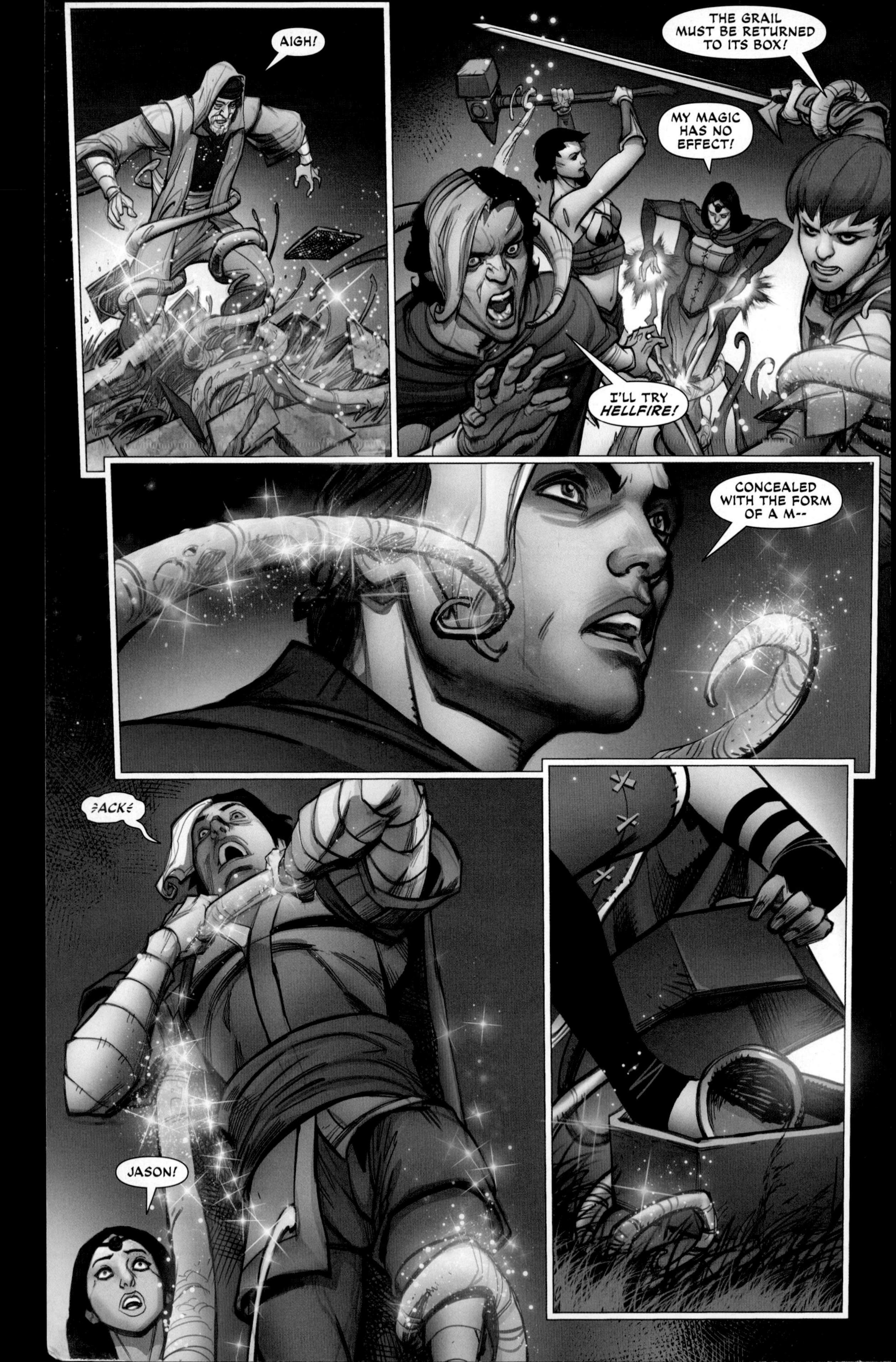
AIGH!
THE GRAIL MUST BE RETURNED TO ITS BOX!
MY MAGIC HAS NO EFFECT!
I'LL TRY *HELLFIRE!*
CONCEALED WITH THE FORM OF A M--
ACK
JASON!

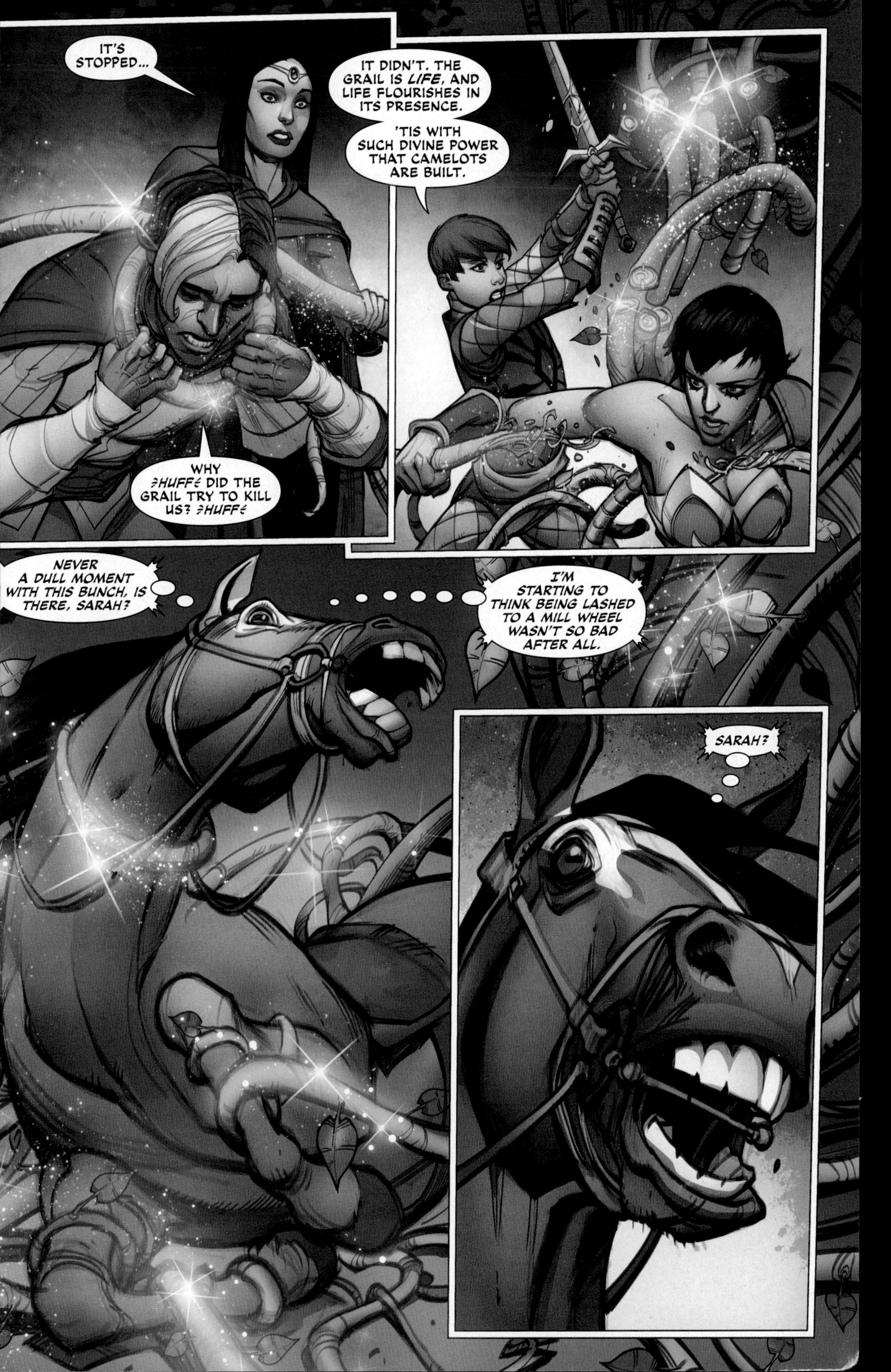
IT'S STOPPED...
WHY ≥HUFF≤ DID THE GRAIL TRY TO KILL US? ≥HUFF≤
IT DIDN'T. THE GRAIL IS *LIFE*, AND LIFE FLOURISHES IN ITS PRESENCE.
'TIS WITH SUCH DIVINE POWER THAT CAMELOTS ARE BUILT.
NEVER A DULL MOMENT WITH THIS BUNCH, IS THERE, SARAH?
I'M STARTING TO THINK BEING LASHED TO A MILL WHEEL WASN'T SO BAD AFTER ALL.
SARAH?

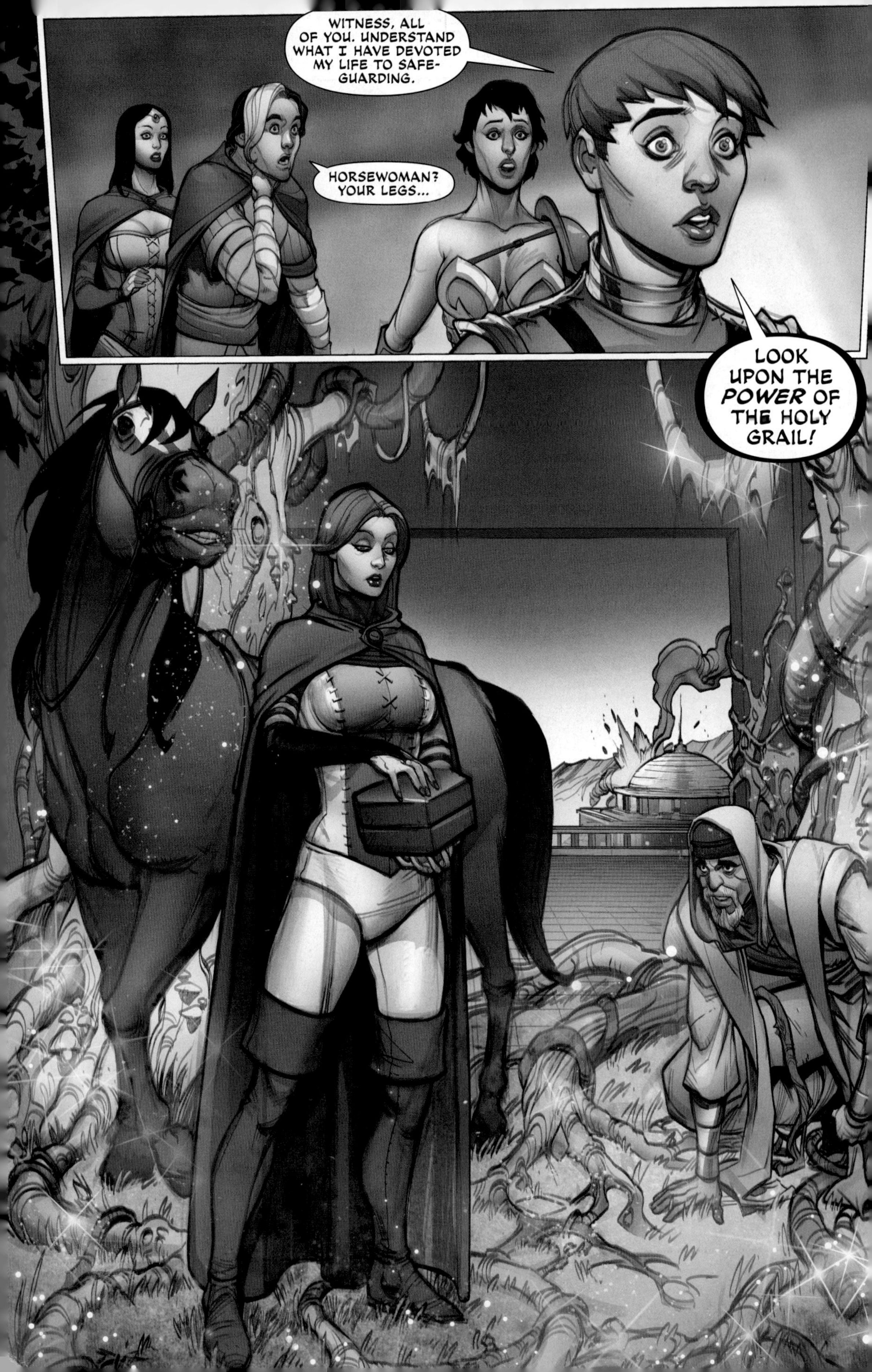
WITNESS, ALL OF YOU. UNDERSTAND WHAT I HAVE DEVOTED MY LIFE TO SAFE-GUARDING.
HORSEWOMAN? YOUR LEGS...
LOOK UPON THE POWER OF THE HOLY GRAIL!

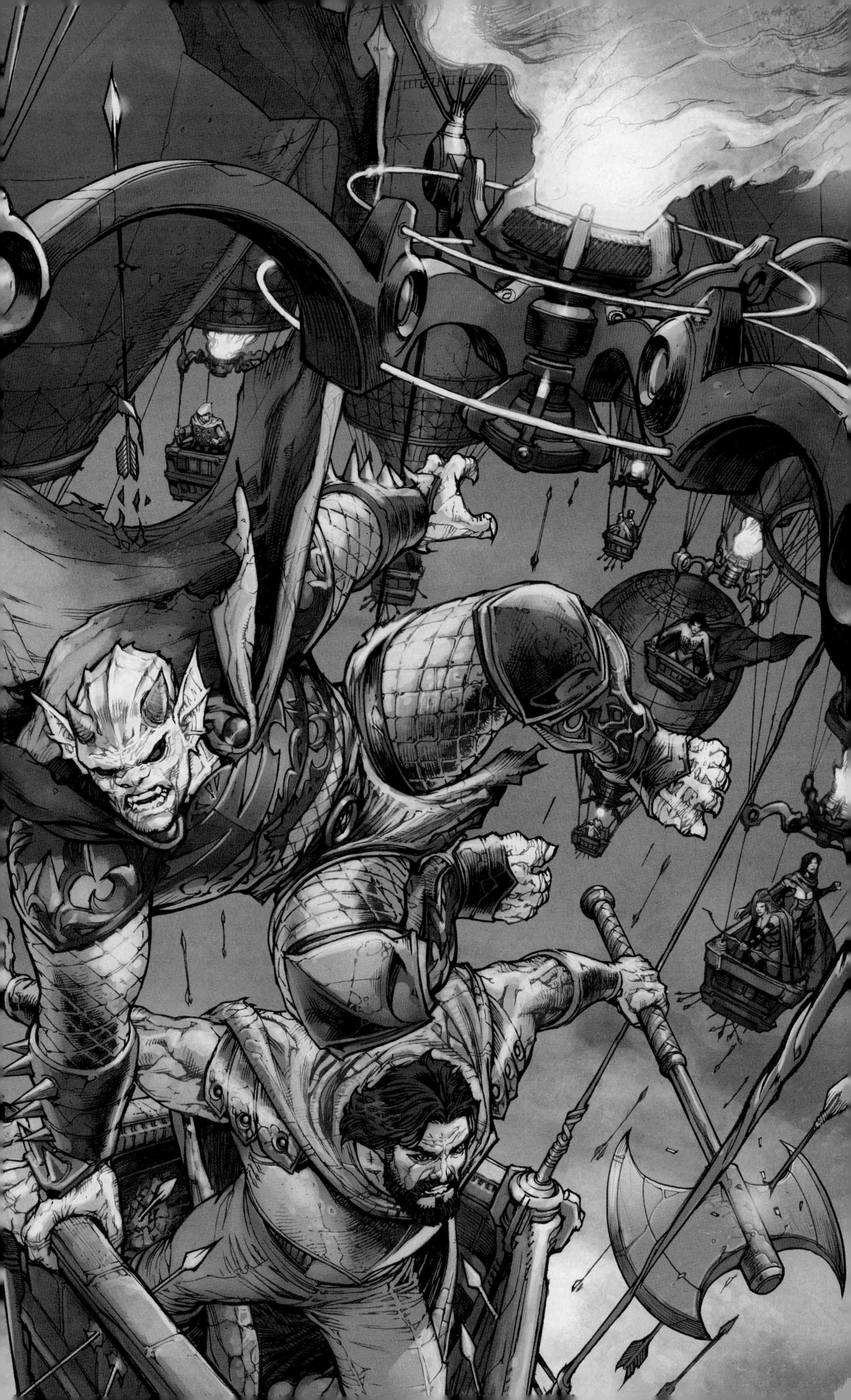

ROBERT VENDITTI
writer

PHIL WINSLADE
artist

HOWARD PORTER
cover artist

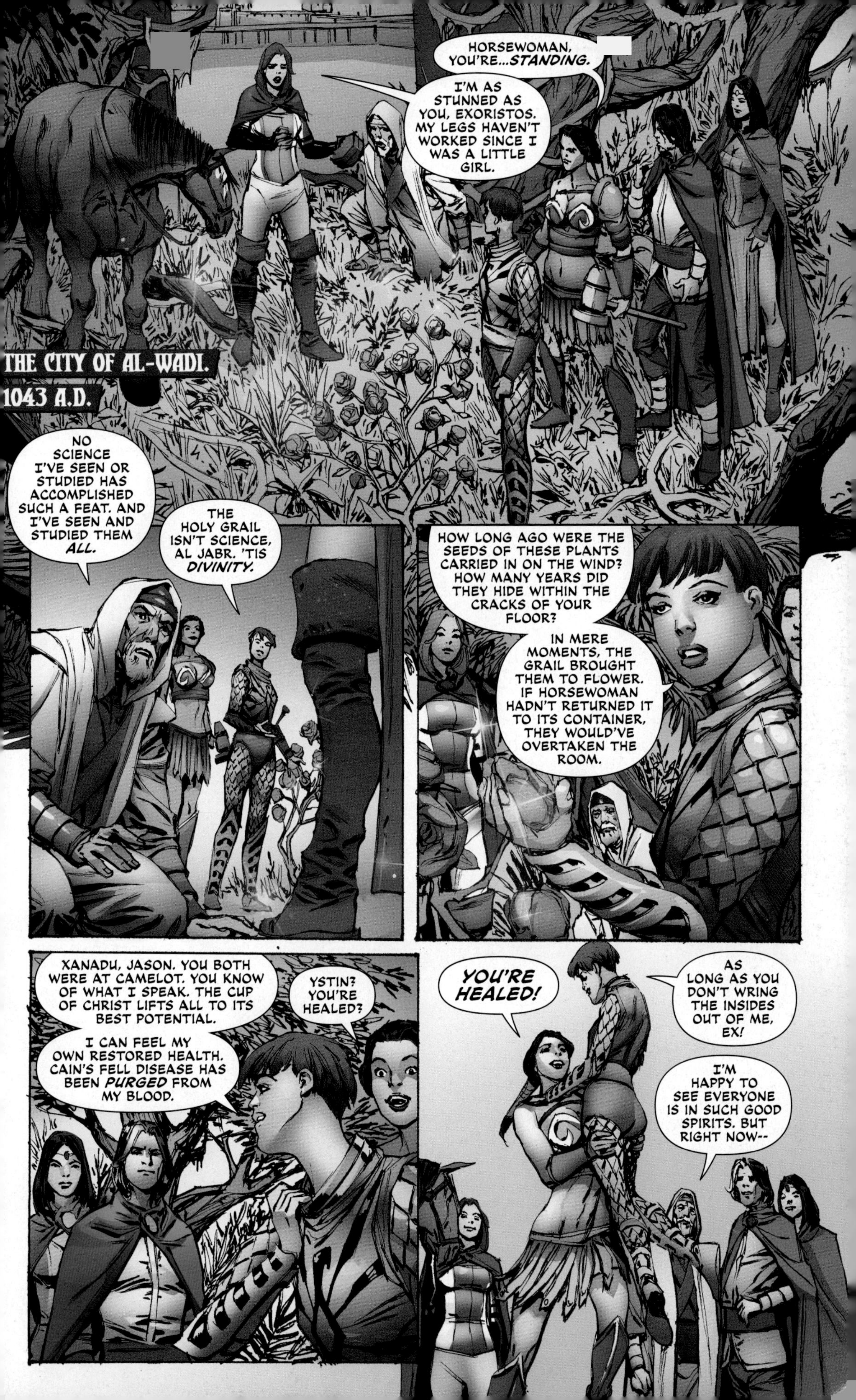

HORSEWOMAN, YOU'RE...STANDING.
I'M AS STUNNED AS YOU, EXORISTOS. MY LEGS HAVEN'T WORKED SINCE I WAS A LITTLE GIRL.
THE CITY OF AL-WADI.
1043 A.D.
NO SCIENCE I'VE SEEN OR STUDIED HAS ACCOMPLISHED SUCH A FEAT. AND I'VE SEEN AND STUDIED THEM ALL.
THE HOLY GRAIL ISN'T SCIENCE, AL JABR. 'TIS DIVINITY.
HOW LONG AGO WERE THE SEEDS OF THESE PLANTS CARRIED IN ON THE WIND? HOW MANY YEARS DID THEY HIDE WITHIN THE CRACKS OF YOUR FLOOR?
IN MERE MOMENTS, THE GRAIL BROUGHT THEM TO FLOWER. IF HORSEWOMAN HADN'T RETURNED IT TO ITS CONTAINER, THEY WOULD'VE OVERTAKEN THE ROOM.
XANADU, JASON. YOU BOTH WERE AT CAMELOT. YOU KNOW OF WHAT I SPEAK. THE CUP OF CHRIST LIFTS ALL TO ITS BEST POTENTIAL.
I CAN FEEL MY OWN RESTORED HEALTH. CAIN'S FELL DISEASE HAS BEEN PURGED FROM MY BLOOD.
YSTIN? YOU'RE HEALED?
YOU'RE HEALED!
AS LONG AS YOU DON'T WRING THE INSIDES OUT OF ME, EX!
I'M HAPPY TO SEE EVERYONE IS IN SUCH GOOD SPIRITS. BUT RIGHT NOW--

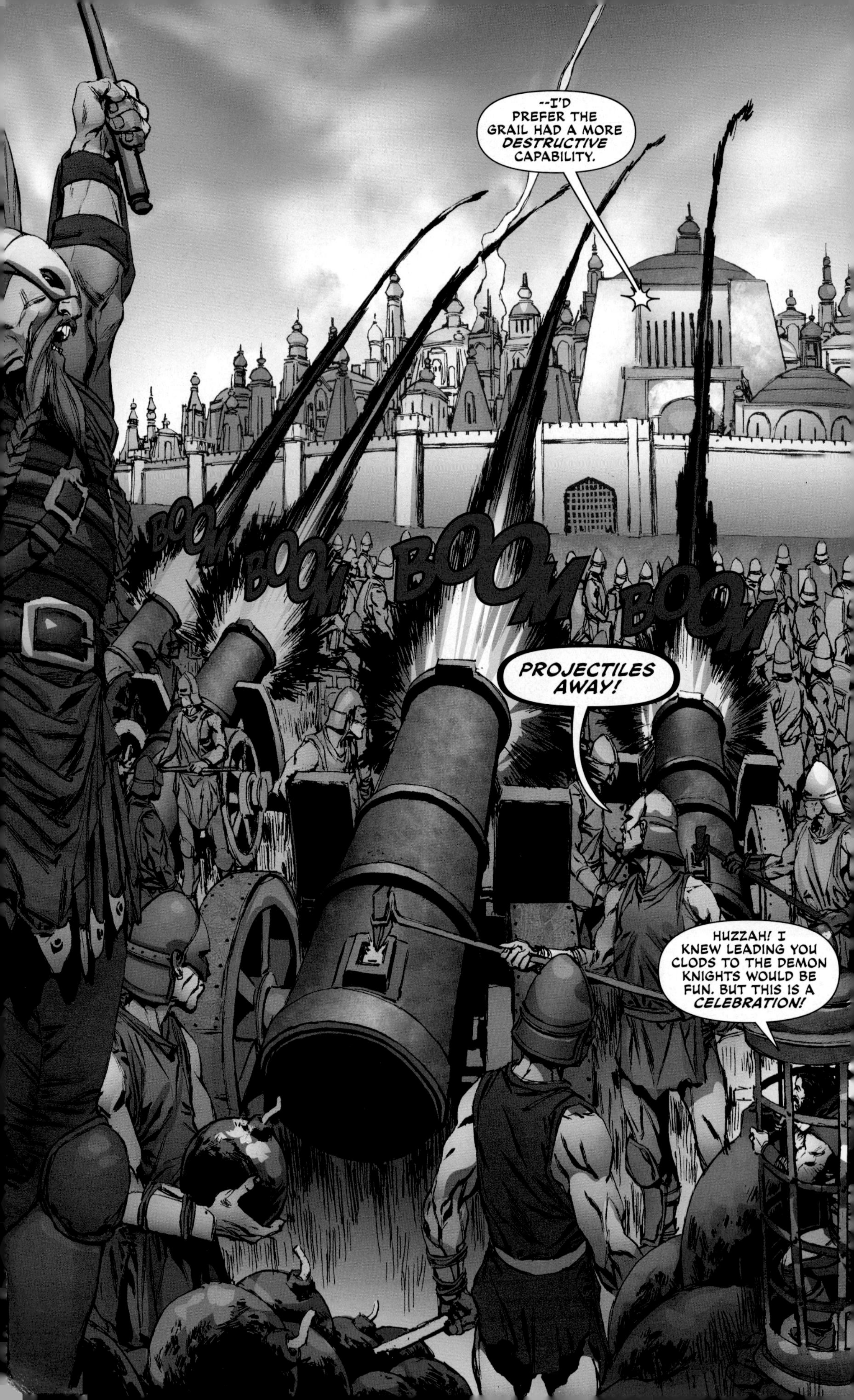
--I'D PREFER THE GRAIL HAD A MORE *DESTRUCTIVE* CAPABILITY.
BOOM
BOOM
BOOM
BOOM
PROJECTILES AWAY!
HUZZAH! I KNEW LEADING YOU CLODS TO THE DEMON KNIGHTS WOULD BE FUN. BUT THIS IS A *CELEBRATION!*

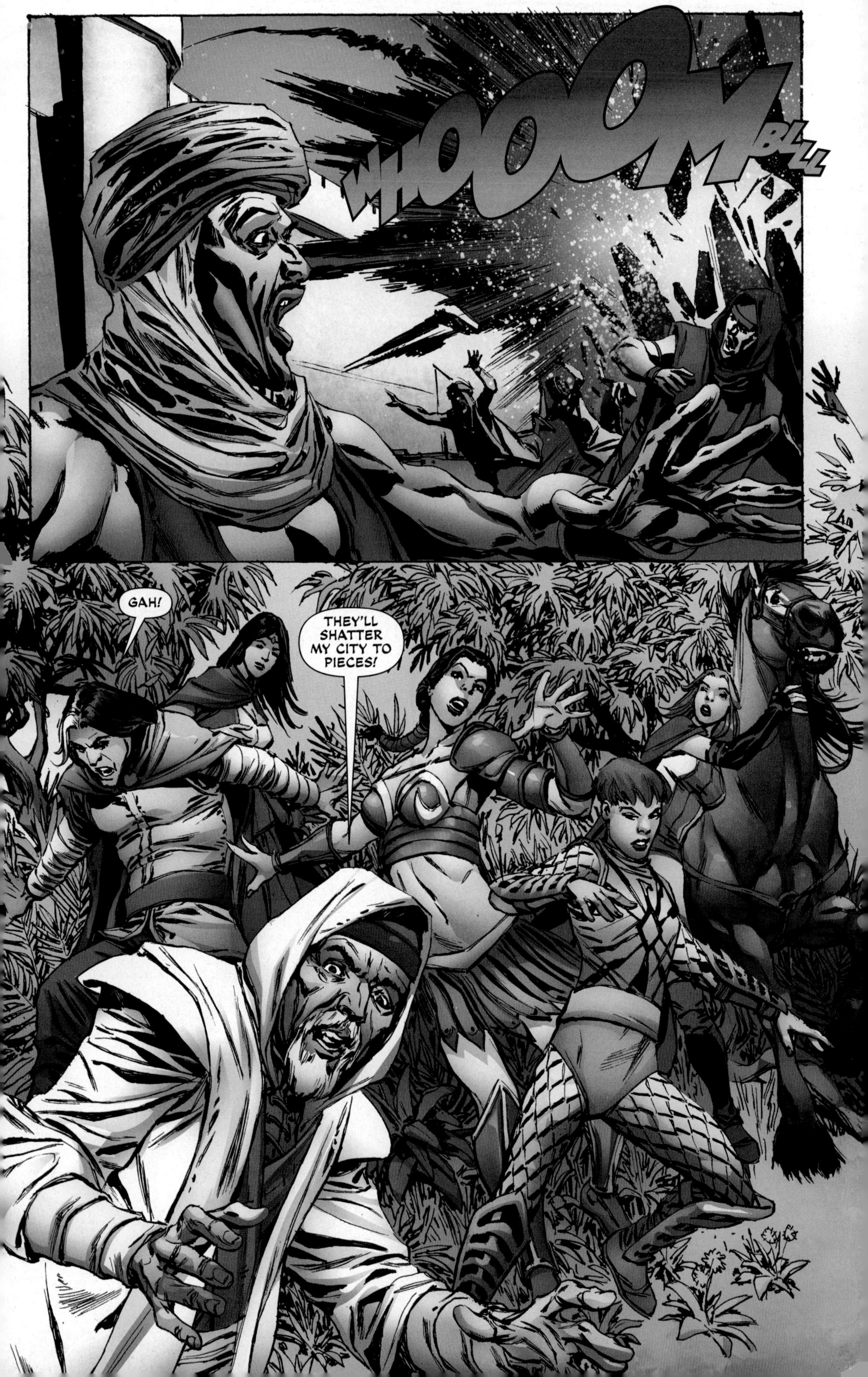
WHOOOM
BLLL
GAH!
THEY'LL SHATTER MY CITY TO PIECES!

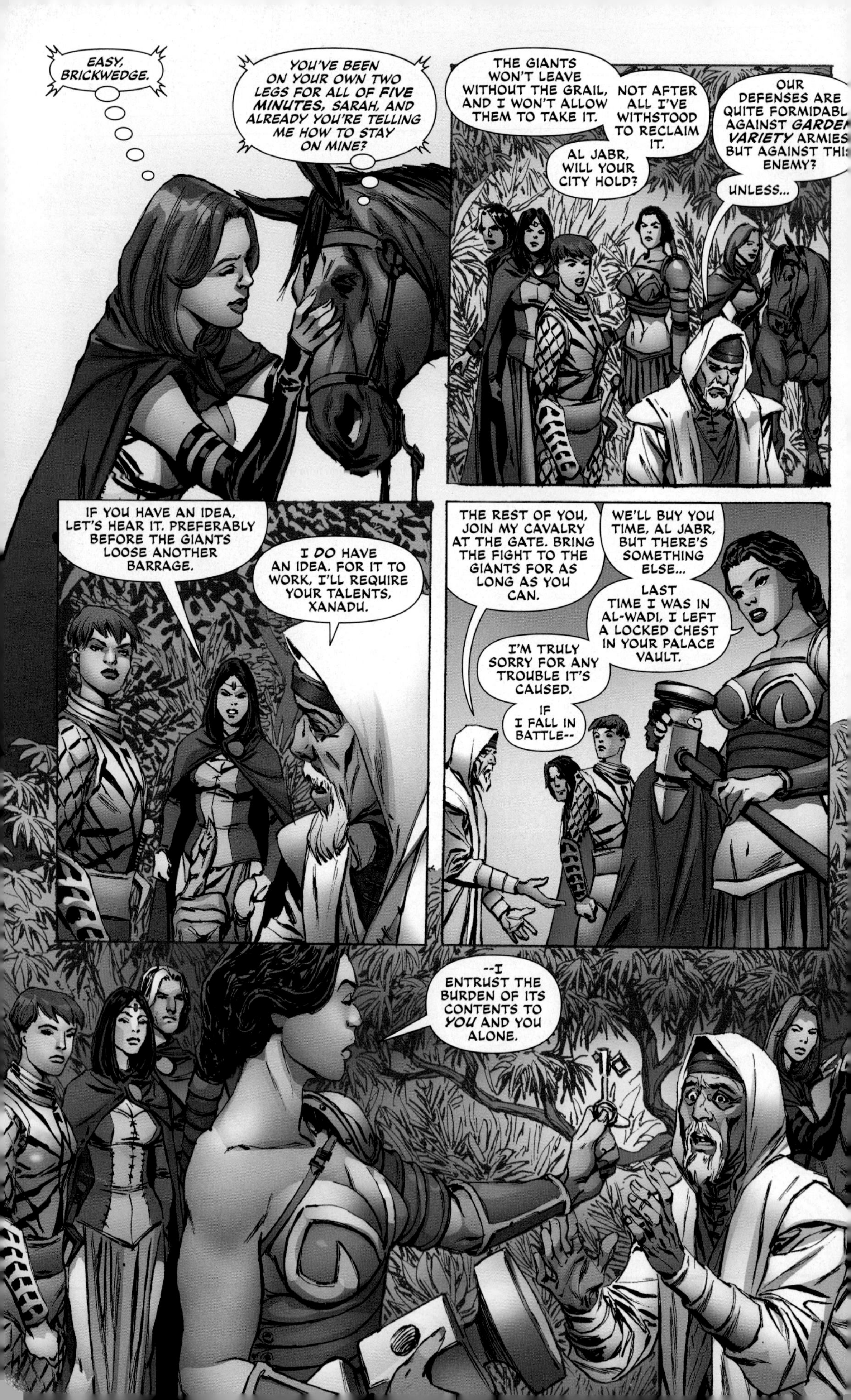
EASY, BRICKWEDGE.
YOU'VE BEEN ON YOUR OWN TWO LEGS FOR ALL OF FIVE MINUTES, SARAH, AND ALREADY YOU'RE TELLING ME HOW TO STAY ON MINE?
THE GIANTS WON'T LEAVE WITHOUT THE GRAIL, AND I WON'T ALLOW THEM TO TAKE IT.
NOT AFTER ALL I'VE WITHSTOOD TO RECLAIM IT.
AL JABR, WILL YOUR CITY HOLD?
OUR DEFENSES ARE QUITE FORMIDABL AGAINST GARDE VARIETY ARMIES BUT AGAINST THI ENEMY?
UNLESS...
IF YOU HAVE AN IDEA, LET'S HEAR IT. PREFERABLY BEFORE THE GIANTS LOOSE ANOTHER BARRAGE.
I DO HAVE AN IDEA. FOR IT TO WORK, I'LL REQUIRE YOUR TALENTS, XANADU.
THE REST OF YOU, JOIN MY CAVALRY AT THE GATE. BRING THE FIGHT TO THE GIANTS FOR AS LONG AS YOU CAN.
WE'LL BUY YOU TIME, AL JABR, BUT THERE'S SOMETHING ELSE...
LAST TIME I WAS IN AL-WADI, I LEFT A LOCKED CHEST IN YOUR PALACE VAULT.
I'M TRULY SORRY FOR ANY TROUBLE IT'S CAUSED.
IF I FALL IN BATTLE--
--I ENTRUST THE BURDEN OF ITS CONTENTS TO YOU AND YOU ALONE.

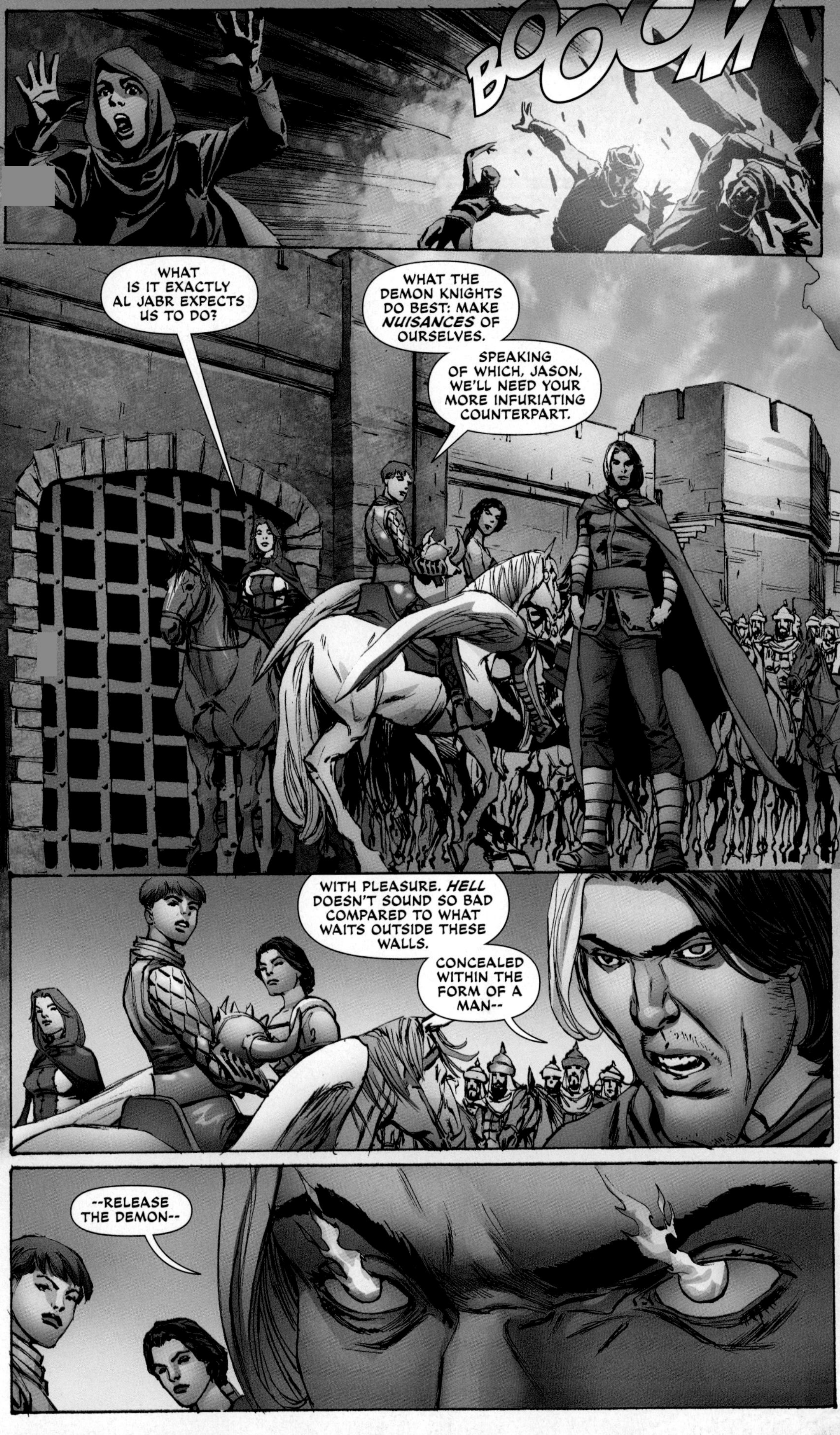
BOOOOM
WHAT IS IT EXACTLY AL JABR EXPECTS US TO DO?
WHAT THE DEMON KNIGHTS DO BEST: MAKE *NUISANCES* OF OURSELVES.
SPEAKING OF WHICH, JASON, WE'LL NEED YOUR MORE INFURIATING COUNTERPART.
WITH PLEASURE. *HELL* DOESN'T SOUND SO BAD COMPARED TO WHAT WAITS OUTSIDE THESE WALLS.
CONCEALED WITHIN THE FORM OF A MAN--
--RELEASE THE DEMON--

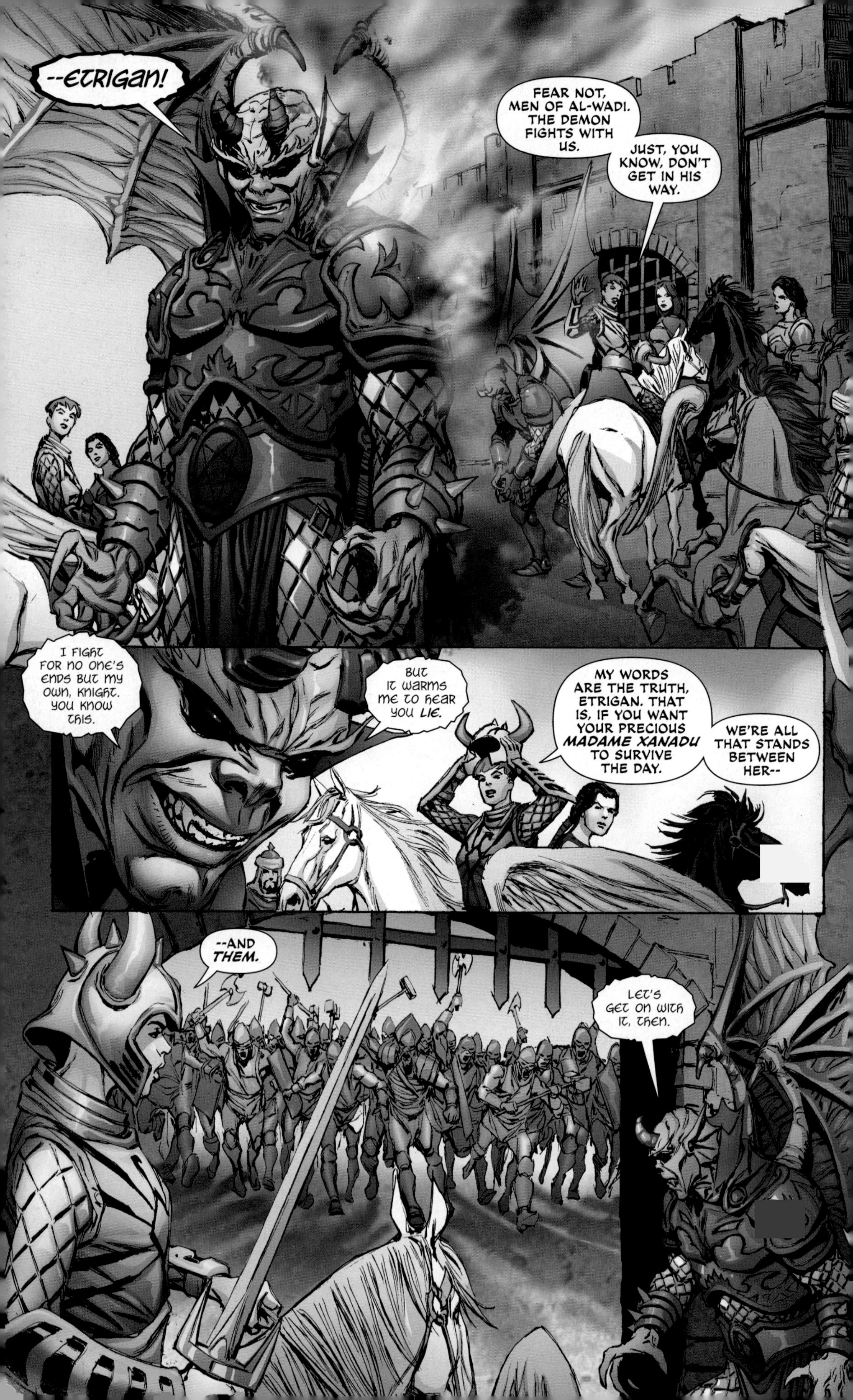
--ETRIGAN!
FEAR NOT, MEN OF AL-WADI. THE DEMON FIGHTS WITH US.
JUST, YOU KNOW, DON'T GET IN HIS WAY.
I FIGHT FOR NO ONE'S ENDS BUT MY OWN, KNIGHT. YOU KNOW THIS.
BUT IT WARMS ME TO HEAR YOU LIE.
MY WORDS ARE THE TRUTH, ETRIGAN. THAT IS, IF YOU WANT YOUR PRECIOUS MADAME XANADU TO SURVIVE THE DAY.
WE'RE ALL THAT STANDS BETWEEN HER--
--AND THEM.
LET'S GET ON WITH IT, THEN.

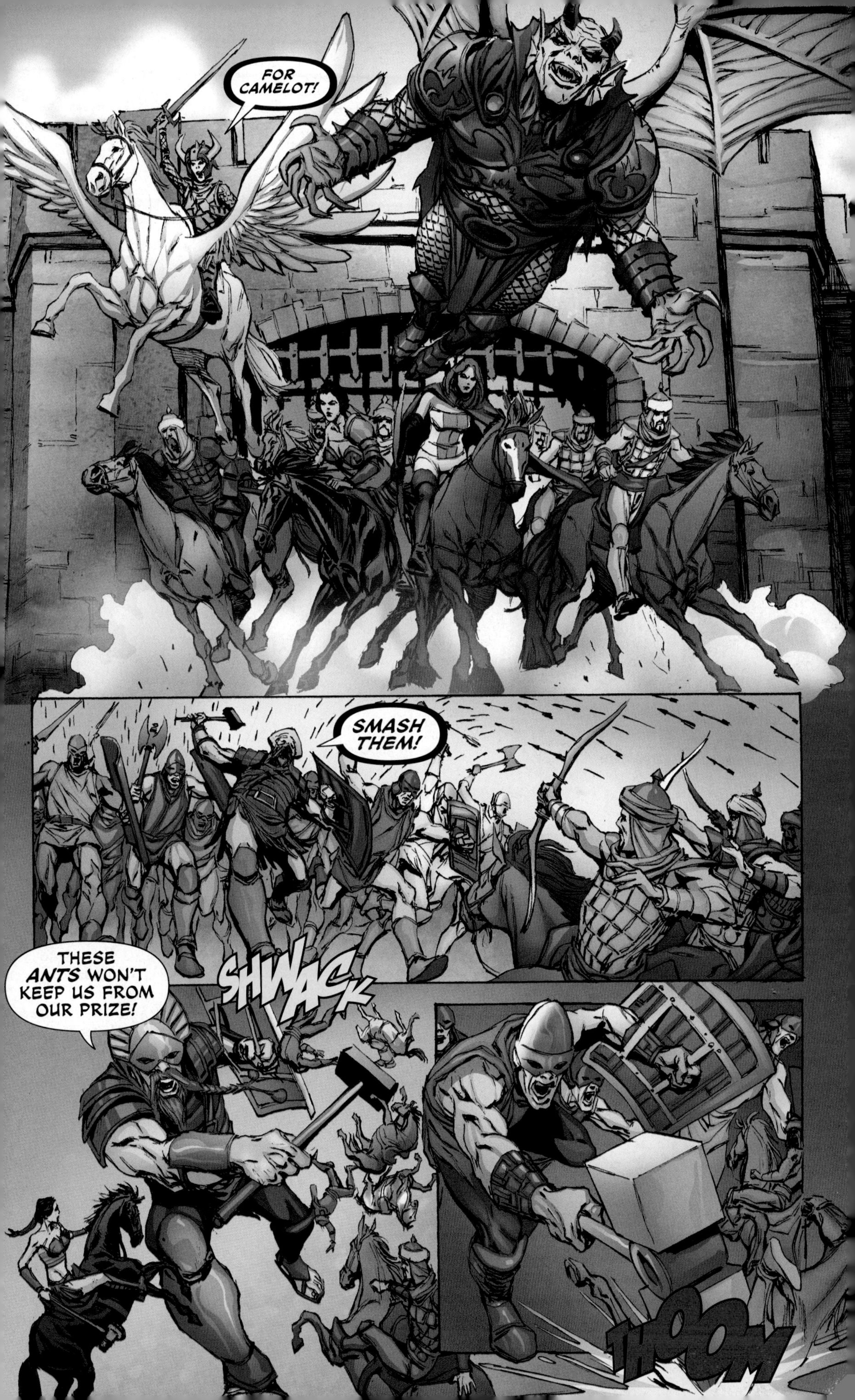
FOR CAMELOT!
SMASH THEM!
THESE ANTS WON'T KEEP US FROM OUR PRIZE!
SHWACK
THOOM

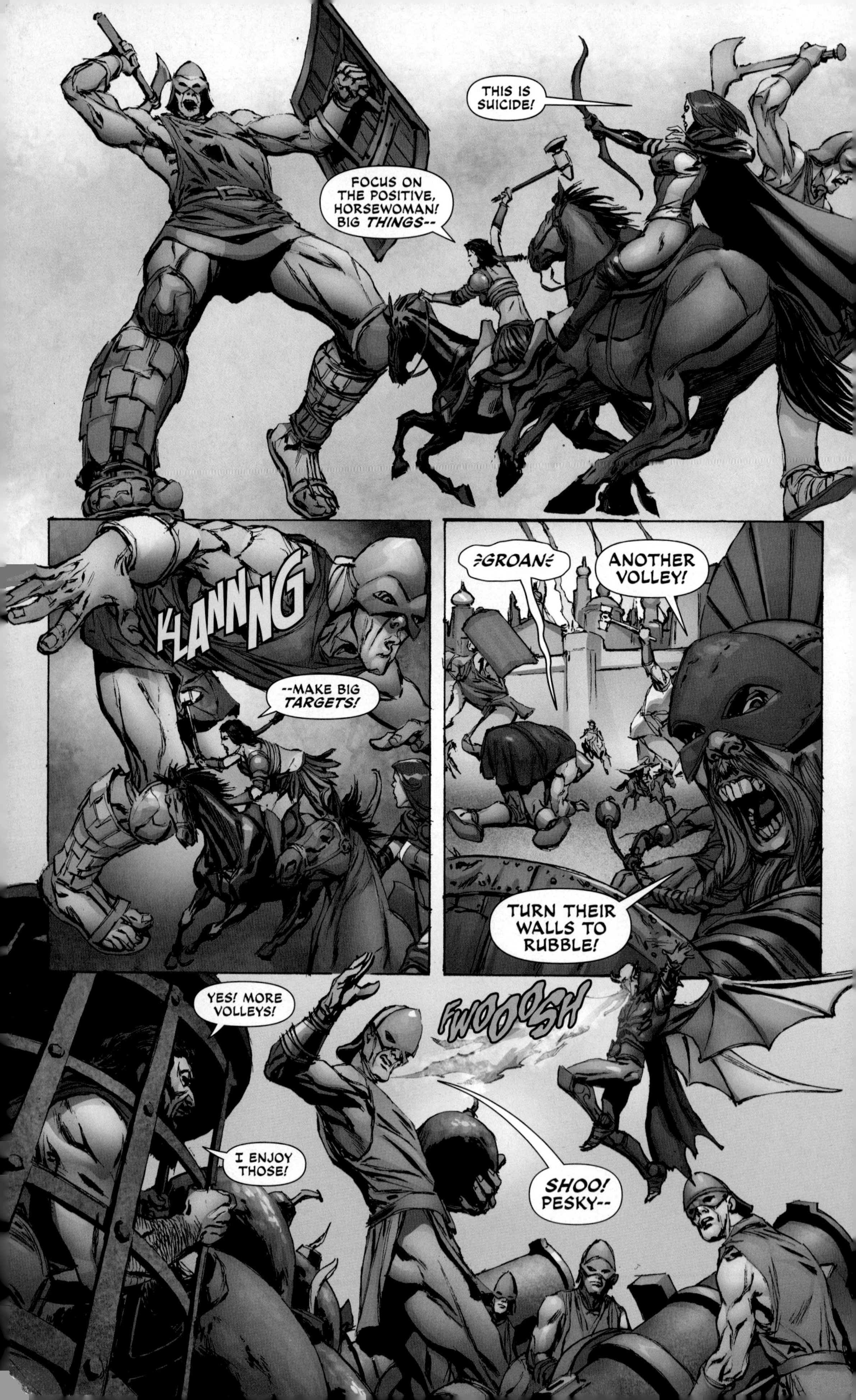
THIS IS SUICIDE!
FOCUS ON THE POSITIVE, HORSEWOMAN! BIG THINGS--
KLANNNG
--MAKE BIG TARGETS!
GROAN
ANOTHER VOLLEY!
TURN THEIR WALLS TO RUBBLE!
YES! MORE VOLLEYS!
FWOOOSH
I ENJOY THOSE!
SHOO! PESKY--

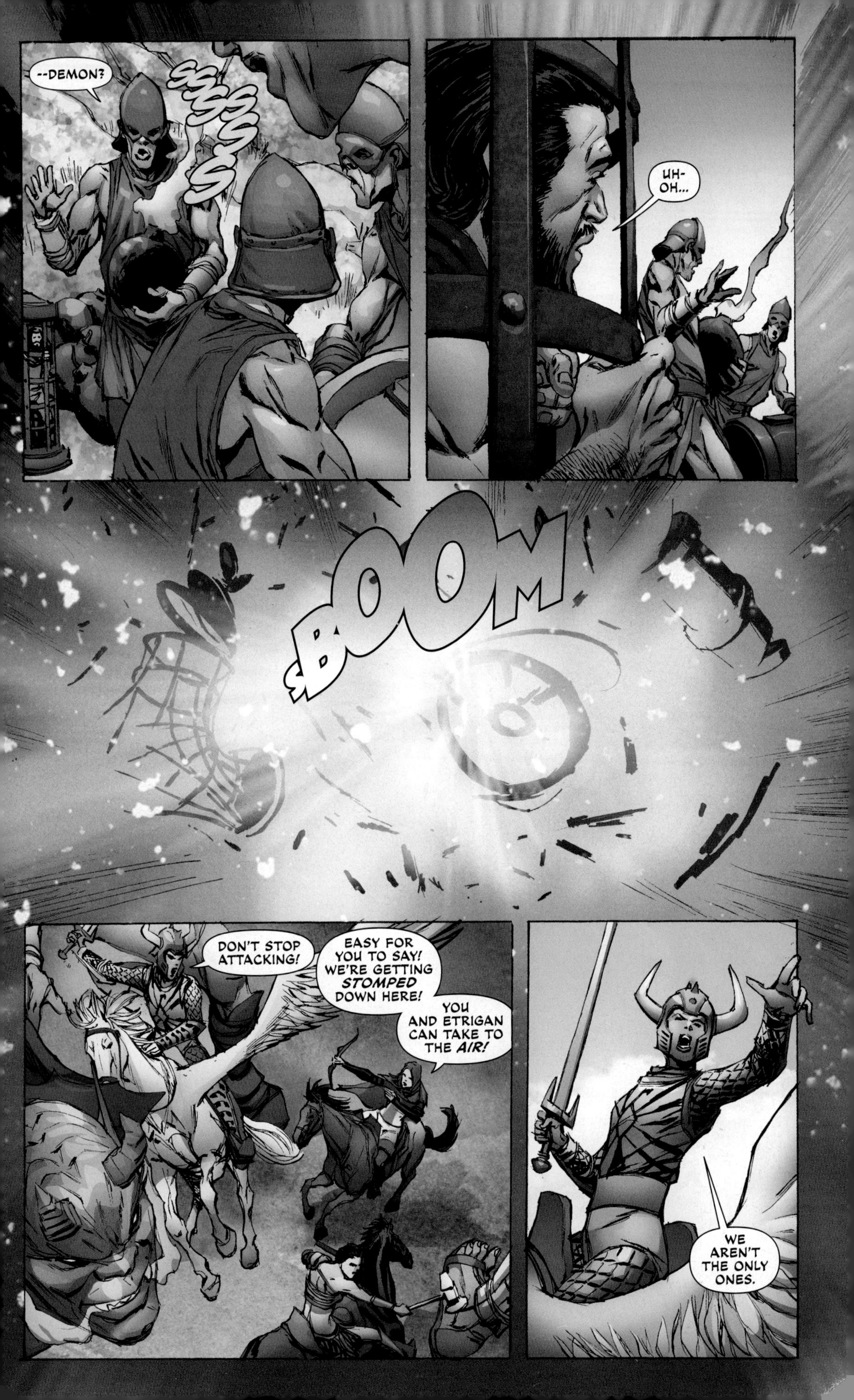
--DEMON?
SSSSSS
UH-OH...
SBOOM
DON'T STOP ATTACKING!
EASY FOR YOU TO SAY! WE'RE GETTING STOMPED DOWN HERE!
YOU AND ETRIGAN CAN TAKE TO THE AIR!
WE AREN'T THE ONLY ONES.

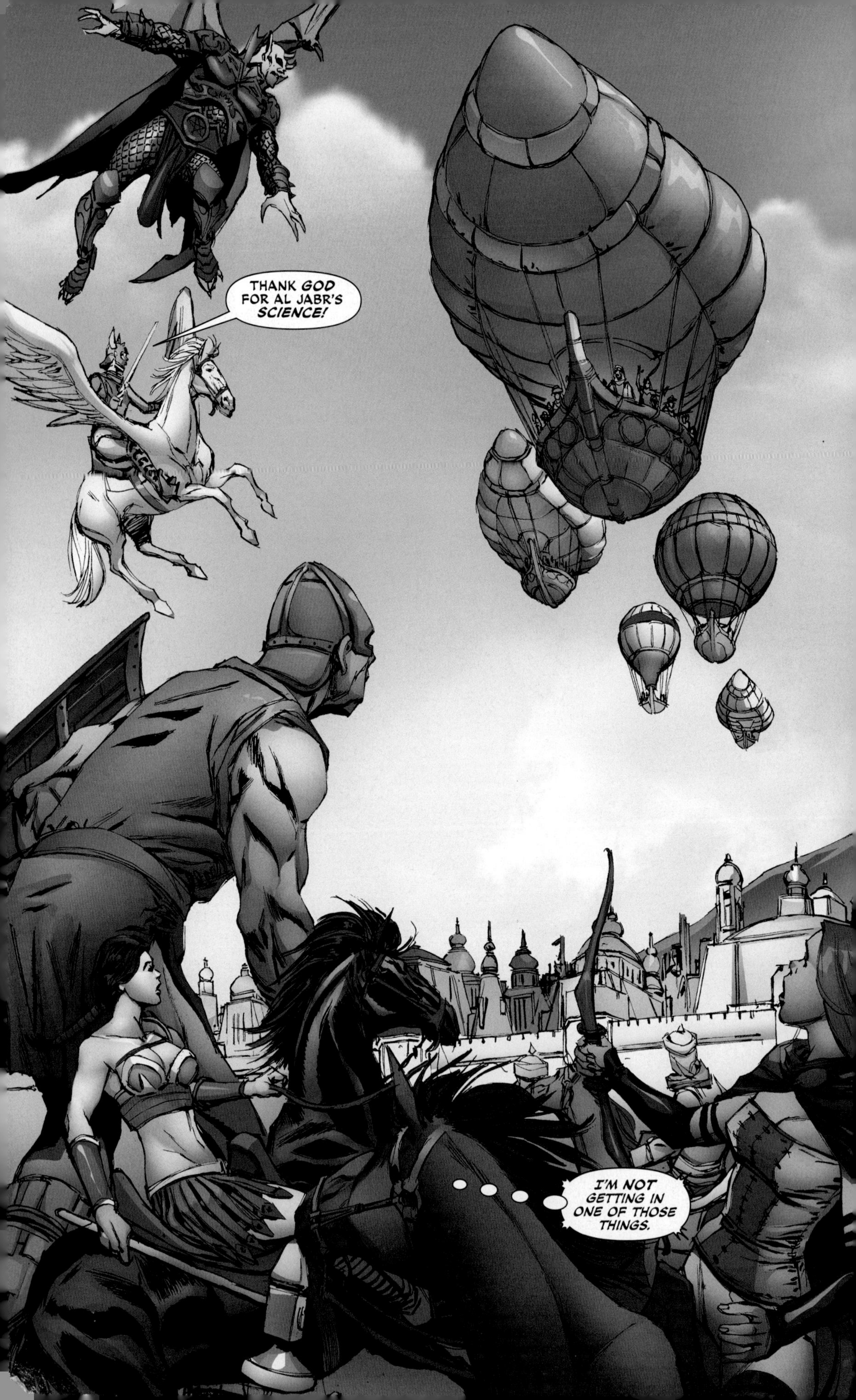
THANK GOD FOR AL JABR'S SCIENCE!
I'M NOT GETTING IN ONE OF THOSE THINGS.

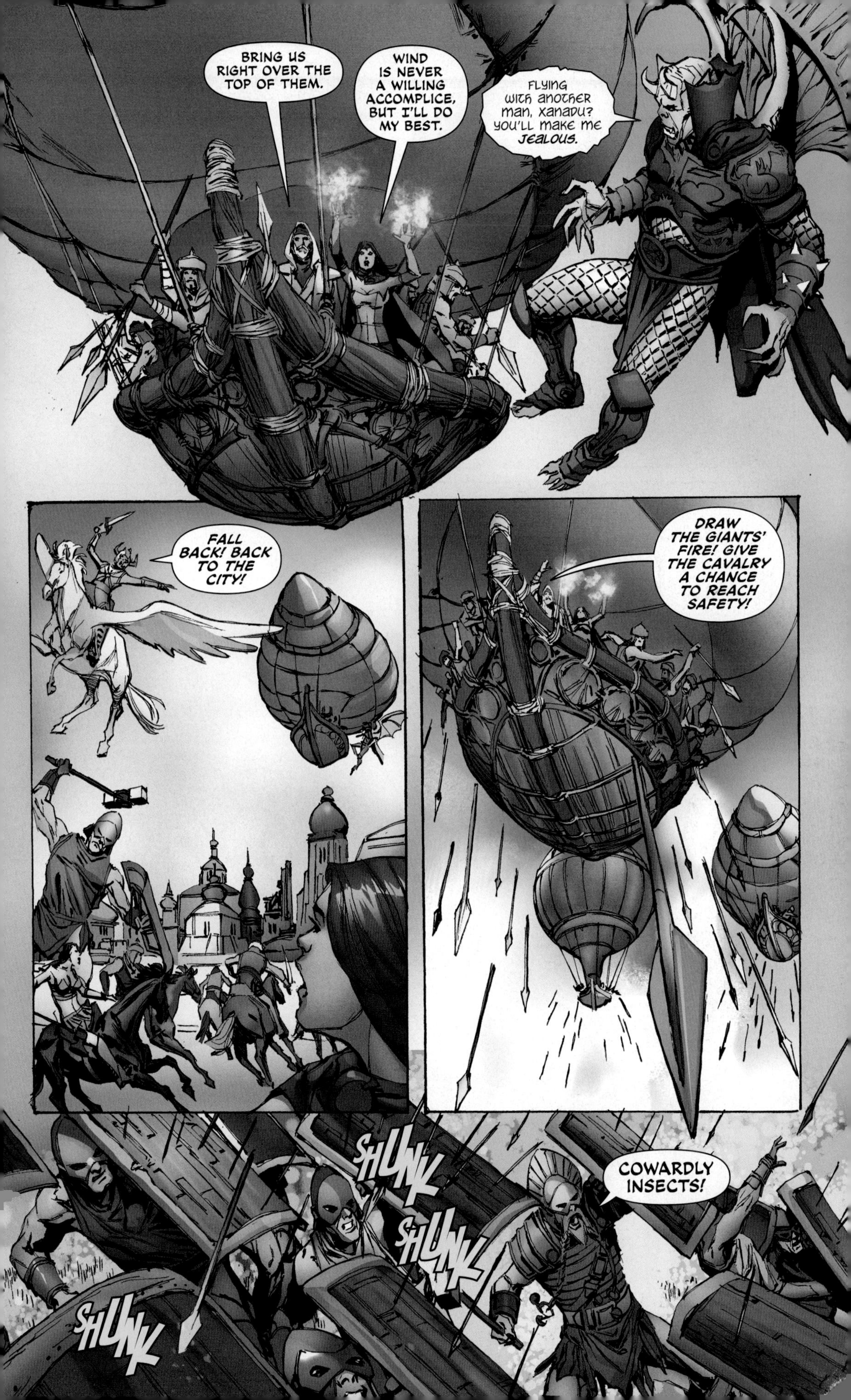
BRING US RIGHT OVER THE TOP OF THEM.
WIND IS NEVER A WILLING ACCOMPLICE, BUT I'LL DO MY BEST.
FLYING WITH ANOTHER MAN, XANADU? YOU'LL MAKE ME JEALOUS.
FALL BACK! BACK TO THE CITY!
DRAW THE GIANTS' FIRE! GIVE THE CAVALRY A CHANCE TO REACH SAFETY!
SHUNK
SHUNK
COWARDLY INSECTS!
SHUNK

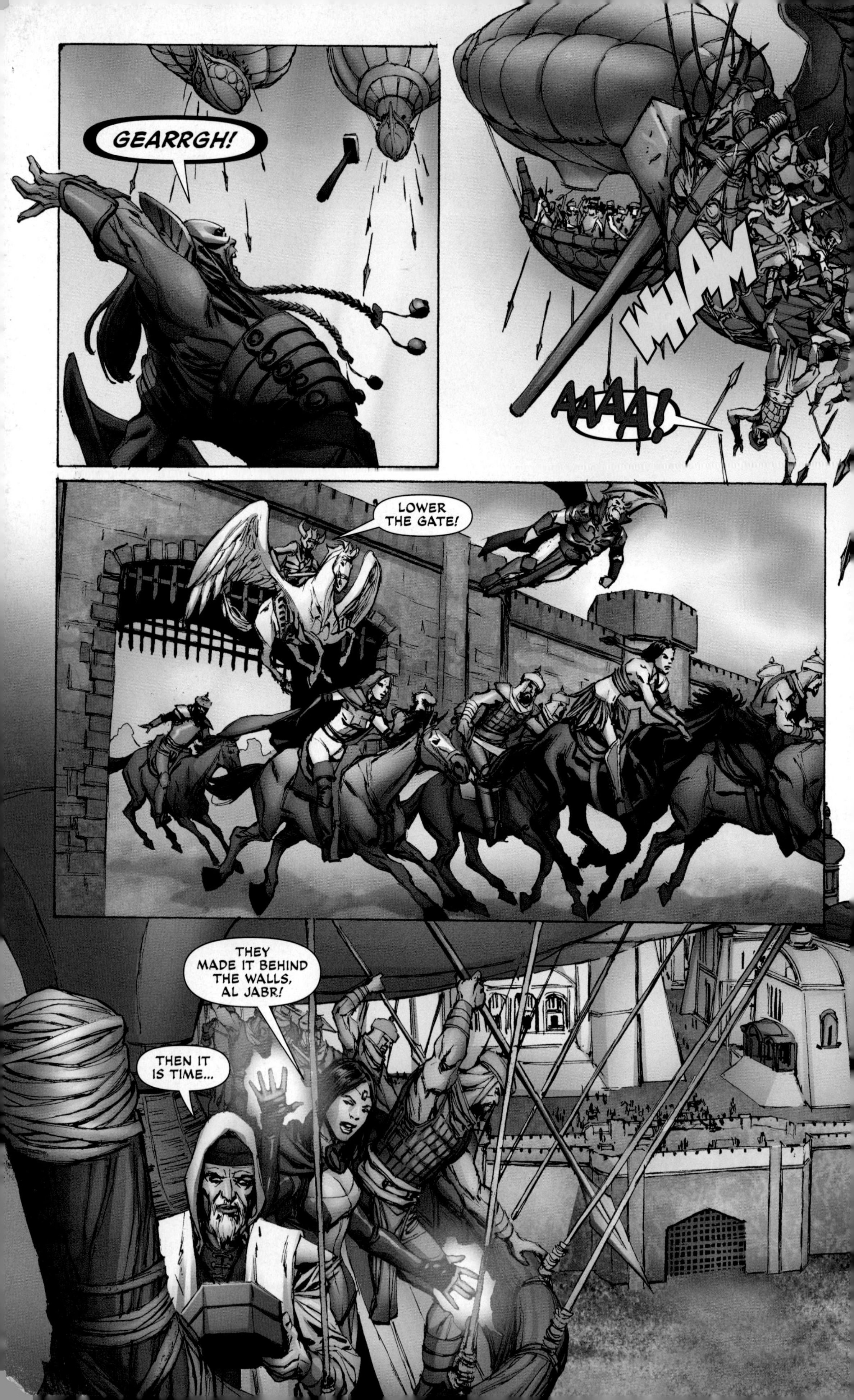
GEARRGH!
WHAM
AAAA!
LOWER THE GATE!
THEY MADE IT BEHIND THE WALLS, AL JABR!
THEN IT IS TIME...

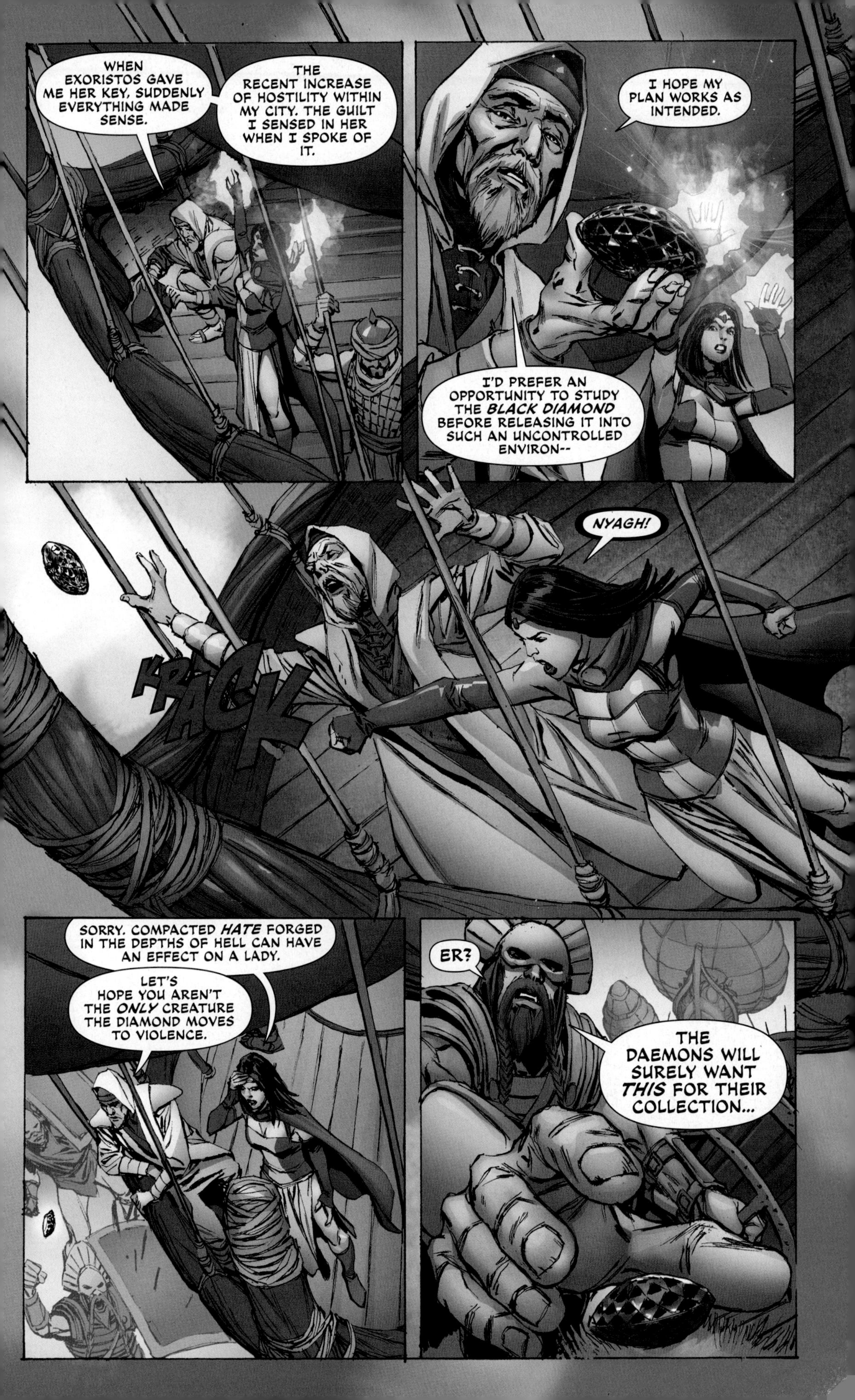
WHEN EXORISTOS GAVE ME HER KEY, SUDDENLY EVERYTHING MADE SENSE.
THE RECENT INCREASE OF HOSTILITY WITHIN MY CITY. THE GUILT I SENSED IN HER WHEN I SPOKE OF IT.
I HOPE MY PLAN WORKS AS INTENDED.
I'D PREFER AN OPPORTUNITY TO STUDY THE *BLACK DIAMOND* BEFORE RELEASING IT INTO SUCH AN UNCONTROLLED ENVIRON--
NYAGH!
K'RACK
SORRY. COMPACTED *HATE* FORGED IN THE DEPTHS OF HELL CAN HAVE AN EFFECT ON A LADY.
LET'S HOPE YOU AREN'T THE *ONLY* CREATURE THE DIAMOND MOVES TO VIOLENCE.
ER?
THE DAEMONS WILL SURELY WANT *THIS* FOR THEIR COLLECTION...

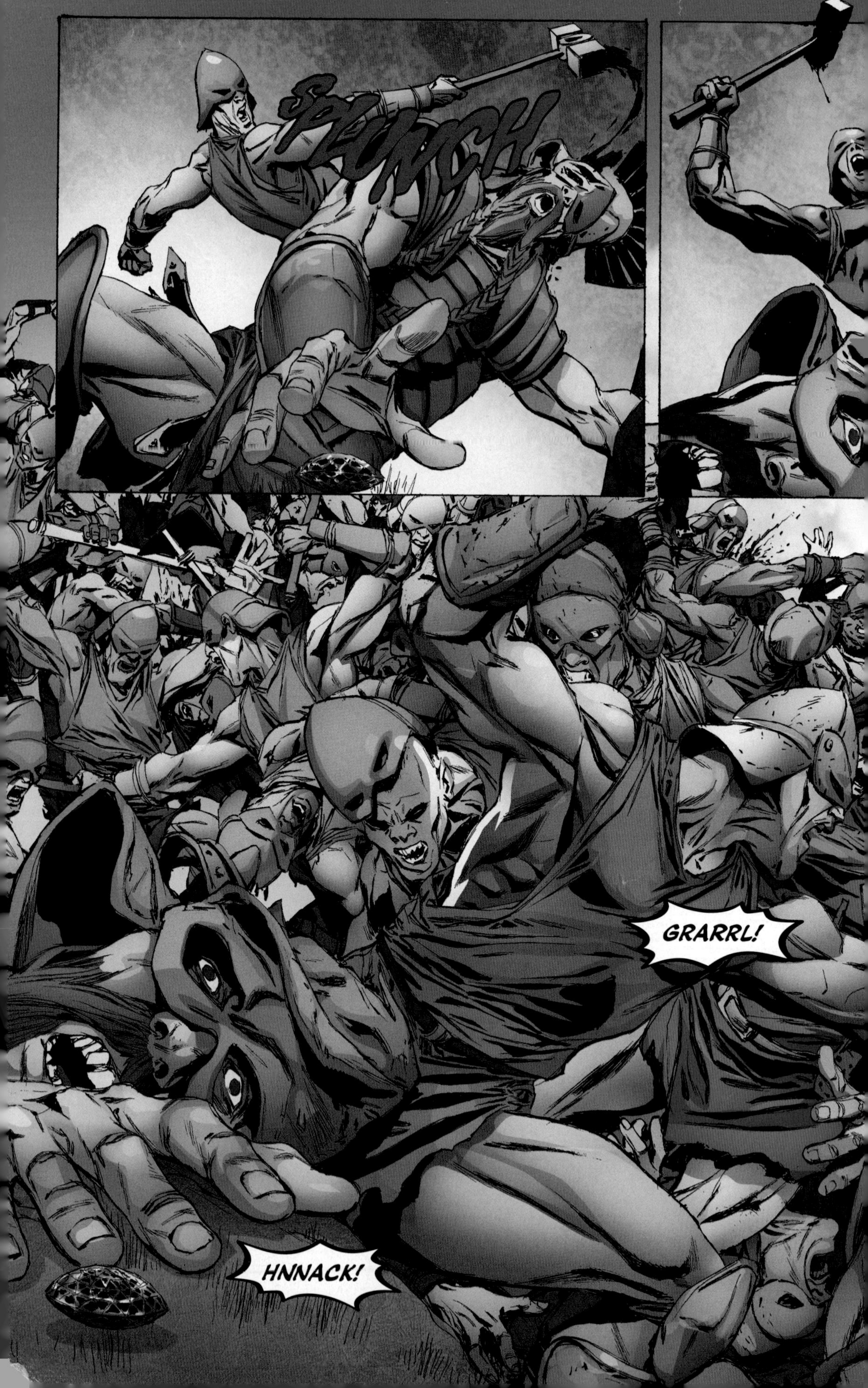
SPLUNCH
GRARRL!
HNNACK!

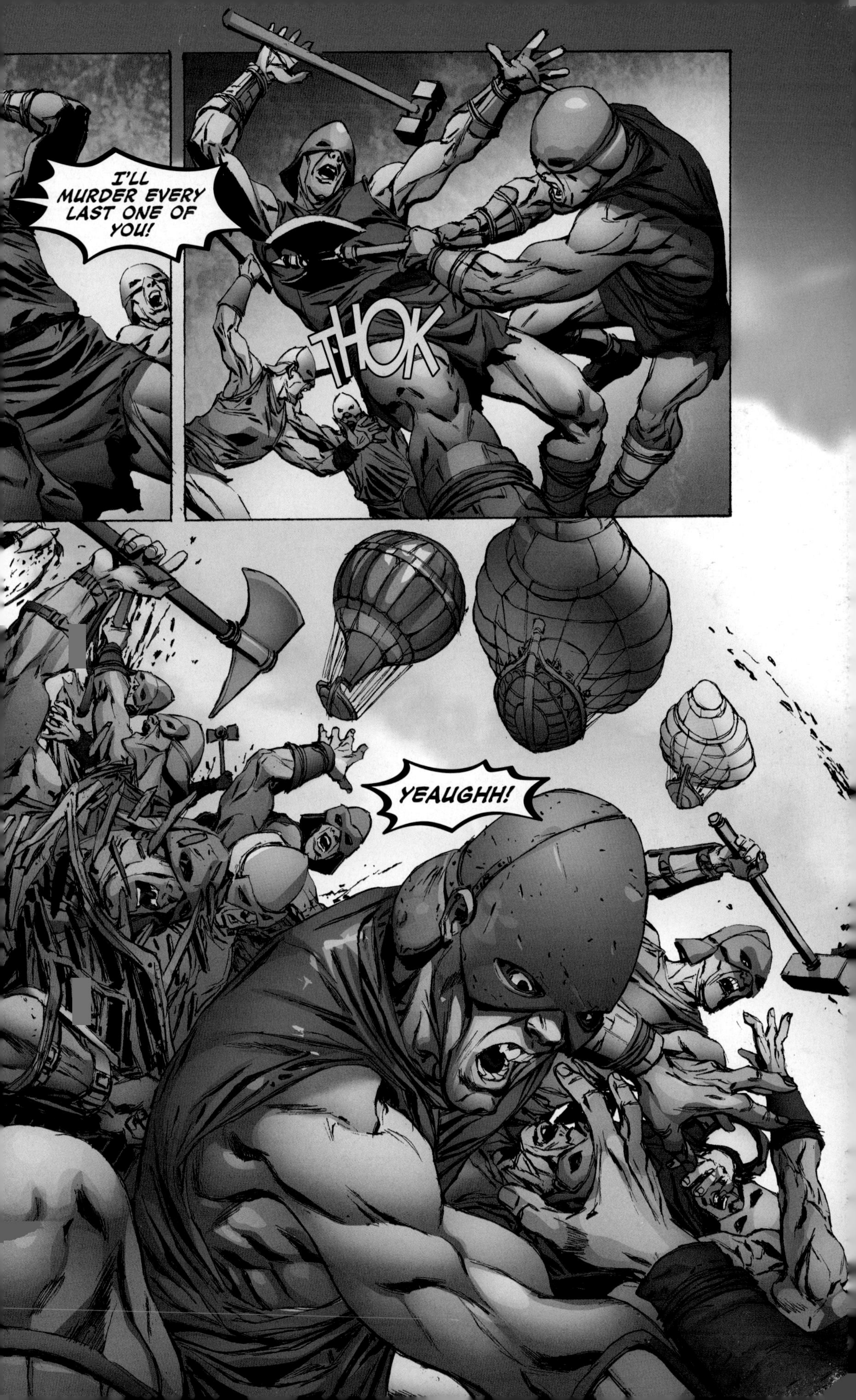
I'LL MURDER EVERY LAST ONE OF YOU!
THOK
YEAUGHH!

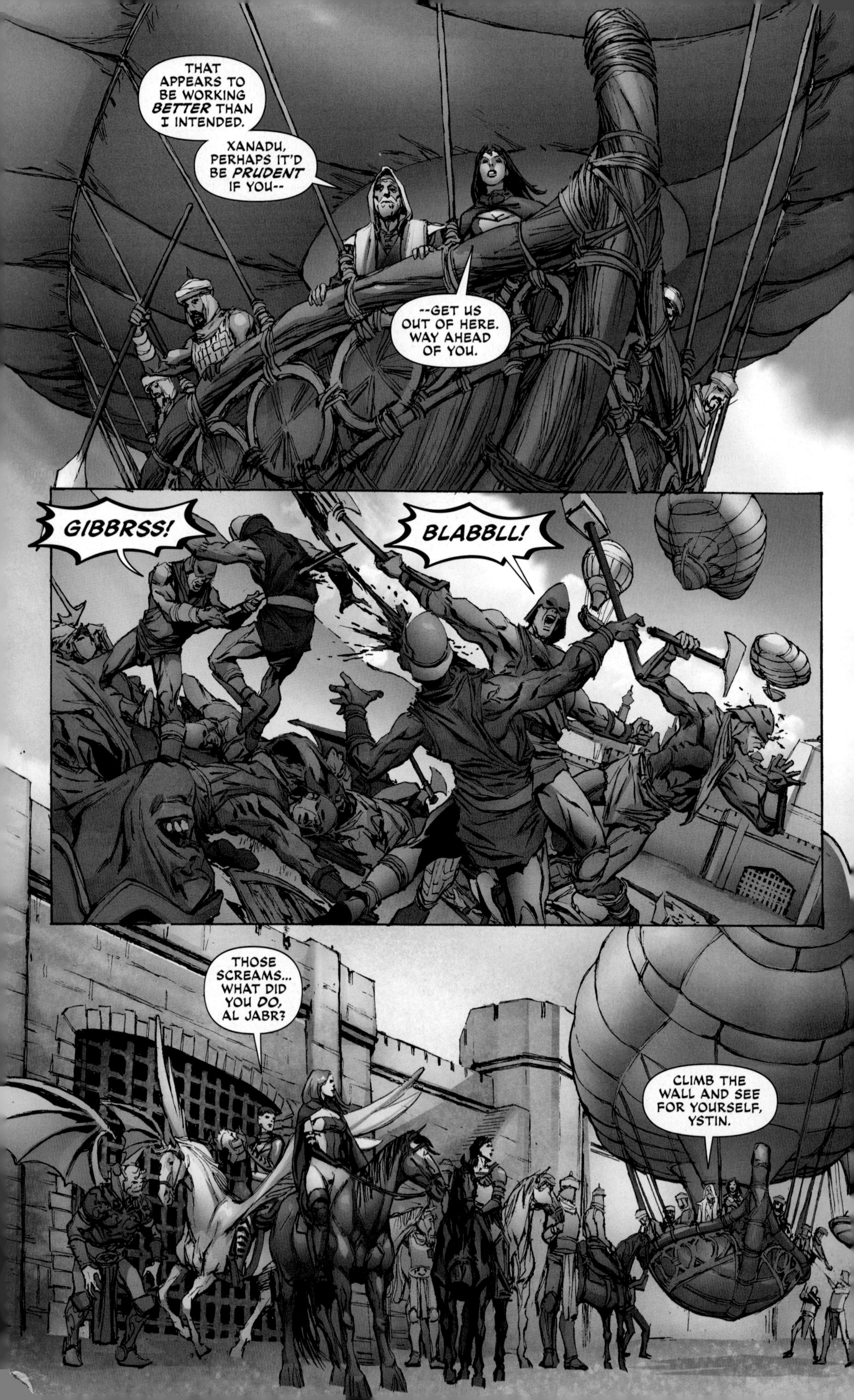
THAT APPEARS TO BE WORKING *BETTER* THAN I INTENDED.
XANADU, PERHAPS IT'D BE *PRUDENT* IF YOU--
--GET US OUT OF HERE. WAY AHEAD OF YOU.
GIBBRSS!
BLABBLL!
THOSE SCREAMS... WHAT DID YOU *DO*, AL JABR?
CLIMB THE WALL AND SEE FOR YOURSELF, YSTIN.

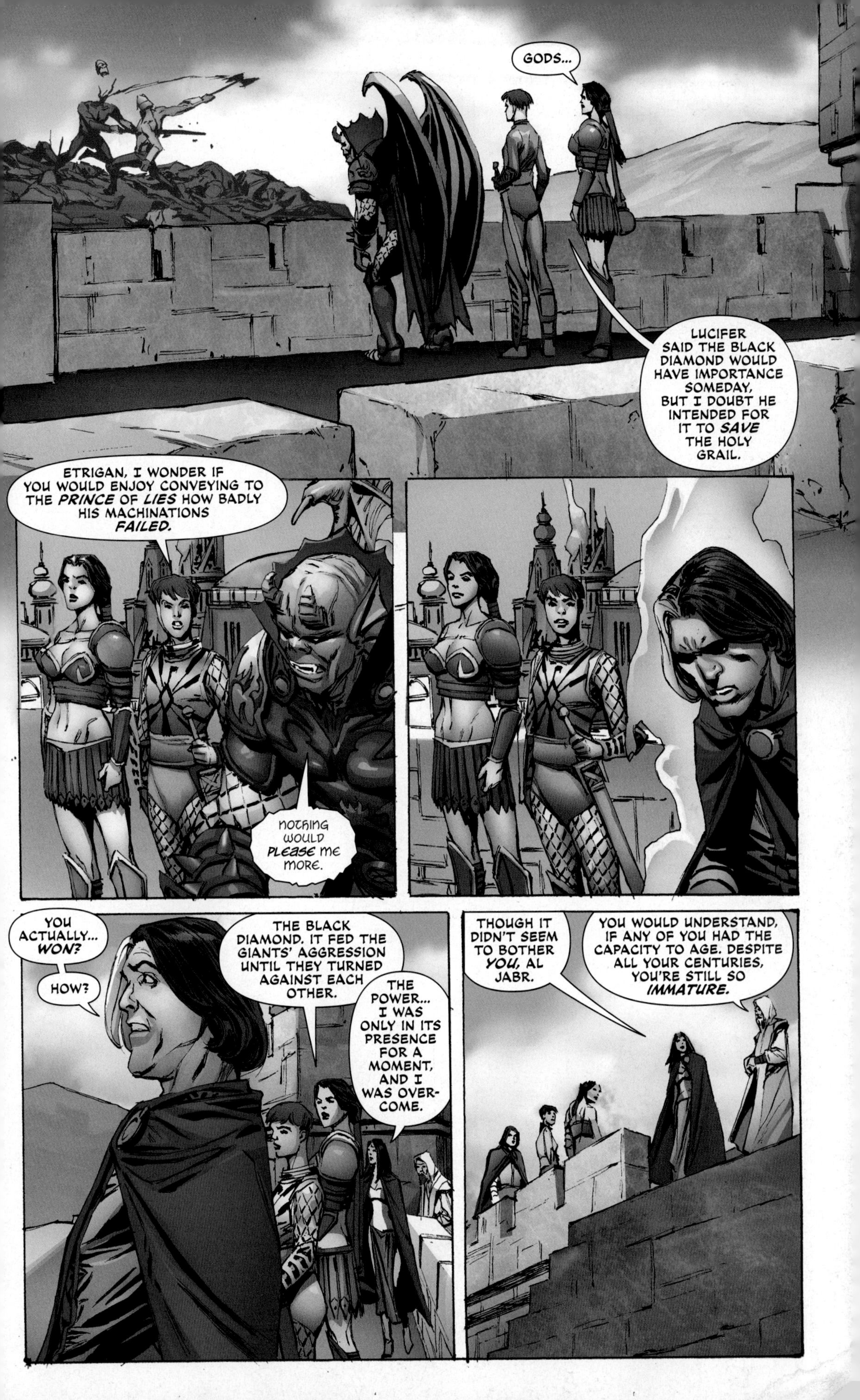
GODS...
LUCIFER SAID THE BLACK DIAMOND WOULD HAVE IMPORTANCE SOMEDAY, BUT I DOUBT HE INTENDED FOR IT TO SAVE THE HOLY GRAIL.
ETRIGAN, I WONDER IF YOU WOULD ENJOY CONVEYING TO THE PRINCE OF LIES HOW BADLY HIS MACHINATIONS FAILED.
NOTHING WOULD PLEASE ME MORE.
YOU ACTUALLY... WON?
HOW?
THE BLACK DIAMOND. IT FED THE GIANTS' AGGRESSION UNTIL THEY TURNED AGAINST EACH OTHER.
THE POWER... I WAS ONLY IN ITS PRESENCE FOR A MOMENT, AND I WAS OVER-COME.
THOUGH IT DIDN'T SEEM TO BOTHER YOU, AL JABR.
YOU WOULD UNDERSTAND, IF ANY OF YOU HAD THE CAPACITY TO AGE. DESPITE ALL YOUR CENTURIES, YOU'RE STILL SO IMMATURE.

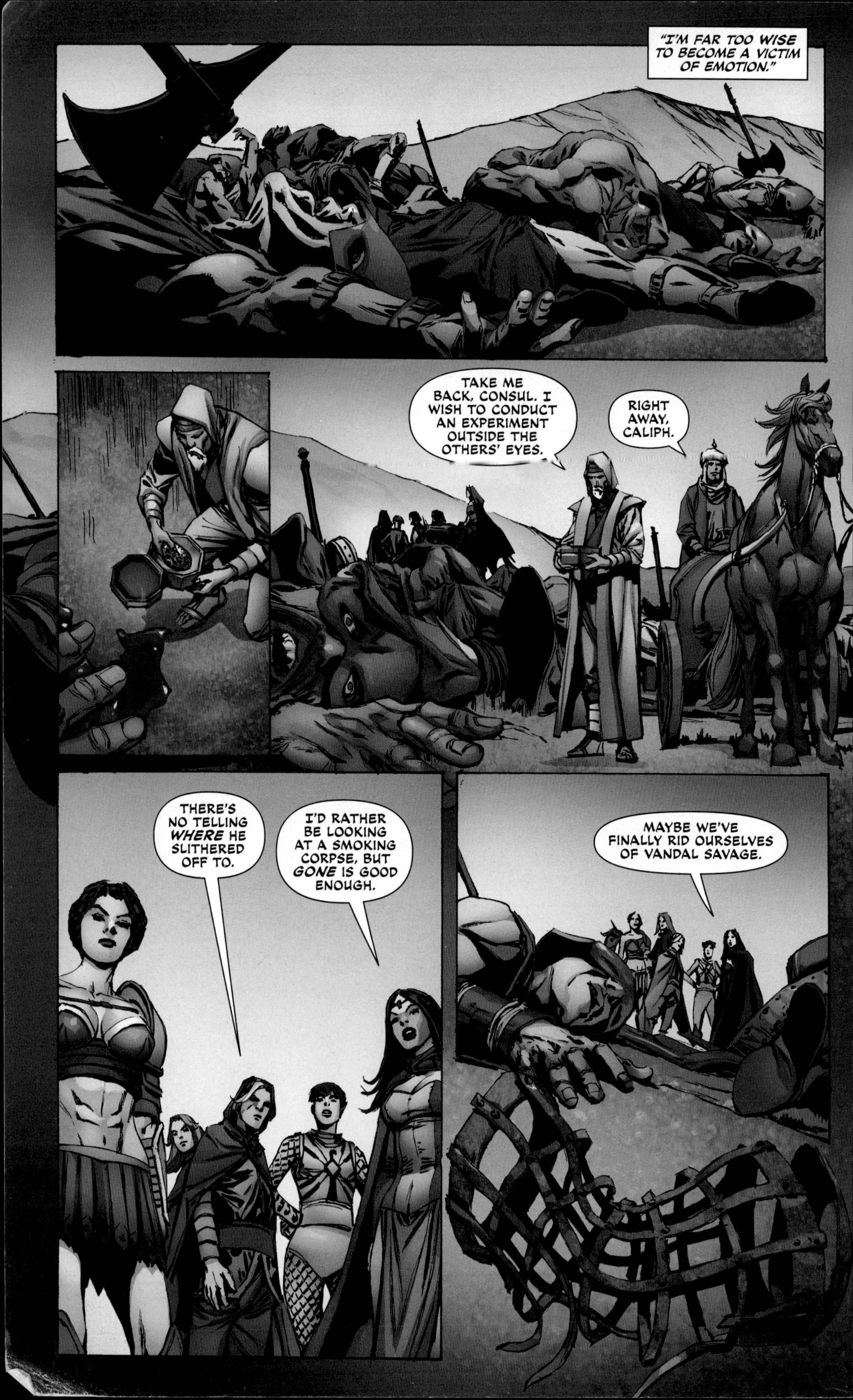
"I'M FAR TOO WISE TO BECOME A VICTIM OF EMOTION."
TAKE ME BACK, CONSUL. I WISH TO CONDUCT AN EXPERIMENT OUTSIDE THE OTHERS' EYES.
RIGHT AWAY, CALIPH.
THERE'S NO TELLING WHERE HE SLITHERED OFF TO.
I'D RATHER BE LOOKING AT A SMOKING CORPSE, BUT GONE IS GOOD ENOUGH.
MAYBE WE'VE FINALLY RID OURSELVES OF VANDAL SAVAGE.

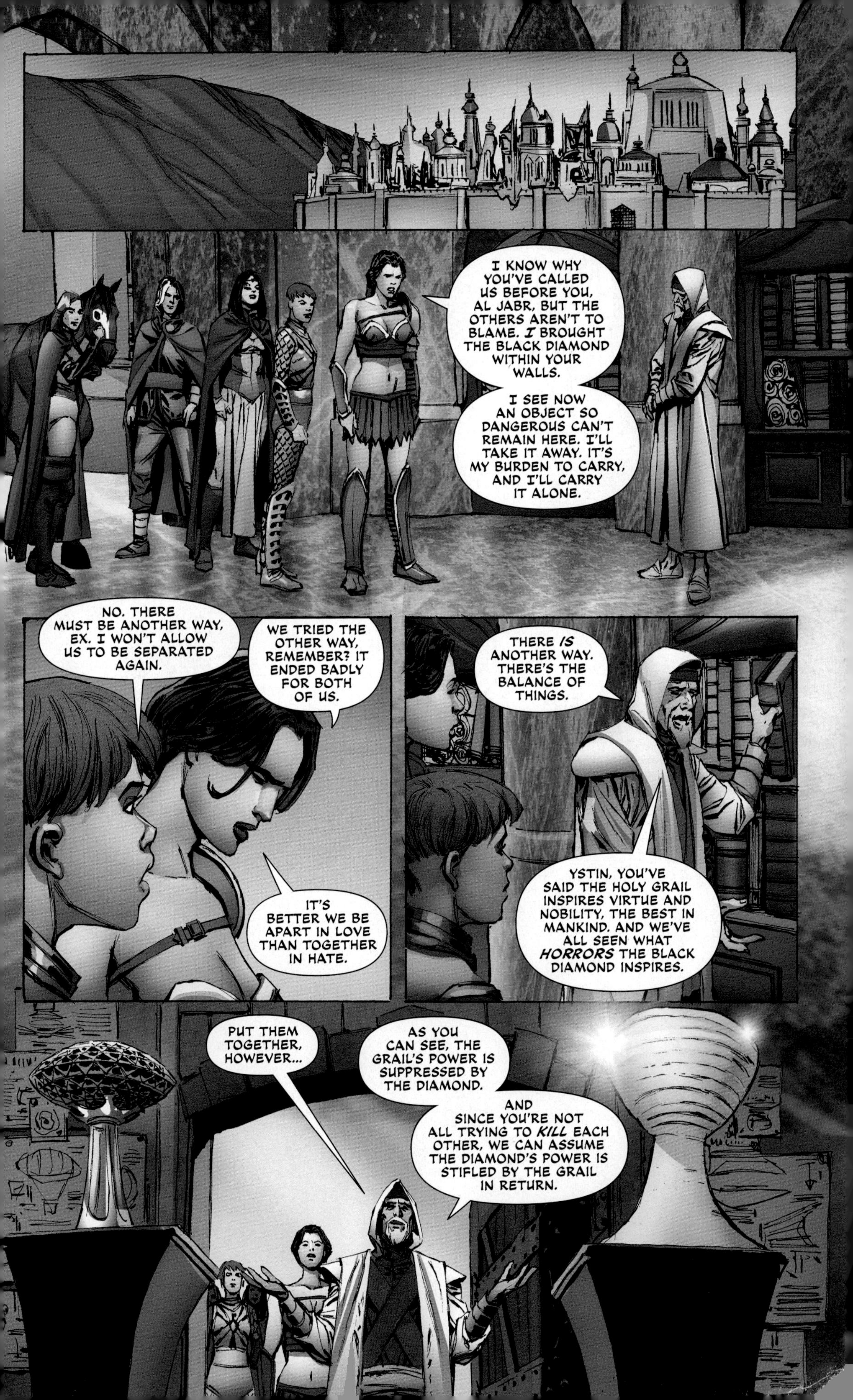
I KNOW WHY YOU'VE CALLED US BEFORE YOU, AL JABR, BUT THE OTHERS AREN'T TO BLAME. *I* BROUGHT THE BLACK DIAMOND WITHIN YOUR WALLS.
I SEE NOW AN OBJECT SO DANGEROUS CAN'T REMAIN HERE. I'LL TAKE IT AWAY. IT'S MY BURDEN TO CARRY, AND I'LL CARRY IT ALONE.
NO. THERE MUST BE ANOTHER WAY, EX. I WON'T ALLOW US TO BE SEPARATED AGAIN.
WE TRIED THE OTHER WAY, REMEMBER? IT ENDED BADLY FOR BOTH OF US.
IT'S BETTER WE BE APART IN LOVE THAN TOGETHER IN HATE.
THERE *IS* ANOTHER WAY. THERE'S THE BALANCE OF THINGS.
YSTIN, YOU'VE SAID THE HOLY GRAIL INSPIRES VIRTUE AND NOBILITY, THE BEST IN MANKIND. AND WE'VE ALL SEEN WHAT ***HORRORS*** THE BLACK DIAMOND INSPIRES.
PUT THEM TOGETHER, HOWEVER...
AS YOU CAN SEE, THE GRAIL'S POWER IS SUPPRESSED BY THE DIAMOND.
AND SINCE YOU'RE NOT ALL TRYING TO *KILL* EACH OTHER, WE CAN ASSUME THE DIAMOND'S POWER IS STIFLED BY THE GRAIL IN RETURN.

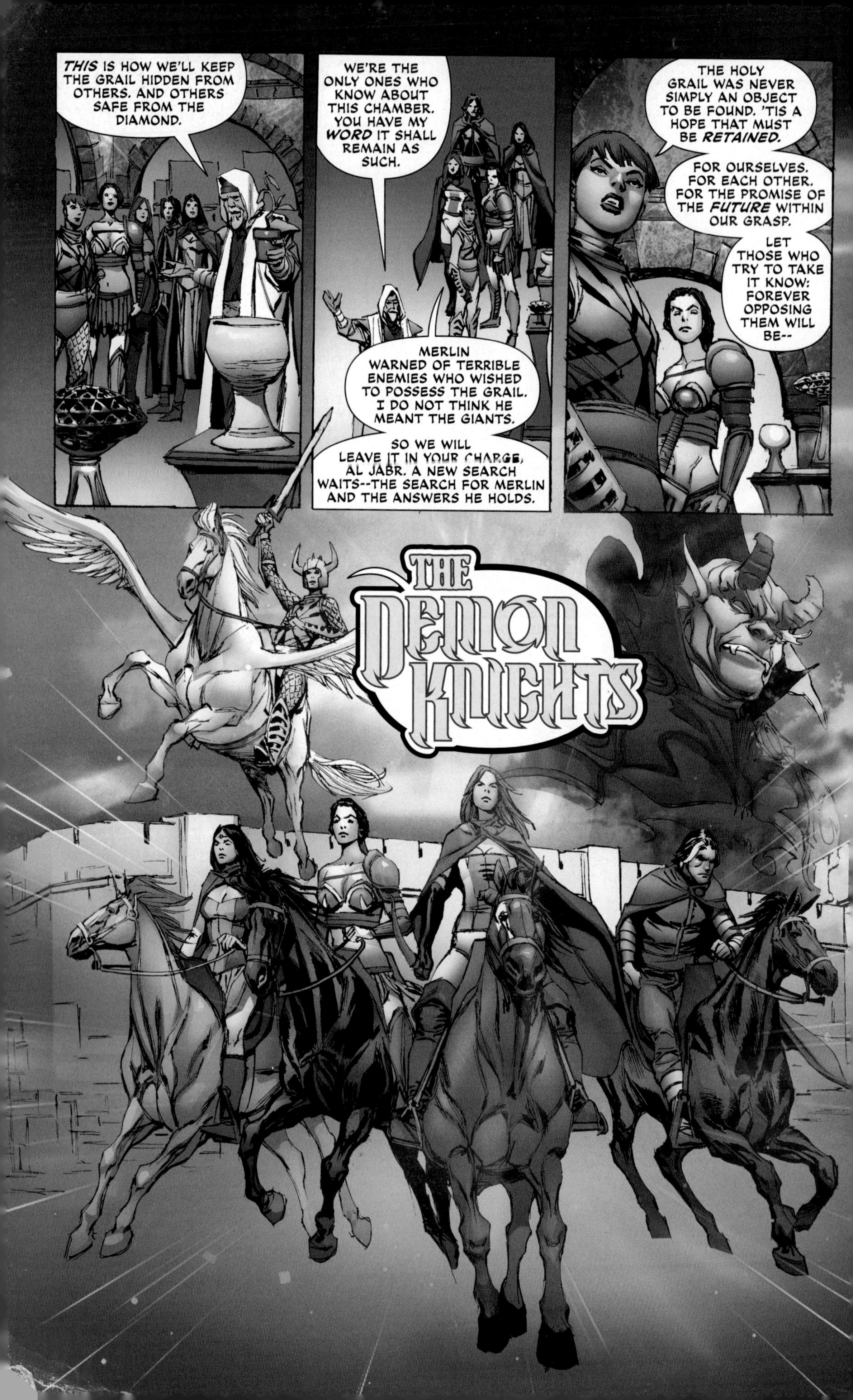
THIS IS HOW WE'LL KEEP THE GRAIL HIDDEN FROM OTHERS. AND OTHERS SAFE FROM THE DIAMOND.
WE'RE THE ONLY ONES WHO KNOW ABOUT THIS CHAMBER. YOU HAVE MY WORD IT SHALL REMAIN AS SUCH.
MERLIN WARNED OF TERRIBLE ENEMIES WHO WISHED TO POSSESS THE GRAIL. I DO NOT THINK HE MEANT THE GIANTS.
SO WE WILL LEAVE IT IN YOUR CHARGE, AL JABR. A NEW SEARCH WAITS--THE SEARCH FOR MERLIN AND THE ANSWERS HE HOLDS.
THE HOLY GRAIL WAS NEVER SIMPLY AN OBJECT TO BE FOUND. 'TIS A HOPE THAT MUST BE RETAINED.
FOR OURSELVES. FOR EACH OTHER. FOR THE PROMISE OF THE FUTURE WITHIN OUR GRASP.
LET THOSE WHO TRY TO TAKE IT KNOW: FOREVER OPPOSING THEM WILL BE--
THE DEMON KNIGHTS

DEMON KNIGHTS #17 cover sketches by Bernard Chang

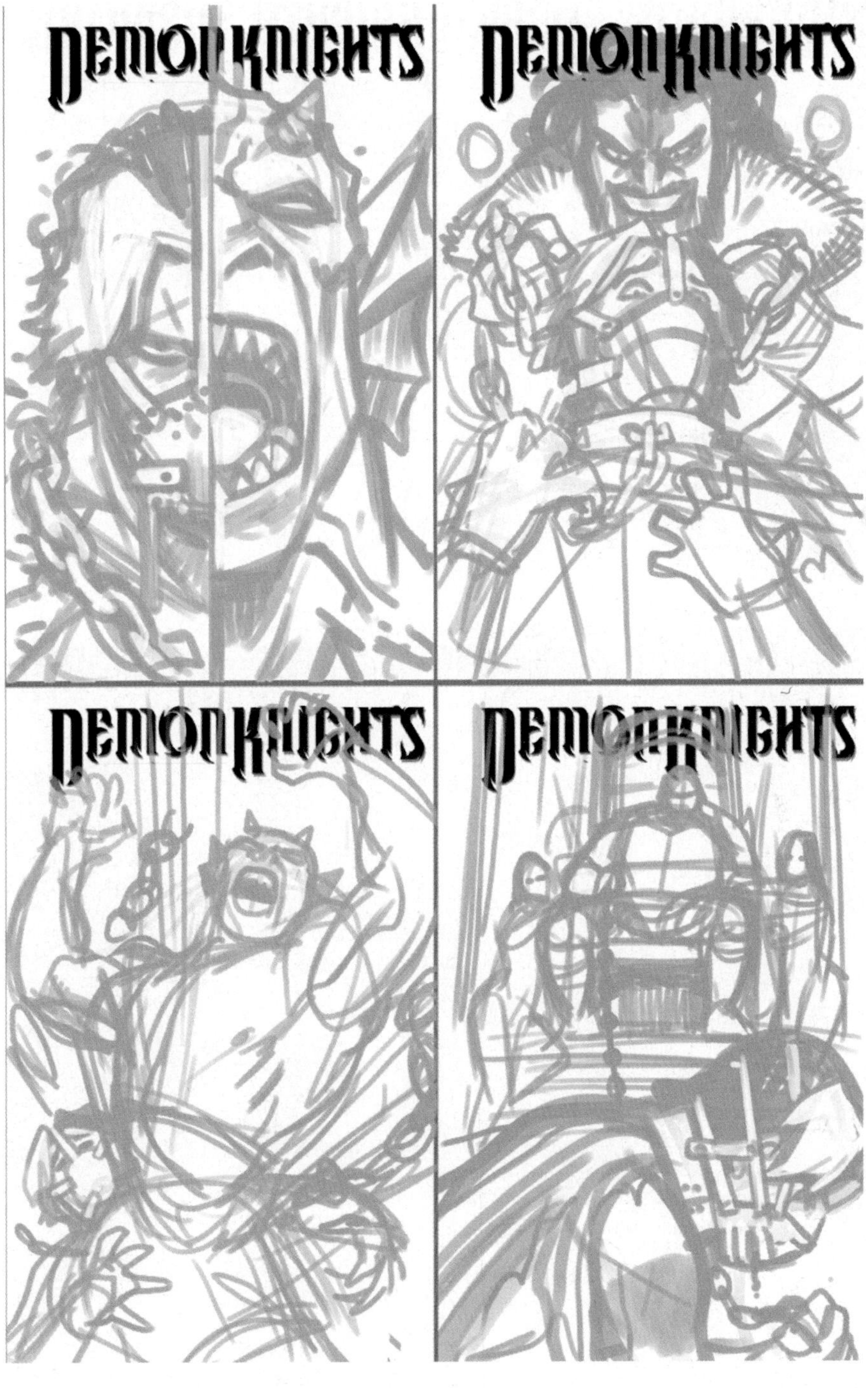
DEMON KNIGHTS
DEMON KNIGHTS
DEMON KNIGHTS
DEMON KNIGHTS

DEMON KNIGHTS #14, #18 cover sketches by Bernard Chang

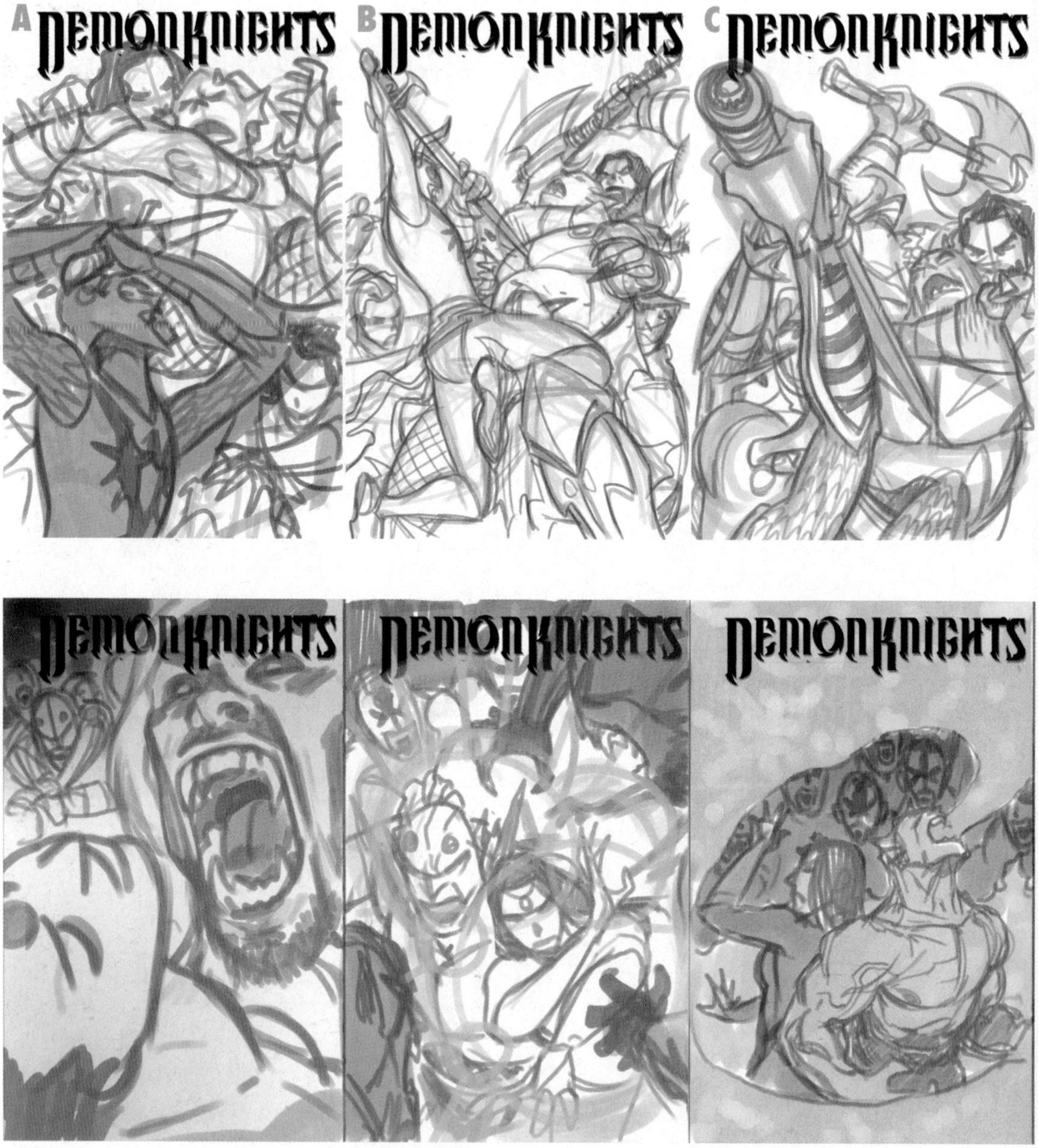
A
DEMON KNIGHTS
B
DEMON KNIGHTS
C
DEMON KNIGHTS
DEMON KNIGHTS
DEMON KNIGHTS
DEMON KNIGHTS

DEMON KNIGHTS #22, #21, #23 cover sketches by Howard Porter

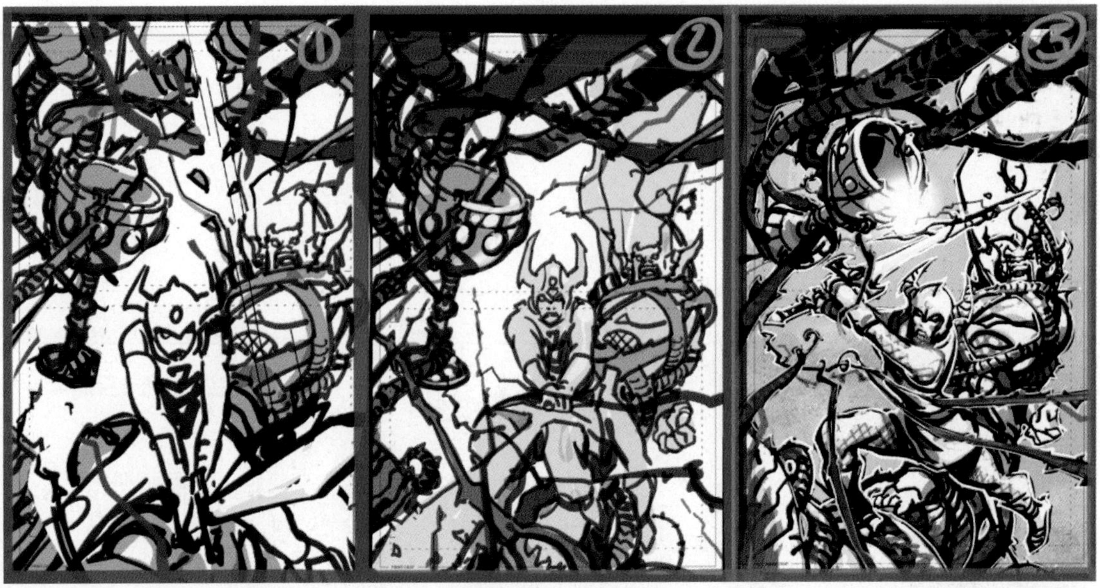
1
2
3

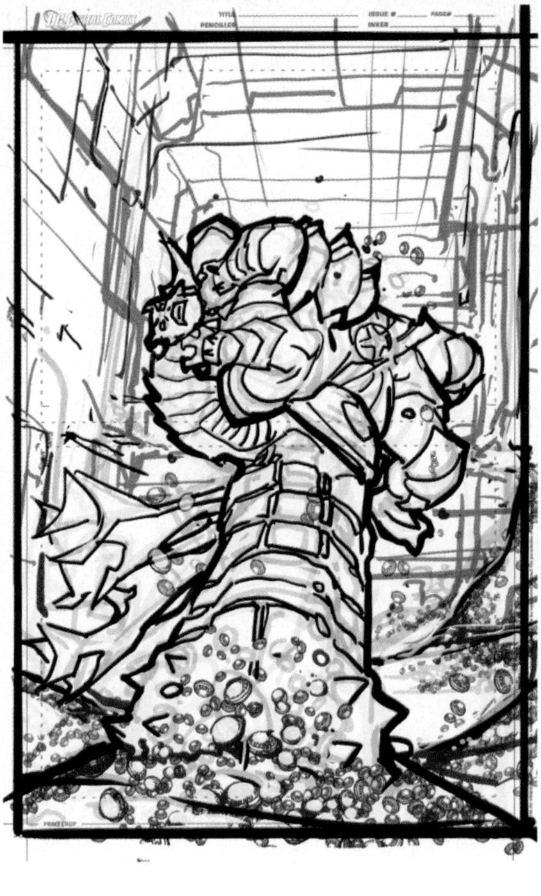

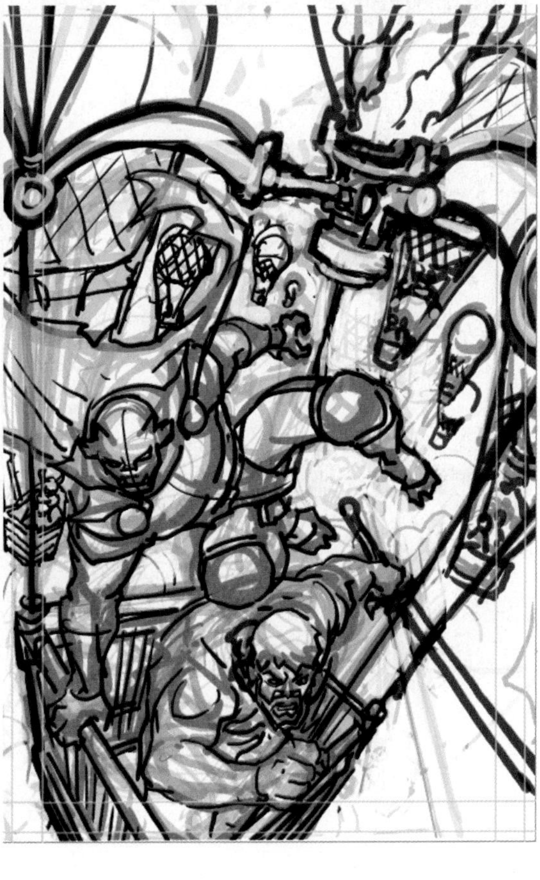

DEMON KNIGHTS #20 pages one and two rough pencils by Chad Hardin

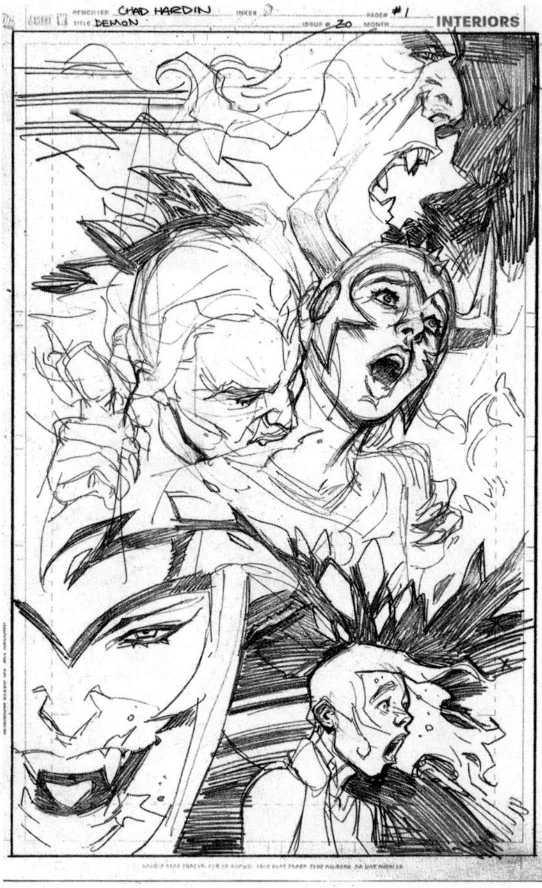
CHAD HARDIN
DEMON
#1
INTERIORS

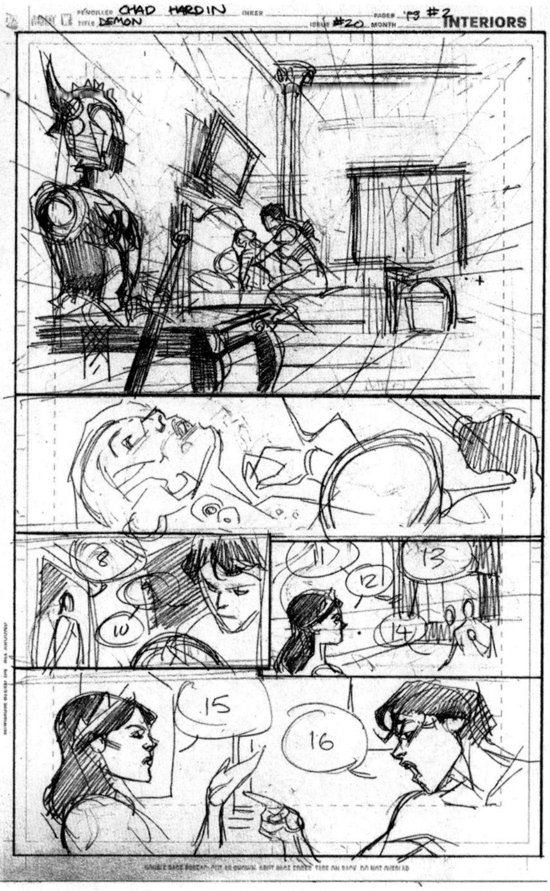
CHAD HARDIN
DEMON
#20
#2
INTERIORS
8
10
11
12
13
14
15
16

DEMON KNIGHTS #20 page one detailed pencils by Chad Hardin

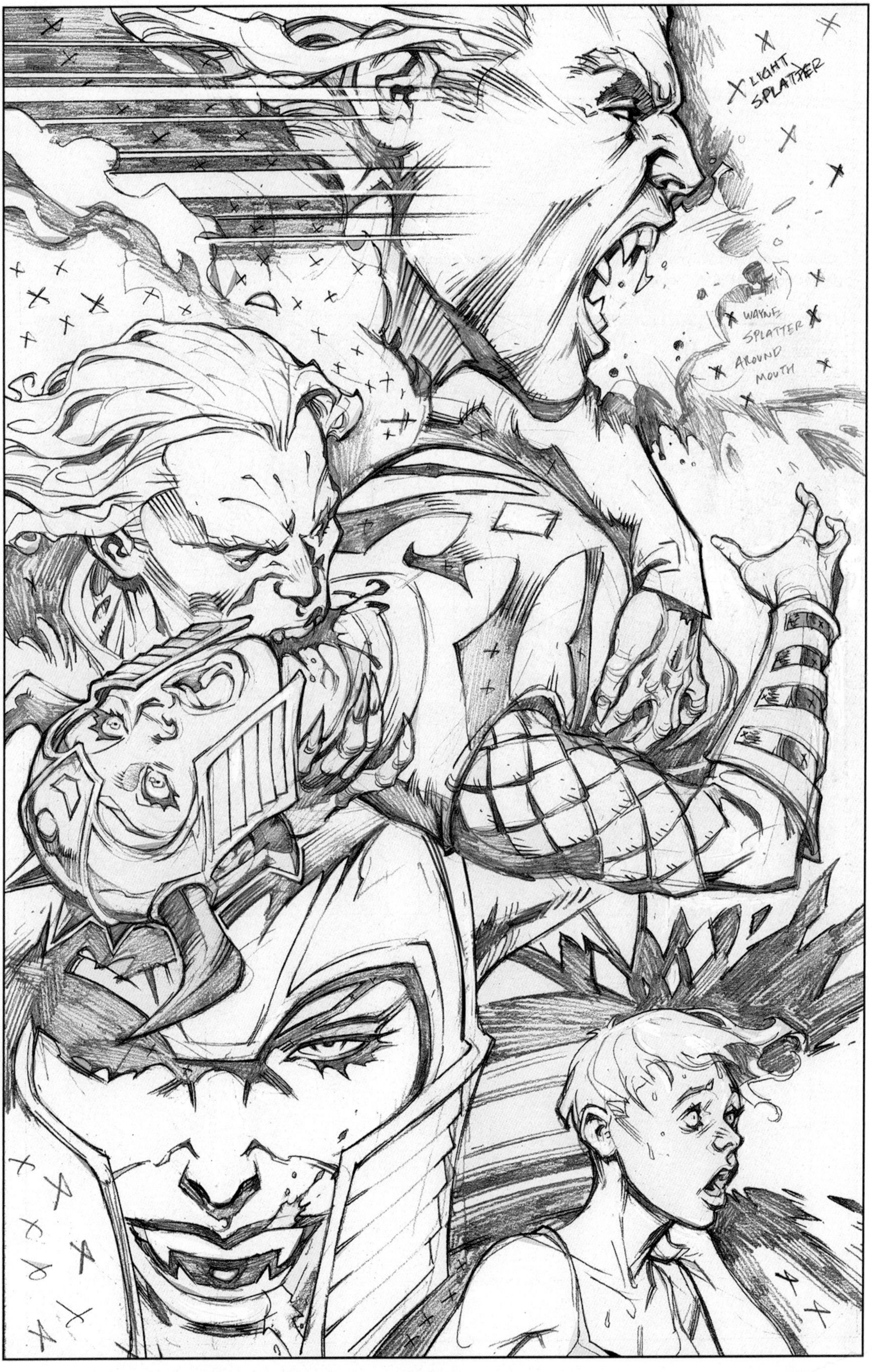

LIGHT SPLATTER
WAYNE SPLATTER AROUND MOUTH

Chad Hardin and Wayne Faucher's page progression from rough sketch to final inks for DEMON KNIGHTS #20 page fourteen

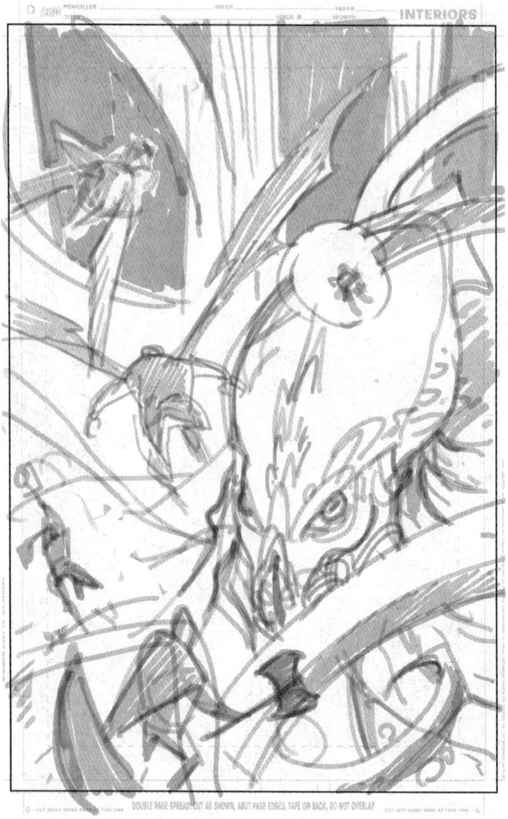
INTERIORS
DOUBLE PAGE SPREAD: CUT AS SHOWN, ABUT PAGE EDGES, TAPE ON BACK, DO NOT OVERLAP

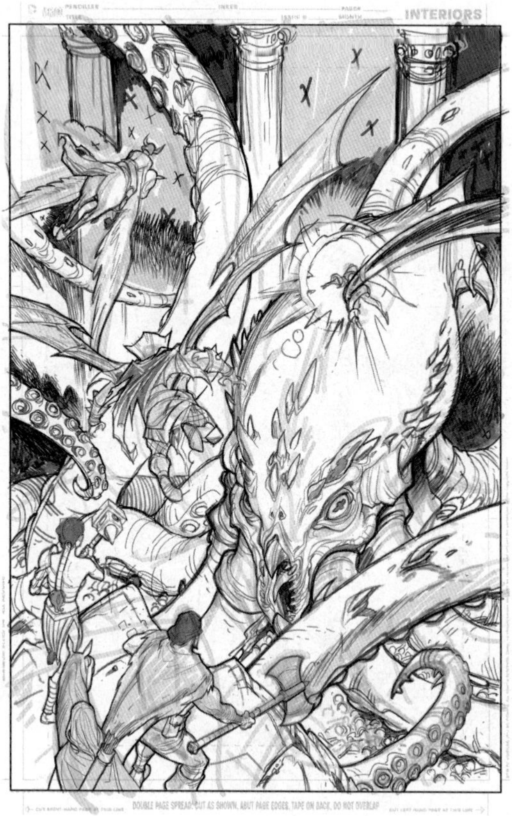
INTERIORS
DOUBLE PAGE SPREAD: CUT AS SHOWN, ABUT PAGE EDGES, TAPE ON BACK, DO NOT OVERLAP

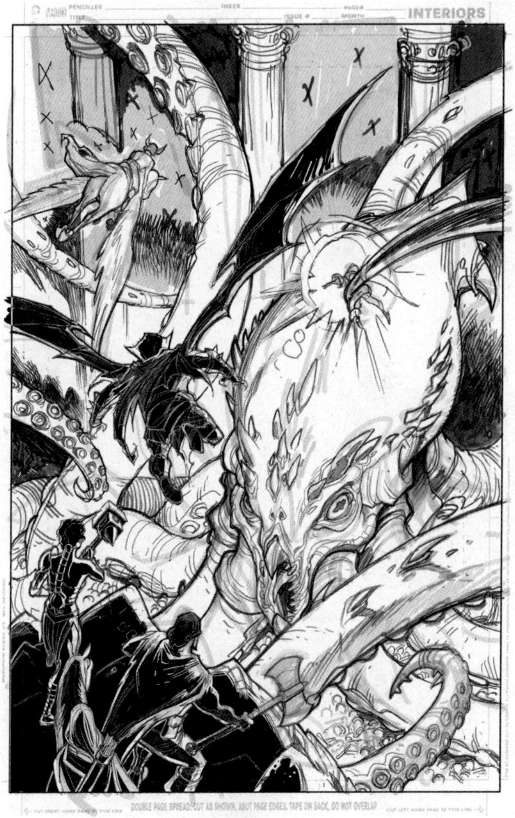
PENCILLER
INKER
PAGE#
TITLE
ISSUE #
MONTH
INTERIORS
DOUBLE PAGE SPREAD: CUT AS SHOWN, ABUT PAGE EDGES, TAPE ON BACK, DO NOT OVERLAP

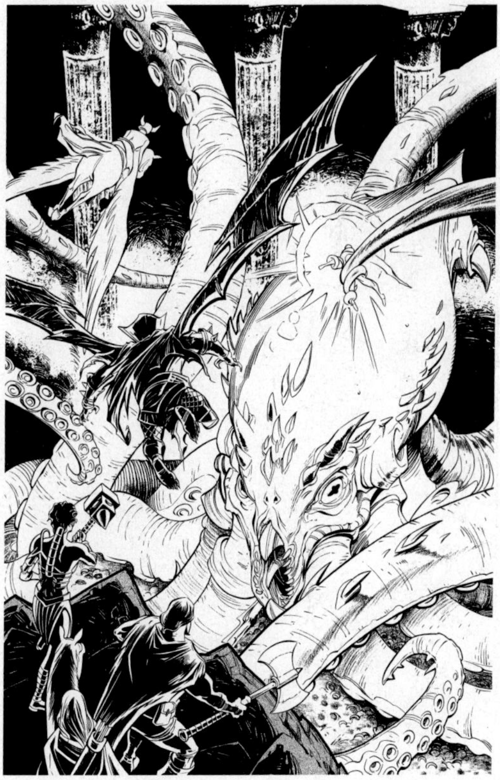

DEMON KNIGHTS #19 Full fold-out cover by Bernard Chang

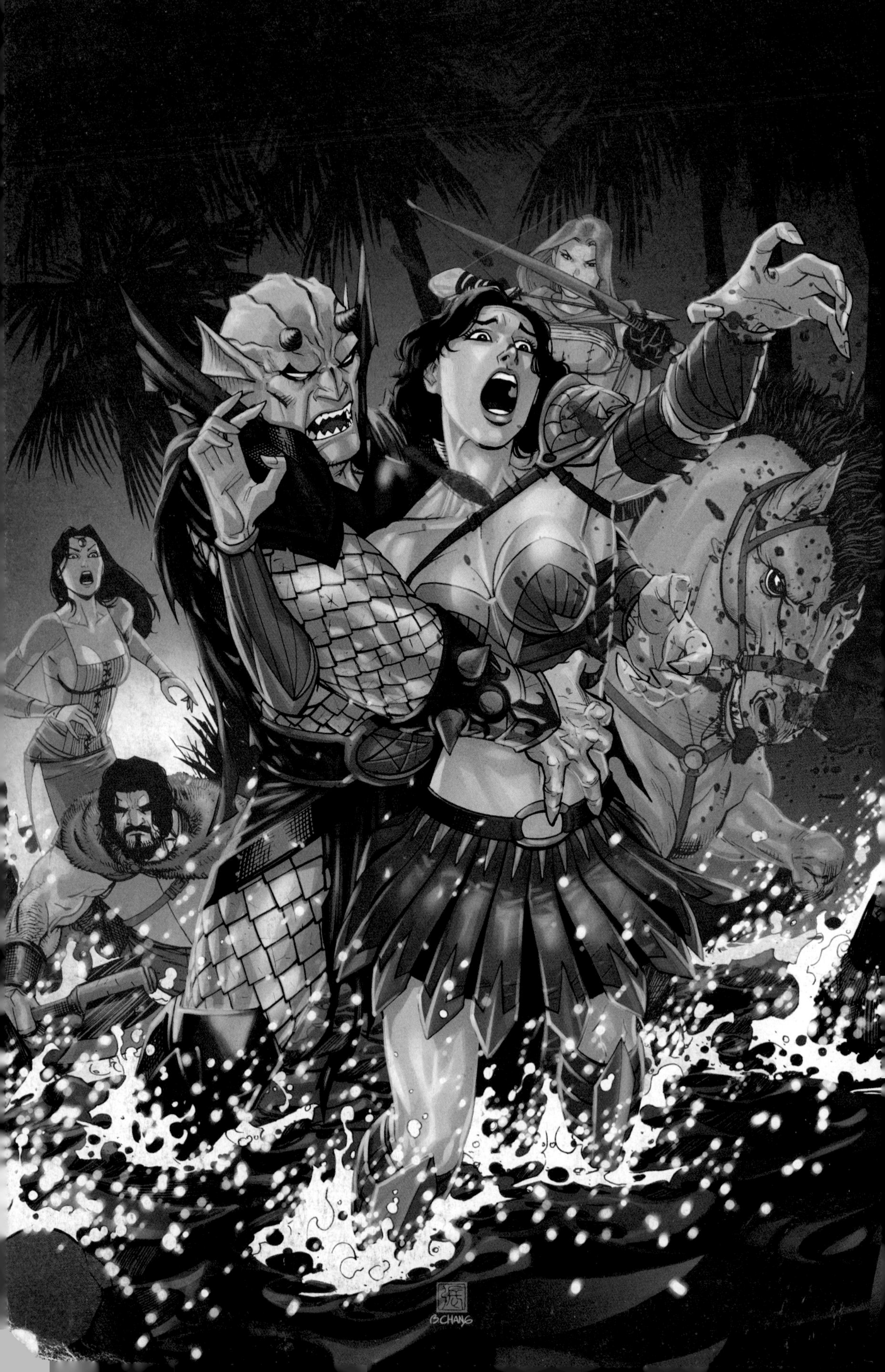

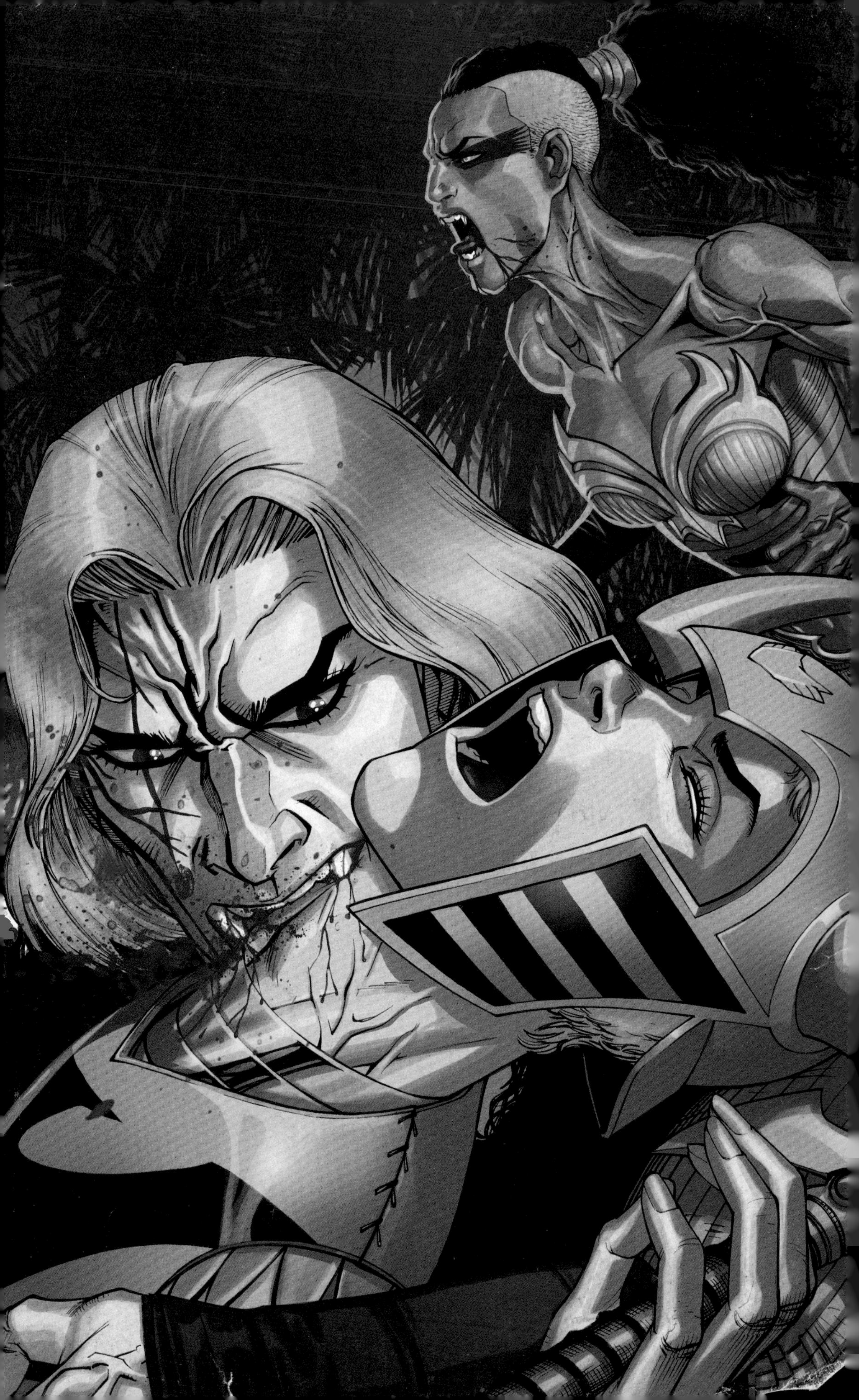

DC COMICS™

"SWAMP THING is a series that you need to be reading, no questions asked."
—IGN

"A thoughtful, well-executed new take on a great character."
—PUBLISHERS WEEKLY

START AT THE BEGINNING!

SWAMP THING VOLUME 1: RAISE THEM BONES

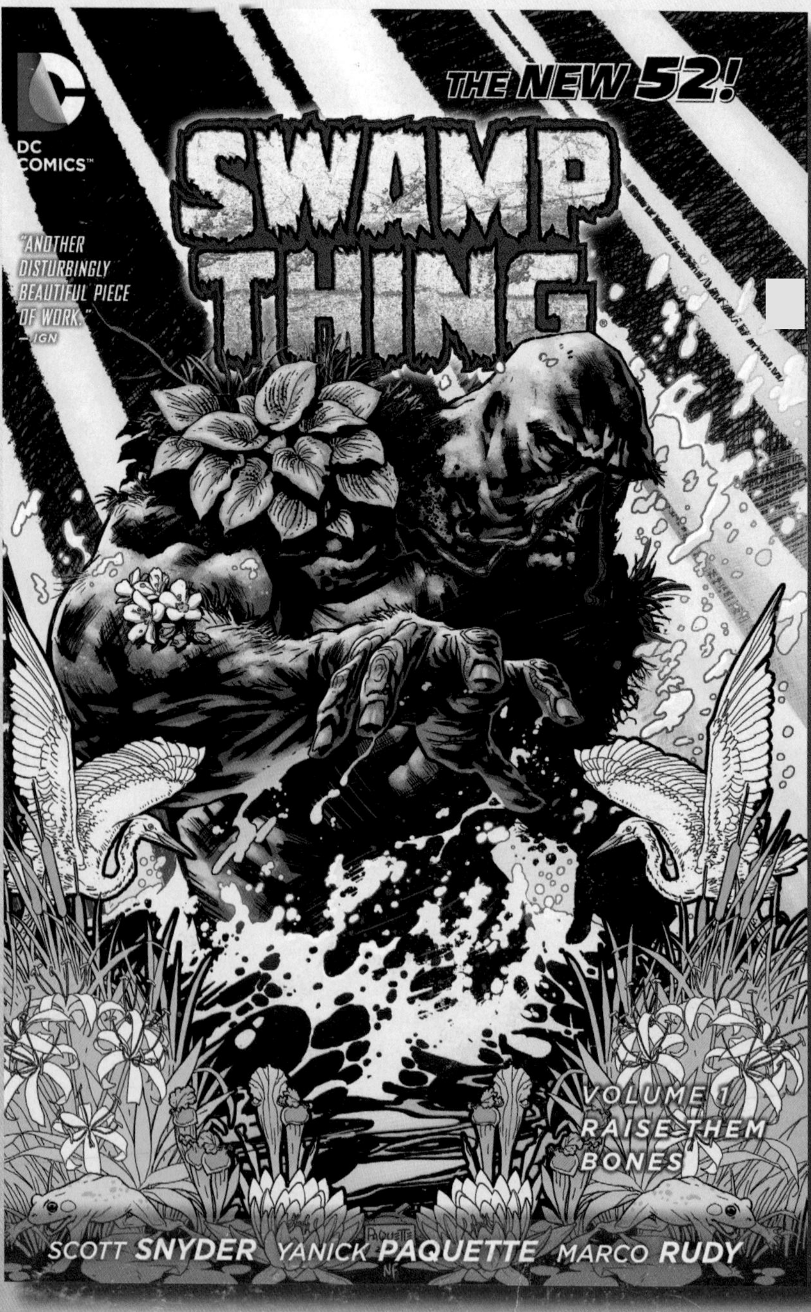

DC COMICS™
THE NEW 52!
SWAMP THING
"ANOTHER DISTURBINGLY BEAUTIFUL PIECE OF WORK." —IGN
VOLUME 1
RAISE THEM BONES
SCOTT SNYDER YANICK PAQUETTE MARCO RUDY

I, VAMPIRE
VOLUME 1:
TAINTED LOVE

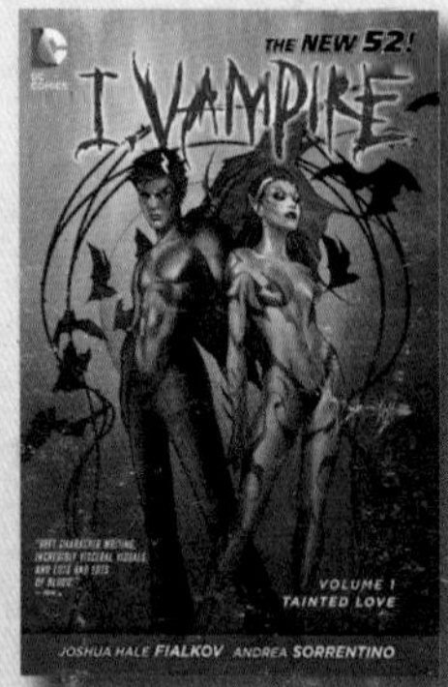

THE NEW 52!
I, VAMPIRE
VOLUME 1
TAINTED LOVE
JOSHUA HALE FIALKOV ANDREA SORRENTINO

DEMON KNIGHTS
VOLUME 1: SEVEN
AGAINST THE DARK

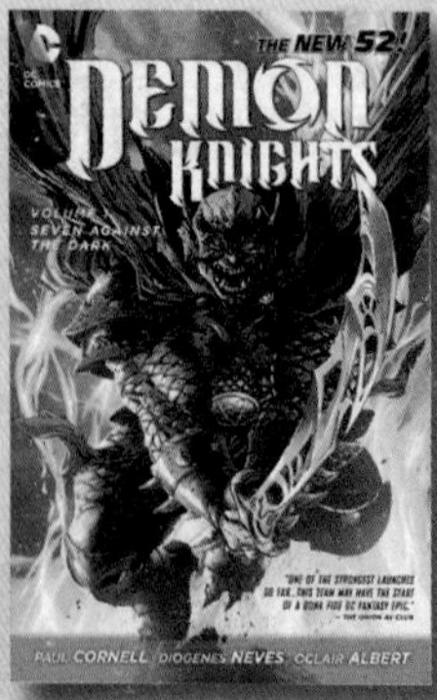

THE NEW 52!
DEMON KNIGHTS
PAUL CORNELL DIOGENES NEVES OCLAIR ALBERT

DC UNIVERSE PRESENTS
VOLUME 1: FEATURING
DEADMAN & CHALLENGERS
OF THE UNKNOWN

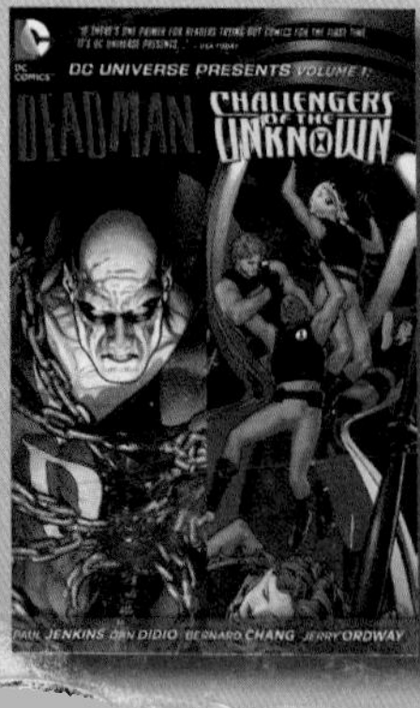

DC UNIVERSE PRESENTS VOLUME 1
DEADMAN
CHALLENGERS OF THE UNKNOWN
PAUL JENKINS DAN DIDIO BERNARD CHANG JERRY ORDWAY